THE
HISTORY OF
ADVERTISING

40
MAJOR BOOKS
IN FACSIMILE

Edited by
HENRY ASSAEL
C. SAMUEL CRAIG
New York University

A
GARLAND
SERIES

THE RELATIONSHIP OF
ADVERTISING EXPENDITURES
TO SALES:

An Anthology of Classic Articles

EDITED BY
AVIJIT GHOSH
C. SAMUEL CRAIG

GARLAND PUBLISHING, INC.
NEW YORK & LONDON
1986

For a complete list of the titles in this series
see the final pages of this volume.

Library of Congress Cataloging-in-Publication Data

Main entry under title:
The Relationship of advertising expenditures to sales.
  (The History of advertising)
  1. Advertising—Costs—Addresses, essays, lectures.
2. Sales—Addresses, essays, lectures. I. Ghosh,
Avijit. II. Craig C. Samuel. III. Series.
HF5811.R45 1985   338.4'36591   84-46070
ISBN 0-8240-6764-9 (alk. paper)

Design by Donna Montalbano

The volumes in this series are printed on
acid-free, 250-year-life paper.

Printed in the United States of America

Contents

Introduction

Reviews

"Aggregate Advertising Models: The State of the Art," John D. C. Little (*Operations Research*, July–August, 1979)

"The Shape of the Advertising Response Function," Julian L. Simon and Johan Arndt (*Journal of Advertising Research*, August, 1980)

Time Series Models

"The Effects of Advertising Carry-Over," Kenneth E. Case and James E. Shamblin (*Journal of Advertising Research*, June, 1972)

"Testing Distributed Lag Models of Advertising Effect," Frank M. Bass and Darral G. Clarke (*Journal of Marketing Research*, August, 1972)

"Measuring Advertising Decay," Ronald W. Ward (*Journal of Advertising Research*, August, 1976)

"Econometric Measurement of the Duration of Advertising Effect on Sales," Darral G. Clarke (*Journal of Marketing Research*, November, 1976)

"Lydia Pinkham Revisited: A Box-Jenkins Approach," P. W. Kyle (*Journal of Advertising Research*, April, 1978)

"The Periodic Pain of Lydia Pinkham," Doyle L. Weiss, Franklin S. Houston, and Pierre Windal (*Journal of Business*, Vol. 51, No. 1, 1978)

"Bivariate Time-Series Analysis of the Relationship Between Advertising and Sales," Dominique M. Hanssens (*Applied Economics*, 12, 1980)

"Modeling Advertising-Sales Relationships Involving Feedback: A Time Series Analysis of Six Cereal Brands," David A. Aaker, James M. Carman, and Robert Jacobson (*Journal of Marketing Research*, February, 1982)

Controlled Experimentation

"Sales Effects of Two Campaign Themes," Peter L. Henderson, James F. Hind, and Sidney E. Brown (*Journal of Advertising Research*, December, 1961)

"Test Marketing Cookware Coated with 'Teflon'," James C. Becknell, Jr., and Robert W. McIsaac (*Journal of Advertising Research*, 3, 1963)

"Advertising Research at Anheuser-Busch, Inc. (1963–68)" Russell L. Ackoff and James R. Emshoff (*Sloan Management Review*, Winter, 1975)

"Advertising Research at Anheuser-Busch, Inc., (1968–74)" Russell L. Ackoff and James R. Emshoff (*Sloan Management Review*, Spring, 1975)

"Analysis of Advertising Experiments," Russell S. Winer (*Journal of Advertising Research*, June, 1980)

Competitive Effects of Advertising

"Advertising and the Sale of Novels," Joel V. Berreman (*Journal of Marketing*, January, 1943)

"Some Correlates of Coffee and Cleanser Brand Shares," Seymour Banks (*Journal of Advertising Research*, June, 1961)

"Predicting Short-Term Changes in Market Share as a Function of Advertising Strategy," Robert D. Buzzell (*Journal of Marketing Research*, August, 1964)

"Individual Exposure to Advertising and Changes in Brands Bought," Purnell H. Benson (*Journal of Advertising Research*, December, 1967)

"Determinants of Market Share," Doyle L. Weiss (*Journal of Marketing Research*, August, 1968)

"A Simultaneous Equation Regression Study of Advertising and Sales of Cigarettes," Frank M. Bass (*Journal of Marketing Research*, August, 1969)

"The Effect of Advertising on Liquor Brand Sales," Julian L. Simon (*Journal of Marketing Research*, August, 1969)

"Optimal Allocation of Competitive Marketing Efforts: An Empirical Study," Jean-Jacques Lambin (*Journal of Business*, 43, 1970)

"Multivariate Analysis of Sales Responses of Competing Brands to Advertising," Neil E. Beckwith (*Journal of Marketing Research*, May, 1972)

"Sales Effectiveness of Automobile Advertising," Robert D. Buzzell and Michael J. Baker (*Journal of Advertising Research*, June, 1972)

"Sales-Advertising Cross-Elasticities and Advertising Competition," Darral G. Clarke (*Journal of Marketing Research*, August, 1973)

"An Analysis of Competitive Market Behavior," Franklin S. Houston and Doyle L. Weiss (*Journal of Marketing Research*, May, 1974)

"Market Share Response to Advertising: An Example of Theory Testing," Dan Horsky (*Journal of Marketing Research*, February, 1977)

Aggregate Response Models

"An Operations-Research Study of Sales Response to Advertising," M. L. Vidale and H. B. Wolfe (*Operations Research*, June, 1957)

"Advertising and Cigarettes," Lester G. Telser (*Journal of Political Economy*, 70, 1962)

"Evaluating and Improving Resource Allocation for Navy Recruiting," Richard C. Morey and John M. McCann (*Management Science*, December, 1980)

"The Advertising-Sales Relationship in Australia," Donald W. Hendon (*Journal of Advertising Research*, February, 1981)

The Optimal Level of Advertising Expenditures

"Optimal Advertising and Optimal Quality," Robert Dorfman and Peter O. Steiner (*American Economic Review*, December, 1954)

"Optimal Advertising Policy Under Dynamic Conditions," Marc Nerlove and Kenneth J. Arrow (*Economica*, May, 1962)

Introduction

The Relationship of Advertising Expenditures to Sales

The over eighty-eight billion dollars that was spent on advertising in the U.S. during 1984 bears mute testimony to the fact that business firms believe that advertising is important for sales. However, the difficulty is in precisely establishing the nature of the relationship between dollars expended for advertising and sales results. This anthology brings together important articles that attempt to shed some light on the relationship between advertising expenditures and sales. The coverage ranges from articles that examine the problem of advertising over time, experimental studies that attempt to measure the relationship in particular instances, and large-scale econometrics studies that look at the phenomenon at the aggregate level.

The anthology is divided into six major sections. In the first section, Reviews, there are two important review articles. Little (1979) provides a comprehensive review of aggregate advertising models. Simon and Arndt (1980) provide an in-depth look at research dealing with the shape of the advertising response function.

The next major section, Time Series Models, examines the effect of advertising over time. The eight articles in this section look at the relationship of advertising expenditures to sales over time. A number of them use the Lydia Pinkham data.

While the econometric time series studies are very useful for looking at aggregate response to advertising expenditures, they all suffer from the limitation common to all correlational approaches. Namely, it is difficult to tell whether the effects are truly causal or simply correlational. This issue is addressed in the third major section, Controlled Experimentation, where experiments that examine the advertising-sales relationship are presented. This section contains four articles that relate the results of particular experiments and one review paper. The two papers by Ackoff and Emshoff (1975), which have become classics in the advertising literature, report the results of a number of studies conducted for Anheuser-Busch on the relationship between advertising expenditures and the sales of Budweiser.

The fourth section, Competitive Effects of Advertising, contains thirteen articles that consider the effect of advertising expenditures in a competitive environment. Most of these papers examine advertising at a brand level or on a market share basis. Also, some of them examine the issue of advertising cross-elasticities.

The fifth section, Aggregate Response Models, considers advertising-sales relationships on a more aggregate level. Essentially, these studies look at the overall response to advertising expenditures rather than the more specific brand share models in the previous section. It includes classic articles by Vidale and Wolfe (1957) and Telser (1962).

Finally, the last section, The Optimal Level of Advertising Expenditures, contains two classic articles, Dorfman and Steiner (1954) and Nerlove and Arrow (1962).

It is hoped that this anthology will provide researchers with a valuable resource. It was not possible to include all that has been written on this subject, but an attempt was made to sample some of the more important and more representative works. These articles, coupled with their bibliographic references at the end of each paper, provide the researcher and practitioner with a wealth of information on the topic.

Avijit Ghosh
C. Samuel Craig

Acknowledgements

The following articles, reprinted from the *Journal of Advertising Research*, are copyright by the Advertising Research Foundation:

"The Shape of the Advertising Response Function," © 1980,

"The Effects of Advertising Carry-Over," © 1972,

"Measuring Advertising Decay," © 1976,

"Lydia Pinkham Revisited: A Box-Jenkins Approach," © 1978,

"Sales Effects of Two Campaign Themes," © 1961,

"Test Marketing Cookware Coated with 'Teflon'," © 1963,

"Analysis of Advertising Experiments," © 1980,

"Some Correlates of Coffee and Cleanser Brand Shares," © 1961,

"Individual Exposure to Advertising and Changes in Brands Bought," © 1967,

"Sales Effectiveness of Automobile Advertising," © 1972,

"The Advertising-Sales Relationship in Australia," © 1981.

The American Marketing Association has granted permission to reprint the following articles from the *Journal of Marketing Research*:

"Testing Distributed Lag Models of Advertising Effect," © 1972,

"Econometric Measurement of the Duration of Advertising Effect on Sales," © 1976,

"Modeling Advertising-Sales Relationships Involving Feedback: A Time Series Analysis of Six Cereal Brands," © 1982,

"Advertising and the Sale of Novels," © 1943,

"Predicting Short-Term Changes in Market Share as a Function of Advertising Strategy," © 1964,

"Determinants of Market Share," © 1968,

"A Simultaneous Equation Regression Study of Advertising and Sales of Cigarettes," © 1969,

Feature Article

Aggregate Advertising Models:
The State of the Art

JOHN D. C. LITTLE

Massachusetts Institute of Technology, Cambridge, Massachusetts

(Received January 1979; accepted April 1979)

Aggregate advertising models relate product sales to advertising spending for a market as a whole. Although many models have been built, they frequently contradict each other and considerable doubt exists as to which models best represent advertising processes. An increasingly rich literature of empirical studies helps resolve these issues by revealing major advertising phenomena that models should encompass. These include: sales responding upward and downward at different rates; steady state response that can be concave or S-shaped and can have positive sales at zero advertising; sales affected by competitive advertising; and advertising dollar effectiveness that can change over time.

A review of aggregate models developed on a priori grounds brings out similarities and differences among those of Vidale and Wolfe, Nerlove and Arrow, Little, and others and identifies ways in which the models agree or disagree with observed phenomena. A Lanchester-motivated structure generalizes many features of these models and conforms to some but not all of the empirical observations. Although econometric studies have revealed important empirical insights, the most frequently used structural forms do not model certain key phenomena, most notably different rise and decay rates. Future work must join better models with more powerful calibration methods.

IGNORANCE of advertising response phenomena, inability to make good measurements, and lack of a theory to organize existing knowledge contribute to great waste in advertising. Contradictions abound. For example, advertising partisans in one company declare that certain markets should receive more advertising because "the brand is strong there and we should take advantage of its momentum." Then, a few minutes later, the same people propose that other markets should also receive more because "industry sales are strong there and our share is low," which, freely translated, means "the brand is weak there and we don't have any momentum." One often sees media scheduled in intensive "flights" so that "the message can be heard through the noise," but, if someone asks why not make the flight half as long and twice as intense,

629

or else twice as long and half as intense, no good answer can be given.

In one company the brand managers push to spend their budgets early in the calendar year. Is this because of product seasonality? Or a belief in the effectiveness of campaigns lasting six months? No, it is because corporate management has a reputation for calling back unspent monies to improve earnings in the fourth quarter. Brand management responds by spending all its money in the spring. One might suspect that management in this company is not quite sure what it is getting for its advertising dollars. In most companies, advertising strategy is subject to intermittent upheavals. Sometimes this happens brand by brand—each year one or two products undergo an agonizing reappraisal. At other times a whole division will go through a convulsion. Perhaps these strategy shifts are appropriate, but rarely is there any clear reason why the reexamination should be taking place for one brand and not another.

After a substantial change, marketing management watches sales carefully and, more often than not, expresses satisfaction. Yet, though a major strategy shift offers a unique opportunity for measurement (say, by holding out some control markets), such steps are virtually never taken.

Advertising also is full of fads. Clearly a company's ads are conspicuous. (They had better be!) Everybody from the president's wife to the newest clerk voices an opinion. Clever copy becomes a conversation piece overnight. ("We try harder," "I can't believe I ate the whole thing.") Innovations perceived as successful are quickly imitated by others, rightly or wrongly. Low key testimonials, comparison advertising and humor have been up and down over the past few years. Mature authority figures seem to be undergoing a revival at the moment. It is an exciting world of good showmanship where strategy changes are conceived, packaged and sold with many of the appeals that characterize advertising itself.

And, to a great extent, this is as it should be. Good strategy requires imagination and style and always will. At the same time, strategy emerges best from a foundation of reliable facts and sound analysis. These are not easy to come by.

The management science/operations research fraternity has nibbled at advertising issues. Moderate heartburn has been a fairly common result. Yet, there have certainly been successes, one or two of which have been widely publicized. See, for example, Weinberg [72], Rao [52] and Ackoff and Emshoff [1]. Other workers have often found these studies hard to duplicate, perhaps because marketing situations differ from company to company or, more likely, because studies to date simply do not supply enough knowledge to provide an adequate foundation for imitation. Quantitative understanding of advertising processes has made some headway but the job is far from done and the available material needs pulling together. This paper takes on part of that job by examining aggregate response models.

A basic OR/MS goal is to find good models. But what is a good model? It depends. We should tailor a model to fit the job at hand. Lilien [32] calls this "model relativism." Urban [70] expresses the same thought when he says the model builder should state the purposes of his model in advance. All right, we want advertising response models that will be useful for (1) tracking and evaluating advertising performance, (2) diagnosing market changes and (3) incorporation into decision models. Although we shall not address decision models per se, they should contain response models with the necessary phenomena to assist meaningfully on (1) annual budgets, (2) geographic allocation and (3) allocation over time. Two other important areas are media and copy. These enter our discussion but will not be treated with the detail required for incorporation into decision models.

In focusing on the response model rather than the decision model, we differ from the many writers who seek to characterize optimal policies once the response model is given. For an extensive review of this literature, see Sethi [59].

Attainment of our goals requires dynamic models that relate advertising spending to sales. We confine attention to established products since they blot up most of the money and since new products use special models. We focus on macro- or aggregate models rather than models of individual customer behavior for two reasons. First, most micromodels so far have been thin on either empirical data or marketing control variables (especially advertising) or both. Second, the most convincing data sources available to companies for calibrating advertising models today are aggregate in nature (historical time series at a national or market level and field experiments). This is not to play down the importance of modeling individual customer response to advertising (see, for example, the media selection models of Little and Lodish [35], Gensch [16], Zufryden [75] and Starr [65]). Rather it is to say that the catalog of advertising effects presented here comes almost entirely from aggregate data and so is inadequate to resolve most micromodeling questions. We note, however, that micromodels will have to reproduce the empirical macroeffects reported here.

I. CONTROVERSIES, CONFUSIONS, AND CONTRADICTIONS

The advertising models in the OR/MS literature are not especially consistent with each other nor with such measurements and data as are available. We identify three areas of controversy: shape, dynamics, and interactions.

Shape. By shape we mean the shape of a curve showing sales response to advertising under steady state conditions. In other words, if a set of different advertising rates were tested with other market influences held fixed and brand sales were measured each time after the market came to equilibrium, what would a plot of sales rate vs. advertising rate look like? *Is such a relationship linear?* Many econometric analyses implicitly assume it to be. *What are sales with zero advertising?* A good many theoretical models imply sales would be zero. *Is response S-shaped?* Most existing models do not permit such a possibility, and yet many media schedules contain "flights" whose justification seems to be based on belief in a threshold or S-shape in the curve. *Do large amounts of advertising depress sales?* So claim some writers but few models accommodate it.

Dynamics. How fast do sales respond when advertising is increased? In the process of calibrating marketing models, the author has often asked marketing managers the following question. What percent of the long run response to an advertising increase would you expect to obtain in the first year? A typical answer would be 60% and the range might run from 30% to 80%. It is interesting to compare these values with the data in the next section.

How fast do sales decay when advertising is decreased? Strong marketing men turn pale when advertising cuts are proposed, even if only for test purposes. "We might lose the brand franchise," they say. Their pallor may be role-playing because companies under financial stress regularly cut budgets drastically, apparently believing that the brand will survive.

Still another question is: *Does hysteresis ever exist?* In other words, are there circumstances under which sales would increase with increased advertising and stay there after withdrawal of advertising? Or, in the opposite direction, could a competitor take away sales and share by increasing advertising, and the brand find it difficult to regain position? Very few marketing models exhibit such a phenomenon, but some people believe it to exist in practice.

Finally, *how does advertising effectiveness change with time* and how can we model it?

Interactions. Is it better to advertise where sales are strong or weak? This is a classical argument, certain to draw proponents to each side. One can be sure that every model contains one or more, often inconspicuous, assumptions relating to this question, and so does any statistical analysis. In a similar vein, *are advertising effects additive with other marketing variables*, e.g., price, promotion, and competitive actions, *or multiplicative, or do they interact in more complicated ways?* All shades of assumptions appear in the model building and statistical literature. They are certainly not all consistent with one another.

2. BASIC PHENOMENA: WHAT CAN BE LEARNED FROM THE DATA?

Measurements must eventually resolve the issues just raised and tell

SALES RATE

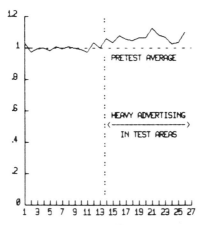

Figure 1. Sales rate of a packaged good responded quickly to increased advertising. Vertical axis shows the ratio of sales in test areas to sales in control areas, normalized to pretest average.

us which advertising phenomena are real and which are only folklore. In this spirit, we present a collection of empirical examples of certain major effects. These will help sort out the models in the next section.

SALES RATE

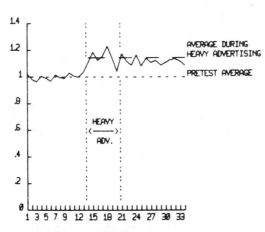

Figure 2. Sales rate of a packaged good rose quickly under increased advertising but declined slowly after it was removed. Vertical axis shows the ratio of sales in test areas to sales in control areas not receiving the heavy advertising.

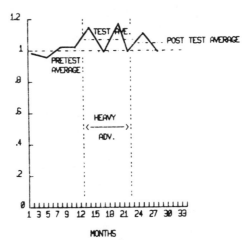

Figure 3. Another example of quick response upward followed by slow decay. Sales show more variance than Figure 2, but same general effect. Vertical axis is again normalized test/control.

Upward Response

Advertising increases sales, or such is the intent. Figures 1–3 show instances of sales before and after the introduction of substantial new advertising dollars. In each case the sales rate increases within a month

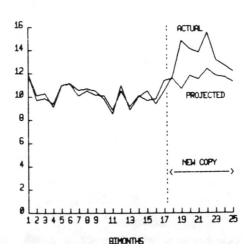

Figure 4. New advertising copy substantially increased Horlick's sales. Actual sales are compared to projections of a model based on market before copy change. Data replotted from Bloom, Jay and Twyman [9].

or two. Observe that this time span is, in each case, shorter than the judgments reported in the previous sections.

Figure 4, taken from data of Bloom, Jay and Twyman [9], is particularly interesting because it shows a jump in sales due, not to an increase in spending, but to a change in copy. Thus "advertising rate" is not necessarily the same as "spending rate." Notice again that sales respond almost immediately. A similar copy change effect appears in the results of Pekelman and Tse [48].

Sales at the New Level

Figures 1-3 show sales leveling off under the new, higher spending rates. Whatever was going to happen in these cases appears to have happened before the advertising stopped. Haley [20], however, has found a further effect shown in Figure 5. The sales increase occurs but its magnitude decreases with time. The leveling off appears to take place at a value lower than the initial gain. Such an effect is common in the case of new products that are purchased frequently. In such cases people learn about the product through advertising and try it, thereby causing a sharp spurt in sales. Only a fraction of the triers become regular purchasers and so sales taper off to a lower rate. In this paper we deal with established brands, but an analogous process seems quite likely: Increased advertising leads a group of nonusers to buy the product for reexamination or just for variety. Some of these customers continue to purchase, others not.

The copy induced sales increase in Figure 4 also seems to fall off. This too may be a new-trier effect, although many advertising people would say that the copy is wearing out. Such a description, however, seems more of a definition than an explanation.

Downward Response

Figures 2, 3, and 5C show sales response to decreased advertising. Notice that sales decay appears to take place more slowly than sales growth. This is particularly evident in Figure 2 and with more variance in Figure 3. In these cases we are able to observe the same product under both increases and decreases of advertising.

A posssible explanation for decay time being longer than rise time is that the rise relates to the advertising communications process, i.e., hearing or seeing the advertising message, absorbing it and acting on it. Since nominal forgetting times for advertising are on the order of a month (Zielish [36] and Strong [66]), it seems reasonable that an established product with good retail availability would show the positive effects of increased advertising within a short time. Krugman [26] argues that 3 exposures may be enough to stimulate action. On the other hand, decay in the absence of advertising seems more a question of experience with the product. Using and liking a brand will have far more influence on a customer than advertising. Although sales decay will depend on compet-

J. D. C. Little

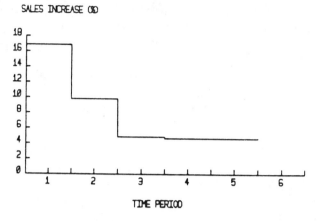

(A) BRAND B : DOUBLED ADVERTISING

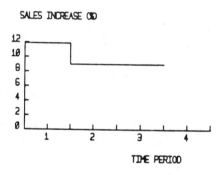

(B) BRAND D : ADVERTISING INCREASED 50%

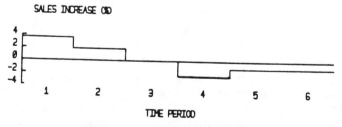

(C) BRAND F : ADVERTISING DECREASED 25%

Figure 5. Field experiments reported by Haley [20] show the erosion of sales increases attained by heavier advertising (Brands B and D) and a relatively slow sales decay following decreased advertising (Brand F). Vertical axis displays the percent sales increase in test areas relative to control areas.

itive activity and other factors, it does not seem surprising (especially when facts stare us in the face) that decay is often much slower than growth.

An essential point, however, is that a good model of sales response to advertising should permit different rise and decay rates.

Sales with Zero Advertising

Figure 6 shows the sales of a line of never-advertised products. Many people do not realize this, but there are literally hundreds of unadvertised products selling happily away in every supermarket and department store. This often occurs when distribution is assured. Thus, chain-store house-brands are guaranteed a place on the shelf. Stores also stock unadvertised "price brands" with unfamiliar names in order to offer the consumer a low cost choice. In other examples, vending machines look out on a captive market and frequently carry unadvertised and virtually

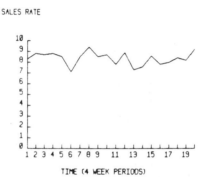

Figure 6. The healthy sales of a line of unadvertised food products show that advertising is not always required in order to sell something.

unknown brands. Department stores stock certain items by function without fanfare, e.g., string, envelopes or thumbtacks. This does not mean that such products would not sell faster with advertising but rather that positive sales with zero advertising are quite reasonable.

We should not be surprised, therefore, that empirical studies of sales response often indicate that a substantial part of the market seems not to be affected by advertising, at least over the medium run. This is noticeable in econometric studies with linear models where positive constant terms are common (e.g., Bass and Clarke [3]).

Thus an advertising response model should admit the possibility of sales with zero advertising (many do not).

Nonlinearity

Suppose advertising is held constant and other market conditions do not change. After some time period the market can be expected to be in steady state. If this were done for a number of different advertising rates, we could make a plot of steady state sales vs. advertising.

What would the curve look like? We would not expect it to be linear, for this would have a variety of nonsensical consequences. (For example, a product with a fixed production cost per unit would have an optimal advertising rate of either zero or infinity.) However, "not linear" covers many possibilities. We describe two important ones.

Diminishing Returns. Figure 7 displays a pair of empirical advertising response curves plotted from data of Benjamin and Maitland [8]. Their data are particularly valuable because of the great range of advertising levels studied. In each case the slope of the curve decreases at high advertising levels, thereby showing concavity or diminishing returns. Less obvious is whether response is better modeled by an absolute ceiling

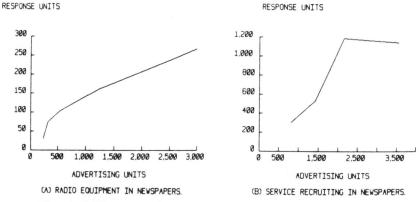

Figure 7. Two examples of nonlinear response exhibit the phenomenon of diminishing returns at high advertising rates. Data replotted from Benjamin and Maitland [8].

(saturation level) or by a function that can surpass any prespecified level, albeit with increasing difficulty. Benjamin and Maitland [8] choose the latter course; they take sales to be the log of advertising. Such a function, however, does not make sense at zero advertising since $\log 0 = -\infty$.

S-Shape. Controversy surrounds the question of whether steady-state sales response to advertising is S-shaped, i.e., whether, at low levels of advertising, increases are increasingly effective up to some point after which diminishing returns set in. Simon [64], for example, says no.

However, as mentioned earlier, many advertising schedules today contain *flights* or *pulses.* A theory that might justify flights is that response is S-shaped, e.g., small advertising rates do little good but medium rates are effective. Published empirical evidence of such relationships is hard to find.

Rao [51] and Rao and Miller [53] display S-shaped response curves which are developed in a three-step process. First Rao analyzes individual market areas by times-series regressions, relating sales to advertising with a linear model. The coefficient of advertising is the slope of the sales vs. advertising curve of the linear model. Often, but not always, he finds a small slope (i.e., less advertising effectiveness) where the average advertising in the market is either very low or very high (Figure 8A). As a second step Rao fits a curve cross-sectionally through the slope data to obtain a relationship between slope and average advertising rate. This is often quadratic. The final step is to integrate the slope vs. advertising relation to obtain sales vs. advertising, i.e., the sales response curve. If the slope is quadratic as in Figure 8A, the sales response will be an S-shaped cubic over the relevant range as shown in Figure 8B. Rao [51] has three or four examples that show generally similar results but also reports that some products show no S-shape.

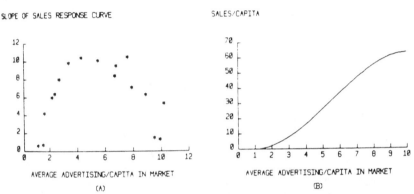

Figure 8. An S-shaped sales response curve developed by Rao's [53] method for a canned juice [51]. (A) Individual market areas analyzed by time series show different advertising response coefficients (slopes). Each point is one market area. (B) Integration of a quadratic fit to (A) yields S-shaped sales response curve. Scaling is arbitrary.

In a similar vein Wittink [74] does time series analyses of individual markets and then cross-sectional studies of the advertising slope coefficients. He too finds larger slopes at larger advertising rates, indicating the lower region of an S-curve. The upper part is presumably guaranteed by ultimate saturation of advertising effect.

On the direct question of the efficacy of pulses (as opposed to whether steady-state response is S-shaped), Ackoff and Emshoff [1] report good results from pulsing. Sethi [58] reports a Milwaukee Advertising Laboratory experiment that seems to show good short run but poor long run effects. In any case, considering current practice, Rao and Miller's work, and the importance of the issue, we argue that advertising models should accomodate S-shaped curves.

Before leaving the empirical evidence on shape, we present certain provocative results from McDonald [38]. He has analyzed panel data that contained not only product purchases but also media exposure. Figure 9 shows a sales measure plotted against an advertising measure. The sales measure is the percentage of brand switches *to* the advertised product as a proportion of switches both *to* and *from* it. Thus 50% would be expected in the absence of an advertising effect and, in fact, Figure 9 averages to 50% if each point is weighted by its number of observations. The advertising measure is the number of opportunities to see ads for the brand in the last four days of the customer's time interval between successive purchases. The curve is an aggregate over several product classes and many brands, all essentially supermarket items. The curve is not comparable to those presented earlier because it deals with individuals, not total market, and because both time interval and sales measure are very

SALES MEASURE

OPPORTUNITIES TO SEE ADVERTISEMENTS

Figure 9. Microlevel evidence for S-shaped sales response is obtained from observing individuals. The sales measure is the number of switches to the advertised brand as a percentage of the total number of switches to and from the brand. Opportunities-to-see include only those in the last 4 days prior to purchase (McDonald [38]).

specialized. However, the results are quite revealing, especially the S-shape, the seeming saturation after just a few exposures and the evidence of immediate advertising effects.

Impulse Response

A standard question about a dynamic system is, "What is its impulse response?" Thus, suppose we put a short burst of advertising into the market, say an expensive TV special, a multipage four-color spread in a magazine, or a massive direct mail drop; what would be the resulting shape of the sales response over time?

Figure 10 shows an example of this. A test group of people was exposed and a control group not exposed to a sharp pulse of advertising. The ratio of test sales/control sales in the following months was recorded. A number of tests have been averaged to give the impulse response shown.

Another type of analysis, common in econometric studies, measures the effect of past advertising on current sales by regression. This yields

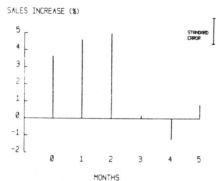

Figure 10. A large impulse of advertising in month zero yields substantial sales increases in months 0, 1 and 2 for an infrequently purchased consumer durable.

an implied impulse response even though the advertising was not actually done in pulses. Figure 11, plotted from the results of Bass and Clarke [3], displays such a case.

Notice that Figures 9–11 corroborate earlier observations that response to advertising is relatively quick. The initial effect of a pulse takes place within 2 months. This is in line with the rise times in Figures 1–3. Ideally, impulse response measurements would also pick up long run effects in the tail. However, if the decay is as slow as those of Figures 2 and 3, the usual statistical methods will have difficulty detecting it.

In examining alternative models in the next section we can determine their impulse responses and compare them to what we observe empirically.

Infrequent Purchases

Figure 10 is especially interesting because it deals with a consumer

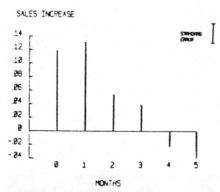

Figure 11. A unit impulse of advertising in month zero produces sales in that and subsequent months. Results determined by econometric methods for a dietary weight control product by Bass and Clarke [3].

durable whose normal time between purchases is measured in years. Some people have argued that the fast advertising response discussed earlier will not apply to infrequently purchased goods. Figure 10 refutes this. The reason such goods can respond quickly is simple enough. At any given point of time some people are in the market, ready to act. Indeed, potential customers often seek information and take a special interest in the advertising for the product class.

However, for infrequent or one-time purchases like houses, refrigerators, books, college educations, or enlistments in the armed services, a new phenomenon is likely to come in: *market depletion.* Figure 12, taken from data of Benjamin, Jolly and Maitland [7], displays the effect. Successive advertisements in a periodical draw fewer and fewer customers, tending toward an asymptotic value where market depletion is

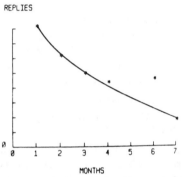

Figure 12. Replies to a series of advertisements in a periodical show evidence of market depletion and temporary rejuvenation. Replotted from Benjamin, Jolly and Maitland [7].

balanced by new entry, or zero if there is none. The authors also observed that when an advertisement was omitted the next one met increased response, indicating a degree of market rejuvenation.

Although statistical significance is not there, the impulse response curves of Figures 10 and 11 hint at a negative sales reaction about four months after the advertising pulse. Such borrowing of future sales is a type of temporary market depletion often found in consumer promotions and one that undoubtedly sometimes occurs with advertising. Becknell and McIsaac [5], for example, report the effect in cookware.

Competition

Companies worry about competition. Surely, if one brand can increase its sales and share by advertising, so can another. Therefore, one brand's advertising will often reduce another brand's sales. Some researchers have studied this phenomenon, for example, Lambin, Naert and Bultez

[31] and Horsky [23]. Figure 13 shows curves derived from data of the former. We argue that an understanding of advertising phenomenon in consumer markets requires competitive models.

Issues Outstanding

For a number of questions raised earlier, straightforward evidence is scanty.

Advertise Where Sales are Strong or Weak? Undoubtedly this question is too simplistic and the right answer depends on conditions. One might expect, for instance, that advertising response would be poor where distribution is weak. On the other hand a concerted marketing program

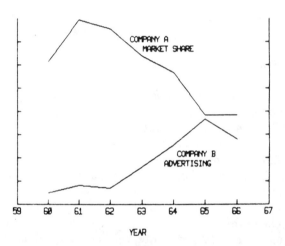

Figure 13. Company A loses share to aggressive Company B marketing that includes heavy advertising. The product is a low price consumer durable. Data derived from Lambin, Naert and Bultez [31].

that includes substantial advertising may be required to gain distribution and the benefits beyond.

The influencing conditions are likely to vary from case to case. Haley [20] produces evidence for better response where sales are already increasing. Rao and Miller [53] report a product for which advertising response is greater where share is greater but Wittink [74] reports the reverse. Competitive advertising can affect response. The various conditions need sorting out.

Hysteresis. Are there situations for established products where advertising can carry sales up to new levels to stay there after. advertising is reduced? Parsons [45] explores what appears to be such a case, but good examples are not generally available.

Interactions. How does advertising interact with other marketing variables? Some models assume additive effects, some multiplicative, and others more complicated relationships. They cannot all be right in a given situation. Interactions are usually much harder to measure than main effects, although some start has been made (Swinyard and Ray [67], Eskin and Baron [14] and Wildt [73]). Almost certainly, advertising response varies over the product life cycle. Some studies have found that advertising response for a product differs from market area to market area. This may result from different product class strength, demographic segmentation, or distribution levels. Much unraveling needs to be done.

Conclusions

The empirical evidence suggests that at least the following phenomena should be considered in building dynamic models of advertising response:

P1. Sales respond dynamically upward and downward to increases and decreases of advertising and frequently do so at different rates.

P2. Steady-state response can be concave or S-shaped and will often have positive sales at zero advertising.

P3. Competitive advertising affects sales.

P4. The dollar effectiveness of advertising can change over time as the result of changes in media, copy, and other factors.

P5. Products sometimes respond to increased advertising with a sales increase that falls off even as advertising is held constant.

All of these effects hold implications for managerial action. Obviously other important phenomena also exist, some of which have been discussed and others of which remain to be discovered. However, parsimony prompts us to keep the list short.

We now look for models that embrace these basic elements. The list does not seem very demanding, and indeed, where there are competing ways to represent the same phenomenon, we shall not be well equipped to distinguish among them. However, even our simple requirements of face validity will find many models wanting.

3. MODELS

For twenty years researchers have been adding marketing models to the literature like grains of sand to the beach. By now the pile, if not a dune, is at least a sand castle. Two rather dramatically different model building traditions coexist uneasily in the literature. One, which we shall call *a priori*, draws heavily on intuition and, although its practitioners are not oblivious to data, the model building goal is to postulate a general structure, not describe a specific application. In this category we place Vidale and Wolfe [71], Nerlove and Arrow [43] and Little [33, 34]. The other tradition is statistical or *econometric* and usually starts from a specific data base, e.g., time series of sales or share and advertising. In this category are Bass [2], Bass and Clarke [3], Montgomery and Silk [41] and Lambin [30] to name a few. In addition some older work and an increasing amount of new work is *mixed* in that it starts with rather more complicated a priori models and endeavors by statistical methods to fit and evaluate them. Examples are Kuehn, McGuire and Weiss [28] and Horsky [23].

A Priori Models

Vidale-Wolfe. In 1957 Vidale and Wolfe [71] published one of the earliest and most interesting of advertising response models. They used three basic ideas: (1) sales rate increases with advertising rate, (2) this effect decreases as sales rate approached a value called saturation and (3) sales constantly erode spontaneously. The authors give empirical illustrations of these phenomena. Let s = sales rate (sales units/period), $\dot{s} = ds/dt$, x = advertising rate (dol/period), ρ = response constant (sales units/dol/period), λ = decay constant (period^{-1}) and m = saturation sales rate (sales units/period). Sales might be measured in kilograms, liters, pounds, cases, etc., periods in weeks, months, years, etc.

The Vidale-Wolfe structure is

$$\dot{s} = \rho x[1 - (s/m)] - \lambda s. \tag{1}$$

The model contains only three constants, yet displays many of the characteristics one would intuitively attribute to advertising response. Since (1) is a first order ordinary differential equation, it has an explicit solution for arbitrary $x(t)$. We shall report it for completeness, but for more intuitive understanding, we shall display (a) sales response to a rectangular pulse, (b) impulse response and (c) steady state response. Suppose that at $t = 0$, $s = s(0)$, and a constant rate of advertising $x(t) = x$ is started which lasts until $t = T$ when it drops to zero. Solving (1) for such a rectangular pulse yields

$$s(t) = \begin{cases} r(x) + [s(0) - r(x)]e^{-[1+(\rho x/\lambda m)]\lambda t} & 0 \le t \le T \\ s(T)e^{-\lambda(t-T)} & T < t \end{cases} \tag{2}$$

where

$$r(x) = m(\rho x/\lambda m)/[1 + (\rho x/\lambda m)]. \tag{3}$$

Equation (2) is sketched in Figure 14a. Notice that the rise time is primarily affected by the constant ρ and decay time by λ.

The impulse response, expressed as the incremental sales generated by an amount, X, of dollars spent in a very short time at $t = 0$, is

$$\begin{aligned} \Delta s(t) &= s(t) - s(0)e^{-\lambda t} \\ &= [m - s(0)][1 - e^{-\rho X/m}]e^{-\lambda t}, \quad 0 < t \end{aligned} \tag{4}$$

J. D. C. Little

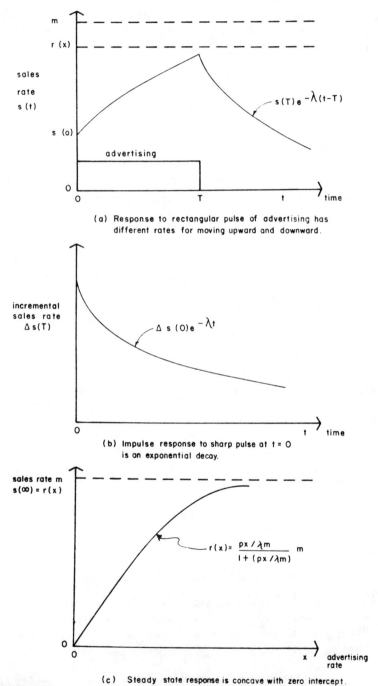

(a) Response to rectangular pulse of advertising has different rates for moving upward and downward.

(b) Impulse response to sharp pulse at t = 0 is an exponential decay.

(c) Steady state response is concave with zero intercept.

Figure 14. Vidale-Wolfe model: Sales response to advertising.

and is sketched in Figure 14*b*. Impulse response is exponential with decay constant λ.

The steady state response to a constant advertising rate x, is

$$s(\infty) = r(x) \qquad (5)$$

with $r(x)$ given by (3) and sketched in Figure 14*c*.

The general solution to the Vidale-Wolfe differential equation for arbitrary $x(t)$ is:

$$s(t) = \left\{ \int_0^t \left[\exp \lambda \int_0^u (1 + \rho x(v)/m\lambda)dv \right] \rho x(u)du + s(0) \right\}$$

$$\cdot \exp\left\{ -\lambda \int_0^t (1 + \rho x(u)/m\lambda)du \right\}.$$

In comparing the Vidale-Wolfe model with our catalog of phenomena, we find that it has different rise and decay times in good agreement with P1. Steady state response, however, is concave, cannot be S-shaped and has zero sales at zero advertising. This is not the flexibility called for by P2. The model does not consider competitive advertising in disagreement with P3. No explicit provision is made for changes in copy or media effectiveness as required by P4, although ρ could be made to perform some of that role. The temporary sales increases of P5 are not handled. The exponential impulse response corresponds weakly to Figures 10 and 11.

Nerlove/Arrow. In a 1962 study of advertising dynamics Nerlove and Arrow [43] employ the term "goodwill," which "summarizes the effects of current and past advertising outlays on demand." Let A = stock of goodwill (dollars), x = advertising rate (dol/period), $\dot{A} = dA/dt$ (dol/period), δ = goodwill depreciation rate (1/period). They postulate that growth and decay of goodwill behave according to

$$\dot{A} = x - \delta A \qquad (6)$$

Goodwill, price and other variables affect sales. Let p = price (dol/unit), z = variables uncontrolled by the firm, $s = s(p, A, z)$ = sales rate (units/period). The authors' purpose is to investigate mathematical conditions required of optimal policies under various circumstances.

Our interest is in sales response. Since sales is presumably a monotone transformation of goodwill, the shape of rectangular, impulse and steady state response for sales will closely depend on that for goodwill. Response to a rectangular advertising input, $x(t) = x$ for $0 \le t \le T$ and $x(t) = 0$ for $t > T$ is

$$A(t) = \begin{cases} A(0)e^{-\delta t} + (x/\delta)[1 - e^{-\delta t}] & 0 \le t \le T \\ A(T)e^{-\delta(t-T)} & T \le t \end{cases} \qquad (7)$$

Incremental response to an impulse of X dollars administered at $t = 0$ is exponential:

$$\Delta A(t) = A(t) - A(0)e^{-\delta t} = Xe^{-\delta t} \qquad 0 < t \qquad (8)$$

Steady state response to constant $x(t) = x$ is linear:

$$A(\infty) = x/\delta \qquad (9)$$

At a later stage of their paper, Nerlove and Arrow investigate the constant elasticity response function, $s = kp^{-\eta}A^{\beta}z^{\xi}$, which, for present purposes, can be written

$$s(t) = kA(t)^{\beta} \qquad (10)$$

with $\beta < 1$ for meaningful functions. Figure 15 sketches rectangular, impulse, and steady state sales responses.

The Nerlove-Arrow model views advertising as piling up goodwill, which continuously leaks away. The current stock of goodwill drives a steady state response function, exemplified as a constant elasticity model. The process is somewhat similar to the Vidale-Wolfe model but the latter differentiates between rise and decay, whereas Nerlove-Arrow does not, since one constant, δ, governs both processes. Thus the model fails on the key phenomenon P1. The constant elasticity model for steady state response has the problem of zero sales at zero advertising and lacks the possibility of an S-shape, thereby lacking the flexibility of P2. There is no consideration of competition (P3), changing effectiveness (P4), or temporary sales increases (P5). With appropriate changes of functions and parameters, most likely P2–P4 could be accommodated but not P1 or P5. The authors give no empirical evidence for their model.

Lanchester Models. We shall give the name Lanchester to a flexible class of competitive marketing models that have a strong resemblance to Lanchester's models of warfare. The basic idea was introduced in 1957 by Kimball [25]. A model of this form has also been considered by Deal and Zionts [13] and a closely related discrete-time version by Schmalensee [57]. We concentrate on a basic two-competitor case and later point out certain generalizations. Let s_1 = sales rate of brand 1 (units/period), s_2 = sales rate of brand 2 (units/period), x_1 = advertising rate of brand 1 (dol/period), x_2 = advertising rate of brand 2 (dol/period), ρ_1 = advertising effectiveness constant of brand 1 (dol^{-1}), ρ_2 = advertising effectiveness constant of brand 2 (dol^{-1}) and m = total market sales rate (units/period):

$$s_1 + s_2 = m. \qquad (11)$$

The basic Lanchester model is

$$\dot{s}_1 = \rho_1 x_1 s_2 - \rho_2 x_2 s_1$$

$$\dot{s}_2 = \rho_2 x_2 s_1 - \rho_1 x_1 s_2. \qquad (12)$$

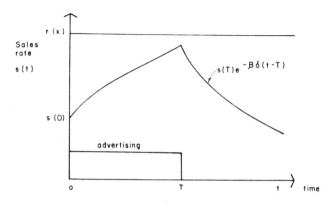

(a) Response to rectangular pulse of advertising has upward and downward movement linked through δ.

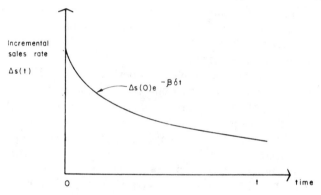

(b) Impulse response to sharp pulse at $t = 0$ is an exponential decay.

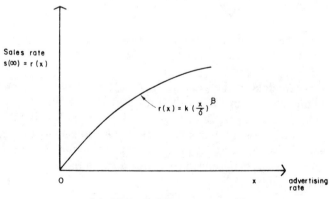

(c) Steady state response is concave ($\beta < 1$) with zero intercept.

Figure 15. Nerlove-Arrow model: Sales response to advertising with constant elasticity response function.

Thus, Company 1 wins sales proportional to its advertising and to Company 2's sales. At the same time Company 1 is losing sales proportional to its own sales and Company 2's advertising. The situation is entirely symmetric for Company 2. The coefficients ρ_1 and ρ_2 permit different advertising dollar efficiencies due to copy, media buying, and other product and market characteristics.

A number of interesting properties of the model emerge from simple analyses. First, we make the substitutions:

$$s_2 = m - s_1 \tag{13a}$$

$$\rho = \rho_1 m \tag{13b}$$

$$\lambda = \rho_2 x_2. \tag{13c}$$

Dropping the now redundant subscript 1, we obtain $\dot{s} = \rho x[1 - (s/m)] - \lambda s$, which is just the Vidale-Wolfe model. Thus, the Lanchester equations (12) form a competitive generalization of Vidale-Wolfe. Note that the decay constant of the Vidale-Wolfe model is now expressed in terms of the competitor's advertising rate.

It follows that, for the case of fixed competitive advertising, appropriate substitutions into (2) to (5) give the rectangular pulse, impulse, and steady state responses and Figure 14 portrays their shapes. The case of time-varying advertising and/or time-varying competitive advertising converts into a first order differential equation which can be solved explicitly if desired.

The steady state response functions help build intuition about the competitive effects of advertising. Solving (11) and (12) yields

$$s_1 = m(\rho_1 x_1)/(\rho_1 x_1 + \rho_2 x_2)$$
$$s_2 = m(\rho_2 x_2)/(\rho_1 x_1 + \rho_2 x_2). \tag{14}$$

Of great interest is the property that one company's response function depends on another company's advertising rate. This is sketched in Figure 16.

Response models of the general type us/(us + them) are well known. In particular Friedman [15] Mills [40] and Bell, Keeney and Little [6] study them. These papers refer to generalizations to N competitors, other functions of advertising, various game theoretic issues, and generalizations beyond advertising. A straightforward expansion of (12) to N competitors with x_j generalized to $x_j^{\zeta_j}$ produces a model with many of the requested phenomena:

$$\dot{s}_i = \rho_i x_i^{\zeta_i} \sum_{j \neq i} s_j - (\sum_{j \neq i} \rho_j x_j^{\zeta_j}) s_i \qquad i = 1, \cdots, N \tag{15}$$

$$\sum_{j=1}^{N} s_j = m. \tag{16}$$

In steady state

$$s_i = m\rho_i x_i^{\epsilon_i}/\sum_{j=1}^{N} \rho_j x_j^{\epsilon_j} \qquad i = 1, \cdots, N \qquad (17)$$

The response function (17) is quite versatile, being S-shaped in x_i for $\epsilon_i > 1$ and concave for $0 \le \epsilon_i \le 1$. Thus, if we think of the ρ_i as carrying media and copy effectiveness, the Lanchester model (15–17) displays phenomena P1–P4 except for nonzero sales at zero advertising. The latter might be treated, at least in principle, by an additive constant. Or, expressed another way, we could say in this and other models that we are dealing with the "advertising affectable market." The model does not display P5, erosion of incremental sales under constant advertising.

A further generalization would be to make each brand's advertising differentially effective against each other brand, e.g., change $\rho_i x_i^{\epsilon_i}$'s, to

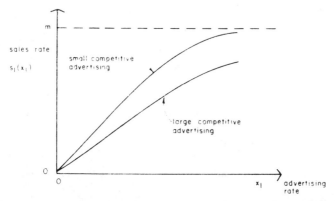

Figure 16. Steady state sales response is affected by competitive advertising in a Lanchester model.

$\rho_i x_i^{\epsilon_i} s_j$. Another feature would be to let the total market size m depend on total industry advertising.

Brandaid. Little [34] presents a general, flexible structure for modeling the effect of the marketing-mix on company sales. The advertising submodel works as follows. Let t = time in discrete units (periods), $s(t)$ = brand sales rate (units/period), $a(t)$ = brand advertising rate (index), $r(a)$ = long run (steady-state) advertising response (units/period) and $\alpha(a)$ = carry-over constant. Customer purchases are presumed to have persistence so that current sales are a weighted combination of previous sales and long run response.

$$s(t) = \alpha s(t - 1) + (1 - \alpha)r(a(t)). \qquad (18)$$

Steady state response is arbitrary; in particular, it can be S-shaped and have a nonzero origin as sketched in Figure 17. The burden of calibration is placed on the user. In applications to date some companies have made empirical measurements that guide the setting of $r(a)$ and some have used managerial judgment or a mix of the two.

The model anticipates that media and copy effectiveness may vary over time. Advertising consists of *messages* delivered to individuals by *exposures* in *media* paid for by *dollars*. These ideas are modeled by

advertising rate
$\qquad$ = (copy effectiveness) × (media efficiency) × (spending rate).

Let $h(t)$ be copy effectiveness, $k(t)$ media efficiency, $x(t)$ spending rate, and h_0, k_0 and x_0 normalizing constants for these quantities. Then the advertising rate, $a(t)$, is given by

$$a(t) = h(t)k(t)x(t)/h_0k_0x_0. \qquad (19)$$

This quantity can drive the response function or, as a further embellish-

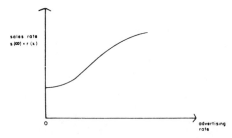

Figure 17. The Brandaid advertising submodel accommodates arbitrary steady state response curves, e.g., an S-shaped curve with nonzero intercept.

ment, a weighted combination of current and past advertising can be used. A simple exponential smoothing model is

$$\hat{a}(t) = \beta\hat{a}(t-1) + (1-\beta)a(t) \qquad (20)$$

where $\hat{a}(t)$ is the effective advertising at t and β is a carryover constant for advertising exposure (units of fraction/period, $0 \leq \beta \leq 1$).

Brandaid treats copy changes by letting a coefficient that multiplies advertising spending vary with time. The same approach can be applied to most of the other models discussed in this paper. The technique seems appropriate for copy changes that communicate the same information better, for example, by using a more attention-getting format or providing a better demonstration of product attributes. Such changes make the advertising dollar go further and so can be considered to affect the scaling of the advertising axis of the sales response curve. On the other hand, copy changes that reposition the product and appeal to different groups of people or suggest new uses affect the sales axis. The basic sales potential of the product may go up or down. This is not modeled explicitly in Brandaid or any other model discussed here, but such a step might be a good one.

We see, therefore, that the Brandaid advertising model meets the criteria of flexibility in dynamic and steady state response (P1, P2) and treats changing effectiveness (P4) to the extent of a changing coefficient. The Brandaid paper also presents a way to model competition that lends itself well to calibration by managerial judgment in decision calculus style but seems less suited to our purposes here. The model has no mechanism for handling the temporary sales increase phenomenon P5.

We now search for unification and show that the previous three models are special cases of Brandaid; or, if you prefer, the previous models have gone out on a limb with specific postulates where Brandaid has refused to make commitments.

Consider first the Vidale-Wolfe model. We convert it to discrete time by the approximation

$$\dot{s} \cong [s(t) - s(t - h)]/h \qquad (21)$$

where h is a small interval of time. Taking the time unit equal to h (i.e. setting $h = 1$) and defining

$$\alpha(x) = 1/[1 + \lambda + (\rho x/m)] \qquad (22a)$$

$$r(x) = (\rho x/\lambda m)/[1 + (\rho x/\lambda m)] \qquad (22b)$$

we obtain, by substituting (21) and (22) into (1) and rearranging, $s(t) = \alpha(x)s(t - 1) + [1 - \alpha(x)]r(x)$. This is just the Brandaid advertising model with $a(t) = x(t)$, the spending rate. Notice in (22) that $0 < \alpha < 1$ and that $r(x)$ is indeed the steady state response of the Vidale-Wolfe model.

The implications of the relation between the two models are several. First, by appropriate specification of $\alpha(x)$, Brandaid can have different rise and decay times. Second, the Brandaid advertising model turns into "our brand" of a two-brand discrete time Lanchester model through substitution of (13b) and (13c) into (22). N competitor generalizations are also possible so that in fact the Lanchester model (15) can be cast into the same form.

The Nerlove-Arrow model in discrete time is a special case too. Set $\alpha = 0$ in (18), suppress $h(t)$ and $k(t)$ in (19) and drive the response function (18) with the effective advertising $\hat{a}(t)$ of (20). Effective advertising corresponds to Nerlove and Arrow's goodwill.

Finally, we note two straightforward generalizations of the lag structure. For (18) $s(t) = \sum_{i=1}^{\infty} \alpha_i s(t - i) + (1 - \sum_{i=1}^{\infty} \alpha_i)r(a(t))$, and for (20) $\hat{a}(t) = \sum_{i=0}^{\infty} \beta_i a(t - i)$ where $\sum_{i=0}^{\infty} \beta_i = 1$. These generalizations are not

especially parsimonious as each added parameter puts more burden on
calibration. A situation in which additional sales lags might be desired is
when sales are measured by factory shipments so that the distribution
pipelines put delays between customer purchase and point of measurement.

Other Models. The literature contains a variety of other a priori
models, a number of which we report here.

Sasieni [54] postulates sales dynamics in the form $\dot{s} = g(s, x, t)$ where
g is a known function that increases with advertising, x, and decreases
with sales, s ($\partial g/\partial x \geq 0$, $\partial g/\partial s \leq 0$). Vidale-Wolfe (1) is a special case.
Schmalensee [56] goes a step further by postulating that, at every
moment, there is an equilibrium demand toward which actual sales are
moving. Equilibrium demand corresponds to our steady state sales rate
with the addition that, in principle, the equilibrium point can change
with time. In our notation, let $r = r(x, p, t)$ be the steady state sales rate
as a function of advertising, x, price, p, and possibly t. Schmalensee
investigates $\dot{s} = F[r(x, p, t), s(t)]$ and assumes $\partial F/\partial r > 0$ and $\partial F/\partial s < 0$.
Again, Vidale-Wolfe can be cast in this form, using (1) and (3): $\dot{s} =$
$[\lambda/(1 - r/m)](r - s)$.

The Brandaid advertising model fits into Sasieni's form but not quite
into Schmalensee's. In continuous time Brandaid becomes

$$\dot{s} = \gamma(x)[r(x) - s] \tag{23}$$

where $\gamma(x) = \lim_{h \to 0}[1 - \alpha(x)]/h$ is the carryover function converted to a
decay factor. The existence of $\gamma(x)$ keeps (23) from being in Schmalensee's
form.

Sasieni and Schmalensee each have as a goal the characterization of
optimal policies and so make as few assumptions as possible about
response. This leads to very general formulations. Both are quite flexible
on·response upward and downward and on the shape of steady response.
At the same time this means they specify relatively little about the
mechanisms of advertising. Sasieni does not explicitly consider competition. Schmalensee introduces it only to the extent of formally indicating
a competitive advertising variable in the equilibrium demand function.

A variety of generalizations and modifications of the Vidale-Wolfe and
Nerlove-Arrow models have been proposed. Mann [37] generalizes the
Nerlove-Arrow exponential weighting of past advertising for determining
goodwill to more arbitrary weightings. Sethi, Turner and Newman [61]
do approximately the same thing to Vidale-Wolfe. They introduce a
variable termed market attitude determined by present and past advertising. Current advertising is thereby replaced in the model by a linearly
weighted combination of present and past advertising.

Sethi [60] proposes a model $\dot{s} = \rho \log x - \lambda s$ which exchanges the

Vidale-Wolfe sales saturation process in (1) for a log function. Steady state response now becomes the strictly concave function $s = (\rho/\lambda)\log x$. From the point of view of our catalog of phenomena this has about the same advantages and disadvantages as Vidale-Wolfe except for the added drawback that the log model makes no sense at zero advertising. Burdet and Sethi [10] also present a discrete time model of Brandaid form with linear steady state response, an undesirable feature.

In the early and mid-1960s researchers created many speculative and often interesting models. Kuehn [27] presents a general marketing mix model motivated by the linear learning description of brand switching. Viewed as an advertising response model, sales consist of a retained fraction of past sales plus new input. The new input is linear in the brand's share of total advertising and in the brand's share of various interaction functions between advertising and other marketing variables. Shakun [62] gives a competitive model in which a firm's market share is share of total advertising but each firm's expenditure is weighted by its market share from the previous period. Industry sales of the product category are a saturating function of effective industry advertising. This in turn is a weighted combination of past effective advertising and new spending, diminished possibly by the spending on competing categories of products. Gupta and Krishnan [19] define effective advertising as a linear weighting of past advertising. Then, in a competitive model, market share equals company share of total effective advertising.

These models are all competitive and so satisfy our phenomenon P3. However, from the vantage point of today, they lack flexibility in rise and decay rate (P1) and have rather inflexible concave steady state response functions (P2).

In a totally different direction of development, Tapiero [68] studies a diffusion model of sales response to advertising. The model views sales as uncertain and the result of a stochastic process. However, the underlying response dynamics are basically Vidale-Wolfe. In still another approach Gould [18] describes the advertising process as a diffusion of information among individuals. His resulting differential equation is identical to Vidale-Wolfe.

Econometric Models

Whereas one group of researchers has proposed and promoted a priori models, another has embraced specific data bases and applied econometric methods to them. Parsons and Schultz [47] describe many of the techniques. The amount of econometric work is large. Clarke [11] finds more than 70 studies and, at that, restricts himself to those amenable to inferences about the cumulative effect of advertising. Lambin [30] alone analyzes 107 brands and reports 291 regressions.

Such studies take the historical data as it comes. The data may or may not contain sufficiently clean changes in advertising to draw solid inferences. Notice that most of our earlier examples of advertising phenomena were drawn from field experiments. It is easier to identify specific effects by direct manipulations than by sifting through the historical record with an econometric sieve. The drawback of experiments, of course, is that they require considerable effort to mount.

Most of the econometric studies use models that are linear or linear in the logarithms of the variables, with or without lagging some of them. Simultaneous equation models are common. Researchers add explanatory variables as available, e.g., other marketing activities, economic indicators, and dummy variables for special circumstances. We examine several major classes of econometric work, focusing, however, only on the advertising response models therein.

Linear in Advertising. Let s_t = sales in period t (sales units). x_t = advertising in period t (dollars). a_i, b_i = constants. A parsimonious linear model used, for example, by Bass and Clarke [3] is:

$$s_t = a_0 + \sum_{i=0}^{L} b_i x_{t-i} \qquad (24)$$

The model has a linear steady state response, given by $s = a_0 + (\sum b_i)x$ and an arbitrary impulse response, represented by the coefficients: b_0, b_i, $\cdots$, b_L (Figure 18).

A related model, used by Palda [44] and others, includes previous sales as well as advertising as explanatory variables.

$$s_t = a_0 + a_1 s_{t-1} + b_0 x_t \qquad (25)$$

Meaningful values of a_1 are in (0, 1). This model also has a linear steady state response function, $s = [a_0/(1 - a_1)] + [b_0/(1 - a_1)]x$, and an exponential (geometric) impulse response with nth term $b_0 a_1^n$.

The two models differ considerably in statistical estimation properties, a fact which has generated considerable discussion (Houston and Weiss [24]) but from our point of view they are similar, since model (25) can be put into the form of (24) with $L = \infty$ by successive substitutions. We note that either model can be cast into the Brandaid format of (18).

These models contain very few of the advertising phenomena described earlier. Linear response is not credible over an indefinite range and obviously fails the requirements of P2.

The impulse response of (24) is versatile but rise times and decay times between steady state levels are essentially the same. To see this, observe that, if sales are in steady state under advertising rate x and we increase the rate by Δ, then n periods later sales will be incremented by $\Delta(\sum_{i=0}^{n} b_i)$. If, after establishing steady state at the new higher advertising, we decrease advertising by Δ back to x, then n periods later sales will be reduced by $\Delta(\sum_{i=0}^{n} b_i)$, the same amount. This is sketched in Figure 19. Thus linear models fail phenomenon P1.

Linear models have been extended to include competitive advertising variables. (See, for example, Picconi and Olson [49] Model 5.) This is desirable but, of course, does not circumvent the difficulties already discussed. We also note that Box-Jenkins model building techniques,

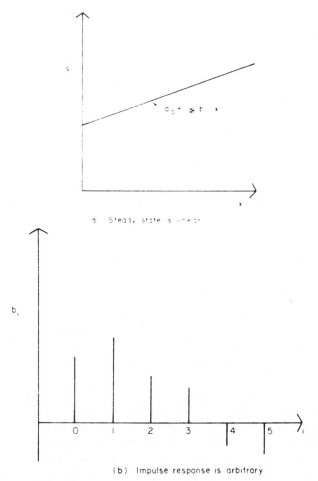

(b) Impulse response is arbitrary

Figure 18. Steady state and impulse response of linear model (24).

although quite different in approach from standard econometric methods, produce models that are linear, or possibly product form (Helmer and Johansson [22]).

Product form Models. Many writers use models of the form

$$s_t = a_0 \prod_{i=0}^{L} x_{t-i}^{b_i} \qquad (26a)$$

which, after taking logs, becomes linear in the constants:

$$\ln s_t = \ln a_0 + \sum_{i=0}^{L} b_i \ln x_{t-i}. \tag{26b}$$

A lagged sales term may be added:

$$s_t = a_0 s_{t-1}^{a_1} \prod_{i=0}^{L} x_{t-i}^{b_i} \tag{27}$$

and sometimes more than one. Logs again linearize the expression with respect to the constants and thereby greatly simplify the task of estimating them from data. Models (26) and (27) are analogs of the linear (24) and (25). The product form is widely used. Examples may be found, for instance, in Montgomery and Silk [41] and many in Lambin [30].

Product form models have an obvious defect, namely, zero advertising produces zero sales and, if lagged advertising terms are included, zero advertising in any lagged period produces zero sales in the current period. The situation is particularly acute for applications with short period

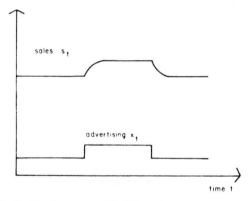

Figure 19. In the linear model (24) and product form model (26) a rapid rise time also means a rapid decay time.

lengths (e.g., months or weeks), since zero advertising in such intervals is quite common. A constant can be added to the advertising variable but an a priori constant represents a strong assumption about the shape of the response function and letting the calibration pick the constant loses the advantages of linearity for estimation (Naert and Weverbergh [42]).

Models in product form fail to conform to our required phenomena in other ways. S-shaped response is precluded. Rise and decay from steady state involve symmetric factors. Thus in (26) if sales are in steady state with advertising x and a jump of Δ is made in advertising, then n periods later sales will be multiplied by a factor $(1 + (\Delta/x))^K$ where $K = \sum_{i=0}^{n} b_i$. If, after reaching steady state with advertising of $x + \Delta$, advertising is reduced to x, then n periods later sales will be divided by the same factor.

Thus we conclude that the usual product form models fail to exhibit the key phenomena P1 and P2.

Models Additive in Nonlinear Functions of Advertising. A number of writers (e.g. Lambin [29]), have used models like (24) with the change that x_t is the share of advertising, i.e., $x_t = $ (brand advertising in t)/(sum of advertising of all brands in t). Often this is coupled with s_t changed to market share. A model of this type satisfies two important goals: it is nonlinear in brand advertising and contains competitive effects. However, the simple share approach does not permit competitors to have different effectiveness and is rather rigid in its nonlinearity. For example, it cannot be S-shaped and so fails P2.

A variant is to use relative advertising, i.e.. the denominator of x_t excludes the brand's own advertising (e.g. Clarke [12]). Also product forms are sometimes used. However, the drawbacks cited above remain. In other cases (Palda [44], Picconi and Olson [49]), equation (25) is used with x_t equal the log of advertising in t. This produces diminishing returns but cannot be S-shaped, has symmetrical rise and decay times, and loses meaning at zero advertising.

Simultaneous Equation Models. A serious problem arises in analyzing historical data because many companies set their advertising budgets, at least in part, on the basis of sales. If the direction of causality between advertising and sales is partly reversed, biased and spurious results can occur (Schmalensee [56]). The problem is potentially quite acute in annual time series data, but such data may have irreparable difficulties anyway in the form of aggregation biases, as discussed by Clarke [11]. Montgomery and Silk [41] argue that simultaneity problems are slight for time periods of, say, a month because companies do not react to competitive advertising on a month-to-month basis. Silk, in private communication, suggests that a more serious simultaneity problem arises in cross-sectional studies because of companies' geographic allocation rules.

In any case, simultaneous equation methods have been brought to bear on sales-advertising time series. Bass [2] and Bass and Parsons [4], for example, use the technique. However, the advertising response models generally used in the equation systems are product form. As a result they have the problems already discussed.

What can we conclude? First, most of the commonly used econometric models of sales response to advertising do not have structures that will accommodate the set of the dynamic phenomena identified earlier. These models are particularly weak in flexibility of shape for the response curve and in allowing different rise and decay rates. None of the models consider phenomenon, P5: sales increases under increased advertising decay with constant advertising. However, a model-builder would be unlikely to hypothesize this phenomenon without experimental evidence like that provided by Haley.

To this writer the standard econometric forms (24 27) are not so much models of advertising as convenient functions fit to the advertising response process in the neighborhood of historical operations. Such a fitting process may be useful. For example a linear model might well be reasonable if the data do not contain a large enough variance in advertising to permit meaningful calibration of a nonlinear model. The coefficient from a linear statistical model might be combined with estimates from other sources about the effects of very large or very small advertising rates to calibrate a decision model. However, the purpose of building the statistical model would then be quite different from our objectives here, which are to find the structure of advertising response that might appropriately be incorporated into the decision model.

The sheer volume of econometric work has led to some empirical generalizations. For example Clarke [11] makes a convincing case for a short term effect of advertising on the order of a few months. He also challenges certain empirically based arguments for long run effects by arguing that they are artifacts of the time period used in the econometric work. Lambin [30] also draws generalizations from his massive study, although some are not entirely persuasive. For example, he says that there is no S-curve because product form and logarithmic models fit better than linear ones. This seems an insufficient argument and, indeed, he seems to contradict himself by later advocating the existence of threshold effects.

A Priori Models with Calibration

A number of researchers have taken the approach of defining advertising models rather independently of standard econometric forms and then devising means to calibrate them on specific historical data bases. This is an important direction of research, although, as with all nonexperimental data, the researcher is dependent on historical variations to make measurement possible. Furthermore, most of the more elaborate models are nonlinear in some of the parameters. This introduces a host of calibration problems, not the least of which is the assessment of the quality of the parameter estimates.

Kuehn, McGuire and Weiss [28] present an early and ambitious example of an a priori model calibrated on historical data. Let s_{it} = market share of brand i in time period t, p_{it} = price of brand i in t, x_{it} = advertising spending of brand i in t and a_{it} = effective advertising in t.

Unknown constants are: α, β = carryover constants for sales and advertising, b = weighting constant reflecting amount of sales not affected by advertising, ϵ = advertising sensitivity exponent, δ = price sensitivity exponent, e_i = brand i advertising effectiveness coefficient and k_i = brand i effectiveness coefficient due to other marketing activities.

$$s_{it} = \alpha s_{i,t-1} + (1 - \alpha)\{bk_i p_{it}^{-\delta}/\sum_j k_j p_{jt}^{-\delta}$$

$$+ (1 - b)k_i p_{it}^{-\delta}a_{it}^\epsilon/\sum_j k_j p_{jt}^{-\delta}a_{jt}^\epsilon\} \tag{28a}$$

$$a_{it} = \beta a_{i,t-1} + (1 - \beta)e_i x_{it} \tag{28b}$$

$$\sum s_{jt} = 1. \tag{28c}$$

By means of nonlinear estimation on historical time series the authors determine twelve constants required in their particular case.

The model has several interesting features. Its general form is that of (18), the Brandaid advertising submodel, but with price effects imbedded in it. The steady state response function is in the braces { } and is essentially the steady state of a Lanchester model with an additive term representing sales at zero advertising. Response can be either S-shaped or concave. It is interesting to note that the fitted value of ϵ was 2.57 so that response is S-shaped in the authors' application. Effective advertising is an exponentially smoothed function of spending (28b). The constraint (28c) forces the market shares to add to one in the model and is an integral part of the estimation. The model contains many, although not all, of the phenomena laid out earlier as desirable.

Horsky [23] builds an interesting model and calibrates it on cigarette data. He considers a two competitor case, one competitor being the brand of interest and the other the rest of the industry. Let s_{it} = market share of Competitor i in period t, x_{it} = advertising spending of Competitor i in t, a_{it} = effective advertising or goodwill of Competitor i in t, β_i = carryover constant for advertising and ρ_i = effectiveness constant for advertising.

Horsky's model for Competitor 1 is $s_{1t} - s_{1,t-1} = \rho_1 a_{1t}s_{2t} - \rho_2 a_{2t}s_{1t}$ with a symmetric equation for Competitor 2. Effective advertising is given by $a_{it} = \beta_i a_{i,t-1} + (1 - \beta_i)x_{it}$, $i = 1, 2$. In our terminology this is a two-competitor Lanchester model in discrete time driven by exponentially weighted past advertising. It can have different rise and decay rates, thereby satisfying phenomenon P1. The steady state response is somewhat inflexible, being concave and having zero sales at zero advertising. Nevertheless, the model is a considerable step up in complexity from most current econometric models and nonlinear estimation is required.

Parsons [46] tackles the problem of time varying advertising effectiveness. Armed with sales and advertising data for a household cleaner from 1886 to 1905 he adds a time varying coefficient to a standard product-form econometric model and finds the change in advertising effectiveness over the product life cycle. Again, nonlinear estimation is required. Pekelman and Tse [48] model copy wearout and replacement as a time-varying coefficient in a Lanchester-like competitive model and track the coefficient with Kalman filter techniques. Turner and Wiginton [69] use nonlinear techniques to calibrate the Vidale-Wolfe model on aggregate industry sales and advertising for filter cigarettes.

These examples show that, when researchers abandon the estimation conveniences of standard econometric models, they can build more realistic models and calibrate them using nonlinear methods.

4. CONCLUSIONS

We have reviewed a large amount of material on the sales effects of advertising for established products. What can we now say about representing these processes with models?

A first conclusion is that advertising is rich with phenomena. We are dealing with communication and its influence on purchase behavior. Perhaps it is presumptuous to expect a regularity that can be reduced to models with only a few parameters. Yet measurements have brought out many recurrent characteristics: an upward response of sales that takes place soon after increased advertising; a relatively slower sales decay on withdrawal that we attribute to customer satisfaction; sales saturation at high advertising levels; a possible threshold-like effect at low levels; a change of effectiveness over time because of media and copy changes; a loss of sales due to competitive advertising; and an effect reported by Haley that an advertising increase sometimes brings only a temporary sales increase. The magnitude and timing of all these effects are of great practical interest in making advertising decisions.

At the same time many other effects remain to be discovered and understood. The S-shaped curve is still on shaky ground. Is pulsing an effective policy and, if so, how long should pulses last? Does the S-shaped curve (essentially a static notion) provide an adequate theory for deriving optimal pulsing policies? What about the reported phenomenon that advertising is more effective when sales are increasing? More measurement and understanding are called for.

A second conclusion is that, although we have an apparent richness of models, many of them are rearrangements of a few key ideas. The Vidale-Wolfe constructs are surviving well, even though generalizations of the original model are very much in order. The competitive Lanchester generalization in which advertising rate is raised to a power looks quite versatile at the moment. It needs a change that will permit positive sales at zero advertising but this could be achieved by defining a component of sales not affected by advertising. The Lanchester model can be used in differential equation form or put in discrete time, in which case it would be compatible with the Brandaid advertising submodel.

We have introduced copy and media effectiveness as a multiplier on spending, and have pointed out that extensions are needed to let copy affect total sales potential. Nowhere have we presented a model for phenomenon, P5, the temporary increase in sales under a permanent increase in advertising. A parsimonious adaptation of a new trier model might help here.

A third conclusion, and possibly a controversial one, is that the commonly used econometric models are of limited value in advertising. Their functional forms generally fail to represent advertising processes except possibly over a limited range. Add to this the problems of collinearity, autocorrelation and simultaneity; an approach that initially appeared easy for learning about advertising by applying standard tools to widely available historical data begins to look more difficult. We should specify more realistic a priori models and calibrate them using the nonlinear and robust estimation tools that are now becoming generally available.

Fourth, we observe that, at least in the literature, there is an underuse of separate calibrations for different parts of a model. Particularly for decision making, we must include in our models all the phenomena that affect the decision. This will often lead to calibrating the model in several parts from eclectic data sources.

Looking ahead, new developments in measurement offer the possibility of resolving some of the outstanding modeling issues. The potential of field experiments is by no means exhausted, although field experiments and historical analysis operating on aggregate data are likely to remain fairly blunt instruments and the greatest opportunities may lie in collecting information at the individual level. Laboratory measurements analogous to those done by Silk and Urban [63] on new product communication are likely to be helpful. Even more promising is the data spinoff of point-of-sale equipment in retail stores. Such equipment can record individual purchases in machine-readable form. Optical scanning of the Universal Product Code for grocery products is one example, and analogous equipment is penetrating department stores. The sheer quantity of data will challenge our computing and analytic resources, but therein lies the potential. The coupling of individual purchase information with observations of media exposure should permit ongoing response measurements of the type pioneered by McDonald [38] and discussed earlier. Individual level measurements also seem required to examine hypotheses being generated from behavioral science (Sawyer and Ward [55]).

At the same time, the measurements must be tied into models. Some of the current structures for describing individual choice behavior appear to be extendable to consider advertising. We note that logit models (e.g. McFadden [39]) are rather similar in form to the steady state of a Lanchester model. Maximum likelihood calibration is available. Hauser [21] provides model testing methods. In another needed direction Givon and Horsky [17] have started to study issues that arise in going from disaggregate to aggregate models.

Much remains to be done. In the next 5 to 10 years there will be abundant opportunities for understanding advertising processes better and putting this knowledge to work in improving marketing productivity.

ACKNOWLEDGMENTS

The author thanks Gary Lilien, Leonard Lodish, Richard Schmalensee, Hermann Simon and Alvin Silk for many helpful comments.

REFERENCES

1. R. L. ACKOFF AND J. R. EMSHOFF, "Advertising Research at Anheuser-Busch, Inc. (1963–68)," *Sloan Management Rev.* **16**, 1–16 (1975).
2. F. M. BASS, "A Simultaneous Equation Regression Study of Advertising and Sales of Cigarettes," *J. Marketing Res.* **6**, 291–300 (1969).
3. F. M. BASS AND D. G. CLARKE, "Testing Distributed Lag Models of Advertising Effect," *J. Marketing Res.* **9**, 298–308 (1972).
4. F. M. BASS AND L. J. PARSONS, "Simultaneous-Equation Regression Analysis of Sales and Advertising," *Appl. Econ.* **1**, 103–124 (1969).
5. J. C. BECKNELL, JR., AND R. W. MCISAAC, "Test Marketing Cookware Coated with Teflon," *J. Advertising Res.* **3**, 2–8 (1963).
6. D. E. BELL, R. L. KEENEY AND J. D. C. LITTLE, "A Market Share Theorem," *J. Marketing Res.* **12**, 136–141 (1975).
7. B. BENJAMIN, W. P. JOLLY AND J. MAITLAND, "Operational Research and Advertising: Theories of Response," *Opnl. Res. Quart.* **11**, 205–218 (1960).
8. B. BENJAMIN AND J. MAITLAND. "Operational Research and Advertising: Some Experiments in the Use of Analogies," *Opnl. Res. Quart.* **9**, 207–217 (1958).
9. D. BLOOM, A. JAY AND T. TWYMAN, "The Validity of Advertising Pretests," *J. Advertising Res* **17**, 7–16 (1977).
10. C. BURDET AND S. P. SETHI, "On the Maximum Principle for a Class of Discrete Dynamical Systems with Lags," *J. Optimization Theory Application* **19**, 445–453 (1976).
11. D. G. CLARKE, "Econometric Measurement of the Duration of Advertising Effect on Sales," *J. Marketing Res.* **18**, 345–357 (1976).
12. D. G. CLARKE, "Sales-Advertising Cross-Elasticities and Advertising Competition," *J. Marketing Res.* **10**, 250–261 (1973).
13. K. R. DEAL AND S. ZIONTS, "A Differential Game Solution to the Problem of Determining the Optimal Timing of Advertising Expenditures," *Proceedings of the Second Annual Northeast Regional AIDS Conference*, American Institute of Decision Sciences, Atlanta, Ga., 1973.
14. G. J. ESKIN AND P. H. BARRON, "Effects of Price and Advertising in Test-Market Experiments," *J. Marketing Res.* **14**, 499–500 (1977).
15. L. FRIEDMAN, "Game Theory in the Allocation of Advertising Expenditures," *Opns. Res.* **6**, 699–709 (1958).
16. D. H. GENSCH, "A Computer Simulation Model for Selecting Advertising Schedules," *J. Marketing Res.* **6**, 203–214 (1969).
17. M. GIVON AND D. HORSKY, "Market Share Models as Approximators of

Aggregated Heterogeneous Brand Choice Behavior," *Management Sci.* 24, 1404–1416 (1978).

18. J. P. GOULD, "Diffusion Processes and Optimal Advertising Policy," in *Microeconomic Foundations of Employment and Inflation Theory*, E. S. Phelps et al. (eds.), W. W. Norton, New York, 1970.

19. S. K. GUPTA AND K. S. KRISHNAN, "Differential Equation Approach to Marketing," *Opns. Res.* 15, 1030–1039 (1967).

20. R. I. HALEY, "Sales Effects of Media Weight," *J. Advertising Res.* 18, 9–18 (1978).

21. J. R. HAUSER, "Testing the Accuracy, Usefulness, and Significance of Probabilistic Choice Models: An Information-Theoretic Approach," *Opns. Res.* 26, 406–421 (1978).

22. R. M. HELMER AND J. K. JOHANSSON, "An Exposition of the Box-Jenkins Transfer Function Analysis with an Application to the Advertising-Sales Relationship," *J. Marketing Res.* 14, 227–239 (1977).

23. D. HORSKY, "An Empirical Analysis of the Optimal Advertising Policy," *Management Sci.* 23, 1037–1049 (1977).

24. F. S. HOUSTON AND D. L. WEISS. "Cumulative Advertising Effects: The Role of Serial Correlation," *Decision Sci.* 6, 471–481 (1975).

25. G. E. KIMBALL, "Some Industrial Applications of Military Operations Research Methods," *Opns. Res.* 5, 201–204 (1957).

26. H. E. KRUGMAN, "Why Three Exposures May Be Enough," *J. Advertising Res.* 12, 11–14 (1972).

27. A. A. KUEHN, "A Model for Budgeting Advertising," in *Mathematical Models and Methods in Marketing*, F. M. Bass et al. (eds.), Richard D. Irwin, Homewood, Ill., 1961.

28. A. A. KUEHN, T. W. McGUIRE AND D. L. WEISS, "Measuring the Effectiveness of Advertising," in *Science, Technology and Marketing*, R. M. Haas (ed.), American Marketing Association, Chicago, 1966.

29. J.-J. LAMBIN, "A Computer Online Marketing Mix Model," *J. Marketing Res.* 9, 119–126 (1972).

30. J.-J. LAMBIN, *Advertising, Competition and Market Conduct in Oligopoly Over Time*, North Holland, Amsterdam, 1976.

31. J.-J. LAMBIN, P. A. NAERT AND A. BULTEZ, "Optimal Marketing Behavior in Oligopoly," *European Econ. Rev.* 6, 105–128 (1975).

32. G. L. LILIEN, "Model Relativism: A Situational Approach to Model Building," *Interfaces* 5, 11–18 (1975).

33. J. D. C. LITTLE, "A Model of Adaptive Control of Promotional Spending," *Opns. Res.* 14, 1075–1097 (1966).

34. J. D. C. LITTLE, "Brandaid: A Marketing-Mix Model, Parts 1 and 2," *Opns. Res.* 23, 628–673 (1975).

35. J. D. C. LITTLE AND L. M. LODISH, "A Media Planning Calculus," *Opns. Res.* 17, 1–35 (1969).

36. L. M. LODISH, "Empirical Studies on Industrial Response to Exposure Patterns," *J. Marketing Res.* 8, 212–218 (1971).

37. D. H. MANN, "Optimal Theoretic Stock Models; a Generalization of Delayed Response from Promotional Expenditures," *Management Sci.* 21, 823–832 (1975).

38. C. McDonald, "What is the Short-Term Effect of Advertising?" *Proceedings of 1970 ESOMAR Conference*, Barcelona, 1970.
39. D. McFadden, "Conditional Logit Analysis of Qualitative Choice Behavior," in *Frontiers in Econometrics*, P. Zarembka (ed.), Academic Press, New York, 1970.
40. H. D. Mills, "A Study in Promotional Competition," in *Mathematical Models and Methods in Marketing*, F. M. Bass et al. (eds.), Richard D. Irwin, Homewood, Ill., 1961.
41. D. B. Montgomery and A. J. Silk, "Estimating Dynamic Effects of Marketing Communications Expenditures," *Management Sci.* **18,** B485–501 (1972).
42. P. A. Naert and M. Weverbergh, "Multiplicative Models with Zero Values in the Explanatory Variables," working paper, University of Antwerp, 1978.
43. M. Nerlove and K. J. Arrow, "Optimal Advertising Policy under Dynamic Conditions," *Economica* **29,** 129–142 (1962).
44. K. Palda, *The Measurement of Cumulative Advertising Effects*, Prentice-Hall, Englewood Cliffs, N. J., 1964.
45. L. J. Parsons, "A Rachet Model of Advertising Carryover Effects," *J. Marketing Res.* **13,** 76–79 (1976).
46. L. J. Parsons, "The Product Life Cycle and Time-varying Advertising Elasticities," *J. Marketing Res.* **12,** 476–480 (1975).
47. L. J. Parsons and R. L. Schultz, *Marketing Models and Econometric Research*, North Holland, Amsterdam, 1976.
48. D. Pekelman and E. Tse, "Experimentation and Control in Advertising, an Adaptive Control Approach," Wharton School Working Paper 76-04-01, University of Pennsylvania, Philadelphia, 1976.
49. M. J. Picconi and C. L. Olsen, "Advertising Decision Rules in a Multibrand Environment; Optimal Control Theory and Evidence," *J. Marketing Res.* **15,** 82–92 (1978).
50. A. G. Rao, Private Communication, March 1979.
51. A. G. Rao, "Productivity of the Marketing-Mix; Measuring the Impact of Advertising and Consumer and Trade Promotions on Sales," paper presented at ANA Advertising Research Workshop, New York, 1978.
52. A. G. Rao, *Quantitative Theories in Advertising*, John Wiley & Sons, New York, 1970.
53. A. G. Rao and P. B. Miller, "Advertising/Sales Response Functions," *J. Advertising Res.* **15,** 7–15 (1975).
54. M. W. Sasieni, "Optimal Advertising Expenditures," *Management Sci.* **18,** 64–72 (1971).
55. A. Sawyer and S. Ward, "Carryover Effects in Advertising Communication; Evidence and Hypotheses from Behavioral Science," in *Cumulative Advertising Effects: Sources and Implications*, D. G. Clarke (ed.), Report 77–111 Marketing Science Institute, Cambridge, Mass., 1977.
56. R. Schmalensee, *The Economics of Advertising*, North Holland, Amsterdam, 1972.
57. R. Schmalensee, "A Model of Advertising and Product Quality," *J. Political Econ.* **86,** 485–503 (1978).

58. S. P. SETHI, "A Comparison between the Effect of Pulse versus Continuous Television Advertising on Buyer Behavior," in *1971 Combined Proceedings*, F. C. Allvine (ed.), American Marketing Association, Chicago, 1971.

59. S. P. SETHI, "Dynamic Optimal Control Models in Advertising: a Survey," *SIAM Rev.* **19**, 685-725 (1977).

60. S. P. SETHI, "Optimal Control of a Logarithmic Advertising Model," *Opnl. Res. Quart.* **26**, 317-319 (1975).

61. S. P. SETHI, R. E. TURNER AND C. P. NEUMAN, "Policy Implications of an Intertemporal Analysis of Advertising Budgeting Models," in *Proceedings 4th Annual Midwest AIDS Conference*, American Institute of Decision Sciences, Atlanta, Ga., 1973.

62. M. F. SHAKUN, "A Dynamic Model for Competitive Marketing in Coupled Markets," *Management Sci.* **12**, B525-530 (1966).

63. A. J. SILK AND G. L. URBAN, "Pretest Market Evaluation of New Packaged Goods: a Model and Measurement Methodology," *J. Marketing Res.* **15**, 171-191 (1978).

64. J. L. SIMON, "New Evidence for No Effect of Scale in Advertising," *J. Advertising Res.* **9**, 38-41 (1969).

65. M. K. STARR, "OR in Marketing: a Case of Failure and Renewal," in *OR'78*, K. B. Haley (ed.), North Holland, Amsterdam, 1978.

66. E. C. STRONG, "The Use of Field Experimental Observations in Estimating Advertising Recall," *J. Marketing Res.* **11**, 369-378 (1974).

67. W. R. SWINYARD AND M. L. RAY, "Advertising-Selling Interactions: an Attribution Theory Experiment," *J. Marketing Res.* **14**, 509-516 (1977).

68. C. S. TAPIERO, "On-Line and Adaptive Optimum Advertising Control by a Diffusion Approximation," *Opns. Res.* **23**, 890-907 (1975).

69. R. E. TURNER AND J. C. WIGINTON, "Advertising Expenditure Trajectories; an Empirical Study for Filter Cigarettes 1953-1965, *Decision Sci.* **7**, 496-509 (1976).

70. G. L. URBAN, "Building Models for Decision-Makers," *Interfaces*, **4**, 1-11 (1974).

71. M. L. VIDALE AND H. B. WOLFE, "An Operations Research Study of Sales Response to Advertising," *Opns. Res.* **5**, 370-381 (1957).

72. R. S. WEINBERG, *An Analytical Approach to Advertising Expenditure Strategy*, Association of National Advertisers, New York, 1960.

73. A. R. WILDT, "Estimating Seasonal Marketing Response using Dummy Variables," *J. Marketing Res.* **14**, 34-41 (1977).

74. D. R. WITTINK, "Exploring Territorial Differences in the Relationship between Marketing Variables," *J. Marketing Res.* **14**, 145-155 (1977).

75. F. S. ZUFRYDEN, "Media Scheduling; a Stochastic Dynamic Model Approach," *Management Sci.* **18**, B145-154 (1973).

*This review of over 100 studies
concludes that diminishing returns characterize . . .*

THE SHAPE OF THE ADVERTISING RESPONSE FUNCTION

Julian L. Simon and Johan Arndt

The general question before us is: What is the effect, for the firm and for society, of a larger rather than a smaller quantity of advertising? As it is stated, however, this question is extraordinarily vague. And the difficulty of putting the right questions in sufficiently precise fashion is the cause of much of the controversy and confusion about the effect of various quantities of advertising.

As passing evidence of this confusion, the entire topic is often treated under the rubric "economies of scale in advertising," even though the situations being discussed seldom (if ever) fit into the economies-of-scale concept. This concept refers to the outcomes of same-proportion increases in *all* inputs; that is, the proportions of all inputs remain the same as the scale of the firm changes. But when discussing advertising quantities, writers inevitably have in mind either an increase in advertising alone, or an increase in the total scale of the enterprise with changing proportions of inputs. And the advertising-sales ratio that is usually adduced as the relevant measurement is worthless for the purpose at hand.

There are at least five interlocking questions about the effects of various quantities of advertising. Some of these questions affect our judgment of advertising's role in the firm's thinking, and all affect our judgment of advertising's impact on the economy as a whole.

(1) Can an increase in the *physical quantity* of advertising—the number of inches in a printed advertisement or the number of seconds in a television or radio commercial—produce a larger-than-proportional number of units sold?

(2) Can an increase in the *expenditure* for advertising produce a larger-than-proportional number of units sold? Because of quantity discounts, the answer to this question could be "yes" even if the answer to question 1 is "no."

Questions 1 and 2 are important on an everyday basis for business decision makers. They also enter into the social questions to come.

(3) Can a same-proportion increase in *all* factors

Julian L. Simon is professor of economics and marketing at the University of Illinois. He is the author of *Issues in the Economics of Advertising, The Management of Advertising, Basic Research Methods in Social Science, The Economics of Population Growth,* and *Applied Managerial Economics.* He has written numerous other books and articles.

11

of the enterprise—including advertising—produce a larger-than-proportional increase in a brand's sales that is traceable to costs in factory production or transportation? This is a true economies-of-scale question—that is, whether a big firm has an advantage over a small firm due to advertising. (There is some inevitable confusion about whether the factors of production and output are measured in physical or monetary terms. But we feel that clarifying the matter is not worthwhile at this point.)

(4) Can an *increase in the number of brands of the same or related products* sold by the firm—with a same-proportion physical increase in all inputs to the enterprise—produce a larger-than-proportional increase in the firm's sales that is not traceable to cost functions in the factory or transportation? That is, are there economies of multibrand operations due to advertising's role?

(5) The hardest question to properly frame concerns dynamic effects and barriers to entry into the industry. Does the existence of advertising as a competitive tool lead to a smaller number of competitors and higher industrial concentration than would otherwise be found if there were no advertising?

After a brief theoretical discussion of the possible shapes of the response function, we will first examine the evidence relating to the physical advertising response function, and next the findings concerning  the monetary response function. The third question by itself constitutes a voluminous—but separable—question; on the other hand, there is little evidence relevant to questions 4 and 5. We shall therefore limit ourselves to a few notes on these latter three issues at the end of the paper.

We will review both recent and not-so-recent evidence, but the reader who wishes more details

Johan Arndt is professor of business administration at the Norwegian School of Economics and Business Administration, Bergen. A graduate of the Royal Norwegian Naval Academy and the Norwegian School of Economics and Business Administration, he holds an M.S. from the University of Minnesota and a D.B.A. from Harvard University. Dr. Arndt has published articles on marketing management and consumer behavior and is the author of *Word of Mouth Advertising* and *Market Segmentation* and the editor of *Insights into Consumer Behavior*.

about older studies is referred to Simon (1965, 1970) so as to conserve space here. (Other reviews covering chunks of this part of the advertising literature may be found in Schmalensee, 1972; Gensch, 1973; Ray, 1975; Aaker and Myers, 1975; and Lambin, 1976.)

What Is the Shape of the Function?

Advertising response function is here used to refer to the quantitative relationship between some *input* of advertising and some *output* or effect of presumed value for the advertiser. Input measures include size and frequency of ads as well as monetary expenditures on advertising. Output measures include sales effects as well as "intermediate" indicators such as ad recall, attitudes, or intention to buy. The advertising response function may refer to the reaction of a given individual (individual response function) or to the reaction of members of a target group (aggregate response function). (While there are important problems in moving from the individual to the group level [see Rao, 1970], these problems of aggregation are not important for the present review.)

Our survey of the literature shows that almost all writers on advertising subscribe to one or the other of the following two proposed shapes of the response function: (1) the concave-downward function and (2) the S-shaped logistic function. The concave function implying monotonically diminishing returns is shown in Figure 1a. Figure 1b shows the S-shaped advertising response function, which first has increasing returns and then, after an inflection point, diminishing returns.

Each proposed response function implies a theory about how advertising operates. Before contrasting the theoretical rationales for the alternative shapes, let us agree that at *some* conceivable point of very low advertising there must be increasing returns. For example, a television commercial too short to identify brand or advertiser can hardly have any positive results. But let us also agree that the relevant range of the function is that over which firms might seriously consider operating, given the accepted technological and commercial restraints. For example, a television commercial shorter than 10 or 15 seconds may not be within the feasible set of alternatives and need not be considered.

The theoretical root of the concave-downward curve is in the microeconomic "law" of diminishing returns to productive inputs (see, for instance, Stigler, 1966). On an aggregate level, the argument is that as the amount of advertising is increased, the unreached prospects will have progressively weaker

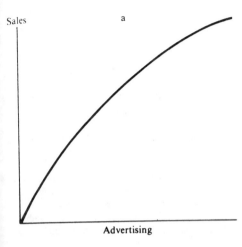

Figure 1
Increasing and Decreasing Returns in Advertising Response Functions

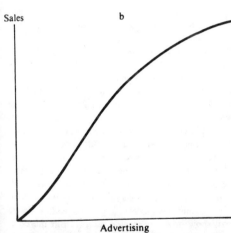

ing returns in manufacturing—indivisibilities of capital goods and organization—is not present to the same extent in advertising. It is true that the minimum of network television time that can be bought is not small in absolute terms, and there are discounts. Advertisers, however, can arrange advertising schedules by purchasing from individual television stations and using regional or local editions of print media in such a fashion that there are no discontinuous jumps from one level of advertising to the next, even in consumer-package-goods advertising.

Despite the above arguments for the concave response function, the great majority of persons interested in advertising—advertising practitioners, media salesmen, economists, and laymen—seem to believe that the advertising response function has an inflection point and is S-shaped. Economists such as Dean (1951), Chamberlin (1962), Comanor and Wilson (1974), and Porter (1976) claim that there are initial increasing returns to scale for advertising. Similarly, some marketing researchers and operations analysts assert that the advertising response curve is S-shaped (Zentler and Ryde, 1956; Vidale and Wolfe, 1957; Rao, 1970).

Psychological arguments are often adduced for the S curve. Sometimes the logistic function is referred to as the "curve of learning." But experimental psychologists have found support for both forms of the curve. Acquisition of complex skills usually can best be described by a concave curve, whereas S-shaped curves have been observed in classical conditioning and in memorizing as well as in the development of skills (Berelson and Steiner, 1964).

Some psychological speculations in favor of the S-shaped response function are based on the notion of a threshold effect. In Chamberlin's (1962) language: "Control of the buyer's consciousness must be gained, and while it is being gained additional expenditure yields increasing returns." Another argument is that "constant repetition would ingrain a stimulus in the mind and eventually lead to a desired effect" (Greenberg and Suttoni, 1973). In the imagery of the advertising-space salesman, the argument is that "You've got to keep dripping the water onto the rock until it cracks."

Krugman's (1965) concept of low-involvement learning may be interpreted as implying an initial threshold for advertising effects. Krugman suggests that consumer response to ads, particularly television ads, may be characterized as passive learning, because much advertising content is learned the same way as is meaningless material. There need not be measurable immediate behavioral or attitudinal effects. Instead, "Stimulus repetition . . . build[s]

buying predispositions (Ozga, 1960). At the level of the individual buyer, the reasoning is that a given message conveys less and less information with each additional exposure (Stigler, 1961). Along this line, Krugman (1972) argues for the special importance of the two or three exposures. He claims that exposure number 1 creates curiosity, number 2 brings recognition, while number 3 clinches a decision; further exposures are said to have little value. This sort of reasoning leads to the hypothesis that there are decreasing returns to both "frequency" and "reach" for advertising.

Furthermore, the most important cause of increas-

a potential for alteration in perceptual structure of advertised brands, i.e., a gradual development of the ability to see the brand differently without being specifically aware of any change'' (Krugman, 1966–1967).

By now it should be clear that there is an abundance of theory, conventional wisdom, and speculation, both economic and psychological, to support a judgment in favor of either an S-shaped or a constant-concave advertising response function. It seems to us that it is not worthwhile to elaborate these theoretical speculations, because inevitably their sum will be inconclusive. Instead we must turn to the data.

The Physical Advertising Response Function

In deciding which empirical studies to review in this and the following section, a key criterion has been whether there are reasonable controls for extraneous and potentially confounding effects. This review distinguishes among three main groups of studies: laboratory experiments, field experiments, and ex post facto studies.

Ideally, a review first presents a representative early bench-mark study in detail and then considers extensions and methodological improvements in subsequent work. On this topic, however, there is little cumulative research. Instead there is little cross referencing, and the literature is fragmented, which constitutes a difficulty for reviewing.

Laboratory Experiments. In a laboratory experiment the researcher can isolate the impact of the advertising variable by manipulating the independent variable and controlling for confounding influences. Yet laboratory experiments have the drawback that the stimulus, response, and setting are far different from market conditions. Also, the use of intermediate variables as measures of effect is questionable because there is little evidence on how such indicators reflect sales or sales opportunities. Therefore, laboratory studies are always weak on *external validity*, generalization of the results to advertising-sales relationships in the world outside the laboratory.

We shall consider the evidence using this (and subsequent) methods, first with respect to increasing *size* of advertisements and then with regard to increasing *repetition*.

Size. Laboratory experiments are unanimous in finding diminishing returns to size (print advertisements) and length (television commercials). The bench-mark study is still that of Strong (1914). Using a dummy magazine, Strong found that recall did not

increase proportionately with the increase in size. The relative recall value for a quarter-page advertisement was 1.0, a half page 1.5, and a full page 2.2. Similar results were found for advertisements that were shown once, twice, and four times at monthly intervals. There is need for new studies using Strong's technique to replicate his results in a wide variety of conditions.

For television commercials ranging from 20 to 60 seconds, Wheatley (1968), Capitman (*Media/Scope,* 1964), Schwerin's theater-lottery method (Hoffman, 1963), and Lodish (1971), reanalyzing Rohloff's (1966) data, all found evidence of sharply diminishing returns. There might, however, be a threshold effect if the time interval in which advertisements are shown is too short for human perception. But in Schwartz's (1975) tachistoscope experiment, the proportion of subjects correctly identifying the brand name rose most at the shortest exposure interval. This suggests that though there *may* be a perception threshold for a given individual, individuals differ sufficiently so that there is no such threshold effect in a *group*.

Repetition. An important ancestor of later experimental advertising repetition studies was Ebbinghaus (1885), who used nonsense syllables as test stimuli, with himself as his only subject. His "acquisition curve" showed that recall increased at a decreasing rate with number of repetitions. A landmark study of advertising in the Ebbinghaus tradition was the well-done experiment by Adams (1916), who worked with dummy magazines containing one, two, or four insertions of the same advertisement. When the same advertisement appeared, there were diminishing returns with repetition. But when different advertisements for the same brands appeared, there were *increasing* returns. Since additional (and different) advertisements may contain new information, it is not implausible that repetition with variation may show initial increasing returns. But more rigorous evidence than the Adams data is needed to test such a hypothesis.

Among the studies on repetition, that of Ray and Sawyer (1971) is the current bench mark because it is the most careful and best controlled. Subjects were told that they were participating in a study of future shopping arrangements via cable television. Then a stream of product advertisements was presented on a screen, with various numbers of exposures for various brands and products. Dependent measures were unaided recall, attitudes toward brands, and purchase intentions. The results showed diminishing returns across numbers of exposure from 0 to 6, a "deviation from a linear trend toward the modified exponential curve of repetition effect on recall . . . very much like the negatively accelerated curve . . . often found for nonsense syllables learning'' (Ray and Sawyer, 1971). The results for the categories of "convenience" and "shopping" goods are shown in Figures 2a and 2b. The smooth curves have been fitted by us to their data points.

Politz's (1960) method of leaving magazines at homes on Monday and Wednesday, then checking recall on Friday, showed conflicting results on various recall measures. Some measures indicated increasing returns, and others indicated decreasing returns. There was a major loophole in this ingenious design, however. Those who received only one magazine received it on Monday, rather than half on Monday and half on Wednesday. Those who received two magazines got them Monday and Wednesday. This meant a longer average time lag between exposure and measurement for the one-magazine group. This study deserves to be repeated with

better controls, because it could produce valuable data.

Studies of repetition in the laboratory using as the dependent variable recall (surveyed by Sawyer, 1974) and intention to buy (Wells and Chinsky, 1965) also do not show increasing returns.

Interesting because of its physiological response measure is Krugman's study (1967), which used an optiscan to record eye movements of a subject exposed to the test ad for 10 seconds in three successive weeks. The results showed that scanning (defined as the proportion of the total ad surface upon which the eye fixated) increased from the first to the second exposure and leveled off with the third exposure. It is not clear what the implications of this finding are for the shape of the advertising response function, but further research could clarify the connection.

In short, laboratory experiments with repetition

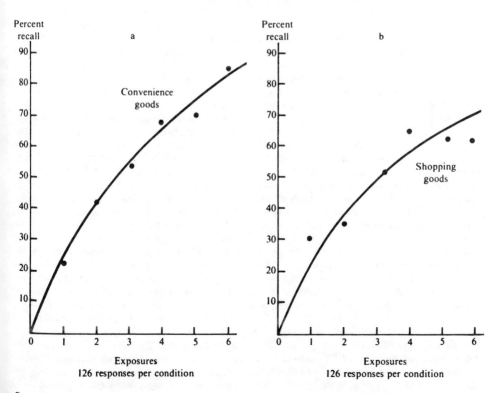

Figure 2
**Relationship between Recall of Advertisement and Number of Exposures
for "Convenience" and "Shopping" Goods**

Source: Ray and Sawyer (1971).

do not give evidence of increasing returns.

Field Experiments. Let us now turn to actual market experiments conducted under realistic conditions. Again, we will distinguish between studies bearing on the effects of size and on the effects of repetition (which will include a few experiments that varied the physical quantity of advertising).

Size. The most impressive evidence on the physical advertising-sales relationship comes from experimentation with mail-order sales. Mail-order data are as nearly perfect as economic data can be, the relationship between advertising and sales being completely measurable with the key that is in every advertisement that reveals the source of each sale that is made. The experiments are well controlled. The modern split-run test (in which every odd magazine in each stack carries advertisement A and every even magazine carries advertisement B) is the most reliable, largest-sample experiment ever carried out in any science. And mail-order tests are realistic because they are real. No links in the logical relationship need to be estimated with judgment, as is the case, say, when one uses readership data to gauge the ultimate sales payoff. Furthermore, in the mail-order business there are no other merchandising efforts that work jointly with advertising—as in the case of dealer-sold products—and that may obscure the effect of advertising. The only reason not to rely completely on mail-order evidence for a judgment about the shape of the advertising response function is that nonmail-order advertising *may* be different from advertising for store-sold and salesman-sold goods and services.

Shryer (1912) provided the earliest and most extensive body of mail-order data—a book-length array of data that is impressive even when compared to any modern study of any type of advertising. These data came from a business that Shryer himself owned and ran, and hence the results of his study affected his own pocketbook. He found conclusively that returns diminish sharply with size. All other reports concur. The only reason for not devoting more space here to these mail-order data is that they are well documented in earlier reviews (Simon, 1965, 1970).

Keyed coupon tests in print advertisements, which are one step further away from realism than are mail-order advertisements, also show diminishing returns (Starch, 1959a). Readership studies, which are not true experiments, also show diminishing returns with size (Rudolph, 1936; Starch, 1966). Engel, Blackwell, and Kollat (1978) have proposed that readership tends to increase in proportion to the square root of the increase in space.

Repetition. Mail-order data from many sources all confirm Shryer's conclusion, based on thousands of keyed advertisements, that "The first insertion of a tried piece of copy in a new medium will pay better, in every way, than any subsequent insertion of the same copy in the same magazine" (Shryer, 1912). In other words, returns decrease with repetition.

Pomerance and Zielske (1958; and especially Zielske, 1959) invented an important new design for comparing the effects of various numbers of advertisements for store-sold products. They mailed 1 to 13 advertisements, at weekly or monthly intervals, to women who were tested for recall of the advertising after the last advertisement had arrived. Reanalysis of the raw data (Simon, 1979) shows that when spread over a longer time period, a given amount of advertising has a larger total impact, measured in recall-weeks. This implies diminishing returns to advertising.

Stewart (1964) used an exposure design similar to that of Zielske (1959) in a massive field-study comparison of the effects of advertising for a bleach and for a food product in four matched quarters of Fort Wayne, Indiana. Stewart concluded that his data showed mixed results with respect to increasing or decreasing returns. But reanalysis of his data suggests that on balance the data are strong evidence *against* increasing returns (Simon, 1970). Similar findings emerge from other recall and coupon studies of repetition (Starch, 1959b; Alfred Politz Research, 1964, 1965). A particularly interesting variation is that of Miller (1976), who studied the response to a poster admonishing readers to contribute to a campaign for the reduction of foreign aid. His subjects (undergraduate college students residing in a dormitory building) were randomly assigned to four treatment conditions: no exposure (pretest), moderate exposure (30 posters), overexposure (170 posters), exposure removal (delayed posttest). Data were collected from a questionnaire. While the design did not provide adequate controls (for instance, contamination in the form of communication among the experimental groups might have occurred), the results showed diminishing returns both for an attitudinal and a behavioral measure (percent volunteering for a campaign). Another study that deserves mention for its novelty of method is that of De Fleur, who dropped a study by De Fleur in leaflets from the air onto eight similar towns in the United States. The number of leaflets dropped per head of population varied over a wide range, being doubled in successive towns. The leaflets requested the finder to note and to pass on a given message. The proportion of the population knowing the message was measured by surveys. Broadbent and Segnit (1972) reanalyzed the data and found that the relationship between number of leaflets dropped per head to proportion knowing the message could be described by a constant-concave geometric response function.

Ex Post Facto Studies. Ex post facto studies try to measure the impact of advertising by comparing subjects' states on indicators of effect by respondents receiving different levels of exposure. Such an ex post facto design is vulnerable to confounding effects by nonadvertising variables because it assumes that subjects can really serve as their own control on nonmeasured potential influences. The design also raises problems as to the direction of causality.

Roberts's (1947) bench-mark study of proprietary-drugs advertising used purchase data over six months on two competing pharmaceutical products for a panel of 2,000 households, who also reported on receipt of advertisement-bearing issues of magazines. Holding constant the effect of important demographic variables, Roberts concluded that "the resulting curve shows plainly the effect of diminishing returns" at all points of the curve. However, Roberts's study suffered from the absence of a measure of prior sales in addition to other difficulties with the cross-sectional approach.

The lack of prior sales data from which Roberts's design suffered was made good by Cerha (1967), who used a panel design to isolate the effect on Swedish gasoline buying behavior of the Esso Tiger campaign, which used a heavy newspaper advertising schedule. Effects of the campaign upon knowledge, attitudes, and behavior (visits to gas stations) were measured as differences (by before and after campaign measures) within strata defined by differences in exposure (defined by opportunity to see the ads, as in the Roberts study). The results showed that the massive campaign, though apparently reaching all members of the target group, failed to sell more Esso gas. Furthermore, Cerha reported that neither knowledge nor attitude changes varied with ad exposure. Yet a remaining unsolved problem in this as well as in an otherwise sound study, the Roberts drug study, is the use of opportunities to see, rather than a direct measure of exposure.

There is a long line of attempts to determine the effect of repetition by measuring the advertising recall by people who have been exposed to different numbers of advertisements in magazines or other media (e.g., the "readership studies" discussed by Britt, 1956; Starch, 1959c; Politz, 1964). But these studies are irreparably flawed by a variety of methodological difficulties.

More recent ex post facto studies using a variety of techniques include an investigation of the effects of movie commercials (Broadbent and Segnit, 1972), a study of airline advertising (Broadbent and Segnit,

1972), a report by McDonald on the relations between reported purchase diary data and media data (Krugman, 1972), and the Morrill study (McGraw-Hill, 1971) of the effect of industrial advertising. They all suggest diminishing returns to advertising, as do three studies cited by Engel, Blackwell, and Kollat (1978): the NBC Hofstra study of television advertising recall, the Tyrex study of product awareness, and a brand-mention study of *Post* magazine readers. The only exception is a German study reported by Geiger and Ernst (1971), who found support for an S-shaped curve for the relationship between reported exposure to magazine advertising and brand awareness. None of these studies seems to us to be sufficiently solid methodologically to be worth examining in depth.

Summary and Conclusion about the Physical Advertising Response Function. The review of the studies on the physical advertising response function has revealed a fragmented and noncumulative research effort. The design and results of the studies reviewed in this section are summarized in Table 1. The independent variable—advertising input—may be size of print advertisement, length of commercial, or number of exposures. The dependent variable may be sales or some "intermediate" effect measure that is conative (e.g., intentions to buy), affective or attitudinal, cognitive (e.g., product awareness or recall of advertisement), or even physiological.

The extreme right-hand column of Table 1 summarizes the findings, indicating whether the study in question showed monotonically decreasing returns over the range covered or increasing returns. Taken together, these studies of the effects of size, repetition, and quantity of advertising show no conclusive evidence of increasing returns in the physical advertising response function. Rather, the evidence massively shows diminishing returns over the ranges studied. In drawing this conclusion, we put special weight on the imaginative and well-controlled experiment of Ray and Sawyer (1971), and on the mail-order data because of their reliability. Geiger and Ernst (1971) claimed to have documented an S-shaped curve, but we find the basis for their conclusion not solid enough to temper our conclusion that the shape of the physical advertising response function is concave downward.

The Monetary Advertising Response Function

Even if there are no increasing returns in the physical advertising response function, there could be increasing returns in the relationship between *expenditure* on advertising and sales in physical or

Table 1
Summary of Design and Findings of Studies of the Physical Advertising Response Function

Research design	Study	Sales	Conative	Affective	Cognitive	Physio-logical	Findings
(1) Laboratory experiments (a) Size	Strong (1914)				x		Decreasing returns
	Wheatley (1968)			x	x		Decreasing returns
	Capitman (1964)				x		Decreasing returns
	Hoffman (1963)		x	x			Decreasing returns
	Lodish (1971)		x				Decreasing returns
	Schwartz (1975)				x		Decreasing returns
(b) Repetition	Adams (1916)				x		Decreasing returns
	Ray and Sawyer (1971)		x	x	x		Decreasing returns
	Politz (1960)				x		In two cases decreasing returns, and in two cases increasing returns
	Sawyer (1974)				x		Decreasing returns
	Wells and Chinsky (1965)		x				Decreasing returns
	Krugman (1967)					x	Decreasing returns
(2) Market experiments (a) Size	Shryer (1912)	x					Decreasing returns
	Simon (1965, 1970)	x					Decreasing returns
	Starch (1959a)		x				Decreasing returns
	Rudolph (1936)				x		Decreasing returns
	Starch (1966)				x		Decreasing returns
(b) Repetition	Shryer (1912)	x					Decreasing returns
	Zielske (1959)				x		Decreasing returns
	Stewart (1964)	x	x	x	x		Decreasing returns
	Starch (1959c)		x				Decreasing returns
	Politz (1964)				x		Decreasing returns
	Politz (1965)		x	x	x		Decreasing returns
	Miller (1976)		x	x			Decreasing returns
	Broadbent and Segnit (1972)				x		Decreasing returns
(3) Ex post facto studies	Broadbent and Segnit (1972)				x		Decreasing returns
	Broadbent and Segnit (1972)				x		Decreasing returns
	Krugman (1972)				x		Decreasing returns
	Morrill (1971)	x		x			Decreasing returns
	Engel, Blackwell, and Kollat (1978)				x		Decreasing returns
	Geiger and Ernst (1971)				x		First increasing, then decreasing returns
	Roberts (1947)	x					Decreasing returns
	Cerha (1967)	x		x	x		No relationship for awareness and attitudes. Linear relationship for behavior.

Dependent measure

money units, because of quantity discounts. And for the enterprise and for society, the monetary relationship is the more relevant.

Quantity discounts are often large in advertising and might lead to increasing returns to advertising. So might these other factors Chamberlin (1962) adduced:

> 1. . . . Improvement in the organization of the expenditure as its total amount is increased . . . the employment of more resources means greater specialization in their use.

> 2. . . . The most effective media may be those whose use requires a large outlay. As expenditure increases, then, a shift may take place to continually more effective media, so that a tendency to increasing returns is imparted to the cost curve.

> 3. . . . The most effective choice of media may involve the use of several in combination. . . .

Let us consider the evidence.

Experimental Studies. For our purposes here, experimental evidence has the large advantage over nonexperimental data in that all other selling conditions can be satisfactorily controlled in an experiment, whereas it is very difficult to do so econometrically. A bench mark is du Pont's 12-market test with amounts of advertising for Teflon corresponding to levels of $1 million, $500,000, and zero (McNiven, 1969). The advertising level was varied in fall and winter so that the results of various combinations of advertising could be seen. The data seem to show that there are *increasing* returns. That is, the $1-million level did much better than the $500,000 level, while the latter did only slightly better than no advertising at all. This set of data constitutes the strongest available evidence for increasing returns, though the generality of the finding is limited by the short range of observations—only three levels of advertising—in the study.

We have found only one near-replication of the du Pont study: Eskin's (1975) test of a new food product with 60 stores in four test markets over six months, which also introduced new methodological twists. There were three price treatments and two advertising treatments allowing tests of interaction effects. Data were collected on various measures of potentially important extraneous factors that could influence the outcome. The proportion of total expenditures allocated to each media class was kept constant. The principal dependent measure was unit sales of the product per store per month.

Advertising had most impact at the lowest price level. At each price level, the proportional increase in sales (adjusted for differences in the covariates)

was smaller than the relative increase in advertising, which suggests diminishing returns. It would be valuable if studies such as the present one and the du Pont experiment were extended so as to include more levels of advertising.

Two other high-quality experiments deserve mention. The American Dairy Association (in cooperation with the Department of Agriculture) ran a well-controlled experiment on the effect of several levels of promotional expenditure upon fluid-milk sales. Over the range of this experiment, there were diminishing marginal returns (Clement, Henderson, and Eley, 1965). And Doyle and Fenwick (1975) conducted an experiment with 32 stores of a company in England which had not advertised in the preceding two years. They subjected stores to three different levels of advertising, plus no advertising for a control group for a six-month period. Doyle and Fenwick concluded: "The advertising response function as developed from the experiment appears to exhibit the classical pattern of diminishing returns."

And last, OHerlihy (1977, 1978a) has described in general terms several large-scale field experiments for British products that he says all show the concave-downward curve rather than the S-curve, though only one of these—for Andrex toilet tissue—has been published in reasonable detail (Branton, 1978).

The admixture of evidence from field experiments requires some judgment. Our evaluation takes note that only one among several studies shows evidence of increasing returns, and that one—like the others—is not reported in sufficient detail for thorough analysis. Hence we are inclined to consider that it is anomalous for any one of many reasons that we do not know. Our reluctance to rely heavily on a single study is reinforced by a recent remark by Corkindale and Kennedy that, in their considerable experience, fully 19 of 20 field studies of advertising expenditures fail to produce valuable information because of a variety of confounding factors and researcher ineptitudes (OHerlihy, 1978b).

In brief, then, we are satisfied that the field experiments as a group show no solid evidence for increasing returns over operating ranges.

Nonexperimental Studies. Ideally, nonexperimental studies of the advertising response function should include the following elements (for a more comprehensive and detailed discussion see Parsons and Schultz, 1976):

(1) marketing-mix interaction effects—i.e., sales impact of other elements of the marketing mix;

(2) competitive effects—i.e., impact of competitors' activities;

(3) carryover effects—i.e., explicit consideration of

lagged responses;

(4) simultaneous relationships (which may be necessary to solve problems of identification or direction of causality: Is advertising causing sales, or are advertising expenditures determined by sales?).

The studies to be reviewed fall far short of this ideal, partly due to limitations in the data available. A purist might exclude cross-sectional and time-series data from this review. But to exclude these econometric studies would mean throwing away much realistic evidence that describes actual buying in response to actual marketing mixes in real-life settings.

We distinguish between time-series and cross-sectional studies, but because some of the studies have pooled these two types of data, the classification of studies into each of the two groups is not neat.

Time-Series Studies. From the earliest days of national advertising for patent medicines, advertisers have striven to relate current advertising expenses to current sales, but without avail because of the lagged effect of advertising. An unusual example of a current-data study that did not suffer fatally from this is that of Buzzell and Baker (1972), who took advantage of the "natural experiment" created by the General Motors strike, which caused firms in the automotive industry to alter their advertising budgets. As may be expected, advertising alone explained only a small proportion of the variation in sales. Finding some support for a logarithmic function, however, the authors concluded that "there appeared to be a diminishing returns phenomenon operating."

An early attempt to allow for competitive effects was reported by Weinberg (1956), who investigated the market effort-sales relationship for a glass-container manufacturer. His data base consisted of observations, over seven years, of annual changes in market share and in the "exchange rate" for marketing expenditures (the firm's marketing expenditures per dollar of sales divided by the corresponding ratio for its competitors). Hence, competitors' activities were to some extent included. A remarkably close fit ($r^2 = .996$) was reported for a logarithmic function, evidence against economies of scale, but the data were described only at a high level of abstraction.

Weiss (1968, 1969) extended the Weinberg study by developing a multiplicative formulation to explain changes in market shares of three national brands of a low-cost consumer food item. The influence of competitive factors was represented with relative advertising and price measures. The estimation resulted in near-zero advertising elasticities, casting

some doubt on Weinberg's excellent fit.

Johansson (1973) made a diligent effort to fit a variety of functions, including semi-log, double-log, and sigmoid, to monthly observations over 13 months of market shares and advertising expenditures in four media for an unidentified product group, but ignored competitive effects. He concluded that "the effect of advertising on market share is best depicted by a curve which is everywhere concave to the origin."

The next group of studies to be reviewed include the effects of lagged advertising in their designs. We concentrate on the single-equation models because most studies using simultaneous-equation models have not explicitly reported investigations of various forms of the response function. For other reviews and discussions of methodological aspects of lagged models, see Clarke (1976), Parsons and Schultz (1976), and Dhalla (1978).

The landmark study that took into account the crucial lagged effect of advertising was that of Telser (1962), who thoroughly investigated the relationship of sales to advertising for the three largest cigarette brands before World War II. He tested several different models, included both competitive effects and price as variables, and concluded that "the level of advertising was high enough to place the companies at the point where there were diminishing returns to advertising."

Telser's conclusion is interesting more as a confirmation than as a discovery, however; one would hardly expect the largest advertisers to stop advertising at a point of increasing returns, if such a point exists. Nor does this finding about the largest brands tell us whether they are operating at a lower per-unit cost than is possible at greatly lower levels of advertising expenditure. This difficulty afflicts all such time-series studies as evidence for or against increasing returns. Once firms have accumulated some knowledge of their response functions, they would never knowingly operate in the region of increasing returns. Hence, the fact that such a region is not *observed* in these studies is not strong evidence that such a region does not *exist*. This caveat also applies to other time-series studies reviewed below, though not to the same degree in most cases.

The best-known single-equation study is that of Palda (1964) on Lydia Pinkham's Vegetable Compound from 1908 to 1960. The product had no known close substitutes, thereby eliminating the complications caused by competitive effects. Palda found that a distributed-lag model with the logarithm of advertising as an independent variable gave the best predictions. This result "tends to confirm the operation of decreasing returns to a variable factor." A large number of studies in the Telser-Palda tradition have confirmed this finding of diminishing returns: analyses of 15 brands of liquor by Simon (1969), of a Swedish drug product by Lohmander and Tufvesson (1975), and of a variety of U.K. products by Cowling *et al.* (1975). Other relevant references are Buzzell (1964), Kuehn, McGuire, and Weiss (1966), Frank and Massy (1967), Lambin (1969, 1970a, 1970b), Sexton (1970, 1972), Hamilton (1972), Montgomery and Silk (1972), Narodick (1972), Schmalensee (1972), Moriarity (1975), and Parsons (1975).

Lambin's exhaustive study (1976) must now be considered the centerpiece single-equation time-series study of the advertising-sales relationship. (The following material on Lambin's work has been drawn from a forthcoming article by Simon [1980].) The econometric techniques are wisely chosen and well used, and the sample covers 107 brands of 16 product classes in 8 countries of western Europe (though all were consumer goods). We shall discuss this study in depth partly because of its comprehensiveness and partly because it produced findings that apparently (but do not really) differ from the general pattern.

Each individual response function that Lambin estimated was best described by a concave-downward diminishing-returns equation. From this, Lambin concluded that "since semilogarithmic (in the advertising variable) and double-log regressions invariably performed better than linear forms, this is evidence that the shape of the advertising response curve is concave downward, i.e., that there is no S-curve and no increasing returns in advertising a given brand by a given firm."

Then Lambin changed course radically and examined the relationship of each brand's advertising share to its market share. This is conceptually related to the relationship between the advertising-sales ratio and the size of the firm, the major difference being the use of brand rather than firm data. The results showed that brands with relatively small market shares had advertising shares larger than their market shares. This Lambin interpreted as indicating that there is a threshold for advertising effectiveness below which advertising expenditures have no effect. Such a threshold constitutes an inflection point, the lower boundary of a region of increasing returns. In the words of Lambin: "Therefore, to reach the level of communication effectiveness, small brands have to keep their advertising shares higher than their market shares."

It is important that we examine this conclusion of Lambin's in detail, because it is susceptible of being cited for many years by those in the advertising business who have a stake in the existence of in-

creasing returns.

Let us be clear. Lambin's overall interpretation must be that there *is* an S curve of increasing returns, though he writes: "Our results present strong evidence that decreasing returns to the advertising factor is the general rule . . . there is no S-curve and no increasing returns." This interpretation is based on the interbrand advertising and market-share relationships. Our task is to go deeper into the meaning of these data to see what interpretation they best support.

Let us first assume with Lambin that smaller brands have higher advertising-sales ratios (advertising shares in the context of his data) than brands with larger market shares. If so, the observed data might be explained as shown in Figure 3. There we see that firms that advertise more have higher response functions. That is, firm E, which is presently advertising at level *E*, has an extrapolated function that produces more sales at any given level of advertising than does the response function for firm D, and so on down the line to firm A. (The observed data cover only the range of the solid lines in Figure 3.)

These data need not indicate a threshold, however, as we shall now explain. It is first important to notice that each separate advertising function shows the returns to advertising with all other (empirically controllable) factors held çonstant. But the comparison of the response functions *from one brand to another* is made with *nothing held constant.* That is, it is reasonable and likely that firm E has a much more extensive distribution network and a larger

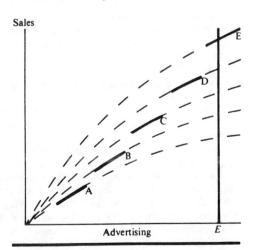

Figure 3
Alternative Interpretation of Lambin's Data

sales force than does firm A. That would explain *both* why firm E has a higher response function *and* why it advertises more in total than does firm A. And, depending on the particular slopes of the functions, the advertising-sales ratio could well be lower for the larger firm for this reason alone. Or the advertising response function might be lower for the larger firm in this situation because it finds that it is best suited with a strategy of a relatively high investment in distribution compared to advertising.

So the logic of Figure 3 is consistent with the observed data without any need of a threshold argument. And if Figure 3 is a sound representation of Lambin's data, then it suggests, plain and simple, that there is no inflection point and no increasing returns, because the response function of the *smallest* firm, A, is concave downward.

There are also additional reasons not to interpret Lambin's data as showing a threshold effect. Lambin used an entirely different sort of argument to explain an inverse relationship between the advertising-sales ratio and market share among the largest firms alone, "because large firms perceive the existence of diminishing returns . . . and therefore set their advertising appropriation at a level where the marginal sales effectiveness of advertising monies is sufficiently high." But the same argument would also apply to small firms. And the resort to several such ad hoc arguments for the same phenomenon under different conditions weakens them all.

Even if Lambin's interpretation of his data as showing a threshold were correct—and we have every reason to think that it is not correct—one would still have to conclude against a threshold being empirically observed. The reason is that in the universe of firms *as a whole*—in contrast to Lambin's convenience sample of 107 brands in 16 product classes—Simon and Crain (1966) found no association between size of firm, as measured by asset value, and the advertising-sales ratio in the various industries (using IRS data on all firms submitting tax returns in 109 industries). Lambin's data are more appropriate than are Simon and Crain's because they are at the brand level. But if the relationship really holds, one would expect to see it at the firm level as well, where it does not appear. This is additional evidence against Lambin's interpretation of his data as showing a threshold effect (and therefore increasing returns at low levels of advertising).

On the multiple-equation studies, these studies (e.g., Bass, 1969; Bass and Parsons, 1969; Samuels, 1970–1971; Lambin, 1970a, 1972; Schultz, 1971; Beckwith, 1972; Clarke, 1973; Comanor and Wilson, 1974; Parsons, 1974; Cowling *et al.*, 1975; and Wildt, 1974) typically work with the advertising variable in

a logarithmic or double-logarithmic form. which implies diminishing returns to advertising. But this form seems to have been chosen by assumption either because the researchers believe it is most realistic or for reasons of mathematical convenience or both. The choice does not, however, throw any light on the shape of the advertising response function. If these studies were to compare various function forms, they could make a contribution.

Cross-sectional Studies. Some of the difficulties with cross-sectional studies were mentioned earlier. An additional problem with cross-sectional studies that measure purchases is that they often fail to control for other marketing variables.

Worth mentioning here because its findings run contrary to most of the other studies reported in this paper, Rao and Miller (1975) obtained bimonthly sales observations of five Lever products in 15 sales districts. For each brand in each district, the coefficients were first estimated for a lagged model relating market share to advertising and various promotional activities. Hence, total incremental sales for each $1 advertising were estimated for each district. Next, the functional relationship between total incremental sales and level of advertising expenditure was established by cross-sectional analysis for the 15 districts. The results indicated "that the relationship of sales to advertising expenditure is approximated by a family of S-shaped curves." Unfortunately, Rao and Miller present only a small part of their data, most of it in graphs which seem to have been smoothed, and they have not responded to requests for the raw data. In light of these factors, together with the fact that no allowance was made for differences in market potential, we are uncertain about how much weight should be placed on this publication.

Summary and Conclusion about the Monetary Advertising Response Function. Of the monetary-variable studies reviewed, almost all show diminishing returns for advertising over the ranges covered. One exception is the experimental study by McNiven (1969); another exception is the Rao and Miller (1975) study. Taken together, these studies support the conclusion from the previous section on the physical advertising response function: there is little evidence for increasing returns to advertising, and considerable evidence for monotonically decreasing returns to advertising over the normal operating range.

Advertising and Economies of Size

Even if there are no physical or monetary increasing returns, advertising could give an advantage to the big spender over the small spender for advertising. This could happen if there is an interaction among various levels of advertising and various other factors of production—for example, in a multiplicative fashion. This leads to the concept of economies of scale.

It is not easy to make sense of the concept of economies of scale with respect to advertising, however. The difficulty is that the concept of economies of *scale* refers to differences in just that: the scale of the enterprise with *all* factors taken together, including their interaction. The concept was not designed to throw light on the operation of a single factor alone.

Because of the conceptual complexity as well as the complexity of interpretation of the advertising-sales ratio, which is the dependent variable in most studies that aim to analyze economies of scale in advertising (and which we regard as useless for this and most other work on advertising; see Simon and Crain, 1966), it would take much space to try to make sense of the matter. We will be happy to supply upon request a longer draft which discusses the matter and concludes that there has never been a satisfactory test of whether advertising is implicated in any economies of scale that operate in any industry. Nor do we find that the question has ever been formulated in a fashion that suggests how it may be answered meaningfully.

Another tricky issue is that of multibrand economies of size stemming from advertising. Such economies are logically similar to geographical economies. One might speculate that a merger of two related-product brands or the development of a related-product brand by a going firm might produce both volume discounts in advertising and communication economies such as the use of a common trademark. And the increase in the number of advertised brands in a majority of consumer categories (Simon, 1970) is consistent with this speculation. (This also represents lessened industrial concentration at the brand level, by the way, an important phenomenon in its own right.)

But a trend toward a larger number of brands sold per firm might also stem from economies of distribution, production, and purchasing (e.g., packaging materials). Hence, this is certainly not strong evidence for multibrand economies of size flowing from advertising. Nor is there other relevant evidence. And it is difficult to think of a sound design to test for this effect.

Advertising might be used as a barrier against potential entrants into the market, just as "stay-out pricing" might be used. The latter has been discussed under the title of "limit pricing," analyzed in

a static manner by Bain (1956), Modigliani (1958), and Sylos-Labini (1962), and in a more dynamic context by Gaskins (1971); for a recent review see Salop (1979).

To our knowledge the dynamic theory of advertising barrier effects has not been spelled out very thoroughly, though for a start see Schupak (1972). And it is not immediately obvious how one would formalize for a mature market the ideas vaguely expressed by the literary concept. For a new product, it seems rather straightforward that a firm making high profits from an innovation might buy advertising beyond what a monopolist would in order to bind customers more closely for the future. And in this way, as well as by simply lowering the prospective profits because of advertising expenditures, a firm with a new product might render entry less attractive. That is, more advertising in period t might mean relatively fewer sales in period $t + 1$ for a potential entrant with given levels of price and advertising.

Working in the other direction is advertising's role as a competitive tool that makes it easier for potential entrants to enter successfully. If one could not advertise, it would be much harder for a potential entrant with a product improvement—a ball-point pen or a rotary engine—or even a potential entrant without a product improvement, to enter the market. In this way advertising has a procompetitive dynamic effect.

Unfortunately, we could find no body of empirical work for us to determine whether the net outcome of advertising is to increase or decrease the rate of market entrance. And it will not be an easy task to design sound research to answer this question.

How May the Basic Questions Finally Be Resolved?

No one study can be considered nearly conclusive on either the physical or monetary response functions. Each of the studies (even Lambin's) offers results for a limited set of conditions, and all have methodological drawbacks of one kind or another. But the near-unanimity of these very different sorts of studies is impressive. If there were increasing returns, *some* of these studies should show it. Yet one hopes that a more comprehensive study will be undertaken.

If one were able to design a study to settle the question once and for all, how should it be done? Of course no study really can answer the question for all products, all media, and all sorts of advertisements, but perhaps a coordinated every-other-house design employing both cable-television and newspaper advertisements would seem to come closest. Using the sort of system available at the Milwaukee Advertising Laboratory and elsewhere, it is possible to give different advertising schedules to even-numbered and odd-numbered houses. An even better design would vary the schedules by blocks, in which case it is easier also to vary the advertising schedules in the newspapers these homes receive. This design makes possible all combinations of schedules of various quantities of advertising.

Purchase diary would likely be the basic mode of effect measurement. But it would be worthwhile to measure product knowledge and attitude at various intervals as well. Experiments should be made with a wide variety of product types to ensure that the findings are not product specific. Wide ranges of amounts of advertising also should be employed to ensure that the results can be very general.

Conclusions and Summary

After completing our review, we agree with Bass (1969) that "there is no more difficult, complex, or controversial problem in marketing than measuring the influence of advertising on sales." In view of the inherent complexities of the subject matter, it is no wonder that no single study can come reasonably close to being definitive.

Despite the methodological problems of the individual studies, the main thrust of the evidence is clear—across product categories, geographical settings, media, methodologies, and researchers. Our findings are as follows.

(1) Studies of the response function linking physical measures of sales impact to physical amounts of advertising consistently indicate diminishing returns to advertising over the ranges of investigation in laboratory experiments and over the normal range of advertising budgets for operating firms. To put it differently, increasing returns have not been reliably observed in the laboratory or in the field.

(2) Studies of the function relating sales in dollars to dollars of advertising, which reflect the role of discounts, also show diminishing returns to advertising, with the exceptions of the McNiven du Pont study (1969) and the Rao and Miller (1975) study.

(3) Taken together, the studies using physical and monetary variables add up to the conclusion that there are not increasing returns to advertising—that is, no S-shaped response function—over the normal operating range.

(4) We hope that a broad concerted attack upon this question is mounted, perhaps by an industry group and perhaps along the lines of the design we have suggested above. Such a piece of work intended primarily to throw light on this subject will provide a more persuasive answer than does the heterogeneous collection of studies upon which we rely for our conclusions.

References

Aaker, David A., and John G. Myers. *Advertising Management.* Englewood Cliffs, N.J.: Prentice-Hall, 1975.

Adams, Henry F. *Advertising and Its Mental Laws.* New York: Macmillan, 1916.

Bain, Joe S. *Barriers to New Competition.* Cambridge: Harvard University Press, 1956.

Bass, Frank M. A Simultaneous Equation Regression Study of Advertising and Sales of Cigarettes. *Journal of Marketing Research,* Vol. 6, No. 3, August 1969, pp. 291–300.

Bass, Frank M., and Leonard J. Parsons. Simultaneous-Equation Study of Sales and Advertising. *Applied Economics,* Vol. 1, May 1969, pp. 103–124.

Beckwith, Neil E. Multivariate Analysis of Sales Responses of Competing Brands to Advertising. *Journal of Marketing Research,* Vol. 9, No. 2, May 1972, pp. 168–176.

Berelson, Bernard, and Gary A. Steiner. *Human Behavior: An Inventory of Scientific Findings.* New York: Harcourt, Brace and World, 1964.

Branton, J. J. The Bowater Scott Approach to Media Phasing. *Admap,* Vol. 14, No. 1, January 1978, pp. 24–26.

Britt, Steuart H. Study Indicates Effective Magazine Ad May Be Repeated without Loss of Readership. *Advertising Age,* May 14, 1956, pp. 63–64.

Broadbent, S. R., and S. Segnit. Response Functions in Media Planning. In *Ten Years of Advertising Media Research, 1962–1971.* London: Thomson Organisation Limited, 1972.

Buzzell, Robert D. Predicting Short-Term Changes in Market Share as a Function of Advertising Strategy. *Journal of Marketing Research,* Vol. 1, No. 3, August 1964, pp. 27–31.

Buzzell, Robert D., and Michael L. Baker. Sales Effectiveness of Automobile Advertising. *Journal of Advertising Research,* Vol. 12, No. 3, June 1972, pp. 3–8.

Cerha, Jarko. *Selective Mass Communication.* Stockholm: Norstedt & Söner, 1967.

Chamberlin, Edward H. *The Theory of Monopolistic Competition.* Cambridge: Harvard University Press, 1962.

Clarke, Darral G. Sales-Advertising Cross-Elasticities and Advertising Competition. *Journal of Marketing Research,* Vol. 10, No. 3, August 1973, pp. 250–261.

———. Econometric Measurement of the Duration of Advertising Effect on Sales. *Journal of Marketing Research,* Vol. 13, No. 4, November 1976, pp. 345–357.

Clement, W. E., P. L. Henderson, and C. P. Eley. *The Effect of Different Levels of Promotional Expenditures on Sales of Fluid Milk.* Washington, D.C.: U.S. Department of Agriculture, Economic Research Service, 1965.

Comanor, William S., and Thomas A. Wilson. *Advertising and Market Power.* Cambridge: Harvard University Press, 1974.

Cowling, Keith, John Cable, Michael Kelley, and Tony McGuinness. *Advertising and Economic Behaviour.* London: Macmillan, 1975.

Dean, Joel. *Managerial Economics.* Englewood Cliffs, N.J.: Prentice-Hall, 1951.

Dhalla, Nariman K. Assessing the Long-Term Value of Advertising. *Harvard Business Review,* Vol. 56, No. 1, January–February 1978, pp. 87–95.

Doyle, Peter, and Ian Fenwick. Planning and Estimation in Advertising. *Journal of Marketing Research,* Vol. 12, No. 1, February 1975, pp. 1–6.

Ebbinghaus, H. *Grundzuge der Psychologie.* Leipzig: Veit, 1885. Quoted in Alan G. Sawyer. The Effects of Repetition: Conclusions and Suggestions about Experimental Laboratory Research. In G. David Hughes and Michael L. Ray (Eds.). *Buyer/ Consumer Information Processing.* Chapel Hill: University of North Carolina Press, 1974.

Engel, James F., Roger D. Blackwell, and David T.

Kollat. *Consumer Behavior,* 3rd ed. New York: Dryden Press, 1978.

Eskin, Gerald J. A Case for Test Market Experiments. *Journal of Advertising Research,* Vol. 15, No. 2, April 1975, pp. 27–33.

Frank, Ronald E., and William F. Massy. Effects of Short-Term Promotional Strategy in Selected Market Segments. In Patrick J. Robinson (Ed.). *Promotional Decisions Using Mathematical Models.* Boston: Allyn & Bacon, 1967.

Gaskins, D. W., Jr. Dynamic Limit Pricing: Optimal Pricing under Threat of Entry. *Journal of Economic Theory,* Vol. 3, 1971, pp. 306–322.

Geiger, S., and O. Ernst. Advertising Pressure: Advertising Response Differentiations of Response Functions According to Target Groups and Media Consumption Groups. *ESOMAR/Wapor Conference,* Part II. Amsterdam: ESOMAR, 1971.

Gensch, Dennis H. *Advertising Planning.* New York: American Elsevier, 1973.

Greenberg, Allan, and Charles Suttoni. Television Commercial Wearout. *Journal of Advertising Research,* Vol. 13, No. 5, October 1973, pp. 47–54.

Hamilton, James L. The Demand for Cigarettes: Advertising, the Health Scare, and the Cigarette Advertising Ban. *Review of Economics and Statistics,* Vol. 54, November 1972, pp. 401–411.

Hoffman, R. M. The 20-Second Commercial. *Media/ Scope,* Vol. 7, No. 7, July 1963, pp. 72, 74, 76.

Johansson, Johny K. A Generalized Logistic Function with an Application to the Effect of Advertising. *Journal of the American Statistical Association,* Vol. 68, No. 343, December 1973, pp. 824–827.

Krugman, Herbert E. The Impact of Television Advertising: Learning without Involvement. *Public Opinion Quarterly,* Vol. 29, No. 3, Fall 1965, pp. 349–356.

———. The Measurement of Advertising Involvement. *Public Opinion Quarterly,* Vol. 30, No. 4, Winter 1966–1967, pp. 583–596.

———. *Looking-with-Learning vs. Looking-without-Learning: An Exploratory Study of Eye Movement Patterns When Viewing Advertisements.* New York: Bureau of Advertising, 1967.

———. Why Exposure May Be Enough. *Journal of Advertising Research*, Vol. 12, No. 6, December 1972, pp. 11–14.

Kuehn, Alfred A., Timothy W. McGuire, and Doyle L. Weiss. Measuring the Effectiveness of Advertising. In Raymond N. Haas (Ed.). *Science, Technology, and Marketing: Proceedings of the 1966 Fall Conference*. Chicago: American Marketing Association, 1966.

Lambin, Jean-Jacques. Measuring the Profitability of Advertising: An Empirical Study. *Journal of Industrial Economics*, Vol. 17, April 1969, pp. 86–103.

———. Advertising and Competitive Behavior: A Case Study. *Applied Economics*, Vol. 2, 1970a, pp. 231–251.

———. Optimal Allocation of Competitive Marketing Efforts: An Empirical Study. *Journal of Business*, Vol. 43, No. 4, October 1970b, pp. 468–484.

———. Is Gasoline Advertising Justified? *Journal of Business*, Vol. 45, No. 4, October 1972, pp. 585–619.

———. *Advertising, Competition and Market Conduct in Oligopoly over Time*. Amsterdam: North-Holland, 1976.

Lodish, Leonard M. Empirical Studies on Individual Response to Exposure Patterns. *Journal of Marketing Research*, Vol. 7, No. 2, May 1971, pp. 212–218.

Lohmander, Bengt, and Ingmar Tufvesson. Studier av marknadsföringens försäljningseffekter: Några bidrag til en forskningstradition. Paper presented at the Seventh Nordic Business Administration Conference in Åbo, Finland.

McGraw-Hill Book Company. *How Advertising Works in Today's Marketplace and Advertising's Challenge to Management: A Second Report on the Morrill Study*. New York: McGraw-Hill, 1971. Quoted in Gary L. Lilien, Alvin J. Silk, Jean-Marie Choffray, and Murlidhar Rao. Industrial Advertising Effects and Budgeting Practices. *Journal of Marketing*, Vol. 40, No. 1, January 1976, pp. 16–24.

McNiven, Malcolm A. (Ed.). *How Much to Spend for Advertising?* New York: Association of National Advertisers, 1969.

Media/Scope. What Is the Best Length for a TV Commercial? Media/Scope, Vol. 8, No. 10, October 1964, pp. 63–66.

Miller, Richard L. Mere Exposure, Psychological Reactance and Attitude Change. *Public Opinion Quarterly*, Vol. 40, No. 2, Summer 1976, pp. 229–233.

Modigliani, Franco. New Developments on the Oligopoly Front. *Journal of Political Economy*, June 1958, pp. 215–232.

Montgomery, David B., and Alvin J. Silk. Estimating Dynamic Effects of Market Communications Expenditures. *Management Science*, Vol. 18, June 1972, pp. B485–B501.

Moriarity, Mark. Cross-sectional, Time Series Issues in the Analysis of Marketing Decision Variables. *Journal of Marketing Research*, Vol. 12, No. 2, May 1975, pp. 142–150.

Narodick, Kit G. Determinants of Airline Market-Share. *Journal of Advertising Research*, Vol. 12, No. 5, October 1972, pp. 31–36.

OHerlihy, C. How to Make a Million from (Almost) Nothing. *Admap*, Vol. 13, No. 7, July 1977, pp. 328–332.

———. Bursting the Myth of the Burst. *Campaign*, Vol. 14, No. 2, February 1978a, p. 35.

———. Halldoor of a Secret Advertising Scandal. *Financial Times*, March 1978b.

Ozga, S. A. Imperfect Markets through Lack of Knowledge. *Quarterly Journal of Economics*, Vol. 74, February 1960, pp. 29–52.

Palda, Kristian S. *The Measurement of Cumulative Advertising Effects*. Englewood Cliffs, N.J.: Prentice-Hall, 1964.

Parsons, Leonard J. An Econometric Analysis of Advertising, Retail Availability, and Sales of a New Brand. *Management Science*, Vol. 20, February 1974, pp. 938–947.

———. The Product Life Cycle and Time-varying Advertising Elasticities. *Journal of Marketing Research*, Vol. 12, No. 3, November 1975, pp. 476–480.

Parsons, Leonard J., and Randall L. Schultz. *Marketing Models and Econometric Research*. New York: North-Holland, 1976.

Alfred Politz Research, Inc. *The Rochester Study* (sponsored by *Saturday Evening Post*). New York:

Alfred Politz Research, Inc., 1960.

———. *Reach and Frequency.* New York: Look Magazine, 1964.

———. *A Study of Advertising Effects in Modern Medicine.* New York: Alfred Politz Research, Inc., 1965.

Pomerance, Eugene, and Hubert Zielske. How Frequently Should You Advertise? *Media/Scope,* Vol. 2, No. 9, September 1958, pp. 25–27.

Porter, Michael E. *Interbrand Choice, Strategy, and Bilateral Market Power.* Cambridge: Harvard University Press, 1976.

Preston, Lee E. Advertising Effects and Public Policy. In Robert King (Ed.). *Marketing and the New Science of Planning: Proceedings of the 1968 Fall Conference.* Chicago: American Marketing Association, 1968.

Rao, Ambar G. *Quantitative Theories in Advertising.* New York: Wiley, 1970.

Rao, Ambar G., and Peter B. Miller. Advertising/ Sales Response Functions. *Journal of Advertising Research,* Vol. 15, No. 2, April 1975, pp. 7–15.

Ray, Michael L. Microtheoretical Notions of Behavioral Science and the Problems of Advertising. Marketing Science Institute Report, No. 75-101, March 1975.

Ray, Michael L., and Alan G. Sawyer. Repetition in Media Models: A Laboratory Technique. *Journal of Marketing Research,* Vol. 8, No. 1, February 1971, pp. 20–29.

Roberts, Harry V. The Measurement of Advertising Results. *Journal of Business,* Vol. 20, No. 3, July 1947, pp. 131–145.

Rohloff, Albert C. Quantitative Analyses of the Effectiveness of TV Commercials. *Journal of Marketing Research,* Vol. 3, No. 3, August 1966, pp. 239–245.

Rudolph, H. J. *Four Million Inquiries from Magazine Advertising.* New York: Columbia University Press, 1936.

Salop, Steven. Strategic Entry Deterrence. *American Economic Review,* Vol. 69, May 1979, pp. 335–338.

Samuels, J. M. The Effect of Advertising on Sales and Brand Shares. *British Journal of Marketing,* Vol. 4, Winter 1970–1971, pp. 187–207.

Sawyer, Alan G. The Effects of Repetition: Conclusions and Suggestions about Experimental Laboratory Research. In G. David Hughes and Michael L. Ray (Eds.). *Buyer/Consumer Information Processing.* Chapel Hill: University of North Carolina Press, 1974.

Schmalensee, Richard. *The Economics of Advertising.* Amsterdam: North-Holland, 1972.

Schultz, Randall L. Market Measurement and Planning with a Simultaneous-Equation Model. *Journal of Marketing Research,* Vol. 8, No. 2, May 1971, pp. 153–164.

Schupak, M. B. Dynamic Limit Pricing with Advertising. Mimeo, Brown University, 1972.

Schwartz, David A. T-Scope Package Test Sample Size. *Journal of Advertising Research,* Vol. 15, No. 3, June 1975, pp. 35–37.

Sexton, Donald E., Jr. Estimating Marketing Policy Effects on Sales of a Frequently Purchased Product. *Journal of Marketing Research,* Vol. 7, No. 3, August 1970, pp. 338–347.

———. A Microeconomic Model of the Effects of Advertising. *Journal of Business,* Vol. 45, January 1972, pp. 29–41.

Shryer, William A. *Analytical Advertising.* Detroit: Business Service Corporation, 1912.

Simon, Julian L. Are There Economies of Scale in Advertising? *Journal of Advertising Research,* Vol. 5, No. 3, June 1965, pp. 15–20.

———. The Effect of Advertising on Liquor Brand Sales. *Journal of Marketing Research,* Vol. 6, No. 3, August 1969, pp. 301–313.

———. *Issues in the Economics of Advertising.* Urbana: University of Illinois Press, 1970.

———. What Do Zielske's Real Data Really Show about Pulsing? *Journal of Marketing Research,* Vol. 16, No. 3, August 1979, pp. 415–420.

———. A Reply to Comanor and Wilson. *Journal of Economic Literature,* forthcoming, 1980.

Simon, Julian L., and George H. Crain. The Advertising Ratio and Economies of Scale. *Journal of Advertising Research,* Vol. 6, No. 4, September 1966, pp. 37–43.

Starch, Daniel. Analysis of 12 Million Inquiries. I. How Size, Color, Position, and Location Affect Inquiries. *Media/Scope,* Vol. 3, No. 1, January 1959a, pp. 23–27.

———. Analysis of 12 Million Inquiries. II. How Thickness of Issue, Season Affect Inquiries. *Media/Scope,* Vol. 3, No. 2, February 1959b, pp. 30–43.

———. How Does Repetition of Advertisements Affect Readership? *Media/Scope,* Vol. 3, No. 11, November 1959c, pp. 50–51.

———. *Measuring Advertising Readership and Results.* New York: McGraw-Hill, 1966.

Stewart, John B. *Repetitive Advertising in Newspapers: A Study of Two New Products.* Boston: Harvard University, Graduate School of Business Administration, Division of Research, 1964.

Stigler, George J. The Economics of Information. *Journal of Political Economy,* Vol. 69, June 1961, pp. 213–225.

———. *The Theory of Price,* 3rd ed. New York: Macmillan, 1966.

Strong, E. K. The Effect of Size of Advertisements and Frequency of Their Presentation. *Psychological Review,* Vol. 21, March 1914, pp. 136–152.

Sylos-Labini, P. *Oligopoly in Technical Progress.* Cambridge: Harvard University Press, 1962.

Telser, Lester G. Advertising and Cigarettes. *Journal of Political Economy,* Vol. 70, No. 5, October 1962, pp. 471–499.

Vidale, M. L., and H. B. Wolfe. An Operations-Research Study of Sales Response to Advertising. *Operations Research,* Vol. 5, No. 3, June 1957, pp. 570–581.

Weinberg, Robert S. Multiple Factor Break-Even Analysis: The Application of Operations-Research Techniques to a Basic Problem of Management Planning and Control. *Operations Research,* Vol. 4, 1956, pp. 152–186.

Weiss, Doyle N. Determinants of Market Share. *Journal of Marketing Research,* Vol. 5, No. 3, August 1968, pp. 290–295.

———. An Analysis of the Demand Structure for Branded Consumer Products. *Applied Economics,* Vol. 1, 1969, pp. 37–49.

Wells, William D., and Jack M. Chinsky. Effects of Competing Messages: A Laboratory Simulation. *Journal of Marketing Research,* Vol. 2, No. 2, May 1965, pp. 141–145.

Wheatley, John J. Influence of Commercial's Length and Position. *Journal of Marketing Research,* Vol. 5, No. 2, May 1968, pp. 199–202.

Wildt, Albert R. Multifirm Analysis of Competitive Decision Variables. *Journal of Marketing Research,* Vol. 11, No. 1, February 1974, pp. 50–62.

Zentler, A. P., and D. Ryde. An Optimum Geographical Distribution of Publicity Expenditure in a Private Organization. *Management Science,* Vol. 2, July 1956, pp. 337–352.

Zielske, Hubert A. The Remembering and Forgetting of Advertising. *Journal of Marketing,* Vol. 23, No. 3, January 1959, pp. 239–243.

To determine its optimal level
of advertising, a firm can safely ignore . . .

The Effects of Advertising Carry-Over

Kenneth E. Case and James E. Shamblin

This paper examines the carry-over effects of advertising on current budgeting decisions. A widely accepted notion of carry-over assumes that exposure is concentrated in a relatively short period of time, but this exposure is distributed, although decayed, over future time periods. The decay rate has been found to vary with the type of advertising, sale-price advertising decaying quickly and institutional advertising decaying at a lesser rate.

We may define carry-over as the propensity of a particular ad to be seen or recalled in periods following its deployment. This includes the building up of favorable attitudes and predispositions to buy in the mind of the consumer.

It is important to differentiate between carry-over and renewal or habitual buying. Retention buying relates to the probability that a consumer is predisposed to favor a previously used brand. The probability that a consumer habitually continues to buy a brand decays with time, the rate depending on the reaction to the currently used product and the extent to which the consumer even considers the purchase of a brand not currently being used.

The motivation for the work conveyed here stems from the paper by Kuehn (1962) and the studies by Julian L. Simon (1965, 1967). Specifically, in validating a model similar to that used by Kuehn, it was noticed that the optimal advertising expenditure was robust with respect to the degree of carry-over present. Although that model is far too complex to present, the two related advertising models by Simon provide a gross but seemingly accurate vehicle for explaining the influence of carry-over on the advertising budget.

Development

In order to develop an extension to Simon's models, a brief review of the basic model concept is presented.

Consider an advertising expenditure A_t which results in a net revenue R_t (the subscript t indicates an arbitrary t^{th} period). Net revenue for a period may be described as total revenue less all costs associated with that revenue except advertising costs. If it can be assumed that a proportion (O < b < 1) of the net revenue will be realized in period $t + 1$ due to renewal buying, such net revenue $(R_{t+1} = bR_t)$ can be credited to A_t. Similarly, if the renewal proportion b remains essentially constant, the present and future net revenue due to expenditure A_t will be:

37

$$\sum_{i=t}^{\infty} R_i = R_t + R_{t+1} + R_{t+2} + \ldots$$

$$= R_t + bR_t + b^2R_t + \ldots$$

$$= R_t \frac{1}{1-b}.$$

If net revenues in future periods are discounted to consider the time value of money, the factor $p (p = \frac{1}{1+i}$, where i is the cost of capital or the applicable interest rate) may be applied as follows:

$$\sum_{i=t}^{\infty} V_i = R_t + p\, R_{t+1} +$$

$$p^2 R_{t+2} + \ldots$$

$$= R_t + p\, bR_t +$$

$$p^2 b^2\, R_t + \ldots$$

$$= R_t \frac{1}{1-p\bar{b}}$$

where V_i is the net present worth of revenue in period i.

The optimizing rule is to advertise up to the point at which an added increment of advertising yields an equal increment of discounted net revenues. This optimizing rule completes the review of the analytical development of Simon.

Consider a graphical representation of the discounted net revenue attributable to advertising during period t versus A_t. The net revenue as a function of advertising exhibits decreasing marginal returns at increasing levels of advertising. Further, as advertising increases without limit (hypothetically), the net revenue will approach a saturation level asymptotically. Such a graphical interpretation is shown in Figure 1.

Now consider advertising carry-over, the degree of which is influenced by the type, mode, copy, etc., of advertising, treated much like the renewal factor. Let q $(O < q < 1)$ represent the fractional amount of advertising carry-over in period t+1 resulting from the advertising expenditure A_t. That is, a carry-over value of qA_t results in period t+1.

Further, if the proportion of various media used in advertising is reasonably stable, the carry-over factor q may be considered constant. Thus, the "composite" advertising $\bar{A}_t$ during the period t can be represented as follows:

$$\bar{A}_t = A_t + qA_{t-1} +$$

$$q^2\, A_{t-2} + \ldots + q^{t-1}\, A_1$$

Kenneth E. Case is an assistant professor of industrial engineering and operations research at Virginia Polytechnic Institute and State University. He obtained the Ph.D. degree in industrial engineering and management at Oklahoma State University. Dr. Case has current interests in advertising research, operations research, and quality control. He is a member of AIIE, ASQC, and is national director of the Quality Control and Reliability Assurance Division of AIIE.

Kuehn noted that q typically lies in the range $0 \leqslant q \leqslant .5$.

The assumption of advertising carry-over implies a period-to-period interdependence relating promotional efforts and corresponding results. As such, consider the effect of carry-over from previous advertising A_t in Figure 2. Notice that at $A_t = O$, there is a positive net revenue due to advertising carry-over from previous periods. It is now of interest to determine what, if any, effect is manifested in the optimal advertising level when the carry-over effect is evident. An associated question is whether increased or decreased spending is motivated by advertising carry-over. In order to assist in determining the effect of advertising carry-over, a simplified mathematical model will be developed.

Due to the asymptotic and decreasing return properties of the net revenue curves in Figures 1 and 2, an exponential approximation can be considered. Let:

$$\sum_{i=t}^{\infty} V_i = S(1 - e^{-\frac{2\bar{A}_t}{S}})$$

where S is the net revenue saturation level and:

$$\bar{A}_t = A_t + qA_{t-1} +$$

$$q^2\, A_{t-2} + \ldots + q^{t-1}\, A_1$$

For purposes of simplification, assume a well developed market where the firm spends the same amount on advertising each period. Thus,

$$\ldots = A_{t-1} = A_t = A_{t+1} = \ldots = A.$$

In order to find the optimal value of A we can let:

$$\bar{A}_t = A + qA + q^2A + \ldots$$

$$= A\frac{1}{1-q}$$

Profit for one of a series of identical time periods may now be expressed as follows:

$$\pi_t = \sum_{i=t}^{\infty} V_i - A$$

$$= S(1-e^{-\frac{2A}{S(1-q)}}) - A$$

Results

Knowing the profit expression, the optimum advertising budget can be determined by setting the partial derivative equal to zero and solving for A:

$$\frac{\partial \pi_t}{\partial A^t} = \frac{2S}{S(1-q)}$$

$$e^{-\frac{2A}{S(1-q)}} - 1 = 0$$

$$A = -\frac{S(1-q)}{2} \ln\left(\frac{1-q}{2}\right)$$

Letting the carry-over coefficient q take on values of 0.0, 0.2, 0.4, and 0.6, the optimal advertising level A can be determined as a fraction of the saturation level,

@ q = 0.0	A = .37 S
@ q = 0.2	A = .37 S
@ q = 0.4	A = .36 S
@ q = 0.6	A = .32 S

Over a wide range of advertising carry-over, the optimal advertising level remains surprisingly constant. That is, under the constrained conditions specified by this model, optimal advertising is extremely robust to changes in carry-over. More specifically, it may be inferred that optimal advertising, considering both carry-over and renewal buying from past periods as well as effects on future periods, is relatively insensitive to the degree of advertising carry-over. However, the above results are based on the assumption of a stable market and a constant advertising expenditure over time.

In order to relax such limiting assumptions, the effect of carry-over has been investigated in a much more generalized model of n competing brands in which product demand is allowed to vary as a function of both time and industry advertising. Habitual buying and carry-over are treated as separate entities.

Many uses have indicated the same result—a rather constant optimal advertising level (or pattern) over the entire range of advertising carry-over ($0 \leqslant q \leqslant .5$). It is also noteworthy that optimal advertising, although varying over time as a function of seasonal demand and competition spending, maintains very similar magnitude and phase levels over all values of carry-over.

The results of this study indicate that a firm need not concern itself with estimating advertising carry-over in order to determine the optimal level of advertising, even if carry-over is felt

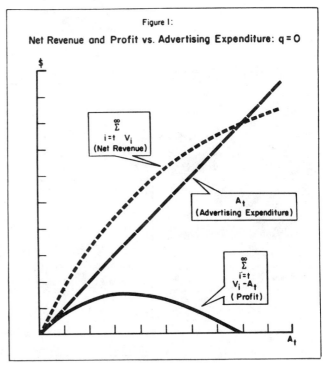

Figure I:

Net Revenue and Profit vs. Advertising Expenditure: q = 0

$\sum_{i=t}^{\infty} V_i$ (Net Revenue)

A_t (Advertising Expenditure)

$\sum_{i=t}^{\infty} V_i - A_t$ (Profit)

to be considerable. On the other hand, as a comparison between Figures 1 and 2 demonstrates, profit is affected by advertising carry-over. Perhaps these results substantiate the reasoning used in most advertising models and business games in which carry-over is not explicitly considered while habitual buying and other parameters are included.

References

Jastram, Roy W. A Treatment of Distributed Lags in the Theory of Advertising Expenditure. *Journal of Marketing,* Vol. 20, July 1955, pp. 36-46.

Kuehn, Alfred A. How Advertising Performance Depends on Other Marketing Factors. *Journal of Advertising Research,* Vol. 2, No. 1, pp. 2-10.

Simon, Julian L. Expenditure Policy for Mail-Order Advertisers. *Journal of Marketing Research,* Vol. 4, 1967, pp. 59-61.

James E. Shamblin is professor of industrial engineering and management at Oklahoma State University. Dr. Shamblin has published and consulted extensively. His B.S., M.S., and Ph.D. are from The University of Texas. His research interests include advertising modelling, operations research, management science, and production control.

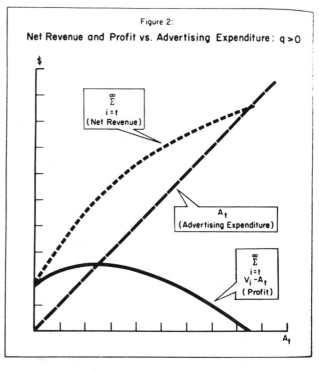

Figure 2:

Net Revenue and Profit vs. Advertising Expenditure: q > 0

$$\sum_{i=t}^{\infty} \text{(Net Revenue)}$$

A_t (Advertising Expenditure)

$$\sum_{i=t}^{\infty} V_i - A_t \text{ (Profit)}$$

Simon, Julian L. New Evidence for No Effect of Scale in Advertising. *Journal of Advertising Research,* Vol. 9, No. 1, pp. 38-41.

Simon, Julian L. A Simple Model for Determining Advertising Appropriations. *Journal of Marketing Research,* Vol. 2, 1965, pp. 285-292.

QUOTABLE

"There is no set solution or pattern for getting your marketing job done. You must be prepared to innovate and create and thereby increase your sales and earnings.

—Warren J. Holmes
Allis-Chalmers Co.

FRANK M. BASS and DARRAL G. CLARKE*

This article deals with estimation and testing of six different distributed lag models, with an example given of sales and advertising data for a dietary weight control product. A distributed lag model more general than the frequently employed Koyck model is shown to be consistent with the evidence.

Testing Distributed Lag Models of Advertising Effect

Time series marketing models often involve some notion of distributed lag, especially in studies of the relationship between sales and advertising. The estimation method employed has not always been the most appropriate method and the models have seldom been tested against plausible alternatives.

It is not difficult to develop a variety of plausible arguments to justify distributed lag theories of advertising effect. While these models have great theoretical appeal, a problem arises if one wants to determine the "best" one. Griliches [11] reviewed statistical methodology associated with distributed lag theories and suggested pessimism about the possibility of discriminating among alternatives on the basis of simultaneous confidence intervals of parameter estimates. Zellner and Geisel [18], building on the ideas of Box and Hill [8], used Bayesian methods to derive posterior odds for a given distributed lag model relative to others.

Our procedure for choosing among alternative models is based on predictive testing. Other researchers [9, 16] have discussed procedures for obtaining maximum likelihood estimates of parameters in distributed lag systems. The availability of sales and advertising data for a dietary weight control product afforded us an excellent opportunity to apply different methods of estimation and predictive tests in a study of alternative distributed lag theories of the effects of advertising.

THE PREDICTIVE TESTING CONCEPT

The concept of predictive testing of econometric hypotheses has been advanced, discussed, and illus-

trated [1, 2, 3], and empirical studies of sales and advertising have appeared which used predictive testing [4, 5, 6, 7]. In spite of the fact that predictive testing falls easily into the framework of logical positivism, the most popular scientific philosophy, the concept is not widely understood or practiced in econometrics. The basic idea is to deduce specific implications from explicit premises; if the premises are true one can make "predictions" about the data. If the predictions are not fulfilled, the data are not consistent with the theory (model) and it is discredited. In attempting to discriminate among alternative models, predictive testing may eliminate some of the candidates. Then if a model survives the tests, even sharper restrictions and premises may be established as a basis for further testing until, hopefully, only one theory survives.

Griliches' article brought up problems inherent in statistical analysis of distributed lag models. Two are central to our analysis: (1) the availability of monthly data makes "the assumption that the greatest response occurs immediately at the beginning of the adjustment period seem rather unfortunate" [11, p. 24], and (2) the confidence intervals obtained for estimates of distributed lag model coefficients are large enough to make determination of the exact lag function very difficult. We agree with Griliches on both counts but shall demonstrate here that predictive testing can eliminate candidate theories by indicating the inconsistency of the evidence with the implications of the theory.

THE GENERAL DISTRIBUTED LAG MODEL

The general form of the distributed lag model is:

$$(1) \quad y_t = \beta_0 x_t + \beta_1 x_{t-1} + \beta_2 x_{t-2} + \cdots + \mu_t,$$

where x_t is an exogenous variable (such as advertising)

* Frank M. Bass is Professor of Industrial Administration, Purdue University, and Darral G. Clarke is Assistant Professor of Marketing, Harvard University. The research reported in this paper was supported by a grant from the Consumer Research Institute.

298

and μ_t is a normally distributed random variable with mean zero, serially independent. Interest is focused here on those models in which the β's are all nonnegative and have a finite sum ($\beta = \sum_i \beta_i < \infty$). On the basis of this last restriction it is possible to rewrite (1) as:

$$(2) \quad y_t = \beta[w_0 x_t + w_1 x_{t-1} + w_2 x_{t-2} + \cdots] + \mu_t ,$$

where:

$$w_i \geq 0 \quad \text{and} \quad \sum_{i=0}^{\infty} w_i = 1.$$

In (2) the current value of the dependent variable (sales, for example) is a function of the current and previous values of the independent variable (advertising, for example). Since the w's are nonnegative and sum to one, they can be thought of as probabilities defined over the set of nonnegative integers. Advertising may attract new customers, some of whom purchase immediately and some of whom delay purchase because of shopping and usage factors. Furthermore, repeat purchase depends on usage rates. The distributed lag effect depends on the distribution of these lag factors over the population of buyers. The relative impact of current and previous advertising in determining current sales can then be described by any member of the family of probability mass functions defined over the set of nonnegative integers.

Probably the best known distribution associated with sales-advertising relationships is the Koyck [13] distribution, often applied in statistical studies of sales and advertising, e.g., [14]. The Koyck specification describes a process in which the impact of advertising on sales decays geometrically with time. Thus if $w_i = (1 - \lambda)\lambda^i$, (2) becomes:

$$(3) \quad y_t = \beta(1 - \lambda)[x_t + \lambda x_{t-1} + \lambda^2 x_{t-2} \cdots] + \mu_t .$$

The popularity of the Koyck specification rests on the fact that its assumption of geometric decay in effectiveness has great intuitive appeal and that an equivalent form to the right-hand side of (3) may be found. This form provides for convenient estimation without the disadvantage of the loss of the several degrees of freedom associated with this right-hand side. Thus lagging (3) by one period and multiplying through by λ gives:

$$(4) \quad \lambda y_{t-1} = \beta(1 - \lambda)[\lambda x_{t-1} + \lambda^2 x_{t-2} \cdots] + \lambda \mu_{t-1} .$$

If (4) is subtracted from (3) and the result rewritten, we obtain:

$$(5) \quad y_t = \lambda y_{t-1} + \beta(1 - \lambda)x_t + \mu_t - \lambda \mu_{t-1} .$$

Therefore, on the basis of the Koyck specification, the distributed lag model may be reduced to one that involves only two variables. The gain in degrees of freedom has not been accomplished without cost, however, since the classical least squares estimators of β and λ are not consistent unless one is willing to make the

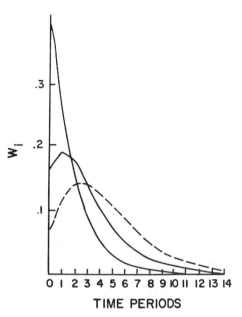

Figure 1
DIFFERENT LAG WEIGHTING SCHEMES

w_i

TIME PERIODS

very strong assumption that $\mu_t = \lambda \mu_{t-1} + \epsilon_t$, with ϵ_t serially independent.

While the Koyck distributed lag model has been the most popular model out of the general class, it is by no means the only reasonable model of distributed lag effect. For example, under some circumstances it would be reasonable to expect the response to advertising to increase at first and then to decline. Figure 1 displays graphically alternative weighting schemes for distributed lag models, each of which might be reasonable under given circumstances.

THE DATA AND BACKGROUND INFORMATION

The data used in this study consisted of a three-year history of sales and advertising for a dietary weight control (DWC) product, aggregated by month. Sales history was measured in multiples of "equivalent serving units" (to account for the different sizes in which the product was distributed) and the advertising history was given in dollar expenditures. Advertising expenditure was recognized in the month in which the advertising occurred, rather than the month in which it was billed to the company.

During the period under study, the product was a

heavily advertised competitor in an active market characterized by large monthly fluctuations in both sales and advertising. These conditions made the DWC market an excellent candidate for a study of the short-run effect of advertising on sales.

The Theory and the General Model

Advertising has been the dominant marketing decision variable for sales of DWC products, since sales are closely related to advertising's success in increasing and directing the consumer's desire to be slimmer. Consumers of the DWC product under study fell into two general classes: (1) those who used the product to help control their weight by consuming it as one of their daily meals and (2) those "on a diet" who consumed practically nothing else but the product.

Consumers in the second group would seem to be the most sensitive to current advertising appeals. Unfortunately, there was no way to distinguish according to these groups' purchases, and advertising may well have affected the two groups differently. Because of extreme fluctuations in advertising expenditures (Figure 2), we expected that multicollinearity of the lagged values of advertising would be less than expected for advertising data or time series data generally. We thus developed a rationale for assuming nonmonotonic, lagged response to advertising.

Letting a_r be the probability of making a first purchase r periods after exposure and b_s be probability of a second purchase s periods after first purchase, the probability of a first or second purchase r periods after exposure is:

$$a_r + a_r b_0 + a_{r-1} b_1 + \cdots + a_r b_r - a_r b_0$$
$$= a_r(1 - b_0) + a_r b_0 + a_{r-1} b_1 + \cdots + a_0 b_r .$$

Credit for the second purchase should be assigned to the expenditure which induced initial trial, and "bumps" in current sales in fact may be the result of repeat purchase resulting from a prior bump in initial purchase. After the first repurchase, the effects of further repeat buying are damped; hence we considered only first and second purchases in the argument above. Since light users (consuming the product only one meal a day) constituted the bulk of the buyers, and since an equivalent serving unit consisted of 24 servings, the modal time to repeat purchase for an average consumer was three weeks or more. Heavy users, on the other hand, tended to respond more quickly to advertising and repurchased the product weekly. The modal total response after exposure obviously depended on the mix of these two groups in the market. Because we used monthly data and because of a modal response time of three weeks, we did not rule out the possibility of the greatest response to advertising occurring in the month following exposure:

$$(6) \qquad S_t = a + \beta(p_0 A_t + p_1 A_{t-1} + \cdots \quad) + u_t$$

where:

S_t = sales at time t
A_t = advertising at time t
p_i = probability of purchase i periods (months) after exposure
β = marginal effect of one dollar of advertising in period t.

We might find $p_1 > p_0$. Thus the Koyck model is not the only reasonable possibility under the circumstances. Estimation of parameters with the Koyck model when this model is inappropriate can lead to serious misinterpretation of the effects of advertising and hence to advertising policies which are not efficient.

Reasonable Distributed Lag Functions

We examine here six possible models within the distributed lag class, and we shall show the transformed version of each and the implications of each in terms of parameter values of the equivalent untransformed lag model.[1] These implied parameter restrictions will then serve as a basis for predictive tests of the models.

Model I. The first model we shall consider is the Koyck model. Thus, the transformed equation to be estimated is:

$$(7) \qquad S_t = a(1 - \lambda) + \lambda S_{t-1} + \beta(1 - \lambda)x_t + \mu_t - \lambda\mu_{t-1}$$

---

[1] The procedure for identifying the parameters of the untransformed model from the estimates of parameters of the transformed model is illustrated briefly in the Appendix.

Figure 2
MONTHLY SALES AND ADVERTISING PATTERNS FOR A DIETARY WEIGHT CONTROL PRODUCT

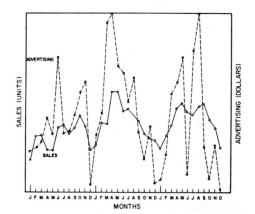

where the condition that $0 < \hat{\lambda} < 1, 0 < \hat{\beta} < 1$ must be satisfied if the data are consistent with the theory and where $\hat{p}_i = \hat{\lambda}(1 - \hat{\lambda}) i = 0, 1, 2, \cdots$.

Model II. A possible alternative to the Koyck model is one in which the geometric decay in the effect of advertising does not begin with the initial period but is delayed—say until period two. The equivalent transformed equation is:

$$(8) \quad S_t = a(1 - \lambda) + \lambda S_{t-1} + \beta a_0 x_t$$
$$+ \beta a_1 x_{t-1} + \mu_t - \lambda \mu_{t-1} .$$

In this case:

$$p_0 = \left(\frac{a_0}{a_0 + a_1}\right)(1 - \lambda) ,$$

$$p_1 = (a_0 \lambda + a_1)\frac{(1 - \lambda)}{(a_0 + a_1)} ,$$

$$p_i = \lambda p_{i-1}, \quad i = 2, 3, \cdots .$$

The restrictions implied by the theory are $0 < \hat{\lambda} < 1$, $0 \leq \hat{p}_0 < 1, 0 \leq \hat{p}_1 < 1$. In order for Model II to differ substantially from Model I, $p_1 > p_0$, implying that $(1 - \hat{\lambda}) < (\hat{a}_1/\hat{a}_0)$.

Model III. The next model is the extension of the Koyck model to a second-order lag function. The appropriate equation is:

$$(9) \quad S_t = a(1 - \lambda_1 - \lambda_2) + \lambda_1 S_{t-1} + \lambda_2 S_{t-2} + \beta a_0 x_t$$
$$+ \mu_t - \lambda_1 \mu_{t-1} - \lambda_2 \mu_{t-2} .$$

For this model:

$$p_0 = 1 - \lambda_1 - \lambda_2 ,$$

$$p_1 = \lambda_1 p_0 ,$$

$$p_i = \lambda_1 p_{i-1} + \lambda_2 p_{i-2} , \quad i = 2, 3, \cdots .$$

In order for (9) to imply a nonnegative lag distribution for x, the following conditions must hold: $0 < \hat{\lambda}_1 < 2$, $-1 < \hat{\lambda}_2 < 1, 1 - \hat{\lambda}_1 - \hat{\lambda}_2 > 0, \hat{\lambda}_1^2 \geq -4\hat{\lambda}_2, (\hat{\beta}a_0) \geq 0$.

Model IV. A natural extension of the second-order lag function in Model III is one in which x is lagged by one period in addition to the lag in the dependent variable. This gives the equation:

$$(10) \quad S_t = a(1 - \lambda_1 - \lambda_2) + \lambda_1 S_{t-1} + \lambda_2 S_{t-2} + \beta a_0 x_t$$
$$+ \beta a_1 x_{t-1} + \mu_t - \lambda_1 \mu_{t-1} - \lambda_2 \mu_{t-2} .$$

For this model:

$$p_0 = \frac{a_0}{a_0 + a_1}(1 - \lambda_1 - \lambda_2),$$

$$p_1 = \frac{a_1}{a_0 + a_1}(1 - \lambda_1 - \lambda_2) + \lambda_1 p_0,$$

$$p_j = \lambda_1 p_{j-1} + \lambda_2 p_{j-2}, \quad j = 2, 3, \cdots .$$

In order for (10) to imply a nonnegative lag distribution for x, the following conditions must hold: $0 < \hat{\lambda}_1 < 2$, $-1 < \hat{\lambda}_2 < 1, 1 - \hat{\lambda}_1 - \hat{\lambda}_2 > 0, \hat{\lambda}_1^2 \geq -4\hat{\lambda}_2 , \hat{\beta}a_0 > 0$, $\hat{\beta}a_1 > 0$. A nonmonotonic lag function would imply $(\hat{a}_1 + \hat{\lambda}_1 \hat{a}_0/\hat{a}_0) > 1$.

Model V. The third-order lag function gives the equation:

$$(11) \quad S_t = a(1 - \lambda_1 - \lambda_2 - \lambda_3) + \lambda_1 S_{t-1} + \lambda_2 S_{t-2}$$
$$+ \lambda_3 S_{t-3} + \beta a_0 x_t + \mu_t - \lambda_1 \mu_{t-1} - \lambda_2 \mu_{t-2}$$
$$- \lambda_3 \mu_{t-3} .$$

For this model:

$$p_0 = (1 - \lambda_1 - \lambda_2 - \lambda_3),$$

$$p_1 = \lambda_1 p_0 ,$$

$$p_2 = (\lambda_1^2 + \lambda_2)p_0 ,$$

$$p_j = \lambda_1 p_{j-1} + \lambda_2 p_{j-2} + \lambda_3 p_{j-3} , \quad j \geq 3.$$

Model VI. The third-order lag function with a period lag in x is the last model considered. The equation which follows from this function is:

$$(12) \quad S_t = a(1 - \lambda_1 - \lambda_2 - \lambda_3) + \lambda_1 S_{t-1} + \lambda_2 S_{t-2}$$
$$+ \lambda_3 S_{t-3} + \beta a_0 x_t + \beta a_1 x_{t-1} + u_t$$
$$- \lambda_1 u_{t-1} - \lambda_2 u_{t-2} - \lambda_3 u_{t-3} .$$

For this model:

$$p_0 = \frac{a_0}{a_0 + a_1}(1 - \lambda_1 - \lambda_2 - \lambda_3),$$

$$p_1 = \frac{a_1 + \lambda_1 a_0}{a_0 + a_1}(1 - \lambda_1 - \lambda_2 - \lambda_3),$$

$$p_2 = \frac{\lambda_1(a_1 + \lambda_1 a_0) + \lambda_2 a_0}{a_0 + a_1}(1 - \lambda_1 - \lambda_2 - \lambda_3),$$

$$p_j = \lambda_1 p_{j-1} + \lambda_2 p_{j-2} + \lambda_3 p_{j-3}, \quad j \geq 3.$$

Parameter Estimates for Models I–VI

Models I–VI pretty well exhaust the range of distributed lag models which it is reasonable or practical to consider. The ordinary least squares regression estimates for Models I through VI are shown in Table 1.

The OLS estimates of Models I–VI were not consistent without a very strong assumption about the form of the disturbance term. Maximum likelihood estimation requires finding solutions to systems of nonlinear equations; some of the variety of methods for this purpose are discussed in the Appendix. The maximum likelihood estimates are shown in Table 2. Notice that the OLS estimate for the coefficient of current advertising was less in every case than the corresponding maximum likelihood estimate; OLS estimates in general were biased upwards for lag effects and biased down-

Table 1

OLS ESTIMATES FOR MODELS I–VI

Model	Estimate	R^2
I	$S_t = 110.294 + .125A_t + .621S_{t-1}$ $(.028) \quad (.104)$ $\lambda = .621, \quad \hat\beta = .329$ $\hat p_0 = .379, \quad \hat p_1 = .235, \quad \hat p_2 = .145, \cdots,$ $\hat p_i = \lambda^i(1 - \lambda), \quad i = 0, 1, \cdots.$	.705
II	$S_t = 147.946 + .113A_t + .077A_{t-1} + .468S_{t-1}$ $(.026) \quad (.032) \quad (.115)$ $\lambda = .468$ $\hat p_0 = .315, \quad \hat p_1 = .357, \quad \hat p_2 = .167, \quad \hat p_3 = .078,$ $\hat p_i = \lambda \hat p_{i-1}, \quad i = 2, 3, \cdots.$	.755
III[a]	$S_t = 143.790 + .115A_t + .829S_{t-1} - .273S_{t-2}$ $(.027) \quad (.148) \quad (.143)$ $\lambda_1 = .829, \quad \lambda_2 = -.273$ $\hat p_0 = .444, \quad \hat p_1 = .368, \quad \hat p_2 = .184, \cdots,$ $\hat p_i = \lambda_1 \hat p_{i-1} + \lambda_2 \hat p_{i-2}, \quad i = 2, 3, \cdots.$	.738
IV[a]	$S_t = 164.487 + .108A_t + .064A_{t-1} + .637S_{t-1} - .188S_{t-2}$ $(.026) \quad (.033) \quad (.172) \quad (.143)$ $\lambda_1 = .637, \quad \lambda_2 = -.188$ $\hat p_0 = .343, \quad \hat p_1 = .422, \quad \hat p_2 = .204, \cdots,$ $\hat p_i = \lambda_1 \hat p_{i-1} + \lambda_2 \hat p_{i-2}, \quad i = 1, 2, \cdots.$	.769
V	$S_t = 126.646 + .116A_t + .867S_{t-1} - .394S_{t-2} + .121S_{t-3}$ $(.027) \quad (.155) \quad (.200) \quad (.139)$ $\lambda_1 = .867, \quad \lambda_2 = -.394, \quad \lambda_3 = .121$ $\hat p_0 = .406, \quad \hat p_1 = .352, \quad \hat p_2 = .144, \cdots,$ $\hat p_i = \lambda_1 \hat p_{i-1} + \lambda_2 \hat p_{i-2} + \lambda_3 \hat p_{i-3}, \quad i = 3, 4, \cdots.$	.745
VI	$S_t = 150.182 + .109A_t + .061A_{t-1} + .675S_{t-1} - .286S_{t-2} + .095S_{t-3}$ $(.026) \quad (.034) \quad (.182) \quad (.201) \quad (.134)$ $\lambda_1 = .675, \quad \lambda_2 = -.286, \quad \lambda_3 = .095$ $\hat p_0 = .330, \quad \hat p_1 = .406, \quad \hat p_2 = .179, \cdots,$ $\hat p_i = \lambda_1 \hat p_{i-1} + \lambda_2 \hat p_{i-2} + \lambda_3 \hat p_{i-3}, \quad i = 3, 4, \cdots.$	.773

[a] The condition $\lambda_1^2 \geqq -4\lambda_2$ does not hold.

wards for current effects. The R^2 statistics were only slightly lower under maximum likelihood estimation than under OLS estimation.

General Implications of Estimates

As indicated in Tables 1 and 2, the estimates of λ_1 and λ_2 for Models III and IV did not satisfy the stability conditions requirements. Of course, these suspicious estimates may have arisen because of chance.

The estimates of the distributed lag weights estimated by OLS for Models I–VI are displayed in Figure 3. The estimates for Models II, IV, and VI suggested nonmonotonic lag functions, while those for Models I, III, and V indicated monotonic decay in advertising effectiveness. The weights shown in Table 2 as derived from maximum likelihood estimates were similar to those based on OLS for Models I–IV, but differed substantially for Models V and VI. In all cases and with both sets of estimates, the weights got close to zero after a lag of three periods.

A PREDICTIVE TEST OF THE AUTOREGRESSIVE ALTERNATIVE

A simple and plausible alternative to Model II is the first-order autoregressive model:

$$(13) \quad S_t = a_0 + aA_t + u_t, \quad u_t = \rho u_{t-1} + \epsilon_t.$$

In testing Model II against this alternative, if (13) reflects the real world, then:

$$S_t = a_0 + aA_t + \rho u_{t-1} + \epsilon_t$$

$$(14) \quad = a_0 + aA_t + \rho(S_{t-1} - a_0 - aA_{t-1}) + \epsilon_t$$

$$= (a_0 - \rho a_0) + aA_t + \rho S_{t-1} - \rho a A_{t-1} + \epsilon_t.$$

Equation (14) implies that the lag effect was due entirely to autocorrelated disturbances. Also, (14) has the same form as Model II, although its interpretation is very different, and if the autoregressive model were appropriate, when the parameters of Model II are estimated we should observe that the product of the

Table 2
MAXIMUM LIKELIHOOD ESTIMATES FOR MODELS I–VI

Model	Estimate	R^2
I	$S_t = 272.6 + .157A_t + .585S_{t-1}$ $\quad\quad\quad\quad (.002) \quad (.083)$ $\lambda = .584, \quad \hat{\beta} = .377$ $\hat{p}_0 = .415, \quad \hat{p}_1 = .242, \quad \hat{p}_2 = .142, \cdots,$ $\hat{p}_i = \lambda^i(1 - \lambda), \quad\quad\quad i = 0, \cdots.$	.650
II	$S_t = 286.2 + .127A_t + .081A_{t-1} + .399S_{t-1}$ $\quad\quad\quad\quad (.026) \quad (.043) \quad\quad (.144)$ $\lambda = .399$ $\hat{p}_0 = .366, \quad \hat{p}_1 = .380, \quad \hat{p}_2 = .152, \cdots,$ $\hat{p}_i = \lambda\hat{p}_{i-1}, \quad\quad\quad\quad i = 2, 3, \cdots.$	.686
III[a]	$S_t = 286.6 + .135A_t + .910S_{t-1} - .305S_{t-2}$ $\quad\quad\quad\quad (.024) \quad (.168) \quad\quad (.150)$ $\lambda_1 = .910, \quad \lambda_2 = -.305$ $\hat{p}_0 = .396, \quad \hat{p}_1 = .360, \quad \hat{p}_2 = .207, \cdots,$ $\hat{p}_i = \lambda_1\hat{p}_{i-1} + \lambda_2\hat{p}_{i-2}, \quad i = 2, 3, \cdots.$	.683
IV[a]	$S_t = 293.6 + .126A_t + .031A_{t-1} + .772S_{t-1} - .250S_{t-2}$ $\quad\quad\quad\quad (.025) \quad (.078) \quad\quad (.439) \quad\quad (.270)$ $\lambda_1 = .772, \quad \lambda_2 = -.250$ $\hat{p}_0 = .384, \quad \hat{p}_1 = .390, \quad \hat{p}_2 = .205, \cdots,$ $\hat{p}_i = \lambda_1\hat{p}_{i-1} + \lambda_2\hat{p}_{i-2}, \quad i = 1, 2, \cdots.$	.692
V	$S_t = 280.6 + .120A_t + 1.14S_{t-1} - .689S_{t-2} + .214S_{t-3}$ $\quad\quad\quad\quad (.020) \quad (.195) \quad\quad (.289) \quad\quad (.167)$ $\lambda_1 = 1.14, \quad \lambda_2 = -.689, \quad \lambda_3 = .214$ $\hat{p}_0 = .181, \quad \hat{p}_1 = 1.59, \quad \hat{p}_2 = -1.14, \quad \hat{p}_3 = .443, \cdots,$ $\hat{p}_i = \lambda_1\hat{p}_{i-1} + \lambda_2\hat{p}_{i-2} + \lambda_3\hat{p}_{i-3}, \quad i = 3, 4, \cdots.$	.691
VI	$S_t = 273.2 + .145A_t - .133A_{t-1} + 1.71S_{t-1} - 1.00S_{t-2} + .260S_{t-3}$ $\quad\quad\quad\quad (.023) \quad (.098) \quad\quad (.628) \quad\quad (.507) \quad\quad (.183)$ $\lambda_1 = 1.71, \quad \lambda_2 = -1.00, \quad \lambda_3 = .260$ $\hat{p}_0 = 1.77, \quad \hat{p}_1 = -.567, \quad \hat{p}_2 = .088, \quad \hat{p}_3 = -.276, \cdots,$ $\hat{p}_i = \lambda_1\hat{p}_{i-1} + \lambda_2\hat{p}_{i-2} + \lambda_3\hat{p}_{i-3}, \quad i = 3, 4, \cdots.$	.735

[a] The condition $\lambda_1^2 \geqq -4\lambda_2$ does not hold.

estimated coefficients of advertising and lagged sales were approximately equal to the negative of the coefficient of lagged advertising. From the estimates in Table 1 we can compare $-(.07708)$ with $(.11259)(.46799) = .052$. These two values differ by more than the estimated standard deviation of any of the involved variables, and if each of the estimates in the product is reduced by three standard deviations the product will still not cover the negative value implied by the autoregressive model. The results are similar if data from Table 2 are used. Thus it seemed reasonable to reject the autoregressive model as representing a complete explanation of the data.

PREDICTIVE TESTING OF MODELS I–VI: PARAMETER ESTIMATE COMPARISONS

The confidence interval basis for discriminating between the different types of lag functions represented in the various regions of the parameter space is conditional upon a given model being an adequate representation of the way nature has generated the data. An alternative test can be developed where the data are such that estimates of one model suggest that another model is inconsistent with the evidence.

The nesting of models in the configuration of models we considered permits a test of one model on the basis of the parameter estimates of another. For example, if Model I is true, we would expect that when Model III is estimated the parameter estimate of the coefficient for sales lagged twice would be sufficiently close to zero that the difference could be attributed to chance. If this is not the case, then Model I would be discredited. Therefore, the predictive test for Model I would be that $\hat{\lambda}_2$ lies within the acceptance region for a test of the hypothesis $H_0: \lambda_2 = 0$. From Tables 1 and 2, we see that $\hat{\lambda}$ in Model III was about two standard deviations away from zero. Thus H_0 was rejected and, along with it, Model I. Similarly, if Model III is an adequate representation of reality, when Model V is estimated, we

Figure 3

DISTRIBUTED LAG WEIGHTS ASSOCIATED WITH
MODELS I-VI, ESTIMATED BY OLS

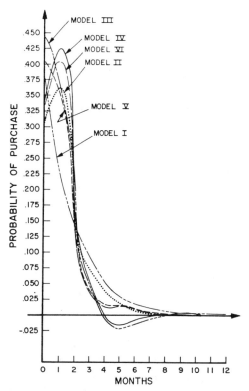

would expect to find that the estimated coefficient for sales lagged three times is close enough to zero that it is easily attributable to chance, to the extent that it differs from zero. Since $\hat{\lambda}_8$ in Model V was close enough to zero, measured in standard deviation units, Model III was not contradicted by the estimates of parameters in Model V. Moreover, the maximum likelihood estimates for the coefficients of lagged advertising and sales lagged three times in Model VI were not large enough relative to their standard deviations to reject Model III. Thus in the nesting of Models I, III, and V in Model VI, Model I was, by conventional standards, rejected, and Model III was not strongly contradicted by the evidence.

The remaining contenders can be tested for consistency with the evidence by a similar approach. If Model

II is an adequate representation of the way the data were generated, then $\lambda_2 = 0$ in Model IV. The estimates of these parameters and their standard deviations for Model IV in Tables 1 and 2 show that by conventional standards the estimates probably (we did not know the exact distributions) did not fall in the critical regions for the tests. Model II, then, was not contradicted by the evidence. Table 3 summarizes the testing of nested models.

The predictive testing led to the rejection of the only model which necessarily implied monotonic response to advertising. This result was, of course, far from conclusive with respect to the shape of the lag distribution, but the evidence against the Koyck model and geometric decay was rather strong.

PREDICTIVE TESTING OF NESTED MODELS I-VI: ANALYSIS OF RESIDUAL VARIANCE

In addition to the absence of knowledge about the exact distribution of parameter estimates, the procedure for discriminating between models discussed in the previous section suffers from the limitation that only one parameter at a time is considered. Scheffe [15] discussed a procedure for testing a regression model against a nested alternative model on the basis of the analysis of residual variance. Since ANOVA is a more robust procedure for hypothesis testing than parameter estimate tests, we supplemented the tests in the preceding section with tests of residual variances.

If Ω is the set of assumptions associated with a regression model with r independent variables; and if ω is the set of assumptions associated with a nested regression model such that ω differs from Ω only by the fact that under ω, q of the variables under Ω have zero regression coefficients, we can test $H_0:\omega$ against $H_1:\Omega$ on the basis of:

$$T = \frac{n - r}{q} \frac{S_\omega - S_\Omega}{S_\Omega}$$

where n is the number of observations, S_ω is the residual sum of squares under ω, and S_Ω is the residual sum of squares under Ω. We reject H_0 only if $T > F_{\alpha,q,n-r}$. The results of the tests are shown in Table 4.

It appears that the additional variable in Model II contributed enough to explained variance to reject Model I, while the additional variables in the other comparisons contributed only negligibly to explained variance.

DIRECT ESTIMATION OF THE ORIGINAL MODEL

Thus far we have used predictive testing in an attempt to eliminate candidate theories for explaining sales behavior. Rejection of the autoregressive disturbance model led us to believe that advertising did indeed have carryover effects. Rejection of the Koyck monotonic

Table 3

PREDICTIVE TESTING OF NESTED MODELS I–VI BY PARAMETER ESTIMATE COMPARISON

Decision rule	Prediction	Evidence	Conclusion
First nest			
Accept Model I if in Model III	$0 < \mid \lambda_2 \mid \hat{\sigma}_{\lambda_2} \mid < 1.65$	$\mid \lambda_2 \mid \hat{\sigma}_{\lambda_2} \mid = 1.90^a$ $\mid \lambda_2 \mid \hat{\sigma}_{\lambda_2} \mid = 2.00^b$	Reject } Reject } Model I
Accept Model III if in Model V	$0 < \mid \lambda_3 \mid \hat{\sigma}_{\lambda_3} \mid < 1.65$	$\mid \lambda_3 \mid \hat{\sigma}_{\lambda_3} \mid = 0.87^a$ $\mid \lambda_3 \mid \hat{\sigma}_{\lambda_3} \mid = 1.28^b$	Accept } Accept } Model III
Accept Model III if in Model VI	$-\infty < \beta\hat{a}_1 \mid \hat{\sigma}_{\beta\hat{a}_1} < 1.65$	$\beta\hat{a}_1 \mid \hat{\sigma}_{\beta\hat{a}_1} = 1.79^a$ $\beta\hat{a}_1 \mid \hat{\sigma}_{\beta\hat{a}_1} = 1.03^b$	Reject } Accept } Model III
Accept Model III if in Model VI	$0 < \mid \lambda_3 \mid \hat{\sigma}_{\lambda_3} \mid < 1.65$	$\mid \lambda_3 \mid \hat{\sigma}_{\lambda_3} \mid = 0.70^b$ $\mid \lambda_3 \mid \hat{\sigma}_{\lambda_3} \mid = 1.42^b$	Accept } Accept } Model III
Second nest			
Accept Model II if in Model IV	$0 < \mid \lambda_2 \mid \hat{\sigma}_{\lambda_2} \mid < 1.65$	$\mid \lambda_2 \mid \hat{\sigma}_{\lambda_2} \mid = 1.31^a$ $\mid \lambda_2 \mid \hat{\sigma}_{\lambda_2} \mid = 0.92^b$	Accept } Accept } Model II
Accept Model I if in Model II	$-\infty < \beta\hat{a}_1 \mid \hat{\sigma}_{\beta\hat{a}_1} < 1.65$	$\beta\hat{a}_1 \mid \hat{\sigma}_{\beta\hat{a}_1} = 2.34^a$ $\beta\hat{a}_1 \mid \hat{\sigma}_{\beta\hat{a}_1} = 1.88^b$	Reject } Reject } Model I

[a] OLS estimates.
[b] Maximum likelihood estimates.

decay model suggests that the process is more general than allowed by the highly restrictive assumptions associated with this frequently employed model. While precise statements about the true shape of the lag distribution are not warranted, at least we can have some confidence in the statement that it is not the Koyck distribution.

One of the reasons for the difficulty in discriminating the shape of the lag distribution is that the parameters of the original model (Equation 1) are nonlinear functions of the parameters of the transformed models. If it were possible to estimate a truncated version of (1) directly where the effects of the truncation were negligible, there would be distinct advantages to this estimation. OLS estimates would be normally distributed, unbiased, and consistent for large samples. Unfortu-

nately, we do not know of a rigorous test for "negligibility of omitted variables." Nevertheless, as a matter of interest, we estimated the parameters of truncated versions of (1) for zero through five-period lags (Table 5). The results were not unlike those for earlier estimates. The estimates of weights after a lag of three periods were small and not significant. Four of the six equations shown suggested a nonmonotonic response function. Looking at the three-period lag equation from Table 5, if $\hat{\beta}$ is taken as the sum of the coefficients, the equation can be rewritten as:

$$(15) \quad S_t = 272.4 + .368\ (.353\ A_t + .359\ A_{t-1} + .179\ A_{t-2} + .109\ A_{t-3})$$

The weight estimates in (15) compare very favorably

Table 4

PREDICTIVE TESTING OF NESTED MODELS I–VI BY ANALYSIS OF RESIDUAL VARIANCE

Model compared $H_0{:}\omega$ vs. $H_1\Omega$	n	r	q	Test statistics			Critical value, $F\ .10, q,$ 33-r	Decision
				S_ω	S_Ω	T		
OLS estimates								
Model I vs. Model II	33	4	1	54,888.511	45,660.380	6.05	2.88	Reject I
Model II vs. Model IV	33	4	1	45,660.380	43,034.691	1.79	2.89	Accept II
Model II vs. Model VI	33	5	2	45,660.380	42,248.377	2.13	2.50	Accept II
Model III vs. Model V	33	4	1	48,755.785	47,472.662	0.79	2.89	Accept III
Maximum likelihood estimates								
Model I vs. Model II	33	3	1	65,211	58,516	3.43	2.88	Reject I
Model II vs. Model IV	33	4	1	58,516	57,384	0.57	2.89	Accept II
Model II vs. Model VI	33	5	2	58,516	53,869	1.21	2.50	Accept II
Model III vs. Model V	33	4	1	59,088	57,704	0.48	2.89	Accept III

Table 5

DIRECT OLS ESTIMATES OF TRUNCATED LAG MODELS

	Lag	R^2
0-Period	$S_t = 362.9 + .173A_t$ $\quad\quad\quad (.039)$	.367
1-Period	$S_t = 321.3 + .121A_t + .148A_{t-1}$ $\quad\quad\quad (.031)\quad\ (.031)$	.624
2-Period	$S_t = 290.4 + .133A_t + .122A_{t-1} + .079A_{t-2}$ $\quad\quad\quad (.029)\quad\ (.031)\quad\ (.030)$	.692
3-Period	$S_t = 272.4 + .130A_t + .132A_{t-1} + .066A_{t-2} + .040A_{t-3}$ $\quad\quad\quad (.029)\quad\ (.032)\quad\ (.032)\quad\ (.031)$	.709
4-Period	$S_t = 294.6 + .124A_t + .131A_{t-1} + .055A_{t-2} + .045A_{t-3} - .028A_{t-4}$ $\quad\quad\quad (.029)\quad\ (.032)\quad\ (.032)\quad\ (.032)\quad\ (.031)$	.722
5-Period	$S_t = 321.4 + .118A_t + .131A_{t-1} + .053A_{t-2} + .036A_{t-3} - .022A_{t-4} - .039A_{t-5}$ $\quad\quad\quad (.027)\quad\ (.030)\quad\ (.031)\quad\ (.030)\quad\ (.033)\quad\ (.038)$	.757

with those of Model II in Table 2: $\hat{p}_0 = .366$, $\hat{p}_1 = .380$, $\hat{p}_2 = .152$, $\hat{p}_3 = .061$. All things considered, there appear to be good grounds for adopting a distributed lag model of the class of models associated with Model II as an explanation of the sales of the DWC product.

SUMMARY AND CONCLUSIONS

Using a variety of estimation and testing procedures on different distributed lag models of sales and advertising data for a dietary weight control product, we demonstrated that statistical models of the dynamics of sales and advertising need not be limited to the highly restrictive Koyck model. Nonmonotonic lag distributions, particularly for monthly data, have strong theoretical appeal and, as we have shown, appeared in this case to be more consistent with the evidence than the Koyck model. Marketing studies which posit distributed lag effects would be more appropriately estimated by maximum likelihood methods than by OLS. When multicollinearity is not great, direct estimation of truncated versions of the lag models is probably meaningful with respect to the shape of the lag function, although there is no theoretical guidance to indicate where the truncation should take place.

APPENDIX

Derivation of Identification Relations

Given the coefficients of the rational lag functions, what is the identity of the associated distributed lag function on the exogenous variables alone?

Let r_i be the response in the dependent variable y in time $t + j$ to a unit impulse in the exogenous variable in period t. The $\{r_i,\ i = 1, 2, \cdots\}$ thus derived differ from the desired lag functions $\{w_i,\ i = 1, 2, \cdots\}$ in that $\sum_{i=0}^{\infty} r_i = \beta \neq 1$. Hence we divide the r_i by β

and obtain the desired lag functions $\{w_i = (r_i/\beta)$, $i = 1, 2, \cdots\}$. It should be noted that the constant plays no role in the identity of the w's, and hence it is not included in the derivations. The following inputs are common to the derivations: $x_t = 1$; $x_k = 0$, $k = -\infty, \cdots, t - 1, t + 1, \cdots \infty$; $y_k = 0$, $k < t$. In Model I, $y_t = ax_t + \lambda y_{t-1}$. Deriving first the responses:

$$r_0 = y_t = a(1) + \lambda(0) = a,$$

$$r_1 = y_{t+1} = a(0) + \lambda y_t = \lambda r_0 = \lambda a,$$

$$r_2 = y_{t+2} = a(0) + \lambda y_{t-1} = \lambda r_1 = \lambda^2 r_0 = \lambda^2 a.$$

In general we find:

$$r_j = y_{t+j} = a(0) + \lambda y_{t+j-1} = \lambda r_{j-1}$$
$$= \lambda^j r_0 = \lambda^j a, \quad j = 1, 2, \cdots.$$

We now require $\beta = \sum_{j=0}^{\infty} r_j$:

$$\beta = \sum_{j=0}^{\infty} r_j = \sum_{j=0}^{\infty} \lambda^j a = a \sum_{j=0}^{\infty} \lambda^j = \frac{a}{1 - \lambda}.$$

Thus $w_i = (r_i/\beta)$, and:

$$w_0 = \frac{r_0}{\beta} = a\left(\frac{1 - \lambda}{a}\right) = 1 - \lambda,$$

$$w_1 = \frac{r_1}{\beta} = \lambda a\left(\frac{1 - \lambda}{a}\right) = \lambda(1 - \lambda),$$

$$w_j = \frac{r_j}{\beta} = \lambda^j a\left(\frac{1 - \lambda}{a}\right) = \lambda^j(1 - \lambda), \quad j = 1, 2, \cdots$$

or

$$w_j = \lambda w_{j-1}, \quad j = 1, 2, \cdots.$$

The derivations for the other models are similar in approach.

Lag-Generating Functions and Lag Operators

For convenience of manipulation, it is useful to have available lag-generating functions and lag operators. If the polynomial function:

$$(16) \qquad A(z) = a_0 + a_1 z + a_2 z^2 + a_3 z^3 + \cdots$$

converges in some interval $-z_0 < z < z_0$, then $A(z)$ is called the generating function of the sequence $\{a_i\}$. The generating function of the Koyck sequence $w_i = (1 - \lambda)\lambda^i$, where $|z| < 1$, is:

$$
\begin{aligned}
(17) \qquad W(z) &= (1 - \lambda)[1 + \lambda z + \lambda^2 z^2 + \lambda^3 z^3 + \cdots] \\
&= \frac{(1 - \lambda)}{1 - \lambda z}.
\end{aligned}
$$

There may be times when one will want to analyze the effect of an advertising input on sales when this effect could be the result of a combination of phenomena, each of which is logically represented by a lag distribution. For example, the effect of advertising could be considered as consisting of time lags caused by two sources: (1) lag between exposure to the advertisement and the first purchase and (2) lag between the initial purchase and a repeat purchase. Each of these lags is not a fixed number but rather is described by a probability distribution. The form of the total lag between advertising and sales is determined by the convolution of the individual lag distributions. The joint probability that independent random variables x and y assume the values i and j respectively is $a_i b_j$ where a_i and b_j are the marginal probabilities. If $S = x + y$ then the event $S = r$ is the union of the events:

$$(x = 0, y = r),$$
$$(x = 1, y = r - 1),$$
$$(x = 2, y = r - 2), \cdots .$$

The probability that $S = r$ is then:

$$c_r = a_0 b_r + a_1 b_{r-1} + a_2 b_{r-2} + \cdots + a_{r-1} b_1 + a_r b_0 .$$

Under these conditions the generating function for the random variable $S = x + y$ is $C(z) = A(z)*B(z)$, where $A(z)$ is the generating function for x and $B(z)$ is the generating function for y. The asterisk denotes the convolution operation.

The lag operator L stands for the operation of shifting backward the index of a variable. Thus:

$$Lx_t = x_{t-1}, \qquad L^2 x_t = x_{t-2}, \qquad \text{and so on.}$$

We are now in a position to rewrite the general distributed lag model utilizing the generating function and lag operator concepts. The general model may then be written as:

$$(18) \qquad y_t = \beta W(L) x_t + u_t .$$

Maximum Likelihood Estimation

Using rational lag functions discussed in some detail in [9, 11], when $W(L)$ is a rational generating function

it can be factored into a ratio of two finite polynomials. In this case the general model can be written:

$$(19) \qquad y_t = \frac{A(L)}{B(L)} x_t + \mu_t, \qquad \mu \sim N(0, \sigma^2 I),$$

where:

$$A(L) = \sum_{i=1}^{m} a_i L^i, \quad B(L) = \sum_{j=0}^{n} b_j L^j, \, b_0 = 1.$$

For estimation purposes we used the transformed model:

$$(20) \qquad B(L) y_t = A(L) x_t + v_t .$$

The problems associated with OLS estimation are, first, that y_{t-k}, $k = 1, \cdots, n$ occur as independent variables and are not uncorrelated with v_t. Second, $v_t = B(L)\mu_t$, and if $\mu \sim N(0, \sigma^2 I)$ it follows that v is not distributed $N(0, \theta^2 I)$. The OLS estimators based on (20) are not consistent. If it were possible to develop maximum likelihood estimates of (19) under general conditions, these estimates would be consistent, asymptotically unbiased, and asymptotically efficient. We employed two methods in the minimization of:

$$(21) \qquad Q = \left(y - \frac{A(L)}{B(L)} x \right)' \left(y - \frac{A(L)}{B(L)} x \right).$$

We minimized Q first by applying the Hooke and Jeeves [12] program developed by Van Wormer and Weiss [17] to the "prefiltering" process [16]. Under the assumption that the disturbances are distributed $N(0, \sigma^2 I)$, the minimization of (21) corresponds to finding the maximum of the likelihood function.

It is apparent that Q is a nonlinear function of $B(L)$; hence OLS is not a feasible estimation procedure for B. For a given B, however, it is obvious that $A(L)$ may be estimated by OLS. The prefiltering process utilizes this fact to find the parameter values which minimize Q:

1. For a given value of $B^0(L)$, calculate:

$$x_t^* = \frac{x_t}{B^0(L)}, \text{ solving recursively for}$$

$$x_t^* = -\sum_{i=1}^{m} b_i x_{t-i}^* + x_t, \quad x_{-1}^* = 0,$$

$$i = 0, \quad 1, \cdots, m - 1.$$

2. Use OLS to calculate the regression:

$$y_t = A(L) x_t^* + \mu_t, \quad \text{find} \quad A^0(L) \mid B^0(L).$$

3. Use $A^0(L) \mid B^0(L)$ to calculate Q^0.
4. Search over the parameter space for $B^0(L)$ which minimizes Q.

The search may be carried out by: (1) partitioning the feasible parameter space into a lattice of trial points, (2) choosing the point which has the minimum value of Q, (3) reducing the area of search to a region around the minimum point chosen in Step 2 and repeating Step 1. The process is continued until the desired accuracy is achieved. It is easy to see that such a process converges to a local minimum of Q and, if the function is well behaved, the global minimum should be found.

The Steiglitz-McBride procedure combines classical calculus and manipulations with lag operators in an iterative scheme to find a solution to the necessary conditions for a maximum of the likelihood function. Thus taking the partials of Q with respect to a_i and b_j:

$$(22) \quad \frac{\partial Q}{\partial a_i} = -2 \sum_t \left(y_t - \frac{A(L)}{B(L)} x_t \right) \frac{L^i}{B(L)} x_t = 0,$$
$$i = 0, 1, 2, \cdots, m$$

$$(23) \quad \frac{\partial Q}{\partial b_j} = 2 \sum_t \left(y_t - \frac{A(L)}{B(L)} x_t \right) \frac{A(L)}{[B(L)]^2} L^j x_t = 0,$$
$$j = 1, 2, \cdots, n,$$

If we define:

$$y_t^* = \frac{I}{B(L)} y_t, x_t^* = \frac{I}{B(L)} x_t, \text{ and } x_t^{**} = \frac{A(L)}{B(L)} x_t^*:$$

$$\mathbf{Y}^* = \begin{bmatrix} y_{m+n}^* & \cdots & y_{m+1}^* \\ y_{m+n+1}^* & \cdots & y_{m+2}^* \\ \vdots & & \vdots \\ y_{T-1}^* & \cdots & y_{T-n}^* \end{bmatrix}, \quad \mathbf{y}^* = \begin{bmatrix} y_{m+n+1}^* \\ y_{m+r+2}^* \\ \vdots \\ y_T^* \end{bmatrix},$$

$$\mathbf{X}^* = \begin{bmatrix} x_{m+n+1}^* & \cdots & x_{n+1}^* \\ x_{m+n+2}^* & \cdots & x_{n+2}^* \\ \vdots & & \vdots \\ x_T^* & \cdots & x_{T-n}^* \end{bmatrix},$$

$$\mathbf{X}^{**} = \begin{bmatrix} x_{m+n}^{**} & \cdots & x_{m+1}^{**} \\ x_{m+n+1}^{**} & \cdots & x_{m+2}^{**} \\ \vdots & & \vdots \\ x_{T-1}^{**} & \cdots & x_{T-n}^{**} \end{bmatrix},$$

and (22) and (23) can be written as:

$$(24) \quad \mathbf{W}^* \gamma = P, \quad \text{where:}$$

$$\mathbf{W}^* = \begin{bmatrix} \mathbf{X}^{*\prime}\mathbf{X}^* & \mathbf{X}^{*\prime}\mathbf{Y}^* \\ \mathbf{X}^{**\prime}\mathbf{X}^* & \mathbf{X}^{**\prime}\mathbf{Y}^* \end{bmatrix}, \quad \gamma = \begin{bmatrix} a_0 \\ \vdots \\ a_m \\ -b_1 \\ \vdots \\ -b_n \end{bmatrix},$$

$$P^* = \begin{bmatrix} \mathbf{x}^{*\prime}\mathbf{y}^* \\ \mathbf{x}^{**\prime}\mathbf{y}^* \end{bmatrix}.$$

Taking an initial value of γ, say $\bar{\gamma}^{(0)}$, then for nonsingular $\mathbf{W}^*$:

$$\bar{\gamma}^{(1)} = \tilde{\mathbf{W}}_0^{*-1} \tilde{P}_0^*.$$

Dhrymes, Klein and Steiglitz showed that if $\bar{\gamma}^{(i)}$ is a consistent estimator of γ, $\bar{\gamma}^{(i+1)}$ also is, and they argue that if the iterative process converges for large samples, the global maximum of the likelihood function has been found. Therefore the fixed point of:

$$(25) \quad [\mathbf{W}^*(\bar{\gamma}^{(k)})]\bar{\gamma}^{(k+1)} = P^*(\bar{\gamma}^{(k)})$$

is taken as the maximum likelihood estimator. The asymptotic distribution of $\hat{\gamma}$ is given by:

$$(26) \quad \sqrt{T}(\hat{\gamma} - \gamma) \sim N(0, \sigma^2 \sum^{-1})$$

and its parameters consistently estimated by:

$$(27) \quad \hat{\sigma}^2 \left(\frac{\mathbf{S}^\prime \mathbf{S}}{T} \right)^{-1},$$

where $\hat{\sigma}^2$ is the global minimum of Q divided by T and $\mathbf{S} = (\mathbf{X}^*, \mathbf{X}^{**})$ is calculated from the maximum likelihood parameter estimates. Therefore, assuming convergence and an initial consistent estimator, there is a basis for computing the estimates of the variance of $\hat{\gamma}$.

REFERENCES

1. Basmann, Robert L. "On the Application of the Identifiability Test Statistic in Predictive Testing of Explanatory Economic Models," *The Econometric Annual of the Indian Economic Journal*, 13 (September 1965), 387–423.
2. ———. "Hypothesis Formulation in Quantitative Economics: A Contribution to Demand Analysis," Papers in Quantitative Economics, University of Kansas, 1968, 143–202.
3. Bass, Frank M. "Application of Regression Models in Marketing: Testing versus Forecasting," Institute Paper No. 265, Institute for Research in the Behavioral, Economic, and Management Sciences, Krannert Graduate School of Industrial Administration, Purdue University, 1969.
4. ———. "A Simultaneous Equation Regression Study of Advertising and Sales of Cigarettes," *Journal of Marketing Research*, 6 (August 1969), 291–300.
5. ——— and Neil E. Beckwith. "A Multivariate Regression Analysis of the Responses of Competing Brands to Advertising," Institute Paper No. 287, Institute for Research in the Behavioral, Economic, and Management Sciences, Krannert Graduate School of Industrial Administration, Purdue University, 1970.
6. Bass, Frank M. and Leonard J. Parsons. "Simultaneous-Equation Regression Analysis of Sales and Advertising," *Applied Economics*, 1 (May 1969), 103–24.
7. ———. "Optimal Advertising Expenditure Implications of a Simultaneous Equation Regression Analysis," *Operations Research*, 19 (May–June 1971), 822–31.
8. Box, George E. P. and W. J. Hill. "Discrimination Among Mechanistic Models," *Technometrics*, 9 (January 1967), 57–72.
9. Dhrymes, P. J., L. R. Klein, and K. Steiglitz. "Estimation of Distributed Lags," *International Economic Review*, 11 (June 1970), 235–49.
10. Goldberger, Arthur S. *Econometric Theory*. New York: John Wiley & Sons, 1964.
11. Griliches, Zvi. "Distributed Lags: A Survey," *Econometrica*, 35 (January 1967), 16–49.
12. Hooke, R. and T. A. Jeeves. "Direct Search Solution of Numerical and Statistical Problems," *Journal of the Association for Computing Machinery*, 8 (April 1961), 212–28.
13. Koyck, L. M. *Distributed Lags and Investment Analysis*. Amsterdam: North-Holland, 1954.
14. Palda, Kristian S. *The Measurement of Cumulative Advertising Effects*. Englewood Cliffs, N. J.: Prentice-Hall, 1964.
15. Scheffe, H. *The Analysis of Variance*. New York: John Wiley & Sons, 1954.
16. Steiglitz, K. S. and L. E. McBride. "A Technique for the Identification of Linear Systems," *IEEE Transactions on Automatic Control*, 4 (October 1965), 461–4.
17. Van Wormer, Theodore A. and Doyle L. Weiss. "Fitting Parameters to Complex Models by Direct Search," *Journal of Marketing Research*, 7 (November 1970), 503–12.
18. Zellner, Arnold and M. S. Geisel. "Analysis of Distributed Lag Models with Applications to Consumption Function Estimation," *Econometrica*, 38 (November 1970), 865–87.

*Polynomial lags can help
show when advertising works*

Measuring Advertising Decay

Ronald W. Ward

The delayed impact of present advertising efforts has received varying degrees of emphasis in the literature. On the one hand, there is general agreement that advertising effectiveness must be analyzed recognizing the decay effect over time (Bass, 1972; Weinberg, 1975; Welam, 1975; Kolter, 1971). Yet analytical treatments of the decay function are generally restrictive in that a priori assumptions about the nature of the decay must be specified.

Recent improvements in the various econometric methods for dealing with distributed lags have particular relevance to the empirical advertising-decay problem. Specifically, the use of polynomial-lag models to estimate the carry-over effect of economic variables can be easily applied with a minimal number of statistical problems (Chen, 1972). This family of lags allows the estimation of more than one series of lags in the same model and does not impose a priori restrictions on the nature of advertising decay. Rather, the method facilitates an estimate of numerous decay

structures and provides a statistical criterion for selecting the appropriate model. Similarly, the lag structure can be applied to numerous forms of the advertising-sales response function.

The polynomial-lag procedure will first be outlined in this article, and then a model of citrus advertising will be used to illustrate its application to advertising research.

Advertising Function

Discussion of advertising functions such as those outlined recently in this journal provides an excellent review of the efforts to improve the quantitative emphasis in advertising (Rao and Miller, 1975). In general, most of the articles encompass various model specifications including restrictive lag structures. Most model specifications are based on both theoretical and empirical studies. For example, the S-shaped advertising function can be argued theoretically while other specifications may be empirically based

(Hochman, 1974; Ward, 1975; Welam, 1975). In both situations, lagged advertising variables are generally part of the model as implicitly assumed where

$$(1) \qquad q_t = f(z_{it}, a_{it}, a_{i,t-1}, a_{i,t-2}, a_{i,t-3}, \dots \varepsilon_t),$$

letting q_t = quantity of sales in period t,

z_{it} = i explanatory variables in period t,

$a_{i,t-j}$ = i-type advertising variables lagged j periods,

and ε_t = random error term.

The empirical problem with equation (1) is the estimation of the advertising parameters once the explicit model is specified.

Assume, for simplicity, that equation (1) is linear and that there is only one exogenous variable z and one type of advertising. Then:

$$(2) \quad q_t = a_0 + a_1 z_t + \lambda_0 a_t + \lambda_1 a_{t-1} + \lambda_2 a_{t-2} + \dots + \varepsilon_t.$$

The advertising parameters measure the carry-over effect and have been historically assumed to be related in a geometric form such as $\lambda_j = \lambda b^{s_i}$

37

(Kolter, 1971). This is the structure used by Rao and Miller (1975), and has proven useful in many studies and should not be disregarded. However, polynomial lags provide an alternative that is less restrictive, easily estimated, and does not lead to the well-known statistical problems inherent in the geometric specification (Almon, 1965; Johnson, 1972). The method is considerably more flexible than those methods used in most past advertising studies. The decay structure is not fixed a priori, and the statistical problems found in the treatments of most geometric-type decay models have been greatly reduced. The polynomial model may in fact show that the geometric decay is representative of the advertising effect. However, the parameters are estimated without violating the assumptions of the regression model.

Polynomial lags provide a distinct advantage over most other decay-estimation techniques where more than one lagged structure is suspected in the same equation. For example, in Rao and Miller's article (1975), both media expen-

Ronald W. Ward is associate professor in the Food and Resource Economics Department, University of Florida. He received his Ph.D. in economics and statistics from Iowa State University. Dr. Ward's major fields of interest are industrial organization and econometrics and his research includes a number of studies on empirical measurement of advertising effectiveness. He has published in the *American Journal of Agricultural Economics* and other professional journals.

ditures and trade deals were treated as lags, and major violations of the regression model are evident in their equations. In contrast, the polynomial procedures could have been easily used to account for the multiple lag structures and still have satisfied the assumptions of the regression model.

Application of Polynomial Lags

The above polynomial procedures have been applied to a model where retail consumption of orange juice is related to citrus advertising. Not only does the study of citrus advertising illustrate the applicability of the polynomial method, it has provided essential empirical measures for making advertising-expenditure decisions for the citrus industry (Ward, 1973).

Specifically, the per-capita retail consumption of orange juice can be explained in part by a distributed lagged advertising model which includes a price effect, seasonality, and a growth variable. Preliminary model analysis suggests that a difference model may be a reasonable specification of the advertising relationship. Hence, define

$$(3) \quad \dot{q}_t = a_0 + a_1 \dot{p}_t + a_2 s + \lambda_1 \dot{a}_t + \lambda_2 \dot{a}_{t-1} + \dots + \varepsilon_t,$$

and let $\dot{q}_t$ = per-capita quarterly changes in consumption of orange juice (single-strength gallons),

t = quarterly time periods (t = 2, summer, 1967; and t = 21, spring, 1972),

$\dot{p}_t$ = change in the deflated retail price per gallon ($/single-strength gallon),

s_t = quarterly seasonal sin function,

$\dot{a}_t$ = change in the quarterly expenditures on national advertising (millions of dollars).

Citrus consumption has shown a strong growth trend and a consistent seasonal fluctuation. These effects are measured with parameters a_0 and a_2 in the dif-

ferential model. Similarly, retail prices would be expected to influence the consumption levels. However, of primary interest to this problem is the estimation of the advertising-decay function.

There is a clear and relatively easy way to estimate the advertising-decay parameters by using polynomial models up to a third degree with both four- and five-quarter maximum lags. All estimates are completed with both restrictive and nonrestrictive conditions imposed on the last decay parameter.

Empirical Estimate. A priori citrus advertising is expected to have a carry-over effect. However, the exact nature of the advertising decay is unknown. The carry-over may be continually declining or there may be reason to expect that the maximum advertising effect may be delayed. Such responses can be approximated by a first-, second-, or third-degree polynomial. There is little theoretical reason for suspecting the carry-over to differ from one of these alternatives.

Using these restrictions, the polynomial approximations are specified as

$$(3a) \; \lambda_j = \beta_0 + \beta_1 j + \beta_2 j^2 + \beta_3 j^3,$$

$$(3b) \; \lambda_j = \beta_0 + \beta_1 j + \beta_2 j^2,$$

or $(3c) \; \lambda_j = \beta_0 + \beta_1 j,$

where $j = 0, 1, 2, 3, 4.$

For an analysis with a four-lag period (i.e., $j \leq 3$), the restricted model is assuming that $\lambda_3 = 0$. Similarly, for the five-period restricted lag model, $\lambda_4 = 0$. For both lag models, one degree of freedom is gained by using the end parameter restriction.

The results from using ordinary least squares on equation (3) under the differential model assumptions are reported in Table 1. First, for most of the equations, a four-period lag assumption was superior to using five lags in that the $\bar{R}^2$ statistic was generally higher for the shorter lag. In all cases, the coefficient associated with more than four lags (i.e., $j = 3$) was statistically insignificant. There were relatively minor differences in the adjusted R^2 for the various degree

38

Table 1

Polynomial Lag Models of Orange-Juice Advertising and Retail-per-Capita Consumption of Orange Juice

Variables (Equation 3)	Nonrestricted Model						Restricted Model					
	Polynomial Third Degree		Polynomial Second Degree		Polynomial First Degree		Polynomial Third Degree		Polynomial Second Degree		Polynomial First Degree	
	Lag = 4	Lag = 5	Lag = 4	Lag = 5	Lag = 4	Lag = 5	Lag = 4	Lag = 5	Lag = 4	Lag = 5	Lag = 4	Lag = 5
	Eq. 3a	Eq. 3b	Eq. 3c	Eq. 3d	Eq. 3e	Eq. 3f	Eq. 3g	Eq. 3h	Eq. 3i	Eq. 3j	Eq. 3k	Eq. 3l
Constant	.00704 (2.144)*	.00888 (2.522)	.00767 (2.095)	.00816 (1.811)	.00763 (2.113)	.00834 (1.996)	.00746 (2.256)	.00974 (2.619)	.00749 (2.027)	.00752 (1.857)	.00739 (2.095)	.00687 (1.697)
Price	-.18566 (3.023)	-.09576 (1.143)	-.18835 (2.738)	-.1886 (1.958)	-.21403 (3.494)	-.17667 (2.054)	-.17536 (2.851)	-.08816 (.9849)	-.21869 (3.436)	-.21523 (3.077)	-.21499 (3.578)	-.23831 (3.532)
Seasonality	.04653 (5.394)	.05743 (5.707)	.04516 (4.689)	.03789 (4.679)	.03830 (7.105)	.03932 (5.845)	.04924 (5.873)	.05306 (5.154)	.03624 (6.939)	.03559 (6.190)	.03666 (7.553)	.03533 (6.084)
Advertising (t)	.01563 (2.714)	.01909 (3.327)	.01845 (2.969)	.01696 (2.327)	.01617 (2.912)	.01845 (3.222)	.01790 (3.283)	.02169 (3.708)	.01661 (2.748)	.01502 (2.771)	.01752 (3.390)	.01606 (2.977)
Advertising (t-1)	.02250 (2.376)	.02363 (2.321)	.01866 (1.803)	.00903 (.844)	.01084 (2.184)	.01255 (2.941)	.02336 (2.443)	.02279 (2.094)	.01096 (1.425)	.00598 (.791)	.01314 (3.390)	.01285 (2.977)
Advertising (t-2)	.00701 (.767)	.00698 (.750)	.00126 (1.307)	-.00270 (.230)	.00551 (1.102)	.00664 (1.602)	.01254 (1.615)	.01009 (1.041)	.00631 (.805)	.0000	.00876 (3.390)	.00963 (2.977)
Advertising (t-3)	.00153 (.298)	-.01117 (1.343)	.00028 (.049)	-.00204 (.213)	.00175 (.0310)	.00074 (.135)	0	-.00536 (.6817)	0	.0000	0	.00642 (2.977)
Advertising (t-4)		-.01109 (1.688)		-.00518 (.658)		-.0056 (.690)		0		0		0
$R^2 =$	.9353	.9461	.9085	.8983	.9009	.8966	.9252	.9294	.8963	.8960	.8951	.8819
$F =$	19.259	20.469	17.877	14.132	22.734	19.517	22.278	21.049	21.599	19.384	31.290	24.901
$DW =$	2.158	2.998	2.144	1.935	1.788	1.919	2.299	2.594	1.638	1.807	1.612	1.465
$n =$	15	14	15	14	15	14	15	14	15	14	15	14
$df =$	8	7	9	8	10	9	9	8	10	9	11	10
	.8868	.8999	.8577	.8347	.8613	.8552	.8836	.8853	.8548	.8498	.8665	.8465

* The *t* statistic is reported within the parentheses.

polynomials and for the restricted and nonrestricted estimation. However, the first-degree polynomial consistently gave the largest *F* statistic as noted with equations (3e) and (3k). Likewise, the restricted model consistently gave more statistically reliable parameter estimates for the advertising decay.

Recognizing the similarity among many of the statistics in Table 1 and the increased significance of the parameters for the restricted first-degree polynomial model, equation (3k) was selected as the best specification among those models considered. This model continually declines like the traditional geometric model, but the empirical results are now free of those statistical problems inherent in the geometric estimates. In particular, all dependent variables are independent of the error term.

Advertising Decay. The decay structure from Table 1 establishes that the full impact of citrus advertising is realized within four quarters from the initial effort. Likewise, the major effect of changes in the advertising effort is realized in the nearest quarter with subsequent declines in the advertising gains.

In the short run, quarterly increases in advertising expenditures can stimulate consumers to increase their consumption levels. For example, suppose the advertising expenditures were increased by $1 million over the previous quarter's efforts. Then the per-capita consumption would be expected to increase by .017 gallons. This gain can easily be converted to total gallons and an economic value of the gains calculated. From these values, an economic decision as to desirable advertising changes can be made. In ad-

dition, the magnitude of the immediate advertising effect provides evidence for deciding if increased advertising programs are large enough to realize short-run inventory problems. For example, a market slump can occur that temporarily reduces consumption and raises inventories. Inventories can be increased, prices can be cut, or advertising can be increased. The model provides guidelines for evaluating the use of price cutting versus increased advertising expenditures to relieve a short-run problem (Ward, 1975).

Over time, a change in advertising has a multiplier effect as measured by the aggregate gains realized from expenditure changes in the present. The carry-over from present changes as calculated in equation (3k) shows that 44.4 per cent of the full impact is felt immediately,

33.3 per cent is realized in the next quarter's changes in sales, and the remaining carry-over is generally realized by the third quarter. In contrast to the short-run effect, a $1-million increase in the advertising expenditures can be expected to raise per-capita consumption by .0394 gallons in the long run. This response would be expected from one initial advertising change in the present period with no subsequent changes in either prices or advertising. A forecast of the full per-capita change over the complete decay period would require assumptions about the prices and advertising programs for each period considered. Recognition of both the correct carry-over effect as well as the potential for later changes is essential for advertising planning.

In contrast to the above situation, where there has been one advertising increase and its impact traced over time, the situation leading to long-run allocations of funds can be analyzed. For simplicity, assume that the citrus industry raised its annual expenditures by $4 million and that these funds were to be expended in quarterly increments according to a long-run advertising plan. Then the expected impact of such policies can be easily calculated. In Figure 1, various allocations of the annual appropriation of funds are considered. Although the actual level of appropriation for advertising would change the magnitude of retail per-capita consumption responses, the patterns of response would vary according to the within-season allocation of the expenditures.

Figure 1.a illustrates the response to an equal distribution of funds over a four-quarter period. Note that the response builds up as a result of the carry-over as estimated from the polynomial lag. The response stabilizes between the increment $t + 3$ and $t + 4$ under this example because the carry-over from the initial change has declined to zero by this time. Similarly, if additional programs are not added after the fourth period, then consumption changes will begin to decline. The positive value in consumption changes is now due en-

Figure 1

Long-run Advertising-Allocation Policies Based on Polynomial-Lag Estimates

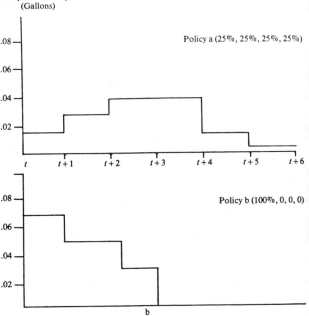

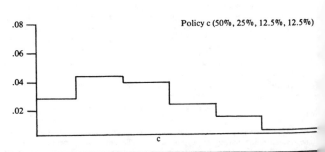

tirely to the advertising carry-over, and this value would decline much more rapidly than did the initial growth from periods t to $t + 3$.

While policy a gives a gradual change in consumption, policy b (Figure 1.b)

represents a much stronger initial stimulant to the consumer. The model suggests that if the additional money were put into one quarter's program, the consumer's per-capita sales would increase substantially. In subsequent periods the per-capita sales would again approach the preadvertising change level.

A third policy (Figure 1.c) emphasizes more advertising early but with funds also distributed throughout the four quarters. This is in contrast to both policies a and b. The peak response here occurs earlier than with policy a but lasts longer than policy b.

The results of Figure 1 are but three of many alternative policies that could be considered. Yet they well illustrate both the importance of having statistical confidence in the decay parameters and planning the advertising allocation. The decay structure determines the type of response that can be expected and when it should occur. For example, if the market needs a quick stimulant with a minimal long-run carry-over, then policy b may be appropriate, whereas if gradual changes are needed, then policies similar to a and c are useful.

Simulation techniques have proven useful when considering policies such as those in Figure 1. Alternative responses can be measured under conditions where other variables such as seasonality and prices are allowed to change. Using the empirical models similar to those adopted above, a processed orange advertising simulation model has been developed for the Florida citrus industry (Ward, 1973).

Conclusion

Polynomial-lag techniques have been applied to a model relating changes in per-capita consumption of citrus juices to both present and past advertising programs. The method and application of polynomial lags are useful for gaining greater flexibility in estimating the type of lag structure that exists. Also, the methods are easily adapted to most lag problems without violation of the basic regression model assumptions. The technique provides an objective statistical method for exploring various decay structures using a minimal number of a priori restrictions.

References

Almon, Shirley. The Distributed Lag between Capital Appropriations and Expenditures. *Econometrica*, Vol. 33, 1965, pp. 178–196.

Bass, Frank, and Darrel G. Clarke. Testing Distributed Lag Models of Advertising Effects. *Journal of Marketing Research*, Vol. 9, 1972, pp. 298–308.

Case, K. E., and J. E. Shamblin. The Effects of Advertising Carry-over. *Journal of Advertising Research*, Vol. 12, No. 3, 1972, pp. 37–40.

Chen, Dean, Richard Courtney, and Andrew Schmitz. A Polynomial Lag Formulation of Milk Production Response. *American Journal of Agricultural Economics*, Vol. 54, No. 1, 1972, pp. 77–83.

Hochman, Eithan, Uri Regev, and Ronald W. Ward. Optimal Advertising Signals in the Florida Citrus Industry: A Research Application. *American Journal of Agricultural Economics*, Vol. 56, No. 4, 1974, pp. 697–705.

Johnson, J. *Econometric Methods*. New York: McGraw-Hill, 1972.

Kolter, Philip. *Marketing Decision Making: A Model Building Approach*. New York: Holt, Rinehart and Winston, 1971.

Rao, Ambar, and Peter B. Miller. Advertising/Sales Response Functions. *Journal of Advertising Research*, Vol. 15, No. 2, 1975, pp. 7–15.

Ward, Ronald W. Processed Orange Advertising Simulation Model. Economic Research Department, Florida Department of Citrus, February 1973.

———. Revisiting the Dorfman-Steiner Static Advertising Theorem: An Application to the Processed Grapefruit Industry. *American Journal of Agricultural Economics*, Vol. 57, No. 3, 1975, pp. 500–504.

Weinberg, Charles B. Carryover Is Important—I. *Journal of Advertising Research*, Vol. 15, No. 3, 1975, pp. 41–42.

Welam, Peter. Carryover and Optimal Advertising—II. *Journal of Advertising Research*, Vol. 15, No. 3, 1975, pp. 43–45.

DARRAL G. CLARKE*

A survey of the econometric literature is undertaken to determine the duration of cumulative advertising effect on sales. The surveyed studies yield conflicting estimates of the duration interval. The data interval is shown to have a powerful influence on the implied duration of advertising effect. The evidence leads to the conclusion that the cumulative effect of advertising on sales lasts for only months rather than years.

Econometric Measurement of the Duration of Advertising Effect on Sales

INTRODUCTION

The most frequent and critical questions of advertising managers are, "How much should I spend?" and "How should I spend it?" Basic to the answers is the question of how long advertising affects sales; it has not been answered very directly with any generality in the marketing or econometric literature. Whereas an individual marketing manager might settle for an answer specific to his own products, public policymakers concerned with regulation of advertising and its effects on competition want a broader answer. And even the marketing manager needs a yardstick against which to assess the reasonableness of the results of studies of his own products.

The purpose of this article is to give the most direct answer possible to the direct question on the basis of the broadest set of evidence available. This is a necessary undertaking because it has not been done and because in articles being published in other areas the results of isolated marketing or economics papers are attributed a breadth of applicability far beyond that intended by their authors. For example, Block [10] assumes that it is a well-established fact that advertising's effect on sales lasts several years and, on the basis of this unproved assumption, concludes that 40 firms avoided an average of $2 million a year in taxes because they were permitted to treat advertis-

ing as an expense rather than an investment. If an advertising manager assumed advertising's effect on sales to last for a period of years, when in fact it only lasted for a period of months or vice versa, poor decisions would necessarily result.

This survey seeks to answer the question of how long the cumulative effect of advertising persists, to assess the scope of the current econometric literature, and to suggest directions for future research. It includes only published econometric studies of advertising effect which are amenable to inference about the duration of cumulative effect. More than 70 such studies were found. Experiments, proprietary commercial research, and other types of studies are not included—not for lack of interest, but rather for lack of present accessibility and a need to restrict the size of the investigation.

Because this is a survey of published results, there is no opportunity to "control" anything. Thus some studies include only advertising as an explanatory variable and others include various elements of the marketing mix also. The studies are based on different competitive situations, different products, and different marketing strategies; hence a large degree of heterogeneity is to be expected in the results. Wherever possible subclassification is attempted to explore the effects of omitted variables.

Such heterogeneity is inherent in cross-sectional studies and must be tolerated where it cannot be reduced if marketing is ever to generate hypotheses which can be used as guidelines in new or diverse situations. Until central tendencies have been isolated, it is difficult to discuss the effect of other variables which might be thought to alter these guidelines.

*Darral G. Clarke is Associate Professor of Management, Brigham Young University. This study was supported jointly by the Marketing Science Institute and the Division of Research, Harvard Business School.

345

ECONOMETRIC MODELS OF CUMULATIVE ADVERTISING EFFECT

The concept that the effect of advertising on sales persists longer than the current period is an intuitively attractive one and various behavioral mechanisms have been hypothesized which support the concept of cumulative advertising effect. These theories are not discussed here because they appear elsewhere in the literature; the focus of this survey of the econometric literature is to ascertain the duration of the effect as implied by that research tradition.

Two definitions simplify the following discussion. A "$p\%$" duration interval is defined as that number of periods during which $p\%$ of the expected cumulative advertising effect has taken place. If the duration interval is derived from a model rather than measured directly, it is called an *implied duration interval*. The time period for which the data are aggregated, i.e. monthly, bimonthly, annually, is called the *data interval*.

The discussion next requires a brief description of econometric models relevant to measuring the duration intervals of cumulative advertising effect.

Direct Duration Interval Models

Direct lag model. The "direct lag" model is the most straightforward way of computing a duration interval. Lagged values of advertising are included as independent variables:

$$(1) \qquad y_t = a_0 + \sum_{j=0}^{n} b_j x_{t-j} + \epsilon_t$$

where:

y_t = sales at time t
x_{t-j} = advertising at time $t-j$
ϵ_t = independent, identically distributed normal disturbances $(0, \sigma^2)$.

The direct lag model is seldom the primary model in a research effort. Its use requires subjective decisions which are arbitrary or, at best, *ex post facto*. The major problem is the necessity of specifying n, the number of lags. For any finite n a truncation bias results which cannot be estimated with mathematical rigor. Another commonly mentioned problem is that the lagged advertising variables will be multicollinear. The fact that most direct lag estimates included in the survey are not significant after three or four lagged periods (see Table 3) could indicate multicollinearity but, because the early lagged advertising coefficients change little with the insertion of the longer lagged periods, it is as likely that the duration interval is short as that multicollinearity is causing the lack of statistical significance.

The direct duration interval estimates and the implied duration intervals derived from more sophisticat-

ed models should agree very closely; if not, both models should be examined for specification error. Bass and Clarke [8] demonstrate a close agreement between the direct and implied duration intervals when the models are correctly specified. From the survey, it appears that the direct lag estimates are neglected more often because of their lack of sophistication than because of the truncation or multicollinearity problems attributed to them.

Weighted average models. It is intuitively appealing to use a moving average of advertising expenditures as a means of measuring cumulative advertising effect. Nerlove and Waugh's [35] study of the demand for oranges is an example of this approach and Reckie's [40] study of a pharmaceutical product produced statistically significant estimates of cumulative advertising effect. The limitation of this method is apparent if the purpose of the study is to determine the length of the duration interval. If the duration interval is shorter than the moving average, significant results are still likely to occur because of aggregation. Thus no evidence about the length of the duration interval is obtained because the approach is not empirical in this respect.

The various polynomial lag models such as the Almon [4] technique or others as applied by Johannson [23] are similarly not empirical with respect to the duration interval

Models Yielding Implied Duration Intervals

Two commonly used families of econometric models imply a cumulative advertising effect. Distributed lag models often are applied to studies of advertising effect and the cumulative nature of their results is widely understood. Less widely used as models of cumulative effect, but nonetheless having implicit cumulative effect, are the partial adjustment models.

Distributed lag models. The family of distributed lag models most commonly used is that of the polynomial lag models represented by

$$(2) \qquad y_t = a_0 + \sum_{k=1}^{m} \lambda_k y_{t-k} + \sum_{j=0}^{n} b_j x_{t-j} + \epsilon_t.$$

Equation (2), with various assumed values for m and n, is discussed by Bass and Clarke [8]. The inclusion of additional lagged values of the dependent variable permits inflection points in the decay function whereas the inclusion of additional lagged advertising terms delays the beginning of the exponential decay by one period per *positive* coefficient. Figure 1 shows the shape of the decay functions obtained from the various distributed lag models computed on the same data.

The Koyck model. The most commonly used polynomial lag model is the Koyck model [24]. It usually is derived from a direct lag function such as (1) in which n is assumed to be infinite and the decay is exponentially declining, i.e. there is a real number

Figure 1
EFFECT OF LAG STRUCTURE ON IMPLIED DURATION
INTERVAL[a]

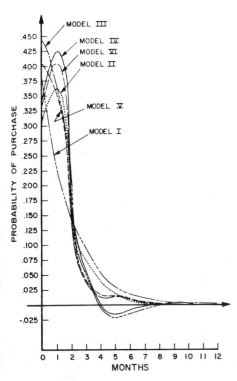

[a] Bass and Clarke [7, p. 304].

Model:

I—lagged sales, advertising (Koyck).
II—lagged sales, advertising, lagged advertising.
III—lagged sales, twice lagged sales, advertising.
IV—lagged sales, twice lagged sales, advertising, lagged advertising.
V—lagged sales, twice lagged sales, triple lagged sales, advertising.
VI—lagged sales, twice lagged sales, triple lagged sales, advertising, lagged advertising.

λ such that $0 \leq \lambda < 1$ and $b_j = \lambda b_{j-1}$ for $j = 1, 2,$ ... Then (1) reduces to

(3) $$y_t = a_0 + \lambda y_{t-1} + b_0 x_t + v_t.$$

It is very important to note that (3) is the reduced form of (1) *only if* the hypothesized number λ exists. If λ does not exist then the strong connection between past advertising and sales cannot be asserted. If the conditions of the Koyck model are satisfied then the computed value of λ measures the decaying effect of advertising over time. If these conditions are not satisfied then model (3) has a somewhat different meaning and probably should be considered as a "partial adjustment model" without the connection to (1).

Partial adjustment model. The partial adjustment model (3) is of interest in its own right and has been used by several authors as a starting point rather than the Koyck hypothesis. The partial adjustment model states that sales in the current period will be much as they were in the previous period plus a response to advertising. There is an implicit carryover effect to advertising just as in the Koyck model, the major difference being that all of the implied carryover effect cannot be attributed to the advertising [13, 21, 34].

The partial adjustment model analogue to the decay function is the adjustment function. Both of these functions and the resultant implicit duration interval or implicit adjustment interval are derived from (3) alone and thus should be the same.[1]

Implied Duration Intervals

It may seem strange to speak of equation (3) as two different models, but the origin of (3), whether it came from (1) or is the conceptual model itself, has important implications in the interpretation of the parameters. In the Koyck model, (3) arises from assumptions about the cumulative effect of advertising by which the role of λ is to measure the rate of decay in the advertising effect.

If (3) is the starting point of the modeling, however, the meaning of λ is not clear at all in the context of cumulative advertising effect. λ is a measure of the inertia in the time series and is as much a function of other marketing mix elements, product loyalty, and other factors leading to a carryover in purchase behavior as it is of advertising. Thus the adjustment period is an aggregate measure of cumulative effects and will be indicative of the duration of cumulative advertising effect only if the effect of advertising persists about the same length of time as do the effects of pricing moves and salesforce efforts, for example. If one of the mechanisms underlying cumulative effects is repeat purchase, for example, then the means by which trial was achieved would not necessarily affect the duration of repurchase and thus the duration

[1] Strictly speaking this statement is not true. The two hypotheses have different implications with regard to the distribution of the disturbances. Thus if estimation procedures were used that recognized the disturbance distributions, the estimates would vary. Only Clarke [14] computes the parameters of the equation and the autocorrelation structure simultaneously.

of cumulative effects of such marketing instruments would seem to be similar.

Distributed lag models computed for the study of pricing effects seem to achieve similar values of λ (and thus similar duration intervals), e.g. [33, 53], and thus this assumption may not be unreasonable. Because few of the surveyed studies are motivated as partial adjustment models, a relatively small liberty with the authors' intent is taken in including them.

Because the duration interval and the adjustment interval are both derived the same way from (3), they are mathematically identical. Having observed the great similarity between the lengths of the duration intervals in Figure 1, the writer decided that only small errors[2] would be introduced if the duration interval were computed for the Koyck model or the Koyck model plus one lagged advertising term, i.e., in equation (2) the cases $m = n = 1$ and $m = 1$, $n = 0$.

If one defines r_ℓ as the response at time $t_{0+\ell}$ to a unit pulse of advertising at time t_0, then $\beta_\ell = \Sigma_{j=0}^{\ell} r_j$ is the cumulative response over ℓ periods. If $\beta = \lim_{\ell \to \infty} \beta_\ell$ then the $p\%$ implied duration interval is defined as the least integer ℓ^* such that $\beta_{\ell^*}/\beta \geq p$.

It is easy to show [see 8, p. 306 for method] that if $m = n = 1$ in equation (2), then

(4)
$$\beta_\ell = \frac{b_0 + b_1}{1 - \lambda} - \frac{\lambda r_\ell}{1 - \lambda},$$

where:

$$r_\ell = \lambda^\ell b_0 + \lambda^{\ell - 1} b_1.$$

So

$$\frac{\beta_\ell}{\beta} = \frac{b_0 + b_1 - \lambda^{\ell-1}(\lambda b_0 + b_1)}{b_0 + b_1}.$$

The smallest non-negative integer ℓ^* such that

$$\frac{\beta_{\ell^*}}{\beta} = 1 - \lambda^{\ell^*-1} \left[\frac{\lambda b_0 + b_1}{b_0 + b_1} \right] \geq p$$

is found as follows:

$$\log(1 - p) \geq (\ell^* - 1)\log\lambda + \log\left[\frac{\lambda b_0 + b_1}{b_0 + b_1} \right]$$

or

(5)
$$\ell^* \leq \frac{\log(1-p) - \log\left[\dfrac{b_1 + \lambda b_0}{b_1 + b_0}\right]}{\log\lambda} + 1.$$

This expression is defined if $p \leq [b_0(1 - \lambda)/b_1 + b_0]$, i.e. unless too much of the advertising effect

is concentrated in the current and immediately following period. It also should be noted that the unit of measurement of ℓ^* is "data intervals," i.e. quarters, years, etc. If $b_1 = 0$, (5) reduces to the familiar expression for the Koyck duration interval $\ell^* \leq [\log(1 - p)/\log(\lambda)]$.

Because the data intervals used in the several studies range from weeks to years it is advantageous to use the continuous analogue of ℓ^* and to compute ℓ^* without restricting it to be an integer. To facilitate further the comparison of results across studies the duration interval here expressed in data intervals is in months. Thus the final expression for the implied duration interval is the product of ℓ^* and the number of months in a data interval.

SURVEY METHODS

A major difficulty in trying to determine what the econometric research tradition indicates about the duration of advertising's effect on sales is that, although many workers have tried to measure the effect of advertising, their emphasis has been methodological rather than substantive. The little substantive content found in the literature generally is not directed toward the duration question. Therefore, in this survey it is necessary to infer meaning from a report which is peripheral to the author's purpose. The Koyck model is often not the preferred model for the authors' purposes, but the model closest to the Koyck model is the most interesting for this study because it provides the most direct comparison of results.

Though a cross-sectional study of the same model in different applications is appealing from a standpoint of consistency, it does raise important questions.

1. How sensitive is the duration interval to the proper specification of the distributed lag model? Even though the shape of the lag function is very sensitive to the distributed lag model specification, it does not appear that the *length* of the duration interval is sensitive to specification error. In Figure 1, which is an application of several distributed lag models to a *single* data base, it is clear visually that the length of the duration interval is about the same for each of the six models (and in any case would vary only by a month or two). Other experience of the writer indicates to him that this result is not atypical, although no more systematic investigation in the surveyed results was made.
2. How sensitive is the estimate of λ to the specification of other nonadvertising independent variables? Here no generalization is possible because the effect of these variables on λ is varied and is not usually explicit in the distributed lag specification.

In the experience of the writer, $\hat{\lambda}$ has been observed to be much more sensitive to autocorrelation bias than it is to variation in the specification of the independent variables. In most instances familiar to the writer, $\hat{\lambda}$ remains remarkably stable whereas various combi-

---

[2] The 90% implied duration intervals are computed for models 1–4 as follows: I—7 months, II—4 months, III—2 months, IV—2 months.

Table 1

SURVEY OF ECONOMETRIC SALES-ADVERTISING ANALYSIS

Researchers	Product	Coefficient of lagged dependent variable λ	90% duration interval (months)
Weekly			
1 Nakanishi [34]	Catsup	.594	1.1
2 Sexton [47]	Frequently purchased grocery product	.480	0.8
Monthly			
3 Bass and Clarke [8]	Dietary product	.468	3.5
4 Beckwith [9]	Low priced food	.990	229.1
5 Montgomery and Silk [32]	Ethical drugs	.348	2.2
6 Palda [36]	Lydia Pinkham	.390	2.4
7 Samuels [41]	Toilet soap	.508	3.4
8 Samuels [41]	Household cleanser	.508	3.4
9 Samuels [41]	Household cleanser	.261	1.7
10 Samuels [41]	Washing up liquid	.423	2.7
11 Samuels [41]	Washing up liquid	.528	3.6
12 Samuels [41]	Washing up liquid	.458	2.9
13 Samuels [41]	Scouring powder	.510	3.4
Bimonthly			
14 Aaker and Day [2]	Instant coffee (mean)	.510	6.8
15 Aaker and Day [2]	Instant coffee (low)	.030	1.3
16 Aaker and Day [2]	Instant coffee (high)	.716	13.8
17 Bass and Parsons [7]	Low priced food	.496	6.6
18 Houston and Weiss [21]	18 low priced food brands (high)	.989	416.3
19 Clarke [14]	18 low priced food brands (low)	.324	4.1
20 Clarke [14]	18 low priced food brands (low)	.324	4.1
21 Clarke [14]	18 low priced food brands (mean)	.825	23.9
22 Wildt [56]	Frequently purchased food firm 1	.498	6.6
23 Wildt [56]	Frequently purchased food firm 2	.272	3.5
24 Wildt [56]	Frequently purchased food firm 3	.502	6.7
Quarterly			
25 Ball & Agarwala [5]	Tea (low) #	.700	19.4
26 Ball & Agarwala [5]	Tea (high) #	.900	65.6
27 Buzzell et al. [11]	Toilet soap	.374	7.0
28 Buzzell et al. [11]	Assorted low priced products	.888	58.2
29 Lambin [28]	Gasoline brand A	.685	19.9
30 Lambin [28]	Gasoline brand B	.785	28.5
31 Lambin [28]	Gasoline brand C	.817	34.2
32 Lambin [28]	Gasoline brand D	.982	381.9
33 Lambin [28]	Gasoline brand E	.291	7.3
34 Lambin [28]	6 gasoline brands	.130	3.4
35 Schultz [45]	Airline frequency share	.420	8.0
Annual			
36 Lambin [25]	Frequently purchased food	.473	36.9
37 Lambin [25]	Frequently purchased food	.507	40.7
38 Palda [36]	Lydia Pinkham	.628	59.4
39 Parsons & Schultz [37]	Aggregate consumption	.567	48.7
40 Parsons & Schultz [37]	Aggregate consumption (services)	.922	340.2
41 Parsons & Schultz [37]	Aggregate consumption (non-durables)	.503	40.2
42 Parsons & Schultz [37]	Aggregate consumption (durables)	.704	78.7
43 Taylor & Weiserbs [51]	Aggregate consumption	.919	339.1
44 Lambin [26]	Small electric appliances area 1	.678	71.1
45 Lambin [26]	Small electric appliances area 2	.366	27.5
46 Lambin [26]	Small electric appliances area 3	.346	26.0
47 Lambin [27]	Gas station share	.701	89.8
48 Simon [51]	Liquor 8 blends	.790	117.2
49 Simon [51]	Liquor bourbon	.750	96.0
50 Simon [51]	Liquor gin	.800	123.8
51 Simon [51]	Liquor vodka	.960	676.9
52 Simon [51]	15 brands (low)	.280	21.7
53 Simon [51]	15 brands (high)	.980	1367.7
54 Dominguez [18]	Filter cigarettes	.140	33.7
55 Dominguez [18]	Non-filter cigarettes	.313	23.8
56 Telser [52]	Lucky Strike	.960	676.9
57 Telser [52]	Camels	.410	31.0
58 Telser [52]	Camels (share)	.736	90.1

Table 1 (Continued)

Researchers	Product	Coefficient of lagged dependent variable λ	90% duration interval (months)
59 Telser [52]	Lucky Strike (share)	.596	53.4
60 Telser [52]	Chesterfield (share)	.657	65.8
61 Schnabel [44]	18 cigarette brands	.661	66.7
62 Schnabel [44]	18 cigarette brands (low)	.190	16.6
63 Schnabel [44]	18 cigarette brands (high)	.896	251.6
64 Schmallensee [43]	Cigarettes (industry)	.841	159.6
65 Schmallensee [43]	Cigarettes company (low)	.602	54.4
66 Schmallensee [43]	Cigarettes company (high)	.748	95.2
76 Peles [39]	Automobiles	.620	57.8
68 Peles [39]	Beer	.493	39.1
69 Peles [39]	Cigarettes	.679	71.4

nations of independent variables result in considerable variation in the estimates of the coefficients of these independent variables.

Regardless of this observation, models containing only lagged sales and advertising have been preferred to models including lagged sales and numerous advertising-related independent variables. When a simple Koyck model was not available, a specification containing a significant lagged sales variable and a significant advertising-related variable was chosen.

In certain applications advertising is not represented by expenditures alone but by advertising awareness, attitude measures, recall, etc. In many of these models multicollinearity among the variables is very likely and may result in none of the advertising variables being significant. If multicollinearity appeared to be a likely cause of lack of significance, the study was included. In this case the length of the duration interval should be interpreted as conditional on the existence of an effect. Such instances were very rare.

On the basis of the foregoing guidelines, a search of the published literature was undertaken in the hope that emerging patterns across applications might compensate somewhat for the methodological problems of individual papers. The results of this study are summarized in Table 1.

SURVEY DISCUSSION

The first impression from Table 1 is that numerous articles deal with distributed lag models and thus implicitly include an estimate of the duration interval. The average coefficient of the lagged dependent variable is .591 and the average implied 90% duration interval is 101 months. A closer inspection shows that the range of the estimated implied duration intervals is very broad; the estimates of the implied 90% duration intervals range from 1.3 to 1,368 months. Considerable variance was expected because of the numerous omitted factors, but this is excessive. For only the cigarette studies, the average implied 90% duration interval ranges from 17 to 677 months. The results of the studies are not consistent and indicate either problems

in the application of the model, or radically varying advertising effect across products or brands. As most of the studies were performed on low-priced, frequently purchased consumer products, one would expect some agreement in the various estimates of the duration of cumulative advertising effect despite the fact that other marketing mix and competitive factors are not controlled.

As a first step in closer analysis of the survey, studies which implied counter-intuitive results were excluded. It seemed unreasonable to expect the effect of an advertisement to last 10 years and therefore results which indicated an implied 90% duration interval in excess of 120 months were removed from further consideration. Furthermore most studies usually involved estimates of λ for which $1 - λ$ is less than one standard error of the estimate of λ. Thus it is likely that the assumptions of the model were violated (i.e. $λ < 1$) and these same studies also were rejected on statistical grounds. This reduced data base is used in Table 2 (11 studies were excluded).

There is no systematic variance of the estimates of λ or the implied duration interval due to the use of market share or sales as the dependent variable. There is also no systematic variance in the estimates of λ or the implied duration interval due to a subjective judgment of the purchase frequency of the products [see 15].

Classifying the studies by data interval (see Table 2) provides statistically different values of $\hat{λ}$, the coefficient of the lagged dependent variable, and produces a distinct pattern in the average implied duration interval.

Notice in Table 2 that the *average implied duration interval derived from annual data is more than 17 times as long as the average implied duration interval derived from monthly data!* This simple split explains 55% of the variance of the estimated implied duration intervals in Table 1. The average estimate of λ computed from annual or quarterly data is larger than the average $\hat{λ}$ computed from monthly data. The bimonthly and weekly values split the difference

Table 2
EFFECT OF DATA INTERVAL ON IMPLIED DURATION INTERVAL

Data interval	Coefficient of lagged dependent variable $(\hat{\lambda})$	90% duration interval	Number of observations
Weekly	.537 (.057)	0.9 (0.2)	2
Monthly	.440 (.027)	3.0 (0.2)	10
Bimonthly	.493 (.076)	9.0 (2.2)	10
Quarterly	.599 (.086)	25.1 (6.9)	10
Annual	.560 (.031)	56.5 (5.1)	27

The amount of variance explained by the categories is significant at the $\alpha = .05$ level for the duration interval only. Pairwise differences significant at the $\alpha = .05$ level are:

	$\hat{\lambda}$					90% duration interval				
Weekly	—					—				
Monthly	NS	—				S	—			
Bimonthly	NS	NS	—			S	S	—		
Quarterly	NS	S	NS	—		S	S	S	—	
Annual	NS	S	NS	NS	—	S	S	S	S	—

The values in parentheses are the sample standard errors of the cell means.

between the monthly, and the quarterly and annual $\hat{\lambda}$'s.

The choice of a data interval and the choice of the dependent variable are statistical artifacts of the research process and have no bearing whatsoever on the actual duration of the cumulative advertising effect. Therefore the disarray in Table 1 is, at least in part, a result of methodological problems. One thing is clear from the survey: *the implied duration interval increases significantly as the length of the data interval increases.*

DATA INTERVAL BIAS

Regardless of what the actual lag structure is, consistent *estimation with different data intervals* would require that the estimate of λ be larger for shorter data intervals than for longer data intervals. Lydia Pinkham's vegetable compound appears in Table 1 both as a monthly and as an annual study and thus serves as an example. The annual λ is .628, the monthly λ is .390; regardless of the true duration interval, these two results cannot be consistent. There must be some bias which affects the estimation procedure. Even though the two data bases cover different time periods, the monthly data are a proper subset of the annual data and there should not be so much difference in the estimated length of the duration intervals.

In the annual study, the implied 90% duration

interval is 59 months, but in the monthly study it is only 4 months. Palda [36] also computes monthly direct lag estimates which indicate a directly measured duration interval of three months. Direct lag estimation on the annual data by Clarke and McCann [16] using spectral techniques shows a duration interval composed of the current and succeeding year only.[3] Their spectral estimates of the monthly lag structure agree closely with Palda's direct lag estimates. The annual direct lag estimates do not agree with the implied duration interval for the annual model.

Table 3 presents a comparison between the direct lag estimates and the implied duration interval for the few studies for which such comparisons are possible. There is greater similarity between the implied duration interval and the direct duration interval for those models computed from monthly data than there is for those computed from quarterly and annual data. Table 3, in the absence of other information, leads one to favor the estimates derived from the shorter data interval models but the evidence is hardly conclusive. Fortunately, a more demanding test is available.

A Test for Data Interval Bias

Although the Koyck model often is used, seldom does an author address the problem of whether the necessary conditions associated with the Koyck model are satisfied, i.e. that in connection with equation (1) there is a real number λ such that

1. $0 < \lambda \leq 1$ and
2. $\beta_k = \lambda\beta_{k-1}$ for $k = 1,2,\ldots$

The importance of the existence of λ is apparent if the equation[4] giving rise to the Koyck model is considered:

$$y_t - \lambda y_{t-1} = (1-\lambda)a + \beta_0 x_t + (\beta_1 - \lambda\beta_0)x_{t-1}$$
$$(6) \qquad + (\beta_2 - \lambda\beta_1)x_{t-2} + \ldots + v_t.$$

Two very important facts about the Koyck model are apparent from (6):

1. The disturbances, v_t, are autocorrelated with parameter λ ($v_t = \epsilon_t - \lambda\epsilon_{t-1}$).
2. The coefficient of x_{t-k} for $k \geq 1$ will be equal to zero only if the hypothesized λ exists. If λ does not exist then equation (6) rather than equation (3) is the reduced form of equation (1). The Koyck model, and its strong hypothesis about the cumulative effect of advertising, depends entirely on the existence of λ.

---

[3]Houston and Weiss [22] compute a model by use of a nonlinear estimation procedure which reduces the estimate of the duration interval derived from the annual data to 24.9 months. Use of their estimation procedure by Clarke and McCann [17] on the monthly data yields an estimate of the duration interval of 5.8 months.
[4]In (1) with $n = \infty$, multiply (1) at time $t-1$ by λ and subtract from (1) at time t.

Table 3
AGREEMENT OF DIRECT LAG ESTIMATES AND IMPLIED DURATION INTERVAL

Researcher(s)	Product	90% duration interval	Maximum lagged advertising with a positive significant coefficient
Monthly			
Palda [36]	Lydia Pinkham	3.4	3
Johansson [23]	Nonseasonal food	—	4
Bass and Clarke [8]	Dietary product	4	3
Montgomery and Silk [32]	Ethical drug	4.2	
Montgomery and Silk [32]	Ethical drug direct mail		2 (gaps)
Montgomery and Silk [32]	Ethical drug samples and literature		4 (gaps)
Montgomery and Silk [32]	Ethical drug journal adv.		5 (gaps)
Sethi [46]	Analgesic	—	3
Quarterly			
Lambin [27]	Gasoline brand A	21.3	3 ($\leq$ 9 months)
Lambin [27]	Gasoline brand B	28.5	($t-2$ only)
Lambin [27]	Gasoline brand C	34.2	0
Lambin [27]	Gasoline brand D	380.	0
Lambin [27]	Gasoline brand F	5.6	($\leq$ 9 months)
Annual			
Peles [39]	Beer	39	2 ($<$ 24 months)
Peles [39]	Cigarettes	78.4	3 ($\leq$ 36 months)
Peles [39]	Automobiles	57.8	1 ($\leq$ 12 months)
Palda [36]	Lydia Pinkham	59.4	
Clarke and McCann [16]	Lydia Pinkham		2 ($\leq$ 24 months)

In his excellent survey of distributed lag models, Griliches [20] discusses a model specification which has a reduced form similar to that of the Koyck model, but a drastically different structural form with very different implications about the duration of cumulative advertising effect: current advertising affects current sales and there is a carryover effect which cannot be attributed solely to advertising. The current effects hypothesis says that *if there is a cumulative effect attributable to advertising, it is of a shorter duration than the data interval.* The current effects model is important in the context of the present survey because the major problem is to decide whether the annual or the monthly results are more consistent with the data. If the cumulative effect of advertising is roughly a year or less, the current effects hypothesis should be satisfied. This would indicate that the duration intervals estimated on annual data are biased by use of data of the wrong data interval. If the cumulative effect of advertising is longer than a year, the current effects hypothesis should be rejected, and the long duration intervals associated with the annual data cannot be rejected as the result of data interval bias.

Considering this "current effects hypothesis" as an alternative to the Koyck hypothesis leads to a very important test. The current effects model can be expressed as:

$$y_t = ax_t + u_t$$
$$(7) \qquad u_t = \rho u_{t-1} + \epsilon_t, \ |\rho| \leq 1.$$

Combining the two equations in (7) results in:

$$y_t = ax_t + \rho u_{t-1} + \epsilon_t$$
$$= ax_t + \rho(y_{t-1} - ax_{t-1}) + \epsilon_t$$
$$(8) \qquad = ax_t + \rho y_{t-1} - a\rho x_{t-1} + \epsilon_t.$$

The similarity of equation (8) to equation (6) suggests a test for the appropriateness of the cumulative effects model or the current effects model. Figure 3 shows the implied lag structure for various values of the test equation:

$$y_t = A_0 + Ax_t + Bx_{t-1} + Cy_{t-1} + v_t$$
$$(9) \qquad v_t = Dv_{t-1} + \epsilon_t.$$

It is seen from (9) and Figure 2 that the Koyck hypothesis is indicated when $B = 0$ and $D = C$. The nonmonotonic declining cumulative effect occurs when $B > 0$ and the current effects model (i.e. if any lagged effect exists it is shorter than the data interval) is indicated when $B = -AC$. The execution of this test in the present survey is necessarily inexact. $\hat{A}$, $\hat{B}$, and $\hat{C}$ are all correlated and thus the distribution of these joint functions involves the correlation matrix of the estimates. This matrix is not published in any of the studies and thus the test cannot be computed here. An approximate test is computed from the parameter estimates.

In Palda's study, the only one that includes both annual and monthly results, the annual duration interval does not agree with the monthly duration interval. Applying the test for data interval bias to the annual results yields the results in Table 4. From these results

Figure 2
LAG STRUCTURE AND THE COEFFICIENT OF LAGGED
ADVERTISING

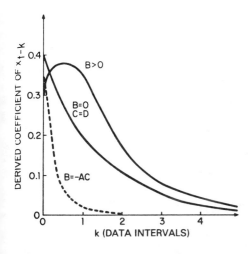

it is seen that the coefficient of lagged advertising is not zero, and thus the Koyck model should be rejected. The test values for the current effects hypothesis are in very close agreement.

Although the distribution of $-\hat{A}\hat{C}$ is not known, the standard error is surely greater than the smaller of the standard errors of $\hat{A}$ and $\hat{C}$. The test values are within one "$\hat{C}$" standard error of each other and because the "degree of falsifiability" [48] of this test

Table 4
ESTIMATES OF TEST EQUATION
$$y_t = A_0 + Ax_t + Bx_{t-1} + Cy_{t-1} + v_t$$
$$v_t = Dv_{t-1} + \epsilon_t$$

	A_0	A	B	C	D	R^2
Estimate	231.6	.609	−.382	.765	.186	.929
Standard error		(.136)	(.156)	(.102)		

Test 1—Koyck and cumulative effects model

Hypothesis	Estimates	Result
$B \overset{?}{=} 0$	$B = -2.45$ std. errors	Reject
$C \overset{?}{=} D$	$.765 \ne .186$	Reject

Test 2—current effects model

Hypothesis	Estimates	Result
$B \overset{?}{=} -AC$	$-.382 = -(.609)(.765)$	
	$-.382 = -.465$	Accept
Min. std. error (A,C)	.102	

is so high. the current effects hypothesis should be accepted. The long implied duration intervals associated with the annual estimates are the result of data interval bias and should be rejected. A more complete discussion of this test is found in [16,17,22].

It is not possible to perform the same test for each of the other studies in Table 1 as the data are not published and the necessary test equation is not always presented. Fortunately, the practice of publishing multiple models has made the test equation available in several studies. Table 5 presents the test values for articles which include the test equation or relevant pieces of it.

Data interval bias is prevalent in the studies based on annual data. In the two studies computed on monthly data the coefficient of lagged advertising is not negative. Of the eight studies computed on quarterly data only one has a negative coefficient of lagged advertising. In this study the coefficient of current advertising was not reported and the test value could not be computed. When the data interval is quarterly or shorter there is no test result which favors the current effects hypothesis. In all but three of the 12 studies computed on annual data the coefficient of lagged advertising is negative and the agreement between the coefficient of lagged advertising and the test value is remarkably close.

Telser's [52] cigarette study indicates the Koyck model is possible but in three other studies of cigarette data the test for data interval bias is satisfied.

The implied duration interval in Lambin's [25] service station share article is 89.8 months, but it should be noted that the implied duration intervals for his five gasoline brands range from 19.9 to 34.2 months and one implied duration interval is 381.9 months. The latter example was deleted in the computation of Table 2 because the computed λ = .982 is within a standard error of 1. Thus, in the gasoline case the evidence is conflicting because the station share result is about three times as long as the published results on the gasoline at a lower level of brand and time aggregation. Only the beer study by Peles [38] indicates an uncontested example of a Koyck model derived from annual data. The implied duration interval of this study is 39 months, one of the shorter implied duration intervals derived from annual data.

The evidence in Tables 3 and 5 strongly indicates that the long implied duration intervals obtained from the annual models are due to data interval bias and the shorter implied duration intervals obtained from the monthly, bimonthly, and quarterly data are more likely to be accurate descriptions of the duration of cumulative advertising effect.

THE KOYCK HYPOTHESIS

In addition to the methodological problems with the Koyck model there are conceptual problems in

Table 5

DATA INTERVAL BIAS: TEST RESULTS

Researcher(s)	Product	Test values		
		B	−AC	Bias
Monthly				
1 Bass and Clarke [8]	Dietary product	+.077	−.053	No
2 Montgomery and Silk [32]	Ethical drugs	NS		No
Quarterly				
3 Lambin [26]	Gasoline brand A	+.034	−.026	No
4 Lambin [26]	Gasoline brand B	NS		No
5 Lambin [26]	Gasoline brand C	NS	−.014	No
6 Lambin [26]	Gasoline brand D	.019	−.014	No
7 Lambin [26]	Gasoline brand F	.016	−.004	No
8 Buzzell [11]	Laundry detergent	+.271	NA	No
9 Buzzell [11]	Hair tonic	−.271	NA	?
Annual				
10 Lambin [25]	Service station share	.035	−.028	No
11 Clarke and McCann [16]	Lydia Pinkham	−.469	−.53	Yes
12 Melrose [30]	Lydia Pinkham	−.199	−.254	Yes
13 Parsons and Schultz [37]	Aggregate consumption	−5.18	−3.47	Yes
14 Parsons and Schultz [37]	Durables	−5.07	−3.56	Yes
15 Parsons and Schultz [37]	Aggregate consumption nondurables	−2.86	−1.2	Yes
16 Parsons and Schultz [37]	Aggregate consumption services	−1.13	−.84	Yes
17 Peles [39]	Automobiles	−.011	−.009	Yes
18 Peles [39]	Beer	NS		No
19 Peles [39]	Cigarettes	−.036	−.15	Yes
20 Telser [52]	Cigarettes (3 brands)	NS		No
21 Schmallensee [43]	Cigarettes	−.14	−.10	Yes

NS = not significant.
NA = not available.

its use in an advertising context. With regard to the structural model (2), it is inconsistent with the marketing concept that the sales of a product would be *solely* a function of advertising, past and present. What about the rest of the marketing mix? Surely there is some effect due to distribution channels, personal selling, and brand loyalty.

If the Koyck hypothesis is literally true, then the reduced form (3) should be observed to be autocorrelated with parameter equal to λ. The Durbin-Watson tests (biased in this case) do not show this to be true. Palda [36] observes that if the disturbance in the structural model (2) is autocorrelated with parameter equal to λ then the reduced form disturbance will not be autocorrelated. This hypothesis implies that the rest of the marketing efforts of the company have the same duration interval as does advertising. Thus in this case the Koyck model has the same implicit hypothesis about carryover effects as does the partial adjustment model. The inclusion of autocorrelated disturbances in the procedures used in estimating equation (3) or (9) is important to avoid forcing the estimates into one or the other of these unlikely models of advertising's effect.

Estimation problems are associated with the Koyck or distributed lag model. It is necessary, from the foregoing argument, to separate autocorrelation from

advertising carryover in order for these models to give an accurate indication of advertising's effect on sales. Houston and Weiss [22] demonstrate an interesting methodology to do this (see also Clarke and McCann [17]). Inability to separate these two factors results in biased estimates of λ, the parameter from which the implied duration interval is computed. The implied duration interval is a rapidly increasing function of λ, especially for λ > .7 and small errors in the estimate of the duration interval. Moreover, it appears that the OLS loss function of the distributed lag models is not very sensitive to changes in λ, further complicating the use of distributed lag models as a vehicle for measuring the length of the duration interval. (For a more complete discussion of these problems see Clarke [15, p. 32-5].)

The distributed lag models are imperfect models for measuring the duration of cumulative advertising effect, but, at a macro level, they are the best available at present.

RELATED STUDIES

Certain other studies provide some information about the duration of advertising effect on sales. Only a few are mentioned here as a supplement to the major focus of the study.

Melrose's study [30] of Lydia Pinkham advertising

as a function of its sales obtains λ values consistent with the surveyed results. Interestingly, the test for data interval bias on his annual model is positive.

Sethi's experiment [46] on analgesic advertising compares a steady advertising expenditure in one market with a pulsed expenditure in another market. The response to the advertising pulse, initially high, declines to the same level as the response to the even advertising in three months.

Frank and Massy's study of promotion [19] shows rapidly declining responses to promotion on the order of three weeks. The STEAM model [31], developed by Massy, forecast the sales of a new product. During the forecast period the company twice engaged in "an intensive promotion program." Sales increased rapidly but decreased to forecasted levels in about six months.

Ackoff and Emshoff [3], reporting on experiments to determine advertising's effect on sales, note no decline after cessation of advertising of Budweiser beer for a period of about 18 months, and a small decline monthly after that. It is interesting that this result corresponds with the only instance in the survey of a longer cumulative effect computed from annual data that is not subject to aggregation bias (Peles' 90% implied duration interval of 39 months).

These few examples also indicate that the duration of cumulative advertising effect is a matter of months rather than years.

SUMMARY AND CONCLUSIONS

To summarize the substantive findings of several papers requires that certain liberties be taken with published results. Most of the studies reported in this survey were not directed primarily at the duration question and thus their use here is not necessarily consistent with the intent of their authors. In isolation, none of the papers gives a satisfactory answer to the question of how long advertising affects sales. By putting them together, as has been done here, one achieves greater confidence in the result. But this compilation process requires compromise in the integrity of the individual papers.

The specific compromise upon which this survey is based is that the implied duration interval is relatively insensitive to changes in the distributed lag specification. If this premise is accepted, then the survey results are a strong statement about the substantive content of a research tradition, and the conclusions drawn about the duration of cumulative advertising effect are as comprehensive as is now possible.

The results of the survey are clear in one sense: *the duration intervals derived from the annual models are too long*. The annual studies show a nearly unanimous presence of data interval bias, whereas the shorter data interval studies do not. In 70 studies the pattern is consistent. The weekly results probably are biased downward because the purchase cycle is proba-

bly longer than the data interval. If one considers the monthly, bimonthly, and quarterly results to be most likely to be free of data interval bias, the duration of cumulative advertising effect on sales is between 3 and 15 months; thus this effect is a short-term (about a year or less) phenomenon.

The estimate of the coefficient of the lagged dependent variable also was found to be biased by use of an annual data interval. This bias may even be in effect on shorter data intervals. The average coefficient of the lagged dependent variable (λ) for the quarterly data studies is .608 in contrast to λ = .430 for the monthly studies. If the data interval for the quarterly data were computed by use of the monthly λ, the implied duration interval would be reduced from 15 to 9 months. The implied 90% duration intervals from the monthly, bimonthly, and quarterly studies would then be 3, 9, and 9 respectively. If this modification is accepted, *the published econometric literature indicates that 90% of the cumulative effect of advertising on sales of mature, frequently purchased, low-priced products occurs within 3 to 9 months of the advertisement. The conclusion that advertising's effect on sales lasts for months rather than years is strongly supported.*

Another critical point, not addressed in this survey, is whether or not distributed lag models (or partial adjustment models) are valid vehicles by which to study advertising's effect on sales. It is apparent that from a managerial point of view these models are lacking in richness of information about controllable variables; but from a technical viewpoint the question is a very difficult one, and is not considered completely here.

A first step in considering the technical applicability question is to observe the frequency with which the distributed lag models are statistically significant and logically signed in the studies listed in Table 1. About 70% of the applications listed have the proper sign for statistically significant coefficients. The articles by Samuels [41], Buzzell [11], and Simon [49], all of which are multiproduct reports, account for most of the insignificant applications. Moriarty [33], however, found advertising significant in only five of 25 sales districts and none of the three aggregate districts which he formed from them. Thus distributed lag models quite broadly obtain statistically significant results. The distributed lag models may not be perfect instruments by which to measure cumulative advertising effects, but careful methodological attention shows that the results of 70 studies are in very close agreement on the duration of the cumulative effect of advertising. Such agreement is indicative of consistency at least, if not validity.

The survey has several important implications for future advertising research.

1. There is a need to perform advertising research on a broader range of products. More than 70% of

the studies in this survey concern mature, frequently purchased, low-priced consumer goods.

2. Advertising studies on annual data should be avoided. There is a bias in the estimate of the coefficient of lagged avertising as well as in the estimate of the implied duration interval. Even if the emphasis is not on measuring duration, the estimates of short-run advertising effect are biased.

3. Researchers who do not include tests for data interval bias should be asked to supply them before their reports are published.

4. Distributed lag models that allow correction for autocorrelation are preferable to those which do not. Whenever possible these estimates should be presented along with the OLS estimates.

5. Alternative models to the distributed lag models should be sought. The models should (1) be more robust in the parameters which measure the cumulative advertising effect, (2) be derived from more realistic models of advertising effect, and (3) be less sensitive to data interval bias.

6. More complete descriptions of the situations in which studies are performed should be required. It is not always easy to find out what data interval is being used. Purchase frequency seldom is presented; competitive situations, product age, and market strategy are very rarely discussed. Without a better description of the factors which could affect the results there is little hope of improving the generality of results or of examining the effect of factors across applications. Because there is no broadly defined cross-sectional data base available for researchers, such cooperation is necessary to combine results and obtain broadly applicable principles.

Too much attention and effort have been spent in finding fault with individual studies, and the focus has too often been to tear down rather than to build upon the work of others. Each of the articles in this survey has flaws. Each could be, and probably has been, rejected in the past by various people for various reasons. But, when taken as a body of research, the articles show remarkable consistency and a good basis for future research.

REFERENCES

1. Aaker, David A. and George S. Day. "Appraising Communications Effects with a Recursive Model," *Proceedings*, AMA, 1971, p. 460.

2. ——— and ———."A Recursive Model of Communication Processes," in David A. Aaker, ed., *Multivariate Analysis in Marketing: Theory and Application*. Belmont, California: Wadsworth, 1971.

3. Ackoff, Russell L. and James R. Emshoff. "Advertising Research at Anheuser-Busch, Inc. (1963-68)," *Sloan Management Review*, 17 (Winter 1975), p. 1-15.

4. Almon, S. "The Distributed Lag Between Capital Appropriations and Expenditures," *Econometrica*, 33 (January 1965).

5. Ball, R. J. and R. Agarwala. "An Econometric Analysis of the Effects of Generic Advertising on the Demand

for Tea in the U.K.," *British Journal of Marketing*, 4 (Winter 1969), 202-17.

6. Bass, Frank M. "Testing vs. Estimation in Simultaneous-Equation Regression Models," *Journal of Marketing Research*, 8 (August 1971).

7. ——— and Leonard J. Parsons. "Simultaneous-Equation Regression Analysis of Sales and Advertising," *Applied Economics*, 1 (May 1969), 103-24.

8. ——— and Darral G. Clarke. "Testing Distributed Lag Models of Advertising Effect," *Journal of Marketing Research*, 9 (August 1972).

9. Beckwith, Neil E. "Multivariate Analysis of Sales Responses of Competing Brands to Advertising," *Journal of Marketing Research*, 9 (May 1972).

10. Block, Harry. "Advertising and Profitability: A Reappraisal," *Journal of Political Economy*, 82 (March/April 1974), p. 267-86.

11. Buzzell, Robert D. "Predicting Short-Term Changes in Market Share as a Function of Advertising Strategy," *Journal of Marketing Research*, 1 (August 1964).

12. ———, Marshall Kolin, and Malcolm Murphy. "Television Commercial Test Scores and Short-Term Changes in Market Shares," *Journal of Marketing Research*, 2 (August 1965).

13. Clarke, Darral G. "An Empirical Investigation of Advertising Competition," unpublished doctoral dissertation, Purdue University, 1972.

14. ———. "Sales-Advertising Cross-Elasticities and Advertising Competition," *Journal of Marketing Research*, 10 (August 1972).

15. ———. "Econometric Measurement of the Duration of the Advertising Effect on Sales," Marketing Sciences Institute Working Paper, #75-106, April 1975.

16. ——— and John M. McCann. "Measuring the Cumulative Effects of Advertising: A Reappraisal," *Proceedings*, AMA, 1973.

17. ——— and ———. "Cumulative Advertising Effect: The Role of Serial Correlation: A Reply," *Decision Sciences*, forthcoming (January 1977).

18. Dominquez, Louis V. and Albert L. Page. "A Note on a Simultaneous-Equation Regression Study of Advertising and Sales of Cigarettes," *Journal of Marketing Research*, 8 (August 1971).

19. Frank, Ronald F. and William F. Massy. "Effects of Short-Term Promotional Strategy in Selected Market Segments," in Patrick J. Robinson, ed., *Promotional Decisions Using Mathematical Models*. Boston: MSI with Allyn and Bacon, 1967.

20. Griliches, Zvi. "Distributed Lags: A Survey," *Econometrica*, 35 (January 1967).

21. Houston, Franklin S. and Doyle L. Weiss. "An Analysis of Competitive Market Behavior," *Journal of Marketing Research*, 11 (May 1974).

22. ——— and ———. "Cumulative Advertising Effects: The Role of Serial Correlation," *Decision Sciences*, 6 (July 1975), p. 471-81.

23. Johansson, Johny K. "On the Estimation of Lagged Effects of Advertising," Working Paper #73, University of Illinois, 1972.

24. Koyck, L. M. *Distributed Lags and Investment Analysis*. Amsterdam: North Holland Publishing Co., 1954.

25. Lambin, Jean-Jacques. "Measuring the Profitability of Advertising: An Empirical Study," *Journal of Industrial Economics*, 17 (April 1969), p. 86.

26. ———. "Optimal Allocation of Competitive Marketing Efforts: An Empirical Study." *Journal of Business*, 43 (October 1970).

27. ———. "A Computer On-Line Marketing Mix Model." *Journal of Marketing Research*, 9 (May 1972), p. 119.

28. ———. "Is Gasoline Advertising Justified?" *Journal of Business*, 45 (October 1972), p. 505.

29. Maddala, G. S. and R. C. Vogel. "Estimating Lagged Relationships in Corporate Demand for Liquid Assets," *Review of Economics and Statistics*, 51 (February 1969), p. 54.

30. Melrose, Kendrick B. "An Empirical Study on Optimizing Advertising Policy," *Journal of Business*, 32 (July 1969), p. 282.

31. Massy, W. F., D. B. Montgomery, and D. G. Morrison. *Stochastic Models of Buying Behavior*, Cambridge: MIT Press, 1970.

32. Montgomery, David B. and Alvin J. Silk. "Estimating Dynamic Effects of Market Communications Expenditures," *Management Science*, 18 (June 1972).

33. Moriarty, Mark. "Cross-Sectional Time-Series Issues in the Analysis of Marketing Decision Variables," *Journal of Marketing Research*, 12 (May 1975), p. 142-50.

34. Nakanishi, Masao. "Advertising and Promotion Effects on Consumer Response to New Products," *Journal of Marketing Research*, 10 (August 1973).

35. Nerlove, Marc and F. V. Waugh. "Advertising Without Supply Control: Some Implications of a Study of the Advertising of Oranges," *Journal of Farm Economics*, 43 (October 1971), p. 813.

36. Palda, Kristian. *The Measurement of Cumulative Advertising Effects*. Englewood Cliffs, New Jersey: Prentice-Hall, Inc., 1964.

37. Parsons, Leonard and Randall L. Schultz. "The Impact of Advertising on the Aggregate Consumption Function: I. Preliminary Results," Institute for Research in the Behavioral, Economic and Management Sciences, Krannert Graduate School of Industrial Administration, Purdue University, Paper #443, March 1974.

38. Peles, Yoram. "Economies of Scale in Advertising Beer and Cigarettes," *Journal of Business*, 44 (January 1971), p. 32.

39. ———. "Rates of Amortization of Advertising Expenditures," *Journal of Political Economy*, 79 (September-October 1971), p. 1032.

40. Reckie, W. Duncan. "Some Problems Associated with the Marketing of Ethical Pharmaceutical Products," *Journal of Industrial Economics*, 19 (November 1970), p. 33.

41. Samuels, J. M. "The Effect of Advertising on Sales and Brand Shares," *British Journal of Advertising*, 4 (Winter 1970-71), 187-207.

42. Sasieni, Maurice W. "Aggregation of Data," unpublished manuscript.

43. Schmallensee, Richard. *The Economics of Advertising*. Amsterdam: North Holland Publishing Co., 1972.

44. Schnabel, Morton. "An Oligopoly Model of the Cigarette Industry," *Southern Economic Journal*, 38 (January 1972).

45. Schultz, Randall L. "Market Measurement and Planning with a Simultaneous-Equation Mobel," *Journal of Marketing Research*, 8 (May 1971), p. 153.

46. Sethi, S. Prakook. "A Comparison Between the Effect of Pulse versus Continuous TV Advertising on Buyer Behavior," *Proceedings*, AMA, 1971.

47. Sexton, Donald E. "Estimating Marketing Policy Effects on Sales of a Frequently Purchased Product," *Journal of Marketing Research*, 7 (August 1970).

48. ———. "A Cluster Analytic Approach to Market Response Functions," *Journal of Marketing Research*, 11 (February 1974).

49. Simon, H. A. "On Judging the Plausibility of Theories," in van Rootselaar and Staal, eds., *Logic, Methodology and Philosophy of Sciences III*. Amsterdam: North Holland Publishing Co., 1968.

50. Simon, Julian. "The Effect of Advertising on Liquor Brand Sales," *Journal of Marketing Research*, 6 (August 1969).

51. Taylor, L. D. and D. Weiserbs. "Advertising and the Aggregate Consumption Function," *American Economic Review*, 62 (September 1972), p. 642-55.

52. Telser, Lester. "Advertising and Cigarettes," *Journal of Political Economy*, 70 (October 1962).

53. ———. "The Demand for Branded Goods as Estimated from Consumer Panel Data," *The Review of Economics and Statistics*, 44 (August 1962), p. 300-24.

54. Weiss, Doyle, L. "Determinants of Market Share," *Journal of Marketing Research*, 5 (August 1968).

55. Wilder, Ronald P. "Advertising and Inter-Industry Competition: Testing a Galbraithian Hypothesis," *Journal of Industrial Economics*, 22 (March 1974), p. 215.

56. Wildt, Albert R. "Multifirm Analysis of Competitive Decision Variables," *Journal of Marketing Research*, 11 (February 1974).

Lydia Pinkham Revisited: A Box-Jenkins Approach

One of the oldest sales/advertising times series (1903-1960) is analyzed here by one of the newest techniques.

P. W. Kyle

Progress in the analysis of marketing time series has not been great over the past 15 years despite the advent of the computer and the increasing sophistication of econometric techniques. The difficulties are immense, particularly any attempt to measure the influence of advertising upon sales. In the past, these difficulties often have been separated into two major categories:

(1) the problem of isolating the form of the relationships between the two time series (the identification problem);

(2) the problem of surmounting the limitations of the various techniques which, in the past, have been used to analyze these series.

These problems are not entirely unrelated, for if we were to assume what is perhaps the most complicated relationship possible between two such series, the inadequacies of the techniques which have been used is made only too clear. If we assume (1) a system composed of a serially correlated sales series, the correlations of which are caused by either the lagged effects of advertising or some inertia in the system, adjustment factors, omitted variables, etc., and (2) that the advertising series is also to some extent serially correlated for those reasons and because of feedback from a serially correlated sales series, then the lack of sophistication of the techniques which have been used in the past is apparent. Simple regression cannot cope. Simultaneous equation methods will be troubled by the inherent serial correlations in both series compounded by the omission of the lagged effects of advertising. The fitting of distributed lag models of the effects of advertising may confuse the inherent serial correlations in both series with the effects of the distributed lags, this error being compounded by the feedback in the system. It is not that there has been no attempt to solve these problems, but that the approach has been to seek a solution to each one individually. Solutions to the serial-correlation problem are well known (Goldberger, 1964; Johnson, 1963), as are those to the problem of feedback (Bass, 1969; Bass and Parsons, 1969; Johnson, 1963), while specific examples of the application of distributed lag analysis to sales and advertising time series can be found in the literature (Bass and Clarke, 1972; Palda, 1963, 1964), and the major criticism made in any one case can often be seen in terms of the fact that the other problems have not been taken into account (Doyle, 1966; Quandt, 1964).

Thus the techniques used must attempt to incorporate all of these problems, and only the work by Bass and Parsons (1969) reflects such an attempt. Alternative techniques which appear to afford such an opportunity are those advanced by Box and Jenkins (1968, 1970). Though present interest in these techniques has centered around their value as a forecasting device, in comparison with either univariate forecasting methods such as exponentially weighted moving averages (Chatfield and Prothero, 1973; Guerts and Ibraham, 1975) or with the forecasting abilities of econometric models (Naylor, Seaks, and Wichern, 1972), these have made use only of the univariate or ARIMA Box-Jenkins models and not their multivariate models, where ARIMA models are fitted to all variables within the system under study and com-

31

bined by a transfer function to yield what Box and Jenkins call their dynamic model. In the view of Naylor, Seaks, and Wichern (1972),

A major field of new investigation in econometrics could centre around combining ARIMA and dynamic models to represent a simultaneous system similar to that handled by traditional econometric methods.

An example of the modeling of such a simultaneous system is the work carried out by Jenkins (1974), which describes the interactions of the mink (predator) and muskrat (prey) populations in northern Canada.

The objectives of this paper are threefold: (1) to illustrate the fitting of a Box-Jenkins ARIMA-type model to a sales time series; (2) to compare this with an econometric-type model which has already been used to explain the same sales data; (3) to record stage 1 of the process by which a Box-Jenkins dynamic model will be fitted to the available data.

Peter Kyle is lecturer in quantitative methods applied to marketing at the University of Lancaster. He is a graduate of Manchester University. In 1970, he spent a year teaching and researching at the Wharton School of Finance and Commerce as a Foundation of Management Education Fellow. Before joining Lancaster in 1966, Mr. Kyle held marketing and research posts in industry.

Application

The data upon which this study is based are taken from Dr. Kristian S. Palda (1964). The objective of this work was to study the cumulative effects of advertising, using the model of distributed lags proposed by Koyk (1954). The product under study was one of the legendary proprietary medicines, Lydia Pinkham's Vegetable Compound, sales of which were first made in the latter half of the nineteenth century. A pioneer user of intensive advertising, this product has been the subject of much interest, and descriptions of the company and its activities are readily available (Palda, 1964). The period under consideration is from 1907 to 1960, when advertising carried almost all the marketing effort. For sales and advertising expenditure, see Figure 1. Further details can be found in Palda (1964). Distributed lag models of various forms were fitted, the best of which were the two designated KOYL 2 and KOYL 2 Yless. The first model included such variables as personal disposable income for the years 1908–1960, a time trend having values 0 to 53 starting in the year 1908, and a dummy variable having a value 1 from 1908 to 1925 and 0 from 1926 on. These, with annual advertising expenditure in the year t (A_t), seek to explain variations in annual sales over the period using the model

$$S_t = -3,649 + .665\ S_{t-1} + 1,180 \log A_t$$
$$ (.063) (243)$$
$$+ 774D + 32T - 2.83Y$$
$$(107) \quad (5.9) \quad (.67)$$
$$R^2 = .941 \qquad n = 53$$

This model had the lowest standard error of residuals, but, in terms of predictive ability rather than goodness of fit, it forecast sales of $1,257,000 for 1961, during which the actual sales were $1,426,000.

The second model, KOYL 2 Yless, excluded disposable income and proved to have slightly less goodness of fit though the predictive ability was improved because, it is thought, disposable income varied widely over the

period of the data and in the year of the forecast was very much higher than its mean. The model was

$$S_t = -3,663 + 0.661\ S_{t-1} + 1.314 \log A_t$$
$$ (.073) (280)$$
$$+ 482D + 9.8T$$
$$(95) \quad (2.9)$$
$$R^2 = .920$$

The forecast sales were $1,453,000 as compared with actual sales of $1,426,000.

R^2 is the unadjusted coefficient of determination, and figures in parentheses are the standard errors of the regression coefficients.

These results indicate the importance of lagged effects in the market for this proprietary medicine, and as such the data provide an interesting basis upon which to test the Box-Jenkins approach. This paper concerns itself with identifying and fitting a univariate Box-Jenkins-type model to the sales series.

The Model

Box and Jenkins have developed a class of stochastic models capable of representing all types of series containing pseudosystematic characteristics. The general form of the models can be written as

$$(1) \qquad \phi_p(B)\ \nabla^d x_t = \theta_q(B)\ a_t$$

where $\phi_p(B)$ and $\theta_q(B)$ are polynomials of the backward shift operator B and are of order p and q respectively. $\nabla^d y_t$ represents the degree of differencing required to ensure stationarity, and a_t is a white-noise series with a mean of zero and constant variance σ_a^2. $\phi_p(B)$ represents an autoregressive process of order p, and $\theta_q(B)$ a moving average process of order q. When combined, they are usually referred to as the ARIMA model of order (p, d, q). A model of order $(1, 1, 2)$ would be written as

$$(1 - \phi_1\ B)\ \nabla y_t = (1 - \theta_1\ B - \theta_2 B^2)\ a_t$$

or, without the backward shift operator, as

$$\nabla y_t - \phi_1 \nabla y_{t-1} = a_t - \theta_1\ a_{t-1} - \theta_2\ a_{t-2}.$$

Figure 1
Annual Sales and Advertising Expenditure, 1907–1960 ($'000)

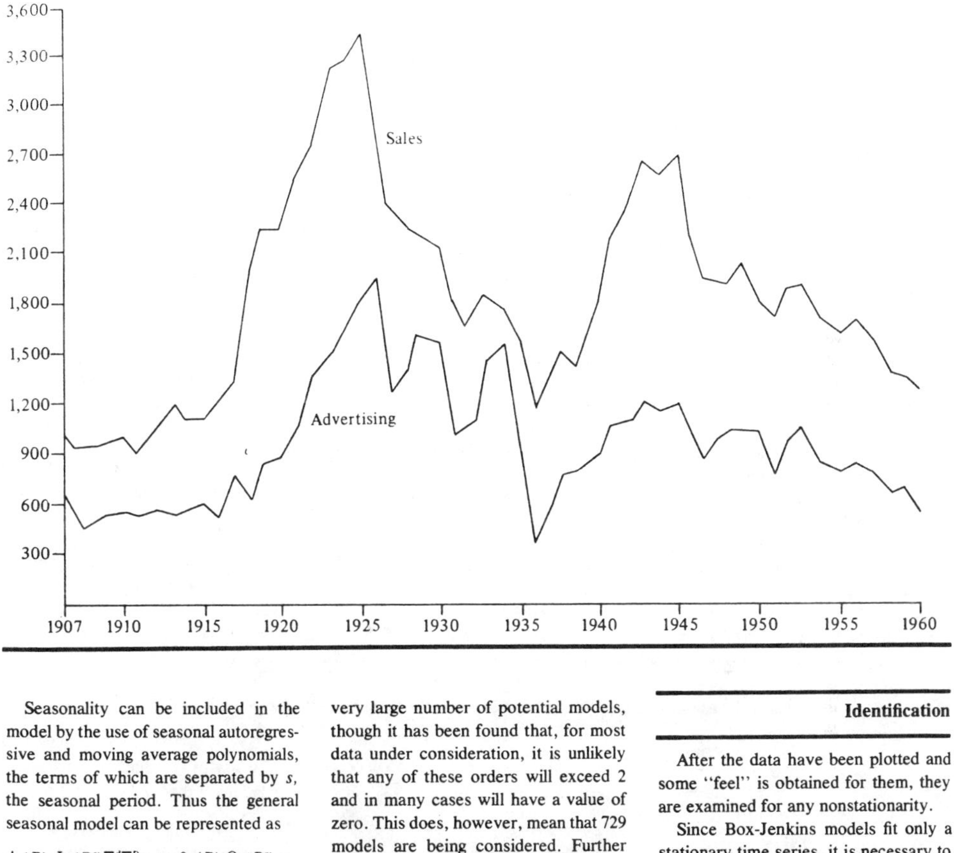

Seasonality can be included in the model by the use of seasonal autoregressive and moving average polynomials, the terms of which are separated by s, the seasonal period. Thus the general seasonal model can be represented as

$$\phi_p(B) \, \Phi_P(B^s) \nabla^d \nabla_s^D y_t = \theta_q(B) \, \Theta_Q(B^s) \, a_t,$$

with s as the seasonal period, D the degree of seasonal differencing, P the order of the autoregressive seasonal operator $\Phi_P(B^s)$, i.e.,

$$(1 - \Phi_1 B^s - \Phi_2 B^{2s} \ldots \Phi_P B^{Ps}),$$

and Q the order of the moving average operator,

$$(1 - \Theta_1 B^s - \Theta_2 B^{2s} \ldots \Theta_Q B^{Qs}).$$

The complete general model can now be described as being of orders $(p, d, q) \, (P, D, Q)$. This obviously encompasses a very large number of potential models, though it has been found that, for most data under consideration, it is unlikely that any of these orders will exceed 2 and in many cases will have a value of zero. This does, however, mean that 729 models are being considered. Further variation in the ability of a particular model to represent the data will depend upon the signs and value of the parameters ϕ_i, Φ_i, θ_i, and Θ_i.

The Box-Jenkins approach to model building, as opposed to that of general econometrics, requires that the particular model, or a subgroup of particular models, first be identified. These models are then fitted, and, through a process of diagnostic checking, further refinements are made. This iterative process continues until no further model inadequacies are found.

Identification

After the data have been plotted and some "feel" is obtained for them, they are examined for any nonstationarity.

Since Box-Jenkins models fit only a stationary time series, it is necessary to detect any nonstationarity within the series and, if it exists, to difference the series until stationarity has been achieved. The plotting of the series is useful in this respect as an early indication if possible nonstationarity of the data can be obtained. The major method by which any nonstationarity is identified and stationarity induced is examination of the estimates of autocorrelations of various differences of the time series. These are defined as

$$r_k(Z) = c_{k/c_0}$$

where

$$c_k = \frac{1}{n}\sum_{t-1}^{n-k}(Z_{t-k}\overline{Z}), \quad k = 0, 1, 2, \ldots$$

is the autocovariance function and where Z_t in this case is either the value of the original series or of any of its differences. If the basic series is nonstationary, the autocorrelations will be large in value and will die out slowly. This will be either at successive lags if the series is nonseasonally nonstationary or, if the series is seasonally nonstationary, in either a cyclical pattern with a period equal to the seasonal period or at lags separated by the seasonal period. If both nonseasonal and seasonal nonstationarity is present, then some combination of these features will be apparent.

In the case of the series representing the sales of Lydia Pinkham, the estimation of the autocorrelation function had those values given in Table 1 and was of the form shown in Figure 2. The autocorrelation function of the base series dies out slowly at successive lags, indicating some nonseasonal nonstationarity and suggesting that differencing the series may induce stationarity. Some evidence of possible seasonal nonsta-

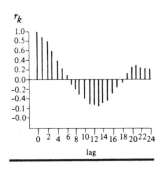

Figure 2
Autocorrelation Figure of x

tionarity is also present since the autocorrelation function has a cyclical form the period of which may be around 12, 13, or 14 years.

In the case of nonseasonal nonstationarity, the autocorrelation function of the first and second differences of the series ($d = 1$ and $d = 2$) are shown in Tables 2 and 3 and in Figures 3 and 4. If stationarity is to be recognized by the fact that the autocorrelation will contain only a few significant autocorrelations and that any overdifferencing which is performed will lead to a more complex pattern of the autocorrelations of the over-

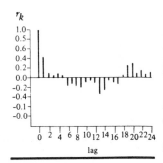

Figure 3
Autocorrelation Function of ∇x

differenced series, then the first differencing of the base series is sufficient to induce stationarity. A further guide is the fact that the variance of the series of the first difference is smaller than that of either the original series or of its second difference.

The autocorrelation function of ∇x still shows some cyclical behavior with a period of 13 years. When, in this case, seasonal differencing of the ∇x series was performed, the resulting variances and autocorrelation functions did not indicate that this series was seasonally nonstationary.

Table 1
Autocorrelations of the Time Series of the Sales of Lydia Pinkham (x)

Mean of Series		
Variance of Series	392,944.0	Approximate Standard Deviation
No. of Observations	54	of Autocorrelations = 0.14
No. of Lags	24	

1–12: 0.91 0.76 0.60 0.43 0.25 0.07 −0.08 −0.22 −0.33 −0.42 −0.49 −0.52
13–24: −0.53 −0.50 −0.42 −0.30 −0.17 −0.01 −0.14 0.23 0.26 0.26 0.24 0.21

Table 2
Autocorrelations of the First Difference of the Sales Time Series (∇x)

Mean of ∇x	5.15	
Variance of ∇x	54,326.9	Approximate Standard Deviation
No. of Observations	54	of Autocorrelations = 0.14
No. of Lags	24	

1–12: 0.43 0.10 0.07 0.11 0.03 −0.16 −0.13 −0.15 −0.21 −0.08 −0.07 −0.08
13–24: −0.33 −0.25 −0.04 −0.05 −0.11 0.02 0.25 0.26 0.09 0.14 0.08 0.10

Table 3
Autocorrelations of the Second Difference of the Time Series ($\nabla^2 x$)

Mean of $\nabla^2 x$	-0.057	
Variance of $\nabla^2 x$	63,053.7	Approximate Standard Deviation
No. of Observations	52	of Autocorrelations = 0.14
No. of Lags	24	

1–12: -0.21 -0.28 -0.05 0.11 0.10 -0.21 -0.05 0.05 -0.17 0.11 0.02 0.20
13–24: -0.29 -0.12 0.21 0.03 -0.16 -0.11 0.19 0.18 -0.22 0.11 -0.08 0.09

Table 4
Partial Autocorrelations of the First Difference of the Time Series (∇x)

1–12: 0.43 -0.11 0.09 0.06 -0.05 -0.19 0.02 -0.14 -0.12 0.11 -0.08 -0.04
13–24: -0.35 0.00 -0.01 -0.06 -0.08 0.15 0.14 0.03 -0.11 0.03 -0.12 0.11

Having established the orders of differencing (d, D) required to achieve stationarity as being (1, 0), initial guesses can now be made of the number of autoregressive parameters (p, P) and moving average parameters (q, Q) required for the ARIMA model to be fitted to the ∇x series. These may be obtained by further examination of the patterns in the autocorrelation function of ∇x and also by examination of the partial autocorrelation function (the partial correlations between ∇x_t and ∇x_{t-k}). The exponential decay behavior (Box and Jenkins, 1970) of the autocorrelation function suggests autoregressive rather than moving average behavior and that the model will require either one or two nonseasonal autoregressive terms. The partial autocorrelation function (see

Table 4 and Figure 5) shows no sign of any nonseasonal moving average behavior (exponential decay in the partial autocorrelation function) of the low-order autocorrelations, only that lag 1 is significant, suggesting one nonseasonal autoregressive term.

Both the autocorrelation function and the partial autocorrelation function have significant values at lag 13. In a series of only 54 terms, it is difficult to judge whether this represents either autoregressive or moving average seasonal behavior, suggesting estimation of models containing each type of behavior. The result of the identification process suggests the fitting of two models of the ARIMA type with orders (p, d, q) (P, D, Q), either of (1 1 0) (1 0 0), giving a model of

Table 5
Model (1 1 0) (1 0 0)
$$(1 - .4128B)(1 + .4258B^{13})\ \nabla x_t = a_t$$
$$(.1268) \qquad (.1178)$$
$$R^2 = .905 \qquad n = 53$$

Model (1 1 0) (0 0 1)
$$(1 - .3780B)\ \nabla x_t = (1 - .8687B^{13})\ a_t$$
$$(.1288) \qquad\qquad (.0513)$$
$$R^2 = .936 \qquad n = 53$$

$$(1 - \phi_1 B)(1 - \phi_1 B^{13})\ \nabla x_t = a_t,$$

or of (1 1 0) (0 0 1), giving a model of

$$(1 - \phi_1 B)\ \nabla x_t = (1 - \phi_1 B^{13})\ a_t.$$

Estimation

In the estimation stage of the model-building process, the parameters are estimated using nonlinear least squares methods developed by Box-Jenkins (1968). In some cases it may be useful to fit rather more elaborate models than those first identified in the identification stage, since the effect of dropping any parameter found to be statistically insignificant can often be adequately guessed while the problem of determining the effect of adding a parameter is more difficult. In the models identified here, which are simple and would appear to account for most of the effects shown in the autocorrelation and partial autocorrelation functions, such elaboration was

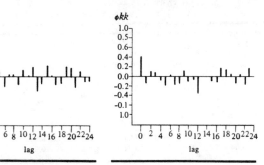

Figure 4
Autocorrelation Function of $\nabla^2 x$

Figure 5
Partial Autocorrelation Function of ∇x

felt to be unnecessary. If, however, any of our models is already overelaborate, this will result in high correlations between the estimates of the parameters themselves.

Table 5 shows the models fitted to the Lydia Pinkham data together with the standard error of the parameters estimated.

Diagnostic Checking

In the third stage of the model-building process, certain diagnostic checks are applied to the model to ascertain whether or not it can be regarded as adequate. This process has two steps, the first of which is to examine the residuals of a fitted model, a_t. If the model is entirely adequate, the residuals should approximate to white noise of variance $\hat{\sigma}_a^2$. If the model is not entirely appropriate, this will result in a pattern of abnormal residuals the existence of which can be detected by determining their autocorrelation function $r_K(\hat{a})$ and comparing the individual autocorrelations at lag k with their standard error $1/\sqrt{n}$. However, since in any random series we might expect one of 20 autocorrelations to be greater than twice its standard error, it is often necessary to test

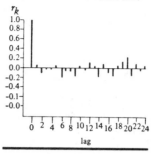

Figure 6
Autocorrelation Function of the
Residuals of the Model (110) (100)

whether or not the autocorrelations, taken as a whole, reveal any inadequacy in the model. If the model is indeed adequate,

$$Q = n \sum_{k=1}^{K} r_k^2(\hat{a})$$

is approximately distributed as a chi-squared distribution with K-p-q degrees of freedom and where n is the number of terms in the different series used to fit the model.

In the case of the first model proposed (1 1 0) (1 0 0), the autocorrelation function of the residuals, as shown in Table 6

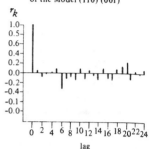

Figure 7
Autocorrelations of the Residuals
of the Model (110) (001)

and Figure 6, reveals no obvious pattern and appears to approximate white noise. Q was found to be 13.0 on 22 degrees of freedom, an acceptably low value revealing the adequacy of the model. That the model is not overelaborate is shown by the extremely low correlation between the parameters ($-$0.083).

The autocorrelations of the residuals of the second mode (1 1 0) (0 0 1) are shown in Table 7 and Figure 7. These, again, appear to represent white noise, and in this case Q was found to be 13.2 on 22 degrees of freedom. Correlation between the parameters was 0.04.

Table 6
Autocorrelations of the Residuals of the Model (110) (100)

Variance of Residuals	37,370
No. of Observations	54
No. of Lags	24
Approx. Standard Error of Autocorrelations	0.14

1–12: 0.04 −0.09 0.00 −0.02 0.04 −0.19 −0.03 −0.03 −0.14 0.02 −0.02 0.13
13–24: 0.02 −0.16 0.09 −0.05 −0.13 0.04 0.17 0.23 −0.12 0.08 −0.03 0.04

Table 7
Autocorrelations of the Residuals of the Model (1 1 0) (0 0 1)

Variance of Residuals	25,286
No. of Observations	54
No. of Lags	24
Approx. Standard Error of Autocorrelations	0.14

1–12: 0.03 −0.06 −0.01 0.01 0.06 −0.29 −0.07 −0.05 −0.09 0.07 −0.05 0.04
13–24: −0.01 −0.11 0.07 −0.04 −0.10 0.05 0.15 0.24 −0.12 0.02 −0.01 0.05

Forecasting

A further criterion exists for evaluating and comparing the results of the foregoing models. It is the ability of these models to predict, and it is on this particular criterion that a powerful school of thought places much emphasis (Friedman, 1953; Stewart, 1965), even though, as Thail (1961) laments, the econometrician is in most cases diverted from making full use of this criterion by the fact that while the number of observations is limited, it is tempting to use everything available for the specification of the model itself, thus removing, or considerably reducing, the possibility of testing the model by forecasting observations lying outside the sample period used.

In considering the predictability criterion, an important distinction should be made between *ex post* and *ex ante* forecasts. In the former, the future values of the endogenous and any lagged exogenous variables are known at the time the forecast is made, and any errors which result are attributable only to the model specification itself. In *ex ante* forecasts, the true values of these variables are unknown and must be estimated; therefore, observed forecasting errors may be due to errors in the estimation of these predetermined variables as well as to errors in model specification. Since it is the *ex ante* forecast which is more likely to be met with in the real world, serious argument has been put forward that the only "true test" of a model is its ability to forecast *ex ante* (Steckler, 1968) and that evaluation of its ability to forecast *ex post* is often little more than a reiteration of the statistical goodness-of-fit criterion already presented.

Palda evaluated his distributed lag models *ex post*. In 1961, disposable income was $365,000,000,000. Pinkham spent $695,000 on advertising, and realized sales of $1,426,000, the latter figures becoming available in June 1962. With these figures the 1961 forecast of sales was $1,257,000 for the KOYL 2 model (a discrepancy of $169,000) and $1,453,000 for the KOYL 2 Yless model

Table 8
Forecasts of 1961 Sales (100) for Lead Times 1 to 5 Years
Actual Sales 1,426

Year	Lead Time	(1 1 0)(1 0 0)	Difference	(1 1 0)(0 0 1)	Difference
1956	5	2,040	+ 616	1,422	− 4
1957	4	2,136	+ 710	1,454	+ 28
1958	3	1,679	+ 253	1,448	+ 22
1959	2	1,393	− 29	1,608	+ 182
1960	1	1,357	− 69	1,410	− 16

(an overestimate of $27,000). The latter forecast in particular appears to give a good result. However, consideration should be given to how these forecasts would actually be made by the company. This is an important factor (Steckler, 1968), particularly when, taking into account the time path of the data necessary to make forecasts, the company would have to forecast with a two-year lead time.

Forecasting using Box-Jenkins method as shown in Box and Jenkins (1970) and Nelson (1970) and summarized in Box and Jenkins (1968) does not necessarily suffer from these problems since the models are univariate and forecasts can be made for any lead time. The results of forecasting the 1961 sales for a lead time of up to five years are shown in Table 8. These show the (1 1 0) (0 0 1) model to be substantially the better, particularly over the longer lead times. When comparing the one-year lead time forecasts with those given by the Palda distributed lag models, Box-Jenkins's models do not appear to be in any way inferior.

Conclusion

These results show that Box-Jenkins methods can be as good as single-equation econometric methods in the examination of marketing time series data. The fact that data of this kind are often heavily serially correlated makes the methods particularly appropriate for examining the structure of the market as well as securing an adequate forecast, though it is their achievements in the latter area for which they have, until

very recently (Chatfield and Prothero, 1973; Johnson, 1963) been known. The fact that the methods are wholly based upon examination of the behavior of residuals, which every good econometrician knows to be a most necessary part of any model-building exercise, means that the methods are very much more than the "black box" which they are often regarded as being.

The performance of Box-Jenkins methods in the present instance raises some interesting points in the measurement of lagged advertising effects. In the case of Pinkham, advertising expenditure was indeed the only major marketing instrument whose control was fully in the hands of the company. To take the next step and to regard the lagged effects of advertising as the only source of the serial correlation in sales is not necessarily justified (Ferguson, 1966; Finton, 1954; Stewart, 1965). Other variables outside the immediate control of the company may have lagged effects (buying habits, word-of-mouth advertising, attitudes to and availability of the appropriate medical care, etc.). If, as Ehrenberg (1974) says, "repeat buying is the main determinant of sales volume," then we are building a model of a system which by its very nature is serially correlated, and inclusion of lagged sales in any model will be much more than a simple surrogate for the residual effects of past advertising expenditures. This could prove to be the case in the present model. The univariate Box-Jenkins model performs just as well as the Koyk models of Palda, which include present advertising expenditure. This could suggest that present advertising has no immediate effect (which is very

37

unlikely when one year is the period of analysis) or that the data reflect a system in which there is feedback, lagged sales being an adequate surrogate for present advertising expenditure.

The problems facing the researcher investigating marketing time series are highly complex, which, if nothing else, this particular example shows. Analysis must be approached in such a way that all possibilities can be considered as the research evolves. In many cases regression analysis and econometric methods require some declaration of faith by the researcher before he proceeds, and this is seldom sufficiently or appropriately modified as the research progresses. Box-Jenkins methods suffer much less in this respect and progress reasonably logically from each stage of analysis to the next (the present paper representing only the first stage). Further stages will be the univariate analyses of both the advertising and disposable income time series and an attempt to combine these into what Box and Jenkins call a dynamic transfer function model.

One criticism which has been made of Box and Jenkins's methods is that they are unnecessarily complicated and thus perhaps expensive (Chatfield and Prothero, 1973). It should be noted that this has occurred when they are being compared with other univariate forecasting methods—e.g., exponentially weighted moving averages—rather than econometric methods. The ability to extend the univariate model into a multivariate one should not be discounted. When compared with conventional econometric methods, this criticism has little or no validity. The ARIMA models shown in this paper were identified very quickly indeed. There was no need for the hundreds of regressions run by Palda in achieving his results nor for the "many regressions to obtain the optimum number of lags and optimum weighting value" which Ferguson (1966) admitted running to test Palda's best-fitting equation (KOYL 2).

References

Bass, Frank M. A Simultaneous Equation Regression Study of Advertising and Sales of Cigarettes. *Journal of Marketing Research*, Vol. 6, August 1969, pp. 291–300.

Bass, Frank M., and Darral G. Clarke. Testing Distributed Lag Models of Advertising Effect. *Journal of Marketing Research*, Vol. 9, August 1972, pp. 298–308.

Bass, Frank M., and Leonard J. Parsons. Simultaneous Equation Regression Analysis of Sales and Advertising. *Applied Economics*, Vol. 1, May 1969, pp. 103–124.

Box, G. E. P., and G. M. Jenkins. Some Recent Advances in Forecasting and Control. *Applied Statistics*, Vol. 17, No. 2, 1968, 91–109.

———. *Time Series Analysis: Forecasting and Control.* San Francisco: Holden Day, 1970.

Chatfield, C., and D. L. Prothero. Box-Jenkins Seasonal Forecasting: Problems in a Case-Study. *Journal of the Royal Statistical Society*, Vol. 136, Part 3, 1973, pp. 295–315.

Doyle, P. Economic Aspects of Advertising. *The Economic Journal*, Vol. 78, September 1966, pp. 570–602.

Ehrenberg, A. S. C. Repetitive Advertising and the Consumer. *Journal of Advertising Research*, Vol. 14, No. 2, April 1974, pp. 25–34.

Ferguson, J. M. Book Review of the Measurement of Cumulative Advertising Effects. *Econometrica*, Vol. 34, No. 4, October 1966, pp. 903–905.

Finton, D. C. Correlation's Last Stand. *Journal of Advertising Research*, Vol. 4, No. 2, June 1964, 50–52.

Friedman, M. *Essays in Positive Economics.* Chicago: University of Chicago Press, 1953.

Goldberger, Arthur S. *Econometric Theory.* New York: John Wiley & Sons, 1964.

Guerts, Michael D., and I. B. Ibraham. Comparing the Box-Jenkins Approach with Exponentially Smoothed Forecasting Model Application to Hawaii Tourists. *Journal of Marketing Research*, Vol. 12, May 1975, pp. 182–188.

Jenkins, G. M. The Interaction between the Muskrat and the Mink Cycles in North Canada. Paper presented to Eighth International Biometric Conference, Constrenta, Romania, August 25–30, 1974.

Johnson, J. *Econometric Methods.* New York: McGraw-Hill, 1963.

Koyk, L. M. *Distributed Lags and Investment Analysis.* Amsterdam: North Holland, 1954.

Naylor, T. H., T. H. Seaks, and D. W. Wichern. Box-Jenkins Methods: An Alternative to Econometric Models. *International Statistical Review*, Vol. 40, 1972, pp. 121–137.

Nelson, C. K. *Applied Time Series Analysis.* San Francisco: Holden Day, 1970.

Palda, K. S. The Evaluation of Regression Results. In Stephen A. Greyser (Ed.). *Towards Scientific Marketing*, Winter Conference of the A.M.A., 1963, pp. 279–290.

———. *The Measurement of Cumulative Advertising Effects.* Englewood Cliffs, N.J.: Prentice-Hall, 1964.

Quandt, R. E. Estimating the Effectiveness of Advertising: Some Pitfalls in Econometric Methods. *Journal of Marketing Research*, Vol. 1, May 1964, pp. 51–60.

Steckler, H. O. Forecasting with Econometric Models: An Evaluation. *Econometrica*, Vol. 36, July–October 1968, pp. 437–463.

Stewart, J. B. Book Review of the Measurement of Cumulative Advertising Effects. *Journal of Marketing Research*, Vol. 2, May 1965, pp. 201–202.

Thail, H. *Economic Forecasts and Policy*. Amsterdam: North Holland, 1961.

Doyle L. Weiss
University of British Columbia

Franklin S. Houston
Temple University

Pierre Windal
University of Sherbrooke

The Periodic Pain of Lydia E. Pinkham

Introduction

In 1964, Palda published the results of the first application of lagged-variable regression models to the question of advertising's sales effectiveness. In doing this he supplied the first empirically supported quantification of the sales-advertising relationship. The purpose of this paper is to reexamine some of the issues which have been raised subsequent to Palda's research and to focus directly on some of the structural issues associated with the class of models examined by Palda (see Schmalensee 1972). As such this paper will focus on these issues by comparing results from the following models: (1) Palda's (1964) original distributed-lag model; (2) a current-effects model (Clarke and McCann 1973); (3) an extension of the above model utilizing a second-order autoregressive structure; (4) a brand-loyalty model, structured after early work by Kuehn (1961); and (5) several Pascal lag distributions (see Kmenta 1971).

Model Development

For convenience, all models have been summarized in table 1, using the compact notation afforded by the lag operator, defined as $BX_t = X_{t-1}$. Before we turn to the discussion of behavioral assumptions underlying the structural form of each model, a comment is in order. If we

This paper examines the Lydia E. Pinkham data and compares a variety of demand models and lag functions. Nonlinear procedures are used to estimate these models and as such are superior to previous studies of the same data base. The current advertising effect as well as the marketing program carryover is shown to be less than found in previous efforts.

Journal of Business, 1978, vol. 51, no. 1)
© 1978 by The University of Chicago
0021-9398/78/5101-0004$01.00

TABLE 1   **Summary of Models**

Structural Form

(1.1) Palda $S_t = b_0 + b_1 \psi(B) A_t + \sum_{i=1}^{3} d_i D_{it} + \epsilon_t$

(1.3) Current effect $S_t = b_0 + b_1 A_t + \sum_{i=1}^{3} d_i D_{it} + \psi(B)\epsilon_t$

(1.9) Second-order autoregressive $S_t = b_0 + b_1 A_t + \sum_{i=1}^{3} d_i D_{it} + \theta(B)\epsilon_t$

(1.5) Brand loyalty $\psi^{-1}(B)S_t = b_0 + b_1 A_t + \sum_{i=1}^{3} d_i D_{it} + \phi(B)\epsilon_t$

(1.7) Pascal lag $S_t = b_0 + b_1 [\psi(B)]^r A_t + \sum_{i=1}^{3} d_i D_{it} + \epsilon_t$

Reduced Form

(1.2) Palda $\psi^{-1}(B)S_t = b_0\psi^{-1}(B) + b_1 A_t + \sum_{i=1}^{3} d_i \psi^{-1}(B)D_{it} + \psi^{-1}(B)\epsilon_t$

(1.4) Current effect $\psi^{-1}(B)S_t = b_0\psi^{-1}(B) + b_1\psi^{-1}(B)A_t + \sum_{i=1}^{3} d_i\psi^{-1}(B)D_{it} + \epsilon_t$

(1.10) Second-order autoregressive $\theta^{-1}(B)S_t = b_0\theta^{-1}(B) + b_1\theta^{-1}(B)A_t + \sum_{i=1}^{3} d_i\theta^{-1}(B)D_{it} + \epsilon_t$

(1.6) Brand loyalty $\psi^{-1}(B)\phi^{-1}(B)S_t = b_0\phi^{-1}(B) + b_1\phi^{-1}(B)A_t + \sum_{i=1}^{3} d_i\phi^{-1}(B)D_{it} + \epsilon_t$

(1.8) Pascal lag $[\psi^{-1}(B)]^r S_t = b_0[\psi^{-1}(B)]^r +$

$$b_1[\psi^{-1}(B)]^r A_t + \sum_{i=1}^{3} d_i [\psi^{-1}(B)]^r D_{it} + [\psi^{-1}(B)]^r \epsilon_t$$

where $\psi(B) = \sum_{i=0}^{\infty} (\lambda B)^i$

$\phi(B) = \sum_{i=0}^{\infty} (\rho B)^i$

$\theta(B) = \sum_{i=0}^{\infty} [B(\lambda + \rho B)]^i$

restrict our attention to the mathematical formulas, the reduced forms of the sales-response functions turn out to be special cases of the general transfer function of time-series analysis (see, e.g., Box and Jenkins 1976).

A naive conclusion would be to consider the econometric models of sales response as special cases of the general transfer function of time-series analysis. This would, however, ignore the fundamental difference in perspective of the two approaches. Time-series analysis is wholly concerned with the reduced forms of the models. The question of whether there exists a structural form that underlies the reduced form of the model is treated as completely irrelevant. The opposite holds for the econometric approach which values a model inasmuch as its structural form follows from proper theoretical considerations. The distinction is one of explanation versus prediction and of a basic difference in philosophy.

The five models are best summarized with the help of three polynomials in the lag operator: $\psi(B)$, $\phi(B)$, and $\theta(B)$. The main difference between the different formulations consists of the particular location of those polynomials within the models. Differences in location correspond to radically different assumptions about the mechanisms at work in the sales-advertising relationship.

Palda model. Palda (1964) postulated that sales (S_t) of a patent medicine (Lydia E. Pinkham's vegetable compound) was a function of the current and prior advertising expenditures (A_t) and can be represented by a geometric decay function, where λ is the advertising-decay constant (see eq. [1.1] of table 1). The reduced form estimated by Palda treated the dummy variables as constants and ignored the autoregressive structure of disturbance term. Thus, Palda estimated a linearized version of (1.2) that ignored the polynomial, $\psi^{-1}(B)$, appearing before the variable D_{it} (dummy variables for advertising copy changes) and the disturbance term ϵ_t. His estimates are reproduced in table 2.

A current-effect model. In constrast to Palda, Clarke and McCann (1973) argue that sales are a function of current advertising expenditures and an autoregressive term which results from a carry-over effect not completely attributed to past advertising expenditures (see eqq. [1.3] and [1.4]). The above model explicitly excludes the geometric decay of advertising's effect as specified by Palda. Clarke and McCann estimated a linear version of (1.4), and their estimates are reproduced in table 2.

Brand-loyalty model. This class of model rationalizes the use of lagged sales as an independent variable attributable to marketing carry-over effects more general than just advertising. Such models do not

TABLE 2   Parameter Estimates for Linear Models by Palda (1964) and Clarke and
                 McCann (1973)

Coefficient Of	Palda Estimate*	Clarke and McCann Estimate†
Advertising (t)	.537	.747
Advertising $(t-1)$	···‡	−.469
Sales $(t-1)$	.628	.712
Intercept	212.	283.

* Estimated by ordinary least squares.
† Linear model, estimated by an iterative procedure.
‡ Parameter not included in estimation.

assume a geometric decay of advertising's effect. Model (1.5) has been proposed by Houston and Weiss (1975) as a generalization of (1.3). This model is of particular interest because it reduces to the linearized form used by Palda when $\rho = 0$. Also, while b_1 represents the current effects of advertising, as in (1.3), equation (1.5) explicitly introduces a carry-over coefficient (λ). While (1.3) generates the lagged sales as a result of the autocorrelated error term.

Pascal models. From time to time, some researchers have argued that distributed-lag models with geometrically declining weights are too restrictive. In the present context we can think of little in the way of the behavior of consumers with menstrual pain which would suggest a lag scheme more complex or more intuitively appealing than the forms already discussed. Nevertheless, we will estimate a model employing the popular Pascal lag distribution to provide some comparisons with the other models.

The Pascal lag distribution is discussed in some detail by Kmenta (1971). The most general form of the model, in our context, is given by equation (1.7), where r is a positive integer and λ is a parameter to be estimated. Notice that for $r = 1$, the model becomes the lag model employed by Palda (1.1). Only the case $r = 2$ will be considered for equation (1.7).

Estimation Procedures

It can be shown that for equation (1.4)

$$E(\epsilon_t\, S_{t-1}) = 0. \tag{2.1}$$

Therefore, maximum-likelihood estimates for the parameters of (1.4) can be calculated by means of nonlinear least-square methods. Likewise, the covariance of the error term and the lagged variables in equations (1.6) and (1.10) are also zero, making both of these equations appropriate for the application of Gauss-Newton nonlinear least-squares procedures as described by Berndt (1973).

Palda's model. With respect to Palda's model (1.2), however, even when the ϵ_t are serially uncorrelated, the covariance of $\psi^{-1}(B)\epsilon_t$ and S_{t-1} is not zero. That is,

$$E[\psi^{-1}(B)\epsilon_t] = -\lambda\sigma^2. \qquad (2.2)$$

This means that ordinary or nonlinear least-squares procedures will produce inconsistent estimates when applied to (1.2). Maximum-likelihood estimates for (1.2) have been developed by Zellner and Geisel (1970). They show the proper estimating equation to be

$$S_t = b_0 + b_1 w_t^{(\lambda)} + \sum_{i=1}^{3} d_i D_{it} + b_2 \lambda^t + \epsilon_t, \qquad (2.3)$$

where

$$w_t^{(\lambda)} = \sum_{i=1}^{t} \lambda^{t-i} A_i$$

and

$$b_2 = S_0 - \epsilon_0 - b_0 - \sum_{i=1}^{3} d_i D_{it}.$$

The value of ϵ_0 and the D_{j0} values are the initial values of these variables and as such are regarded as parameters of the model. Under these circumstances the logarithmic likelihood function for S_1, S_2, ... , S_T is

$$L = -T/2 \ln(2\pi\sigma^2)$$
$$- (1/2\sigma^2) \sum_{t=1}^{T}\left\{S_T - [b_0 + b_1 w_t^{(\lambda)} + \sum_{j=1}^{3} d_j D_{jt} + b_2\lambda^t]\right\}^2. \quad (2.4)$$

For known value of λ, the above likelihood function can be maximized with respect to b_0, b_1, b_2, and the d_{jt}'s by means of the Gauss-Newton procedure mentioned above. Since λ is known to be between zero and one, a grid-search procedure may be used to find the value of λ which globally maximizes L. The subsequent values of λ and the other parameters will be maximum-likelihood estimates and therefore asymptotically efficient. The estimates resulting from this procedure are shown in table 3.

If there is suspicion that the disturbances in (1.1) are not serially independent, then that assumption may be replaced by

$$\epsilon_t = \rho\epsilon_{t-1} + u_t. \qquad (2.5)$$

Maximum-likelihood estimators for the serially correlated case can be developed in a manner similar to that for the serially independent case.

TABLE 3   Parameter Estimates

Models	$\hat{\rho}$	$\hat{\lambda}$	$\hat{b}_1$	$\hat{b}_2$	$\hat{b}_3$	$\hat{b}_0$	$\hat{d}_1$	$\hat{d}_2$	$\hat{d}_3$	$\ln \hat{\Sigma}$
1. Palda (1.2, 2.3)	...	.250	1.647 (12.8)	370.9 (.28)	...	421.73 (3.26)[b]	-252.9 (-1.52)	171.7 (1.70)	-458.0 (-4.60)	781.7
2. Palda (2.8)	.880	.350	1.000 (5.75)	-372.6 (-.72)	...	1027 (3.53)	172.7 (.51)	-14.03 (-.05)	-195.5 (-1.09)	741.6
3. Autoregressive (1.4)	.902 (14.2)	...	.6419 (4.992)	...	...	1394 (14.4)	55.3 (.15)	-112.5 (-.40)	-210.3 (-1.10)	746.0
4. Autoregressive (1.10)	1.29 (9.08)	-.394* (-2.83)	.4378 (3.62)	...	...	1577 (5.35)	-115.3 (-.37)	-286.6 (-1.18)	-146.0 (-.84)	741.0
5. Pascal, $r = 2$ (1.7, 3.2)	...	.150	1.65 (12.7)	5631. (.39)	-4931. (-.33)	414.4 (3.17)	-215.8 (-1.10)	175.8 (1.72)	-461.6 (4.59)	781.5
6. Pascal, $r = 2$ (3.2)	.840	.190	1.025 (5.89)	2981. (.56)	-3702. (-.72)	1006. (3.99)	247.5 (.74)	36.3 (.15)	181.4 (-1.04)	740.8
7. Brand loyalty (1.6) with $\rho = 0$	...	.659 (7.97)	.562 (3.93)	...	...	140.4 (1.43)	-59.89 (-.58)	173.6 (2.51)	-227.8 (-3.27)	741.8
8. Brand loyalty (1.8)	.79 (4.91)	.368 (2.17)	.554 (4.12)	...	...	698.0 (1.80)	118.3 (1.40)	-14.1 (-.19)	-221.9 (-1.35)	737.2

Note.—Sample size for all models is 52 observations; numbers in parentheses are asymptotic t-statistics.
* The λ for model 4 is the first-order autocorrelation coefficient resulting from $u_t = \lambda u_{t-1} + \rho u_{t-1} + \epsilon_t$.

The estimating equation can be shown to be

$$S_t - \rho S_{t-1} = (1 - \rho)b_0 + \sum_{i=1}^{3} d_i(D_{jt} - \rho D_{jt-1}) +$$

$$b_1 w_t^{(\lambda,\rho)} + b_2 \lambda^t + u_t, \quad (2.6)$$

where

$$w_t^{(\lambda,\rho)} = (A_t - \rho A_{t-1}) + \lambda(A_{t-1} - \rho A_{t-2}) + \lambda^2(A_{t-2} - \rho A_{t-3}) + \ldots$$
$$+ \lambda^{t-2}(A_2 - \rho A_1) + \lambda^{t-1}A_1, \quad (2.7)$$

$$b_2 = \epsilon_0 - \rho S_{-1} - (1 - \rho)b_0 - (\rho b_1/\lambda)A_0$$

$$- \sum_{j=1}^{3} d_j(D_{j0} - \rho D_{j-1}). \quad (2.8)$$

Because of the first differences involved, the resulting logarithmic likelihood function is set up for $S_2, S_3, \ldots, S_T$ and is

$$L = -[(T - 1)/2]\ln(2\pi\sigma_u^2) - (1/2\pi\sigma_u^2) \sum_{t=2}^{T} [S_t - \rho S_{t-1} - b_0(1 - \rho)$$

$$- b_1 w_t^{(\lambda,\rho)} - b_2 \lambda^t - \sum_{j=1}^{3} d_j(D_{jt} - \rho D_{jt-1})]. \quad (2.9)$$

As before, for given λ and ρ, the likelihood L can be maximized as a function of the remaining parameters by means of nonlinear least-squares methods. In this case a double-grid search (λ and ρ) will reveal the parameter values which result in a global maximum for L. These values will be maximum-likelihood estimates. The results from the grid-search procedure are presented in table 3.

Pascal distribution r = 2. Maximum-likelihood procedures for (1.7) and its auto regressive case can be found in Kmenta (1971) or in Windal and Weiss (1975). After some algebraic manipulation, (1.7) can be transformed and written ready for estimation as

$$S_t = b_0 + b_1(1 - \lambda)^2 w_t^{(\lambda)} + \sum_{j=1}^{3} d_j D_{jt} + b_2 \lambda^t + b_3 t \lambda^t + \epsilon_t, \quad (3.1)$$

where

$$w_t^{(\lambda)} = A_t + 2\lambda A_{t-1} + 3\lambda^2 A_{t-2} + \ldots + t\lambda^{t-1}A, \quad (3.1a)$$

$$b_2 = S_0 - b_0 - \sum_{j=1}^{3} d_j D_{j0}, \quad (3.1b)$$

and

$$b_3 = S_0 - \lambda S_{-1} - b_0(1 - \lambda) - \sum_{j=1}^{3} d_j (D_{j0} - \lambda D_{j-1}). \quad (3.1c)$$

The terms D_{j0}, D_{j-1}, S_0, and S_{-1} are treated as constants and estimated as part of the composite terms b_2 and b_3.

The estimating equation for the first-order autocorrelation case of the Pascal lag ($r = 2$) can be shown to be

$$S_t - \rho S_{t-1} = b_0(1 - \rho) + b_1(1 - \lambda)^2 w^{(\lambda, \rho)}_t + \sum_{j=1}^{3} d_j(D_{jt} - \rho D_{jt-1})$$

$$+ b_2\lambda^t + b_3 t\lambda^t + \epsilon_t, \quad (3.2)$$

where

$$w_t^{(\lambda \rho)} = (A_t - \rho A_{t-1}) + 2\lambda(A_{t-1} - \rho A_{t-2}) + \ldots + t\lambda^{t-1}A_1,$$

$$b_2 = S_0 - \rho S_{-1} - b_0(1 - \rho) - \sum_{j=1}^{3} d_j(D_{j0} - \rho D_{j-1}), \quad (3.2b)$$

$$b_3 = (S_0 - \rho S_{-1}) - \lambda(S_{-1} - \rho S_{-2}) - b_0(1 - \lambda)(1 - \rho)$$

$$- \sum_{j=1}^{3} d_j[(D_{j0} - \lambda D_{j-1}) - \rho(D_{j-1} - \lambda D_{j-2}) + (b_1/\lambda)(1 - \lambda^2)\rho A_0].$$

$$(3.2c)$$

As before, the values S_0 and S_{-1} along with D_{j0}, D_{j-1}, and D_{j-2} are assumed to be constants and estimated as part of the composite terms b_2 and b_3.

As with Palda's model, the absolute values of ρ and λ fall between zero and one, and a grid-search procedure was used to find their optimum values. Nonlinear least-squares procedures were used to calculate maximum-likelihood estimates for the parameters of (3.1) and (3.2) for grid values of λ and ρ. The optimum parameters are presented in table 3.

Current effects: second-order autocorrelation. Finally, the current-effects model, equation (1.4), has been extended to include second-order autocorrelation effects. The equation of the error term is

$$u_t = \lambda u_{t-1} + \rho u_{t-2} + \epsilon_t. \quad (3.3)$$

The results of this estimation are presented in table 3, along with estimated values for all of the models discussed.

Model Comparisons

Models (1.4) and (1.5) are nested models in the sense that (1.5) collapses to a form identical to (1.4) when $\lambda = 0$. As a result, the two models can be compared by means of the likelihood ratio statistic

$$\eta = \Sigma_0^{-T/2}/\Sigma_1^{-T/2}, \quad (4.1)$$

where $\hat{\Sigma}_0$ = sum of squared residuals associated with the restricted model or null hypothesis ([1.4] in this example), and $\hat{\Sigma}_1$ = sum of squared residuals associated with the alternative hypothesis or the unrestricted model ([1.5] in this example). Under the null hypothesis, the statistic $-2 \ln \eta$ is asymptotically distributed $\chi^2 (P_1 - P_0)$, where P_1 is the number of parameters associated with the alternative hypothesis and P_0 is the number of parameters associated with the null hypothesis. (In the present example, the more general specification [1.5] is the alternative hypothesis and [1.4] forms the null hypothesis.) The null hypothesis is to be rejected when $-2\ln \eta$ exceeds the critical value of $\chi^2(P_1 - P_0)$ at the chosen level of significance. (For convenience in making nested comparisons, the values of $T \ln \hat{\Sigma}$ have been calculated and presented in table 2.) To complete the present example, $-2 \ln \eta \sim \chi^2(1)$ and is approximately equal to 8.8 (746.0–737.2). Model (1.4) is rejected in favor of the more general specification (1.5). (Because of its complexity, the whole expression for b_2 [2.13c] was estimated as a constant.)

Except for models (1.4) and (1.5), the other nested pairs result from incorporating autocorrelation effects into the basic behavioral model. The total set of nested pairs from table 2 and their related statistics are shown in table 4. Looking down the left-hand column of table 4 it is easy to see that the case for serial correlation being present in each of the models is a strong one.

The methodology for comparing nonnested pairs of models is not nearly as well developed as the likelihood ratio test described above for nested pairs. The basic method for comparing nonnested models is outlined with considerable detail in McGuire, Weiss, and Houston (1974) and will only be briefly described here. Essentially, the comparison of nonnested models amounts to choosing the model with the "higher" likelihood value.

The statistics suggested by McGuire et al. and modified for comparison involving single-equation models with identical dependent variables are:

$$\eta^* = [(T - p_1)/(T - p_0) \, (\hat{\Sigma}_0/\hat{\Sigma}_1)]^{-T/2}. \tag{4.2}$$

The model "in the numerator" is accepted if $\eta^* > 1$, and the denominator model is chosen if $\eta^* < 1$.

The calculations for η^* have been carried out in terms of $\ln \eta^*$ to ease the computational task. These values are presented in table 5. Looking across the last row of table 5 one can see that model (1.6) is superior to all of the other models analyzed when equation (4.2) is the basis of the comparison. The critical value of $\chi^2(1)$ at the .005 level of significance is 7.879.

TABLE 4   Nested Model Comparisons

Model Pair		$-2 \ln \eta$	Degrees of Freedom	Significance Level*
Null	Alternative			
1(2.3)	2(2.8)	40.1	1	<.00001
3(1.4)	4(1.10)	5.0	1	.025
5(3.2)	6(3.2)	40.7	1	<.00001
7(1.6, $\rho=0$)	8(1.6)	4.6	1	.032
3(1.4)	8(1.6)	8.8	1	.005

* Level at which the null hypothesis would be rejected.

TABLE 5   Values of $\ln \eta^*$

Numerator Model (Null)	Denominator Model (Alternative)				
	Pi	2(2.8)	4(1.0)	6(3.2)	8(1.6)
2(2.8)	8	$\cdots$	$-.88$	.20	-2.78
4(1.10)	7	.88	$\cdots$	.98	-1.9
6(3.2)	9	$-.20$	$-.98$	$\cdots$	-2.98
8(1.6)	7	2.78	1.9	2.98	$\cdots$

* Accept the numerator model (null hypothesis) when $\ln \eta^* > 0$ (1,p, $\eta^* > 1$) and accept the denominator model (alternative hypothesis) when $\ln \eta^* < 0$ (i.e., $\eta^* < 1$).

Results and Discussion

The previous section demonstrates the superiority of model (1.6) over the remaining model forms. Although obtained from a different background, this model is parallel to Palda's (1964) original reduced-form equation before adjustments for serial correlation.

A comparison of the parameter estimates for the various models highlights a number of interesting points. First, all of the models with the exception of model (1.5) (without autocorrelation effects) show dramatically smaller values for $\hat{\lambda}$ than found by Palda. This is true even for the estimated values of λ from the reformulation of the original Palda equation (1.2). The latter results are likely due to the more realistic estimation done here with nonlinear procedures and the use of time-dependent dummy variables. The parameter estimates for models (2.8) and (1.6) show that what was previously described as a carry-over effect is largely accounted for by serial correlation. (The negative $\hat{\lambda}$ for model 4 in table 3 may be misleading. In this one instance, λ is used to represent the second serial correlation coefficient.)

A comparison of the estimates for the coefficient of current advertising expenditures b_1 shows radical differences across the various models. The Palda models and the Pascal models show parameter estimates for b_1 greater than one, while the autoregression models and the brand-loyalty models show estimates for b_1 about one-half as large (table 3). The statistically superior model (1.5) suggests that the lower advertising estimates are in fact the more appropriate ones.

Finally, a minor but surprising and unexplained point is that when serial correlation is included in any of the models examined, the importance of advertising copy (d_i) is diminished.

Conclusion

In summary, the results show that of the wide variety of models examined, model (1.5), the brand-loyalty/serial correlation model, best explains the Pinkham data. The parameter estimates indicate that what was previously felt to be a high advertising carry-over effect can be in part attributed to serial correlation. Finally, the estimates for current advertising effects are surprisingly close to the estimates from Palda's original model, and Palda still appears correct in his generalization about advertising's cumulative effect.

References

Berndt, E. R. 1973. Notes on a computational algorithm for estimating parameters in a system of linear or nonlinear equations by method of least squares. Working Paper, Economics Department, University of British Columbia.

Box, G. E., and Jenkins, G. M. 1976. *Time Series Analysis*. Rev. ed. San Francisco: Holden-Day.

Clarke, Darral G., and McCann, John M. 1973. Measuring the cumulative effects of advertising: a reappraisal. In Thomas V. Greer (ed.), *1973 Combined Proceedings*. Chicago: American Marketing Association.

Houston, Franklin S., and Weiss, Doyle L. 1975. Cumulative advertising effects: the role of serial correlation. *Decision Sciences* 6 (July 1975): 471–88.

Kmenta, Jan. 1971. *Elements of Econometrics*. New York: Macmillan.

Kuehn, Alfred A. 1961. A model for budgeting advertising. In Frank Bass et al. (eds.), *Mathematical Models and Methods in Marketing*. Homewood, Ill.: Irwin.

McGuire, Timothy W.; Weiss, Doyle L.; and Houston, Franklin S. 1974. The multinomial logit as a logically consistent market share model. Working Paper no. 254, University of British Columbia.

Palda, Kristian S. 1964. *The Measurement of Cumulative Advertising Effects*. Englewood Cliffs, N.J.: Prentice-Hall.

Schmalensee, Richard. 1972. *The Economics of Advertising*. Amsterdam: North-Holland.

Windal, P. M., and Weiss, D. L. 1975. Distributed lag models, consistent estimators and circular transformations. Working Paper no. 334, Faculty of Commerce, University of British Columbia.

Zellner, A., and Geisel, M. S. 1970. Analysis of distributed lag models with applications to consumption function estimation. *Econometrica* 38 (November): 865–88.

Applied Economics, 1980, 12, 329–339

Bivariate time-series analysis of the relationship between advertising and sales

DOMINIQUE M. HANSSENS

University of California, Los Angeles, U.S.A.

This paper focuses on empirical model building of the sale–advertising relationship at the aggregate response level. Arguments are presented in favour of a combined Box–Jenkins econometric approach to model this relationship. The approach is illustrated and the resulting model is compared to competing models with respect to descriptive and forecasting performance.

I. INTRODUCTION

The successful introduction of the method of Box and Jenkins for univariate time-series model building has raised an important controversy about the value of integrated autoregressive-moving average models (*ARIMA*) versus econometric models. In the context of forecasting, *ARIMA* models sometimes outperform econometric equations, as reported, e.g. by Nelson (1972). This is a surprising finding, in light of the fact that *ARIMA* models use the information of only one time series for forecasting. However, it is known by now that *ARIMA* and econometric models are related to each other. This relationship removes much of the original controversy, but, more importantly, it creates some unique opportunities for empirical causal model building and testing on longitudinal data. In Trivedi's (1975) words, "... time series and structural models need not be thought of as competing approaches."

The purpose of this paper is to use the integration of structural models and time-series analysis to investigate empirically the relationship between product sales and advertising expenditures. In the literature this problem has been approached primarily with econometrics. For example, Clarke (1976) lists no less than 69 econometric sales–advertising studies performed between 1962 and 1975. Although this approach has certainly been successful, one has to be aware of its limitations and dangers. With respect to parameter estimation, the frequently occurring problems such as multicollinearity, heteroskedasticity and autocorrelation are well known and many technical solutions for them have been proposed. With respect to model specification, the critical factor is the availability of a tested theory to generate a model, e.g. price theory in economics. In the case of advertising, about the only element of theory on which there is general agreement is that it has some

positive effect on sales, which is of rather low magnitude and possibly distributed over time
i.e. a carryover effect. In addition, there is evidence of a feedback effect, i.e. past sales may
partially determine the level of future advertising expenditures (e.g. Bass, 1969). In con
clusion, a substantial portion of sales–advertising model building is left to empirical research
i.e. to the search for statistical regularities in the data. While this inductive approach t
research has its powerful advocates, e.g. Ehrenberg and Simon, caution is required wit
longitudinal data. As early as 1926 the dangers of correlational techniques on time-serie
data have been pointed out (Yule, 1926), yet in practice they are often neglected.

This brief description serves as a background for the present research which proposes
use multiple time-series analysis in conjunction with econometric model building for th
study of the sales–advertising relationship. Specifically, the issues of *causality detection* (
grangian sense) and *lag specification* from data analysis are at stake. The opportunity fo
this research comes from recent advances in theoretical time-series analysis and focus
around the well known method of Box and Jenkins. The reader who is not familiar with th
methodology is referred to Box and Jenkins (1976) and Haugh and Box (1977).

II. DATA

A multiple time-series model for advertising and sales will be developed for the Lydia Pinkha
vegetable compound data. This product was introduced in 1873 as a remedy against men
pausal malaise and menstrual pain and has been in the market ever since. The history of t
company gained strong publicity on several occasions because of controversies around t
product's components and a large court case which made an excellent company data ba
public. This history is described in full in Palda (1964), who also lists annual data on doll
sales and advertising for 1907 through 1960 and monthly data for January 1954 throu
June 1960.

This data base was selected for several reasons. First, the product is a frequently purchase
low-cost consumer nondurable, which is a category of substantial interest to empiri
researchers in marketing and economics. Secondly, advertising was almost the exclusi
marketing instrument used by the company; price changes were small and rare, whereas t
distribution, mainly through drug wholesalers remained fairly constant. Furthermore, the
were no direct competitors for this product, so that the market under study can be label
as a closed sales–advertising system. Thirdly, the data series are sufficiently long to perfo
a meaningful statistical analysis and reserve a portion of the data for forecasting.

Since the Lydia Pinkham data are publicly available and of excellent quality they ha
been used by several researchers for various purposes. For example, Palda (1964) introduc
the first empirical evidence of the advertising carryover effect on sales using this data. Clar
and McCann (1977) and Houston and Weiss (1975) argued about the role of serial cor
lation in the error term. Helmer and Johansson (1977) provided an application of Box–Jenk:
transfer function analysis, Caines, Sethi and Brotherton (1977) presented a new syst
identification algorithm and Melrose (1969) did an empirical study on optimizing advertis
policy.

In spite of these and other literature sources this study can not benefit too much fr
earlier findings. The reason is that virtually all previously published Lydia Pinkham mod

are based on the annual data series. In an important review of the field, Clarke (1976) found that such models are seriously affected by temporal aggregation bias. For example, sales response models to advertising based on yearly data suggest advertising carryover effects of several years, whereas models on monthly or quarterly data indicate that the effects last only a few months. Clarke presents strong arguments for using the shorter interval data, especially in the case of frequently purchased products. In this paper only the monthly data are considered.

III. EMPIRICAL ANALYSIS

Univariate models

The first part of the empirical analysis is the fitting of univariate time-series models to the two sets of observations. Since numerous examples of this process exist in the literature, this step is not discussed in great detail. It was found that the series exhibit a strong seasonal pattern, so the twelfth-order seasonal differences (∇^{12}) are taken first. A Prothero–Wallis (1976) test on the transformed series confirmed that they are stationary. The *ARIMA* models are

$$\nabla^{12} A_t = (1 - 0.477 \, B^{12}) \alpha_{A_t}, \, RSS = 2 \, 199 \, 000, \, \chi^2(23) = 10.890,$$

$$\nabla^{12} S_t = -44.98 + (1 - 0.257 \, B^{12} - 0.621 \, B^{15}) \alpha_{S_t}, \, RSS = 1 \, 083 \, 800, \, \chi^2(21)$$

$$= 9.407 \tag{1}$$

where RSS is the residual sum of squares and $\chi^2(k)$ is the Box–Pierce Chi-square statistic for white noise.

Causality Detection

The first important conclusion from the *ARIMA* model building is that the autoregressive operators of the two variables are the same. Following Quenouille (1957), this implies that it is possible that a two-way causal structure between these series exist, i.e. advertising and sales can be both endogenous variables.

To test whether, in fact, there is empirical evidence of a two-way structure, the estimated *ARIMA* residuals α_A and α_S are cross-correlated at various lags. These cross-correlations are shown in Table 1; for comparison purposes we list the values for the original, non-whitened data. The patterns on the whitened data differ substantially from these on the raw data, which are very irregular and would suggest strong interrelationships between the two series at various lags. However, as Granger and Newbold (1974) and others have pointed out, many of the correlations on the original data are likely to be spurious, so that model specification should be performed on the white-noise series only.

First, the hypothesis of series' independence is tested using Haugh's M statistic:

$$M = N \sum_{i=-k}^{k} r^2 \alpha_A \alpha_S(i).$$

Haugh (1976) has shown that, under the null hypothesis of independence, the value M is

Table 1 *Cross-correlograms*

Lag[a]	Original Data	Whitened Model
−12	0.46	0.24
−12	0.57	0.08
−10	0.25	−0.08
−9	−0.09	0.01
−8	−0.31	−0.13
−7	−0.08	0.06
−6	0.40	0.01
−5	0.20	−0.09
−4	0.03	−0.02
−3	−0.28	0.22
−2	−0.42	0.18
−1	−0.12	−0.07
0	0.40	0.25
1	0.62	0.29
2	0.32	0.35
3	−0.11	0.04
4	−0.31	−0.24
5	0.02	−0.26
6	0.37	−0.17
7	0.31	0.19
8	−0.03	−0.10
9	−0.33	−0.15
10	−0.46	0.11
11	−0.11	0.14
12	0.23	−0.12

[a]Negative lags: $\alpha_S \rightarrow \alpha_A$. Positive lags: $\alpha_A \rightarrow \alpha_S$.

approximately Chi-square distributed with $(2k + 1)$ degrees of freedom. Using $k = 12$ the test result is

M	d.f	*Verdict* ($\alpha = 0.05$)
39.539	25	*reject* H_0

so that the possibility of series independence need not be considered further.

Next, the cross-correlograms are used to determine possible shapes of the dynamic shock model (Haugh and Box, 1977) relating α_A and α_S. Bearing in mind that individual coefficients in the neighbourhood of 0.25 $(2/\sqrt{N})$ or more in absolute value can be considered significant, the conclusions are: − the only possible feedback effect is at lag twelve, i.e,

$$\alpha_{A_t} = \omega'_{12} B^{12} \alpha_{S_t} + u'_{1t},$$

where u'_1 is the added noise term. Advertising appears to have a carryover effect on sales, a east in the first few periods. This effect can be represented explicitly, e.g.

$$\alpha_{S_t} = (\omega'_0 + \omega'_1 B + \omega'_2 B^2)\alpha_{A_t} + u'_{2t},$$

or implicitly through a Koyck formulation, which assumes geometric decay of the advertising impact on sales, i.e.

$$\alpha_{S_t} = \frac{\omega'_0}{(1 - \delta'_1 B)} \alpha_{A_t} + u'_{2t}.$$

For parameter estimation we make use of the fact that a dynamic shock model is a special case of Wall's Rational Lag Distributed Structural Form (*RSF*) for which a full information maximum likelihood (*FIML*) estimation method was developed (Wall, 1976). What makes this procedure more attractive than, say, ordinary least squares is the fact that it allows to estimate the added noise parameters and that several equations can be parameterized simultaneously.

Experiments with various dynamic shock model specifications yielded an interesting result: the contemporaneous effect of α_A on α_S is not significant. Since a contemporaneous effect in the other direction is ruled out on logical grounds, a model with lagged effects is specified. The strongest advertizing impact occurs at period one, after which there is a monotone decay. The fully parameterized dynamic shock model with standard errors of parameters between brackets is

$$\alpha_{A_t} = 0.396 \, B^{12} \, \alpha_{S_t} + e_{1t}, \qquad (2a)$$

$$(0.239)$$

$$\sigma^2_{e_1} = 36\,570,$$

$$\alpha_{S_t} = \frac{0.271 \, (0.111) \, B}{1 - 0.492 \, B} \, \alpha_{A_t} + e_{2t}, \qquad (2b)$$

$$(0.190)$$

$$\sigma^2_{e_2} = 21\,010.$$

Overall, the relationships suggested by the cross-correlograms are confirmed. With respect to the error terms e_1 and e_2, they are not significantly correlated. Strictly speaking one expects an $AR(1)$ process on e_2 (see, e.g. Haugh and Box, 1977), but since its coefficient was not significant it was deleted from the analysis.[1]

The equations for sales, including an $AR(1)$ noise process were

$$\alpha_{S_t} = \frac{0.244 \, (0.121) \, B}{1 - 0.529 \, B} \, \alpha_{S_t} + \frac{1}{1 - 0.163 \, B} \, e_{2t}$$

$$(0.208) \qquad\qquad (0.181)$$

$$\sigma^2_{e_2} = 21\,020.$$

Structural Model Building

The last step in model development consists of transforming the dynamic shock model into a structural form. This transformation is done quite easily in theory, since it amounts only to substituting the *ARIMA* Equations 1a and b in Equation 2

$$\alpha_{A_t} = \omega'_{12} B^{12} \alpha_{S_t} + e_{1t}$$

$$\alpha_{S_t} = \frac{\omega'_1 B}{1 - \delta'_1 B} \alpha_{A_t} + e_{2t}$$

becomes

$$\frac{1 - B^{12}}{1 - 0.45 B^{12}} A_t = k' + \omega'_{12} B^{12} \frac{1 B^{12}}{1 - 0.26 B^{12} - 0.62 B^{15}} S_t + e_{1t},$$

$$\frac{1 - B^{12}}{1 - 0.26 B^{12} - 0.62 B^{15}} S_t = \frac{\omega'_1 B}{1 - \delta'_1 B} \frac{1 - B^{12}}{1 - 0.45 B^{12}} A_t + e_{2t}, \tag{3}$$

or

$$\nabla^{12} A_t = k + \frac{\omega'_{12} B^{12} (1 - 0.45 B^{12})}{1 - 0.26 B^{12} - 0.62 B^{15}} \nabla^{12} S_t + (1 - 0.45 B^{12}) e_{1t},$$

$$\nabla^{12} S_t = \frac{\omega'_1 B}{1 - \delta'_1 B} \frac{1 - 0.26 B^{12} - 0.62 B^{15}}{1 - 0.45 B^{12}} \nabla^{12} A_t + (1 - 0.26 B^{12} - 0.62 B^{15}) e_2 \tag{4}$$

This theoretically derived structural form is quite complex unless a few simplifying assumptions are made. In particular the high-order autoregressive denominator processes implied by the model are unrealistic for economic data and expensive to parameterize. Therefore a structural form on the seasonally differenced data ($\nabla^{12} z_t$) is specified and the assumption is made that the *MA* processes of advertising and sales cancel each other out. The structural model then becomes:

$$\nabla^{12} A_t = k_1 + \omega_{12} B^{12} \nabla^{12} S_t + \psi_A (B) e_{1t},$$

$$\nabla^{12} S_t = k_2 + \frac{\omega_1 B}{1 - \delta_1 B} \nabla^{12} A_t + \psi_S(B) e_{2t}$$

where ψ_A and ψ_S are the added noise factors.

The estimation of this *RSF* model consists of two steps. First, the transfer function parameters are parameterized, using *FIML*. Then, the residuals are examined, in order to find the added noise processes, $MA(12)$ for ψ_A and $MA(1, 2, 3)$ for ψ_S. The resulting model is

$$\nabla^{12} A_t = 0.416 B^{12} \nabla^{12} S_t + (1 - 0.568 B^{12}) e_{1t}, \tag{5}$$

$$\sigma^2_{e_1} = 34\ 481.$$

[2] This assumption implies primarily that the $MA(15)$ term is ignored, which may result in a slightly more complex added noise level.

$$\nabla^{12}S_t = \frac{0.374\,(0.126)\,B}{1 - 0.546\,B}\;\nabla^{12}A_t + (1 + 0.082\,B - 0.068\,B^2 + 0.372\,B^3)e_{2t}, \qquad (5b)$$

$$\qquad\qquad (0.188) \qquad\qquad\qquad (0.177)\quad (0.184)\quad (0.193)$$

$$\sigma_{e_2}^2 = 25\,600.$$

IV. FORECASTING PERFORMANCE

The development of a structural model has requested a substantial research effort and the question is raised immediately whether this effort has been worthwhile. The answer can only be furnished by performing a model evaluation. Specifically, we would like to know whether Equation 5 is a superior forecasting tool and whether it provides better insight into market structure than competing approaches. The second evaluation is done verbally in the conclusions section. The forecasting evaluation is the subject of this section, using the eighteen holdout observations mentioned earlier.

Several sources in the literature (e.g. Nelson, 1972) have demonstrated the superiority of so-called naive *ARIMA* models over econometric models for forecasting, so it is logical to compare the forecasting performance of the *ARIMA* Equation 1 to our model. In addition, two econometric models developed on the same monthly data are selected for the test (see Palda, 1964, pp. 37–8). Since Palda used all 78 observations for model development and since his data were deseasonalized, the equations are re-estimated using *OLS* first

$$S_t = 1112.831 + 0.188A_t + 170A_{t-1} + 0.041A_{t-2} + u_t(R^2 = 0.368) \qquad (6)$$

$$\qquad\quad (0.63)\qquad (0.070)\qquad (0.062)$$

$$S_t = 616.763 + 0.435S_{t-1} + 0.206A_t + u_t(R^2 = 0.377) \qquad (7)$$

$$\qquad\quad (0.107)\qquad (0.046)$$

Since there are no published advertising models on the monthly data the *ARIMA* Equation 1a will be used to generate forecasts of the explanatory variables in Equations 6 and 7. The results of this comparison are shown in Table 2.

Table 2 *Comparison of forecasting performance*[a]

	Advertising	Sales
ARIMA, Equation 1	678 863	357 772
RSF Equation 5	489 985	354 577
ARIMA Equation 1 on Advertising, *PALDA* Equation 6 on Sales	678 863	870 023
ARIMA Equation 1 on Advertising, *PALDA* Equation 7 on Sales	678 863	885 713

[a]Table entries are sums of squared forecast errors for eighteen holdout observations.

All models perform satisfactorily in predicting future patterns of sales and advertising. However, there are differences in the quality of this performance which can be measured by overall forecast errors. Equation 5 performs best on both series, reducing the forecast error for advertising by 28 percent and the error in sales by 1 to 60 percent. One should not make too strong inferences about a forecasting sample of only eighteen observations, but at least the conclusion can be made that Equation 5 performs consistently better than its competitors, sometimes substantially better.

Table 2 also shows that the 'naive' *ARIMA* models provide good forecasts. In fact, in a few experiments on one-step ahead forecasting, the univariate models occasionally out-performed all the causal models. These findings are not in conflict with reported results in the literature and, using Pierce and Haugh's terminology (1977), indicate the importance of examining the 'intrastructure' of time series as thoroughly as the 'interstructure.'

V. CONCLUSIONS

In this paper a structural model for monthly Lydia Pinkham advertising and sales was developed, combining the time-series properties and the causal relationships of the two series. This model has proven superior forecasting performance against several univariate and multivariate alternatives. What remains to be done is to evaluate Equation 5 as a description of the relationship between sales and advertising. The discussion centres around three contributions: the modeling of a feedback relationship, the specification of carryover effect of advertising and the distinction between time-series effects and exogenous effects on sales.

The *RSF* Equation 5 is the first one to acknowledge the feedback relationship between sales and advertising in the monthly Lydia Pinkham series. This relationship was found after the systematic elements in sales and advertising were removed, consistent with the causality detection framework of Granger—Newbold and Haugh. From an econometrician's standpoint it implies that a simultaneous-equation model is needed, a point which has been discussed and illustrated at length by Bass and Parsons (1969). In addition to the discovery of feedback, the combined time-series econometric model also assesses the relative importance of the feedback function, which can be derived from the following summary of structural error variances

Model	Error Variance
Mean	202 833
$\nabla^{12} A_t$	48 620
Feedback Function	40 770
Feedback plus Noise model	34 481

A substantial portion of total variability in advertising is due to systematic, in this case seasonal, variation. As a result, it can be said that the sales feedback on advertising is important only to the extent that it explains deviations from the expected seasonal pattern in advertising. Especially in the absence of inside information about managerial decision making, the combined feedback—time series model for advertising provides a reliable picture of the aggregate outcome of the advertising budgeting process in this organization.

As a second contribution, the *RSF* model reveals a clear, empirically determined shape of the advertising carryover effects. The main difference with other published results is the absence of a contemporaneous effect, since Equation 5 suggests that the first advertising effect occurs after a one-period lag. This result is plausible because the Lydia Pinkham sales figures are recorded when the goods are shipped, whereas advertising expenditures are made when the advertisements actually appear. In itself, this finding may not be too important, but it does illustrate the risk of modeling spurious relationships among variables when one fails to take into account their time-series properties first. Finally, the magnitude of the carryover effect, which is measured by the output lag coefficient 0.518, suggests that the 90 percent duration interval of advertising is 4.5 months. This finding is in agreement with Clarke's conclusion that 'the published econometric literature indicates that 90 percent of the cumulative effect of advertising on sales of mature, frequently purchased, low-priced products occurs within 3 to 9 months of the advertisement' (Clarke, 1976).

Last but not least, this modeling approach allows one to compare the importance of the 'intrastructure' and the 'interstructure' for monthly sales. Again, consider the following list of structural error variances

Model	Error Variance
Mean	36 856
$\nabla^{12}S_t$	30 433
Advertising Effects	27 610
Advertising plus noise model	25 600

The situation is quite different from the advertising case. First, it appears that neither past sales nor the advertising history are very successful in reducing the variance in the series. In the literature on sales and advertising, several sources report R-squares of 0.70 and more, which leads one to observe that (1) R-square is not a good measure of association on longitudinal data (see Pierce, 1977) and (2) that one should not expect very good fit with a limited information set such as the one used in this study. Secondly, one can conclude that the exogenous influences and the added noise are about equally important in explaining deviations from the seasonal pattern in sales ($\nabla^{12}S_t$). The results also indicate that, while the advertising effects are significant, they do not have a very important influence upon month-to-month variations in sales.

Although this study of combined time-series and economic model building is limited because only two series were considered, it is hoped that it generates insight, not only into the empirical research opportunities offered by this relatively new methodology, but also into the value of the information captured in the history of an economic time series before inferences are made about causal relationships.

ACKNOWLEDGEMENTS

The author would like to thank Professor Kent D. Wall for making his computer program available.

REFERENCES

Bass, F. M. and Parsons, L. J. (1969) Simultaneous-Equation Regression Analysis of Sales and Advertising, *Applied Economics*, 1, 103–124.

Box, G. E. P. and Jenkins, G. M. (1976) *Time Series Analysis, Forecasting and Control*, Holden–Day, Inc. San Francisco.

Cains, P. E., Sethi, S. P. and Brotherton, T. W. (1977) Impulse Response Identification and Causality Detection for the Lydia Pinkham Data, *Annals of Economic and Social Measurement*, 6, 147–63.

Clarke, D. G. (1976) Econometric Measurement of the Duration of Advertising Effect on Sales, *Journal of Marketing Research*, 13, 345–57.

Clarke, D. G. and McCann, J. M. (1977) Cumulative Advertising Effects: The Role of Serial Correlation; A Reply, *Decision Sciences*, 8, 33–43.

Granger, C. W. J. and Newbold, P. (1974) Spurious Regressions in Econometrics, *Journal of Econometrics*, 2, 111–120.

Granger, C. W. J. and Newbold, P. (1977) Identification of Two-Way Causal Systems, *Frontiers in Quantitative Economics*, III A, North-Holland Amsterdam.

Haugh, L. D. (1976) Checking the Independence of Two Covariance–Stationary Time Series: A Univariate Residual Cross-Correlation Approach, *Journal of the American Statistical Association*, 71, 378–85

Haugh, L. D. and Box, G. E. P. (1977) Identification of Dynamic Regression (Distributed Lag) Models Connecting Two Time Series, *Journal of the American Statistical Association*, 72, 378–85.

Helmer, R. M. and Johansson, J. K. (1977) An Exposition of the Box–Jenkins Transfer Function Analysis With An Application to the Advertising–Sales Relationship, *Journal of Marketing Research*, 14, 227–39

Houston, F. S. and Weiss, D. L. (1975) Cumulative Advertising Effects: The Role of Serial Correlation, *Decision Sciences*, 6, 471–81.

Melrose, K. B. (1969) An Empirical Study of Optimizing Advertising Policy, *Journal of Business*, 32 282–92.

Nelson, C. R. (1972) The Prediction Performance of the *FRB–MIT–PENN* Model of the U.S. Economy, *American Economic Review*, 62, 423–6.

Newbold, P. (1978) Feedback Induced by Measurement Errors, *International Economic Review*, 19, 787–91

Pack, D. J. (1977) Documentation for a Computer Program for the Analysis of Time Series Models Using the Box–Jenkins Philosophy, *Automatic Forecasting Systems*, Hatboro, PA.

Palda, K. S. (1964) *The Measurement of Cumulative Advertising Effects*, Prentice-Hall Englewood Cliffs N. J.

Pierce, D. A. (1977) Relationships – and the Lack thereof – between Economic Time Series, with Special Reference to Money and Interest Rates, *Journal of the American Statistical Association*, 72, 11–22

Pierce, D. A. and Haugh, L. D. (1977) Causality in Temporal Systems: Characterizations and a Survey, *Journal of Econometrics*, 5, 265–93.

Prothero, D. L. and Wallis, K. F. (1976) Modeling Macroeconomic Time Series, *Journal of the Royal Statistical Society A*, 139, 468–486.

Quenouille, M. H. (1957) *The Analysis of Multiple Time-Series*, Hafner Publishing Co., New York.

Schwert, W. G. (1977) Tests of Causality: The Message in the Innovations, *Working Paper*, University of Rochester Graduate School of Management, GBP 77–4, p. 53.

Trivedi, P. K. (1975) Time Series Versus Structural Models: A Case Study of Canadian Manufacturing Inventory Behavior, *International Economic Review*, 16, 587–608.

Wall, K. D. (1976) FIML Estimation of Rational Distributed Lag Structural Form Models, *Annals of Economic and Social Measurement*, 5, 53–64.

Yule, G. U. (1926) Why Do We Sometimes Get Nonsense Correlations Between Time Series? *Journal of the Royal Statistical Society A*, 89, 1–64.

Zellner, A. and Palm, F. (1974) Time Series Analysis and Simultaneous Equation Econometric Models, *Journal of Econometrics*, 2, 17-54.

DAVID A. AAKER, JAMES M. CARMAN, and ROBERT JACOBSON*

A time series analysis of the advertising-sales relationship is conducted for six cereal brands under the assumption that feedback is potentially present. This relationship is found to be very weak. The danger of applying a misspecified Koyck model is illustrated.

Modeling Advertising-Sales Relationships Involving Feedback: A Time Series Analysis of Six Cereal Brands

The description of the nature of the current and cumulative effects of advertising has long been recognized by both managers and public policymakers as an important but difficult problem in marketing. Theory-based normative models are available (Sethi 1979), but must assume some model of the dynamic process of carryover effects. The specification and estimation of such a model in a given empirical context are indeed difficult. A brief review of some of the previous modeling efforts illustrates the difficulty and provides background for the research we describe.

One of the difficulties in developing a structural model of the process is to specify the particular form of the lag structure. One approach is the classic geometric decay specification of Koyck (1954). In reduced form, the model is:

$$(1) \qquad S_t = a + \lambda S_{t-1} + bA_t + e_t.$$

Clarke (1976) provides an excellent review of the substantial number of Koyck model applications through 1974. As Griliches (1967), Clarke (1976), and others have observed, this widely used model involves serious difficulties. First, two very different structural models give rise to the same reduced form. In one, the original Koyck specification, the lagged sales term coefficient is assumed to represent only the effect of past advertising. In the other, termed a "partial adjustment model" by Clarke (1977, Ch. 2), λ is assumed to be measuring the "goodwill" created by brand usage and the total mar-

keting program, not just advertising. Second, if the lag structure differs from the hypothesized geometric decay, serious biases can occur (Bass and Clarke 1972). Third, the model assumes there is no simultaneous relationship between sales and advertising. When this assumption fails, the results could be very misleading. Fourth, the nature of the Koyck transformation probably generates serial autocorrelation. Fifth, a successful model application requires not only that the specification be correct, but that the data involve a frequency appropriate to the context. Clarke (1976) suggests, for example, that monthly data are often appropriate and that use of annual data instead can cause greatly exaggerated carryover effects.

Since the development of the Koyck model in 1954, considerable advances have been made in econometric estimation techniques and in the introduction of lag structures other than Koyck's. Bass and Clarke (1972) and Montgomery and Silk (1972) introduced additional lagged advertising terms that served to delay the start of the geometric decay. Ward (1976) considered a polynomial lag structure and Mann (1975), Weiss, Houston, and Windal (1978), and Bultez and Naert (1979) used a Pascal lag structure. Both structures allow the effect of advertising to increase in later periods before it begins to decay. In the Bultez and Naert application of the Pascal lag model, the lagged sales or goodwill term is explicitly hypothesized to be generated solely by advertising, just as in the original Koyck formulation.

Two other structural formulations are of interest. Clarke and McCann (1973) postulate that sales are a function of current advertising expenditures, but include an autoregressive error term to model carryover effects not completely attributable to past advertising expenditures:

---

*David A. Aaker is J. Gary Shausby Professor of Marketing Strategy, James M. Carman is Professor, and Robert Jacobson is Lecturer, University of California at Berkeley.

Journal of Marketing Research
Vol. XIX (February 1982), 116–25

(2) $S_t = a + bA_t + u_t$

where:

$$u_t = \rho u_{t-1} + e_t.$$

The reduced form is identical to equation 1 except it also has a lagged advertising term. Houston and Weiss (1975) have developed a "brand loyalty" model that is identical to Clarke's "partial adjustment" model, except that the lagged sales term is hypothesized to represent only the effect of purchase experience. They also explore a brand loyalty model in which an autoregressive term is included. In its reduced form, it is the same as equation 1, except it includes a lagged advertising term and a second lagged sales term. Bass and Clarke (1972) also tried models with two and three lagged sales terms.

Time Series Analysis

One approach to modeling the advertising-sales relationship, which could be called an econometric approach, is to postulate one of the available model structures and estimate the parameters. However, as the preceding review makes clear, a host of structural models are available and an associated group of assumptions to be made about the environment to be modeled. The reality is that it is very difficult in a given context to make judgments with confidence about those sensitive assumptions.

In an alternative approach, termed time series analysis, the data are allowed to specify the relationship as much as possible. In time series analysis a series of procedures are employed to detect a wide variety of possible relationships, including the possibility of no relationship at all. Time series analysis is not an end in itself. Its value is in the insights it provides in describing reduced form relationships. In this role, it provides a mechanism for testing structural models of the advertising-sales relationships.

One particular time series test of interest explores the possible presence of a sales-to-advertising influence as well as (or instead of) an advertising-to-sales influence. The advertising-sales simultaneity issue has been neglected in many structural models. However, given the nature of the advertising budgeting decision process, the reverse causal flow often has the potential to be present. Hanssens (1980), for example, found a sales-to-advertising influence in the Lydia Pinkham data, but many researchers have used these data under the assumption of no such relationship.

Several times series tests for causal direction are based on a causality definition by Granger (1969) known as "Granger causality." Briefly, a variable X is said to "Granger cause" another variable Y if Y can be better predicted from the past of X and Y together than from the past of Y alone, other relevant information also being used in the predictions. The most commonly used tests for Granger causality are one developed by Sims (1972)

and another sometimes termed the Pierce-Haugh (1977) test.

Purposes of the Article

One purpose of this article is to explore the nature of the advertising-sales relationship for six cereal brands with more than 16 years of monthly data. The cereal industry is of interest because it is relatively stable yet highly competitive and because it has been the focus of a major antitrust suit, one issue of which involves the advertising-sales relationship. Because of the richness of the data and the context and because it is far from obvious which model structure would be appropriate, a time series analysis is employed. A second purpose is to illustrate time series analysis when two-way causation is possible. Our study differs from several others in the area, e.g., Bass and Pilon (1980) and Hanssens (1980), in that it does not rely solely on the Pierce-Haugh test for the direction of causation. Because the Pierce-Haugh test does have serious limitations, a second causal detecting test is discussed and employed. A third purpose is to illustrate the dangers of using a misspecified model by applying the widely used Koyck model to the data base. The fourth purpose is to discuss the use of accounting data in this marketing research context. For many organizations it is difficult to justify analysis efforts based on alternative data sources which can be extremely costly. Before we present the results, we outline the modeling process, describe the data, and discuss the advantages and disadvantages of accounting data.

THE MODELING PROCESS

Transfer function analysis developed under the framework of Box and Jenkins (1976, Ch. 10) is not appropriate when the possibility of feedback is present, as Granger and Newbold (1977) and Helmers and Johansson (1977) have noted. Feedback is said to be present when a variable X is influencing another variable Y while Y is also influencing X. Because the possibility of feedback is present in most advertising-sales relationships, the Box-Jenkins approach to transfer function analysis is inappropriate. A procedure allowing for the identification and estimation of a variety of lag structures while also allowing for the possibility of feedback was developed by Haugh (1972).[1] Hanssens (1980) used this pro-

---

[1]Another representation of a time series model allowing for feedback is described by Tiao and Box (1979) who propose estimating a multiple ARMA model of the form:

$$\phi(B)\mathbf{Z}_t = \theta(B)\boldsymbol{\epsilon}_t$$

where $\mathbf{Z}_t$ is a vector of mean stationary series, $\boldsymbol{\epsilon}_t$ is a vector of white noise errors, and

$$\phi(B) = I - \phi_1 B' - \ldots - \phi_P B^P, \; \theta(B) = I - \theta_1 B' - \ldots - \theta_q B^q.$$

A variety of other approaches can be used to estimate dynamic reduced forms including vector autoregressions (Sims 1980) and state space modeling (Akaike 1976).

cedure to identify a feedback in the Lydia Pinkham data and Bass and Pilon (1980) used it to explore a price-sales relationship.

The assumed model has the form:

$$A_t = c_1^* + \frac{\omega_1^*(B)}{\delta_1^*(B)} S_t + \frac{\theta_1^*(B)}{\phi_1^*(B)} \eta_{1t}$$

(3)

$$S_t = c_2^* + \frac{\omega_2^*(B)}{\delta_2^*(B)} A_t + \frac{\theta_2^*(B)}{\phi_2^*(B)} \eta_{2t}$$

where:

S_t is sales at time t,

A_t is advertising at time t,

$\omega_i^*, \delta_i^*, \phi_i^*, \theta_i^*$ $i = 1,2$ are polynomials in the backward shift operator B ($B^k X_t = X_{t-k}$). The ratio involving ω_i^* and δ_i^* is used to approximate a higher order polynomial representing how the left variable is influenced by the right variable. The ratio of ϕ_i^* and θ_i^* is used to approximate a higher order polynomial representing the error structure.

c_i^* is a constant.

η_{it}^* is a white noise error term.

The modeling procedure, explicitly detailed by Granger and Newbold (1977), involves five steps.

Step 1. Convert both the sales and the advertising data to white noise by building two separate, autoregressive moving average (ARMA), univariate models. The purpose of this step is to remove that part of the series which can be explained in terms of its own past behavior.

$$\phi_1(B)S_t = c_1 + \theta_1(B)\xi_{1t}$$

(4)

$$\phi_2(B)A_t = c_2 + \theta_2(B)\xi_{2t}$$

Step 2. Calculate the cross-correlations between the prewhitened series. Use the cross-correlations to identify relationships between the prewhitened series. Though it may appear initially that the prefiltering of the data would destroy any possible relationship between the series, Pierce-Haugh (1977) and Granger-Newbold (1977) show that if a relationship is present between the untransformed series it will be present between the prefiltered series. Of course, deciding which correlations are really relevant is often difficult. Difficulties are associated with small sample properties, interpreting groups of coefficients that are individually marginally significant, interpreting an isolated significant coefficient; and identifying chance-caused significant coefficients. The process involves judgments based on experience and *a priori* feelings about the plausible forms of the relationship. The resulting model can be represented as:

$$\xi_{1t} = c_1^{**} + \frac{\omega_1^{**}(B)}{\delta_1^{**}(B)} \xi_{2t} + \frac{\phi_1^{**}(B)}{\theta_1^{**}(B)} \eta_{1t}$$

(5)

$$\xi_{2t} = c_2^{**} + \frac{\omega_2^{**}(B)}{\delta_2^{**}(B)} \xi_{1t} + \frac{\phi_2^{**}(B)}{\theta_2^{**}(B)} \eta_{2t}$$

where the double asterisks indicate polynomials different from those in equation 3.

Step 3. Estimate the model linking the prewhitened series, equation set 5, and check the adequacy of the representation by testing for whiteness of residuals and by determining the effect of deletion and addition of parameters on the fit. Modify and reestimate if necessary.

Step 4. Combine the model estimated in step 3 with the univariate models' fit in step 1 to formulate the interrelationships between the original series. Thus, equation set 3 is created.

Step 5. Estimate the complete model, check the adequacy of the representation, and modify and reestimate if necessary. One of the structures reviewed at the beginning of the article could emerge.

THE DATA

In 1972, the Federal Trade Commission issued a complaint against the four leading ready-to-eat cereal companies—Kellogg, General Mills, General Foods, and Quaker Oats—charging them with practicing a "shared monopoly" (Quaker Oats later obtained release from the case). The complaint alleged that the four did not compete on a price basis, enjoyed monopoly profits, and made it difficult for other firms to enter the industry because of their large advertising budgets, brand proliferation, and control over retail shelf space. These charges suggest that price competition would not be an important element of the marketing mix.

In the process of discovery for this litigation, the FTC requested and obtained—with a few exceptions, to be noted—monthly data on factory shipments, factory sales dollars, and manufacturer's advertising expenditures (excluding production and research expenditures) for each brand in the industry for the period October 1949 to May 1974. Data were incomplete and of poor quality for the brands of the defendant, General Mills, and for the nonlitigants.

Six cereal brands were selected for study: Kellogg's Corn Flakes, Special K, Life, Rice Krispies, Alpha Bits, and Sugar Frosted Flakes. This brand set included two major adult cereals, two nutritional cereals, and two presweetened children's cereals. All brands selected had

Table 1
SALES AND ADVERTISING MEANS AND STANDARD DEVIATIONS

Brand	Advertising (in thousands of current dollars)		Sales (in millions of current dollars)	
	Mean	Standard deviation	Mean	Standard deviation
Corn Flakes	501	243	3.41	.85
Special K	321	132	2.05	.69
Life	137	137	.96	.17
Rice Krispies	387	132	2.89	1.04
Alpha Bits	136	116	.74	.18
Sugar Frosted Flakes	303	137	2.21	.99

substantial levels of both advertising and sales and also substantial variation in advertising and sales over time (Table 1). They also had complete data over several years. The length of the monthly data ranged from 7.8 years for Life to 16 years for Kellogg's Corn Flakes, Special K, and Rice Krispies. In each case, the data terminated at December 1972.

Because the analysis involves only six cereals, it is not appropriate to explore models including competitive responses to a brand's advertising effects. Thus, any elasticities on response coefficients that are estimated are "total advertising elasticities" in the Lambin, Naert, Bultez (1975) sense.

ADVANTAGES AND DISADVANTAGES OF ACCOUNTING DATA

The data base has several advantages and also some shortcomings. Some of the shortcomings are unique to this data base; others may apply generally to accounting data. It is useful to make these advantages and disadvantages explicit for a better understanding of the results, of the use of accounting data in academic research, and of when accounting data could be useful to the marketing manager.

The sales data represent invoiced factory shipments. The quality of the data should be high because invoicing is a high-visibility activity for internal accountants and auditors. Though some small systematic and random errors may be present—e.g., returns or back-dating of invoices at the end of the month—this series should have high reliability and validity in comparison with most marketing data. From the marketing manager's standpoint, they are the lowest cost and most available movement data.

A disadvantage of the sales data is the need to estimate the distribution of the lag (or lead) between retail sale

and factory sale. After consultation with marketing people in the grocery field, we conclude that, on average, factory sale follows retail sale by about one month. That is, an order on the cereal manufacturer is in response to an out-of-stock condition created by sales, and the sales, out-of-stock, order-entry, shipment, and invoice cycle takes about one month. Thus, in this article, sales at time t actually represent factory shipments at time $t + 1$. Because the analysis to be used examines a large number of lags, this assumption is not as critical as one might initially think. If the lag between shipments and retail sales were other than one month, the estimated relationship between advertising and sales would appear with a different lag but it would still appear. It is important that the lag be relatively consistent over time for each brand.

The advertising data create other problems. The data are dollars of advertising, not gross rating points, which would be a measure of physical quantity of advertising. All dollars are current dollars for both sales and advertising. One might argue intuitively that deflating advertising to constant dollars is appropriate, but both theory and empirical evidence suggest otherwise. On the theoretical side, we have no reliable deflator for advertising; an incorrect one may do more harm than good. In addition, because sales are also not deflated, inflation is allowed to work on both series. On the empirical side, Schmelensee's (1972) analysis of the relationship between consumption and advertising at the national level gave the same result with both constant and current dollars. Picconi and Olson (1978, 82–92) found current dollar advertising expenditures were superior to the constant dollar form.

A second concern is the differences in the time of recognizing an advertising expenditure in accounting records. The media have different billing practices. For

Table 2
UNIVARIATE MODELS[a]

Brand	No. of observations	Advertising	Sales
Corn Flakes	192	$(1 - .43B - .44B^{12})A_t = 468.510 + \epsilon_t$ (7.2) (6.9) (4.6)	$(1 - .66B^{12})S_t = 3,509,700 + (1 + .21B - .31B^2)\epsilon_t$ (12.1) (29.3) (2.9) (4.1)
Special K	192	$(1 - .44B - .26B^{12})A_t = 338,600 + \epsilon_t$ (6.5) (3.8) (12.7)	$(1 - .24B - .75B^{12})S_t = 9,843,800 + \epsilon_t$ (5.1) (14.7) (.3)
Life	94	$(1 - .24B^3)A_t = 143,360 + (1 + .26B)\epsilon_t$ (2.3) (6.3) (2.5)	$(1 - .32B^3 - .59B^{12})S_t - 134,500 + (1 + .20B)\epsilon_t$ (3.6) (6.4) (3.2) (2.0)
Rice Krispies	192	$(1 - .24B - .27B^2 - .26B^{12})A_t = 424,410 + \epsilon_t$ (3.4) (3.6) (3.8) (10.7)	$(1 - .17B^3 - .82B^{12})S_t = 10,315,000 + \epsilon_t$ (3.8) (17.6) (.8)
Alpha Bits	131	$(1 - .16B^{12})A_t = 130,510 + (1 - .20B)\epsilon_t$ (1.7) (2.5)	$(1 - .42B - .27B^3 - .22B^{12})S_t = 751,450 + \epsilon_t$ (5.4) (3.4) (3.1) (5.3)
Sugar Frosted Flakes	192	$(1 - .47B - .34B^{12})A_t = 347,400 + \epsilon_t$ (7.4) (5.7) (9.3)	$(1 - .28B^{13})(1 - B^{12})S_t = 148,970 + (1 - .62B^{12})\epsilon_t$ (3.3) (8.1) (7.5)

[a] The t-statistics are in parentheses.

Table
CROSS-CORRELATIONS OF
CORRELATION OF FILTERED ADVERTISING

	Effective no. of obs.	Std. error	k = −12	−11	−10	−9	−8	−7	−6	−5	−4
Corn Flakes	180	.075	.095	−.098	−.023	.028	−.020	.020	.158*	.015	−.060
Special K	180	.075	−.045	−.039	.082	−.031	.073	−.051	.035	.072	−.116
Life	82	.110	.118	.193*	.016	.000	.022	.162	.249*	.000	−.032
Rice Krispies	180	.075	.034	−.071	−.076	−.013	−.019	.179*	.099	−.067	−.052
Alpha Bits	119	.092	−.000	−.008	−.015	.064	−.021	−.182*	.093	.165*	.085
Sugar Frosted Flakes	167	.077	.043	−.050	.049	−.063	−.023	.038	.070	−.058	.018

*Significant at the .10 level (two-sided test).

example, network television is more likely to be billed in the period in which it is run (or even earlier) than is spot television, radio, or print. Of course, advertising agencies could also create differences in the time between advertising and billing to the advertiser, but the media appear to be the biggest source of variation. If differences do exist, advertiser accountants may not recognize the expenditure in a consistent fashion. Specifically, the advertising expenditure could be recognized when the advertising is contracted, when it is run, or when it is billed. We believe most firms try to recognize the expenditure when it is run, but even a well-meaning accountant can have problems.

In particular, television rate rebates cause a problem. The media bill at contracted rates. These rates are based on gross rating points delivered and are often fixed months before an advertisement actually appears. Some contracts call for rebates for nondelivery of audience, based on the results of rating services that report well after a show has run. Does the accountant recognize the rebate credit in the month it is received or is an adjustment made in the period when the advertisement ran? Our data appear to reflect both practices. Specifically, Kellogg, which produces four of the six cereal brands analyzed, never reported negative advertising expenditures. However, the brands Life and Alpha Bits did report negative advertising expenditures, although both the size and frequency were modest. In our analysis, the data received from the FTC were not adjusted. Several adjustments were explored with the Life series but did not provide any useful insights. Further, the data represent real information—undelivered messages. The only question is when they were undelivered. If the adjustment is consistent over time, the analysis will find it; if it is a random event, it will be white noise. Certainly it is better to leave it in than to guess at some arbitrary adjustment.

FINDINGS

The Univariate Models

The first step was to develop the ARMA filters for both the advertising and the sales times series. The re-

sults are shown in Table 2. Consider first the advertising filters. Each brand shows a 12-month seasonal component, except Life, for which a three-month seasonal term is present. In addition, there is either a moving average or an autoregressive term with a one-month lag for each brand. One possible interpretation is that the advertising budget responds to past advertising budget decisions. Another is that the univariate models are reduced-form representations of structural models relating advertising to other variables. Similar model characteristics emerged for the sales data. The models for all brands included a 12-month seasonal term. In addition, the models for three of the brands also had a three-month seasonal term. The model of every brand except Sugar Frosted Flakes had either an autoregressive or a moving average one-month lag term. All the models are parsimonious, in keeping with the objective of univariate time series analysis, yet give no indication of model inadequacy on the basis of a variety of diagnostic checks, including several tests to ensure the residuals approximated white noise.

Cross-Correlations

Table 3 shows the cross-correlations between the filtered advertising and filtered sales. The correlations with a positive lag represent causal flows from advertising to sales and those with a negative lag represent a causal flow from sales to advertising. Under the null hypothesis of no relation, the correlations are known to be asymptotically, independently, normally distributed with zero mean and variance $1/N$, where N is the sample size.

Several observations can be made from Table 3. First, there does not seem to be any lag structure at all. Neither the Koyck geometric lag assumption nor any other lag pattern (such as the Pascal) appears to be present. Second, the significant correlations are relatively few. Among the 150 correlations, only 20 are significant at the 0.10 level and six of those are either negative or adjacent to a large correlation of the opposite sign. One would expect 15 significant correlations even if the two series were independent. Of the 72 correlations involving lagged advertising, only seven are significant at the .10 level and two of those are negative or adjacent to a large negative correlation. One would expect seven

3

FILTERED MONTHLY SERIES
$(t - k)$ AND FILTERED SALES (t)

-3	-2	-1	0	1	2	3	4	5	6	7	8	9	10	11	12
.058	.106	.151*	-.045	.075	.075	.047	.182*	.133*	-.060	-.092	.097	.054	.082	.034	.084
.155*	.002	.073	.185*	.042	.067	-.125*	.029	.026	-.098	.086	.021	-.006	.151*	.018	-.102
.086	.156	.237*	.011	.143	.052	-.102	.113	-.162	-.057	.213*	-.185*	-.060	.070	-.092	-.093
-.027	.154*	-.136*	-.026	.126*	.045	-.054	.040	.007	-.025	.053	.061	.083	-.073	.046	.021
.076	-.016	.067	-.004	-.056	.006	.013	.031	.035	-.007	.078	.049	-.081	-.096	-.011	-.071
.079	.100	-.074	.143*	-.082	.006	.085	.042	-.031	-.068	.026	.038	-.045	.049	.082	-.076

under chance. These observations suggest that the hypothesis test of no causal relationship might be appropriate. Certainly no universal model relating advertising and sales emerges.

The Pierce-Haugh Test

The basic logic of what is here termed the Pierce-Haugh test is that if Y does not Granger cause X, then the cross-correlations between filtered X and lagged values of filtered Y should, as a group, be insignificantly different from zero. If, in fact, advertising does not cause sales, the statistic

(6)
$$Q = n^2 \sum_{k=1}^{m} (n-k)^{-1} \hat{\rho}_k^2$$

where:

n is the effective number of observations,
m is the number of correlations to be summed,
k is the lag period, and
$\hat{\rho}_k$ is the estimated cross-correlation with lag k,

should be asymptotically distributed as chi square with m degrees of freedom.[2] If sales do not cause advertising, the statistic for negative values of k will have this distribution. Table 4 shows that, for all brands, the null hypothesis of advertising not influencing sales cannot be rejected at the 0.05 level, although for Corn Flakes this null hypothesis can be rejected at the 0.10 level. The null hypothesis of sales not influencing advertising is rejected only for Life at the .05 level although it is rejected for Rice Krispies at the 0.10 level. As 12 statis-

tical tests were employed, the relationships suggested seem relatively weak if they are present.

The Sims Test

For several reasons, a second test by a different method is a useful supplement and check on the Pierce-Haugh test. Citing the work of Durbin (1970), Sims (1977a) concluded that the Pierce-Haugh procedure for testing for causality is not a valid test, i.e., the Type I error is incorrect, for there is an asymptotic bias in the variance estimate of $1/n$ for the residual cross-correlations once causation in one direction is detected. The test is biased against finding a feedback relationship. Thus the conclusion of unidirectional causality based on the Pierce-Haugh test (or variations of it) that has appeared in several articles is unwarranted. However, the findings of no relationship in either direction fit the special case in which the information matrix is diagonal and the standard error based on the null hypothesis of no relationship is appropriate.

There are additional reasons for including a second test. One is the problem that has become known as spurious independence. In general, the relationship between the residuals will be weaker than the relationship between the original series. The series are first related to their own past values, which may act as proxies for past values of the other series, before the interseries relationship is examined. The performance of the Pierce-Haugh test in past studies suggests that the test has a tendency to be unable to reject the null hypothesis of no relation-

---

[2]The contemporaneous term is not typically used in the calculation of Q, as one cannot be sure whether it represents one variable influencing the other, or both series influencing each other. In this case sales are unlikely to be influencing advertising within a month. However, a contemporaneous correlation can occur if a third factor is influencing both series. Because such a condition could exist in our context, we, too, do not place the contemporaneous term in the Pierce-Haugh statistic.

Much discussion has evolved around asymptotically equivalent versions of this statistic (Davies, Triggs, and Newbold 1977). The version used in this study is one suggested by Ljung and Box (1978).

Table 4

THE PIERCE-HAUGH TEST—THE Q-STATISTIC[a]

Brand	$A(t - k) \rightarrow S(t)$	$S(t - k) \rightarrow A(t)$
Corn Flakes	20.4	17.1
Special K	14.8	13.4
Life	18.1	24.4
Rice Krispies	8.7	20.5
Alpha Bits	4.9	12.4
Sugar Frosted Flakes	7.5	7.9

[a]All statistics should be compared with a 0.05 critical value of $\chi^2(12) = 21.0$. The 0.10 critical value of $\chi^2(12)$ is 18.6.

ship. Second, analyst judgment is involved in the choice between autoregressive and moving average parameters, the way in which to model the seasonal factors, and how parsimonious the parameterization should be. These judgments may influence the results of the Pierce-Haugh tests. The Sims test does not involve estimating ARMA filters and thus is much simpler to use.

The Sims test of causality involves regressing a variable Y on past, current, and future values of another variable X. Given that the future cannot cause the past, if Y does not influence X, the coefficients for the future values of X should, as a group, be insignificantly different from zero. The Sims test is simpler to use than the Pierce-Haugh test in that it does not involve identifying and estimating ARMA filters but is for the most part restricted to causality detection. In contrast, the analysis of prewhitened cross-correlation on which the Pierce-Haugh test is based does include a procedure for identifying the dynamic interactions of the variables.

Because the Sims test calls for an F-test on a coefficient group, the residuals must approximate white noise. However, the regression just described does not ensure white noise residuals. To alleviate this problem, Sims used generalized least squares to transform the data by a filter common to all variables, so that the residuals would be white noise. A similar but easier way that the residuals can be guaranteed to approximate white noise is to input lagged dependent variables on the right side of the regression to "soak up" any serial correlation. This approach, involving six lagged dependent variables,[3] was employed and is here termed a "modified Sims test." The regression underlying the test that advertising does not cause sales was thus:

$$(7) \quad A_t = \sum_{i=1}^{6} a_i A_{t-i} + \sum_{i=0}^{12} b_i S_{t-i} + \sum_{i=1}^{12} c_i S_{t+i} + \sum_{i=1}^{12} d_i D_i$$

where:

A_t is advertising in period t,
S_{t-i} is sales in period $t - i$, and
D_i is a seasonal dummy variable for month i.

Under the null hypothesis, the coefficients associated with future sales should, as a group, be insignificantly different from zero. The regression associated with the other hypothesis, that sales do not cause advertising, was:

[3]The choice of the lengths of the lags was somewhat arbitrary. The lengths selected were thought to remove serial correlation and yet be able to detect possible relationships. However, the findings of the analysis were relatively insensitive to different lag lengths.
[4]The companion advertising equation was also run. A significant coefficient was found for a one-month sales lag but in terms of ex-

Table 5
MODIFIED SIMS TEST—THE F-STATISTIC

Brand	0.05 critical value	$A(t) \rightarrow$ $S(t + k)$	$S(t) \rightarrow$ $A(t + k)$
Corn Flakes	$F(12,125) = 1.83$	1.90*	.69
Special K	$F(12,125) = 1.83$	1.48	.78
Life	$F(12,27) = 2.13$	1.17	1.46
Rice Krispies	$F(12,125) = 1.83$	1.30	2.06*
Alpha Bits	$F(12,64) = 1.90$	.69	.81
Sugar Frosted Flakes	$F(12,125) = 1.83$	1.19	1.52

*Significant at the 0.05 level.

$$(8) \quad S_t = \sum_{i=1}^{6} a_i S_{t-i} + \sum_{i=0}^{12} b_i A_{t-i} + \sum_{i=1}^{12} c_i A_{t+i} + \sum_{i=11}^{12} d_i D_i.$$

The null hypothesis is that the coefficients associated with future advertising are zero.

The results of the Sims test are reported in Table 5. Of interest is the fact that the Life sales-to-advertising relationship is not significant. However, the relationships involving Rice Krispies and Corn Flakes, which in the Pierce-Haugh test are significant at the 0.10 level, are significant in the Sims test. Table 3 suggests that the sales-to-advertising relationship in the Rice Krispies data could probably be traced to correlations corresponding to lags of one, two, and seven in the filtered data. Similarly, Table 3 reveals Corn Flakes correlations corresponding to lags at periods four and five in the filtered data. Again, because of the number of statistical tests used, a conclusion that the relationships are weak seems justified.

The Corn Flakes Relationship

To explore further the extent of the advertising-to-sales relationship in the Corn Flakes data, we estimated the following model, drawing on the analysis of the prewhitened cross-correlations and a variety of diagnostic checks.[4]

planatory power it was negligible. The estimated two-equation model for Corn Flakes is specified below.

$$\left(\begin{bmatrix} 1 & 0 \\ 0 & 1 \end{bmatrix} - \begin{bmatrix} .40 & \cdot \\ (.06) & \cdot \end{bmatrix} B - \begin{bmatrix} \cdot & \cdot \\ .41 & \cdot \\ (.17) & \end{bmatrix} B^4 - \begin{bmatrix} .20 & \cdot \\ (.06) & \cdot \end{bmatrix} B^6 \right.$$

$$- \begin{bmatrix} .35 & \cdot \\ (.07) & .66 \\ \cdot & (.05) \end{bmatrix} B^{12} \left) \begin{bmatrix} A \\ S \end{bmatrix}_t = \begin{bmatrix} 24846 \\ (39271) \\ 989517 \\ (196700) \end{bmatrix} + \left(\begin{bmatrix} 1 & 0 \\ 0 & 1 \end{bmatrix} \right.$$

$$- \begin{bmatrix} -.05 \\ (.02) \\ -.17 \\ (.07) \end{bmatrix} B - \begin{bmatrix} \cdot \\ .34 \\ (.07) \end{bmatrix} B^2 \right) \begin{bmatrix} \epsilon_1 \\ \epsilon_2 \end{bmatrix}_t,$$

$$(1 - .66B^{12})S_t = 989,517 + .41A_{t-4}$$
$$\phantom{(1 - .66B^{12})S_t =} (.05) \quad (196,700) \quad (.17)$$
(9)
$$+ (1 + .17B - .34B^2)\xi_t$$
$$ (.07) \quad (.07)$$

(standard errors are in parentheses)

The equation suggests that advertising lagged four months has an impact on current sales. Though this impact may represent the underlying behavioral relationship, we are skeptical and make two observations. First, the advertising-to-sales relationship, to the extent that it does exist, is relatively weak in that the lagged advertising variable is able to reduce the error variance of sales by 2.8% from that of the univariate sales equation of Corn Flakes. Second, there is a strong possibility that the significant four-month lag coefficient in Table 3 simply reflects sampling error and the process of considering so many cross-correlations. The four-month lag does not seem intuitively reasonable.

To investigate further the latter possibility, the data set was split into two halves and equation 9 was estimated for each half; only for the second half was the advertising coefficient significant. It was very small and insignificant for the first half of the data set. This finding suggests that, at the very least, the relationship was not present throughout the sample.

Conclusions

The net conclusion is that, with respect to the six cereal brands as represented by the described data, little relationship between advertising and sales is detectable. No discernible, intuitively plausible lag structure emerges across the brands or even for one of the brands by itself. Further, when the two causal tests were applied, the null hypothesis was rejected only for the sales-to-advertising direction for Rice Krispies and Life (only in the Pierce-Haugh test) and for the advertising-to-sales direction for Corn Flakes. The Corn Flakes relationship is found to be relatively small in terms of variance explained and does not appear in the first half of the data set.

Several explanations for these findings are possible. First, the problems with accounting data may have masked the relationships. Second, the causal-detection method could have low power and/or may be unable to detect certain types of relationships. Third, it is certainly possible for a structural model relating advertising and sales to give rise to a reduced form with "small coefficients." Modeling the underlying behavioral relationship between advertising and sales may be much more complicated than typically assumed and may involve constructs such as awareness and attitudes and the partitioning of the data into groups such as loyal and nonloyal buyers. Structural models based on the assumption that sales are influenced solely by advertising may simply be inadequate. Fourth, as Sims (1975) has noted, one can find a spurious causal ordering if one variable such as advertising is used to optimally stabilize another

variable such as sales. However, cereal manufacturers seem extremely unlikely to know how to utilize advertising to "control" sales in this fashion. Further, a pattern of negative correlations between lagged sales and current advertising which would be expected under the optimal stabilization scenario is not in evidence.

Another possibility is that the relationship between advertising and sales is indeed weak or nonexistent in this context. Such a conclusion is substantively most interesting but is not as unintuitive and unexpected as it might seem. An extensive review of empirical studies by Aaker and Carman (1981) reveals that findings of no significant advertising effects are not uncommon. Among the cited reasons is the probable "overadvertising" among advertisers of established brands and the difficulty of modeling the relationship.

APPLYING THE KOYCK MODEL

Even given the qualifications, the results discussed seem rather clear. An analyst might postulate a structural model, apply it to this same data base, and come to a very different conclusion. We suggest that the possibility of misspecification should be investigated. Further, if managerial recommendations were made on the basis of

Table 6
KOYCK DISTRIBUTED LAG MODEL

Brand		Advertising effect $b/1 - \lambda$
The model	$S_t = bA_t + \lambda S_{t-1} + \sum_{i=1}^{12} d_i D_i + \epsilon_t$	
Corn Flakes	$S_t = .17A_t + .23S_{t-1} + \sum_{i=1}^{12} d_i D_i + \epsilon_t$ $ (.88) \quad (3.14)$	.22
Special K	$S_t = .60A_t + .81S_{t-1} + \sum_{i=1}^{12} d_i D_i + \epsilon_t$ $ (2.83) \quad (18.69)$	3.16
Life	$S_t = .02A_t + .50S_{t-1} + \sum_{i=1}^{12} d_i D_i + \epsilon_t$ $ (.18) \quad (4.89)$	.04
Rice Krispies	$S_t = .66A_t + .84S_{t-1} + \sum_{i=1}^{12} d_i D_i + \epsilon_t$ $ (2.20) \quad (21.47)$	4.13
Alpha Bits	$S_t = .07A_t + .65S_{t-1} + \sum_{i=1}^{12} d_i D_i + \epsilon_t$ $ (.64) \quad (9.29)$	.20
Sugar Frosted Flakes	$S_t = .75A_t + .85S_{t-1} + \sum_{i=1}^{12} d_i D_i + \epsilon_t$ $ (2.80) \quad (21.73)$	5.00

where:

D_i are seasonal dummy variables,

$b/1 - \lambda$ is the total impact of an increase in advertising of $1 on sales, including both immediate (b) and carryover effects under the Koyck assumption that "goodwill" is generated solely by advertising.

The t-statistics are in parentheses.

the misspecified model, the outcome could be very damaging.

To illustrate, the Koyck distributed lag model represented in reduced form by equation 1 was applied to this data base. The results are shown in Table 6. Note that the 12 dummy variables serve to deseasonalize the data, a refinement often neglected in past published studies.

Consider the Koyck assumption that the lagged sales term is due solely to advertising carryover effects. Under that assumption, rather dramatic advertising effects are found for Special K, Rice Krispies, and Sugar Frosted Flakes, yet we can be fairly confident that the lagged advertising effect for these brands is very low. Note also that the lagged advertising effect for Corn Flakes, the only brand for which the hypothesis of no causal relationship from advertising to sales is rejected, is essentially zero.

Of course, in this context, even without observing the failure of the geometric lag to emerge in the cross-correlations and the results of the causality tests, we see clearly that the Koyck assumptions will not hold. Advertising is surely not the only cause of the lagged sales term. In this market, distribution, premium promotions, brand loyalty, and product characteristics will certainly be important influences.

The possibility remains that the model in Table 6 could be interpreted as a "partial adjustment model," in which the lagged sales term is due to brand loyalty and to the total marketing effort. The advertising effect is now limited to the coefficient of contemporaneous advertising, b, and lagged advertising effects are zero. A comparison of Table 3 and Table 6 leads to the following observations.

1. The Table 6 finding that, under the partial-adjustment assumption, there is a contemporaneous effect of advertising on sales for Special K and Sugar Frosted Flakes is compatible with the significant correlation at zero for the two brands in Table 6.
2. The fact that no contemporaneous effect of advertising on sales for Corn Flakes, Life, and Alpha Bits is found in the partial adjustment model is compatible with the Table 3 low correlations for the contemporaneous terms.
3. The Table 3 significant correlations at lags of four and five periods for Kellogg's Corn Flakes are not modeled in the partial-adjustment model and thus are not found.
4. The significant partial-adjustment-model contemporaneous advertising coefficient for Rice Krispies, for which there is no corresponding Table 3 significant contemporaneous correlation, is probably related to the fact that Rice Krispies is the one brand for which an indication of sales leading advertising was detected.

Analysis of residuals suggests the presence of serial correlation at various lags. This finding again suggests the Koyck models are misspecified. However, the misspecification is not as blatant as suggested by Granger and Newbold (1974) as the lagged sales term "soaks up" much of the autocorrelation. In fact, the misspecification is difficult to detect by using standard regression diagnostics, as the Durbin-Watson statistic checks only

for first-order serial correlation and is biased toward two in the presence of a lagged dependent variable.

Additional evidence is available that the structure of equation 1 represents a misspecification regardless of the interpretation of the lagged sales term. If a univariate advertising model of Table 2 is substituted into equation 1, the resulting structure should be similar to the corresponding Table 2 univariate sales model. Clearly such matches do not occur.

Given a structural model for the relationship between advertising and sales, we can stipulate what the reduced form should be. For example, for a Koyck model written as equation 10 and an advertising model of the form shown in equation 11,

$$(10) \qquad (1 - \phi_1 B)S_t = b_1 A_t + \xi_{1t}$$

$$(11) \qquad (1 - \phi_2 B)A_t = \xi_{2t}$$

one can determine what the univariate model for sales should look like. Multiplying equation 10 by $(1 - \phi_2 B)$ yields:

$$(12) \quad (1 - \phi_1 B)(1 - \phi_2 B)S_t = b(1 - \phi_2 B)A_t + (1 - \phi_2 B)\xi_{1t}.$$

Combining equations 11 and 12 and expanding yields:

$$(13) \qquad (1 - \phi_1^* B - \phi_2^* B^2)S_t = b_1 \xi_{2t} + (1 - \phi_2 B)\xi_{1t}.$$

If we ignore the seasonal components, equation 11 is not an unreasonable assumption based on the pattern of the data as reflected by Table 2. Equation 13 shows S_t having a second-order autoregressive representation and a moving average term that is the sum of zero and first-order moving average processes. Ansley, Spivey, and Wrobleski (1977) have shown that the sum of a finite moving average representation is a moving average of order less than or equal to the maximum of the orders of the individual moving average terms. Therefore, we can write equation 13 as:

$$(16) \qquad (1 - \phi_1^* B - \phi_2^* B^2)S_t = (1 - \theta_1^* B)\eta_t.$$

Thus, under the proposed model, sales should be represented as an ARMA (2, 1) model. The comparison is seen most sharply for Corn Flakes. If we ignore the seasonal components, under the Koyck hypothesis, the univariate model for Corn Flakes sales should be of this form. The fact that the representation in Table 2 is different seems to cast doubt on the Koyck structural model.

SUMMARY

A time series analysis was conducted for six cereal brands. The analysis proceeded on the assumption that feedback was potentially present, but the relationship was found to be extremely weak. No lag structures are evident. In fact, the hypothesis test of no causal relationship cannot be rejected except in the advertising-influencing-sales direction for Corn Flakes and in the sales-influencing-advertising direction for Rice Krispies.

The danger of applying a misspecified structural model is shown by estimating the Koyck distributed lag model with the data base. Our conclusion is that in situations where lag structure is important, the *a priori* assumption of a particular structure—e.g., geometric—in a structural model analysis can produce grossly misleading results. A superior procedure may be to conduct a time series analysis first, to obtain some insight into lag structure, and then to test a reasonable, theory-based structural model.

REFERENCES

Aaker, David A. and James M. Carman (1981), "Are You Overadvertising?" working paper, University of California, Berkeley (February).

Akaike, H. (1976), "Canonical Correlation Analysis of Time Series and the Use of an Information Criterion," in *System Identification: Advances and Case Studies*, R. K. Mehra and D. G. Lainotis, eds. New York: Academic Press.

Ansley, C. F., W. A. Spivey, and W. Wrobleski (1977), "On the Structure of Moving Average Processes," *Journal of Econometrics*, 6 (July), 121–34.

Bass, Frank M. and D. G. Clarke (1972), "Testing Distributed Lag Models of Advertising Effect," *Journal of Marketing Research*, 9 (August), 298–308.

——— and Thomas L. Pilon (1980), "A Stochastic Brand Choice Framework for Econometric Modeling of Time Series Market Share Behavior," *Journal of Marketing Research*, 17 (November), 486–97.

Box, G. E. P. and G. M. Jenkins (1976), *Time Series Analysis, Forecasting, and Control*. San Francisco: Holden Day.

Bultez, Alain V. and Phillipe A. Naert (1979), "Does Lag Structure Really Matter in Optimizing Advertising Expenditures?" *Management Science*, 25 (May), 454–65.

Clarke, D. G. (1976), "Econometric Measurement of the Duration of Advertising Effect on Sales," *Journal of Marketing Research*, 13 (November), 345–57.

——— (1977), "Cumulative Advertising Effects: Sources and Implications," Marketing Science Institute Report 77-111 (September).

——— and John M. McCann (1973), "Measuring the Cumulative Effects of Advertising: A Reappraisal," in *Proceedings*, Thomas V. Greer, ed. Chicago: American Marketing Association.

Davies, N., C. M. Triggs, and P. Newbold (1977), "Significance Levels of the Box-Pierce Portmanteau Statistic in Final Samples," *Biometrika*, 64 (December), 517–22.

Durbin, J. (1970), "Testing for Serial Correlation in Least-Squares Regression When Some of the Regressors Are Lagged Dependent Variables," *Econometrica*, 38 (May), 410–21.

Granger, C. W. J. (1969), "Investigating Causal Relations by Econometric Models and Cross-Spectral Methods," *Econometrica*, 37 (July), 424–38.

——— and P. Newbold (1974), "Spurious Regressions in Econometrics," *Journal of Econometrics*, 2 (July), 111–20.

——— and ——— (1977), *Forecasting Economic Time Series*. New York: Academic Press.

Griliches, Zvi (1976), "Distributed Lags: A Survey," *Econometrica*, 35 (January), 16–49.

Hanssens, Dominique M. (1980), "Bivariate Time-Series Analysis of the Relationship Between Sales and Advertis-

ing," *Applied Economics*, 12, 329–39.

Haugh, L. D. (1972), "The Identification of Time Series Interrelationships with Special Reference to Dynamic Regression," unpublished doctoral dissertation, Department of Statistics, University of Wisconsin–Madison.

Helmers, Richard M. and J. K. Johansson (1977), "An Exposition of the Box-Jenkins Transfer Function Analysis with an Application to the Advertising-Sales Relationship," *Journal of Marketing Research*, 14 (May), 227–39.

Houston, Franklin S. and Doyle L. Weiss (1975), "Cumulative Advertising Effects: The Role of Serial Correlation," *Decision Sciences*, 6 (July), 471–88.

Koyck, L. M. (1974), *Distributed Lags and Investment Analysis*. Amsterdam: North Holland Publishing Company.

Lambin, J. J., P. A. Naert, and A. Bultez (1975), "Optimal Marketing Behavior in Oligopoly," *European Economic Review*, 6 (April), 105–28.

Ljung, G. M. and G. E. P. Box (1978), "On a Measure of Lack of Fit in Time Series Models," *Biometrika*, 65 (August), 297–303.

Mann, D. H. (1975), "Optimal Theoretic Advertising Stock Models: A Generalization Incorporating the Effects of Delayed Response from Promotional Expenditures," *Management Science*, 21 (March), 823–32.

McGuire, Timothy W., D. L. Weiss, and F. S. Houston (1977), "Consistent Multiplicative Market Share Models," in *Proceedings of the American Marketing Association*. Chicago: American Marketing Association, 129–34.

Montgomery, David B. and Alvin J. Silk (1972), "Estimating Dynamic Effects of Market Communication Expenditures," *Management Science*, 18 (June), B485–B502.

Picconi, Mario J. and Charles L. Olson (1978), "Advertising Decision Rules in a Multibrand Environment: Optimal Control Theory and Evidence," *Journal of Marketing Research*, 15 (February), 87–92.

Pierce, D. A. and L. D. Haugh (1977), "Causality in Temporal Systems: Characterizations and Survey," *Journal of Econometrics*, 5 (May), 265–93.

Schmelensee, Richard R. (1972), *The Economics of Advertising*. Amsterdam: North Holland Publishing Company.

Sethi, S. P. (1979), "A Survey of Management Science Applications of the Deterministic Maximum Principle," in *Applied Optimal Control*, TIMS Studies in Management Science, 9. Amsterdam: North Holland Publishing Company, 33–68.

Sims, C. A. (1972), "Money, Income, and Causality," *American Economic Review*, 62 (September), 540–52.

——— (1977a), "Comment on Pierce's Paper," *Journal of the American Statistical Association*, 72 (March), 23–4.

——— (1977b), "Exogeneity and the Causal Ordering in Macroeconomic Variables," in *New Methods in Business Cycle Research: Proceedings from a Conference*, Federal Reserve Bank of Minneapolis, 23–44.

——— (1980), "Macroeconomics and Reality," *Econometrica*, 48 (January), 1–48.

Tiao, G. C. and G. E. P. Box (1979), "An Introduction to Applied Multiple Time Series Analysis," Technical Report No. 582, Department of Statistics, University of Wisconsin–Madison.

Ward, Ronald W. (1976), "Measuring Advertising Decay," *Journal of Advertising Research*, 16 (August), 37–41.

Weiss, Doyle L., Franklin S. Houston, and Pierre M. Windal (1978), "The Periodic Pain of Lydia E. Pinkham," *Journal of Business*, 51, 91–101.

Sales Effects of Two Campaign Themes

PETER L. HENDERSON, JAMES F. HIND and SIDNEY E. BROWN

U.S. Department of Agriculture

Advertising is only one of many factors influencing purchase. Here is an experiment which took the most significant factors into account and permitted a sales comparison of the themes employed.

SOUND PLANNING AND CONTROL of advertising requires improved measurement of advertising effectiveness.

PETER L. HENDERSON heads the Development Analysis Section, Market Development Branch, Marketing Economics Division, U. S. Department of Agriculture. He has served on the staffs of the University of Georgia, Cornell University, and Virginia Polytechnic Institute, where he taught and conducted research in marketing. He has authored and co-authored various research reports on the merchandising and promotion of fruit. He received a Ph.D. from Cornell in 1952; for his dissertation he adapted the double change-over experimental design for use in marketing research. This application, reported as "Special Promotional Programs for Apples —Their Effects on Sales of Apples and Other Fruit" by the USDA in January 1961, forms the basis for this article.

JAMES F. HIND received a B.S. in 1954 and an M.S. in 1958 from the University of Tennessee where he studied marketing and applied statistics. An agricultural economist in the USDA's Market Development Branch, he has used experimental designs in advertising research to evaluate the sales effectiveness of the promotion of agricultural products. He belongs to the American Marketing Association and the American Statistical Association.

The purpose of this study was to evaluate the sales effectiveness of a specific promotional campaign. While the research techniques and statistical analyses were developed by physical scientists, the adaptation of these methods to advertising research has resulted in improved measurement of advertising effectiveness.

The basic experimental design and analysis was employed in the biological sciences as early as 1911 (Cochran et al., 1941). It was later adapted and applied to problems in market research by Henderson (1952) as cited by Federer (1955) and in *Wood Chips* (1959).

A recent article published in this *Journal* discussed the theory and concept of an experimental design as applied to a specific problem in advertising research (Jessen, 1961). A mathematical model

SIDNEY E. BROWN has a B.A. (1953) in liberal arts from the University of Richmond and an M.S. (1955) in agricultural economics from Virginia Polytechnic Institute. A member of the American Farm Economics Association, he has sought to develop more effective ways of reporting movement of products into consumption. Like Mr. Hind, he has been an agricultural economist at the USDA since 1958 and co-author of several of its publications.

2

FIGURE 1
USE-THEME DISPLAY
"MAKE A WONDERFUL WALDORF
SALAD TONIGHT"

FIGURE 2
HEALTH-THEME DISPLAY
"KEEP 'EM HEALTHY"

of market simulation was described and computations made on simulated data. This paper reports the use of this design in a refined and extended form with real market data. It also discusses an entirely new technique for evaluating the effects of price, display allocation and customer traffic on the sales of advertised products.

The study was done in cooperation with the Washington State Apple Commission. During past years the Commission had developed a promotional program employing two advertising themes. One stressed the various uses of apples (fruit combination salads, baked apples, other dishes), while the other emphasized the healthful qualities of apples (builds strong bodies, dental benefits, etc.). Supermarket displays using these themes are shown in Figures 1 and 2 above.

The objectives of the study were to determine:

1. the over-all sales effectiveness of the promotional program relative to no promotion;

2. the relative sales effectiveness of the two promotional themes;

3. the short-time residual or carry-over effects, if any, of each theme;

4. the effects of the promotional activities for Washington apples on sales of apples from competing areas, and other selected fruits; and

5. the influence on sales of apples and other fruits of various merchandising and advertising practices (e.g., price cuts, display space and newspaper advertising) employed by stores to promote apples and other selected fruits.

TABLE 1

EXTRA-PERIOD LATIN SQUARE CHANGE-OVER EXPERIMENTAL
DESIGN USED IN APPLE ADVERTISING STUDY OF 72
SUPERMARKETS IN SIX MIDWESTERN CITIES

Four-week time periods	Sequence (cities)					
	Square I			Square II		
	City 1	City 2	City 3	City 4	City 5	City 6
1	A	B	C	A	B	C
2	B	C	A	C	A	B
3	C	A	B	B	C	A
4	C	A	B	B	C	A

Treatment A = General health theme; Treatment B = Apple use theme; Treatment C = No advertising and promotion (control group). For a discussion of the concepts underlying analysis of variance in general, and of Latin square designs in particular, please see page 40.

METHOD

Experimental Design

Items tested, called treatments, included: an apple use advertising and promotional theme, a general health advertising and promotional theme and a control with no advertising or promotion. The control treatment was used to provide a basis for comparison. The experimental design to evaluate treatment effects was an extra-period double change-over design (see Table 1). Designs of this type are sometimes referred to as switch-back, switch-over or cross-over designs.

The basic design (three time periods) consists of two replications of orthogonal Latin squares in which the sequence of treatments is reversed in the two squares. This design makes it possible to obtain estimates of direct and subsequent one-period carry-over effects of each treatment as well as the combined (direct plus carry-over) effects of each treatment with sustained use. The fourth time period, in which the treatments in the previous period are repeated, increases the precision of estimation of carry-over effects, which in turn results in greater accuracy for the estimates of the combined effects.

Treatments were assigned to successive four-week time periods (rows) and cities (columns). Since each treatment occurred once in each row and column within a basic square, systematic errors resulting from constant variations among time periods and cities were equalized.

The mathematical model which forms the basis for the analysis is:

$$Y_{ijkt} = \bar{Y} + S_i + C_{ij} + P_{ik} + D_t + R_{t(k-1)} + e_{ijk}$$

where:

Y_{ijkt} = observed sales for the jth city in the ith square during the kth period;

$\bar{Y}$ = over-all average sales of apples for all treatments and time periods;

S_i = effect of the square;

C_{ij} = effect of the city;

P_{ik} = effect of the period in that square;

D_t = direct effect of treatment;

$R_{t(k-1)}$ = the carry-over (residual) effect of the immediately preceding treatment, and;

e_{ijk} = experimental error.

This is the analysis of variance model, and its underlying assumptions must be reasonably met for it to be properly employed in experimental research. These assumptions are reviewed elsewhere (Eisenhart, 1947). It is sufficient to note two basic assumptions: that constants in the model can be estimated without entanglement with each other, that is, they are additive; and that the experimental errors are independently and normally distributed.

Sample

Six midwestern cities, ranging in population from 100,000 to 150,000 and relatively free of sustained and intensive promotional campaigns for apples, were selected for the test. These cities were roughly comparable in major economic characteristics and supply considerations and overlapping of

,heir local newspaper and television facilities was negligible.

Twelve self-service food stores were selected in each city to represent establishments of different sizes, different types of management and ownership (chain voluntary chains and nonaffiliated independents), and different geographical areas of the city. Trade sources estimated that the panel stores in each city accounted for approximately 50 to 80 per cent of retail food sales.

Intensity of promotion for the two promotional test themes (apple use and general health) featuring Washington State apples was as nearly equal as possible. Promotion included sponsored television programs Wednesday and Friday of each week and special tie-in advertising by retailers in media they normally used. During nonpromotional periods, retailers co-operated by following their normal merchandising and promotional practices for apples in the absence of a promotional campaign by a commodity group. To insure reliable measurement of advertising themes, sample stores were asked to maintain: comparable apple displays for both test promotional themes; approximately equal store-sponsored promotion of apples by each test theme (special displays and features in newspaper ads); and comparable competition from selected fruits for each test theme in price, display area and feature advertising.

Weekly tonnage sales data for Washington State apples, apples from other areas, oranges, grapefruit and bananas were collected from each store by the standard audit method:

(Beginning inventory + weekly receipts) − (ending inventory + transfers + withdrawals + spoilage) = sales.

Additional data collected for each store on a weekly basis included total dollar sales in the produce department, and the amount of newspaper advertising by retailers for apples and selected fruits. Supplemental information on merchandising practices employed by the stores, such as prices and amount of display area for apples and other fruits, and the use of point-of-sale materials and special displays was collected by observation on Monday and Friday each week.

Analysis of Variance

Analysis of variance was used to separate the variations in sales of each fruit studied (Washington State apples, all apples, oranges, grapefruit and bananas) that were attributable to cities, time periods, direct effects, carry-over effects and experi-

mental error. For illustration, the subdivision of the sum of squares for these attributes will be shown only for sales of all apples; the subdivision of sums of squares is similar for each fruit.

In the analysis of variance, only the partitioning of the sum of squares for direct and carry-over effects of treatments require special consideration. The conventional computations for the sums of squares for the other factors stratified in the experimental design and experimental error are given in textbooks on experimental design (Federer, 1955; Lucas, 1957).

Following the notation of Table 1, the sums of squares for the direct effects of treatments is given as:

$$\frac{1}{mn(n+1)(n+2)} \left\{ \left[(n+1)(\Sigma A) - (\underline{C_2} + \underline{C_3}) - G.T. \right]^2 + \left[(n+1)(\Sigma B) - (\underline{C_3} + \underline{C_1}) - G.T. \right]^2 + \left[(n+1)(\Sigma C) - (\underline{C_1} + \underline{C_3}) - G.T. \right]^2 \right\}$$

with m being the number of squares (two), n the common number of rows, columns and treatments (three) in a square of the basic three time-period design, and G.T., the grand total of all observations.

Obviously, since no treatments involving promotion preceded those applied in the first time period, there are no carry-over effects of treatments in the first period. Thus, in computing the sum of squared deviations associated with carry-over effects, the numerical calculations should not include the data generated in the first period. The sum of squares for carry-over effects is computed as follows:

$$\frac{1}{mn} \left[(B_{12} + A_{24} + B_{33} + C_{42} + C_{33} + A_{64})^2 + (C_{13} + C_{23} + B_{34} + B_{44} + A_{52} + A_{63})^2 + (C_{14} + A_{23} + A_{32} + B_{43} + C_{54} + B_{62})^2 \right]$$

$$- \frac{1}{mn^2} (G.T. - \text{total period 1})^2$$

where the first subscript for each letter indicates the city and the second subscript indicates the time period.

The treatments designed in the first set of parentheses represent all treatments immediately following treatment A in cities one through six; similarly, treatments in the second parentheses represent those following treatment B, etc.

The complete partitioning of degrees of freedom and sums of squares for total apple sales (sales of apples from all areas combined) are given in Table

2. Carry-over effects in the analysis of total apple sales did not approach statistical significance. Thus, the degrees of freedom and sums of squares associated with the carry-over effect were subsequently pooled in the error term as shown in a later table.

TABLE 2
ANALYSIS OF VARIANCE, TOTAL APPLE SALES IN POUNDS

Source of variation	Degrees of freedom	Sums of squares	Mean square	F
Squares	1	2,417,070,246	2,417,070,246	55.83*
Periods within squares	6	2,437,012,149	406,168,692	9.38*
Between periods	(3)	(2,422,596,446)	(807,532,149)	18.65*
Periods x squares	(3)	(14,415,703)	(4,805,234)	0.11
Cities within squares	4	1,613,017,480	403,254,371	9.32*
Direct effect treatments	2	492,948,044	246,474,022	5.69†
Carry-over effect treatments	2	7,062,739	3,531,370	.08
Error	8	346,325,670	43,290,709	—
Total	23	7,313,436,328	—	—

Under certain experimental conditions, the statistician might argue to pool the sums of squares and degrees of freedom for period x squares interaction (when insignificant) in the error term. However, when to pool and when not to pool is controversial and may tend to inflate the significance of treatment effects as in this case. Thus, for conservative estimates of treatment effects, this was not done.
* Significant at the .01 probability level.
† Significant at the .05 probability level.

When significant carry-over effects are present, the following computational procedures are employed for estimating the direct and carry-over effect of each treatment.

Estimates of the direct effect per treatment, $\overline{D}_a \ \overline{D}_b \ \overline{D}_c$ are:

$$\overline{D}_a = \overline{Y} + \frac{1}{mn(n+2)}\left[n + 1 \ (\Sigma \ A) - (\underline{C}_2 + \underline{C}_3) - G.T.\right]$$

$$\overline{D}_b = \overline{Y} + \frac{1}{mn(n+2)}\left[n + 1 \ (\Sigma \ B) - (\underline{C}_3 + \underline{C}_4) - G.T.\right]$$

$$\overline{D}_c = \overline{Y} + \frac{1}{mn(n+2)}\left[n + 1 \ (\Sigma \ C) - (\underline{C}_1 + \underline{C}_2) - G.T.\right]$$

Estimates of carry-over effects per treatment, $\overline{R}_a, \ \overline{R}_b, \ \overline{R}_c$, are:

$$\overline{R}_a = \frac{1}{mn^2}\left[n(B_{12} + A_{24} + B_{33} + C_{42} + C_{53} + A_{64}) \right.$$
$$\left. - (G.T. - Total \ period \ 1)\right]$$

$$\overline{R}_b = \frac{1}{mn^2}\left[n(C_{13} + C_{22} + B_{34} + B_{44} + A_{52} + A_{63}) \right.$$
$$\left. - (G.T. - Total \ period \ 1)\right]$$

$$\overline{R}_c = \frac{1}{mn^2}\left[n(C_{14} + A_{23} + A_{32} + B_{43} + C_{54} + B_{62}) \right.$$
$$\left. - (G.T. - Total \ period \ 1)\right]$$

with symbols defined as before.

The estimate of the combined and direct carry-over of a particular treatment is the sum of the means of the direct and carry-over effects for that treatment, $\overline{D}_t + \overline{R}_t$, computed by the preceding formulae. Since advertising investment is usually spread over a sustained period of time, the combined direct and carry-over effects of treatments would appear to provide better estimates of treatment differences than direct effects alone (i.e., when carry-over effects are significant).

For treatment contrasts, the standard error of a difference for direct, carry-over, and combined (direct plus carry-over) effects is given respectively as the square root of:

$$\frac{2(n+1)}{mn \ (n+2)} \ S^2, \ \frac{2}{mn} \ S^2, \ and \ \frac{2(2n+3)}{mn \ (n+2)} \ S^2$$

where S^2 is the error mean square obtained in the analysis and m and n are as defined previously.

In the illustrative study, only the direct effects of treatments are considered, since carry-over effects were negligible. Estimates of direct effects of treatments, and the accompanying sample statistics, are given in Table 3 at this stage of the analyses (i.e., before covariance analysis).

TABLE 3
TREATMENT MEANS AND SAMPLE STATISTICS BEFORE AND AFTER COVARIANCE ANALYSIS[1]

Item	Before covariance analysis — Direct effect $(\overline{D}_t)$	After covariance analysis — Direct effect $(\overline{D}_t)$
Treatment means: (Direct effects)		
Apple use theme	75,461	77,267
General health theme	71,575	69,722
No advertising or promotion	64,176	64,222
Sample statistics:		
Standard deviation[2]	5,945	5,333
Coefficient of variation (%)[2]	8.4	7.6
Standard error of a difference[3]	3,070	2,751

[1] Treatment means are expressed as average sales per city per four-week time period.
[2] Based on pooled degrees of freedom and sums of squares for carry-over effects in the experimental error.
[3] Between two treatment means.

Analysis of Covariance

The sales data for Washington State apples and all apples were also adjusted for nonconstant sources of variation in sales that were not taken into account by the experimental design. These included variation in weather conditions among cities within one periods. The store's total dollar sales in the produce department were used in covariance analysis as an index of number of customers and purchasing power of customers in making adjustments. Produce sales did not completely satisfy the requirements of a concomitant observation, because produce sales and apple sales were not independent of each other since produce sales are affected to some extent by apple sales. However, apple sales contribute a relatively small percentage of the store's total produce sales. This was the best index for which data were available to reflect customer traffic and purchasing power.

The covariance correction for the regression of sales of all apples on total produce sales increased the precision of the findings because results were then based upon a constant number of customers and customer purchasing power in each city during each treatment. A brief description of the mathematical computations follows.

The analysis of sums of squares of produce sales, and the sums of products of produce sales and the sales of apples, is analogous to the analysis of variance previously described. The only difference is that in computing the cross products corresponding values of produce and apple sales are multiplied instead of squared in each stage of computation.

If Y_{ijkt} is defined as before and X_{ijkt} is the corresponding concomitant observation for produce sales and b is the constant multiplier for the deviations of the concomitant variable from its over-all mean, the previous analysis of variance model takes the form:

$$Y_{ijkt} = \overline{Y} + S_i + C_{ij} + P_{ik} + D_t + D_{t(k-1)} +$$

$b\,(X_{ijkt} - \overline{X}) + e_{ijk}$, with the symbols as defined before and $\overline{X}$ the over-all mean of produce sales.

The effects of the regression of produce sales (X) are removed from the sums of squares for error and direct effects treatment + error of apple sales (Y) by using the respective sums of squares for X and corresponding cross products (XY) shown in Table 4 in the formula:

$$S_Y^2 - (S_{XY})^2/S_X^2$$

A degree of freedom is associated with regression and subtracted from degrees of freedom for error and treatment + error. The sum of squares of direct effect treatments, adjusted for produce sales, are then obtained by subtracting the corrected sum of squares for error from the corrected sum of squares for treatment + error. Degrees of freedom for treatments are similarly obtained. The complete computations can be followed in Table 4. A more detailed description of the standard computations involved are given in *Biometrics* (Cochran, 1957).

Adjusted treatment means are computed by: $\overline{D}_t - b\,(\overline{X}_t - \overline{X}_{ijk})$ where $\overline{D}_t$ is the mean apple sales of the tth treatment, $\overline{X}_t$ is the corresponding mean for produce sales and $\overline{X}_{ijk}$ is the over-all mean of produce sales. The adjustment factor or regression coefficient b is given by the formula, $b = \dfrac{S_{XY}}{S_X^2}$ where S_{XY} and S_X^2 are the error sums of cross products (of X and Y) and the error sum of squares (for X) respectively, as shown in Table 4.

Adjusted treatment means, and other sample statistics computed before and after the covariance analysis are shown in Table 3. The increase in accuracy due to covariance analysis is demonstrated by the ten per cent reduction in the size of the

TABLE 4

ANALYSIS OF COVARIANCE, TOTAL APPLE SALES IN POUNDS (Y), PRODUCE SALES IN DOLLARS (X)

| Source of variation | Degrees of freedom | Sum of squares and products | | | Error of estimate[1] | | |
		S_{X^2}	S_{XY}	S_{Y^2}	Sum of squares	Degrees of freedom	Mean square
Direct effects of treatments	2	36,021,777	42,438,284	492,948,044	—	—	—
Error[2]	10	69,926,512	—82,535,043	353,388,409	255,971,376	9	28,441,264
Treatments + error	12	105,948,289	—40,096,759	846,336,453	831,161,596	11	—
Adjusted for produce sales	—	—	—	—	575,190,220	2	287,595,110[3]

[1] Sum of Squares for error: $S_{Y^2} - \dfrac{(S_{XY})^2}{S_{X^2}} = 353,388,409 - \dfrac{(-82,535,043)^2}{69,926,512} = 255,971,376$

Sum of Squares for treatments + error: $S_{Y^2} - \dfrac{(S_{XY})^2}{S_{X^2}} = 846,336,453 - \dfrac{(-40,096,759)^2}{105,948,289} = 831,161,596$

[2] Carry-over effects are insignificant and are pooled in error terms.
[3] This treatment mean square with two degrees of freedom tested against error mean square with nine degrees of freedom is significant at the .005 per cent probability level.

standard error of a difference. The use of the concomitant variable in the covariance analysis had almost the same effect as an additional Latin square in reducing the size of the difference between two treatment means which would be statistically significant. That is, at least one more replication of the four-period Latin square design would be required to attain the same precision in detecting significant differences if covariance were not used.

The F test was used to determine if differences in sales among the three treatment means were statistically significant. The least significant difference (LSD) test was used to determine significance between any two treatment means. These tests will not be discussed in detail, since they are commonly used methods (Cochran, 1957). It should be noted, however, that a prerequisite to using the LSD test is the finding of significant differences among treatments by the F test.

Multiple Covariance Analysis

An extension of the covariance technique discussed previously was used to determine the nature and extent of the influence of retail merchandising practices and pricing policies on sales of apples (Washington State and other areas), oranges, grapefruit and bananas. Merchandising factors evaluated were price, display space and newspaper advertisement space. Produce sales, as before, were used to reflect number of customers and relative purchasing power of customers. These merchandising factors are referred to hereafter as quantitative factors. It was not possible to measure the direct effects on sales of such nonquantitative factors as variety, size and quality of fruits, size of pricing unit, type of display (prepackaged, bulk or combination) and packaging material.

Data for quantitative factors were tabulated for each city by weeks and plotted on scatter diagrams against sales of each fruit. Thus, a general indication was obtained of the factors related to volume of sales of each fruit. Factors which had no apparent relation to sales were eliminated.

Arithmetical computations in multiple covariance analysis are most laborious and complex. Ostle (1954) reviews them briefly. It would be quite boring and rather lengthy to discuss and illustrate the many iterative computations involved. These analyses are better explained by symbolizing a basic regression model and then following with some discussion of the adaptations and extensions of this basic model as used in the study.

The basic regression model is:

$$Y = \mu + b_1x_1 + b_2x_2 + \ldots + b_nx_n + e$$

where Y is the sales observation in a city during any week for a particular fruit, μ the over-all mean and b_1, b_2 ... b_n regression coefficients, estimates of the effects of the x_1, x_2 ... x_n selected quantitative factors. The residual e is made up of city-time period and treatment effects, and random or experimental error. The regression model assumes that such quantitative factors as price, display area and newspaper advertisement space for the particular fruit remain constant between cities and four-week time periods. That is, none of the variation in sales is due to the influence of other variables associated with city and time period differences such as income levels, population characteristics and seasonal trends. This is highly unrealistic, since the influence of such variables vary considerably between cities and over time.

However, by combining the concepts of regression and analysis of variance, a more discriminating analysis can be made in which place and season effects are removed. This technique, covariance analysis, permits the measurement of the net effects of these specified quantitative factors on sales. The analysis of variance model is:

$$Y_{ij} = \mu + P_i + C_j + e_{ij}$$

where Y_{ij} and μ are defined as before, P_i and C_j, the city and time period respectively. In this model the residual e_{ij} consists of the effects of the quantitative factors $b_1x_1 + b_2x_2 + \ldots b_nx_n$ and the random noncompensating errors of measurement. Combining the regression and analysis of variance models we have the covariance model:

$$Y_{ij} = \mu + P_i + C_j + b_1x_1 + b_2x_2 + \ldots b_nx_n + z_{ij}$$

where z_{ij} represents the random and noncompensating errors and the effects of the unidentified factors. This model, unlike the previously stated regression model, defines and accounts for the effects of city and seasonal differences. Thus, the estimates of the effects b_1, b_2 ... b_n of the quantitative factors x_1, x_2, ... x_n on sales are free of the place and season effects.

Based on the covariance model, a multiple analysis of covariance was first used to adjust the sales variation for each fruit for the variations associated with cities and time periods. A multiple regression analysis was then made of the adjusted data (i.e., the residual sums of squares and cross products) to identify and quantify the net effects of the merchandising factors significantly affecting sales. The

8

TABLE 5

MULTIPLE COVARIANCE ANALYSIS

Source of variation	Degrees of freedom	Sums of squares	Mean squares	F[1]
Total	863	412,284,650	—	—
Nonquantitative factors:				
Cities and time periods	17	129,383,870	7,610,816	44.8
Residual 1	816	282,900,780	334,398	—
Quantitative factors:[2]				
Display space for Washington State apples	1	48,705,457	48,705,457	286.6
Produce sales[3]	1	41,561,786	41,561,786	244.5
Display space for other apples	1	4,861,877	4,861,877	28.6
Price of Washington State apples	1	3,630,474	3,630,474	21.4
Display space for grapefruit	1	2,558,838	2,558,838	15.1
Newspaper advertisement space for Washington State apples	1	2,113,867	2,113,867	12.4
Joint effects of above factors (interactions)	4	36,697,381	—	—
Residual 2	840	142,771,100	169,996	—

[1] All significant at the 0.01 per cent probability level.
[2] Quantitative factors adjusted for effects of each other and nonquantitative factors of cities and time periods.
[3] Used as an index to reflect changes in the number of customers patronizing the store and changes in the relative purchasing power of customers.
[4] Degrees of freedom entangled with residual degrees of freedom.

multiple regression analysis was repeated until only those factors affecting sales remained which attained statistical significance at the 0.05 probability level. The practical utility of a factor based upon the magnitude of its regression coefficient (b value) and coefficient of determination (R^2) was also a criterion for retaining it in subsequent analysis. The complete analysis for Washington State apple sales is shown in Table 5.

RESULTS

There were substantial differences in sales of both Washington State and all apples between pe-

riods with promotional themes (apple use and health) and periods of no promotion (see Table 6).

When sales of apples were combined, the apple use theme was significantly more effective in promoting sales than the health theme. However, the nine per cent sales difference between the two themes for Washington State apples was not large enough to be statistically significant.

The themes used in the four-week test period significantly affected neither Washington State nor total apple sales during the next four-week period without advertising.

TABLE 6

SALES OF APPLES FROM WASHINGTON STATE AND OTHER AREAS DURING NO APPLE PROMOTION AND TWO APPLE PROMOTIONAL THEMES[1]

Source of apples	Average sales per store per four-week period			Difference in sales between no promotion and—[2]					
	With no promotion	With apple-use theme	With health theme	Apple-use theme		Health theme		Apple-use theme and health theme	
	Lb.	Lb.	Lb.	Lb.	%	Lb.	%	Lb.	%
Washington State	3,124	4,117	3,784	993**	31.8	660*	21.2	333	8.8
Other areas (Midwestern and Eastern States and Canada)	2,227	2,322	2,026	95	4.3	—201	—9.1	295	14.6
Total or average	5,351	6,439	5,810	1,088***	20.1	459*	8.6	629**	10.8

[1] All sales data were adjusted for variations among treatments (themes and no promotions) which might be attributed to differences in number of customers and purchasing power per customer. While there were price reductions associated with weekly specials featured by retailers, average prices (weighted by sales) did not differ significantly among treatments.
[2] Differences required for statistical significance for apples from Washington State and from other areas are ± 735 pounds at the five per cent probability level**; ± 596 pounds at the 10 per cent probability level*. Differences required for statistical significance for apples from all areas combined are ± 748 pounds at the one per cent probability level***; ± 520 pounds at the five per cent probability level**; and ± 422 pounds at the 10 per cent probability level*.
The economic implication of these probability levels is that the chances or odds of obtaining sales differences of these magnitudes are less than 1, 5 or 10 in 100 from random sales flucuations and non-constant experimental errors.

TABLE 7

SALES OF SELECTED FRUITS DURING NO APPLE PROMOTION AND TWO APPLE PROMOTIONS[1]

Fruit	Average sales per store per four-week period			Difference in sales between no promotion and—[2]	
	With no promotion	With apple use theme	With health theme	Apple use theme	Health theme
	Lb.	Lb.	Lb.	%	%
Oranges	5,516	5,680	5,784	3.0	4.9
Grapefruit	5,272	5,156	5,996	—2.2	13.7
Bananas	5,944	5,836	5,752	—1.8	—3.2
Total	16,732	16,672	17,532	—0.4	4.0

[1] All sales data were adjusted for variations among advertising treatments which might be attributed to differences in number of customers and purchasing power per customer. Sales data were further adjusted for the effects of prices, display space, and other significant merchandising and promotional practices employed by stores. The regression coefficients obtained in the multiple regression analysis were used in adjusting means. Computations are similar to those made in obtaining the adjusted means in the covariance analysis.

[2] Differences required for statistical significance at the five per cent probability level are ± 10.8 per cent for oranges; ± 17.5 per cent for grapefruit; and ± 10.0 per cent for bananas. Differences required for statistical significance at the 10 per cent probability level are ± 8.7 per cent for oranges; ± 14.2 per cent for grapefruit; and ± 8.1 per cent for bananas.

Advertising Washington State apples exerted only a minor influence on sales of oranges, grapefruit and bananas. The effect of the advertising seemed to vary among the fruits depending on the theme employed. The sales differences were too small to determine whether the promotional themes for apples significantly improved the sales of these fruits or not. The differences that were found corresponded to findings of previous research studies, namely, that advertising and merchandising practices which increase sales of apples also benefit sales of oranges, as suggested by the data in Table 7. Also, the decrease in sales of bananas when either apple theme was advertised compared to no promotion was similar to findings of previous studies which have indicated that apples and bananas are competitive products (Henderson, 1952, 1955, 1955).

Changes in sales of apples, oranges, grapefruit, and bananas were significantly related to changes in some but not all of the practices employed by stores in merchandising and promoting these fruits, such as amount of display area, newspaper advertising, and prices (see Table 8).

Sales of each fruit were generally affected by the merchandising and promotional practices used with it. The major exception was the amount of display space devoted to each fruit, which affected the fruit displayed and also had some influence on other fruits. Variation in the amount of display space used for grapefruit affected all fruit except bananas. Grapefruit sales varied directly with the amount of space in grapefruit displays, while sales of apples and oranges varied inversely with the amount of space for grapefruit displays. Banana sales increased and orange sales decreased when the size of banana displays was increased. Similarly, a decrease in ba-

nana sales and an increase in orange sales were associated with a decrease in the amount of space devoted to banana displays. These findings indicate that grapefruit competes with apples and oranges for display space and sales, while bananas compete with oranges for display space and sales.

Price and display space devoted to each fruit exerted the most influence on sales. Sales for each fruit varied directly with the amount of display space and inversely with price. The variation in sales of each fruit from week-to-week was also generally related to the week-to-week variation in amount of newspaper advertising space devoted to each fruit by retailers.

Sales of each fruit were significantly and directly related to the volume of produce sales. Produce sales reflect the combined effects of promotional and merchandising practices employed by stores on the sales of individual products, and the influence of such practices in drawing additional customers into the stores.

OTHER APPLICATIONS

While the notation and terminology used refer to this specific experiment, the design and analyses presented would be valid in other areas of advertising research where measurable carry-over effects of promotional techniques are likely to occur. Some general applications are given in the following illustrations.

This experimental design could be used to predict the most efficient promotional alternatives from consumer or trade media advertising, personal selling, point-of-purchase effort, cooperative advertising and premium offers, and to determine the place of each in the total promotional effort for a

TABLE 8

MERCHANDISING AND PROMOTIONAL PRACTICES WHICH SIGNIFICANTLY AFFECTED
SALES OF WASHINGTON STATE APPLES, APPLES FROM OTHER AREAS, AND OTHER SELECTED FRUITS

Factors significantly affecting sales of—[1]

Factors	Washington State apples	Other apples[2]	Oranges	Grapefruit	Bananas
Promotive sales (dollars)	+ 0.3	+ 0.3	+ 0.7	+ 0.8	+ 0.7
Price (cents per pound)					
Washington State apples	−25.9	—	—	—	—
Other apples	—	− 8.8	—	—	—
Oranges	—	—	−93.9	—	—
Grapefruit	—	—	—	−122.1	—
Bananas	—	—	—	—	−86.6
Display space: (square feet)					
Washington State apples	+21.8	− 8.4	—	—	—
Other apples	− 6.8	+25.8	—	—	—
Oranges	—	—	+16.2	—	—
Grapefruit	− 4.8	− 6.4	− 7.3	+ 10.7	—
Bananas	—	—	−14.9	—	+15.6
Newspaper advertising space: (square inches)					
Washington State apples	+ 5.0	—	—	—	—
Oranges	—	—	+ 6.5	+ 8.5	—
Grapefruit	—	—	—	—	—
Bananas	—	—	—	—	+19.6

[1] A plus sign indicates that a positive change (increase) in the value of a factor is accompanied by an increase in sales of a fruit and a negative change by decrease in sales. For example, on the average, an increase of one square foot in the display space for Washington State apples was accompanied by an increase of 21.8 pounds in Washington apple sales. A negative sign signifies that a positive change in the factor results in decreases in Washington apple sales and a negative change (decrease) in the factor results in an increase in Washington apple sales. Thus, on the average an increase of one cent a pound in the price of Washington apples resulted in a decrease of 25.9 pounds in sales of Washington apples.
[2] Apples from areas other than Washington State.

product. At the same time, holding promotional expenditures relatively constant for each technique tested, promotional outlay could be related to sales returns. Using a more complicated arrangement of this design, the optimum levels of promotional outlay under different conditions could also be found.

With these alternative uses of the design the multiple covariance technique could be used to obtain estimates of sales responses (for a product sold at retail) to changes in prices, display space and other merchandising practices employed by retail stores. This information could be used in deciding what combination of price and merchandising practices will tend to maximize returns from advertising and promotional activities. The covariance technique could also determine relationships between sales of a product and such factors as price of the product, price of related or competing products, and consumers' incomes, in order to forecast sales in a market from measurements on a sample. The estimated parameters for such quantitative variables could be applied to other market areas with similar socio-economic characteristics, since these estimates would be corrected for place and season effects.

REFERENCES

COCHRAN, W. G. et al. A Double Change-over Design for Dairy Cattle Feeding Experiments. *Journal of Dairy Science*, Vol. 24, No. 11, November 1941, pp. 937-951.

COCHRAN, W. G. Analysis of Covariance: Its Nature and Uses. *Biometrics*, Vol. 13, No. 3, September 1957, pp. 268-269.

COCHRAN, W. G. *Experimental Designs.* Second Edition. New York: John Wiley & Sons, Inc., 1957, p. 76.

EISENHART, CHURCHILL. The Assumptions Underlying the Analysis of Variance. *Biometrics*, Vol. 3, No. 1, March 1947, pp. 1-21.

FEDERER, WALTER T. *Experimental Design.* New York: The Macmillan Company, 1955, pp. 148-149 and 449-452.

HENDERSON, PETER L. Application of the Double Change-over Design to Measure Carryover Effects of Treatments in Controlled Experiments. *Methods of Research in Marketing. Paper No. 3.* Ithaca: Cornell University, 1952.

HENDERSON, PETER L. *Marketing Services Affecting Apple Sales.* Unpublished Ph.D. Dissertation. Ithaca: Cornell University Library, 1952.

HENDERSON, PETER L. Merchandising Apples. *Virginia Fruit.* Virginia Horticultural Society, Vol. 42, May, 1955, pp. 34-36.

HENDERSON, PETER L. The Effect of Advertising and Point of Sale Aids on Apples. *Virginia Fruit*, Vol. 42, June 1955, pp. 30-34.

JESSEN, RAYMOND J. A Switch-over Experimental Design to Measure Advertising Effect. *Journal of Advertising Research*, Vol. 1, No. 3, March 1961, pp. 15-22.

LUCAS, H. L. Extra-period Latin Square Change-over Design. *Journal of Dairy Science*, Vol. 40, No. 3, March 1957, pp. 225-239.

OSTLE, BERNARD. *Statistics in Research.* Ames: The Iowa State College Press, 1954, pp. 406-408.

WOOD RESEARCH CORPORATION. The Experimental Method in Marketing Research. Philadelphia: *Wood Chips.* February 1959.

Test Marketing Cookware
Coated with "Teflon"[1]

JAMES C. BECKNELL, JR. AND ROBERT W. MCISAAC

E. I. du Pont de Nemours & Company

Du Pont TV commercials expanded the
total cookware market 21 per cent, and
doubled purchases of the type advertised.

BEGINNING in early 1962, sales of cookware coated
with a "Teflon" finish followed a pattern characteristic of fad products. The early sales activity
involved frying pans, most of them imported from

JAMES C. BECKNELL, JR. is a
research psychologist in the Advertising Research Section of E. I.
du Pont de Nemours & Company.
He has worked for R. H. Macy as
an assistant buyer, and for the
A. J. Wood Research Corporation
as a project director. He received
a B.S. in economics from the University of Pennsylvania in 1952,
an M.A. in psychology from the
University of Arkansas in 1957,
and has done further graduate
work in psychology at the University of Pennsylvania. He is a
member of the American Psychological Association, the American Statistical Association, and other professional groups.

ROBERT W. McISAAC is a research associate in the Advertising
Research Section of the Du Pont
Company. He received his A.B.
degree in economics and statistics
in 1958 from Syracuse University.
Previously he was a statistician
for the Economics Department of
Mutual Federation of Independent Cooperatives, Inc., Syracuse,
New York. His main vocational
interests have been in the fields of
marketing and advertising research, in both the consumer and
industrial areas. He is Du Pont's
representative to the Federal Statistics Users' Conference.

France and Italy. The introduction came at a time
when the controversy over saturated versus non-
saturated fats and their relation to cholesterol
counts was getting a great deal of publicity. The
low friction coefficient of the "Teflon" finish eliminated the need for using any fat to prevent food
from sticking to the pan. This attribute was promoted as a health aid. Du Pont was not involved in
consumer promotion for the cookware but the Du
Pont name and the trademark "Teflon" were both
heavily used by retailers and manufacturers in their
promotions.

The cookware used as a base for coating was of
a lower gauge and poorer quality aluminum than
the American housewife was accustomed to. All too
often the "Teflon" finish was poorly applied and
would peel or scratch off the pan. More and more
cookware of inferior quality reached the U.S. market. The scare over fats began to wane and the
limited market of those persons worried over high
cholesterol became saturated with frypans coated
with "Teflon". Sales dropped and returns to retailers of the inferior cookware that had given unsatisfactory service increased drastically. Retailers
were caught with large inventories of low quality
pans. By midsummer 1962, the only sales of cook-

[1] Du Pont's registered trademark for its TFE fluorocarbon
resin finish.

ware coated with "Teflon" were at distress prices. Naturally, retailers were not anxious to reorder. It appeared at this point that cookware coated with a "Teflon" finish was all but dead.

Meanwhile, the Du Pont Fabrics & Finishes Department had developed an improved "Teflon" finish in several colors and a new method of application which virtually eliminated the peeling problem. Thus the technical problems were pretty well overcome and a truly satisfactory product was now possible, but the market had disappeared.

Under these market conditions manufacturers showed very little interest in producing cookware of this type. If a market were to be developed for cookware coated with "Teflon", it would clearly have to be done by Du Pont.

Marketing Strategy

Industrial Finishes Sales and Advertising personnel developed a marketing and advertising strategy which consisted of four major ingredients:

1. Standards of finishing were set that would insure quality coatings of "Teflon". The use of a Du Pont "Seal of Approval" was offered under license to manufacturers who met the standards.

2. A consumer advertising campaign was created that promoted the ideas of "easy cleanup" and the quality of cookware items bearing the Du Pont "Seal of Approval." /

3. A heavy public relations program on "Teflon" was initiated that made use of "The Marketing Group" and a barrage of news releases in each of the test markets.

4. An experimental test marketing of the product at three different levels of advertising during each test period was designed.

The program was presented to cookware manufacturers for their consideration. Some domestic manufacturers agreed to come in on the program and produce and market some cookware coated with "Teflon". The test marketing program was set up in accord with the methodology outlined below.

METHOD

The test marketing-advertising experiment was designed to discover whether or not the market for non-stick cookware could be resurrected with the improved product and a television consumer advertising program. If so, what level of advertising would be necessary to move the product in significant quantities?

The basic design called for 13 cities to receive three levels of television advertising during the fall 1962 product introduction (Table 1).

TABLE 1
FALL 1962 PRODUCT ADVERTISING

10 Daytime Commercial Minutes Per Week	5 Daytime Commercial Minutes Per Week	No Ads
Detroit	Dayton	Wichita
Springfield	St. Louis	Philadelphia
Columbus	Bangor	Grand Rapids
Omaha	Youngstown	Rochester
	Pittsburgh	

A cross-over experimental design was employed so that if there were any continuing effect from the fall television advertising it could be detected. Therefore in the winter the same cities received the levels of advertising shown in Table 2.

TABLE 2
WINTER 1963 PRODUCT ADVERTISING

7 Daytime Commercial Minutes Per Week	3 Daytime Commercial Minutes Per Week	No Ads
Detroit	Columbus	Omaha
Springfield	St. Louis	Pittsburgh
Dayton	Bangor	Philadelphia
Wichita	Youngstown	Grand Rapids
	Rochester	

Combining the fall and winter advertising treatments we have a full factorial experimental design. An experiment of this type is very efficient in that it permits the testing of several strategies at the same time under controlled conditions, getting not just information on the effect of each advertising level, but on the combined effect of all sequences of levels (Table 3).

TABLE 3
EXPERIMENTAL DESIGN
Fall 1962

Winter 1963	10 Daytime Ads Per Week	5 Daytime Ads Per Week	No Ads
7 Daytime Ads Per Week	Detroit Springfield	Dayton	Wichita
3 Daytime Ads Per Week	Columbus	St. Louis Bangor Youngstown	Rochester
No Ads	Omaha	Pittsburgh	Philadelphia Grand Rapids

The major research measurement of sales during each test period was a wave of telephone interviews conducted with samples of 1,000 female heads of households in each of the test markets. The samples were drawn randomly from the phone book on a no-callback basis.

An extensive audit of stores was planned but had to be curtailed because of the inability of the research supplier to gain the cooperation of heavily trafficked stores in many of the test markets.

The first wave of interviews was conducted in the first week of January, 1963, the second wave between April 12 and 16, 1963. All interviewing was done by National Certified Interviews of Chicago.

The questionnaire asked the housewife questions in the following areas:

1. Had she acquired cookware in the past three months?

2. What type of cookware: Glassware? Metalware?

3. What kind of cookware? Frypans? Saucepans? Cookie sheets? (etc.), and how many of each?

4. Was any of the cookware she obtained of the non-stick variety, and if yes, which ones? What was the name of the material that made that item non-stick?

5. What was the name of the store where the cookware was purchased?

6. What type of store did she consider it to be?

During preliminary analysis of the data from the first wave, the proportion of respondents who didn't know the name of the non-stick material was higher than anticipated. Therefore respondents who claimed to have purchased non-stick items but did not know the name of the material that made them non-stick were telephoned again and asked, "Does the inside finish of the (name of item) look and feel the same as the finish on the outside of the pan, or is the finish on the inside of the pan different from the finish on the outside?" Cookware reported to be different was assumed to be "Teflon". This modification was incorporated into the questionnaire for the winter test so that it would cover all types of non-stick cookware.

General Market Information

This report covers the research conducted during the fall of 1962 and the winter of 1963. The study generated the following market information.

During the fall (including Christmas) 15 per cent of the female heads of households acquired some new cookware, either through their own purchases or as a gift. This figure dropped to nine per cent during the winter (January through March). The average number of items acquired per thousand female heads of households dropped in approximately the same ratio from 360.8 in the fall to 246.8 in the winter.

If the assumption is made that half the year's purchases of cookware occurred during the six-month period studied, the data indicate that approximately 30 per cent of the annual purchases of cookware occur in the fall and 20 per cent occur in the winter. These figures match housewares sales reports by department stores (Department Store Trade, 1963).

An average of 2.4 units of cookware were acquired in the fall versus 2.7 units in the winter. About 70 per cent of the cookware obtained was reported to be metalware. The remaining 30 per cent was either glassware or some form of ceramic. Table 4 shows the types of cookware obtained and the relative amounts.

TABLE 4

COOKWARE ITEMS PER 1,000 FEMALE HEADS OF HOUSEHOLDS—WINTER 1963

| | Number per 1,000 | | | |
	Metal	Glass & Ceramic	Total	Per Cent of Grand Total
Sauce pans	73.8	17.0	90.8	36.8
Frying pans, Skillets	44.3	6.5	50.8	20.6
Casserole dishes	3.3	37.1	40.4	16.4
Cake pans, Pie plates	11.3	4.7	16.0	6.5
Loaf pans, Roasters, Dutch ovens	12.9	3.1	16.0	6.5
Cookie sheets	8.3	—	8.3	3.4
Muffin tins	6.1	—	6.1	2.5
Griddles, grilles	3.2	—	3.2	1.3
All other	9.4	5.7	15.1	6.1
Total	172.6	74.1	246.8 =	100.0

Test Marketing Problems

The test marketing program had its problems; these are stated here so they may be kept in mind when looking at the results. Some of the problems created nonmeasurable biases in the results.

The chief problem was in distribution or product availability. Distribution was spotty during the fall introduction and improved slightly during the winter months. Shipments of merchandise fell behind orders from retailers and created out-of-stock situations in markets where sales were strongest. We are therefore unable to predict accurately how well cookware coated with "Teflon" would sell if it were readily available. This study should be viewed as indicating what can be expected if introductory marketing conditions at the national level are similar to those encountered by the introduction of the product into the test markets last fall and winter.

A lesser problem was the loss of one of our control study markets (Rochester, New York) because of a heavy cookware advertising campaign run during the fall by a local retailer.

As they became aware that a test marketing program with an improved product was under way, retailers in all the test markets tried to sell off as much of their inventories of distress merchandise as they possibly could. This may have had the effect of inflating sales of skillets and griddles coated with "Teflon" by some unknown quantity. When the introduction of the improved cookware into the test markets started, it became evident that the Du Pont advertising program for cookware coated with "Teflon" had to accomplish the following marketing tasks:

1. It had to convince the cookware manufacturers that the new improved cookware coated with "Teflon" would sell in quantities large enough to go into more than limited production.

2. It had to overcome and reverse a growing prejudice against "Teflon" in the retail trade.

3. It had to move enough of the low quality merchandise that retailers had in inventory to persuade them to order the new merchandise.

4. It had to sell housewives on the notion that "Teflon" had a place in cookware other than frypans and that the product had benefits other than fat-free frying.

These tasks could not be accomplished until the commercials were actually being run in the test markets, since cookware manufacturers and retailers who had had experience with cookware coated with "Teflon" adopted a "let's wait and see what happens" attitude. Limited quantities of cookware coated with "Teflon", other than skillets and griddles, were produced and shipped to retailers during the early part of the test program. This makes the fall data of limited interest, so most of the emphasis will be placed on the results of the research done for the winter 1963 phase of the program. In terms of sales the "low level of advertising" did no better than the "no advertising level," so the data generated in the "no advertising" and the "low advertising" markets are combined to give a more substantial basis for the averages.

RESULTS

We were principally interested in answering two questions:

1. Could we increase the total size of the cookware market?

2. Could we sell more cookware items coated with "Teflon", either through increased market size or increased share of market for "Teflon"?

In Table 5, for fall 1962 we see that 1) the total market was increased by the high advertising level from 317 units to 404 units per thousand persons, an increase of 27 per cent; 2) the number of units of "Teflon" sold per thousand women more than doubled, 16 units to 38 units; 3) the "Teflon" market share almost doubled, going from five to nine per cent of total cookware; 4) in the low advertising condition almost all "Teflon" sales were restricted to skillets and griddles, whereas in the high advertising condition approximately 25 per cent of the sales were items other than these.

TABLE 5

COOKWARE UNITS PER 1,000 FEMALE HEADS OF HOUSEHOLDS

	Fall 1962		Winter 1963	
	High Adver- tising	Low or No Adver- tising	High Adver- tising	Low or No Adver- tising
Total Units (all types)	404	317	268	221
Units coated with "Teflon" (all types)	38	16	59	27
Skillets and griddles coated with "Teflon"	28	16	27	13
"Teflon" Market Share	9%	5%	22%	12%

Table 5 also shows the results for winter 1963. Here again we see 1) a significant increase in the total number of cookware units sold in the markets with high advertising compared to the markets with low or no advertising (221 up to 268), an increase of 21 per cent; 2) more than double the number of "Teflon" units sold per thousand women, up from 27 to 59. Again the ratio of skillets and griddles coated with "Teflon" was lower in the high advertising cities than in the low or no advertising cities; however, significantly some nonskillet and griddle material was moving in the low advertising cities by this time.

Possibly the most meaningful comparison in Table 5 is between fall 1962 and winter 1963, where the trend of sales for the items coated with "Teflon" can be seen.

By the time the second phase of the test marketing program was completed, distribution was improving and back orders decreasing as production and shipments to retailers increased. Although sales of cookware in total fell off seasonally during the first quarter of the year, the sales pattern within the quarter varied according to the advertising treatment being imposed during the winter.

Table 6 shows the interaction or "carry-over" effect of the fall advertising on the winter sales, as well as the effect of the winter advertising on the winter sales. The data in Table 6 are for all cookware; two unexpected outcomes were observed. In cities which received high advertising in the winter of 1963 but little or no advertising in the fall of 1962, the market expansion was greater than in cities where the advertising had been maintained at a constant high level. Also, in areas with a high level of fall 1962 advertising but where the advertising had been reduced or cut out in the winter of 1963, the total market size actually fell below the market size in areas where practically no advertising effort had been exerted.

TABLE 6

TOTAL COOKWARE UNITS PER 1,000 FEMALE HEADS OF HOUSEHOLDS—WINTER 1963

Winter Advertising Treatment	Fall Advertising Treatment		Average Winter Purchases
	High	Low or No	
High	255	282	268
Low or No	205	229	221

We may be reasonably certain that the market expansion in both the fall and winter was a real phenomenon caused by the advertising for cookware coated with "Teflon". The chance of observing differences as large as these is less than 5 in 100 (chi square = 4.3).

This market expansion may be only temporary. When the data are looked at in terms of both the fall and the winter advertising treatments, it appears that the high level of advertising probably borrows future sales. Purchases were highest, 282 per thousand, in markets that had been exposed to low or no advertising in the fall and a high level during the winter. Purchases were lowest, 205 per thousand, in the group of markets that were exposed to a high level in the fall, followed by low or no advertising in the winter.

The cookware market logically breaks into two segments, metal cookware and glass cookware. Tables 7 and 8 show what happened to the total market size for each of these segments of the market. Obviously, only sales of metal cookware were affected by the advertising for "Teflon".

The difference (52) between the groups exposed to the winter high level and low or no advertising represents an expansion of approximately 36 per cent. The gross difference is statistically significant (chi square = 8, p < .005). However, there is again strong evidence that it may be only a temporary expansion if advertising pressure is not maintained. We cannot predict how long this expansion will last even *with* advertising pressure.

TABLE 7

NUMBER OF METAL COOKWARE ITEMS OBTAINED IN PAST THREE MONTHS PER 1,000 FEMALE HEADS OF HOUSEHOLDS—WINTER 1963

Winter Advertising Treatment	Fall Advertising Treatment		Average Winter Purchases
	High	Low or No	
High	185	205	195
Low or No	128	148	143

The advertising did not seem to have any effect on the glassware market in total (see Table 8). A negative difference of four units per thousand housewives occurred on the average. This difference is not statistically significant (chi square = 0.11).

TABLE 8

NUMBER OF GLASSWARE ITEMS OBTAINED IN PAST THREE MONTHS PER 1,000 FEMALE HEADS OF HOUSEHOLDS—WINTER 1963

Winter Advertising Treatment	Fall Advertising Treatment		Average Winter Purchases
	High	Low or No	
High	70	78	74
Low or No	78	78	78

It appears that the Du Pont advertising had a considerable effect on the cookware market but that up to now this effect has been to expand total metal cookware sales without having any expansion effect on total glassware sales. Expanding the total market is of interest to cookware manufacturers but Du Pont's profit comes through sales of "Teflon" coated items alone.

Purchases of cookware coated with "Teflon" in the winter high advertising group are more than double purchases in the winter low or no advertising group (Table 5). This difference is statistically significant (chi square = 11.9). The data in Table 9 also indicate that there was a definite "carry-over sales effect" from the fall advertising at the high advertising level.

TABLE 9

NUMBER OF COOKWARE ITEMS COATED WITH "TEFLON" OBTAINED PER 1,000 FEMALE HEADS OF HOUSEHOLDS—WINTER 1963

Winter Advertising Treatment	Fall Advertising Treatment		Average Winter Purchases
	High	Low or No	
High	70	49	59
Low or No	32	25	27

Purchases in the group of markets exposed to a high level of advertising during both the fall and the winter test periods were almost three times purchases in the group of markets where little or no advertising was done during either test period.

The data in Table 9 show a strong interaction in a positive direction where the advertising was maintained at a high level, and again there appears to be a negative effect in the subsequent period when a high level of advertising of this product is followed by nothing. A regression line was fitted to these data, taking into account the amounts of advertising in the fall of 1962 and in the winter of 1963, and the interaction between them. The empirically derived equation is:

Unit sales of cookware coated with "Teflon" $= 30.76 - 1.24$ (fall advertising) $+ .90$ (winter advertising) $+ .57$ (winter advertising) $\times$ (fall advertising)

The multiple correlation is .64, which means we can explain 40 per cent of the unit sales of cookware coated with "Teflon" by Du Pont national advertising alone.

Metalware accounted for most of the purchases of cookware coated with "Teflon" (see Table 10). Purchases of metal cookware coated with "Teflon" in the group of markets exposed to a high level of advertising in the winter were more than double purchases of the group of markets exposed to little or no advertising in the winter (51 vs. 24 units per thousand female heads of households).

TABLE 10

METAL COOKWARE ITEMS COATED WITH "TEFLON" PER 1,000 FEMALE HEADS OF HOUSEHOLDS—WINTER 1963

| Winter Advertising Treatment | Fall Advertising Treatment | | Average Winter Purchases |
	High	Low or No	
High	65	38	51
Low or No	28	22	24

Again a "carry-over effect" from the fall advertising is evident. Purchases were significantly higher (chi square $= 7.7$) in the group of markets exposed to a high level of advertising in both test periods than they were in the group of markets exposed to the high level of advertising only in the winter.

Few purchases of glassware coated with "Teflon" were reported (see Table 11). The difference in average purchases between the advertising levels is not large enough to be statistically significant but the direction of the difference is consistent with the rest of the results, so we can at least suspect that the winter advertising did have a positive effect on purchases of glassware coated with "Teflon".

Although market share figures are of less interest in markets with proved elasticity of demand, they still offer a perspective not found in gross unit figures (see Table 12). The average market share

TABLE 11

AVERAGE GLASSWARE ITEMS COATED WITH "TEFLON" OBTAINED PER 1,000 FEMALE HEADS OF HOUSEHOLDS—WINTER 1963

| Winter Advertising Treatment | Fall Advertising Treatment | | Average Winter Purchases |
	High	Low or No	
High	5	10	7.5
Low or No	4	2	2.5

for all the markets exposed to a high level of advertising in the winter phase was 10 percentage points (or 1.8 times) higher than the average for markets not exposed to advertising in the winter. The effect is even more graphic when the "Teflon" market share in markets exposed to high levels of advertising during both the fall and winter phases of the study (27 per cent) is compared to the market share in markets exposed to very little or no advertising in either period (11 per cent). Again the "carry-over effect" from the fall advertising is evident, indicating that the advertising does help build market share.

TABLE 12

SHARE OF TOTAL PURCHASES FOR COOKWARE COATED WITH "TEFLON"—WINTER 1963

| Winter Advertising Treatment | Fall Advertising Treatment | | Share of Average Purchases, Winter Advertising Treatment |
| | High | Low or No | |
	%	%	%
High	27	17	22
Low or No	16	11	12

The same pattern is evident for metal cookware coated with "Teflon" alone, as seen in Table 13. Cookware coated with "Teflon" achieved a market share of 26 per cent on the average in markets exposed to a high level of winter advertising versus a 16 per cent average market share in markets with little or no winter advertising. When the average market share for the markets exposed to advertising in both seasons is compared with the group of markets exposed to little or no advertising in either season, we find a difference of 20 market share points. The difference between the group of markets exposed to high advertising in the fall and winter and the group exposed to a high level in the winter

TABLE 13

METAL COOKWARE COATED WITH "TEFLON" SHARE OF METALWARE MARKET—WINTER 1963

| Winter Advertising Treatment | Fall Advertising Treatment | | "Teflon" Share of Average Purchases, Winter Advertising Treatment |
| | High | Low or No | |
	%	%	%
High	35	18	26
Low or No	21	15	16

only is 17 market share points. This again indicates the presence of a "carry-over effect" from the fall promotion. It should be remembered that this increase in market share came in markets where market expansion took place as well.

As shown in Table 14, glassware coated with "Teflon" achieved a higher share (12 per cent) of the glassware market in markets exposed to the high level of advertising in the winter than in markets exposed to little or no "Teflon" advertising (5 per cent). There appears not to have been any "carry-over effect" on glassware sales from the fall advertising. Distribution was poor for glassware coated with "Teflon" and this may in large measure account for its poor showing.

TABLE 14

GLASSWARE COATED WITH "TEFLON" SHARE OF
GLASSWARE MARKET—WINTER 1963

Winter Advertising Treatment	Fall Advertising Treatment		"Teflon" Share of Average Purchases, Winter Advertising Treatment
	High %	Low or No %	%
High	11	13	12
Low or No	5	4	5

SUMMARY

The Du Pont advertising of cookware coated with "Teflon" worked at the high level but had no discernible effect at the lower levels, both in fall 1962 and winter 1963. The advertising and promotional efforts expanded the total cookware market by about 21 per cent. This expansion came almost entirely through expanded purchases of metalware. There is some evidence that this market expansion comes through a borrowing of future sales unless the advertising pressure is maintained.

The successful advertising strategy more than doubled purchases of cookware coated with "Teflon". Purchases went from 27 units in markets exposed to low or no advertising to 59 units per thousand female heads of households. A "carry-over effect" from the fall advertising occurred at the high level of advertising, i.e., purchases were significantly higher in markets exposed to a high level of advertising in both fall and winter than they were in markets exposed to a high level of advertising in either the fall or winter tests alone.

These differences account for both market expansion and gains in market share for cookware coated with "Teflon". There is strong evidence of an advertising "carry-over effect" from season to season in terms of building market share.

In markets with no Du Pont television advertising for "Teflon", cookware coated with "Teflon" accounted for about 11 per cent of the market. In markets with only one season of advertising, the market share reached about 16 per cent, and where advertising was run for two seasons "Teflon" market share reached 27 per cent. It should be remembered that the increase in market share for cookware coated with "Teflon" occurred in markets where an expansion in cookware sales also occurred.

Most of the gains for cookware coated with "Teflon" were in the metalware segment of the market. Gains in the glassware coated with "Teflon" share of the market also occurred in those markets exposed to a high level of advertising, but they were spotty and may be a result of the differences in the distribution. There is no evidence of an advertising "carry-over effect" in the market share data for glassware coated with "Teflon".

CONCLUSIONS AND RECOMMENDATIONS

The market for cookware coated with "Teflon" has been brought to life with an improved product and a $1,000,000 level of advertising. This is particularly true of the metal cookware coated with "Teflon". The glassware market does not seem to respond nearly as well to the advertising program as the metalware does. This may be a result of poor distribution or a basic problem with the product itself.

The national introduction of the product in the fall will require at least ten daytime TV spots a week during the fall season and seven or more spots during the winter or the equivalent season, if a profitable level of sales is to be achieved.

Continued measurements should be made in Detroit, Springfield, Omaha, and Columbus, since these markets will be one year ahead of the national market this fall. They should be watched closely because the cookware coated with "Teflon" market could very well expand rapidly, only to contract rapidly soon afterwards. These markets, being one year ahead of the rest of the country, would warn of this and give Du Pont Fabrics & Finishes Department management and "Teflon" customers time to modify their marketing strategy appropriately.

REFERENCE

Department Store Trade, United States. *Distribution of Annual Sales by Month for 1962.* Issued by the Board of the Federal Reserve System, May, 1963. Code: C.7.3.1.

Advertising Research at Anheuser-Busch, Inc. (1963-68)*

Russell L. Ackoff, University of Pennsylvania
James R. Emshoff, University of Pennsylvania

This is the first part of a two-article series in which Professors Ackoff and Emshoff describe almost eleven years of management science research and implementation in the marketing area of Anheuser-Busch, Inc. From their unique vantage point the authors illuminate the process by which issues of experiment design and theory validation must be tempered by pragmatic considerations of cost and risk to the company involved. Further, they demonstrate a contingency approach to implementation which stresses the continuous education and involvement of the managers concerned. In this first article the authors describe their early work concerning the total amount of money to be spent on advertising, the distribution of advertising across time and the relative and absolute effectiveness of different media. Their second article, to be published in the Spring issue of the *Review*, will describe ongoing work in message evaluation and the modelling of consumer behavior. *Ed.*

The association with Anheuser-Busch, Inc. (A-B) that is described here began in 1959. Over the last fifteen years research has been carried out on almost every aspect of A-B's operations and planning. The company's view of this association has appeared in several articles.[1] *Business Week* and *Fortune*[2] have described aspects of this work and some of the theoretical output has also appeared.[3] This article, however, is the first case study to be published. It provides an account of a sequence of investigations involving advertising of the company's principal product, BUDWEISER beer.

Background

A-B's original contact was made by E. H. Vogel, Jr., then manager of business planning. Work over the first few years was devoted to determining when new breweries would be required, where they should be located, and what size they should be. Facility plans were developed to cover a ten-year period. Capital requirements for these facilities were estimated and a financial model

---

* The authors acknowledge the major roles of Drs. Eli S. Marks and Maurice Sasieni in the work reported in this article.
    1 See Busch [2] and Vogel [6].
    2 See "Computers Can't Solve Everything" [3], "Wharton Analyzes the Beer Drinker" [8] and "While Big Brewers Quaff, the Little Ones Thirst" [9].
    3 See Ackoff and Emery [1], Curtis [4], and Rao [5].

1

of the firm was developed and used to predict capital availability. The model showed that not quite enough capital would have been available to finance the building program without increasing the company's traditional debt to debt-equity ratio. Research then turned to ways of making more capital available when needed.

Production operations involving scheduling and allocation of demand to breweries already had been studied and modified to yield much of the potential savings. Marketing, which involved a major share of the company's expenditures, had not yet been analyzed. An initial examination into this area revealed that the largest category of marketing cost involved advertising. Therefore, in 1961 we first recommended research into it. The proposal was turned down because of the widespread satisfaction with the company's advertising. Responsible managers were unwilling to evaluate and modify a successful program. Research turned instead to distribution and inventories.

Advertising Expenditures

Just before mid 1961 August A. Busch, Jr., then president and chairman of the board, asked us if we would evaluate an advertising decision he was about to make. In that year BUDWEISER was budgeted to receive about $15,000,000 worth of advertising. Mr. Busch had been approached by the vice president of marketing with a request for an additional $1,200,000 to be spent on advertising in twelve of the 198 areas into which the company divided its national market. The vice president had defended his proposal on the basis of the projected increase in sales that he believed would result. Mr. Busch explained that he was confronted with such a proposal every year and that he always had accepted it. He intended to do the same again, but he asked, "Is there any way I can find out at the end of the year whether I got what I paid for?" We said we would think about it and make some suggestions.

The proposal we presented to Mr. Busch shortly thereafter consisted of allowing the Marketing Department to select any six of the twelve areas initially proposed and giving it $600,000 for additional advertising. The remaining six areas would not be touched and would be used as controls. This biased selection procedure was intended to overcome some of the opposition that the Marketing Department felt toward any effort to evaluate its proposal.

Earlier we had developed an equation for forecasting monthly sales in each market area. Our plan now was to measure the deviation of actual monthly sales from the forecast for each market area in the test. Using the statistical characteristics of the forecasts we estimated that we had a 95 percent chance of detecting a 4 percent increase in sales in the areas with additional advertising. Since the increase predicted by the Marketing Department was in excess of this amount, Mr. Busch authorized the test and it was initiated.

The test was conducted over the last six months of 1961 yielding 72

(12 × 6) observations. The analysis of these data failed to reveal a significant difference between the test and control areas. Nevertheless, the control areas did better on average than was forecast. Therefore, we assumed that all the sales above those forecasted were attributable to the increased advertising and evaluated the results accordingly. Even under this assumption the increased amount of advertising was *not* justified by the deliberately overestimated increase in sales attributed to it.

Encouraged by these results, Mr. Busch asked us to design research directed at determining what amount should be spent on advertising. However, he wanted to proceed with caution, because he believed that much of the success of BUDWEISER, which was leading the beer market with a share of 8.14 percent in 1962, was due to its quality and the effectiveness with which this was communicated through its advertising. When we suggested research involving experimentation with market areas he authorized use of fifteen such areas provided they did not include any of the company's major markets.

Constrained in this way we sought an experimental design that would maximize learning about advertising expenditures. Our design effort was guided by two methodological principles. First, we knew that the company advertised for only one reason: *to increase sales*. Therefore, we were determined to measure the effect of advertising *on sales* and not on more easily measured intervening variables such as recall of messages or attitudes toward the product. For this reason we decided to continue to use deviations of actual from forecast sales as the variable to be observed. This allowed us to cancel out much of the effect on sales due to factors other than advertising. Accordingly, efforts to improve forecasting of monthly market-area sales were continuous.

Secondly, we were committed to an attempt to *explain* the causal effect of advertising on consumer purchases and not merely to find statistical correlations between them. Our search of the marketing literature for such an explanation was futile; it only revealed correlations and regressions between advertising and sales. These usually showed that increases (or decreases) in the former were associated with increases (or decreases) in the latter. From such associations it was almost universally inferred, and incorrectly, that increases in advertising yield increases in sales almost without limit. We believed that what these analyses really showed was that most companies forecast next year's sales quite accurately and then set their advertising budgets as a fixed percentage of predicted sales. In other words, forecasts of increased sales produce increased advertising.

Our commitment to experimentation derived from a determination to find a causal connection between advertising and sales, not merely an association between them, and to develop an ability to manipulate advertising so as to produce desired effects on sales that could be observed.

Since we knew of no tested theory, we fabricated our own. Our hunch was that advertising could be considered to be a stimulus and sales a response to it. Much is known about the general nature of stimulus-response functions. They usually take the form shown in Figure 1. Therefore, we formulated the following hypotheses:

> A small amount of advertising has virtually no effect on sales but as the amount is increased it pushes the response through a *threshold* after which it produces an increasing effect. This effect decreases and flattens out once the respondents are *saturated;* that is, they either turn off further exposure to the stimulus or are consuming up to their capabilities or capacities. Response to further increases in advertising remains relatively unchanged until the respondents reach *supersaturation,* a point beyond which they respond negatively.

In an earlier study conducted for the Lamp Division of the General Electric Company[4] we had found such a relationship between frequency of sales calls (stimulus) and purchases (response). In the sales-call context the idea of supersaturation is not as shocking as it is in advertising. Clearly, there is an amount of a salesman's presence that is intolerable to a buyer. Beyond this one would expect the buyer to try to get rid of the salesman by discontinuing his purchases. Similarly, we felt reasonably sure that, for example, if all television advertising were for only one product, the public would react negatively.

---

[4] See Waid, Clark and Ackoff [7].

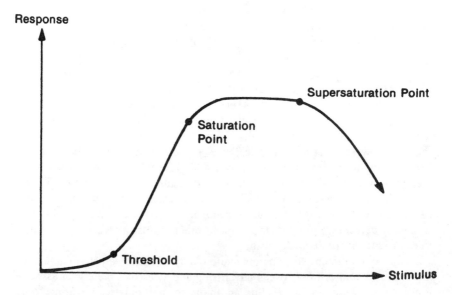

Figure 1   A Typical Stimulus-Response Function

The First Experiment

A minimal experiment would have involved applying the same percentage change in advertising expenditure to each of the fifteen market areas allotted to us and comparing the results obtained from them with those obtained from an equal number of control areas. But we needed only nine areas to obtain the level of accuracy set as our target: to be able to detect a 2 percent difference in sales 95 percent of the time. The introduction of two different treatments, one involving an increase and the other a decrease in advertising expenditures, required eighteen test areas, three more than were available to us. However, even an experiment with two different treatments would yield only three points: the average effect of each treatment and that of the control group. The difficulty this presented derived from the fact that every configuration of three points except one, V-shaped, could be fitted to the relationship (Figure 1) that we wanted to test. Therefore, there was a very low probability that even a three-level experiment would disprove our hypothetical relationship; hence, it was a very poor test of the validity of this relationship.

For these reasons we decided to ask for three different treatments and a control group even though this would require twenty-seven markets plus nine under control. Four experimental points could disprove our theory as easily as it could confirm it and, therefore, would have provided a reasonable test of it.

We had nothing to go on but our intuition in selecting the experimental treatment levels: a 50 percent reduction, and 50 and 100 percent increases in budgeted levels of advertising. We wanted to make changes large enough to produce observable effects on sales, assuming such changes had any such effect, and large enough so that if there were no observable effects this fact could not be dismissed because the changes were believed to be too small. Two increases rather than decreases were selected to make the experiment more palatable to the Marketing Department.

When this four-level design was presented it was rejected because it involved the use of too many market areas. However, Mr. Busch agreed to our use of eighteen rather than fifteen areas provided that we change the reduction in advertising we had proposed from 50 to 25 percent. He felt that a 50 percent reduction might irreparably damage the areas so treated. This left us with a three-level experiment: −25%, 0%, and +50% changes from budget.

Although we were not completely happy with this outcome because it did not provide an adequate test of our theory, we were pleased that we had the opportunity to conduct even a limited experiment. We were reasonably sure that if it produced interesting results, restrictions on future experiments would be lifted.

A 3 × 3 × 3 factorially designed experiment was prepared in which two other important marketing variables were explicitly controlled: *the amount spent on sales effort* (salesmen) and *the amount spent on point-of-sales displays and signs.* We also would have liked to control pricing but this was precluded. This design is illustrated in Figure 2.

Market areas were selected randomly from the "permissible list" and randomly assigned to the twenty-seven treatments. Use of the "permissible list" could obviously bias our results but again our hope was that the results would justify further experimentation and that it would not be so restricted.

The experiment was carried out over the calendar year 1962 thereby yielding twelve observations of each market area. We were able to reach a conclusion at the end of six months, but the experiment was continued to build up confidence in the results. The results, however, attracted little confidence; they were too much at variance with expectations within the company and its advertising agency. The three points shown in Figure 3 fell into the only configuration, V-shaped, that was inconsistent with our theory because the relationship being tested (Figure 1) had no V in it. In addition, we found no significant interaction between advertising, sales effort, and point-of-sales expenditures, a surprising but not an unacceptable result, and the results indicated that current levels of sales effort and point-of-sales expenditures were close to optimal. This last result was readily accepted.

No one found much difficulty in believing that a 50 percent increase in

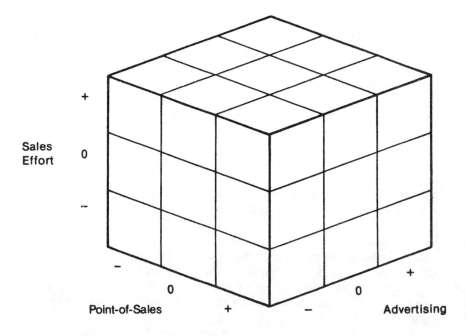

Figure 2   The 3 x 3 x 3 Experiment

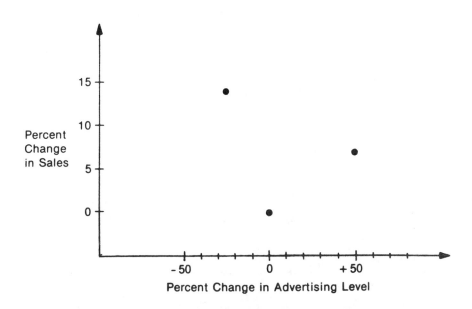

Figure 3   Results of First Experiment (1962)

advertising produced a 7 percent increase in sales, but only Mr. Busch and Mr. Vogel were willing to consider seriously the possibility that a 25 percent reduction of advertising could produce a 14 percent increase in sales. Even they were not ready to act on this finding but they did want to analyze the situation further. Therefore, they asked us to design another experiment that would check these results and that would be more convincing to others.

We had to revise our theory before designing the next experiment. On the surface it appeared necessary to reject the theory but we had grown very fond of it. Therefore, we sought a modification of the theory that would make it consistent with the experimental results.

It occurred to us that there might be two or more distinct consuming populations in each market area with a response curve like the one we had assumed but that these might be separated along the horizontal scale (see Figure 4). The aggregated response curve would then have a V in it. When this possibility was presented to Mr. Vogel, he thought it quite reasonable and suggested that the markets might be segmented into three parts: heavy, moderate, and light beer drinkers. This made sense to us. One would expect heavy users of a product to be more sensitive to its advertising than moderate users, and moderate users more sensitive than light users. We looked for some way of testing this assumption and we found one.

It would have been very time-consuming and costly to determine how many beer drinkers of each type there were in each market area. We had

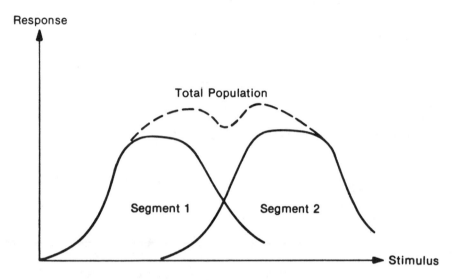

Figure 4   Response Function of Segmented Population

neither the time nor the money required to do so. But we did know from previous studies that beer consumption correlated positively with discretionary income within the range of such income in which most beer drinkers fall. Therefore, we determined the average discretionary income in each market area that had been used in the previous experiment and compared it with the average deviations from forecasted sales in each area. There was a positive correlation between these deviations and average discretionary income, thereby lending some credence to the user-level segmentation assumption.

We revised our theory to incorporate three response functions for each market area. This meant that the aggregated response functions for markets as a whole could differ significantly because of different proportions of heavy, moderate, and light beer drinkers.

The Second Experiment

In order to test the revised theory we decided that we needed seven different advertising treatments. We wanted to repeat the earlier experiment and add treatments further out on both ends of the scale. Seven treatments were selected: −100% (no advertising), −50%, −25%, 0%, +50%, +100%, and +200%. Because of improvements in our forecasting methods only six areas were required for each treatment. This design was accepted with only slight modification: the number of test areas in the two extreme treatments was reduced.

The experiment was conducted over twelve months in 1963 and 1964. Again data were collected monthly. The results obtained confirmed the findings of the first experiment. When plotted the seven points fell on a curve such as is shown in Figure 5. There were two deviations from our expectations. First, only two, not three, peaks appeared. But this was not serious because the points out on the right were so far apart that there could well be a third hump concealed by the interpolation between the points. It was harder to explain the finding that the areas in which all advertising had been eliminated (—100%) survived the year with no significant difference in performance from the control areas (0%). Hardly anyone believed this result. Those who did attributed it to the long history, strength, and exposure of BUDWEISER in the marketplace. We suggested further tests of the effect of complete elimination of advertising.

Although a willingness to act on our findings had not yet developed, there was growing agreement on the desirability of continuing the research. The 1963-64 experiment was continued with particular attention given to the areas from which all advertising had been removed. The objective was to determine how long it would take before any deterioration of sales could be detected, at what rate it would take place, and how easily lost sales could subsequently be recaptured. We also initiated some research into the relative effectiveness of different media. While this research was going on, the first opportunity to apply the results already obtained presented itself.

Application of Results

In mid 1964 Mr. Busch wanted to make more cash available to meet some commitments he had made. He asked Mr. Vogel and us if this could be done. We jointly proposed that advertising be reduced by 15 percent in twenty-five

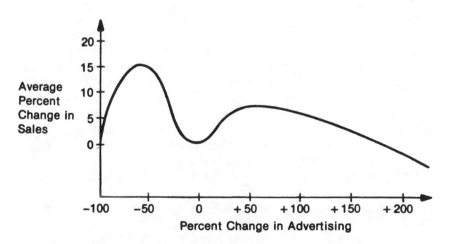

Figure 5   Results of Second Advertising-Level
Experiment (1963)

of the smallest markets. The smallest markets were chosen in order to mini-mize any possible long-run harmful effects. The proposed change was capable of yielding more than the amount Mr. Busch asked for. We also pointed out that we could maintain very close watch over the areas affected and report immediately on any reduction of sales that might occur in them. We pre-dicted, however, that the proposed decrease in advertising would produce about a 5 percent increase in sales. Mr. Busch decided to go ahead.

The predicted results were obtained by the end of the year. As a conse-quence, the number of reduction areas was increased to fifty and the amount of the reductions was increased to 25 percent. From then on more and more areas were similarly treated and the reductions were gradually increased until the advertising expenditure per barrel was $0.80 in contrast to $1.89 which it had been when the research was initiated. During this period (1962-68) sales of BUDWEISER increased from approximately 7.5 million to 14.5 million barrels and its market share increased from 8.14 to 12.94 percent.

Timing of Advertising

Returning to the experiment involving complete deprivation of advertising, the areas thus deprived showed no response until more than a year and a half later. From then on a small decline was noted each month. This was allowed to continue only long enough to provide good estimates of the deterioration rate. Moves to correct these markets were then made. They were restored to their normal growth rate in about six months with only their normal amount of advertising.

These results led to a new line of speculation. Would it not be possible to pulse advertising, using an on-and-off pattern, and obtain the same effective-ness that is obtained by continuous advertising? We came to think of adver-tising as a motion picture which, of course, is really a sequence of motionless pictures. If sixteen still photographs are taken and projected per second, the appearance of motion is created because images are retained in the retina between exposures. We felt the same should be true of advertising.

Two types of pulsing were considered. In one, advertising expenditures in all media are on or off together. In the other, only one medium is used at any time but the media are alternated. We designed an experiment to test the first of these types of pulse. It involved four treatments: one control (I) and three pulsing patterns (II, III, and IV) shown in Table 1. In addition, the level of expenditure in each was varied as is shown in Table 2. The market areas used in this experiment were classified by median income and growth rates.

One of the pulsing patterns was found to be significantly better than the others and slightly better than normal advertising when accompanied by a high level of expenditure. Another pattern was found to be best when accompanied by a low level of expenditure. In addition, the pulsing patterns

	I	II	III	IV
Spring	X	X	0	X
Summer	X	0	X	X
Autumn	X	X	0	0
Winter	X	0	X	0

Table 1   Pulsing Patterns

were found to interact significantly with median income level and the growth rate of the market area. Subsequent experimentation revealed no significant difference between time-pulsing and media-pulsing. Media-pulsing, however, was easier to administer.

These results were cautiously incorporated into small reductions of advertising expenditures that were made in series. It was only after one change was demonstrated to have the predicted effect that the next change was made. Regular monthly checks on the performance of each market area were initiated and continue to this day.

Media Selection

In the early experiments on advertising expenditures, the budgets for experimental areas were set by the research team but the way in which additional moneys were allocated or reductions were made was left entirely in the hands of the advertising agency. Five media were involved: billboards, magazines, newspapers, radio, and television. We examined the relationship between the actual changes in media allocations and changes in sales. This preliminary analysis indicated no significant difference in effectiveness between magazines, newspapers, and radio, but it suggested that television was slightly superior and that billboards were substantially inferior.

An experiment was designed to test these tentative findings (see Table 3). Magazines were not included in this experiment because they could not

Advertising Level	Pulsing Pattern			
	I	II	III	IV
High	150%	100%	100%	100%
Low	100%	50%	50%	50%

Table 2   Percent of Local Budget Spent by Pulsing Pattern and Advertising Level

	Local TV	Billboard	Radio	Newspaper
No National TV	5	5	5	5
National TV	5	5	5	5

Table 3   Media Experiment (1967-68): Number and Treatment of Market Areas

be controlled within small areas. A distinction was made between *local* and *national* television. In each of twenty areas only one medium was used; in another twenty each medium was combined with national television. The results showed that national television was slightly superior to any local medium. Local television (with or without national television) and radio were more effective than newspapers or billboards. Billboards were the least effective.

To explain the poor showing of billboards, a number of observations were made to determine how much information could be conveyed by a billboard. We found that little more than the product name and a slogan could be communicated. This meant that billboards can do little more than remind one of the existence of an already familiar product; they cannot convey much, if any, new information about it. A second set of observations showed that the typical urban dweller in the United States saw but did not necessarily notice the word "BUDWEISER" on signs, displays, or beer containers almost ten times per day. He hardly needed additional reminding of its existence. On the basis of these findings virtually all billboard advertising was discontinued. The company had been spending about 20 percent of its advertising budget through this medium.

Conclusion

To summarize the results obtained by 1968, we note that volume had approximately doubled, market share had increased from 8.14 to 12.94 percent, and advertising expenditures were reduced from $1.89 to $0.80 per barrel, a 58 percent reduction. It would be foolish, of course, to claim that this improvement in performance was due entirely to changes in advertising. Other types of changes, some based on research and some not, were also made during this period. But one thing is clear: the changes induced by the research described here did not hurt Anheuser-Busch.

The strength of the opposition to the results of our early experiments is less surprising in retrospect than it was at the time. These results contradicted the strong beliefs of people who had good reason to believe they understood advertising and who had the success of the products involved to prove it.

Furthermore, these people did not understand the logic of experimental design and the statistical analysis of the data yielded by experiments. They were convinced that sales were affected by a large number of complexly interacting and inherently qualitative variables and, therefore, that the effect of any one of these on sales could not be isolated or measured.

The greatest resistance came from those managers who had direct responsibility for the decisions to which the research was addressed and from the advertising agency people who were attached to the account. It was clear that the agency people felt that our research cast doubt on their competence and creativity. It also threatened the agency's income.

For these reasons it became apparent to us that three things had to be done if we were to gain acceptance, let alone support, of our efforts. First, we would have to bring those who had to deal with the research results to an understanding of the logic of experimental design and statistical analysis. Second, we would have to involve them actively in the design of the experiments and in the analysis and interpretation of their results. Finally, we would have to try to change the method of compensating the advertising agency so that its fee was not decreased as the efficiency of advertising was increased.

The process of education and involvement took time. It was carried out both informally and formally in sessions conducted specifically for this purpose. Managers at the highest levels were generally the first to approve of experimentation. They sometimes became impatient with their subordinates and tried to force early research results on them. Such pressure slowed acceptance at the lower levels. But in general, when top managers felt compelled to act, as Mr. Busch did on the first reduction of advertising expenditures, they worked hard to make the implementation itself experimental and to carry it out as gradually and nondisruptively as possible. In all, it took about three years (1962-65) for the educational efforts to begin to pay off.

These efforts were facilitated by two other important changes. First, we proposed that the basis for the agency's compensation be changed so that it would benefit financially when the company did. As long as the agency was paid a percentage of A-B's expenditures on advertising, it naturally resisted research that had the potential of reducing its earnings. Therefore, we suggested a scheme by which the agency's fee was increased if either sales increased with no increase in advertising or advertising expenditures decreased with no decrease in sales. The agency was persuaded to try this scheme for a year with assurances that it would receive no less in fees during the trial year than it had in the previous year. In the trial year advertising expenditures decreased but since sales increased the agency's compensation also increased. The scheme was continued for another year with repetition of this outcome and then became permanent. Because of it the agency became increasingly interested in research, strengthened its research department, and encouraged it to collaborate with us. This was done to our mutual benefit. By 1968 the difficulties with agency acceptance of research results were largely a thing of the past. The agency has since initiated such a compensation scheme with other clients.

Acceptance of research as an instrument of management was greatly facilitated by the establishment of two very competent in-house groups, one in marketing and the other in corporate planning. Leon Pritzker, who was the initial director of the group in marketing, had a major role in the later phases of the research reported here. August A. Busch, III, then executive vice president but now president, observed: "The University and company units work together very closely. . . ."[5] E. H. Vogel, Jr. continued: "Today we hardly make any decision of any consequence that does not involve our researchers in one way or another. This blending of research and management did not occur overnight. It developed slowly under careful guidance."[6]

Research results were built up slowly but accumulatively. The results of each piece of research were integrated with previous results where they were consistent. Where they were not, a more general explanation was sought, one that made integration possible, and then the integrating principle was thoroughly tested. No result was ever taken to be true for all time. As Mr. Vogel observed:

> We did not try to impose [research-based] recommendations as though we had suddenly gained possession of ultimate truth. We usually initiated the application of recommendations on a small scale with close controls imposed on them. As confidence in results developed, we extended applications.
>
> No matter how generally management accepted a research result it was never applied without a well-designed control system to tell us whether the recommendations worked as expected. We have learned as much from the feed-back such control provided as we have from the research that produced the initial recommendations.
>
> More important, perhaps, is that we now design controls for evaluating decisions which management reaches without the benefit of research. This enables us to learn more rapidly and accurately from experience, and it has indoctrinated management with an experimental approach to decision making.[7]

References

[1] Ackoff, R. L., and Emery, F. E. *On Purposeful Systems*. Chicago: Aldine-Atherton, 1972, Chapter 8.

[2] Busch, A. A., III. "The Essentials of Corporate Growth." Address given to Charles Coolige Parlin Marketing Award Banquet, May 9, 1973.

[3] "Computers Can't Solve Everything." *Fortune*, October 1969, p. 126 ff.

[4] Curtis, K. P. *The Modelling of Con-*

---

[5] See Busch [2].
[6] See Vogel [6], p. 24.
[7] See Vogel [6], pp. 24-25.

sumer Purchase Behavior. Unpublished Ph.D. dissertation, University of Pennsylvania, 1969.

[5] Rao, A. G. *Quantitative Theories in Advertising.* New York: John Wiley & Sons, 1970.

[6] Vogel, E. H., Jr. "Creative Marketing and Management Science." *Management Decision,* Spring 1969, pp. 21-25.

[7] Waid, C.; Clark, D. F.; and Ackoff,

R. L. "Allocation of Sales Effort in the Lamp Division of the General Electric Company." *Operations Research* 4 (1956): 629-647.

[8] "Wharton Analyzes the Beer Drinker." *Business Week,* 24 March 1973, p. 44.

[9] "While Big Brewers Quaff, the Little Ones Thirst." *Fortune,* November 1972, p. 103 ff.

Advertising Research at Anheuser-Busch, Inc. (1968-74)

Russell L. Ackoff, University of Pennsylvania
James R. Emshoff, University of Pennsylvania

This is the second of a two-article series in which Professors Ackoff and Emshoff describe almost eleven years of management science research and implementation in the marketing area of Anheuser-Busch, Inc. In this article the authors describe their first attempts to evaluate advertising message content and their subsequent work aimed at developing and validating a theory of drinking behavior. They go on to describe the usefulness of the theory in the evaluation of message content and in market segmentation and media selection problems. Throughout the article the power of theory-based marketing research is illustrated. *Ed.*

In part I of this two-part paper we described research conducted for Anheuser-Busch (A-B) on three aspects of advertising: the amount to be spent overall, media mix, and timing. This research was conducted during the period 1963-1968. By 1968 significant improvements in the use of advertising had been made at A-B as a result of this research. The volume of A-B's sales approximately doubled over seven years, its market share increased from 8.14 to 12.94 percent, while its advertising expenditures were reduced from $1.89 to $0.80 per barrel, a 58 percent reduction.

Early Attempts at Message Evaluation

Early in 1968 E. H. Vogel, Jr., then vice president of marketing, asked that we turn our attention to the content and quality of advertising messages. We began by surveying organizations that offered message-evaluation services. Much information was collected about each. Using this data we selected about six organizations that most impressed us for closer examination. Each was visited and questioned at length. Finally, we selected one agency that seemed to have the soundest procedures and the following proposition was made. We would carry out an experimental test of the agency's message evaluations with the understanding that if the results were favorable, the agency could use them as it wished; if they were not, we would not release information about the study. The message-evaluation agency agreed.

A-B's principal advertising agency was asked to select about fifty of its television commercials and to include about equal numbers of those that they considered to be effective and ineffective. They were not restricted to selecting commercials which actually had been used. The message-evaluation agency

1

then conducted tests of these commercials in three cities which we selected. The agency was asked to identify six commercials that were evaluated as superior in all three cities and six that were evaluated as inferior in the same cities.

The message-evaluation agency obtained consistent evaluations in two of the three cities, but the third yielded results that were inconsistent with the other two. The city with the inconsistency was one in which A-B had a large brewery. We suspected that the message evaluations obtained in this city were greatly influenced by the company's presence. Through discussion with others who had conducted similar message evaluations, we learned of similar experiences in cities in which a company was a major economic force. This suggested that most of the public in such cities already had strong favorable or unfavorable opinions of the company and its products and were not subject to significant influence by company advertising.

This finding led to two actions. First, another city was selected to replace the brewery city in the message-evaluation effort. Second, a sequence of carefully monitored reductions in advertising was introduced in the brewery city. Reductions of about $250,000 in annual expenditures were made over a relatively short time with no effect on sales.

The message-evaluation agency, using the new third city, was able to identify the required number of consistently superior and inferior commercials. These were then used in a designed experiment in which a number of market areas were exposed to only the superior commercials, and an equal number were exposed to only the inferior commercials. The amounts spent on advertising in these areas were carefully controlled. As in the research previously reported, the deviation of actual from forecast sales was used as the measure of performance.

We found no significant difference between the performance of the two sets of advertisements. Therefore, we concluded that the message evaluations were not related to the effectiveness, or ability to affect sales, of the messages. The only positive value of this conclusion was that it led A-B to discontinue its use of such message-evaluation services. Doing so yielded a modest saving, but the problem originally raised remained unsolved.

This experience convinced us that we would not be able to evaluate advertising messages adequately without knowing *why* people drink beer and, more generally, alcoholic beverages. When we mentioned this conviction to a marketing manager in another company, he said that it was clear why people drank beer: they drank it because they liked it. When we asked him how he knew this, he replied, "They wouldn't drink it if they didn't." We sought a less circular and more illuminating explanation of drinking behavior.

Typology of Drinking Behavior

A literature search uncovered a number of drinking theories all of which dealt with abuse rather than normal use of alcohol. Furthermore, not one of them had been adequately tested; most were supported by only a small number of clinical observations. To design and conduct tests of these theories would have required more time, money, and patience than we had. Fortunately we found someone else who had done this.

Emery's Drinking Types

Dr. Fred E. Emery and his colleagues at the Human Resources Centre of The Tavistock Institute in London, an organization with which we had collaborated over a number of years, had tested most of the available theories of drinking and none had proven adequate. Emery and his coworkers then devoted their efforts to producing a detailed description of drinking behavior and to extracting underlying patterns in such behavior which might provide a basis for theoretical speculation. They collected a large amount of psychological and drinking data from regular drinkers in England, Ireland, and Norway.[1] Analysis of these data revealed three distinctive drinking types which Emery named and described as follows:

> *Reparative*. Generally middle-aged of either sex. Has not achieved as much as he or she had hoped to by that stage of his or her life, although usually far from being a failure. Believed they were capable of achieving what they wanted but also believed that doing so would require sacrifices by others about whom he or she cared greatly. For example, achievement might require a move that would displease his wife and/or children. Therefore, he or she sacrificed his or her aspirations in the interest of others. Well adjusted to this situation.
>
> Most drinking occurs at end of work day rather than on weekends, vacations, and holidays. Usually drinks with a few close friends or members of the family. A controlled drinker who seldom becomes high or drunk and very rarely an alcoholic. Drinking is associated with the transition from work to nonwork environment and is seen as a type of self-reward for sacrifices made for others.
>
> *Social*. Generally a younger adult of either sex. Has not yet attained level of aspiration but believes he or she will and that doing so requires approval and support of others. Driven by desire to get ahead.
>
> Drinking heaviest on weekends, holidays, and vacations. Usually in larger groups consisting of acquaintances in social settings. Generally a controlled drinker but less so than reparative. Drinking associated with friendliness and acceptance of and by others, as a lubricant of social situations.
>
> *Indulgent*. Of any age and either sex. Has not attained level of aspiration and never expects to. Considers self an irretrievable failure. Life viewed as tragic.
>
> Drinking heaviest when subjected to pressure to achieve. Associated

---

[1] Defined as consuming an average of two or more ounces of alcohol per day. Because of lower per capita consumption of alcohol in the U.S., we subsequently used one ounce or more to define regular drinking here.

with escape. Least controlled drinker; most likely to become high, drunk, or alcoholic.

We at Wharton found these categories exciting and suggestive, but we were disturbed by the fact that there were *three* of them. The only explanation for this could be that there was a single underlying scale on which the three categories represented low, medium, and high ranges. But Emery and we agreed that there must be more than one underlying scale.

Ackoff and Churchman's Personality Types

We suspected that there were two underlying scales because two of Emery's drinking types appeared to be special cases of two of four personality types that C. West Churchman and Russell L. Ackoff had identified in the late 1940s. In their analysis of C. G. Jung's personality types (introvert-extrovert), Churchman and Ackoff had uncovered two underlying scales, each divided into two ranges (low-high). The combination of these scales resulted in four possible types (low-low, low-high, high-low, high-high) of which introversion and extroversion were only two.

Introversion and extroversion deal with an individual's relationship with his environment. An individual is related to his environment in two ways: the way his environment affects him and the way he affects his environment. Churchman and Ackoff had constructed a scale on which measurements could be made of an individual's sensitivity to his environment. Probability of response was plotted against the strength of environmental stimuli. (See Figure 1.) The response space was divided in half by a diagonal from the lower left to the upper right. An individual whose probabilities of response in general fall above the diagonal was said to be sensitive to his environment because he is responsive to even weak environmental stimulation. He was called an *objectivert*. An individual whose probabilities of response in general fall below the diagonal is insensitive to his environment. He was called a *subjectivert* because, if not responding to his environment, he has to be responding to something else, something internal. Therefore, he is sensitive to his self, his own thoughts, feelings, beliefs, and attitudes.

An objectivert finds it easier to remember names, phone numbers, and addresses than a subjectivert; he or she will observe furnishings or the dress of others more carefully and be more aware of their feelings and desires. The subjectivert thinks ahead, plans his or her activities in an anticipated situation, and tends to stick to his or her plan whatever happens; the objectivert tends to go in without a plan but responsively. An objectivert is easily distracted by noise or other external stimuli and feels compelled to listen to anyone who speaks to him or her; a subjectivert tends to ignore possible distractions and frequently does not hear what is said to him or her because he or she is lost in his or her own thoughts.

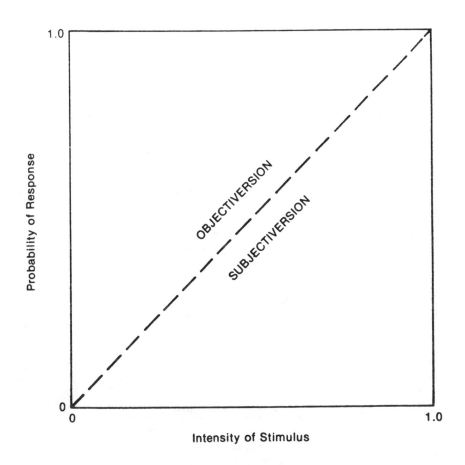

Figure 1   The Environmental Response Function

Objectiversion and subjectiversion are tendencies, not rigid commitments. Hence an objectivert may act like a subjectivert in some circumstances
and vice versa. The less extreme a person's position in this space is, the more
likely he is to respond to both internal and external stimuli. In some circumstances, perhaps a social gathering, a subjectivert is likely to behave more
like an objectivert than he usually does. On the other hand, an objectivert
working in his or her study may look like a subjectivert.

A second scale was constructed that could be used to measure an
individual's effect on his environment. (See Figure 2.) Here the cumulative
probability of responding with varying degrees of effect on the environment
is plotted. This space was also divided by a diagonal into two equal areas,
one representing *internalization,* an inclination to act on oneself, to adapt
oneself and modify one's own behavior to solve problems; and one representing

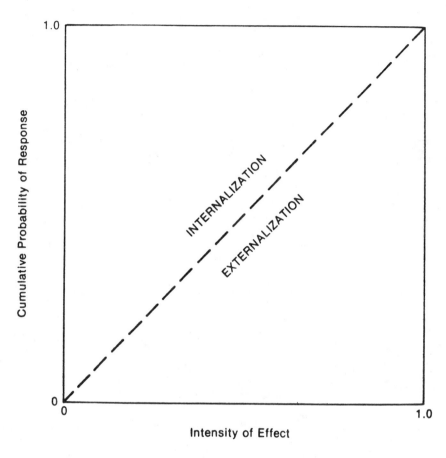

Figure 2   The Environmental Effect Function

externalization, an inclination to act on and modify the environment in problem-solving efforts.

If someone enters an externalizer's environment and annoys or distracts him, he is likely to try to stop the intrusive behavior. An internalizer in the same position is more likely to try to ignore the intruder or move to another place. The externalizer will try to organize a group of which he is part, to lead it; the internalizer is more likely to be a follower. If cold in a house, the externalizer will try to turn up the heat; the internalizer is more likely to add clothing.

Combining these two scales yields the four types shown in Figure 3. In their work of the 1940s Churchman and Ackoff had observed that most people were neither introverts (subjective internalizers) nor extroverts (ob-

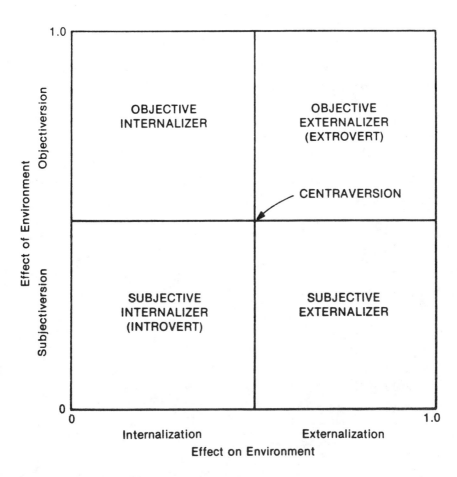

Figure 3   Personality Types

jective externalizers) but one of the two *mixed* types (objective internalizers or subjective externalizers).

The Matching Hypothesis

Now the initial hunch relating Emery's drinking types to the personality types identified by Churchman and Ackoff was as follows:

1. Emery's *reparative* drinkers appeared to be a subclass of *objective internalizers*, because they were sensitive and responsive to the needs of others and adapted to these needs by sacrificing their own aspirations.

2. Emery's *social* drinkers appeared to be a subclass of *subjective externalizers*, because they were primarily driven by their own ambitions and attempted to manipulate others to get what they wanted.

It also occurred to us that Emery's *indulgent* drinkers were divisible into two groups corresponding to the types classified introvert and extrovert. If this were so, we hypothesized, introverted drinkers blamed their failures on their environment and tried to escape this environment by drinking; the extroverted drinkers blamed their failures on their own shortcomings and drank to escape these. At our suggestion Emery reentered his data on the indulgent and found that, indeed, the two drinking types we had inferred from our personality types did exist. He retained the term *indulgent* for the introverted drinker and called the extroverted drinker an *oceanic*. This result considerably reinforced our conviction that we were on the right track.

Emery had found that most regular drinkers were in the social and reparative groups which were subclasses of our mixed types. Recall that

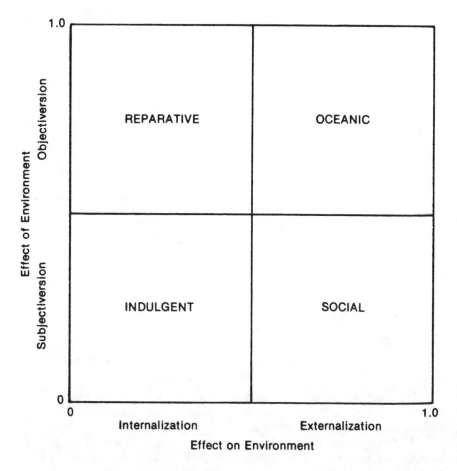

Figure 4   The Matching Hypothesis

Churchman and Ackoff had found that more individuals fell into the mixed types than into the pure. This was also reinforcing.

Emery also had found that most alcoholics were indulgents or oceanics (although most indulgents and oceanics were not alcoholics). Using our typology and the Environmental Interaction Theory (EIT) which began to emerge from it, we hypothesized two very different types of alcoholics. The first, an introverted (indulgent) alcoholic, would tend to drink himself into a catatonic state, a lack of consciousness of and interaction with his environment. He would tend to drink in virtual isolation. The second, an extroverted (oceanic) alcoholic, would tend to drink himself into unselfconsciousness and hyperactivity, into a manic or orgiastic state. Consistent with our theory was the fact that many orgies (for example, the Mardi gras) involved masks and costumes which facilitate escape from self by providing anonymity. Subsequently, this hypothesis and others led us into studies of alcoholism.

Our matching hypothesis that Emery's drinking types were subgroups of our EIT types had to be rigorously tested. This was done by establishing a laboratory into which regular drinkers were brought for observation and interview. Since independent classifications of drinkers into the EIT and Emery drinking types were to be based in part on judgments made by clinical psychologists, it was first necessary to teach them how to use both classification schemes. Training was continued until there was a high degree of consistency in judgments made independently by different clinicians and these in turn agreed with those made by the researchers responsible for the types and theory. Even after the interviewers were "calibrated" several made independent judgments on each subject, using tapes of the interviews.

The results of a test of the matching hypothesis, one which used 125 subjects, are shown in Table 1. Seventy-six percent of the observations fit the hypothesis. This is relatively strong confirmation. The cases that do not match are most likely to be due to lack of perfect precision of the classification procedures.

Measurement Tools

Having established the link between the Emery drinking types and the personality dimensions in the EIT, we were ready to direct research towards the

Drinking Types	Objective Internalizer	Subjective Externalizer	Objective Externalizer	Subjective Internalizer
Reparative	30%	5%	7%	1%
Social	4%	31%	1%	3%
Oceanic	0%	1%	10%	0%
Indulgent	1%	0%	1%	5%

Table 1   Results of a Test of the Matching Hypothesis (125 subjects)

development and testing of a hypothesis formulated to *explain* drinking behavior. Before we could seek such an explanation, however, we had to develop and validate instruments for measuring the dimensions of our personality types. Although the clinical interviewing procedures had been demonstrated to have high reliability, their cost was too great to employ them on larger samples drawn from multiple locations. Each of the 125 interviews referred to above cost approximately $300, and these were conducted in 1968. Even if we were to cut these costs in half, they would have been too large to deal with large samples drawn from multiple locations. Consequently, we turned our research to the development of less expensive typing procedures. One direction we took involved use of a behavioral laboratory in which we hoped to be able to reduce or eliminate clinical interviewing costs by collecting data on an individual's personality by observing his behavior in specially constructed situations. The other direction we took involved the design of self-administered paper-and-pencil tests that a subject could take without supervision.

We designed and tested several situations for the behavioral laboratory. The most successful was a waiting room situation. In this situation subjects were not aware that they were in a test environment, hence their behavior was relatively normal. We found it easy to confront subjects with choices that appeared to be a normal part of this environment. For example, two comfortable chairs were placed around a coffee table in the center of the room facing a TV set, and two old straight-backed chairs were placed in a corner of the room from which the TV could not be seen. We piled papers and open notebooks on the comfortable chairs so that when two subjects entered the room they would be in a dilemma; they could either remove the clutter from the comfortable chairs and use them (an externalizing action) or use the old chairs (an internalizing action). The TV set was on but out of focus so we could observe if a subject tried to adjust it. In total, there were about a dozen such stimuli in the environment.

Occasionally we obtained unexpected but very revealing observations from the waiting-room situation. For example, in one session involving a husband and wife, the wife moved the papers from the cluttered chairs and sat in one of them but the husband went to a straight-backed chair. When he sat in it, one of the rungs in a leg accidently came out. This made it impossible for him to use it. He rose and stood in the corner. His wife, however, came over and fixed the chair for him so he could resume his seat. Not surprisingly, our later tests showed her to be an externalizer and him to be an internalizer.

The waiting-room environment provided rich and reliable readings on both personality scales. It had an additional advantage: observations could be made by individuals who had no particular training in our theory, thus substantially reducing costs. However, we found that the time and expense required to make our observations in this situation were too great, particularly when we had to operate in different cities. Nevertheless, we found that the information obtained from the behavioral laboratory enabled us to design a substantially more efficient and shorter interviewing procedure for the clinicians. Eventually we were able to shorten the clinical procedure so that a subject could be accurately and reliably typed for thirty-five dollars.

Development of an acceptable self-administered paper-and-pencil test took more than two years. Two criteria of acceptability were imposed on this effort. First, there had to be at least a 75 percent agreement between the results of the test and clinical evaluations. Second, there was to be no bias in the classification of those subjects about whom there was disagreement between test and clinic. This would assure us of acceptable collective accuracy when we went into the field and used large numbers of subjects. Fortunately, A-B's management understood the methodological issues and did not press us into going into the field prematurely.

A Theory of Drinking

Once valid measurement instruments were developed, we began a more intensive research program aimed at establishing the causal links between our personality theory and the purposes served by consumption of alcohol among the types. The hypothesis formulated to explain drinking behavior was suggested by the earlier hypothesis about the two types of alcoholics and by the fact that most alcoholics came from the pure rather than the mixed types. In addition, it made use of the following intermediate maturation hypothesis:

> As those in the pure types (introversion and extroversion) grow older they tend to become *more* introverted and extroverted, to move *away* from the point of centraversion. As those in the mixed types mature they tend to move *toward* centraversion.

By interviewing spouses of middle- and older-aged couples in the clinic and extracting from each descriptions of the change in personality that occurred in the other over the years, data were obtained which supported this hypothesis. This led to our drinking hypothesis:

> *Alcoholic beverages are used to produce short-run transformations in personality of the same type produced by maturation in the long run.*

This hypothesis implies that introverts and extroverts drink to become more introverted and extroverted, respectively, and therefore less like each other; but the mixed types drink to become more centraverted and therefore more like each other.

Testing the Theory

We did not feel that we could test this hypothesis by interviewing techniques because we doubted that most drinkers were aware of their reasons for drinking (not to be confused with their rationalization for doing so), and, if they were, they might be unwilling to reveal their reasons in an interview. Therefore, James Emshoff designed a rather complex but very effective behavioral test of this hypothesis.

Through a field survey 250 regular drinkers were identified and invited to participate in an effort by Anheuser-Busch to select one of four newly developed beers to bring out on the market. They were invited to a meeting place where, when they arrived, they were first given the paper-and-pencil personality typing test previously referred to. They were then told that they would be given an opportunity to taste and test the four new beers but before doing so they would be shown the television commercials that had been prepared for each brand.

The television commercials had been prepared by the advertising agency in story-board form. Each commercial consisted of three scenes. In the first a person was shown who was clearly one of the four types in a situation that was characteristic of that type. In the second scene the same person was shown drinking one of the four new brands of beer while its virtues were extolled by an announcer. Each brand had been given a three-letter name selected from a list of names that had been demonstrated to have no value connotations. The names used were BIX, ZIM, WAZ, and BIV. In the third scene the same person was shown with his personality significantly transformed in the direction predicted by our drinking hypothesis.

After being shown these commercials the subjects were allowed to taste the beers in the quantity and manner that they wished and to discuss them with each other. Each brand was contained in the same type of bottle with identical labels except for the name printed on them. Furthermore, and most important, was a fact unknown to the subjects: all four of the beers were the same brew from the same brewery.

The subjects were not only asked to express their preferences, which they did with no difficulty, but they were also asked to select a case of one of the brands which they would be given to take home. The percentage that chose the brand corresponding to their personality type was much larger than one would expect by chance. Furthermore, all the subjects believed that the brands were different and that they could tell the differences between them. Most felt that at least one of the four brands was not fit for human consumption.

These results not only confirmed the drinking hypothesis but also suggested an important direction for further research. A survey was designed and carried out in which beer drinkers were asked to characterize those whom they believed typically drank each major brand of beer marketed in their areas. This survey was carried out in six cities; 1200 subjects were interviewed. The results clearly revealed that each beer was perceived as having an appeal to particular personality clusters. Further research showed that those who drink each brand of beer do in fact fall into these perceived clusters. The personalities associated with each brand not surprisingly corresponded to

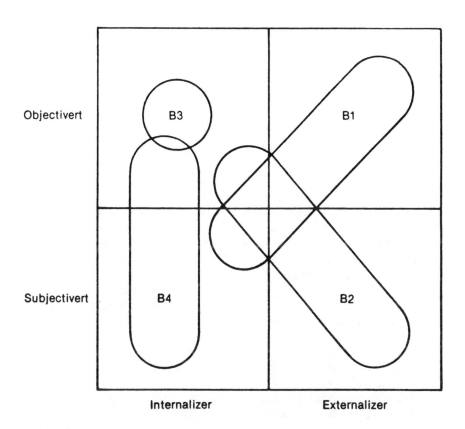

Figure 5   Personality Segments Associated with Different Brands of Beer

those of the people usually shown in the brand's commercials. The personality segments found to be associated with four major brands of beer are shown in Figure 5.

Applications of the Theory

Using this knowledge it was possible to determine by further surveys what personality types drink each of the three brands A-B produces: MICHELOB, BUDWEISER, and BUSCH. Although these were found to have some overlap, mainly they were found to appeal to different personality segments of the market. This enabled us to determine which segments of the beer market each brand was and was not reaching. From these surveys we also were able to estimate what portion of the beer consumed was consumed by each type. The portions varied significantly. Using this information we then were able to specify target market segments to be reached by either existing brands or new ones, and now we knew what kind of advertising messages would be most effective in doing so.

For example, although it was found that MICHELOB had most of its market in one part of the personality space, a small portion of its consumers were drawn from a different part of this space, a part in which the largest percentage of beer drinkers fell. This led to an advertising campaign directed at the second segment. The campaign appears to have succeeded in increasing this brand's share of the target market.

The implications of these results to the preparation of advertising messages are clear, but the typology and the theory based on it could be used in another, less apparent way. We hypothesized different usage of different media by different personality types. For example, we predicted that reparative drinkers (objective internalizers) would watch more television than social drinkers (subjective externalizers), because reparatives are more likely to observe others and socials are more likely to be doing things and participating. The chances that a reparative will watch at least six hours of television on a nonwork day, for example, are more than two-and-a-half times greater than for a social. This ratio is even higher for indulgents, as one would expect. It is also possible to predict which magazines appeal to each type. For example, *Playboy* is almost twice as likely to be read by an oceanic as it is by an indulgent; the reverse is true for *Reader's Digest*. Objectives (oceanics and reparatives) read newspapers more regularly and thoroughly than subjectives. By combining information on the segmentation of the market with the information gained about use of media, it became possible to combine messages and media in such a way as to direct advertising messages at particular market segments in a more effective way.

Our typology and personality theory has also enabled A-B to gain insights into marketing phenomena that do not involve advertising. For example, research was undertaken for the company to determine what happens in a market when a new competitor enters it. In particular, the company was interested in identifying the personality characteristics of those who are most likely to try a new brand when it is introduced, those who switch to it as their regular brand, and the way others subsequently learn about the brand and gain information about it. Research was conducted in a number of markets that had experienced new brand entries in the relatively recent past. This work revealed that different personality types have significantly different likelihoods of trying new products. One of the types purchases new products 30 percent faster than the overall average. A second type does so slightly more than average, a third type slightly less, and the fourth type 40 percent below average. Furthermore, we found that those who are identified as early triers are influenced by advertising differently than those people who switch to the product after it becomes established. The understanding thus gained has enabled A-B to develop more effective advertising and other marketing tools at appropriate points before, during, and after the introduction of new products into the market.

Conclusion

The research described herein began in 1968 and continues today. It was the early 1970s before it yielded any usable results but the results it eventually yielded show how much can be done with even a little understanding of the consumer. It also shows the potential power of theory in gaining such understanding. Most market research tends to be descriptive, not explanatory. Therefore, what is observed is seldom understood and cannot be used to serve either the producer or the consumer more effectively. Understanding must be rooted in theory and theory must be tested experimentally by determining whether predictions deduced from it are valid. Description may enable an organization to adapt to market conditions but not to affect them in the way it desires. Only explanations based on theory can do that.

The personality theory discussed herein obviously applies to other products which have psycho-dynamic effects; that is, modify the personality of the user. With the encouragement of A-B and at times its support, other applications of the theory have been pursued. It has been applied to studies of alcoholism and also to other addictive behavior, particularly that involving narcotics. The theory also is being used to study the use of legal drugs. Emery has used these concepts in the study of tobacco and caffeine consumption. The potentialities of the theory have only begun to be explored.

*To careful design and execution
must be coupled appropriate . . .*

Analysis of Advertising Experiments

Russell S. Winer

In a recent article in this *Journal* (Enis and Cox, 1975), the authors argued that experimentation is a useful tool for evaluating advertising effectiveness. They also felt that a limitation on the use of experiments is due to managers' lack of skill in interpreting results. This paper points out that the interpretation of experimental results is not straightforward for several reasons.

(1) There are various modeling approaches available for evaluating experiments.

(2) There are various levels of aggregation at which the observations may be analyzed.

(3) Several different response variables may be employed.

(4) Different combinations of the above three points and other factors may produce different results and thus different interpretations of the efficacy of the experiment.

The focus of this study is on the analysis of experiments, not on design or implementation. Even if the utmost care is given to experimental execu-

tion, the researcher must be careful at the data-analysis stage that the approaches used are congruent to the questions being asked. This paper does not discuss forecasting implications since emphasis is inferential in nature.

To address this issue of experimental analysis, I have divided the paper into three main parts. The first part reviews the major advertising experiments that have appeared in the literature. This review differs from Enis and Cox's article in that the papers focused on here are on field-advertising experiments where the consumers are exposed to the treatments in as natural an environment as possible. I do not consider laboratory tests. This paper evaluates the literature on two levels: level of aggregation and analytic model used. Second, I apply several models of the type used in previous studies to a field experiment and compare the results. Finally, I develop a systematic approach of analyzing experiments that account for management information needs.

Previous Studies

In evaluating the analyses performed in previous studies, one of the criteria used is the level of aggregation of the analysis. On a continuum of aggregation levels, the endpoints are individual consuming unit (e.g., panel) data and firm-level measures. From the former we can obtain purchase and/or attitude information. The firm-level measures are usually in terms of sales or market share. Between the endpoints, we can analyze information on the basis of market areas, sales territories, or some similar basis.

The level of aggregation of the analyzed data may differ from the collection level. When this occurs, the ability to discern disaggregate effects is lost. Therefore, in a review of previously published experiments we must note not only the level of data analyzed, but also whether it had been aggregated from a more disaggregate base.

A second attribute of previous studies that I examine is the method of analysis used. There are two broad categories of analysis. The first consists of those methods that are not theory- or model-based. Two examples are some form of pre/post-test contrast between control and experimental groups and a tabulation method. Neither method utilizes a model for testing for advertising effects, although this is not to say that statistical inference cannot be performed.

We can find alternatives to examining the test results in methods utilizing some type of model. The most common methods for such analysis are analysis of variance (ANOVA) and regression. In fact many regression models used are ANOVA-type, where the independent variables are dummy variables representing various treatment levels. For a discussion of the ANOVA-regression relationship, see Melnick and Shoaf (1977).

This group of model-based approaches can be subdivided into ANOVA/ANOVA-type regression models and regression/econometric models that are theory-based. The former are actually statistical models that are not developed from any consumer- or market-behavior basis. There are many instances when a more behavioral model is of interest. For example, creative methods for determining the extent and nature of carryover effects could be incorporated. Also, marketing effects such as price and distribution may influence response to the advertising test. Finally, in a competitive market, firms' marketing policies affect each others' sales or market share. In such a situation, a simultaneous equation model might be specified (see Beckwith, 1972).

Table 1 presents the results of the literature review. These works represent only those published studies where a field experiment in a natural setting was examined. Also, only one study from an experiment that produced several is reported. When the description "regression" is used in the "Analysis method" column, this implies that a behavioral-modeling approach was utilized. The column entitled "Level of data analyzed" shows the response variable used.

We can make several comments based on Table 1. First, a wide variety of data levels and analysis methods have been used. But the cases where theoretically based models have been utilized are few. Second, only 3 of the 11 studies have analyzed consumer-level data without aggregation. In fact no regression model or behavioral model has been used to analyze consumer-level data. Also, there was a gap between 1964 and 1971 in field-advertising experiments of the type described here. The recent trend to more experiments supports the contention voiced in Enis and Cox that experimentation would make a comeback.

A Field Experiment

I will now apply several methodologies to a field experiment for the purpose of comparing results. I obtained the data utilized in these analyses from a split-cable television panel. Split-cable TV is analagous to split-run tests in print media—i.e., researchers can test different advertising in terms of timing, copy, or quantity in an experimental situation with large samples of families.

Split-cable TV is cable television with two different cables delivering programming to a test city. This allows wiring of homes to either of the cables,

Table 1
Review of Previously Published Field-Advertising Experiments

Author(s)	Level of data analyzed	Level of data collected	Analysis method
Becknell, McIsaac (1963)	Sales	Consumer	ANOVA-type regression
Bogart, Tolley, Orenstein (1970)	Consumers (various measures)	Same	Tabulation
Buzzell (1964)	Market area, market share	Consumer	Regression model
Doyle, Fenwick (1975)	Store sales	Same	ANOVA
Eskin (1975)	Store sales	Same	ANOVA-type regression
Henderson, Hind, Brown (1961)	Store sales	Same	ANOVA, ANACOVA
Hoofnagle (1963)	Sales	Consumer, supermarket	ANOVA, regression
McGuire (1977)	Consumer purchases	Same	ANOVA
Prasad, Ring (1976)	Market share	Consumer	Regression model
Rao (1970)	Market-area sales	Same	ANOVA, regression
Sethi (1971)	Market share	Consumer	Control-experimental group before-after contrast
Stewart (1964)	Consumers (various measures)	Same	Tabulation
Woodside, Waddle (1975)	Store sales	Same	ANOVA

thus permitting a checkerboard pattern of families on alternate cables A and B throughout the city. Thus, two families shopping at the same stores and living in the same neighborhood can receive different schedules of commercials. This establishes a controlled field experiment with no visible controls.

I recruited a sample of nearly 4,000 families matched on a demographic basis to form a panel. They were almost evenly divided between test group and control group. Because some families either dropped out at various stages or reported infrequently, I instituted a minimum reporting rule per 12-week interval. This produced a subset of 830 families—411 test, 419 control. This subset exhibited characteristics almost identical to the total sample.

The data covered 200 weekly periods. The first year of data (52 periods) provided pre-test information. The advertising test itself covered two years, and the final 44 weeks provided information pertaining to post-test behavior. The test itself was an increase in weight to the experimental families of an average of 50 percent in terms of

Russell S. Winer is an assistant professor at the Graduate School of Business, Columbia University. He received a Ph.D. in industrial administration from Carnegie-Mellon University. His publications have appeared in the *Journal of Marketing Research, Journal of Business, Decision Sciences,* and *Management Science.*

GRPs over the two years.

The product studied is a frequently purchased, low-cost, branded consumption item that can be bought in a wide variety of locations; several sizes and quantities are available of each brand. Sales of the product are seasonal.

The product class can be divided into flavor categories. The brand being tested is in the category that has the best-known and most widely advertised brands in the product class. Each flavor division is relatively homogeneous in that if someone is searching for a flavor, the market is well defined in terms of competition and advertising vis-à-vis each brand in the category. The flavor class containing the tested brand comprises 61 percent of the total product-class market, with three brands being dominant.

Analysis of the Data: Aggregate

The first analysis is a simple control-group-versus-experimental-group before-and-after test contrast on the data *after* aggregating the panel purchases to compute sales measures. Let X_1^C and X_2^C represent before and after measurements on the control group, and let X_1^T and X_2^T be the measurements on the test group. Then D, the post-test minus pre-test difference, can be expressed

$$D = (X_2^T - X_1^T) - (X_2^C - X_1^C),$$
$$= (X_2^T - X_2^C) - (X_1^T - X_1^C).$$

In this analysis, the X_1 measures are market shares of volume (ounces) from the 52 weeks of pre-test data. The X_2 measures are 8-week market shares, thus giving 13 measures during the test period and 5 post-test measures. The last 4 weeks of data are not examined in order to maintain consistency in the period definitions. Eight-week periods provide sufficient time for repurchase to occur and opportunity to trace the path of the advertising effects. Table 2 shows the results for the tested brand.

The advertising-test effects show a positive trend. The positive difference

Test weeks	D	Significance
1–8	1.3	NS
9–16	3.7	NS
17–24	5.7	<.05
25–32	0.5	NS
33–40	3.4	NS
41–48	5.8	<.05
49–56	6.5	<.05
57–64	2.9	NS
65–72	6.6	<.05
73–80	8.7	<.01
81–88	7.7	<.01
89–96	6.0	<.05
97–104	9.9	<.01

Table 2
Control-Experimental-Group Contrasts

Post-test weeks

1–8	10.1	<.01
9–16	3.7	NS
17–24	2.4	NS
25–32	6.7	<.05
33–40	3.4	NS

lasted for the first eight weeks but then tapered off. From these results, the experiment appears to have been successful.

A second method used with the aggregated sales data is the ANOVA-type regression model. The model is

$$S_t = a_0 + a_1 G + a_2 Q_1 + \ldots a_8 Q_7 +$$
$$a_9 P Q_1 + a_{10} P Q_2 +$$
$$a_{11} P Q_3 + \epsilon_t,$$
$$t = 1, \ldots, 50,$$

where S_t is sales in four-week period t; G is 1 if observation is from the experimental group, 0 otherwise; Q_1 is 1 if observation is from the experimental group and in four-week period 1, 2, 3, or 4, 0 otherwise; . . . Q_7 is 1 if observation is from the experimental group and in four-week period 25 or 26, 0 otherwise; $P Q_1$ is 1 if observation is from the experimental group and in post-test four-week period 1, 2, 3, or 4, 0 otherwise; . . . $P Q_3$ is 1 if observation is from the experimental group and in post-test four-week period 9, 10, or 11, 0 otherwise. There is a total of

Table 3
ANOVA-Type Regression Results

Coefficient		Estimate	t value	Significance
a_1:	group	.112	4.433	<.01
a_2		$-.336 \times 10^4$	$-.721$	NS
a_3		$.719 \times 10^3$	.155	NS
a_4		$.849 \times 10^4$	1.825	<.01
a_5	adv.	$.182 \times 10^4$	.391	NS
a_6	test	$.674 \times 10^4$	1.449	<.10
a_7		$.105 \times 10^5$	2.255	<.05
a_8		$-.103 \times 10^4$	$-.167$	NS
a_9		$-.931 \times 10^3$	$-.200$	NS
a_{10}	post-	$-.336 \times 10^4$	$-.721$	NS
a_{11}	test	$-.215 \times 10^5$	-4.131	<.01

$\overline{R}^2 = .43.$

100 observations—50 from each group. The model removes any basic group differences with the variable G, and the advertising effects over time are represented by Q_1 through Q_7 in the test weeks and PQ_1 to PQ_3 in post-test weeks. Table 3 shows the results.

When sales is the response examined, the results are different. The treatment is not as positively significant during the test weeks, and in fact sales decreased post-test compared to the pre-test figures.

We could also use a third method on the experimental data after aggregation. As mentioned earlier, an alternative to an ANOVA-type model is a formulation that is more theoretically based. We could develop such a model as follows. Although competitive activities cannot be controlled in a field experiment, the variable that changes most often (and therefore the most important to the model) is price. Sales is often included in such models to account for either

(1) an inertia or momentum effect that implies lagged sales affect current sales or

(2) the fact that the underlying process generating sales is a distributed lag model.

Assuming the former, a model describing market behavior in this situation could be

$$S_t = a_0 + a_1 S_{t-1} + a_2 G +$$
$$a_3 A + a_4 PA + a_5 T +$$
$$a_6 RP_t + \epsilon_t,$$
$$t = 2, \ldots, 50,$$

where S_t and G are defined as previously; A is 1 if observation is during the test weeks for the experimental group's sales, 0 otherwise; PA is 1 if observation is during the post-test weeks for the experimental group, 0 otherwise; T is 1 during seasonal periods for the product, 0 otherwise; RP_t is the relative price of the brand in four-week period t.

I specified the equation for each brand in the market and estimated these equations as "seemingly unrelated" (Zellner, 1962). This is based on

the feeling that sales of brands in the product class are affected by competitive policies as well as their own. I mentioned this modeling approach earlier. Table 4 shows the results for the tested brand only.

We may conclude from this analysis that the advertising test has positive effects on sales while post-test sales are lower than pre-test sales. These support the ANOVA-type regression. Price has the expected sign, and there is a seasonality effect. The sign on a_1 is puzzling, but the coefficient, while significant statistically, is of low magnitude.

Analysis of Data: Consumer Level

I performed the previous three analyses on the panel data after aggregation. Earlier in this paper, I mentioned that no studies have been done using family-level data. In this section, I describe a model that attempts to fill this gap.

First, the response variable examined is weekly consumption of each family. It is felt that consumption is more appropriate than, say, purchases since it is the desire to consume that motivates purchase. Therefore, consumption is a more basic behavioral variable. Second, advertising can have two types of effect on consumption behavior: transitory (where the effects are short-lived) and permanent (where a new consumption level is attained). In order to assess the efficacy of the

Table 4
Results from Model of Market Behavior

Coefficient		Estimate	t value	Significance
a_1:	lagged sales	$-.102$	-1.700	<.05
a_2:	group	1.202×10^4	6.565	<.01
a_3:	advertising	4.663×10^3	2.492	<.05
a_4:	post-test	-4.936×10^3	-2.185	<.05
a_5:	seasonality	1.966×10^3	1.787	<.05
a_6:	price	-1.381×10^5	-11.320	<.01

$\overline{R}^2 = .76.$

treatment, we must separate these two effects. Third, there is a momentum or feedback mechanism operative that implies that current behavior is determined in part by the consumption behavior of the previous week.

I will not reproduce the total model development. The equation for the experimental families is

$$C_{it} - C'_{it} = a_1(C_{i,t-1} - C'_{i,t-1}) +$$
$$A_t + P_t + V_i + \epsilon_{it},$$
$$t = 1, \ldots, 104,$$

where C_{it} is consumption of family i in test week t; C'_{it} is consumption had there been no extra advertising; A_t is transitory advertising effect; P_t is relative price; V_i is permanent advertising effect on family i. A similar equation exists for the tested brand for the post-test weeks. The equation is written in general form with no coefficients on the advertising and price variables.

We must take several steps to estimate the equation. We compute consumption by smoothing purchases in a linear fashion. We estimate the C'_{it} variable utilizing an auxiliary regression equation that uses pre-test average weekly consumption information from the experimental families plus an estimate of how these families' average consumption may have changed in the absence of the test. We use the control group to derive this figure. The price variable is represented by separate prices for each brand in the competitive set. Note that since the analysis is on the experimental and post-test data, P_t is an advertising price interaction. Finally, the advertising variables need structure. We can represent the permanent effect by an individual family dummy variable. We used various functions to represent the transitory effects. The best-fitting function was a square-root curve.

The coefficient of a_1 was .37 ($p < .01$) for the test weeks and .28 ($p < .01$) for the post-test weeks. The transitory effects varied from .45 ounces in week 1 of the test to 4.6 ounces in the last test week. After the test, there were no transitory effects. Permanent

influences on family consumption were not significant. The advertising-price interaction effects were not significant. A more detailed description of the results can be found in Winer (1977).

Discussion

Let us first compare the results of the three aggregate approaches. The two sales models results provide different implications than the simple market-share analysis. The latter indicated that there were positive market-share effects from the experiment for both test and post-test. The sales results for the test weeks were also positive, but were negative for the post-test period. Such a post-test discrepancy could arise from product category sales declining and the tested brands' share of the lower sales increasing. But beyond the fact that the ANOVA-type regression model has sales as a dependent variable, it is theoretically no different from the before-after comparison. The simultaneous equation model is a richer and more theoretically based approach than the other two since it incorporates competitive influences and other variables and therefore yields more information. The effects of the advertising test in ounces, determined by the three aggregate approaches, differ markedly. The simple before-after

analysis indicated an average four-week sales increase of 8,970 ounces, the ANOVA-type model 3,411 ounces, and the market model 4,663 ounces. These figures were averages from the 104 experimental weeks.

Upon comparing the aggregate and disaggregate models, the differences occur in two areas. First, implications of the coefficients differ. The simultaneous-equation model had a negative sign on the lagged dependent variable, while the family-level model indicated positive momentum. The test influences cannot be directly compared due to the different models. The permanent effects in the family model are different from carryover effects measured by post-test dummy variables since the former can be created during the test. Thus the sum of the permanent and transitory effects represents the test-period effects of the aggregate model. This is a second discrepancy between the approaches since separating permanent and transitory effects of the advertising experiment required the additional degrees of freedom from the cross-sectional time-series panel data. Therefore aggregation causes the ability to model at the family level to vanish.

As a result of this discussion, I developed a guideline for the analysis of advertising experiments according to managerial information needs. This is

Table 5
Analytic Approach versus Experimental-Information Use

Methodology	Information use		
	Customer analysis	*Strategic/tactical*	*Budgetary*
Aggregation level	• Individual	• Individual • Firm	• Firm
Appropriate model type	• Behavioral	• ANOVA • ANOVA-type regression • Pre-test, post-test comparison	• Behavioral
Dependent variable of interest	• Consumption • Purchase	• Market share	• Sales

displayed in Table 5. Three of the most common uses of the advertising information with respect to marketing planning are for analyzing customer behavior, for making strategic or tactical decisions on copy, timing, etc., and for determining budget levels. Three analysis decisions are the aggregation level of the data, the appropriate modeling approach, and the type of dependent variable used.

For doing a customer analysis, the approach is relatively straightforward. Individual-level data should be analyzed with a behavioral model. The dependent variable should also represent possible consumer response and should be consumption or purchase. Information obtainable at this level is usually descriptive and may pertain to how heterogeneous the response to the advertising is, any advertising-price interactions, strength of brand loyalty, etc.

If we were to analyze the experiment for strategic/tactical purposes, we could utilize individual- or firm-level data since the focus is now more on the experimental variable. Since the problem revolves only around the question of whether or not the strategy/tactic is a good one, a more general appraisal produced by ANOVA and the other nonbehavior approaches should suffice. The dependent variable selected reflects the fact that strategy development should be competitively based; thus knowing only the level of sales shift is not sufficient. Also, it is important to know when an experimental advertising approach positively affects competitors' sales.

The final application of the experiments deals with budgetary decisions. In this case, only the behavior of the market is important, which implies that firm-level data are appropriate. But since the most accurate results are necessary, we should use a market-behavior model. Since the outlay for additional advertising expenditures will be compared to incremental revenues, sales is the appropriate dependent variable for budget purposes.

Conclusion

I have shown that different methods of analyzing an advertising experiment can produce different results. I made no attempt to develop a systematic method for evaluating the different modeling approaches, aggregation levels, time periods, or response variables. The analysis should be tailored to the needs of management. That is, the use to which the results will be put should be the determining factor in selecting the analytic approach. The way the results will be used should determine the aggregation level, modeling approach, and particular variables included in the analysis.

References

Becknell, James C., and Robert W. McIsaac. Test Marketing Cookware Coated with "Teflon." *Journal of Advertising Research,* Vol. 3, No. 3, September 1963, pp. 2–8.

Beckwith, Neil E. Multivariate Analysis of Sales Responses of Competing Brands to Advertising. *Journal of Marketing Research,* Vol. 9, No. 2, May 1972, pp. 168–176.

Bogart, Leo, B. Stuart Tolley, and Frank Orenstein. What One Little Ad Can Do. *Journal of Advertising Research,* Vol. 10, No. 4, August 1970, pp. 3–13.

Buzzell, Robert D. *Mathematical Models and Marketing Management.* Boston: Harvard University Press, 1964.

Doyle, Peter, and Ian Fenwick. Planning and Estimation in Advertising. *Journal of Marketing Research,* Vol. 12, No. 1, February 1975, pp. 1–6.

Enis, Ben M., and Keith K. Cox. Ad Experiments for Management Decisions. *Journal of Advertising Research,* Vol. 15, No. 2, April 1975, pp. 35–41.

Eskin, Gerald J. A Case for Test Market Experiments. *Journal of Advertising Research,* Vol. 15, No. 2, April 1975, pp. 27–33.

Henderson, Peter L., James F. Hind, and Sidney Brown. Sales Effects of Two Campaign Themes. *Journal of Advertising Research,* Vol. 1, No. 5, December 1961, pp. 2–11.

Hoofnagle, William S. The Effectiveness of Advertising for Farm Products. *Journal of Advertising Research,* Vol. 3, No. 4, December 1963, pp. 2–6.

McGuire, Timothy W. Measuring and Testing Relative Advertising Effectiveness with Split-Cable TV Panel Data. *Journal of the American Statistical Association,* Vol. 72, No. 360, December 1977, pp. 736–745.

Melnick, Edward L., and F. Robert Shoaf. Multiple Regression Equals Analysis of Variance. *Journal of Advertising Research,* Vol. 17, No. 3, June 1977, pp. 27–31.

Prasad, V. Kanti, and L. Winston Ring. Measuring Sales Effects of Some Marketing Mix Variables and Their Interactions. *Journal of Marketing Research,* Vol. 13, No. 4, November 1976, pp. 391–396.

Rao, Ambar G. *Quantitative Theories in Advertising.* New York: Wiley, 1970.

Sethi, S. Prakash. A Comparison between the Effect of Pulse vs. Continuous TV Advertising on Buyer Behavior. *Proceedings of the American Marketing Association.* Chicago: American Marketing Association, 1971.

Stewart, John B. *Repetitive Advertising in Newspapers: A Study of Two New Products.* Boston: Harvard University Press, 1964.

Winer, Russell S. An Econometric Analysis of the Effect of Advertising on Consumer Behavior. Paper No. 198 (rev.). Columbia University, Graduate School of Business, 1977.

Woodside, Arch G., Gerald L. Waddle. Sales Effects of In-Store Advertising. *Journal of Advertising Research,* Vol. 15, No. 3, June 1975, pp. 29–33.

Zellner, Arnold. An Efficient Method of Estimating Seemingly Unrelated Regressions and Tests for Aggregation Bias. *Journal of the American Statistical Association,* Vol. 57, No. 298, June 1962, pp. 348–368.

RESEARCH STUDY

STORE-AND-FORWARD VOICE SWITCHING

- Reviews probable development of systems and services of "non-interactive" voice message transmission and reception, with detailed discussion of the current state of the art of store and forward voice systems.

- Discusses in detail expected new S&FV service from AT&T with a new dimension "Advance Calling", which provides a "one-to-many" calling feature capable of delivering a message to one or many parties and other novel characteristics.

- Analyzes key opportunities for common carriers and private system vendors and describes numerous potential applications of S&FV systems and "Voice Mail" in detail.

- Ten year market projections with relationship of expected market developments in S&FV systems to electronic mail and the "office of the future".

- 161 pages; 27 illustrations; published January 1980; price $895.00.

For free descriptive literature and detailed table of contents, contact:

International Resource Development Inc.
30 High Street
Norwalk, CT 06851 U.S.A.

Phone (203) 866-6914
WU Telex 64-3452

ADVERTISING AND THE SALE OF NOVELS

JOEL V. BERREMAN
Stanford University

EDITOR'S NOTE: *Mr. Berreman here investigates some aspects of a little-explored area of marketing.*

I

GEORGE H. DORAN, looking back on a lifetime of varied and successful publishing, remarked, "The great profession of publishing has measurably degenerated into a business of mass production where each highly enterprising publisher of the new era seeks by advertising and other ultra-modern methods to out-yell his contemporaries of this new dispensation."

The book industry in this new role has certain characteristics which create for it a unique marketing problem. Competitive organization, a limited and unstable market, a product which changes every season and defies standardization, and over-production in relation to the effective demand, are among the problems which confront the publisher. In addition to this, the industry seeks to satisfy a public taste, thought to be wholly unpredictable.

A glance at the output and average sale per title of the book industry will illustrate the problem of over-production. In 1935 there were 215 publishing houses in the United States which put out five or more books each. Together they placed on the market 6,914 new titles and 1,852 new editions. Of these, 1,362 titles were new fiction.

That these figures represent a wasteful over-production of new titles which is injurious to the industry is suggested by the small number of copies of most of them sold. Of a sample list from the same year the average sale per title was 5,523 copies, the median sale was only 2,500 copies, and 32 per cent of the books sold less than 1,500 copies each.

Since, according to publishers' estimates, a book does not begin to yield a profit until its sales pass the four or five thousand mark, the above figures demonstrate that a large proportion of the fiction published contributes nothing to the financial success of the publisher. In fact, it is generally recognized in the book industry that good sellers have to carry the poor ones, and profits depend upon the appearance of the occasional best seller. Accordingly publishers incur a great deal of expense in attempts not only to select appropriate books for publication but also to promote their books and secure for them long and favorable reviews.

Under such circumstances it is vital to the industry that the value of promotional and other methods of stabilizing demand, or of predicting and producing the profitable "best sellers," be appraised. The problem to which this paper is addressed is the determination of the extent to which advertising is capable of producing best sellers in the field of fiction.

II

It is generally believed in the book industry that advertising alone cannot sell books. Publishers claim that they advertise their wares for three reasons: (1) To keep authors contented by convincing them that their books are being duly pushed. (2) To convince book dealers that the titles they have stocked are being supported fully by the publisher. (3) To boost the sales of a book that is already selling, serving rather to reinforce than to create or initiate sales popularity.[1]

This scepticism regarding the effectiveness of book advertising has been based largely upon the practical experiences of publishers and others in the industry. Anyone acquainted with the marketing of books can cite striking examples in which extensive and well planned promotion has failed to produce commensurate sales success.

One determined publisher in England is reported to have spent 2,500 pounds to advertise a book of which he sold only 40,000 copies at a gross price of 2,800 pounds. Stanley Unwin at one time gave a dissatisfied author the privilege of doing all the advertising and hiring all the agencies he liked under an agreement that the publisher would pay all the cost if gross receipts from sales exceeded two-thirds of the money spent on advertising. The offer was accepted, but the proceeds were less than half the advertising cost.[2]

A more recent example was the spectacular failure of the 1938 Hervey Allen book, *Action at Aquila*. It received early and extensive promotion by the use of every selling device known to the industry. Because of this and the spectacular success of the author's previous *Anthony Adverse*, it was stocked heavily by book stores. A month before publication it claimed advance orders of 75,000 copies. This figure soon rose to 80,000, and the publisher printed over 100,000 copies. But after an initial sale of perhaps 45,000 to the ultimate consumer, the book almost completely stopped moving. Such a lesson is not soon forgotten by either book sellers or publishers who were left with large unsold surpluses.

On the other hand, instances can be cited where books, even those by quite unknown authors, have achieved outstanding sales with almost no prior advertising.

In the literature of the trade such cases bulk large, and they have led to the conclusion that it is impossible to sell books by advertising. To the scientist, however, this evidence is inconclusive. It is based essentially upon the "anecdotal" method, long since abandoned by science because it tends to focus attention upon, and draw conclusions from, the unique and the exceptional rather than the more significant rule. It is to overcome this difficulty that an attempt has been made here to apply statistical methods to the problem.

III

The data used in this study consist of sales and advertising figures on 234 books selected from publishers' lists between 1933 and 1938.

This number included three major sample groups of importance to the present study. Eighty-three titles were selected at random from the 1935 spring fiction lists of the 22 publishers who were willing to co-operate. For most of these titles monthly sales totals and monthly advertising expense were obtained from the publishers. Fifty-eight titles were likewise selected from the spring fiction of 1938, and their sales were checked weekly in 5 outlets in a local trade area. Fifty titles of outstanding best-sellers in fiction were selected from the period of 1935–38. On the last group it was impossible to obtain data from publishers, so that advertising had to be determined by direct measurement of that appearing in a representative sample of advertising media, and sales had to be determined from best seller reports in the *New York Herald Tribune Books* and *Publishers*

[1] Stanley Unwin, *The Truth About Publishing*, p. 228.
[2] Unwin, pp. 229–230.

Weekly. A method of scoring these reports was devised; the results correlated highly with sales figures furnished by publishers themselves on a sample group, and the sample of advertising media measured also correlated well with publishers' data.

With these data it was possible to determine the statistical relationship between amount of advertising and number of copies sold by the method of correlation. This correlation was found to be both high and reliable. From the 1935 sample a product moment coefficient of correlation of .79±.03 was obtained between total amount spent for advertising and total sales. Coefficients of .93, .67, and .77 were obtained when other sample lists were treated in the same manner. Thus, a close relationship exists between those two variables. But the nature of this relationship can not be determined without further analysis. Before it can be inferred that advertising causes sales, or that sales can be predicted on the basis of advertising, it is necessary to know the time relationship between the two. If advertising follows sales success it obviously cannot be construed as a cause of that success.

The following table will show that the sales and advertising of books, both best sellers and those of low average sales, are very closely coordinated in time.

But the cause and effect relationship is not yet apparent. For further light on this point advertising on each book has been segregated into the following time categories:

(1) Advance advertising, i.e. that appearing in published form a week or more prior to publication date of the book.
(2) Advertising appearing the first month after publication.
(3) Advertising after the first month.

The correlation between the amount of

TABLE I. DISTRIBUTION OF RETAIL SALES AND ADVERTISING BY WEEKS. FIFTY-THREE BOOKS OF 1938 LIST, LOW AND AVERAGE SELLERS

Weeks after Publication	% of Copies Sold	% of Advertising Appearing
Pre-publication	0	7.
1 to 4 weeks	56.1	60.
5 to 8 weeks	19.7	18.
9 to 12 weeks	11.4	4.5
After 12th week	12.9	8.4

Four Best Sellers, 1938 Sample List

	% of Copies Sold	% of Advertising Appearing
Pre-publication	1.5	1.5
1 to 4 weeks	16.7	24.5
5 to 8 weeks	10.	11.6
9 to 12 weeks	10.6	8.3
After 12th week	61.5	54.

advertising in each of these categories and total sales is shown in the table for both the average and low sellers of the 1935 list, and for fifty best sellers drawn from a five year period.

CORRELATION BETWEEN ADVERTISEMENTS APPEARING AT VARIOUS TIME INTERVALS AND TOTAL SALE OF BOOKS

Variables	1935 List			Best Sellers		
	N	r	P.E.	N	r	P.E.
Advance advertisements and total sales	77	.60	.04	50	.25	.09
Advertisements first month and total sales	77	.79	.03	50	.30	.09
Advertisements after first month and total sales	77	.73	.03	50	.75	.04

The first thing to be noted is the consistently high and reliable relationship between advertising and sales in respect to the 1935 list of low and average sellers. Since advertising in advance cannot be interpreted as resulting from sales, the correlation here clearly implies that such advertising is either predictive or causative of subsequent success of books in this group. The meaning of this correlation will be clarified by a glance at the quartile distribution chart shown below.

PROBABILITY CHART, SALES AND ADVANCED
ADVERTISING BASED ON 83 CASES
OF 1935 BOOKS

Amount of Advance Advertising	Sales Totals (Copies)			
	0-1199	1200-2499	2500-5999	6000-up
$120 up (4th quartile)	5%	5%	15%	75%
$50-$119 (3rd quartile)	0	33%	44%	23%
$20-$49 (2nd quartile)	27%	53%	20%	0
$0-$19 (1st quartile)	47%	27%	13%	13%

Stated in terms of probability, this means that if a book has received, up to a week before publication date, a total of $120 or more of advertising (in the sample media) there is a three to one chance that it will reach an ultimate sale of over 6,000 copies; whereas if it has received in the same time less than $20 in advertising, it has only a little less than an even chance of reaching a sale of 1,200 copies. Since a sale of 2,500 copies is close to the average sale of all fiction in this sample, it may be said that books advertised as much as $120 in advance have nine chances to one of selling above average, whereas those receiving less than $20 have only one chance in four of exceeding the average. It seems that this represents roughly the publisher's prediction of the probable success of a book. Since 6,000 copies or over is a profitable sale under present publishing conditions, a publisher could assure himself a profitable sale on 75% of his titles by simply eliminating those on which he is unwilling to risk $120 in advance advertising.[3] Thus, in this class of low and average sellers, those which

[3] It should be recognized that this is only a sample of advertising and does not include other promotional expense. It should be interpreted in a relative rather than an absolute sense, say as the least advance advertising accorded a book among the 25% receiving the greatest amount.

receive the most early advertising can generally be counted upon to have superior sales.

A further fact of importance is revealed by a comparison of the amount of advance advertising received by the 1935 sample and the best-seller lists. The range of variation in advance advertising among the 1935 volumes is much narrower than that among the best sellers, and the amount was generally less. Almost 80% of the best sellers received more advance advertising than 75% of the 1935 list, and fully half of the best sellers received more than any book in the lower selling sample. Were the two samples thrown together on a single probability chart most best sellers would therefore fall in the highest category in respect to advance advertising. This simply means that most books which later become best sellers have had the advantage of superior advance advertising. The complete surprise successes are therefore not the rule.

Again with reference to the correlations above, one may note that the fifty books in the list of best sellers show no significant correlation between sales and any category of advertising except late advertising, that appearing after their first month. With probable errors of .09 these r's would have to exceed .36 to be statistically significant. This fact strongly suggests that the bulk of advertising of best sellers *accompanies* or *follows* sales rather than precedes them, and it is impossible to predict from advertising, even a month after publication date, the relative success which best selling novels will achieve.

IV

The evidence thus far presented indicates that the probable sale of poor and average sellers can be predicted with some accuracy from advance and early advertising; that it is possible to predict with somewhat better than chance accuracy which books will become good or high sellers, but that it is impossible to predict (or apparently to control) on the basis of advertising the wide variability in sales which occur among books that sell from 10,000 to a million copies and comprise the highly profitable bestsellers.

The relationship between advertising and sales of best sellers seems therefore to be a reciprocal one. Whereas advertising may increase sales, or increase a book's chances of success, it is clear that sales success results in increased advertising. From these facts, and a study of weekly advertising and sales of particular books, the advertising policy of most publishers may be stated somewhat as follows:

On the basis of their judgment of a book's sales possibilities, publishers assign an initial amount for promotion and advertising. If early response from dealers and reviewers is favorable, this may be increased. A little of this goes for advance publicity, but the bulk of it is spent during the first two or three weeks after publication date. Subsequent advertising depends largely on the success of the book. If a book at once begins to sell, whether advertised much or not, the publisher becomes enthusiastic and begins another campaign. If a few months later it is still selling, another group of advertisements appear. This intermittent and irregular advertising will continue as long as the book continues to sell. Thus initial advertising precedes but subsequent advertising follows and depends on sales success. Thus a close reciprocal relation exists between advertising and book sales.

It is evident, however, that advertising cannot be properly considered alone as a causative factor in book sales. The advertiser needs something to work on. Most advance promotion is given to books which the publisher believes he can sell. Name prestige of an author, selection by a book club, special timeliness of a book, or its appeal to what the publisher believes to be the interests of a large public, not to mention extensive and favorable reviewing, generally also characterize a book which is heavily promoted. Several of these factors are almost always present in the total situation out of which best sellers emerge.

An examination of specific cases of surprise successes which are often cited as evidence of the essentially unpredictable nature of best sellerdom reveals that most of them possess a number of these advantages. *Anthony Adverse*, hailed as one of the great surprises of the past decade, received an unusual amount of pre-publication advertising, occasioned in part by a postponement in its publication date and its selection by the Book of the Month Club. The club selection itself is almost a guarantee of superior sales. It received reviewing 25 per cent in excess of the average for club selections and two and a half times as extensive as the average for the 1935 unselected list.

The now famous *Gone With the Wind*, though a first novel, also received an unusual amount of early publicity. This was followed by more advertising in its first month than any other book in the entire five-year period, and by reviewing exceeded by only one. It, too, was a selection of the Book of the Month Club, and after its first ten months its author was awarded the Pulitzer prize. Thus, while these cases stand out as the most spectacular among surprise successes, they by no means achieved that success unaided or unheralded. Many other books of outstanding success have the advantage of a well-known author

Books which do not enjoy a number of such special advantages furnish an almost negligible proportion of best sellers.

V

Although the data of this paper do not furnish a final answer to the question of whether advertising causes sales, they furnish enough evidence to justify some tentative conclusions on the point.

(1) It may first be concluded that early (i.e. advance and pre-publication) advertising along with other factors which generally accompany it, in large part determine the initial sale of a book. Since the initial sale of four to six weeks is a very large part of the total sale of most books, those which do not become best sellers show a total sale proportional to the amount of such early advertising. The high correlation between early advertising and total sales is evidence for this conclusion. It may be that the advance publicity persuades the dealers that the publisher has confidence in particular books and intends to push them heavily. If the dealer stocks a book he will make every effort to dispose of his stock. At the same time the early publicity brings the book to the attention of especially interested persons, those who make up the author public or other interest group to which the book may be expected to appeal on the basis of its promise of personal satisfactions.

(2) The greater the amount of pre-publication advertising a book receives the greater the chance that it will become a best seller. This early advertising is largely to the trade, and represents but a small cost, yet it bears as close a relationship to outstanding sales success as does the much larger volume of advertising generally placed during the first month after publication. From this it appears that an increase in advertising at this point would increase the chances of such success with the least outlay of advertising funds. In many cases a hundred dollars or so might even be drawn from the post-publication appropriation. While lowering that larger fund very little proportionately, it would often more than double the pre-publication outlay, and thus greatly enhance the prospects of outstanding sales. If the first conclusion above is correct such an increase in advance advertising to the trade would also tend to increase sales of all books, whether they become best sellers or not.

(3) Although the situation which includes large initial advertising and publicity appears to be favorable to the emergence of best sellers, no criteria have yet been found by which the relative sales of best selling novels can be predicted or accounted for. This conclusion emerges from the fact that although large early advertising is followed in a majority of cases by superior sales, the wide variation in the total sales of different best sellers shows no significant correlation with the amount of early advertising.

(4) Finally, it is evident that advertising which appears after the first month is in large part the *result* of early sales success. Whether it causes further success in some cases cannot be determined from the present data. Many persons in the book industry believe it does. The reliable correlation between late advertising and the sale of best sellers could result, however, either from sales resulting from advertising, or from advertising resulting from sales.

VI

The phenomena of best-sellerdom would appear to fall in the realm of social behavior characterized by fads, fashions, and related processes. The sale of a book depends heavily upon the prestige which attaches to the book and incidentally to the person who has read or can talk about it. Successful sales may accrue from any factor or combination of factors capable of bestowing upon a book and its reader the requisite prestige or attention-getting power. One of these factors appears to be an extensive and unusual advertising and promotional campaign. Others are selection by a book club, a literary prize, extensive and favorable reviews, recommendation by some person of prominence, the reputation of an author based on prior success, or any combination of these factors. Moreover, success is cumulative. Once a book begins to sell it receives added publicity and the prestige that success itself affords. When by virtue of such factors as these a book gets to be widely talked about, when it becomes the thing to do to read it or have it on the table, when the person who has not read it feels it necessary to apologize for the fact, then the book is on its way to become a best seller.

It does not appear that any one of the prestige giving factors is indispensable to achieve this result. Neither does it seem that these favorable factors affect sales as wholly independent causes, but rather as parts of a total favorable situation from which best sellers generally emerge. Advertising, however, generally accompanies any favorable combination of factors, since they lead the publisher to hope for successful sales and induce him to place the advertising.

It is not inconceivable that a single factor such as advertising alone might give a book sufficient prestige to make it sell, but it would have to be so extravagant or unique as to make the book stand out conspicuously among the season's other offerings. This has in some cases been done, but not always profitably. That best sellers could be indefinitely created at will by advertising seems quite out of the question. Publicity methods may be expected to lose their attention-getting or prestige value just in proportion to the frequency with which they are employed. In the midst of a bedlam of extravagant promotion schemes it is next to impossible to attract much attention by further extravagances. When many competitors promote their respective lists with equal gusto they tend to cancel each other out, especially when the market is limited as is the market for books. Though advertising in the book field may perform some informative function, it seems doubtful whether it alone retains much prestige-giving power, and if indefinitely increased in amount it may be expected to produce rapidly diminishing returns.

Some Correlates of
Coffee and Cleanser Brand Shares

SEYMOUR BANKS
Leo Burnett Company

From an analysis of purchases, prices, preferences and promotion of two everyday products, Dr. Banks is able to find some factors likely to be important in explaining a brand's share of the market.

A THEORY OF MARKET DEMAND for brands must consider two major elements: first, the choice process within the mind of the consumer; and second, the marketing environment in which purchase takes place. This paper describes a model of market demand for brands of convenience goods and reports the results of a test of this model.

All discussion of demand in this paper is in terms of ratios, i.e., a brand's share of the market. If one attempted to deal with demand in an absolute sense, these ratios would have to be multiplied by a base which would consider such factors as the importance of the product in consumers' budgets and the level of national income. This is a task far greater than seems desirable at the moment, and one which is not necessarily required for realism.

SEYMOUR BANKS is a vice president of the Leo Burnett Company where he manages two sections: media planning and research in the media department, and copy and creative research in the research department. Before joining Burnett he was associate professor of marketing at DePaul University from 1946 to 1951. He received a B.S. in chemical engineering from Iowa State College in 1939, and an M.B.A. in 1942 and a Ph.D. in 1949, both in marketing from the University of Chicago. Past president of the Chicago chapter of the American Marketing Association, he is presently chairman of ARF's Audience Concepts Committee, whose report was published last month. He is the author of 11 articles on marketing and advertising research in the *Journal of Marketing, Public Opinion Quarterly, Journal of Applied Psychology* and *Journal of Business.* As president of the Hyde Park Cooperative Society, he helps direct the operations of a large supermarket.

Many businesses consider primary demand trends to be out of their control, and evaluate their relative success in terms of selective demand position.

The general demand model may be written:

$$P_1 = f_c \underset{C_1}{(A_1, A_2, \ldots)} + f_r \underset{R_1}{(B_1, B_2, \ldots)} + f_w \underset{W_1}{(D_1, D_2, \ldots)} + f_m \underset{M_1}{(E_1, E_2, \ldots)}$$

where P_1 is a brand's share of the market. Market share is taken to mean a brand's share of the total volume of sales of the given product class in a certain geographical area.

The terms on the right of the equation are of two types. The first term (C_1) deals with consumer evaluation of the intrinsic attributes of a brand, and the remainder with the marketing efforts of the component elements of the channel of distribution: R for retailer, W for wholesaler and M for manufacturer.

The A's in the consumer term of the above equation are criteria by which consumers evaluate the intrinsic qualities of various brands of a given type of merchandise. For coffee, these criteria might include flavor, flavor consistency, bouquet, type of grind, and size and type of package. These criteria will differ from person to person in number and importance. Furthermore, since judgment is subjective, individuals with identical criteria may have different evaluations of a given brand. The evaluation of each brand on all criteria considered by a consumer leads to a consolidated judgment of that brand at that time.

This mental evaluation of brands by a consumer can be visualized as an archipelago with some peaks rising out of a sea while others are visible below the surface. Sea level corresponds to a level of acceptability for brands of a given product. The peaks represent scalar evaluations of the qualities of the various brands at a given time. Brands are considered acceptable in the sense that, by their intrinsic qualities alone, they would be considered as possible purchases. For example some brands of coffee may not be acceptable because they have too mild or too strong a flavor or do not come in the desired grind.

But the above picture holds only temporarily. As time passes, brands may lose their acceptability, either because their qualities have actually deteriorated or because other brands have been improved. Brands previously unacceptable may rise to acceptability by product improvement. A scouring cleanser, for example, which was changed from an abrasive to a detergent increased sales considerably.

Then too, the *level* of acceptability is subject to change. In times of shortage, consumers take almost any brand. But in a buyer's market, they will not accept substitutes for favored brands.

A purchase is made from among the acceptable brands but is not mechanically determined by an evaluation of value, either ordinal or cardinal. An acceptable product may cease to be bought because the customer who used it previously desires a change for change's sake. This satiation phenomenon appears to be random and is relevant only for individual decision; its effect probably washes out in groups (Banks, 1950).

The number of brands considered depends in part upon the extent of the consumer's experience and in part upon the nature of the product. The more experienced the consumer, the more brands he knows, but limits are imposed by attention and memory. Generally the consumer is more familiar with convenience goods than with shopping goods. In the case of shopping goods like appliances, a complete picture of brands is seldom available—the consumer shops not only to learn which brands are for sale, but often to discover the criteria by which he might evaluate the brands he has discovered.

The term of the demand equation starting with R represents selling effort by retailers for each brand considered. The B's represent their performance of activities like special displays, demonstrations, recommendations to consumers, services rendered (large stock, credit and repair), return privileges, etc., on the brands he carries. The next term deals with efforts of wholesalers to push different brands, training courses for retailer salesmen, demonstrations, special price or credit concessions and so on. Finally, we have the term which represents the selling efforts of the manufacturers for each of their brands.

The rather simple assumptions implied by the form of equation used are not really satisfactory in representing the effect of a manufacturer's sales efforts. A sound marketing program calls for working at several levels simultaneously. Manufacturers merchandise new consumer advertising campaigns to wholesalers and retailers; retailers are affected by advertising campaigns addressed to the general public; price changes affect margins throughout the channel of distribution. The manufacturer's selling efforts and those of his wholesalers and retailers are often closely related. Because of this, the plus signs in the equation should be interpreted as general logical conjunctions rather than as arithmetical additions. Possibly multiplication signs would represent reality more closely.

Customers, retailers, wholesalers and manufacturers vary greatly in scope of activity and our equation must not be interpreted as giving equal weight to each of the terms. Formally, the f_c, f_r, f_w and f_m in the equation represent quite general functions of the factors inside the brackets.

METHOD

Two research techniques which are often used to determine the effect of marketing variables upon sales of brands are experimentation and regression analysis. In the first, the researcher controls the way in which the independent variables affect his test units. One example might be a sales test of a new package design versus an old, each package being used in a comparable sample of stores.

In the regression procedure, the researcher assumes a simple relationship between the market share of a brand and prices, promotional efforts, point of purchase advertising, etc., for it. The assumption is that the market share of a brand can be expressed as an equation, usually linear, which is of the form:

Brand share = a (price of the brand)
        + b (consumer's preference rating) + etc.

By mathematical techniques we choose values of the coefficients a, b, c, etc., which best fit the observed facts. The researcher cannot control factors such as preference ratings for all the brands, but his mathematical procedures enable him to estimate the effect of each while the effects of the others are accounted for statistically. The regression procedure has administrative advantages, but will not yield the functional relationship among the variables studied.

The user of regression analysis assumes that:

1. The values of the independent variables are fixed and may be looked upon as population parameters. Often particular values are deliberately chosen.
2. For a given set of values of the independent variables, the resulting values of the dependent variable are normally distributed.
3. That the sample be drawn by a process of random selection (Anderson and Bancroft, 1951).

The research situation which we shall discuss has an additional complication in that all variables, both independent and dependent, are subject to error. Bartlett (1949), and more recently Acton (1959), have discussed procedures for dealing with this type of situation, but few applications have appeared in the literature.

In evaluating the results of tests of significance of regression coefficients, caution will be used. In a numerical example presented by Bartlett (1949), the 95 per cent confidence interval of the regression coefficient is 16 per cent larger, assuming both variables are subject to error, than when assuming the independent variable is stated or measured without error.

Our data were collected in early December 1950 from 165 Chicago housewives selected by area sampling procedures. Blocks were chosen at random and four respondents picked at random in each block. Purchases were measured about a week before information was collected on other variables but it was felt that the situation prevailing at the time of purchase could not differ materially from that a week later.

For both scouring cleanser and coffee, the interview covered the respondent's knowledge and use of the various brands, preference ratings on the brands she knew, and brands, quantities, and place of her last purchase. Information was also obtained on possibilities for exposure to advertising in terms of ownership of a radio or TV set, subscription or regular readership of magazines and Chicago newspapers. Respondents were classified into high, medium and low economic strata on the basis of the

1940 rent data for the block in which they lived; this last rating was subject to revision by the interviewer after inspection of the household furnishings and equipment.

The respondents were asked to state their preferences for brands of scouring cleanser and coffee by means of a thermometer rating device. One-half of the respondents made preference statements before the question of purchases was raised and the other half made similar preference statements after the interviewer had determined the brands on hand. The two preference distributions differed insignificantly; from which we inferred no bias induced by the order of questioning and the returns of both halves were combined.

Only the highest preference ratings made by respondents were considered. If a respondent placed several brands in the highest category she used, each brand received an equal fractional share of the rating. The sum of these ratings for all respondents gave the total number of highest-choice ratings per brand. This procedure is described elsewhere (Banks, 1950).

To obtain data on purchases, the interviewer asked to see all containers of the last purchase under the guise of obtaining code numbers. Only when the containers were reported destroyed (e.g., when coffee packed in bags had been put into canisters and the bag discarded) were housewives asked to tell what brand they had bought last. Brand shares were of total amount bought in last purchases.

After discussing brand preference and purchase with a respondent, it was easy to discover where her last purchase of scouring cleanser and coffee had been made. The interviewer then went to the designated store or stores (not infrequently the scouring cleanser and coffee were bought in different stores) as soon as possible after finishing a given block assignment of interviews, and for each of the brands carried observed the price (in cents per package for scouring cleanser, in cents per pound for coffee), the amount of stock displayed, and the presence of promotional effort and point of purchase displays.

The formal model of demand discussed at the beginning of this article must be simplified drastically for empirical research because it deals with a very large number of variables, most of which are extremely difficult to measure. The model became, after appropriate simplification, one of multiple linear regression. The following equation was set

24

up to study the forces affecting market shares of brands of scouring cleanser and coffee.

$$P_i = aX_1 + bX_2 + cX_3 + dX_4 + eX_5 + fX_6 + gX_7,$$
where

P = Each brand's share of the sample's last purchase of the product.

X_1 = Consumer preference in terms of number of highest ratings per brand.

X_2 = Average price in cents per unit.

X_3 = Store coverage =
$$\frac{\text{No. stores stocking each brand, weighted by number shopping these stores}}{\text{Total number of users}}$$

X_4 = Index of stock display =
$$\frac{1 \text{ (no. good shelf displays)} + 2 \text{ (no. special displays)}}{\text{Total number of ratings}} \times 100$$

X_5 = Index of promotional effort =
$$\frac{\text{No. stores where brand carried offers of price deals or premium}}{\text{No. of stores stocking}} \times 100$$

X_6 = Index of Point of Purchase Advertising =
$$\frac{\text{No. stores where brand had POP effort}}{\text{No. of stores stocking}} \times 100$$

X_7 = Dollar expenditure for advertising in the three major media (newspaper, radio and magazines), Chicago, June through November 1950.

a, b, c, d, e, f, g are the regression coefficients which were computed mathematically.

Information on consumer advertising expenditures was obtained from three sources. A. C. Nielsen Company made available (in private correspondence) radio, newspaper and magazine advertising expenditures for brands of scouring cleanser and coffee in metropolitan Chicago from June through November 1950. This was satisfactory for scouring cleanser but gave no information on advertising of chains' private brands of coffee. The Chicago Tribune made available unpublished data on total advertising expenditures of these chains in Chicago in newspapers during this period. Some chains were willing to state, also in private correspondence, what share of their local advertising budget was allocated to their private brands of coffee; for the others, a sample of newspapers was selected and the ratio of space found to be allocated to their private brands of coffee was used as the share of their total advertising budget allocable to their private brands of coffee.

RESULTS

The data were analyzed to determine first, how successfully—as measured by the coefficient of multiple correlation—the research model fitted the actual purchase pattern; and second, the relative importance of the different elements of the model, as measured by the size of their regression coefficients.

First we considered how closely each factor separately was related to brand shares. For this we examined the simple correlations. For both coffee and scouring cleanser, consumer preference rating and store coverage, themselves highly correlated, showed the highest simple correlation with market shares. For scouring cleanser, promotional effort was highly correlated with market shares, while advertising expenditure was poorly correlated. The reverse was true for coffee. For both products, advertising expenditure was more highly correlated with store coverage than with market share or any other variable.

Table 1 shows the regression coefficients which permit direct evaluation of the relative effect of the independent variables on the dependent variable, brand shares.

TABLE 1

REGRESSION COEFFICIENTS BETWEEN BRAND SHARES AND SEVEN MARKETING ACTIVITIES

Marketing Activity	Cleanser (N = 9) (Multiple R = .999)	Coffee (N = 21) (Multiple R = .792)
Brand Preference (a)	.368*	1.108†
Average Price (b)	− .436*	− .202
Store Coverage (c)	.150*	.609
Stock Display (d)	.224*	− .364
Promotional Effort (e)	.416*	.067
POP Advertising (f)	− .242*	− .207
Advertising Expenditure (g)	.143*	− .536*

* Significant at the five per cent level.
† Significant at the one per cent level.

For Cleanser:
$$P_1 = .368X_1 - .436X_2 + .150X_3 + .224X_4 + .416X_5 - .242X_6 + .143X_7$$

For Coffee:
$$P_1 = 1.108X_1 - .202X_2 + .609X_3 - .364X_4 + .067X_5 - .207X_6 - .536X_7$$

For the scouring cleanser equation, all coefficients were significant at the five per cent level of confidence. The most important factors in determining market shares of brands were price, promotional effort and brand preference. As might be expected, price is negatively related, while promotional effort and brand preference are positively related to market share. One apparent anomaly was that point of purchase advertising was negatively related.

For coffee, the regression model produced a coefficient of multiple correlation of .972, significant at the one per cent level of confidence. However, in contrast to the scouring cleanser data, only two of the marketing factors studied, brand preference and advertising expenditure, were found to have significant effects upon the share position of brands of coffee, while store coverage approached significance.

For scouring cleanser it was observed that there were relatively high correlations between the brand preference ratings and several of the variables measuring marketing activity. The question arose—need we consider preference at all in such a demand equation?

The question was answered by dropping preference as an independent variable and noting what happened to the fit of the regression equation. This made little difference: R^2 dropped from .9997 to .9903, a change of less than one per cent. The reason for this may be found in the results of the regression of these marketing variables on the preference. Ninety-three per cent of the variance in preference for brands of scouring cleanser was accounted for by variance in the six external marketing variables. All of the regression coefficients were significant beyond the five per cent level, with those of price, promotional effort and stock display being highest. Differences among these three were not significant.

For coffee, on the other hand, dropping the preference variable reduced R^2 from .9456 to .6063, a change of 35 percentage points. Although the six-variable regression equation without preference for various brands of coffee still yielded a statistically significant multiple correlation coefficient, it is clear that these customers were more sensitive to the qualities of coffee brands than to the qualities of cleanser brands.

The linear equation based on six marketing variables did a satisfactory job of "explaining" shares of brands of scouring cleanser and coffee. However, there are advantages in reducing the number of variables. Other sets of regression equations were developed, using only the three marketing variables found to have the strongest relation to brand shares.

For scouring cleanser, the three used were price, store coverage and promotional effort. These three variables were quite effective in fitting the data; R^2 dropped from .9903 to .8892, only 10 per cent.

Because of the ease with which this three-variable equation could be computed, it was applied to various segments of the total sample. On the basis of information collected during the interview, respondents could be classified in the following ways: by income group; by whether they were exposed to much advertising; and by whether they shopped mostly at chain or independent stores.

Income was determined from 1940 Census rent data and modified by interviewer's evaluation of homes. To be considered as being "exposed to much advertising" they had to be exposed to three advertising vehicles other than radio programs. Type of store usually shopped was determined by questioning.

In a cross-classification of respondents by income level and stores shopped (see Table 2), it was found that the low income groups patronized independents

TABLE 2

REGRESSION COEFFICIENTS BETWEEN CLEANSER BRAND SHARES AND THREE MARKETING ACTIVITIES: BY STRATA

Group	Regression Coefficients			Multiple Correlation Coefficient
	Average Price	Weighted Store Coverage	Promotional Effort	
Entire Sample	−.291†	.491†	.603†	.943†
Chain Store	.083	−.049	1.016†	.977†
Independents	−.015	.601*	.343	.832*
Adv. Prone	−.338†	.587†	.530†	.938†
Non-Prone	−.037	.164	.831†	.936†
High Income	.044	.210	.837†	.919†
Medium Income	.974	.130	.867†	.935†
Low Income	.029	.162	.809†	.909*

* Significant at the five per cent level.
† Significant at the one per cent level.

to a much greater degree than did the two upper income groups. This was largely because few chains have units in the Negro and low income areas. There was no clear relationship between income and availability to advertising exposure.

Even when the total sample was split up, the regression coefficients for the scouring cleanser data remained significant except for respondents shopping at independent grocery stores. Promotional effort and distribution apparently were more important than price in "explaining" variations in scouring cleanser brand shares for the entire sample as well as for its different segments. However, all three coefficients were still significant beyond the one per cent level.

Between the various segments of the sample, some differences in importance of the three variables did emerge. Apparently chain store shoppers were more susceptible to promotional offers and deals for brands of scouring cleanser than housewives who shopped at independent stores; for the latter, availability was the most important factor. Those open

advertising exposure were equally affected by the distribution of brands and the use of promotional effort.

Price also had a strong effect. Promotional effort was the only variable among the three tested to affect market share among those respondents not available to heavy advertising exposure.

Income seemed to have no effect upon the weights of the variables in the demand equation. This seems plausible since scouring cleanser is relatively cheap. It is interesting to note that disguised price reductions—in terms of special deals or offers—had a much stronger effect upon scouring cleanser brand shares than did actual price differences. This was equally true for all income groups.

A three-variable regression model was also fitted to the coffee data using the variables found to have highest correlation with market shares: price, store coverage and past six months' advertising expenditure.

It was found to yield a statistically significant fit; the coefficient of multiple correlation was significant at the one per cent level. However, the fit of the three-variable equation for coffee was substantially poorer than that for scouring cleanser. There are at least two reasons for this: the greater diversity of marketing patterns among the 21 brands of coffee than among the nine brands of scouring cleanser; and the greater importance of brand quality for coffee than for scouring cleanser.

For the entire sample, only store coverage had a statistically significant relation with market shares of coffee brands. Neither price nor advertising expenditure was found to have a significant effect upon market shares when the other two factors were held constant.

The three-variable model was applied to various segments of the sample and statistically significant fits were obtained among chain store shoppers, those advertising prone and those in the high income group. Probably these three sub-groupings overlapped so that the same respondents showed up under different headings.

Although the data were not statistically significant, an interesting situation held among the "manufacturer's brand" buyers. Among those people who bought a manufacturer's brand (Hills Brothers, Chase & Sanborn, Stewarts, etc.), advertising actually appeared to have a negative relation with sales. Examination of the raw data indicated that, during the period studied, Maxwell House was spending 40 per cent of the total advertising volume in Chicago for these six brands, but was receiving

only 16 per cent of their total sales. In contrast, Manor House was spending only nine per cent of the total advertising volume, but receiving almost 30 per cent of total sales.

CONCLUSIONS

The more general model discussed at the beginning of this paper has illustrative value for teaching purposes. It formulates problems of demand in marketing terms by dealing with market share data obtained by differentiated brands whose owners compete with all the tools in their respective arsenals. Students are thus presented with a device for considering the major variables affecting sales.

The demand model easily accommodates the familiar discussion of convenience, shopping and specialty goods. For example, the demand model for convenience goods would likely show store coverage, point of purchase display and promotional effort to be most important in affecting sales. On the other hand, for specialty goods preference would probably be the only variable of major importance.

The model tested by the data presents more of a mixture of values. Such a regression model can approximate the importance of various factors affecting market shares, and the relationships between these factors. Surveys are less helpful on this point since people seldom can evaluate the relative importance of the factors impinging upon their purchase decisions.

The results of regression analysis should be considered as first approximations for several reasons. Foremost is the fact that they show only co-variation, not cause and effect. The regression analysis is useful to point out the factors to be used in experimentation, but should not be considered as a substitute for it.

Findings from the regression model hold only for the range of observations available in the data. Promotional effort was found to have a stronger relationship than price with brand shares of scouring cleanser. But the range of prices was quite narrow, 8.6 to 12.9 cents per can. Whoever breaks through these limits may well find price to have a great effect upon market shares.

Another caution in the use of the regression analysis is that it yields only over-all relationships. In any market, some brands are declining in market shares, others are rising, while still others are merely holding their own. The regression procedure gives coefficients which are actually averages of the coefficients for the individual brands. These results may not apply to any one brand.

Marketing strategies usually call for manipulating several variables simultaneously. Manufacturers merchandise their coming advertising campaigns to their retailers, who respond by improving stock holdings and displays and by putting up point of purchase advertising sent them. Private brands are usually offered in only a few stores; but in these stores they are usually given the best locations, largest stock displays and massive point of purchase advertising displays. Manufacturers' brands, especially in convenience goods, tend toward 100 per cent coverage but with less prominence of display within stores. Regression analysis is not the best way to cope with these different relationships between several independent variables.

Finally, regression analysis is a quantitative procedure and uses essentially quantitative evaluations of data. It is quite likely that many relationships are distorted by the units we use to express these quantities. Advertising is the most important case in point though the problem also arises with premiums and deals. If the effect of advertising were proportional to expenditure on it, then the firm which spent the most for advertising would sell the most product. However, this does not happen (Borden, 1942). Advertising effect depends not only upon magnitude of expenditure but also upon the motivating power of the copy and upon the media used. Failure of advertising expenditure to correlate with sales does not mean that advertising is ineffective, but may mean only that the measuring procedure failed to evaluate properly the strengths of various campaigns.

Implicit in the model presented is the assumption that all variables act instantaneously. This assumption is open to serious doubt. An effort was made to take differing time lags into consideration by considering advertising expenditures for the previous six months, while all other variables were assumed to be acting at the time of the research. This was a guess. It was found that the correlation of brand sales with the previous year's advertising was slightly higher than with the data of the shorter period, but the improvement was not significant. The varying time lag of different variables is certainly one of the most important matters of concern to marketing directors yet little or no research has been devoted to it.

I have said much of the limitations of the regression model but little of its value. I believe it offers real advantages. For relatively little expenditure, a substantial amount of material can be collected and evaluated. The simple correlations between market shares and the independent marketing variables will give a picture of the marketing strategies being used for the brands of a given product class, plus relationships between consumers' appreciation of the qualities of brands and external marketing variables. Finally, the findings of the multiple regression analysis can be considered a first approximation of the relative importance of these marketing variables—especially if more faith is put in findings of no effect than in findings of much effect.

REFERENCES

ACTON, F. S. *The Analysis of Straight Line Data.* New York: John Wiley and Sons, 1959, Chapter 5.

ANDERSON, R. L. AND T. A. BANCROFT. *Statistical Theory in Research.* New York: McGraw-Hill Book Company, 1951.

BANKS, SEYMOUR. The Relationships Between Preference and Purchase of Brands. *Journal of Marketing,* Vol. 15, No. 2, October 1950, pp. 145-157.

BARTLETT, M. S. Fitting a Straight Line when Both Variables are Subject to Error. *Biometrics,* Vol. 5, 1949, pp. 207-212.

BORDEN, N. H. *The Economic Effects of Advertising.* Chicago: R. I. Irwin, Inc., 1942, Chapter 8.

EZEKIEL, M. *Methods of Correlation Analysis,* 2nd ed. New York: John Wiley and Sons, 1941, Chapter 21.

As an instance of the nonsense or spurious correlation that is a real statistical fact someone has gleefully pointed to this: There is a close relationship between the salaries of Presbyterian ministers in Massachusetts and the price of rum in Havana. Which is the cause and which the effect? In other words, are the ministers benefiting from the rum trade or supporting it? All right. That's so far-fetched that it is ridiculous at a glance. But watch out for the other applications of post hoc logic that differ from this one only in being more subtle.

—DARRELL HUFF

Predicting Short-Term Changes in Market Share as a Function of Advertising Strategy

ROBERT D. BUZZELL*

➤ This article presents the results of a series of multiple regression analyses in which past market share, advertising expenditure share, and test scores for television commercials were used to predict changes in market shares. The results suggest that the quality of advertising message content-and-presentation, as measured by the test scores, is closely related to short-term changes in market shares for food and drug products. This relationship implies that marketing models based on dollar expenditures alone cannot provide sufficient explanations of market response to advertising.

The search for more rational methods to plan and evaluate advertising has been almost as long, and nearly as fruitless, as the quest for the Philosopher's Stone. For nearly 100 years, businessmen have bemoaned their inability to measure returns from advertising efforts. In recent years, there have been numerous attempts to develop mathematical models of relationships between advertising and sales or profits [1, 2]. Many different approaches have been used in these models. Some have been developed by a process of deduction from a few "plausible" assumptions; others are based on large-scale field experiments in which various advertising "treatments" are applied to geographic areas. Nearly all mathematical models of advertising, however, have one property in common: they omit the so-called "creative" aspects of the advertising process from consideration.

In most cases, mathematical models of advertising consist of equations purporting to express functional relationships between advertising expenditures and sales. Either expenditures or sales, or both, may be expressed in *dollars,* as *fractions* of industry totals, as percentage *changes* from a base° period, or as deviations from average or "normal" levels. In models designed to aid managers in selecting advertising media, advertising may be measured in terms of numbers of "impressions" or "exposures" delivered to an audience. Whatever the manner of expressing the variable,

the underlying logic is usually the same—namely, that in advertising "it's not what you say or how you say it, but *how often* you say it."

To be sure, this assumption is seldom stated explicitly. Typically, nothing at all is said about message content and presentation. If the question is raised, many model-builders—and a few experienced advertising men —will assert that, with a few notable exceptions, effects of message content and presentation do not vary enough to influence observed sales results. After all, there are only so many things to say about a product, and similar creative techniques are used by most or all advertising agencies. Consequently, any company employing a competent advertising agency can expect to get about the same "quality" in advertising as its major competitors, and this quality will change but little from year to year. The exceptions to this general rule are the rare creative triumphs—like Volkswagen—and the even more rare creative flops.

Apart from the supposition that the "creative variable" does not vary, there are some other reasons for the typical neglect of message content and presentation in models of advertising. The most important is the belief that no reliable way exists to *measure* the effects of message content and presentation. Certainly there is considerable disagreement in the advertising world on *how* such effects should be measured. Most national advertisers use tests of various kinds to evaluate their creative strategies, both before and after the advertising appears. Measures of "effectiveness" used for this purpose include awareness of a brand, recall of advertisements, attitudes toward products, coupon returns or inquiries, and various psychological techniques [6, 7]. Most of these measures are open to criticism, and critics delight in pointing to instances in which an increase in awareness or an improvement in attitude is *not* accompanied by an increase in sales [3]. Critics usually content themselves, however, with one or a few examples of this kind, and conclude by dismissing the idea of measuring the effects of message content

* Dr. Buzzell is associate professor in Harvard University's Graduate School of Business Administration. The analysis described in this paper was initiated by Mr. Malcolm P. Murphy of Schwerin Research Corporation and carried out by the author and Mr. Murphy. Earlier versions of the analysis based on a somewhat different model, were presented at the Operations Research Discussion Group of the Advertising Research Foundation and at the Workshop on Planning and Evaluation of the Association of National Advertisers in December, 1963. This version was presented to the Eleventh International Meeting of The Institute of Management Sciences in Pittsburgh, March 12, 1964.

and presentation. There have been very few attempts to relate measures of creative quality to sales results on a systematic basis.

ARE "CREATIVE" FACTORS IMPORTANT?

While message content and presentation have generally been neglected in mathematical models of advertising, there are reasons to believe that these factors *do* have significant effects on consumer purchasing behavior. The most convincing piece of evidence is the fact that the great majority of marketing executives *believe* creative factors to be important. In effect, they are willing to bet that $1,000,000 spent on one type of campaign *will* produce more sales than $1,000,000 spent on another type of campaign. It can be argued, of course, that this conviction is just a form of self-delusion and, perhaps, puffery by advertising agencies. Apart from executives' beliefs, there are some assorted scraps of evidence to support the argument that creative factors affect sales. For example, Daniel Starch has demonstrated a relationship between recall of magazine advertisements and purchasing of the advertised brands during the week following exposure [4]. Of course, the relationship between reading and buying runs both ways [5], so that readership figures cannot be interpreted purely as measures of creative quality. But this and similar evidence seems to suggest that there *are* variations in the sales effects of different advertising messages.

If we assume for a moment that the sales effects of advertising *do* depend on message content and presentation, then it is clear that mathematical models based on dollar expenditure alone leave much to be desired. Suppose, for example, that we examine historical time series data for sales and dollar expenditures, and try to ascertain some general relationship between the two. Even if we are successful in adjusting for the influence of non-advertising variables such as prices, the relationship may be seriously distorted if the creative quality of advertising in different time periods has changed. Similarly, if we conduct an experiment to determine the sales effects of different levels of expenditure, using the *same* message in each territory, the results may still be misleading when a different message is used in a subsequent period. Thus, the effect of omitting "creative factors" from models of advertising is to distort observed relationships, leading to serious errors in prediction and, possibly, in policy decisions based on the predictions.

A MEASURE OF MESSAGE EFFECTS

If message content-and-presentation is an important factor in the advertising process, then it is desirable to incorporate some measure of this factor into any mathematical model of the process. As mentioned above, there are many different methods of "copy testing" that might be used for this purpose. The analysis described below was based on data from one of the most widely-used services for testing *television commercials,* the Schwerin Research Corporation (SRC).[1] Briefly, the procedure used in testing commercials is as follows:

1. Names are randomly selected from residential telephone directories in a metropolitan area. (Tests are conducted mainly in New York, and also in five other cities in the U.S.A., two in Canada, and in London.) Respondents are invited to attend a theater preview of a television program. The average audience size is around 350.
2. Prior to the film, the respondent is asked to select the brand in each of three product categories which she would prefer to receive if she wins a lottery drawing to be conducted later.
3. The audience is exposed to a television program film which includes test commercials for one brand in each of the three product categories.
4. After exposure to the film, respondents are again asked to indicate their brand preferences in each of the three product categories.

This testing procedure yields two basic statistics: the percentage of respondents expressing preference for a brand *before* exposure to a test commercial ("Pre-Preference") and the percentage expressing preference *after* exposure ("Post-Preference"). The net change (Post-Preference minus Pre-Preference) is one measure of the effect of the commercial message. A subsidiary statistic is the *average* change in preference associated with exposure to commercials in a given product class. SRC compiles averages or "norms" for each product class on an annual basis.

Space does not permit an extended discussion of the SRC testing procedure, sample selection, possible biases arising from commercial position, night of week, and so on. In this analysis, we have simply assumed that the test scores for commercials *do* reflect differences in message content and presentation, and then proceed to investigate the apparent *effects* of these differences on consumer purchasing. For obvious reasons, the analysis is limited to product classes, brands, and time periods for which test data were available. Typically, advertisers have tests made of several alternative commercials, and then use the same basic type of message in an advertising *campaign* lasting from three months to a year or more. In our analysis, we have used test scores as measures of an advertiser's message content and presentation during the *four-month period*

[1] The Schwerin test procedure is not, of course, the only technique available for measuring the effectiveness of television commercials. Gallup & Robinson, Inc., conducts aided-recall tests following the broadcasting of commercials, and Batten, Barton, Durstine, & Osborn, Inc., utilizes an "on-the-air" testing procedure in its "Channel One" test facility. The distinctive feature of the SRC test is its simulation of a purchasing situation.

following the date of the test. Because SRC tests television commercials, we deal only with television advertising, and the analysis involves only products for which television is the dominant advertising medium.

REGRESSION ANALYSIS OF CHANGES IN MARKET SHARE

The data derived from SRC commercial tests were used in a regression analysis of changes in market shares in six product classes: light duty liquid detergents, margarines, toilet soaps, hair tonics, stomach remedies, and analgesic products. Producers in all of these product fields rely very heavily on television advertising as a means of competition. The major competing brands in each field are generally very similar, except when one brand gains a temporary advantage through product improvement. Major brands also generally have roughly equal distribution, pricing, and field sales support. The purpose of this analysis was to determine the relationship between a brand's market share and three other variables: *past market share, television advertising expenditures,* and *message content and presentation* as measured by the SRC test scores.

Before results of the regression analysis are discussed, some general considerations should be mentioned. *First,* changes in the market shares from 1 four-month period to the next are typically very small. In statistical terms, market share figures exhibit a high degree of auto-correlation. Consequently, we can expect that most of the variance in current market share will be explained by market share in one or more past periods. *Second,* to complicate matters, both measures of market share and advertising expenditures used in the analysis are subject to measurement error. The market share data were derived from store audits in a sample of outlets, and the periods covered by the audits do not correspond exactly to the months for which the figures are reported. Advertising expenditures were estimated from published sources. While both estimates are subject to error, there is no reason to suspect any consistent bias in one direction or the other. *Third,* we can expect significant correlations among the independent variables in the analysis; for instance, consumer's expressed brand preferences naturally depend in part on their past purchases, so that Pre-Preference is highly correlated with previous market share. No claim is made, therefore, that the explanatory variables in the regression equations are independent of one another.

These facts of life are obviously at variance with the classical assumptions one would *like* to make in regression analysis, but such an analysis nevertheless seemed useful in exploring the effects of message content and presentation on sales. The specific questions we sought to answer were these:

1. Is message content and presentation—as measured by the SRC test score—a significant factor in explaining short-term changes in market share? If it were *not,* then we would expect the test scores to be of little value in predicting share changes.
2. If the "creative variable" is significant, then in what *form* should it be expressed? As mentioned previously, the net change in the fraction of respondents expressing preference for a brand (Post-Preference minus Pre-Preference) has been used as a measure of message effect. This can be further modified by subtracting the Norm or average preference change from the observed change, as an approximation of "how much better" a given commercial is than the average competing commercial.
3. How important is advertising message relative to advertising expenditure? That is, which seems to contribute most to observed changes in market shares?
4. Does the relative importance of advertising message content-and-presentation vary among product classes?
5. Is there any evidence that changes in market share are governed in part by the trend in market share prior to the beginning of a period? If so, we would expect the accuracy of prediction to be increased by utilizing information on market share for at least *two* past periods rather than just one.

FORM OF THE ANALYSIS

The regression analysis was based on 60 observations, representing all of the brands and time periods for which SRC test data were available in the six product classes mentioned earlier.

Three different regression models were tested. In the first, the dependent variable was a brand's market shares during the current period, while the independent variables were the brand's market shares during the two preceding time periods and its share of total industry television advertising expenditures in the current period and preceding time periods. That is,

$$MS_{1,\ t} = a + b_1 MS_{1,\ t-1} + b_2 MS_{1,\ t-2} + b_3 AS_{1,\ t} + b_4 AS_{1,\ t-1} + u.$$

The purpose of this regression was to determine how accurately we could predict changes in market share using only past market share and a brand's share of industry advertising *expenditures.*

The second and third models included the same independent variables *plus* the three statistics derived from SRC commercial tests—Pre-Preference for the brand, Post-Preference, and the Norm (average) preference change for all tested brands in a given product field. In Model II, we pooled the data for all six product fields and inserted a dummy variable d_j for each product field. Thus, the regression equation was:

$$MS_{1,\ t} = a + b_1 MS_{1,\ t-1} + b_2 MS_{1,\ t-2} + b_3 AS_{1,\ t} + b_4 AS_{1,\ t-1} + b_5 Pre_1 + b_6 Post_1 + b_7 Norm + \sum_{j=1}^{5} d_j + u.$$

where $d_j = 1$ if $i \, \epsilon \, j$, 0 otherwise.[2] Model III was identical to Model II except that the analysis was made separately for each product class and the dummy variables were eliminated.

RESULTS OF THE ANALYSIS

The results of the analysis can best be described in relation to the questions we sought to answer. To deal with the most general question first, it appears that advertising *message content-and-presentation is significantly related to changes in market share.* In Model II, which included both dollar expenditures and test scores, the pertinent statistics were as follows:

Independent Variable	Regression Coefficient (b)	$t = \dfrac{b}{\sigma_b}$ (54 d.f.)	Partial Correlation Coefficient
$MS_{i, \, t-1}$	.8733	42.56	.9854
$Post_i$	.1094	6.16	.6425
$Norm_i$	−.1076	−2.45	−.3167
Dummy (Hair Tonics)	−.7183	−2.40	−.3103
AS_i	.0155	1.32	.1767

R^2 (corrected) $= .993$ $\sigma_u = .6757$ share pts.
Avg. Absolute Error $= .5106$ share pts.

Since the partial coefficient for the Post-Preference score implies that it explains about 40 percent of residual variance, and the "t" value is obviously significant, it is clear that this variable helps to explain market share changes. This can also be seen by comparing the results of Model II with those of Model I, which did not include the test score data. When we predict market share changes on the basis of dollar expenditures only, the errors in prediction are considerably greater:

	Model I (Dollars only)	Model II (Dollars and Test Scores)
R^2 (corrected for d.f.)	.9887	.9930
σ_u (share points)	.8595	.6757
Avg. absolute error (share points)	.6753	.5106

The very high coefficients of multiple correlation reflect the high degree of correlation between current market share and past market share ($r_{MSt, \, MSt-1} = .926$). Consequently, a more meaningful measure of the goodness of fit for either of the two regression equations is the percentage of *residual* variance explained, after allowance for past market share. In

these terms, the multiple correlation coefficients were the following:

Model I (dollars only)	$R^2 = .0825$
Model II (dollars and test scores)	$R^2 = .4329$

The regression coefficients estimated for Model II shed some light on *how* the test score figures can best be used to measure the probable effect of message content and presentation. The Pre-Preference score does not enter into the equation at all.[3]

As to the form of the "creative variable," it may be noted that the regression coefficients for Post-Preference and the product class Norm are almost exactly in absolute value and opposite in algebraic sign - - -. 1094 *vs.* —.1076. In a predictive equation, it would be legitimate to use the *difference* between the two (Post-Preference minus Norm) as a measure of message quality.

RELATIVE IMPORTANCE OF MESSAGE QUALITY

The relative importance of advertising message quality and advertising expenditure may be judged by a comparison of their respective regression coefficients and partial correlation coefficients in Model II:

Coefficient	Post-Preference	Advertising Share
b	.1094	.0155
β (Standardized)	.1345	.0199
r (Partial correlation)	.6425	.1767

The implication is clear that message quality was of substantially greater importance than advertising expenditure in explaining the observed changes in market share for the brands and time periods included in this study.

VARIATION AMONG PRODUCTS

Model III included the same variables as Model II, but the regression analysis was made separately for each of the six product classes. In doing this, of course, we were forced to use very small samples, ranging in size from 6 for Hair Tonics to 12 for light duty liquids and upset stomach remedies. The results of this analysis suggest that *there are important differences among*

---

[2] The "dummy" variables for the first 5 product classes represented the differences, if any, between each product class and the sixth product (analgesics). Any one of the 6 product classes could have been used as the "base class."

[3] Although no pre-determined "F" level was set for adding or dropping independent variables, the computer program used in the analysis will stop adding new variables when the determinant of the inverse matrix for the next step is within a prescribed (and very small) distance from zero. In Model II, the computation stopped before "Pre-Preference" was entered. The reason for this may be the high simple correlation, .849, between Pre-Preference and past Market Share. This, in turn, suggests that *if* predictions had to be made before market share data became available, Pre-Preference might be a suitable proxy. We have not tested this idea directly as yet.

product classes in the effects of advertising strategy. Least-squares estimates of the regression coefficients (standardized Betas) were as follows:

Independent Variable	Product Field				
	L.D. Liquids	Margarine	Toilet Soap	Hair Tonic	Stomach Remedies
Constant	6.911	−0.266	−11.570	−11.018	−1.429
MS_{t-1}	.577*	.895	.374	.818*	.957*
Post	.526*	.173†	.082	.405†	.351†
Pre			.728		−.280†
Norm		−.046	.055		
AS_t			.212		
AS_{t-1}	−.111			.271	
R^2 (corrected)	.970	.992	.992	.981	.990
$σ_e$ (share pts.)	.454	.571	.332	.392	.436
Sample size	12	11	8	6	12

* Significant at .01 level.   † Significant at .05 level.

No figures are shown for the analgesics field because in this instance the analysis yielded extremely implausible results and none of the estimates was statistically significant even at the .10 level.

Because of the small sample sizes, the results for individual product fields are merely suggestive. The coefficients for MS_{t-1} suggest relatively high retention or "brand loyalty" rates in the margarine, hair tonic, and stomach remedy fields but very *low* loyalty in the toilet soap field.

The lower standard errors of estimate within product fields are to be expected because of the inherently lower variability of market share within a more homogeneous grouping. The percentage of variance explained by regression is about the same or lower in the individual fields as in the pooled analysis. About all that can be said on the basis of this evidence is that there probably *are* significant differences among product fields, but the available data are not adequate for reliably estimating the parameters in each field.

TREND IN MARKET SHARE

The results of the analysis do *not* indicate a significant association between current market share and the share trend prior to the beginning of a period. If there were, we would expect MS_{t-2} to appear in the equation as a significant explanatory variable. Since it did not, the implication is that, on an aggregate level, changes in market share can safely be treated as a first-order process. This does not imply that individual

customers' brand choices can be treated as a first-order Markov process: indeed, the evidence against this is overwhelming.

SUMMARY

To sum up, the analysis of market share changes, test score data, and advertising expenditures suggests the following:

1. The content and presentation of advertising messages, as measured by the SRC commercial tests, is related to short-term changes in market share.
2. If anything, advertising message quality is *more* important than the level of advertising expenditure. Message quality is neither insignificant nor invariant, as has often been assumed in models of the advertising process.
3. There appear to be differences in the effects of advertising among product fields, but presently available data do not permit reliable estimation of the magnitude of these differences.
4. Trend in market share does not appear to carry over two or more campaign periods.

All of these conclusions are tentative, of course, and subject to modification as more data become available. But a good Bayesian would certainly have to take these findings into account in setting his "priors" for further research.

REFERENCES

1. Robert D. Buzzell, *A Basic Bibliography on Mathematical Methods in Marketing*, AMA Bibliography Series No. 7, Chicago: American Marketing Association, 1962.
2. Robert D. Buzzell, "Operations Research for Measurement of Advertising Effectiveness: The First Five Years," *Proceedings, 9th Annual Conference*, Advertising Research Foundation, 1963.
3. Scott Paper Company, "Industrial Packaged Goods Advertising Effectiveness Evaluation 1960-61," mimeographed report, 1962.
4. Daniel Starch, "Do Ad Readers Buy the Products?" *Harvard Business Review*, 36 (May-June 1958), 49-58.
5. ———, "Advertisement Readership by Brand Users and Non-Users," *Starch Tested Copy*, No. 101 (December 1963).
6. Harry D. Wolfe, *et al.*, *Measuring Advertising Results*, Studies in Business Policy No. 102, New York: National Industrial Conference Board, 1962.
7. ———, *Pretesting Advertising*, Studies in Business Policy No. 109, New York: National Industrial Conference Board, 1963.

Individual Exposure to Advertising and Changes in Brands Bought[1]

PURNELL H. BENSON
Rutgers, The State University

Per dollar of advertising, magazines apparently can sell more toothpaste than television can.

The quest for cause and effect relationships between advertising and sales is strewn with the wreckage of serial correlation. Companies whose sales are increasing usually put more money into advertising. Of sales and advertising, which is cause and which is effect?

The research design examined in this paper utilizes variations in exposure of each individual consumer to advertising. Changes in advertising exposure for the individual consumer, as contrasted with changes which affect an entire market, are of several kinds. 1. The individual shifts her selection of media because of reader interest or viewer interest. 2. The availability of media to the consumer changes according to circumstances. Her TV set may not be operating, or she may go visiting instead of watching TV. She may forget to pick up her favorite magazine at the newsstand. 3. The advertiser alters his selection of media to carry his message. In changing from medium to medium, he

alters exposure for individuals who see one medium, but not the other.

Are these variations in individual exposure to advertising reflected in measurable changes in individual buying habits? If research can answer this question, a new avenue for testing the effects of advertising upon sales is opened.

The Approach

The only data amenable to studying changes in individual advertising exposure and changes in

PURNELL H. BENSON is associate professor of marketing at the Graduate School of Business Administration, Rutgers, The State University. He is also director of developmental research with Grudin Research Corporation, and president, Consumer and Personnel Studies, Inc., a firm specializing in mathematical analysis of consumer and market data. He has served such companies as General Electric, General Mills, Johnson and Johnson, and Scott Paper. In 1935 he graduated Phi Beta Kappa from Princeton, received an M.A. in sociology from Harvard in 1936, and a Ph.D. in sociology from the University of Chicago in 1952. Previously he taught sociology and social psychology at Temple University. At Drew University he was chairman of the Division of Social Studies.

[1] The author wishes to acknowledge the assistance of Dr. Charles E. Swanson, professor of marketing at New York University. When he was chairman of the Research Committee of the Magazine Advertising Bureau, Dr. Swanson proposed the research design, helped convince the Magazine Advertising Bureau to proceed with the project, and made beneficial comments on the first draft of the research report. Mr. Paul Hefner was responsible for the computer program.

individual brand purchase are re-interview data which include, for each consumer, reports of media read or viewed and reports of brand purchases. The consumer panel data collected in 1963-64 by the Brand Rating Research Corporation are of this type (Garfinkle, 1963).

The exposures reported by consumers to media carrying brand advertising involve changes in the amount of advertising by the manufacturer from time period to time period, as well as media variation by him. Similarly, changes in brand purchase incorporate trends in sales activity for the manufacturer's brand. These trends must be eliminated from the data if the problem of serial correlation is to be avoided. After eliminating the trend in brand purchase by the panel from the individual's report of brand purchase, the variability which remains is the individual's purchase pattern about the trend as the base line. Likewise, after eliminating, from the individual's report of exposure to advertising media, the trend in amount of advertising, the variability in individual exposure which remains is that due to individual circumstances.

Analysis of the Data

Toothpaste, as a widely used and heavily advertised product, was selected for study. The December 1963 and May 1964 waves of data collected by the Brand Rating Research Corporation were used in the analysis of three leading brands of toothpaste. Two-thirds of the respondents interviewed during the first wave were re-interviewed during the second wave. The present study includes 2,639 cases of female toothpaste users, mostly housewives, reporting in both waves of interviews.

Panel participants are asked to give their first choice for brand purchase, their second choice, brands also bought during the past six months, and brands not bought at all during the six months. These levels of buying preference were assigned numerical values of 1, 2, 3, and 4 as the sales variable for each of the three brands, prior to the analysis.

The exposure to magazines is recorded in terms of having read 4 out of 4 of the previous issues, 3 out of 4, 2 out of 4, 1 out of 4, and 0 out of 4. A sixth category of not having read any of the past 4 issues, but having read occasionally in the past six months, was assigned a numerical value of .5. Also, respondents report television shows as having watched 4 out of 4 previous broadcasts, 3 out of 4, 2 out of 4, 1 out of 4, 0 out of 4, and watch occasionally but not the last 4 episodes, assigned .5.

The exposure of the individual to the magazine or television show is not an exposure to advertising unless advertising is carried in the magazine or on the show. The exposure to the medium must be weighted by the amount of advertising carried. An index to this amount is provided by the amount of money spent by the advertiser for his advertising in the medium. The periods of advertising considered in the study are five months long. The amounts spent on individual magazines and television shows used in the analysis of toothpaste are from audits by the Magazine Advertising Bureau and by the National Association of Broadcasters.

Since spot TV advertising data were not available by time period of viewing, spot TV advertising was omitted from consideration. Also omitted from the study are all other sales influences, such as copy themes, product changes, premiums, coupons, pricing, and packaging, which induce brand buying. To the extent that these variables exert any trend influence, their effects upon brand preference are removed by the analysis. The only promotional effects which remain are random ones about the trends, and also remaining are joint effects of copy content and forms of promotion used concurrently with expenditures upon magazine or sponsored TV advertising. Magazine and sponsored TV shows are the two advertising media examined in the analysis made of the consumer panel data. Since the study is an exploratory one to investigate the feasibility of a method of analysis, the conclusions reached about these two types of media are not considered to have general application.

The money spent by the advertiser in each medium, converted to cost per unit exposure, is multiplied by the exposure of each consumer to the medium. This is done separately for each consumer for each of the three brands advertised in each of 15 magazines and on each of 72 television shows. The products of magazine cost per individual and amount of individual exposure are accumulated for the individual consumer to yield a measure of the extent of her exposure to magazine advertising by each of the three brands. Similar arithmetic products are accumulated to yield a measure of the extent of her exposure to television advertising by each of the brands.

Next, for each consumer, the weighted exposure to the brand advertised in the first time period is subtracted from the weighted exposure in the second time period. This is done separately for magazine and for television advertising of the brand involved. Also, the buying preference for each brand is differenced from the first to the second time periods to obtain the change in buying pattern. The foregoing two million pieces of arithmetic required 10 minutes of computer time.

Using age, education, income, and each of 11 geographic regions as demographic variables, all of the trends in each dependent and in each independent variable for each individual consumer which can be accounted for by the demographic variables were removed by multiple regression analysis. The computer required an hour for this part of the analysis. The residual changes in each of the sales and advertising variables for each consumer are used as data input during the final regression analyses to relate advertising exposure to changes in brand purchase. In the final regressions, the variables included are magazine and television advertising in behalf of each of the three brands (six independent variables) and changes in brand purchase for each brand (three dependent variables).

Use of the Discriminant Function

The question arises of whether the intervals for buying levels 3 and 4 are equivalent to those between 1 and 2. That is, for a brand to move from bought-very-little to not-bought-at-all may not mean the same thing as for a brand to move from first buying choice to second buying choice, which is the criterion of a brand switch. This question was answered by calculating, as part of the regression analysis, what scale separation 3 and 4 should have on the buying preference scale if the independent variables exert the same effect per scale unit of buying preference at levels 3 and 4 as they do at levels 1 and 2. The calculation is made by the rationale of the discriminant function originated by R. A. Fisher, which estimates the statistically best fitting scale values for a set of categories (Guttman 1941).

The arithmetic device is to include entries for a dummy independent variable which are 1 when the dependent variable is 3, and 0 when it is not 3. Similar entries are made for a second dummy variable which are 1 when the dependent variable is 4, and 0 when it is not 4. These entries are made in the analysis prior to differencing variables and calculating residuals. The regression coefficients obtained for the dummy variables after the final multiple regressions, subtracted from the corresponding scale values, give the best fitting estimates for the scale values.

The final multiple regression analyses of brand purchase in relation to advertising exposure were also performed without correction by the discriminant function procedure. The final set of regressions consumed another 20 minutes, or a total of about an hour and a half on the machine.

Results and Discussion

The levels of correlation obtained with and without the discriminant rationale are similar. With this component of the analysis, the multiple correlations between brand purchase-preference and the six advertising variables are .049, .022, and .039 for the brands identified as A, B, and C. Without the discriminant effect upon scale values 3 and 4, the multiple correlations are .047, .037 and .040. Five of the multiple correlations are significant at about a 95 per cent level of confidence, their standard errors being .019 with an N of 2,639 cases. Taken together, the correlations seem convincing indication that individual exposure to advertising is correlated with individual brand purchase.

Why is the correlation between individual exposure to advertising and brand buying preference no higher than what was found? One reason is that the elimination of trend variation removes some of the baby's skin with the bath water. Not only is the serial correlation removed, but also some genuine cause and effect influences contained in the correlation of trends are discarded from consideration.

A more obvious reason is that brand purchase is affected by numerous other things besides individual exposure to advertising. Prominent among these is whether the copy or commercial content is apt or inept. A further limitation is that the audit of individual exposure covers only 4 weeks to 4 months of the total period of 5 months considered at the time of each wave of interviews.

The results seem more dependable for comparing relative effects of different types of advertising than they do for estimating the optimum total amount of advertising to be carried for maximum profit from sales. The circumstance that one of the types of advertising appears to merit more money being expended upon it relative to the other type does not imply from this analysis that the amount of money spent on the other type exceeds profitability.

At least, the results show that consumer re-interview data have the leverage to demonstrate measurable effects of advertising upon buying behavior. More frequent and more detailed audits of advertising exposure, or the use of experimental designs in

TABLE 1
CHANGES IN PERCENTAGE BRAND SHARE OF THREE TOOTHPASTES OVER A FIVE MONTHS' PERIOD IN
RELATION TO CHANGES IN ADVERTISING EXPOSURE
MEASURED IN $100,000'S SPENT PER FIVE MONTHS' PERIOD OF ADVERTISING

Advertising Variable	Amount Spent by Brand During 5 Months' Period. $100,000's	Brand A			Brand B			Brand C		
		Regression Coefficient	Standard Error	t Value	Regression Coefficient	Standard Error	t Value	Regression Coefficient	Standard Error	t Value
Magazine advertising by Brand A	20	−.08 (−.39)	.11 (.41)	−.8 (−.9)	−.04 (−.06)	.13 (.39)	−.3 (−.1)	−.16 (.11)	.12 (.39)	−1.4 (.3)
Magazine advertising by Brand B	9	.08 (−.02)	.20 (.74)	.4 (−.0)	.05 (−.23)	.24 (.71)	.2 (−.3)	.27 (−.39)	.22 (.70)	1.2 (−.6)
Magazine advertising by Brand C	2	−.23 (−.30)	.46 (1.68)	−.5 (−.2)	−.82 (−2.37)	.54 (1.61)	−1.5 (−1.5)	.76 (.32)	.49 (1.59)	1.5 (.2)
TV sponsor advertising by Brand A	40	.03 (−.29)	.05 (.17)	.6 (−1.6)	−.08 (.12)	.06 (.16)	−1.4 (.8)	.01 (.25)	.05 (.16)	.2 (1.5)
TV sponsor advertising by Brand B	52	−.00 (.24)	.04 (.15)	−.1 (1.6)	−.00 (.04)	.05 (.14)	−.1 (.3)	.01 (−.11)	.04 (.14)	.3 (−.8)
TV sponsor advertising by Brand C	29	.03 (.09)	.07 (.26)	.4 (.3)	.14 (.04)	.08 (.25)	1.7 (.2)	−.04 (−.29)	.08 (.25)	−.5 (−1.2)

Note: Figures in parentheses are results from regression analysis without assignment of optimum scale values to levels 3 and 4 of brand preference.

media allocation, or the aggregation of data over more than one time interval or over more than one product class, can each be expected to improve the leverage which the consumer panel operation gives to defining the relationship between sales and advertising.

Table 1 contains the regression coefficients, standard errors of coefficients, and t values for the influences of each of six types of advertising (magazine and television by each of three brands) upon the buying preferences for each of the three brands. The coefficients have been scaled to show the absolute change in percentage brand share expected in five months from a change in advertising expenditure of $100,000 during two succeeding five-month periods. Owing to the low levels of multiple correlation, the magnitudes of the regression coefficients are under-estimates of the actual sales-advertising relationships.

The individual regression coefficients scarcely achieve statistical significance. One-third of them for the discriminant regression are 1.2 or larger; the expected number with no correlation would be one-fourth this size or larger.

Also worth noting is that the largest improvements from magazine advertising exposure are found for Brand C, whose magazine advertising is at the lowest level, where increases in exposure would be expected to have larger effects. The abso-

lute magnitude of the regression coefficients for all magazine advertising is several times larger than that for television advertising. This result adumbrates a pattern of low levels of advertising in magazines possessing advertising potential from increased expenditure.

An F test with 2 by 2 degrees of freedom to allow for intercorrelated results shows that the regression coefficients for magazine advertising exposure have greater magnitude, plus or minus, than coefficients for television advertising, with 97.5 per cent confidence. With this degree of confidence it may be stated that magazine advertising produces greater effects per dollar upon brand sales than does television advertising. These effects are favorable or unfavorable, depending on the quality of advertising.

Figure 1 charts the relationship between alteration in brand share per $100,000 change in 5 months' level of advertising and the level of advertising during 5 months. Students of advertising will recognize that the six points plotted conform to the expected logarithmic relationship between total sales and total advertising. Letting S stand for brand share and X for amount spent upon advertising, the points show the relationship between dS/dX and X. This relationship is approximated by $dS/dX = 1/X$. The integration of this differential equation gives $S = \log X$.

Although the relationship charted is only ap-

FIGURE 1

AVERAGE CHANGES IN BRAND SHARE OF
PRIMARY AND COMPETING BRANDS OF
TOOTHPASTE PER $100,000 CHANGE IN
LEVEL OF 5 MONTHS' ADVERTISING, AS A
FUNCTION OF ADVERTISING LEVEL

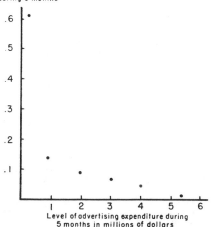

Tenths of a per cent change in
brand share per $100,000
change in level of advertising
during 5 months

Level of advertising expenditure during
5 months in millions of dollars

proximate, the value of the coefficient of correlation for the data fitted to the relationship is .995. The value of t is 20, and the degree of confidence that the diminishing returns relationship prevails in the universe from which consumers were sampled is 99.99 per cent. The low levels of advertising in magazines indicate that more advertising effect can be accomplished by increasing this type of advertising than by increasing television advertising, per $100,000 of expenditure. The relationship merits more detailed examination with larger amounts of data, aggregated by product class or by time period.

In aggregating product classes, the relative effects of the advertising by one company in behalf of its brands compared with the advertising by a second company seem discernible with the present design of analysis applied to consumer reinterview data. Also, comparisons between the average effectiveness of one group of advertising campaigns in relation to a second group of campaigns seem within the scope of this analysis. More detailed comparisons of brands or media do not yet appear to be practical.

REFERENCES

GARFINKLE, N. S. A Marketing Approach to Media Selection. *Journal of Advertising Research*, Vol. 3, No. 4, December 1963, pp. 7-15.

GUTTMAN, L. The Quantitative Prediction of a Qualitative Variate. In Paul Horst, *The Prediction of Personal Adjustment*. New York: Social Science Research Council, 1941, pp. 271-275.

Only as we examine and test our theoretical assumptions can we hope to make them more adequate, to remove inconsistencies, and thus to improve our ability to predict.
—DOUGLAS MCGREGOR

DOYLE L. WEISS*

The economic well-being of a business firm can often be summarized in terms of its market share. Market share responds to price, advertising expenditures, retail availability, and product characteristics. Marketing managers are compelled to understand the dynamics of market share behavior in these terms. This article is an analysis of market share movements for a low-cost, frequently purchased consumer product. It represents a first effort in understanding such movements for marketing management's major decision variables.

Determinants of Market Share

The efficient conduct of all consumer-based enterprise requires an understanding of the relationships between consumer behavior and the short-term movements of a firm's market share. Changes in market shares are a function of consumer-purchasing decisions, influenced by a variety of factors, both economic and psychological. In the short run, however, the marketing manager can manipulate four major variables to influence consumer-purchasing behavior and his brand's market share: (1) price, (2) advertising expenditures, (3) retail availability, and (4) physical product characteristics. The critical question for the marketing manager in the short run is: What is the optimum mix for these marketing variables? This question can only be answered after the form of the relationship between market share and these variables is established. The purpose of the following study was to investigate this relationship for a low-cost, frequently purchased, brand-identified consumer product.

DATA SOURCES

The raw data supporting the subsequent empirical analysis were provided by the *Chicago Tribune's* Family Survey Bureau, the Harvard Business School, and the marketing policy group of one of the industry's principal firms. The material contained four years of family purchase records and estimates of competitive advertising expenditures for the Chicago metropolitan market area. At the request of the cooperating company, the name of the product class and identities of the participating brands are withheld. The product class is a low-cost consumer food item with high brand identification and is sold in food markets and delicatessens.

* Doyle L. Weiss is assistant professor of industrial administration, Purdue University.

The four years of data represented the purchasing activities of 899 panel families who purchased 123 different brands. The participating families were originally selected by the Family Survey Bureau through a modified, stratified sampling plan.[1] However, several problems developed with the panel's composition; and therefore, the 1960–63 data cannot be considered to result from a strict probability sample.

As expected, difficulty with nonresponse was present. Some families selected by the sampling plan would not be panel members and keep records of their daily purchases. Alternate families with similar characteristics had to be recruited. Moreover, some families, though they joined the panel and consented to keep the necessary records, failed to. Thus, their records are erroneous, incomplete, or missing for periods of time.

The attrition of panel families was also not uniform across membership by age. Newer family members had a higher dropout rate than did older members.

[1] The *Chicago Tribune* panel was started in 1947 with 800 families. The panel families were selected from an area sample conducted for the Chicago Consolidated Area, which involved a complete census of residential blocks in the Chicago SCA using census tracts and Sanborn maps. Blocks were then stratified by area, using population as a control, and sampled on a random basis. A complete enumeration of the dwelling units within the selected blocks was made, and 5,813 households were randomly chosen to form a household pool. From this pool a stratified random sample (strata being race, family size, and family income) of 800 families was selected to form the first panel. This pool of 5,813 households was used to replace families as needed. Because of aging, changing income, and changing size of families in the 1947 pool, it was necessary in 1955 to add 3,900 families to the pool by similar procedures. Since 1955, the pool has occasionally not contained families with certain critical characteristics. Families with these characteristics have been recruited from lists of families created by the *Tribune* for other consumer surveys, occasionally by random recruitment in specific neighborhoods or suburbs, and by referrals through other panel members for family types extremely difficult to locate.

Journal of Marketing Research,
Vol. V (August 1968), 290–5

Since the compensation offered to participating families was small, attrition among newer members might be more concentrated in the upper income levels, causing continuity problems for this important group.

Besides these effects, panel data are often criticized because panel membership is thought to influence economic behavior. Some marketing researchers argue that the act of recording the attributes of each purchase[2] makes the family hypersensitive to price differentials compared with the balance of the population.

Despite these difficulties, the sample is large and represents a continuous record of consumer-purchasing behavior for a long time. Also, the research tradition associated with the use of panel data is well established in marketing research literature.

THE PRODUCT CLASS

Although purchases were reported for 123 brands over the four years, most were extremely weak local brands. The product class contains four strong brands (three national and one regional) that dominate the market and control about 65 percent of the total panel volume. Evidence of this dominance can be seen in Figure 1, which shows market share movements for the nine largest brands and an "all other" classification.

Figure 1 shows that Brand 1 is consistently the strongest brand in the market with Brands 2, 3, and 4 having about equal shares.[3] Brand 1 shows some decline from this dominant position for the sample period, however, with its share changing erratically from approximately 30 percent of the market at the beginning of the period to nearly 24 percent at the end.[4] It appears that much of this change was associated with the dramatic increase in Brand 3's share during the last four periods.

Besides the four years of family purchase data, bimonthly estimates of advertising expenditures were made available for the same period. These data were expenditure estimates in the Chicago metropolitan area for the three nationally advertised brands. As a result of the availability of such advertising data, relative prices and shares were summarized and aggregated for bimonthly periods from the family purchase records in preparation for the subsequent three brand analysis. The data for the three national brands are graphed in Figures 2, 3, and 4.

The advertising expenditure data represent estimates of newspaper, magazine, radio, network television,

---

[2] Panel members are required to keep a detailed diary of their purchases. For each purchase they record date of purchase, item purchased, its price, number of units, size of a single unit, store where purchase was made, and whether the item was bought on a "deal" or promotion. The diaries are periodically collected and processed by the Bureau.

[3] Brands 1, 2, and 4 are nationally advertised brands, but Brand 3 is a regional brand.

[4] Brand 1's management noted that the period from the last half of 1962 through 1963 represents a modern low point in the brand's performance.

Figure 1
SEMI-YEARLY MARKET SHARE
(1960 THROUGH 1963)

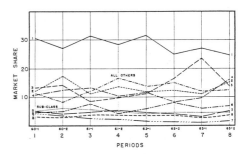

and spot television advertising activities for the Chicago metropolitan market. They do not include expenditure estimates for billboard, transit card, direct mail, or other such forms of advertising. These estimates are based on monitoring reports from at least two agencies (Rorabaugh and BAR) that track advertising expenditures by all advertisers.

Economic theory and marketing knowledge dictate that price and advertising are two of the primary influences on sales (and market share) of competing consumer products. The importance of these variables in relation to others such as retail availability, product quality, and packaging in determining a brand's sales is not easily determined a priori. It will depend on whether product differentiation along the dimensions of these last attributes can be achieved and whether the market considers such differentiation to be important. For the data studied, package size and configuration were not widely used as competitive weapons by the industry. The standard size was well-known, medium-sized container of traditional shape. Moreover, the proliferation of flavors that exist in the market was

Figure 2
COMPARATIVE PRICES FOR THREE NATIONAL BRANDS
(1960 THROUGH 1963)

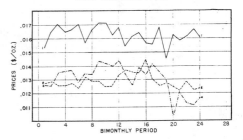

RESULTS OF ANALYSIS ON LINEAR MODELS 1 THROUGH 9

Model	Constant a_0	Price a_1	Advertising a_2	Dummy variables		R^2 [a]	Error variance
				Brand 2 a_3	Brand 1 a_4		
1. No transformation on data	−.600[c]	62.9[c]	.00654[c]	—	—	.656	.0087
2. Differences from mean	.372[c]	64.5[c]	.00956[c]	—	—	.733	.0068
3. Ratio to mean	−.567[c]	.843[c]	.0926[c]	—	—	.740	.0066
4. Log of ratio with mean	−1.40[c]	2.31[c]	.499[c]	—	—	.749	.0066[b]
5. Dummies, no transformation	.702[c]	−37.8[c]	.00144	.020	.433[c]	.900	.0026
6. Dummies, differences from mean	.121[c]	−61.8[c]	.00178	.0157	.509[c]	.925	.0019
7. Dummies, ratio to mean	1.01[c]	−.895[c]	.0154	.00878	.501[c]	.922	.0020
8. Dummies, ratio to mean, logs	−1.86[c]	−2.56[c]	.0723	.0524	1.44[c]	.935[b]	.0016[b]
9. Dummy variables only	.218[c]	—	—	.027	.318[c]	.850	.0038

[a] R^2 adjusted for degrees of freedom; all are significantly different from zero at the .95 confidence level.
[b] Based on antilogs of estimates from the model.
[c] Significantly different from zero at the .95 confidence level.

not present from 1960 through 1963.[5] As a result, the data are clean of these hard-to-measure influences. However, product quality has always been a strong competitive issue among the major manufacturers and advertisers. It influences the major theme of almost all advertising messages and is the dominant image projection of national brands. Also, distribution systems and retail availability are certain to vary among brands and exert a differential influence on sales.

Unfortunately, data necessary to support a comprehensive study of all these variables are not available although the subsequent analysis provides some insights into their interrelationships and relative strengths.

ECONOMETRIC MODELS OF MARKET SHARE

To explain the market share movement for the three national brands, several familiar econometric formulations of the demand relationship were fitted to the data. (See the table.)

In the subsequent analysis the three national brands are treated as a three-brand market. Four simple linear forms with market share as the dependent variable were fitted to provide an emprical basis with which the results from the more complicated forms could be compared.[6] In the first model, volume-weighted average price and advertising expenditures for bimonthly periods were used as independent variables without transformation.[7] The explained variation resulting

[5] Two distinct flavor classes were sold, however, from 1960 through 1963. The vanilla flavor accounted for about 95 percent of the volume during this period.
[6] For a detailed examination of the results of these four models, see [5].
[7] The basic variables in the four models are defined as follows:
$S_{B,t}$ is market share for Brand B at time t
$P_{R,t}$ is price (dollars per ounce) for Brand B at time t
$A_{B,t}$ is advertising expenditures (thousands of dollars) for Brand B at time t.
Because market share was the dependent variable, the residuals

from the regression accounted for approximately 66 percent of the total variance in the market share movements for the three national brands. Both the price coefficient and coefficient for advertising expenditures were significantly different from zero at the .95 level of confidence. The regression coefficient on price, however, was estimated to be positive and was significantly different from zero at the .95 confidence level.

The same pattern of coefficients appearing in this first regression model appeared, without substantial change, in the other three simple models tried. The second model accounted for 73 percent of the variance in the dependent variable and used the differences from the period averages of both price and advertising as independent variables. The third model transformed the independent variables by dividing them by the appropriate mean value for the period. The relative influence of the ratio variables on market share did not change significantly from that of the two previous models. The value of R^2 moved only slightly, from .73 to .74. A logarithmic transformation (Base e) made on the variables (including the dependent variable) of the ratio model produced approximately the same result as the ratio model, itself. A comparable R^2 and F value was calculated for the logarithm model by regressing market shares for the sample period on estimates of these values produced by the model.[8]

associated with each bimonthly subset of observations are related by an identity. Consequently, ordinary least-squares estimates are inefficient although they are consistent and unbiased. For a complete discussion of the problems of estimating parameters in these and subsequent models, see [3].
[8] To arrive at comparable R^2 and F values, however, it was first necessary to solve for the antilog of the market share estimates produced by this model, that is:

$$\hat{S}_{B,t} = e \exp [Ln (S_{B,t})],$$

where
e is the base of the natural logarithms,
$\hat{S}_{B,t}$ is the estimate of market share implied by the logarithm model for Brand B.

The appearance of the positive price coefficient in all four models was disturbing. The data are historical and, as such, present a temporal record of equilibrium points. Under these conditions economic theory suggests that the positive price coefficient could result from upward shifts in the demand curve, brought about by one or a combination of factors. The suspected movement could easily have been caused by an exogenous increase in total demand, affecting all three brands equally. If this were true, however, the effects of the change would not be reflected by models using market share as the dependent variable. For the same reasons, one would not expect shifts resulting from an increasing intensity or effectiveness of the industry's total advertising expenditures to have caused the problem. Also, any changes in the effectiveness or intensity of advertising expenditures by individual brands would be expected to be reflected in the advertising coefficient and not through a positive price coefficient.

A more likely explanation for this positive coefficient is the existence of other variables, not in the analysis, having a positive association with both market share and price and manifesting their influence spuriously through the price variable. Several variables operating through Brand 1 could be responsible for the price coefficient's positive sign, such as product quality differences, superior in-store promotional activities, preferential shelf-space allocations within stores, cumulative effects of past advertising efforts, or more effective use of advertising expenditures.

ANALYSIS WITH DUMMY VARIABLES

Because proper data for these missing variables were not available for the three brands, dummy variables were added to the models as their proxies. Because the proxy variables' regression coefficients are intercepts rather than slopes, they are correctly associated with slowly changing, long-run inputs to the demand function. Of the missing variables, product quality, retail distribution, and advertising capital (cumulative effects) are most often considered as long-run attributes.

Although the proxies must represent the combined effect of all missing variables, product quality seems to be the most important. This view is supported by one brand's management that thinks quality greatly affects a brand's long-run market performance. The company's advertising copy reflects management's opinion on this point and exploits a quality theme. Also, limited data would suggest that their efforts with distribution and in-store promotional activities in the sample market are not greatly superior to those of the other national brands and are not responsible for Brand 1's superior market share and higher price.

The notation "exp" means raised to the power.

As mentioned, the values used in the estimation procedure were generated by sampling methods and may contain errors. Hence, the estimation procedures are influenced by the well-known problems associated with errors in the variables, see [1, Chapter 6].

Figure 3
COMPARATIVE ADVERTISING EXPENDITURES FOR THREE NATIONAL BRANDS
(1960 THROUGH 1963)

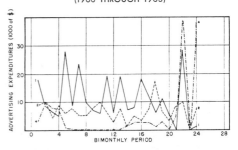

The models with dummy variables added are Models 5 through 8:

Model 5

$$S_{B,t} = a_0 + a_1 P_{B,t} + a_2 A_{B,t} + a_3 Q_1 + a_4 Q_2,$$

where

Q_1 is 1 when B is 2 and 0 otherwise

Q_2 is 1 when B is 1 and 0 otherwise,

and the other variables remain as previously defined (see Footnote 6).

Model 6

$$S_{B,t} = a_0 + a_1 (P_{B,t} - \overline{P}_t) + a_2 (A_{B,t} - \overline{A}_t) + a_3 Q_1 + a_4 Q_2,$$

where

$\overline{P}_t$ is average price (weighted by volume) for all three brands for period t,

$\overline{A}_t$ is $\sum_B A_{B,t}/3$,

and the other variables remain as previously defined.

Model 7

$$S_{B,t} = a_0 + a_1 (P_{B,t}/\overline{P}_t) + a_2 (A_{B,t}/\overline{A}_t) + a_3 Q_1 + a_4 Q_2.$$

Model 8

$$S_{B,t} = a_0 \{ (P_{B,t}/\overline{P}_t)^{a_1} \} \{ (A_{B,t}/\overline{A}_t)^{a_2} \} \{ e^{(a_3 Q_1 + a_4 Q_2)} \},$$

When a log transformation (Base e) is made on Model 8 it becomes:

$$\log (S_{B,t}) = \log (a_0) + a_1 \log (P_{B,t}/\overline{P}_t) + a_2 \log (A_{B,t}/\overline{A}_t) + a_3 Q_1 + a_4 Q_2.$$

Figure 4

RELATIVE MARKET SHARE FOR THREE NATIONAL BRANDS
(1960 THROUGH 1963)

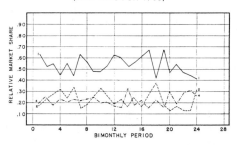

In this form, regression estimates for a_0, a_1, a_2, a_3 and a_4 can be obtained.

Because of zero advertising expenditures for some brands, a translation of the expenditure data by one unit was necessary before Model 8 could be fitted. Therefore, direct interpretation of the regression coefficients as elasticities is not directly possible.

REGRESSION RESULTS

The addition of dummy variables as proxies for quality and distribution measures considerably improved the explanatory power of the models. The dummy variables also cleared the confusion among quality, price, and the dependent variable, market share. In all cases, the linear relationships are significantly different from zero at the .95 level of confidence. Models 6, 7, and 8, however, produced the best fits with determination coefficients of .925, .922 and .935,[9] respectively. Model 5 (no transformations on price and advertising, but with dummy variables) yielded an R^2 of .900.

The dummy variables' marginal contribution to the explanation of variance in the dependent variable is significantly different from zero at a confidence level far past .95 in all cases.

Another and perhaps stronger test of the significance of the influence of price and advertising on relative share can be made by reversing the previous analysis, postulating the following naive model, and observing how much its explanatory power can be improved by adding price and advertising variables:

Model 9

$$S_{B,t} = a_0 + a_3 Q_1 + a_4 Q_2,$$

where

Q_1 is 1 when B is 2 and 0 otherwise,

[9] Antilogs were taken, and the coefficient of determination was calculated by regressing the estimate against the actual values of market share.

Q_2 is 1 when B is 1 and 0 otherwise,
$S_{B,t}$ is Brand B's share in period t.

This model postulates that the best prediction of a brand's market share is provided by the average value of its share.[10] The results of the regression fitting this model to the data are included in the table. The regression produced an R^2 of .850 that is significantly different from zero at the .95 confidence level.

The computed values of the appropriate F statistic measuring the significance of the contribution of price and advertising to the explanation of variance in the dependent variable measured against Model 9 are:

Model	Computed F	D.F.
9. Dummy variables only	194.8	2,69
5. No transformations	15.7	2,67
6. Differences from mean	33.6	2,67
7. Ratio to mean	30.5	2,67
8. Log of ratio to mean[11]	4.25	2,67

The addition of price and advertising has explained a significant amount of the remaining variance from Model 9. As indicated in the table, however, the contribution of advertising in Models 5, 6, and 7 is not significant at the .95 level of confidence.

COEFFICIENTS OF DUMMY VARIABLES AS INTERCEPTS

The method of adding dummy variables to the models forced the effect of Brand 3's proxy variable into the common intercept and caused a_3 to represent the difference between Brand 2's influence and Brand 1's influence on product quality (and other variables); a_4 represents this difference between Brand 2 and Brand 3. Following the analysis suggested by Suits [4], the dummy variables' coefficients may be interpreted, in each of the models, as differences in intercepts caused by the absent variables they represent. For three of the models containing dummy variables (5, 6, and 7) the resulting intercepts for the different brands are:

	Brand		
	1	2	3
5. No transformations	1.135	.704	.702
6. Difference from period mean	.630	.137	.121
7. Ratio with period mean	1.602	1.02	1.02

The coefficients for the dummy variables are different intercepts for regression lines with otherwise identical slopes. The fact that a_3 is not significant (see the table)

[10] In contrast, the implied null hypothesis for testing this influence in the previous analysis was "the best prediction of a brand's market share is the average share for all of the brands."

[11] Model 9 does not provide the proper explained sum of squares for the contribution of the dummy variables alone for the logarithm model 8. To get the appropriate sum of squares for this model, the following regression was run, and the antilogs of its estimates were used:

$$\text{Log } (S_{B,t}) = a_0 + a_1 Q_1 + a_2 Q_2.$$

means that the difference in quality (perceived or actual as reflected by the market) between Brand 3 and Brand 2 is not significantly different from zero. This relationship remains essentially stable in all three models (5, 6, and 7); the hypothesis that the two brands are similar is supported.

The behavior of Brand 1 in this respect is different. The computed t value for Brand 1's dummy variable coefficient (a_4) is highly significant in all three models. This means a significant quality difference exists between Brand 1 and Brand 3 as measured by the difference in their respective intercepts.[12] Moreover, this relationship is consistent for the three models. It is also entirely reasonable to infer from this fact a significant difference between the quality index for Brand 1 and Brand 2 in the same direction as for Brand 1 and Brand 3. The validity of this inference is supported by the stability of the computed t statistic for a_3 and a_4 over all three models.[13]

The table indicates that adding dummy variables to the analysis requires a different interpretation of the influence of advertising on market share. Although its influence was less than that of price in the first four models, it was significantly different from zero at the .95 level of confidence. However, with addition of the dummy variables, the coefficient of advertising is not significantly different from zero at this confidence level.

DISCUSSION AND CONCLUSIONS

In some respects this article is another of several demand studies designed to investigate the underlying structural relationships and price responsiveness of a product market. In important dimensions, however, it is different from almost all demand studies previously reported. First, it is concerned entirely with the demand for individual brands for a single consumer product

---

[12] Note that the t statistic is not being used to test for significant difference between the regression coefficients of the proxy variables but to determine whether the implied intercept of Brand 3 is different from that of Brands 1 and 2.

[13] To further test this proposition, it would be necessary to compare the regression sum of squares for the following two models:

(1) $S_{B,t} = a_0 + a_1 P_B' + a_2 A_B' + a_{3,4} Q_{1,2}$;

$Q_{1,2} = 1$, if $B = 1$ or 2 and zero otherwise, and

(2) $S_{B,t} = a_0 + a_1 P_B' + a_2 A_B' + a_3 Q_1 + a_4 Q_2$.

class. Second, the article deals necessarily with competitive models of the demand relationship and thereby acknowledges this fundamental market characteristic.

The superior fit of Model 8 to the data supports Kuehn's [2] contention that price and advertising interact and does not produce linear effects on either market share or volume. Kuehn's argument that larger advertising expenditures will support higher prices is appealing since economists have long felt that advertising expenditures cause the demand curve to shift upward. The multiplicative structure of Model 8 allows this joint influence of price and advertising on sales to be examined.

Two implications of the research to marketing managers are:

1. When cost structures are added to the analysis and their parameters estimated, the models become normative models of firm behavior and descriptive models of market share behavior. As such they may be examined for short-run optimal price and advertising decisions.
2. The models may be used as forecasting mechanisms to examine the probable effect of current merchandising policies on market share position and company profits.

Unfortunately the models' forecasting ability is still unknown. Advertising expenditure data for 1964 and later has not yet been released by the cooperating firm's management, and I can only imperfectly assume relative predictive accuracy from the models' determination coefficients.

REFERENCES

1. J. Johnston, *Econometric Methods*, New York: McGraw-Hill Book Company, Inc., 1960.
2. Alfred A. Kuehn and Doyle L. Weiss, "How Advertising Performance Depends on Other Marketing Factors," *Journal of Advertising Research*, 2 (March 1962), 2–10.
3. Timothy W. McGuire, *et al.*, "Estimation and Inference for Linear Models in Which Subsets of the Dependent Variables are Constrained," Carnegie-Mellon University, Working Paper No. 3, Pittsburgh, Pennsylvania.
4. Daniel B. Suits, "Interpreting Regressions Containing Dummy Variables," Speech to Research Seminar in Quantitative Economics, University of Michigan, May 1962.
5. Doyle L. Weiss, "An Analysis of Market Share Behavior for a Branded Consumer Product," Unpublished Ph.D. dissertation, Graduate School of Industrial Administration, Carnegie Institute of Technology, June 1966.

FRANK M. BASS*

This article demonstrates the application of simultaneous equation regression methods in analyzing limited time series data for sales and advertising. In testing a model with sales and advertising relationships for filter and non-filter cigarette brands, we could not reject a model in which the advertising elasticity for filter brands is substantially greater than that for nonfilter brands.

A Simultaneous Equation Regression Study of Advertising and Sales of Cigarettes

INTRODUCTION

There is no more difficult, complex, or controversial problem in marketing than measuring the influence of advertising on sales. There is also probably no more interesting or potentially profitable measurement problem than this one. The difficulties involved in measuring the influence of advertising may generally be separated into three major categories:

1. isolating advertising effects from the many other variables that affect sales
2. measuring the quantity of advertising, considering that advertising dollar expenditures reflect alternative choices of media, psychological appeals, and copy
3. identifying the relationship that reflects the influence of sales on advertising, as well as that which reflects advertising's influence on sales—the so-called identification problem.

Quandt [17] has analyzed these and other difficulties at length. Kuehn and Rohloff [12] have argued that because of the severity of these measurement difficulties, greater progress in studying advertising effectiveness can be made by analyzing household or individual consumer behavior than aggregative data. Simple regression studies are particularly susceptible to criticism because of the serial correlation in sales and advertising [5].

There have been several interesting brand-switching studies [7, 9, 10]. However, only a few of these studies have attempted to relate changes in brand-switching

activity to marketing decision variables [11, 14, 15, 24]. Furthermore, no known published work deals with the identification problem in advertising. Telser [18, 19], Palda [16], Weinberg [23], and Vidale and Wolfe [22] have applied single-equation regression models to macro sales and advertising data. Besides failing to solve the identification problem, these single-equation regression studies permit only a weak or ambiguous test of the model.

This article suggests that progress can be made in studying advertising effectiveness by: (a) trying various approaches and models, (b) devising models that must pass an unambiguous test, in a scientific sense, to be found to agree with the data and, (c) publishing enough detail to permit and foster debate and criticism.

The study presented in this article is not without limitations. The scarcity of data not only hinders model formulation but also poses unknown dangers associated with errors in the equations. Because data are only available annually, the number of observations is restricted, and short-term variations are concealed.

This study deals with aggregative sales and advertising data, the form in which data are commonly available to management. The model must pass a severe test to be acceptable. Furthermore, it takes into account the simultaneous nature of the relationship between sales and advertising, a serious omission in previous studies. Not only is sales influenced by advertising, but advertising is also influenced by sales. Advertising decision rules, whether rigid or flexible, certainly account for sales. Therefore, single-equation regression models cannot adequately identify advertising-sales and sales-advertising relationships. The multiple-equation regression model explored here deals explicitly with these simultaneous relationships.

* Frank M. Bass is professor of industrial administration, Purdue University. The author is indebted to Robert L. Basmann for his advice, criticism, and contribution of ideas. Thomas H. Bruhn, Gordon Constable, and Marvin Margolis provided computational assistance. The author assumes full responsibility for this article.

Journal of Marketing Research,
Vol. VI (August 1969), 291–300

ORGANIZATION

The organization of this study closely follows that suggested by Basmann [3]. The model is formulated in terms of a system of equations including endogenous and exogenous variables—the structural relations. Besides the set of structural equations, the model comprises restrictions on the parameters of structural relations which are determined theoretically and provide the basis for testing the model. As indicated by Basmann [3] ". . . the testing of theoretical premises about an economic parameter is logically prior to its estimation."

The system of structural equations is uniquely related to a set of reduced-form equations in which each endogenous variable is separately related to the exogenous variables. Assumptions that restrict the structural parameters necessarily imply limits on the parameters in the reduced-form equations. Estimates of the reduced-form parameters taken in conjunction with the implied boundaries on these parameters constitute the test of the model.

This model was constructed to explain recent sales levels of groups of competitive cigarette brands for which given initial conditions and background assumptions are met. The initial conditions for this explanatory model are described by sequences of two exogenous variables, disposable personal income and prices. The background conditions imply the absence of external perturbations.

Each structural equation explains a part of the system of relations being studied when that part is isolated from the rest of the system. We shall construct the model by building the parts and then assembling the components to derive the system.

SYSTEM AND ASSUMPTIONS

The model consists of two demand equations for two competing groups of cigarette brands and two equations that describe the advertising relations for these groups of brands. The sales of the major filter cigarette brands have been aggregated to give one demand equation for this group. Similarly, there is one demand equation for the major nonfilter brands. The system's two remaining equations describe the behavior of advertising for the two competing groups of cigarette brands. The filter brands are: Winston, Kent, Marlboro, Herbert Tareyton, Viceroy, L&M, and Parliament; the nonfilter brands are: Pall Mall, Camel, Lucky Strike, Chesterfield, Old Gold, and Philip Morris. Sales and advertising data for 1953–1965 were obtained from *Advertising Age* [1, 2].

Since the prices of filter brands are identical as are the prices of nonfilter brands, the aggregation of brand sales in each class is justified theoretically. The Leontieff-Hicks theorem [8, 13, 25] establishes that if the prices of a group of goods change in equal proportion, that group can then be treated as a single commodity. Basmann [4] has shown that this theorem applies when the parameters of the consumer's utility function depend on advertising of competitive commodities. Since the Leontieff-Hicks theorem justifies aggregation in this study, concepts of complementarity, substitutability, price elasticity, income elasticity, etc., apply to the grouped commodities just as the corresponding concepts and measures apply to single goods.

In developing a test of the model we shall require specification of the structural equations as well as hypothesized limits on the values of the structural parameters (see the appendix). Although the estimates of parameters are not restricted by the hypotheses, we shall test the hypothesis that the structural parameters lie within certain intervals by making predictions about the reduced-form parameters. We shall therefore give the hypothesized limits on each structural parameter and discuss the reasons for establishing these limits.

Table 1
ENDOGENOUS AND EXOGENOUS VARIABLES

Year	Y_1	Y_2	Y_3	Y_4	X_1	X_2
1953	2.39851	3.50465	−1.26117	−0.28369	3.41653	−0.60906
1954	2.60060	3.45582	−0.90035	−0.37119	3.41876	−0.60906
1955	2.83890	3.42632	−0.62703	−0.43061	3.44491	−0.60206
1956	2.97883	3.38979	−0.43572	−0.44389	3.46147	−0.60033
1957	3.09065	3.33810	−0.34364	−0.55378	3.46451	−0.59176
1958	3.15067	3.30278	−0.34605	−0.53839	3.46304	−0.59860
1959	3.18361	3.30251	−0.30510	−0.54141	3.47986	−0.57349
1960	3.19626	3.29920	−0.33548	−0.53467	3.48502	−0.57675
1961	3.20779	3.29484	−0.34157	−0.54432	3.49358	−0.57675
1962	3.21945	3.27891	−0.36206	−0.54872	3.50804	−0.57840
1963	3.23843	3.25720	−0.28542	−0.54580	3.51834	−0.56543
1964	3.22329	3.20154	−0.29571	−0.54809	3.54063	−0.55596
1965	3.23099	3.21304	−0.31297	−0.49872	3.56335	−0.53910

Sources: See [1, 2, 20, 21, 26].

DEMAND FOR MAJOR BRANDS OF FILTER AND NONFILTER CIGARETTES

Demand Equation for Filter Brands

For every year t, if the demand for filter brands is considered in isolation from the rest of the system,

$$(1) \quad y_{1t} = \beta_1 y_{3t} + \beta_2 y_{4t} + \gamma_1 x_{1t} + \gamma_2 x_{2t} + \gamma_3 + \mu_{1t},$$

where

y_{1t} is logarithm of sales of filter cigarettes (number of cigarettes) divided by population over age 20

y_{3t} is logarithm of advertising dollars for filter cigarettes divided by population over age 20 divided by advertising price index

y_{4t} is logarithm of advertising dollars for nonfilter cigarettes divided by population over age 20 divided by advertising price index

x_{1t} is logarithm of disposable personal income divided by population over age 20 divided by consumer price index

x_{2t} is logarithm of price per package of nonfilter cigarettes divided by consumer price index

$E(\mu_{1t}) = 0$, and

$$\text{Var } (\mu_{1t}) = E(\mu_{1t}^2) = \omega_{\mu_1}^2.$$

We therefore postulate that the per capita sales of filter cigarettes is a nonlinear function of the ratio of per capita advertising for the two competitive types of cigarettes and the two exogenous variables. Advertising dollars have been deflated by an advertising price index developed by Yang [26]. Although it might have been desirable to include prices of the filter and nonfilter cigarettes as variables, the nonfilter price is available as a component of the consumer price index, but the filter price is not.

Premises About Equation 1 Parameters:

$\beta_1 + \beta_2 = 0$. This premise implies that the ratio of filter advertising to nonfilter advertising governs the influence of advertising on the demand for filter cigarettes. Since Equation 1 is expressed in logarithms of the quantities, it may be written in terms of the original quantities as:

$$Y_{1t} = Y_{3t}^{\beta_1} Y_{4t}^{\beta_2} X_{1t}^{\gamma_1} X_{2t}^{\gamma_2} 10^{\gamma_3 + \mu_{1t}}.$$

If $\beta_1 = -\beta_2$, this equation is then:

$$Y_{1t} = (Y_{3t} \mid Y_{4t})^{\beta_1} X_{1t}^{\gamma_1} X_{2t}^{\gamma_2} 10^{\gamma_3 + \mu_{1t}}.$$

The premise that $\beta_1 + \beta_2 = 0$ is therefore consistent with the idea that the demand for filter cigarettes is influenced by the ratio of advertising for the two different types of cigarettes. This premise and the others which follow were derived from theory and judgment. Regardless of the origins of the premises, they are explicit and testable.

$.5 \leq \beta_1 \leq .6$. The assumptions that demand elasticity with respect to advertising is inelastic and that advertising has a positive effect on sales imply that β_1 is be-

tween zero and one. This range has been substantially narrowed to test rigidly the premises.

$1.0 \leq \gamma_1\ 1.3$. Filter and nonfilter cigarette brands are clearly highly substitutable commodities, the filter brand being favored. The income elasticity of filter brands is assumed to reflect the income effect over the historical period analyzed.

$0 < \gamma_2 \leq .8$. Consistent with the previous premise, it is logical to assume that the cross-elasticity of demand for filter brands with respect to the price of nonfilter brands should be nonnegative and possibly high.

$-1.25 \leq \gamma_3 \leq -.75$. The intercept term is the most difficult parameter to interpret economically. The restrictions on this parameter have therefore been established residually, using the other restrictions and typical values of the other variables.

Demand Equation for Nonfilter Brands

For every year t, if the demand for nonfilter brands is considered in isolation from the rest of the system,

$$(2) \quad y_{2t} = \beta_3 y_{3t} + \beta_4 y_{4t} + \gamma_4 x_{1t} + \gamma_5 x_{2t} + \gamma_6 + \mu_{2t},$$

where

y_{2t} is logarithm of sales of nonfilter cigarettes (number of cigarettes) divided by population over age 20

y_{3t}, y_{4t}, x_{1t}, x_{2t} are as defined previously

$E(\mu_{2t}) = 0$, and

$$\text{Var } (\mu_{2t}) = E(\mu_{2t}^2) = \omega_{\mu_2}^2.$$

Premises About Equation 2 Parameters:

$\beta_3 + \beta_4 = 0$. This premise implies, as in Equation 1, the ratio of the advertising hypothesis.

$.2 \leq \beta_4 \leq .3$. In keeping with the premise that nonfilter cigarettes are inferior, we shall test the hypothesis that the advertising elasticity for this group of brands is approximately one-half that of filter brands.

$0 \leq \gamma_4 \leq .8$. The income elasticity of nonfilter brands is assumed to be less than unity (less than the corresponding elasticity for filter brands) and possibly near zero. This restriction is consistent with the premise that income effects differentially favor filter brands.

$-3.0 \leq \gamma_5 \leq -1.0$. The demand for nonfilter cigarettes is assumed to be price elastic and possibly high. This premise is consistent with the assertion that nonfilters are inferior to filters. An increase in the price of nonfilters therefore induces a more than proportionate decline in demand.

$-1.25 \leq \gamma_6 \leq -.75$. The limits on the intercept term are deduced residually.

ADVERTISING RELATIONSHIPS FOR MAJOR BRANDS OF FILTER AND NON-FILTER CIGARETTES

Equation Describing Advertising Behavior of Filter Brands

For every year t, if the advertising of filter cigarettes is considered in isolation from the rest of the system,

(3) $\qquad y_{1t} = \beta_5 y_{2t} + \beta_6 y_{3t} + \gamma_7 + \mu_{3t}$

or,

$$y_{3t} = \frac{1}{\beta_6} y_{1t} - \frac{\beta_5}{\beta_6} y_{2t} - \frac{\gamma_7}{\beta_6} - \frac{1}{\beta_6} \mu_{3t}$$

$E(\mu_{3t}) = 0,$ $\qquad$ and

$$\text{Var}(\mu_{3t}) = E(\mu_{3t}^2) = \omega_{\mu_3}^2.$$

Premises About Equation 3 Parameters:
$.6 \leq \beta_6 \leq .7.$
$-1.0 \leq \beta_5 \leq -.9.$ Equation 3 postulates that advertisers consider the sales of both types of cigarettes in determining the advertising budget for filter cigarettes. The restriction on β_5 implies that the advertising of filter cigarettes responds positively to increases in filter cigarette sales. The advertising response is assumed to be more than proportionate to the increase in filter cigarette sales and possibly smaller for nonfilter cigarettes.
$5.0 \leq \gamma_7 \leq 7.0.$ The limits on the intercept term are deduced residually.

Equation Describing Advertising Behavior of Nonfilter Brands

For every year t, if the advertising of nonfilter cigarettes is considered in isolation from the rest of the system,

(4) $\qquad y_{2t} = \beta_7 y_{1t} + \beta_8 y_{4t} - \gamma_8 - \mu_{4t}$

or,

$$y_{4t} = \frac{1}{\beta_8} y_{2t} - \frac{\beta_7}{\beta_8} y_{1t} - \frac{\gamma_8}{\beta_8} - \frac{1}{\beta_8} \mu_{4t}$$

where
$E(\mu_{4t}) = 0,$ $\qquad$ and

$$\text{Var}(\mu_{4t}) = E(\mu_{4t}^2) = \omega_{\mu_4}^2.$$

Premises About Equation 4 Parameters:
$-1.0 \leq \beta_7 \leq -1.5.$
$-3.0 \leq \beta_8 \leq -3.5.$ The advertising of nonfilter cigarettes is assumed to respond negatively to higher levels of sales of both filter and nonfilter cigarettes, but the response is possibly slightly greater to the sales of filter than to nonfilter cigarettes.
$5.0 \leq \gamma_8 \leq 7.0.$ The limits on the intercept term are deduced residually.

MODEL OF SALES AND ADVERTISING OF FILTER AND NONFILTER CIGARETTES

The model's parts produce the system of structural equations that describe the sales and advertising of the two competing products:

$$-y_{1t} + 0y_{2t} + \beta_1 y_{3t} + \beta_2 y_{4t} + \gamma_1 X_{1t}$$
$$+ \gamma_2 X_{2t} + \gamma_3 + \mu_{1t} = 0$$

$$0y_{1t} - y_{2t} + \beta_3 y_{3t} + \beta_4 y_{4t} + \gamma_4 X_{1t}$$
$$+ \gamma_5 X_{2t} + \gamma_6 + \mu_{2t} = 0$$
$$-y_{1t} + \beta_5 y_{2t} + \beta_6 y_{3t} + 0y_{4t} + 0X_{1t}$$
$$+ 0X_{2t} + \gamma_7 + \mu_{3t} = 0$$
$$\beta_7 y_{1t} - y_{2t} + 0y_{3t} + \beta_8 y_{4t} + 0X_{1t}$$
$$0X_{2t} + \gamma_8 + \mu_{4t} = 0,$$

or

$$\beta y_t + \Gamma X_t + u_t = 0.$$

REDUCED-FORM EQUATIONS

The system of structural equations

$$\beta y_t + \Gamma x_t + \mu_t = 0$$

is equivalent to the system of equations

$$y_t = -(\beta)^{-1}\Gamma x_t - (\beta)^{-1}\mu_t$$

if β is nonsingular. The reduced-form equations (see the appendix) are:

$$y_{1t} = \alpha_1 X_{1t} + \alpha_2 X_{2t} + \alpha_3 + \eta_{1t}$$
$$y_{2t} = \alpha_4 X_{1t} + \alpha_5 X_{2t} + \alpha_6 + \eta_{2t}$$
$$y_{3t} = \alpha_7 X_{1t} + \alpha_8 X_{2t} + \alpha_9 + \eta_{3t}$$
$$y_{4t} = \alpha_{10} X_{1t} + \alpha_{11} X_{2t} + \alpha_{12} + \eta_{4t}.$$

The parameters α_i, $i = 1, 2, \cdots, 12$ and η_{it}, $i = 1, \cdots, 4$ are functions of the structural parameters. Therefore the premises about the structural equations may be used to make predictions about the reduced-form parameters. Unless all the reduced-form parameter estimates lie within the acceptable limits of their predicted values as implied by the structural premises, at least one of the premises is discredited. For this predictive test to be valid, the determinant of β, Δ, must not be zero. Therefore it is necessary to show that the structural premises exclude the possibility of a zero Δ.

No empirical test can prove conclusively that a theory is true, but it can disprove a theory. Under certain circumstances structural parameters may be estimated without testing the model; however, if the structural equations are unidentified or over-identified, estimation procedures are debatable. In any case the predictive test shows whether a theory agrees with the empirical evidence.

TEST OF THE MODEL

To test the model, the implied maximum and minimum values of the reduced-form coefficients were calculated[1] and appear with the estimated values in Table 2.

[1] These calculations were made using the gradient projection method with the computer program Share Distribution #1399 SDGP 90.

Table 2

MAXIMA AND MINIMA OF REGRESSION PARAMETERS
ADMISSABLE UNDER STRUCTURAL PREMISES AND
ESTIMATES OF REGRESSION PARAMETERS

Minimum value	Coefficient estimate	Maximum value
2.30	α_1 (8.75)	39.85
−49.50	α_2 (−7.82)	−0.32
−148.25	α_3 (−31.96)	−7.92
−12.05	α_4 (−2.34)	−0.47
−1.24	α_5 (0.78)	13.50
3.69	α_6 (11.94)	55.75
2.17	α_7 (10.11)	48.34
−62.25	α_8 (−10.90)	−1.19
−215.12	α_9 (−42.01)	−14.13
−15.91	α_{10} (−2.64)	−0.43
0.25	α_{11} (2.77)	20.25
2.83	α_{12} (10.33)	69.87
−1.61	Δ	−0.12

A more complete test of the model could have been conducted by making explicit assumptions about the covariance terms of the structural equations and solving for maxima and minima of the reduced-form covariance terms. This was not done for this study. The results in Table 2 clearly show that the model satisfies the conditions implied by the structural premises. All 12 reduced-form coefficient estimates lie within the acceptable region. For this test, the model is in good agreement with the data.

IDENTIFIABILITY AND STRUCTURAL PARAMETER ESTIMATION

Since the model satisfies the test conditions associated with the reduced-form equations, we may proceed to structural estimation and further testing, if necessary (see the appendix). Since

$$y_i = -(\beta)^{-1}\Gamma x_i - (\beta)^{-1}\mu_i,$$

$$A + (\beta)^{-1}\Gamma = 0 \quad \text{and} \quad \beta A + \Gamma = 0.$$

In this study the structural parameters β_5, β_6, β_7, β_8, γ_7, and γ_8 are uniquely identified, i.e., estimates of these parameters are implied by estimates of the reduced-form parameters. Estimates of the remaining structural parameters were developed by two-stage least squares regression, but the significance of this estimation was not determined. The unidentified parameters remain unidentified except for the limits of restrictions placed on them. The estimated parameter values are:

$$\beta_1 = \quad .594 \qquad \hat{\gamma}_1 = \quad 1.173$$
$$\beta_4 = \quad .247 \qquad \hat{\gamma}_2 = \quad .305$$
$$\beta_5 = -\ .924 \qquad \hat{\gamma}_3 = -\ .874$$
$$\beta_6 = \quad .651 \qquad \hat{\gamma}_4 = \quad .815$$

$$\hat{\beta}_7 = -1.222 \qquad \hat{\gamma}_5 = -2.607$$
$$\hat{\beta}_8 = -3.158 \qquad \hat{\gamma}_6 = -1.027$$
$$\hat{\gamma}_7 = \quad 6.425$$
$$\hat{\gamma}_8 = \quad 5.496$$

Comparisons of the fitted equations with actual observations of sales of both types of cigarette brands are shown in Figure 1.

MANAGERIAL IMPLICATIONS

Having developed a model that satisfies test conditions, we will now explore the model's managerial implications. Because the demand equations in this study aggregate the sales for several brands and no direct information is provided here about the advertising elasticities of individual brands, the following managerial implications are only tentative and suggestive.

We consider a segment of the model in isolation from the system. There are several profit functions which an

Figure 1

COMPARISON OF ACTUAL AND ESTIMATED SALES,
FILTER CIGARETTES AND NONFILTER CIGARETTES

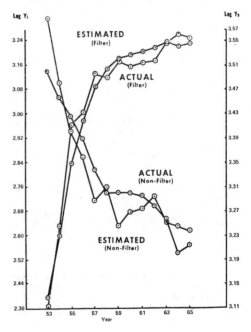

advertiser might adopt, e.g., game theoretic models, return on investment functions, aspiration level decision rules. The profit function considered here is current annual profit given the values of all variables (including competitive advertising), except the decision variable, advertising.

The profit function is:

$$\pi(A_t) = pq(A_t) - C(q) - A_t,$$

where

p is price
$q(A_t)$ is current sales as a function of current advertising
$C(q)$ is total production cost as a function of the sales volume
A_t is current advertising.

Maximizing, we have:

$$\frac{\partial \pi}{\partial A_t} = \left(p - \frac{\partial C}{\partial q}\right)\frac{dq}{dA_t} - 1 = 0.$$

Defining the advertising elasticity of demand in the usual way,[2] as:

$$\beta_1 = \frac{dq}{dA_t}\frac{A_t}{q},$$

we may write the profit maximization condition as:

$$\left(p - \frac{\partial C}{\partial q}\right)\beta_1 \frac{q}{A_t} = 1, \quad \text{or}$$

$$\frac{A_t}{q} = m\beta_1,$$

if unit production costs are constant, where m is unit gross margin exclusive of advertising costs. The advertising elasticity of demand, β_1, in general is not necessarily constant, but is constant in models such as the one developed here in which the logarithm of demand is a linear function of the logarithm of other variables, including advertising.

Using the demand equation developed earlier for filter cigarettes (Equation 1) and assuming that unit production costs are constant, the following profit function applies to filter cigarettes:

$$\pi(A_{1t}) = mq(A_{1t}) - A_{1t} = mP_t\left(\frac{A_{1t}}{C_t}\right)^{\beta_1}\left(\frac{A_{2t}}{C_t}\right)^{-\beta_1}$$
$$(Y_t)^{\gamma_1}(P_t)^{\gamma_2}(10)^{\gamma_3} - A_{1t},$$

where

m is unit gross margin, exclusive of advertising costs
P_t is population at time t over the age of 20
A_{1t} is dollar advertising expenditures for filter brands at time t

___
[2] For comparison, see [6].

Figure 2
COMPARISON OF OPTIMAL AND ACTUAL ADVERTISING
EXPENDITURES, FILTER CIGARETTES

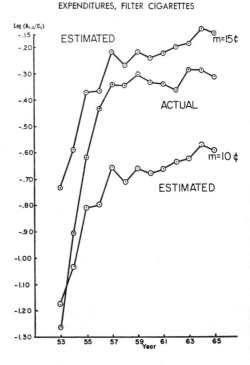

A_{2t} is dollar advertising expenditures for nonfilter brands at time t
C_t is P_t times advertising price index at time t
Y_t is disposable personal income divided by P_t times consumer price index at time t
p_t is price of nonfilter cigarettes divided by consumer price index at time t.

Then, $A_{1t}^* = m\beta_1 q(A_{1t}^*)$, and

$$\left(\frac{A_{1t}^*}{C_t}\right) = \left[\frac{m\beta_1 P_t}{C_t}\left(\frac{A_{2t}}{C_t}\right)^{-\beta_1}(Y_t)^{\gamma_1}(P_t)^{\gamma_2}(10)^{\gamma_3}\right]^{1-\beta_1}.$$

The logarithm of this quantity has been calculated and measured against the comparable figure for actual advertising expenditures during 1953–1965. Gross margin for cigarettes is between 10 and 15 cents per carton. Calculations have therefore been made for both of these figures and are shown in Figure 2.

The results are perhaps somewhat surprising. Actual expenditures are bracketed by the optimal expenditures calculated at the two different gross margin levels.

Figure 3

COMPARISON OF OPTIMAL AND ACTUAL ADVERTISING EXPENDITURES, NONFILTER CIGARETTES

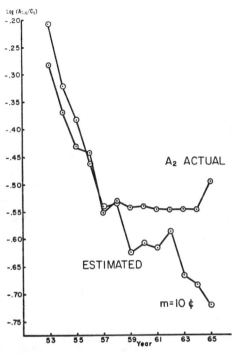

There is also a startling coincidence of direction and magnitude of change between the optimal and actual advertising expenditures. These results suggest that the advertising expenditure policy of the average filter brand was nearly optimal according to at least one criterion of optimality. This criterion assumes, among other things, that profit maximization for filter brands is independent of profit maximization for nonfilter brands. However, these results tell little about the optimal advertising strategy for an individual filter brand

since the advertising elasticity for an individual brand may differ from that for the group.

Optimal expenditures have also been calculated using the demand equation and parameter estimates for nonfilter brands and assuming ten cents gross margin per carton. Figure 3 provides a comparison of these calculations with the actual expenditures. The optimal and the actual expenditures follow parallel paths from 1953 until 1958, after which the actual is stable though the optimal continues to decline. It is possible that there was nonoptimal over advertising of nonfilter brands after 1958 associated with an attempt to maintain minimum market share levels.

Although this implication about the group's advertising may not apply to every brand, it appears that at least some nonfilter brands were pursuing nonoptimal strategies during the period. The increase of nonfilter advertising in 1965 was associated with the introduction of filter cigarettes under brand names traditionally associated with nonfilters. This product policy has increased and accelerated in the industry since 1965, thus blurring the distinction between the two types of cigarettes and tending to destroy the possible future managerial uses of this study.

SUMMARY AND CONCLUSIONS

Despite its limitations, the simultaneous-equation regression model, developed and tested in this article, suggests that it may be successfully applied to advertising problems of this kind and may aid in shaping managerial decisions. Additional data on such variables as media, special sales promotions, distribution, and quality measures of advertising would add greatly to the credibility and rigor of aggregative statistical studies such as this one. However, this information can be obtained within companies. Further study within the framework suggested here may lead to significant managerial benefits.

Although results of this study are tentative with respect to the general applicability to advertising problems of the methodological framework, they suggest the possibility of designing formal, testable models to process the kinds of aggregative information generally available to management. The simultaneous regression model discussed here is the first known published model of its kind. However, a few firms are developing similar models.

APPENDIX

Structural Equations and Premises

The system of structural equations is:

$$
\begin{bmatrix}
-1 & 0 & \beta_1 & -\beta_1 \\
0 & -1 & \beta_3 & -\beta_3 \\
-1 & \beta_5 & \beta_6 & 0 \\
\beta_7 & -1 & 0 & \beta_8
\end{bmatrix}
\begin{bmatrix}
y_{1t} \\ y_{2t} \\ y_{3t} \\ y_{4t}
\end{bmatrix}
+
\begin{bmatrix}
\gamma_1 & \gamma_2 & \gamma_3 \\
\gamma_4 & \gamma_5 & \gamma_6 \\
0 & 0] & \gamma_7 \\
0 & 0 & \gamma_8
\end{bmatrix}
\begin{bmatrix}
X_{1t} \\ X_{2t} \\ X_{3t}
\end{bmatrix}
+
\begin{bmatrix}
\mu_{1t} \\ \mu_{2t} \\ \mu_{3t} \\ \mu_{4t}
\end{bmatrix}
= 0,
$$

$$E(\mu_t) = 0,$$

$$E(\mu_t^2) = \omega_{u_t}^2 .$$

The premises to be tested about the parameters are:

$\beta_1 + \beta_2 = 0$	$-3.0 \leq \gamma_5 \leq -1.0$
$\beta_3 + \beta_4 = 0$	$-1.25 \leq \gamma_6 \leq -.75$
$.5 \leq \beta_1 \leq .6$	$-1.0 \leq \beta_5 \leq -.9$
$.2 \leq \beta_4 \leq .3$	$.6 \leq \beta_6 \leq .7$
$1.0 \leq \gamma_1 \leq 1.3$	$5.0 \leq \gamma_7 \leq 7.0$
$0 \leq \gamma_2 \leq .8$	$-1.0 \leq \beta_7 \leq -1.5$
$-1.25 \leq \gamma_3 \leq -.75$	$-3.0 \leq \beta_8 \leq -3.5$
$0 \leq \gamma_4 \leq .8$	$5.0 \leq \gamma_8 \leq 7.0$

Reduced-Form Equations

The assumption that β is nonsingular is equivalent to the assumption that the determinant of the matrix, Δ, is non-vanishing within limits of the possible values of the matrix elements. The implicit limits on

$$\Delta = \beta_6\beta_8 + \beta_3\beta_5\beta_8 + \beta_3\beta_6 - \beta_1\beta_8 - \beta_1\beta_6\beta_7$$

have been calculated by maximizing and minimizing this function subject to the restrictions assumed for the variables. Thus,

$$-1.61 \leq \Delta \leq -0.12.$$

Since the Jacobian is implicitly nonvanishing at every point of the hypothetical structural parameter space, the reduced-form equations are deduced with the aid of the implicit function theorem. Thus

$$y_t = -(\beta)^{-1}\Gamma X_t - (\beta)^{-1}\mu_t ,$$

where

$$-\beta^{-1} = (1/\Delta) \begin{bmatrix} (\beta_6\beta_8 + \beta_3\beta_5\beta_8 + \beta_3\beta_6) & -\beta_1(\beta_6 - \beta_5\beta_8) & -\beta_1\beta_8 & \beta_1\beta_6 \\ \beta_3(\beta_8 + \beta_6\beta_7) & (\beta_6\beta_8 - \beta_1\beta_8 - \beta_1\beta_6\beta_7) & -\beta_3\beta_8 & \beta_3\beta_6 \\ (\beta_3 + \beta_8 - \beta_5\beta_7) & -(\beta_5\beta_8 + \beta_1 - \beta_1\beta_5\beta_7) & -(\beta_8 + \beta_3 + \beta_1\beta_7) & (\beta_1\beta_3\beta_5) \\ (\beta_3 - \beta_6\beta_7 - \beta_3\beta_5\beta_7) & (\beta_6 - \beta_1 + \beta_1\beta_5\beta_7) & -(\beta_3 - \beta_1\beta_7) & (\beta_1 - \beta_3\beta_5 - \beta_6) \end{bmatrix}$$

$$\Delta = \beta_6\beta_8 + \beta_3\beta_5\beta_8 + \beta_3\beta_6 - \beta_1\beta_8 - \beta_1\beta_6\beta_7 ,$$

and

$$y_{1t} = \alpha_1 X_{1t} + \alpha_2 X_{2t} + \alpha_3 + \eta_{1t}$$

$$y_{2t} = \alpha_4 X_{1t} + \alpha_5 X_{2t} + \alpha_6 + \eta_{2t}$$

$$y_{3t} = \alpha_7 X_{1t} + \alpha_8 X_{2t} + \alpha_9 + \eta_{3t}$$

$$y_{4t} = \alpha_{10} X_{1t} + \alpha_{11} X_{2t} + \alpha_{12} + \eta_{4t} ,$$

where

$$\alpha_1 = [(\beta_6\beta_8 + \beta_3\beta_5\beta_8 + \beta_3\beta_6)(\alpha_1/\Delta) - \beta_1(\beta_6 + \beta_5\beta_8)(\gamma_4/\Delta)]$$

$$\alpha_2 = [(\beta_6\beta_8 + \beta_3\beta_5\beta_8 + \beta_3\beta_6)(\gamma_2/\Delta) - \beta_1(\beta_6 + \beta_5\beta_8)(\gamma_5/\Delta)]$$

$$\alpha_3 = [(\beta_6\beta_8 + \beta_3\beta_5\beta_8 + \beta_3\beta_6)(\gamma_3/\Delta) - \beta_1(\beta_6 + \beta_5\beta_8)(\gamma_6/\Delta) - \beta_1\beta_8(\gamma_7/\Delta) + \beta_1\beta_6(\gamma_8/\Delta)]$$

$$\alpha_4 = [\beta_3(\beta_8 + \beta_6\beta_7)(\gamma_1/\Delta) + (\beta_6\beta_8 - \beta_1\beta_8 - \beta_1\beta_6\beta_7)(\gamma_4/\Delta)]$$

$$\alpha_5 = [\beta_3(\beta_8 + \beta_6\beta_7)(\gamma_2/\Delta) + (\beta_6\beta_8 - \beta_1\beta_8 - \beta_1\beta_6\beta_7)(\gamma_5/\Delta)]$$

$$\alpha_6 = [\beta_3(\beta_8 + \beta_6\beta_7)(\gamma_3/\Delta) + (\beta_6\beta_8 - \beta_1\beta_8 - \beta_1\beta_6\beta_7)(\gamma_6/\Delta) - \beta_3\beta_8(\gamma_7/\Delta) + \beta_3\beta_6(\gamma_8/\Delta)]$$

$$\alpha_7 = [(\beta_3 + \beta_8 - \beta_3\beta_5\beta_7)(\gamma_1/\Delta) - (\beta_5\beta_8 + \beta_1 - \beta_1\beta_5\beta_7)(\gamma_4/\Delta)]$$

$$\alpha_8 = [(\beta_3 + \beta_8 - \beta_3\beta_5\beta_7)(\gamma_2/\Delta) - (\beta_5\beta_8 + \beta_1 - \beta_1\beta_5\beta_7)(\gamma_5/\Delta)]$$

$$\alpha_9 = [(\beta_3 + \beta_8 - \beta_3\beta_5\beta_7)(\gamma_3/\Delta) - (\beta_5\beta_8 + \beta_1 - \beta_1\beta_5\beta_7)(\gamma_6/\Delta) - (\beta_8 + \beta_3 - \beta_1\beta_7)(\gamma_7/\Delta) + (\beta_1 - \beta_3\beta_5)(\gamma_8/\Delta)]$$

$$\alpha_{10} = [(\beta_3 - \beta_6\beta_7 - \beta_3\beta_5\beta_7)(\gamma_1/\Delta) + (\beta_6 - \beta_1 + \beta_1\beta_5\beta_7)(\gamma_4/\Delta)]$$

$$\alpha_{11} = [(\beta_3 - \beta_6\beta_7 - \beta_3\beta_5\beta_7)(\gamma_2/\Delta) + (\beta_6 - \beta_1 + \beta_1\beta_5\beta_7)(\gamma_5/\Delta)]$$

$$\alpha_{12} = [(\beta_3 - \beta_6\beta_7 - \beta_3\beta_5\beta_7)(\gamma_3/\Delta) + (\beta_6 - \beta_1 + \beta_1\beta_5\beta_7)(\gamma_6/\Delta) - (\beta_3 - \beta_1\beta_7)(\gamma_7/\Delta) + (\beta_1 - \beta_3\beta_5 - \beta_6)(\gamma_8/\Delta)].$$

The random vectors $\eta_t = (\eta_{1t}, \eta_{2t}, \eta_{3t}, \eta_{4t})$ for every t are independently and identically normally distributed with $E(\eta_t) = 0$ and covariance matrix $\sum = [\sigma_{hi}]$. The reduced-form covariance matrix depends on β and the covariance matrix of the structural equations.

Identifiability and Structural Parameter Estimation

The relations between the structural and reduced-form parameters are:

$$\begin{bmatrix} -1 & 0 & \beta_1 & -\beta_1 \\ 0 & -1 & \beta_3 & -\beta_3 \\ -1 & \beta_5 & \beta_6 & 0 \\ \beta_7 & -1 & 0 & \beta_8 \end{bmatrix} \begin{bmatrix} \alpha_1 & \alpha_2 & \alpha_3 \\ \alpha_4 & \alpha_5 & \alpha_6 \\ \alpha_7 & \alpha_8 & \alpha_9 \\ \alpha_{10} & \alpha_{11} & \alpha_{12} \end{bmatrix} + \begin{bmatrix} \gamma_1 & \gamma_2 & \gamma_3 \\ \gamma_4 & \gamma_5 & \gamma_6 \\ 0 & 0 & \gamma_7 \\ 0 & 0 & \gamma_8 \end{bmatrix} = 0,$$

and the twelve given identifying functions are:

$$\Phi_1 = -\alpha_1 + \beta_1(\alpha_7 - \alpha_{10}) + \gamma_1 = 0$$

$$\Phi_2 = -\alpha_2 + \beta_1(\alpha_8 - \alpha_{11}) + \gamma_2 = 0$$

$$\Phi_3 = -\alpha_3 + \beta_1(\alpha_9 - \alpha_{12}) + \gamma_3 = 0$$

$$\Phi_4 = -\alpha_4 + \beta_3(\alpha_7 - \alpha_{10}) + \gamma_4 = 0$$

$$\Phi_5 = -\alpha_5 + \beta_3(\alpha_8 - \alpha_{11}) + \gamma_5 = 0$$

$$\Phi_6 = -\alpha_6 + \beta_3(\alpha_9 - \alpha_{12}) + \gamma_6 = 0$$

$$\Phi_7 = -\alpha_1 + \beta_5\alpha_4 + \beta_6\alpha_7 = 0$$

$$\Phi_8 = -\alpha_2 + \beta_5\alpha_5 + \beta_6\alpha_8 = 0$$

$$\Phi_9 = -\alpha_3 + \beta_5\alpha_6 + \beta_6\alpha_9 + \gamma_7 = 0$$

$$\Phi_{10} = \beta_7\alpha_1 - \alpha_4 + \beta_8\alpha_{10} = 0$$

$$\Phi_{11} = \beta_7\alpha_2 - \alpha_5 + \beta_8\alpha_{11} = 0$$

$$\Phi_{12} = \beta_7\alpha_3 - \alpha_6 + \beta_8\alpha_{12} + \gamma_8 = 0.$$

If the vectors $\begin{bmatrix} \alpha_4 \\ \alpha_5 \end{bmatrix}$ and $\begin{bmatrix} \alpha_7 \\ \alpha_8 \end{bmatrix}$ are independent and the vectors $\begin{bmatrix} \alpha_1 \\ \alpha_2 \end{bmatrix}$ and $\begin{bmatrix} \alpha_{10} \\ \alpha_{11} \end{bmatrix}$ are independent, then from the identifying relations Φ_7 through Φ_{12}, the structural parameters $\beta_5, \beta_6, \beta_7, \beta_8, \gamma_7$ and γ_8 are uniquely identified. Since in this study the identified parameters are uniquely determined by the identifying relations, there is no need to apply identifiability test statistics.

The reduced-form regression results are:[a]

$$y_{1t} = 8.75X_{1t} - 7.82X_{2t} - 31.96 + \hat{\eta}_{1t} \qquad (R = .793)$$

$$t = (2.07) \qquad (-.90) \qquad (-1.63)$$

$$y_{2t} = 2.34X_{1t} + .78X_{3t} + 11.94 + \hat{\eta}_{2t} \qquad (R = .930)$$

---

[a] The data were processed by the ECOMP-2 Computer Program, General Electric RM 61 TMP-12 Vol. 4, written by Clee L. Childress.

$$t = (-2.72) \quad (.44) \quad (2.98)$$

$$y_{3t} = 10.11X_{1t} = 10.90X_{2t} - 42.01 + \hat{\eta}_{3t} \quad (R = .710)$$

$$t = (1.91) \quad (-1.01) \quad (-1.71)$$

$$y_{4t} = -2.64X_{1t} + 2.78X_{2t} - 10.33 + \hat{\eta}_{4t} \quad (R = .634)$$

$$t = (-1.57) \quad (.81) \quad (1.32)$$

REFERENCES

1. Advertising Publications, Inc., "Costs of Cigarette Advertising: 1952–1959," *Advertising Age*, 31 (September 19, 1960), 126–7.
2. ———, "Costs of Cigarette Advertising: 1957–1965," *Advertising Age*, 37 (July 25, 1966), 56–8.
3. Robert L. Basmann, "On the Application of the Identifiability Test Statistic in Predictive Testing of Explanatory Economic Models," *Econometric Annual, Indian Economic Journal*, 13, No. 3, (1965), 387–423.
4. ———, "A Theory of Demand with Variable Consumer Preferences," *Econometrica*, 24 (January), 1956, 47–58.
5. Frank M. Bass, "A Dynamic Model of Market Share and Sales Behavior," in Stephen A. Greyser, ed., *Toward Scientific Marketing*, Chicago: American Marketing Association, 1963, 263–76.
6. Robert Dorfman and Peter O. Steiner, "Optimal Advertising and Optimal Quality," *The American Economic Review*, 44 (December 1954), 826–36.
7. Ronald E. Frank, "Brand Choice as a Probability Process," *Journal of Business*, 35 (January 1962), 43–56.
8. John R. Hicks, *Value and Capital*, Oxford: Clarendon Press, 1946, 312–3.
9. Ronald A. Howard, "Stochastic Models of Consumer Behavior," in Frank M. Bass, *et al.*, eds., *Application of the Sciences in Marketing Management*, New York: John Wiley & Sons, Inc., 1967.
10. Alfred E. Kuehn, "Consumer B and Choice—A Learning Process?" in Ronald E. Frank, *et al.*, eds., *Quantitative Techniques in Marketing Analysis*, Homewood, Ill.: Richard D. Irwin, 1962.
11. ———, "A Model for Budgeting Advertising," in Frank M. Bass, *et al.*, ed., *Mathematical Models and Methods in Marketing*, Homewood, Ill.: Richard D. Irwin, 1961.
12. ——— and Albert C. Rohloff, "On Methods: Fitting Models to Aggregate Data," *Journal of Advertising Research*, (March 1967), 43–7.
13. Wassily Leontieff, "Composite Commodities and the Problem of Index Numbers," *Econometrica*, 4 (January 1936), 39–59.
14. Richard Maffei, "Advertising Effectiveness, Brand Switching and Market Dynamics," *Journal of Industrial Economics*, 9 (April 1961), 119–31.
15. William F. Massy and Ronald E. Frank, "Short Term Price and Dealing Effects in Selected Market Segments," *Journal of Marketing Research*, 2 (May 1965), 171–85.
16. Kristian S. Palda, *The Measurement of Cumulative Advertising Effects*, New York: Prentice-Hall, 1964.
17. Richard E. Quandt, "Estimating Advertising Effectiveness: Some Pitfalls in Econometric Methods," *Journal of Marketing Research*, 1 (May 1964), 51–60.
18. Lester G. Telser, "The Demand for Branded Goods As Estimated from Consumer Panel Data," *The Review of Economics and Statistics*, 44 (August 1962), 300–24.
19. ———, "Advertising and Cigarettes," *The Journal of Political Economy*, 70 (October 1962), 471–99.
20. U.S. Census Bureau, *Statistical Abstract of United States*, Washington, D.C.: Government Printing Office, 1965, 327; 360–1.
21. U.S. Department of Agriculture, *Agricultural Statistics*, Washington, D.C.: Government Printing Office, 1965, 111–2.
22. M. L. Vidale and H. B. Wolfe, "An Operation-Research Study of Sales Response to Advertising," *Operations Research*, 5 (June 1957).
23. Robert S. Weinberg, "The Uses and Limitations of Mathematical Models for Market Planning," in Frank M. Bass, *et al*, eds., *Mathematical Models and Methods in Marketing*, Homewood, Ill.: Richard D. Irwin, 1961.
24. Doyle Weiss, Alfred A. Kuehn, and T. McGuire, "Measuring the Effectiveness of Advertising," in Ray Haas, ed., *Science, Technology and Marketing*, Chicago: American Marketing Association, 1966.
25. Herman Wold, *Demand Analysis: A Study in Econometrics*, New York: John Wiley & Sons, Inc., 1953, 108–9.
26. Charles Yang, "A Theoretical and Empirical Investigation of Advertising Cycles," Unpublished Ph.D. thesis, New York University, 1962.

JULIAN L. SIMON*

This study estimates the revenue and profit generated by increments of advertising expenditures for liquor brands. Various distributed-lag regressions were fitted to ten-year periods for 15 brands ranging from small to largest. Found were annual retention rates around .75, and a logarithmic response function. Perhaps most important, this technique, pioneered by Telser and Palda, is again found useful.

The Effect of Advertising on Liquor Brand Sales

INTRODUCTION

A mail-order merchant can easily measure the effect of his advertising; he counts the dollars that come in in response to each coded advertisement. But distributors of branded consumer goods do not find it so easy to determine the effect of their advertising, and hence they are uncertain about how much to advertise. There are two causes of their measurement difficulty: (a) the distributor has no simple way to find out which sales result from which advertisements in which media; and (b) the effects of consumer-goods brand advertising are diffused over a relatively long time. The second difficulty is the more troublesome, and is largely the cause of the first one.

The effect of liquor advertising is among the harder advertising effects to measure, as will be seen later. Liquor executives commonly say that no one knows, and no one *can* know, the effect of liquor advertising. Yet liquor firms do advertise. Indeed, expenditures for advertising exceed production costs for many brands.[1]

THE DATA

Having *any* data at all for this sort of study is unusual. The liquor industry was chosen for study because advertising data is available. A detailed discussion of these data is available on request from the author. Briefly, exact sales data are available for 17 government liquor monopoly states (MSD), about 25 percent of all-US

consumption. *Business Week* estimates for all-US consumption are also available, but their reliability is questionable and they do not cover all brands and years. In this article the monopoly-state data are used unless it is noted otherwise. The *Business Week* data (BWD) are useful mostly to tell how to inflate the monopoly states' sales data to the United States as a whole to compute total profit or loss. Advertising expenditure data are estimated from commercial services that count ads in magazines and newspapers, but the estimates understate substantially; and point-of-purchase and other important media are not counted at all. Price and proof data come from the state of Washington's annual reports of state wholesale purchases.

The sample consists of 15 of the largest-selling brands, chosen because at least some BWD were available for each brand to provide a basis for generalization to the entire United States. Brands of Scotch and Canadian whiskey were omitted because blends cause extra difficulty in estimating costs. Also omitted were brands that shifted from blends to bourbons or to bonds during the study period and brands that were sold as bonds and bourbon straights at the same time.

Bias might arise because brands that were unsuccessful over the sample period were excluded for lack of data. But there was sufficiently little entry and exit from the *Business Week* list so the problem is not great.

The study period is 1953 to 1962. Data were not available before 1952; that year was omitted because no lagged values exist for it. Access to monopoly states' data ended with 1962.

* Julian L. Simon is associate professor of economics and marketing, University of Illinois. The author thanks Professor James M. Ferguson for the opportunity of reading his paper on the same subject, though Ferguson's approach is quite different from that discussed here.

[1] Production costs for a case of whiskey fifths might run $2 to $5. Bottling costs might be $2. Anywhere from $1 to $10 might be spent for advertising. Federal tax (86 proof) is $21.67. The wholesale selling price might be $27 to $35.

Journal of Marketing Research,
Vol. VI (August 1969), 301-13

PROCEDURE AND RESULTS

The general model follows:

(1) $S_{j,t} = f(S_{j,t-1}, A_{j,t}, R_{k,t}, P_{j,t}, F_{j,t}, \ldots)$,

where

$S_{j,t}$ is sales of Brand j in Year t
$A_{j,t}$ is advertising expenditures for Brand j in Year t
$R_{k,t}$ is sales of all brands of the same type k as Brand j, e.g., blended whiskey, gin, etc.
$F_{j,t}$ is proof of Brand j in Year t
$P_{j,t}$ is price of Brand j in Year t.

The key concept in the general model is geometrically distributed lags, which allows one to summarize in the single term $S_{j,t-1}$ the present effect of all selling forces in all prior years that influence $S_{j,t}$. This concept comes from the work of Koyck [8], building on an earlier idea by Fisher [2, 3]. It was first discussed in connection with advertising by Jastram [7], and its first empirical use for advertising was by Telser [19]. The concept is explained particularly clearly by Palda [12].[2] But there are many possible specific models in which this general concept can be applied, and for any given research situation most of the forms will yield unsatisfactory results.

Estimation of Decay Rate or Retention Rate (b_j)

This section aims to estimate the proportion of customers in Year t that will continue to be customers in Year $t+1$, net of the effect of advertising in Year $t+1$. The retention rate serves two important purposes. First, it provides a baseline above which one can estimate the effect of advertising in a given year. Second, it can be combined with the short-term estimate of advertising effectiveness to estimate the long-term effect of advertising (see [15]).

Equation 2 is the simplest model that includes some allowance for trend and for sales of the product class, e.g., bourbon:

(2) $S_{j,t} = a_j + b_j S_{j,t-1} + c_j A_{j,t} + h_k R_{k,t}$,

where

$S_{j,t}$ is sales of Brand j in monopoly states in adjusted cases (1,000's) in Year t
$R_{k,t}$ is sales of product-type k in monopoly states in adjusted cases (1,000's) in Year t

[2] Briefly, we assume that (ignoring disturbance terms and intercept)

(1a) $S_{j,t} = c_j A_{j,t} + k c_j A_{j,t-1} + k^2 c_j A_{j,t-2} \ldots k^n c_j A_{j,t-n}$.

The same relationship holds for the prior period:

(1b) $S_{j,t-1} = c_j A_{j,t-1} + k c_j A_{j,t-2} + k^2 c_j A_{j,t-3} \ldots k^n c_j A_{j,t-n-1}$.

Then multiply each term in (1b) by k and subtract (1b) from (1a) giving:

(1c) $S_{j,t} - k S_{j,t-1} = c_j A_{j,t}$,

or

(1d) $S_{j,t} = k S_{j,t-1} + c_j A_{j,t}$.

$A_{j,t}$ is advertising (\$1,000's) of Brand j in Year t
b_j is retention rate.

But the matrix of observed simple correlation coefficients showed very high multicollinearity between S_{t-1} and R_t. And stepwise multiple regressions run with this form showed extreme instability in the coefficients b and h because of the multicollinearity.

Another possibility is:[3]

(3) $\dfrac{S_{j,t}}{R_{k,t}} = a_j + b_j \left(\dfrac{S_{j,t-1}}{R_{k,t-1}}\right) + c_j A_{j,t}$.

Another possibility is to force a function like Equation 3 through the origin as in Equation 4:

(4) $\dfrac{S_{j,t}}{R_{k,t}} = b_j \left(\dfrac{S_{j,t-1}}{R_{j,t-1}}\right) + c_j A_{j,t}$.

Preliminary exploration indicated that regressions such as (3) often have intercepts large enough to swamp the rest of the estimates. These intercepts can be positive or negative; the large size probably stems from the fewness of the observations and the poor quality of the data. Not only does a constrained-through-origin "CON" model promise coefficients with more correct signs, but it makes better theoretical sense. If we assume that a brand's sales are created almost entirely by advertising (which is not implausible for liquor; this considers price and proof as parameters), then a regression that contains S_{t-1} and A_t terms on the right-hand side allows for no sensible meaning to be attached to slope-intercept constants. S_{t-1}, A_t and current variables, such as price, should account for all the variation in S_t.[4]

Equation 5, a variant of Equation 4 that uses the *logarithm* of advertising, is an important possibility for two reasons. First, there is reason to think that there are monotonically diminishing returns to scale in advertising [14], and the logarithmic is among the simpler

[3] The ratios of S/R in Equation 3 are not intended to represent market shares. Rather, this is a device for standardizing the brands' sales for general trends such as increases in population or taste shifts exogenous to the product type. It is reasonable to think that if there is an increase in population, say, the sales of each brand could be expected to be larger in proportion to the population increase. The sum of such demand expansion for the product is represented in the sales for the product as a whole, which is the rationale for including R in the equation. A similar form that shows more clearly that this is not a market-share concept is to standardize each sales term by multiplying with the ratios

$$\dfrac{\frac{1}{10}\sum_{t=1}^{10} R_{k,t}}{R_{k,t}} \quad \text{or} \quad \dfrac{\frac{1}{10}\sum_{t=1}^{10} R_{k,t-1}}{R_{k,t-1}}$$

respectively.

[4] Telser's work with cigarettes contains an example of this phenomenon. In his regressions for Camels and Lucky Strikes, of the form $S_t = a + b S_{t-1} + c \log A_t + d \log \text{income} + f \log \text{price} + g$ time, estimates of the constant a are -60 billion cigarettes and -143 billion cigarettes, respectively. Sales in the biggest year in Telser's sample were 48 billion Camels and 44 billion Lucky Strikes [19, p. 481].

functions that are concave to the origin. Second, previous work has found the logarithmic function to be a good fit for the advertising response function, e.g., [12, 19].

$$(5) \qquad \frac{S_{j,t}}{R_{k,t}} = b_j \left(\frac{S_{j,t-1}}{R_{k,t-1}} \right) + c_j \log A_{j,t}.$$

None of the above models has included price or proof terms, because one or both of these variables were constant over the full period for some of the brands, and for some of the other brands the signs of the variables were not theoretically acceptable. (A related investigation of price effects will be discussed at another time; the results of the most plausible model are shown in Table 1 but without discussion.)

Selecting the "best" regression form is neither easy nor perfectly objective. There are several possible philosophical criteria—prediction, explanation, etc. and many statistical tests, such as R^2, t, and others, as well as less formal statistical devices. Telser relied primarily on the criterion of goodness of fit. Palda used several criteria including explanation of variance (R^2), prediction (standard error of prediction, and accuracy of prediction of a few peculiar observations), and study of the t ratio (regression coefficient/standard error of coefficient). The criteria used here are less formal, partly because this study considers 15 sets of data, i.e., 15 brands, compared to Palda's one series and Telser's two or three. Therefore, there is less danger of a specious post facto choice of model that might only be the extreme observation in various randomly generated series. Also, the criteria used here are less formal because unlike both Telser and Palda this author attempts to estimate one constant at a time and is willing to use different regressions for the different constants. (On the other hand, the shortness of the time series puts this study at a comparative disadvantage compared with Telser's and Palda's studies.)

The models just mentioned, as well as several other models with constrained-through-origin and unconstrained variants, and some using both monopoly-state and all-US (*Business Week*) data, were compared. The model represented by Equation 5 (LOG-CON) using MSD generally seemed best for estimating the b_j retention coefficients. Though I think methodological issues are as important as the article's substance, the criteria used to select this model as best are relegated to the appendix. The reader interested in method may also wish to examine Tables 1 and 2, which present the results for several of the more likely models.

One important characteristic of the LOG-CON model (5) is its logarithmic advertising function rather than a linear advertising function. This finding is discussed later. A second important characteristic is the constraint through the origin. Such a model makes good theoretical sense, as well as producing the best results by most criteria (see the appendix).

The most important substantive result of this section

is that liquor brands have a very high retention rate from year to year (say .75), almost as high as the retention rate calculated by Telser for cigarettes before World War II. Combined with the observation that advertising is the overwhelmingly important cause of sales (because taste is generally indistinguishable between brands, the label and bottle shape are probably not influential, and no push money can be given in state stores) we then can deduce that the effect of advertising on liquor sales is diffused over a relatively long time, three quarters of it in years following the year in which the advertising appears.

Differences in Brand Retention Rates

Grouping b_j's for the LOG-CON model in Table 1, Column 3, we find these results: $b_{\text{blends}} = .79$ ($n = 8$), $b_{\text{straight bourbons}} = .75$ ($n = 4$), $b_{\text{gins}} = .80$ ($n = 2$), and $b_{\text{vodka}} = .96$ ($n = 1$). The results are almost identical when we look at the b_j's in the unconstrained LOG-CON version taken as groups.

The absence of differences in b between product types must not, however, be allowed to mask the important fact that the unstandardized retention rates will necessarily differ among product types. And it is the unstandardized retention rate that is the relevant economic quantity to firms. The b_j's estimated by LOG-CON may be the same for blends and straights, but if straights are selling more and blends less, a retention rate of .75 for a straight brand means more sales next year than for the blend brand with the same retention rate.

An independent forecast of the future sales of each product type is therefore necessary accessory information for a decision that is to be based on retention rates. Though the concept of b_j standardized as in LOG-CON may be confusing in some ways, it forces the explicit recognition of the need for product forecasts. And such forecasts cannot, or at least should not, be derived from the kind of regression analysis used here that is blind to all changes in taste. We have no statistical basis to assure us that next year blends will not begin to grow in popularity again while straights lose popularity.

There also does not seem to be any relationship between b_j and either price range or mean volume. (Note, however, that the sample excludes the experience of brands with small sales volume.) This finding does not agree with Telser's conclusion about the volume retention rate relationship in cigarettes, "... the rate of depreciation of advertising capital [1 — retention rate] is not a constant since it depends on relative advertising expenditure" [19, pp. 492–4]. It is worth noting that Telser drew his conclusion from his transition probability model of market share, and he was working with only the three largest brands. This is an issue on which we can use much further information.

Based on the findings in this section, from here on we can pool the standardized estimates of b for different brands and product types to constitute a broadly

Table 1
RESULTS FOR VARIOUS REGRESSION MODELS BY BRAND—MONOPOLY STATES DATA

Brand	Equation Log-Con $\frac{S_{j,t}}{R_{k,t}} = b \frac{S_{j,t-1}}{R_{k,t-1}} + c_j \log A_{j,t}$ Step 1 b_j	Step 2 b_j	Step 2 c_j	Equation Log-Not $\frac{S_{j,t}}{R_{k,t}} = a + b_j \frac{S_{j,t-1}}{R_{k,t-1}} + c_j \log A_{j,t}$ Step 1 b_j	Step 1 a intercept	Step 2 b_j	Step 2 c_j	Step 2 a intercept	$\frac{S_{j,t}}{R_{k,t}} = b_j \frac{S_{j,t-1}}{R_{k,t-1}} + c_j A_{j,t}$ b_j	c_j
Guckenheimer (blend)	1.00^b	.87^b	.00069^c	.76^b	.0039	.1	.00099^c	−.0050	.95^b	.000028^b
Carstairs (blend)	.97^b	.67^b	.0014^d	.68^b	.0094	.68	.0025	−.0079	.80^b	.000057^d
Four Roses (blend)	^a	.44	.0026^d	.37^d	.023	.62	−.0031	−.038	1.20^b	−.0000029^d
Kessler (blend)	1.10^b	.98^b	.0011^b	.99^b	.0065	.98	.0012	−.00032	.96^b	.000015^c
Seagrams 7 (blend)	1.00^b	.75^b	.0078^d	.50^a	.13	.51	−.00076	.14	1.00^b	−.000000043^c
Corby's Reserve (blend)	.99^b	.74^b	.0036^d	1.10^b	−.010	.96	.0071^c	−.010	.90^b	.000015^c
Imperial (blend)	1.00^b	.88^b	.0016^d	.99^b	.0032	.67	.014^b	−.073	.88^b	.000084^b
Old Thompson (blend)	.96^b	.83^b	.00027	.84^b	.0015	.82	.00012	.0011	.98^b	−.00000082
Ancient Age (bourbon)	1.00^b	.67^b	.0019^c	.75^b	.011	.53	.0070^d	−.031	.86^b	.000047
Echo Springs (bourbon)	.97^b	.84^b	.0014	.91^b	.0040	.94	.019^c	−.11	.80^b	.000026^d
Kentucky Gentleman (bourbon)	1.10^b	.89^b	.0021^d	.99^b	.0047	.80	.0019^d	.0040	.90^b	.000073^d
Bourbon Supreme (bourbon)	1.10^b	1.00^b	.0066^c	.57^b	.029	.50	.0029^d	.021	1.00^b	.000021
Gordon's (gin)	.98^b	.73^b	−.0068	^a	.64	.49	−.037	.36	1.00^b	−.000055
Gilbey's Gin (gin)	.99^b	.61^b	.0068^b	.46^a	.098	.28	−.0062	.17	.91^b	.000012^d
Smirnoff (vodka)	.95^b	.96	−.00047	.95^b	−.00043	.64	−.037	.32	.95^b	−.0000013
Number + (or −)	15						10		15	10
		($n = 15$)		($n = 15$)			($n = 15$)		($n = 15$)	($n = 15$)
Mean		.79							.94	

Brand	$\frac{S_{j,t}}{R_{k,t}} = b_j \frac{S_{j,t-1}}{R_{k,t-1}} + c_j \log A_{j,k} + d_j P_{j,t}$ b_j	c_j	d_j	$\frac{S_{j,t}}{R_{k,t}} = a_j + b_j \frac{S_{j,t-1}}{R_{k,t-1}} + c_j \log A_{j,t} + d_j P_{j,t}$ b_j	c_j	d_j	a intercept	$\frac{S_{j,t}}{R_{k,t}} - .75 \frac{S_{j,t-1}}{R_{k,t-1}} = a + c_j \log A_{j,t}$ c_j	a intercept
Guckenheimer (blend)	1.1^b	.00096^a	−.0000017^d	.97^b	.00043	−.000015^d	.044	.00065^d	.21
Carstairs (blend)	.63^b	.0082^a	−.000016^d	.49^d	.0051^a	−.000043^b	.11	.0025	−.97
Four Roses (blend)	.36	.0040^d	−.0000022	.50^d	−.0037^d	−.0000086^b	.016	−.0039^d	3.9
Kessler (blend)	.98	.0020	−.0000018	1.10^b	−.0026	−.000068^c	.21	.014^b	−6.9
Seagrams 7 (blend)	.68^c	.0072^d	.0000078	.51^c	−.00099	−.0000020	.14	−.0015	8.0
Corby's Reserve (blend)	Price was constant over study period							.0080^c	−2.9
Imperial (blend)	Price was constant over study period							.012^b	−6.5
Old Thompson (blend)	.82^b	.00013	.00000031	.77^b	.00024	−.0000032	−.010	.023	.13
Ancient Age (bourbon)	.52^c	.0058^d	−.0000060^d	.85^b	−.020^a	−.00005^b	−.36	.0027	−.85
Echo Springs (bourbon)	1.0^b	.019^a	−.000037^a	1.0^c	−.019^a	−.000042	−.017	.018^c	−9.6
Kentucky Gentleman (bourbon)	Price was constant over study period							.0022^b	.45
Bourbon Supreme (bourbon)	Price was constant over study period							.0013	1.5
Gordon's (gin)	1.0^b	.0015	.0000076	.74^b	−.022^a	−.000083^b	−.45	−.024^b	22.
Gilbey's Gin (gin)	.59^c	.0043	.000016	−.71^d	−.048^d	−.00012^d	−.99	.0052	.81
Smirnoff (vodka)	Price was constant over study period							−.026^b	26.
Number + (or −)								($n = 15$)	
Mean									

^a Indicates advertising (log $A_{j,t}$) came into stepwise regression first. Otherwise lagged sales ($S_{j,t-1}/R_{k,t-1}$) entered first.
^b t ratio greater than 3. ^c t ratio between 2 and 3. ^d t ratio between 1 and 2.

Table 2
SUMMARY OF PERFORMANCES OF VARIOUS REGRESSION MODELS

Data (1)	Equation number in text (2)	Regression equation (3)	Number of correctly signed sets of coefficients (4)	Number of cases in which lagged sales come into stepwise regression first (5)	Mean b_j (6)	Range of b_j (7)	Mean $\frac{b_j}{\sigma_b}$ (8)	Mean $\frac{c_j}{\sigma_c}$ (9)
1) MSD	5, LOG-CON	$\frac{S_{j,t}}{R_{k,t}} = b_j \frac{S_{j,t-1}}{R_{k,t-1}} + c_j \log A_{j,t}$	13 ($n = 15$)	14 ($n = 15$)	.79	.56	6.76[a]	3.30[a]
2) MSD		$\frac{S_{j,t}}{R_{k,t}} = b_j \frac{S_{j,t-1}}{R_{k,t-1}} + c_j \log A_{j,t} + d_j P_{j,t}$	13 ($n = 14$)	Not applicable	.78	.74	3.57[a]	1.43[a]
3) MSD	LOG-NOT	$\frac{S_{j,t}}{R_{k,t}} = a_j + b_j \frac{S_{j,t-1}}{R_{k,t-1}} + c_j \log A_{j,t}$	10 ($n = 15$)	14 ($n = 15$)	.70	.82	4.93	0.76
4) MSD	4	$\frac{S_{j,t}}{R_{k,t}} = b_j \frac{S_{j,t-1}}{R_{k,t-1}} + c_j A_{j,t}$	10 ($n = 15$)	15 ($n = 15$)	.94	.40	17.31[a]	0.83[a]
5) BWD	LOG-NOT	Same as Row 3	10 ($n = 14$)	11 ($n = 14$)	.60	1.09	4.00	0.50
6) BWD	5, LOG-CON	Same as Row 1	13 ($n = 15$)	13 ($n = 14$)	.75	.79	5.67[a]	1.50[a]
7) MSD		$S_t = b_j S_{t-1} + c_j \log A_{j,t}$	14 ($n = 15$)	14 ($n = 15$)	.76	.53	6.90[a]	2.00[a]
8) BWD	4	Same as Row 4	11 ($n = 14$)	14 ($n = 14$)	.92	.55	12.10[a]	0.73[a]

[a] Figures cannot be compared to unconstrained model data, because the constraint through the origin inflates these statistics.

based estimate of b, which can then be used to improve estimates of other coefficients. The estimate used for the retention rate for a brand whose sales are stable from year to year will be .75. Substituting this estimate into Equation 5, the results are generally sensible, as will be discussed later:

$$(6) \qquad \frac{S_t}{R_t} - .75\left(\frac{S_{t-1}}{R_{t-1}}\right) = a + c_j \log A_t.$$

Choice of Model for Estimating c_j

The great effect of retained sales on present sales makes it difficult to develop good estimates of the effect of advertising. Because so much of the variance is explained by S_{t-1} (or its standardized equivalent), the effect of A_t is obscured. In fact, for a particular brand, in those models in which b_j is higher, c_j is lower and vice versa. However, because the retention rate is high, a given amount of short-run advertising effect necessarily stands for a larger long-run effect. The short-run effect of advertising is heavily levered, but our lever's purchase is very small, which means that error is heavily levered, too.

Taking several criteria together (also discussed in the appendix), the LOG-CON model (Equation 5) is "best" for estimating c_j as it was also found to be for b_j. The acceptance of the logarithmic advertising function in preference to linear functions implies that there are diminishing returns to advertising over the range of advertising expenditure with which we are dealing. Logarithmic functions were compared with linear functions in many otherwise identical models, and the logarithmic functions usually did better. This finding agrees with those of Telser and Palda [12, 19] and with the general idea that there are no economies of scale in advertising [14]. The findings of Telser and Palda apply to narrow ranges of advertising expenditures, whereas the data in this study cover a variety of expenditure ranges, i.e., big as well as little brands. From this we can conclude (to the extent that our data are good) that there are diminishing returns at all advertising expenditure levels, at least in the liquor industry.

Now it is again necessary to consider, in the context of estimating c_j, whether there is justification for using a model constrained through the origin. The major justification for doing so when estimating b_j is that it was not theoretically reasonable to accept a large intercept. But when estimating c_j it does not matter whether most of the variance is explained by lagged sales, or by some other force, or by a combination of the two.

Looking at the c_j in the LOG-NOT model shown in Table 1, we see that 5 of the 15 c_j's are negative, compared with 2 of 15 in the LOG-CON version. This suggests that the more reasonable results in the LOG-CON version may be specious. The question, then, is whether some of the c_j's are really negative. To answer this, we must explore the results of other models.

The results of LOG-NOT with BWD are roughly the same (4 of 14 negative), but this is not surprising because the BWD were adjusted with MSD. Nevertheless, Seagrams 7 and Gilbey's Gin have positive c_j's in the all-US regression of LOG-NOT. Because some of the negative c_j's are not consistently negative lessens belief that they are really negative.

Another model examined was:

$$(7) \qquad \frac{S_{j,t}}{R_{k,t}} - .75\left(\frac{S_{j,t-1}}{R_{k,t-1}}\right) = a_j + c_j \log A_{j,t}.$$

This model uses the pooled information on b_j to ensure that quirks in a b_j from any cause will not cause quirks in the corresponding c_j. In this model only 3 of 14 c_j's were negative.

Further reason to disbelieve in negative c_j is that the c_j's in LOG-NOT are more variable than in LOG-CON, but for seven of the brands the c_j's were higher in LOG-NOT whereas eight were lower. This suggests that even if the LOG-CON form reduces dispersion artificially, it does not bias the estimate upwards or toward more positive values. It would seem wise to estimate c_j with the logarithmic form of the model constrained through the origin, LOG-CON.

Now c_j for each Brand j can be estimated. But theory and general considerations give us the nerve to go a little farther. First, we can reject negative c_j's, because they are against all theoretical considerations and because signs of some c_j's are different in the different models. We will not work further with brands with negative c_j's in our basic model.

A reasonable business economist would probably go further. He would either re-estimate "bad" c_j's from other models or use pooled estimates. Using estimates from other models seems like specious selection, but it might not be bad, for example, to estimate c_j for Gordon's gin from an expanded LOG-CON model that includes price, especially since price seems more important for Gordon's gin than other brands.

As to pooled estimates, it probably would make good sense to adjust the c_j toward the mean c_j of similar brands, but this will not be pursued.

A reader who is familiar with the literature on advertising budget decisions might ask whether the effect of A_t could be estimated better with a pair of simultaneous equations in which S_t and A_t would both be endogenous variables. This issue has not been raised by previous writers (e.g., Telser and Palda), and perhaps it deserves to be mentioned at least in passing.

The single equation approach makes most sense here because the purpose of this article is to estimate control parameters rather than to predict equilibrium values. As Wold argues, "the relations of interdependent systems [of simultaneous equations] being predictive and the relations of causal chains (being) causal . . . interdependent systems do not allow an interpretation in terms of causal flows, at least not in the same immediate sense as causal chains" [21, p. 37]. This implies the use of a single least-squares regression.

Effects of Advertising as a Function of Other Variables

Now we can investigate how the effectiveness of advertising is related to such variables as price range and sales volume. The first step is to translate the estimated regression coefficients into net dollars by way of numbers of cases, transforming the variables back from their logarithmic form. The appropriate statistic for each brand is the dollars of long-run net revenue (equal to total revenue less all costs except advertising) created by a marginal dollar of advertising for the brand at the mean expenditure level over the period of our study.

The device of evaluating the effect of an incremental change at the midpoint(s) of a variable(s) was previously used by Telser and Palda, but makes several troubling assumptions. First, the midpoint only has special meaning for a curvilinear function; the evaluation of a change in a linear advertising function is the same at any point as at the midpoint. Second, why use the midpoint at all? Why not the last year, the first year, or each year? Assuming a stable environment, then the midpoint is at least a starting point; we can tell whether a given advertising expenditure at the midpoint is too large or too small. A more complete treatment would consider each year as a sample observation and compute the most profitable point as described in [15].

The statistic we seek first is the marginal number of case sales in the short run (MVH_j), which can be used immediately to compare brands and then as the foundation for the rest of the analysis in a model such as:

$$(8) \qquad S_{j,t} = b_j S_{t-1} + c_j A_{j,t}$$

$$(9) \qquad MVH_j = c_j Z,$$

where Z is a factor of conversion to all-US data.[5]
For the equation standardized by product type the translation is more complex. Substituting $(R_t + R_{t-1})/2$ for each R_t and R_{t-1}, an approximation that should not be far wrong, for Model 3 (linear advertising function, not constrained through origin):

$$(10) \qquad MVH_j = c_j Z R_{k,t} .$$

For LOG-NOT, Equation (4),

$$(11) \qquad MVH_j = c_j z \bar{R}_k \frac{\log \bar{A}_j}{\bar{A}_j} ,$$

where $\bar{A}$ and $\bar{R}$ are mean values.
The data in Table 3 show very clearly that the estimate of whether a given brand is at a profitable or unprofitable advertising level is extremely sensitive to the

estimates of c_j and b_j, but the estimates of c are much more variable.[6]

The large variation in MVH_j among brands at the same volume and price range is somewhat questionable because the effectiveness of liquor advertising seems less likely to vary among brands than any other type of advertising; tight legal constraints control what can be said and shown in liquor advertising. A brand owner might therefore want to modify the point estimate for his brand toward the mean of estimates for similar brands or toward estimates made with other equations for the same brand.

Now we can compare the efficiency of advertising for the various brands. In Table 3, Column 11 shows MVH_j measured in (adjusted to fifths) cases sold at the mean advertising expenditure during 1953–1962, i.e., for each brand MVH_j is the incremental number of cases that would be sold if one dollar more were spent for advertising than the mean expenditure from 1953–1962.

If $b_j = .75$, the long-run effect (MVL_j) is approximately four times MVH_j. MVL_j is the total effect (in cases) of an incremental dollar of advertising at the mean expenditure; it includes the cases sold in Year t and in all succeeding years. The brands with the smallest advertising expenditure (Guckenheimer, Bourbon Supreme, Corby's, Kentucky Gentlemen) have the largest MVL_j. This finding is not an artifact caused by use of a logarithmic function; rather, c_j is calculated separately for each brand. However, each of these brands is low priced in its product category. Also, the companies may spend a relatively larger share of their total promotion on personal selling and hidden discounts than do those of other brands. And this study may suffer from sample selection bias because the only brands with small advertising expenditures that could enter the sample had sales large enough to place them among the largest selling brands.

The next transformation is to obtain marginal dollar sales per advertising dollar at the mean advertising expenditure, MDL, by multiplying by the mean distributor's case price.

$$(12) \qquad \begin{array}{l} \text{Marginal Dollar Sales Effect, Long Run } (MDL_j) \\ = \text{price} \times MVL_j \approx 4 \times \text{price} \times MVH_j . \end{array}$$

Because the dispersion among brand prices is small compared with the dispersion in the marginal case effect, a similar MDL position prevails among the brands as noted for MVL.

The transformation from revenue to profit is most important. It depends on estimates of distributor's

---

[5] $$z = \frac{\dfrac{S_{j,t}(\text{in BWD})}{S_{j,t}(\text{in MSD})} + \dfrac{S_{j,t-1}(\text{in BWD})}{S_{j,t-1}(\text{in MSD})}}{2}$$

[6] Because of the logarithmic transformation of A_t, the c_j's from LOG-CON must be transformed before they can be compared for size, i.e., a brand at a higher volume with the same c_j as a smaller volume brand has a lower MVH.

Table 3

EFFECTS OF ADVERTISING ON REVENUE AND PROFIT ESTIMATED WITH LOG-CON (MSD)

Brand J	Type of liquor	Mean proof	c_i	Mean advertising ($1,000) A_i	$\log A_i$ / Log (5)	Mean product sales (1,000 cases) $\bar{R}_k$	Mean brand U.S. sales $\bar{S}_i$ (BWD)	Mean brand monopoly state sales $\bar{S}_i$ (MSD)	Multiplier (Z) [(8)÷(9)]	Marginal cases per dollar short run (MV'H) $Z = \frac{(c_i)(\log A_i)(\bar{R}_k)(Z)}{A_i}$ = (4)×(6)×(7)×(10)÷(5)
(1)	(2)	(3)	(4)	(5)	(6)	(7)	(8)	(9)	(10)	(11)
Guckenheimer	Blend	86	.00069	31	1.4914	29,037	696	163	4.27	4.08
Carstairs	Blend	86	.0014	973	2.988	29,037	836	304	2.75	.34
Four Roses	Blend	86.3	.0026	2233	3.351	29,037	1079	357	3.02	.34
Kessler	Blend	86	.0011	504	2.702	29,037	809	491	1.65	.28
Seagrams 7	Blend	86.3	.0078	4653	3.668	29,037	6943	2602	2.67	.48
Corby's	Blend	86	.0036	567	2.754	29,037	1689	882	1.91	.97
Imperial	Blend	86	.0016	1335	3.126	29,037	2521	785	3.21	.35
Old Thompson	Blend	86.3	.00027	319	2.504	29,037	670	117	5.73	.35
Ancient Age	Bourbon	86	.0019	1324	3.122	19,507	1174	180	6.52	.57
Echo Springs	Bourbon	86	.0014	433	2.637	19,507	731	282	2.59	.43
Kentucky Gentleman	Bourbon	87.2	.0021	72	1.857	19,507	492	157	3.13	3.30
Bourbon Supreme	Bourbon	90.3	.0066	92	1.964	19,507	458	284	1.61	4.42
Gordon's	Gin	93	.0015*	1263	3.10	7,601	1781	383	4.65	.13
Gilbey's Gin	Gin	90	.0068	1076	3.032	7,602	1531	349	4.39	.64
Smirnoff	Vodka	80	negative	2046	3.312	4,731	1584	288	5.50	negative

Brand J	Type of liquor	Mean proof	Marginal cases per dollar long run (MVL) = (11)÷0.25	Mean price $\bar{P}_i$	(MDL) (12)×(13)	Mean cost per case of fifths to brand owner (Ex. adv.)	Mean case net (13)−(15)	Profit per marginal dollar of advertising long run (MNL) (12)×(16)−$1	$\frac{R_{k,55} - R_{k,62}}{R_{k,55}} \div 10 = Q$	MNL adjusted for trend and money discount $\frac{(11)\times(16)}{1 - .75x \times .90 \times (18)}$
(1)	(2)	(3)	(12)	(13)	(14)	(15)	(16)	(17)	(18)	(19)
Guckenheimer	Blend	86	16.32	$28.17	$459.73	$26.50	$1.67	$26.25	.976	22.09
Carstairs	Blend	86	1.36	29.09	39.56	26.50	2.59	2.52	.976	2.85
Four Roses	Blend	86.3	1.36	34.23	46.55	26.58	7.65	9.40	.976	8.43
Kessler	Blend	86	1.12	29.31	32.83	26.50	2.81	2.15	.976	2.55
Seagrams 7	Blend	86.3	1.92	33.04	63.44	26.58	6.46	11.40	.976	10.05
Corby's	Blend	86	3.88	29.70	115.24	26.50	3.20	11.42	.976	10.06
Imperial	Blend	86	1.40	29.75	41.65	26.50	3.25	3.55	.976	3.69
Old Thompson	Blend	86.3	1.40	29.90	41.86	26.58	3.32	3.65	.976	3.77
Ancient Age	Bourbon	86	2.28	37.10	84.59	28.95	8.15	17.58	1.030	15.24
Echo Springs	Bourbon	86	1.72	32.60	56.07	28.95	3.65	5.28	1.030	5.15
Kentucky Gentleman	Bourbon	87.2	13.20	32.65	430.98	29.25	3.40	43.88	1.030	36.82
Bourbon Supreme	Bourbon	90.3	17.68	32.75	579.02	30.00	2.75	47.62	1.030	39.88
Gordon's	Gin	93	.52	27.77	14.44	27.57	0.27	−0.86	1.072	0.12
Gilbey's Gin	Gin	90	2.56	28.17	72.11	26.79	1.38	2.53	1.072	3.19
Smirnoff	Vodka	80	—	30.03	—	24.19	5.84	—	1.991	—

* The estimate of c_i for Gordon's gin was taken from a regression that included price as well as advertising and lagged sales, because the estimate of c_i was otherwise negative.

cost for each brand:

Marginal Profit per Advertising Dollar (MNL_j)

(13)   = (price—all costs except advertising -1)

$$\times \ (MVL_j).$$

The estimates of costs per case used here are: gin or vodka, $25.75; blended whiskey, $26.50; bourbon, $28.45. Bases of the estimates are available on request from the author. The MNL_j shown in Table 3, Column 18 indicate that estimates of marginal profit from advertising are extremely sensitive to cost estimates. An important conclusion to be drawn from this article is that in the determination of advertising's economic effect, cost estimation may be as important as the estimation of advertising's sales effect. For example, the tax reduction from Seagrams' tiny shift from 86.8 to 86 proof in 1957 increased net revenue by 20 cents per case, totaling about $1,300,000—more than one-third the company's advertising expenditure in that year. Changes in bottling and packaging costs or in the allocation of joint costs could also produce large changes compared with advertising.

Also important in advertising expenditure decisions is the effect on brand sales of long-term trends in the product's sales. The basic LOG-CON model estimates are b_j and c_j for a world made static by using S_t/R_t and S_{t-1}/R_{t-1} as dependent and independent variables, respectively. But if product sales are rising and if a given brand's sales can be expected to rise ceteris paribus—a reasonable assumption unless the number of brands increases—then the brand's prospects are better, and the marginal profit effect is greater, than is shown in Table 3, Column 18.

If a product type's case sales are expected to rise five percent each year, say, we can make an appropriate adjustment simply by multiplying b_j by 1.05. This affects the multiplier in this way:

$$\frac{1}{1 - 1.05b_j} \approx \frac{1}{1 - .75 \times 1.05} = 4.45.$$

If, however, a product's sales are expected to decline (like blended whiskey from 1953–62), the adjustment will be less than 1 and the multiplier will be less than 4. A firm forecasts the future of a product type by considering the general trend in liquor sales (as affected by population, for example) and the taste changes for the particular product. Both considerations are included in the adjustment to the multiplier. Of course, the correctness of the adjustment depends on the accuracy of the forecasts.

A firm's last adjustment is for the interest discount on money; a dollar of sales five years in the future is worth less today than a dollar of sales today. Adjusting the multiplier allows for the decrease in dollar value. For example, if the firm's interest rate $(r) = .10$, its

discount rate $(\rho) = .90$, and

$$\frac{1}{1 - b_j \times \text{product} - \text{trend} \times \rho}$$

$$= \frac{1}{1 - .75 \times 1.05 \times .90} = 3.4.$$

The results appear in Column 20 of Table 3.

A few observations about the profit-and-loss situations of brands are:

1. Seagrams 7 Crown was making a fortune over the period of analysis. Though its MNL was lower than smaller brands, its volume was very large and its profit per case was very substantial. Why this was so is not clear. However, the method can be checked with a crude approximation. If one assumes that Seagrams 7 Crown sales and advertising for the middle year (1957) are rough indexes of long-term equilibrium, then a distributed-lag analysis should equal an analysis based on the current period. Seagrams spent $.55 in advertising per case sold, leaving ($6.46 − .55) $5.81 profit (before overhead costs) per case sold.

2. Four Roses advertising was very profitable despite its low MVL because of the very high net revenue per case sold.

3. The difference in profit results between Corby's and Kessler must stem from a difference in advertising copy effectiveness, or a difference in variables such as distribution effectiveness which were not allowed for, or errors in the data. The last seems the likeliest explanation to me, in which case the pooled estimates would be the best estimates for the individual brands.

4. The rise in advertising expenditures relative to the case sales over the study period suggests that firms may have revised upwards their estimates of profitability of various amounts of advertising. Firms may also feel that an industry-wide escalation of advertising may be unprofitable for all firms in the long run, and this belief may have worked to reduce expenditures below levels that are apparently optimum for individual firms. If so, the decrease in industry concentration [1] that accompanied the rise in advertising expenditures over the study period may suggest a structural relationship between the two variables.

CONCLUSIONS

Abstracting from product type trends, the retention rate from year to year (i.e., the brand loyalty), is in the neighborhood of .75. The retention rate does not seem to be a function of price range, sales volume, or advertising volume.

A logarithmic function represents the effects of advertising expenditure better than a linear function. This is equivalent to stating that there are diminishing returns to advertising at all expenditure levels investigated.

The marginal profit effect of advertising is higher for the smaller advertisers in the sample. This also suggests that there are diminishing returns to advertising over the wide range of expenditure levels included in our sample.

If one considers their mean expenditure levels, all brands in the sample appear to have spent too little for advertising.

If the estimates are modified to take account of secular shifts in taste among liquor types, plus population growth, and if it is assumed that advertisers knew as of 1953 what the trends would be over the next 10 years, i.e., assuming trends over the ten years of the study period can be extrapolated linearly from any year in the sample period, profitability estimates are altered slightly.

Perhaps the most important finding is the reaffirmation of Telser's and Palda's findings that this is a feasible technique for estimating the retention rate of sales custom as well as advertising's long-run effect. It is noteworthy that plausible results were obtained despite grave flaws in the data; indeed, it seems a small miracle that anything turned out at all. This suggests that a firm can make even better use of the technique than can the outside academic investigator, because the firm's own data will furnish a better foundation for the analysis.

The application of this technique cannot be automatic. Examination of the particular firm, its environment, and many regression approaches are important. Otherwise the technique may have worse results than crude reckonings of current period sales and expenditures, because complicated techniques can be illusory in promising more than they deliver.

APPENDIX: CRITERIA USED IN SELECTING MODELS

The following are the criteria and the decision process used in choosing the basic model for estimating b_j—Model 4, LOG-CON—which is constrained through the origin and uses a logarithmic function of advertising.

The first criterion for designating LOG-CON was that for more brands than almost any other equation—13 in 15—the signs of b_j and c_j are both positive. (See Table 2, Column 4. Table 1 shows a sample of a less-summarized form of the data.) Also, lagged sales come into the stepwise regression before advertising in 14 of 15 cases.

The regressions with ratios on the left and right sides of the equations do much better than equations of the form

$$(A1) \qquad S_t = h_j R_{k,t} + b_j S_{t-1} + c_j A_{j,t},$$

or

$$(A2) \qquad S_t = h_j R_{k,t} + b_j S_{j,t-1} + c_j \log A_{j,t},$$

because of the very high collinearity between S_{t-1} and R_t. R_t is in the regression only to allow for the relatively slight effects of product trends, but it often swamps the effect of S_{t-1}, causing b to become wildly unreliable. On the other hand, if R_t is omitted,

$$(A3) \qquad S_t = b_j S_{t-1} + c_j \log A_{j,t}.$$

Model A3 does better on the first criterion (and the following criterion, too) than does LOG-CON, showing 14 of 15 correctly signed coefficients. Nevertheless, LOG-CON was chosen, primarily because it is theoretically more reasonable to choose a model that allows for the overall influence of product sales. But if product sales are influential, why should a model such as LOG-CON that includes them do apparently worse than Model A3, which ignores them? Table 4 gives a clue; it contains data on Smirnoff vodka, one of two brands (Gordon's gin is the other) whose coefficients were correct in A3 but wrong in LOG-CON. (Corby's whiskey had correct coefficients in LOG-CON but wrong ones in A3.) R_t undeniably affects S_t in Table 4. But the "trend" in vodka sales was sufficiently consistent over the entire period so that the linear trend in S_{t-1} "explains" the trend in S_t better than R_t. But this is spurious. If the changes from year to year were random, R_t would show influence, but S_{t-1}'s only influence would be from "retained" sales. This is why we prefer LOG-CON—because if one has no reason to forecast a continuation or change in an overall product sales trend for a given year, it would seem wiser to allow for the influence of R_t rather than ignore it or hope that a trend extrapolation would include its effect.

The comparison of LOG-CON and A3 also shows how sensitive these short time series are when considered individually; a slight inaccuracy in the data or a coincidental or extraneous relationship between variables can completely alter the individual results. This is why this investigation gains strength from considering many series and then pooling the results. Again note that the ratios S_t/R_t and S_{t-1}/R_{t-1} are not to be interpreted as market shares but as a device for standardizing S_t and S_{t-1}.[7]

Table 4
DATA FOR SMIRNOFF VODKA

| Year | Monopoly states | | | All-US[a] |
	S_t	S_{t-1}	R_t	A_t
1952 (Pre-Study Period)	033	000	084	495
1953	066	033	162	776
1954	091	066	242	676
1955	159	091	461	1042
1956	285	159	936	2105
1957	358	285	1287	2443
1958	360	358	1332	2908
1959	394	360	1512	2291
1960	393	394	1608	2662
1961	383	393	1650	2683
1962	394	383	1768	2873

[a] Source: *Business Week*.

[7] It might make better sense to employ the statistic $R_{k,t} - S_{j,t}$ as a standardizing denominator for the jth firm instead of R_t. It would not make much difference except for brands like Seagrams 7 that account for a large proportion of the product type's sales. And for such large brands, $R_{k,t} - S_{j,t}$ might indicate more about the brand's market share but less about the general trend for the product, which is what we are interested in.

Table 5

COEFFICIENTS OF LOG-CON (MSD) UNDER VARIOUS KOYCK ASSUMPTIONS

Brand	Direct estimate	e						
		0	.4	.5	.6	.8	.9	.95
Guckenheimer	1.11	.88	.87	.87	.87	.87	.86	.85
Carstairs	.68	.76	.74	.72	.70	.57	.37	.24
Four Roses	.62	1.68	3.46	6.47	35.74	−6.20	−4.40	−3.92
Kessler	.98	.99	.99	.99	.99	.99	.99	.98
Seagrams 7	.51	.85	.83	.82	.81	.73	.61	.52
Corby's Reserve	.96	.86	.85	.84	.82	.50[a]	1.46[a]	13.49
Imperial	.67	.90	.89	.89	.89	.89	.88	.86
Old Thompson	.82	.96	.96	.96	.95	.90	.64	−.30
Ancient Age	.53	.76	.73	.72	.70	.59	.48	.41
Echo Springs	.94	.92	.92	.91	.91	.88	.41[a]	−.39[a]
Kentucky Gentleman	.80	.95	.95	.95	.94	.92	.88	.68
Bourbon Supreme	.50	.63	.62	.61	.61	.58	.55	.53
Gordon's Gin	.49	1.03	1.03	1.03	1.03	1.03	1.03	1.04
Gilbey's Gin	.27	.79	.77	.77	.76	.71	.67	.64
Smirnoff Vodka	.64	.97	.97	.97	.97	.97	.96	.96

[a] Negative square-root argument.

The second criterion was the amount of variation in the estimates of the b coefficients among the various brands, i.e., the ratio:

$$\frac{\frac{1}{n}\sum_{j=1}^{n} b_j}{\sigma\, b_j}.$$

If the ranges of b_j in the various regressions (see Table 5, Column 2) are used as a handy estimate of dispersion in b_j, MSD does better than BWD in LOG-CON regressions. However, the superiority of LOG-CON with MSD to the regression with BWD is because of the greater accuracy of the MSD. The higher MSD median coefficient of .83 compared with .76 may also result from the MSD regressions having better sales data and poorer (actually, less relevant) advertising data. One might object to comparing the two series because MSD is used to interpolate where BWD is missing. To the extent that the two series are using the same data, however, they would converge, so a difference between them must derive from the differences in the series.

This second criterion becomes somewhat less attractive when we consider that the various brands have different characteristics that might sensibly produce true variation in their b_j. A third criterion therefore avoids pooling elements that might be unlike; we compare the ratios (regression coefficient/standard error) in Table 1, Column 4 or Table 2, Column 8. By this test, comparing MSD to BWD on LOG-CON, in nine cases MSD values exceed BWD values, while in six cases BWD values are higher. (Note that we cannot make this test between constrained and unconstrained models because the interpretation of the t value in the constrained regression is not clear.)

Like all other criteria, this third criterion cannot be applied without some ad hoc judgment. For example,

in more than half the cases the t values for b_j are higher in the linear MSD version (LIN-CON) than in the logarithmic MSD version (LOG-CON). However, this is mostly because of the poorer performance of advertising in the linear versions. The t values for c_j are higher in the logarithmic versions, and in some cases in which the linear b_j exceeds its logarithmic counterpart the sign of advertising is wrong.

It is the constrained-through-the-origin feature of our chosen model that is most interesting. None of the criteria used so far helps to make a fair comparison of constrained and unconstrained forms. The test of the number of positive coefficients is loaded in favor of the constrained version because the constraint almost forces a positive b_j. Similarly, the test of variation in b is loaded in favor of the constrained form, and the t and R^2 values cannot be compared because of the computer program's quirks. (However, R^2 and t values in a fair comparison would have to be lower for a constrained version because the constraint warps the regression surface away from the position that would otherwise give the best fit.)

The best justification for selecting the constrained model is that it is simpler and makes the best theoretical sense, as discussed earlier. The observed coefficients for constrained and unconstrained models reassure us, however, because the mean b_j is similar. And the b_j's change wildly in unconstrained models in the stepwise regressions, whereas they are more stable from step to step in constrained forms. (See Table 1.) If the constraint merely reduced the dispersion, we might suspect it of removing true dispersion among the b_j's. But the b_j's for individual brands are sometimes high and sometimes low in different models, which suggests that the variation is largely error, from the choice of model as well as other sources, rather than true dispersion.

Though it is true that the b_j's estimated by LOG-

CON with MSD are plausible in that they are high but less than 1, one might think that we are receiving exactly what our inputs are forcing the equation to put out. However, the c_j's give evidence for the method's validity. Given that the b_j's are positive, the c_j's are not forced to be positive or negative; nevertheless, the c_j's show the more sensible sign more often in this equation than in any other equation.

We can also compare the order in which variables come into the stepwise multiple regressions. The form chosen as best, LOG-CON with MSD, has the order of variables entering as: (a) lagged sales, (b) advertising, and (c) price (where applicable) more often than any other form. This order makes the most theoretical sense and it is not forced by the constraint.

The results of LOG-CON with price as an added variable are also shown in Table 2. The addition of price shifts the sign of one of the two negative c_j's, and an added variable decreases the likelihood that the constraint through origin is forcing the results we expected to find. Nevertheless, three of the ten c_j's are positive.

The reader may question the validity of estimates of the structural parameters of advertising and the retention rate on the basis of the tiny sample sizes—ten observations in each sample. A sample this size often provides little statistical power because of the small amount of information, and the results of a ten-observation regression may be biased because of a lagged independent variable. If it were not for the potential bias, we could simply pool the results of our 15 samples of 10 observations each with the confidence that we would be boosting our statistical power to respectable levels. But 15 biased samples are little better than one in estimating the true parameters, though they will have a smaller sampling variation.

There is considerable literature on the extent and danger of the bias [5, 6, 11]. This literature suggests an a priori argument against a very bad bias in this case: when the true coefficient of the lagged variable is high, the bias will be less than when the true coefficient is low. And there is considerable reason to believe that in the case of liquor brands the lagged coefficient will be high. Reasons include trade surveys that show high consumer loyalty, and the evidence on an analogous product (cigarettes) developed by Telser [19]. But I cannot rest on such a priori argument. To do so would be to bootstrap one's way to the conclusion; if we knew that the coefficient was high, we would not need to prove it statistically.

The coefficients generated by the various functions also provide an empirical reason to believe that bias is not important. As can be seen in Koyck's formulas [8, p. 36ff], the smaller the residuals, the smaller the bias, ceteris paribus. And intuitively, the smaller the disturbances, the less the danger of autocorrelation among the disturbances. Hence, one can compare the

coefficients in the function that includes another variable (price) in which the disturbances will therefore be reduced. Table 1 (Step 2) shows the basic function but unconstrained through the origin. The median lagged coefficient is *higher* in the equation with the added variable. The fact that the median coefficient is similar in a wide variety of other functions also supports the argument. All this suggests that there is no upward bias, and that is the only direction in which there is reason to fear a bias.

To go further, Koyck's method can be applied to explore the possible biases under various assumptions about the autocorrelation in the disturbance term. The inputs were the residuals and lagged coefficients from LOG-NOT. The results can be seen in Table 5. Only if one assumes that $e = .9$ or above, is the median coefficient below the best direct estimate of .75, and then the medians are .65 ($e = .9$) and .57 ($e = .95$). And it seems farfetched that the actual e would be as high as .9. Therefore, this sensitivity analysis suggests that the direct estimates found here for the individual brands are not seriously biased upwards.

If, then, one discounts the likelihood of serious inconsistency of the individual brand estimates, one can then rely on the pooled estimate from the brands, subject to the sampling variation of the individual means. One then can say that there is as much statistical power as might be derived from a sample larger than ten observations.

The inclusion of price does not have a large effect on most of the b_j's, and within the LOG-CON model that otherwise appears best for estimating b_j, several of the d_j's have the wrong sign. This, together with the absence of any price changes for some brands, motivates the omission of price from models for estimating b_j.

It was also necessary to set up criteria to choose the best estimator of c. (Note that different regressions may be "best" for estimating b_j and c_j.)

The first criterion was the same as in choosing an estimating equation for b_j: the largest number of combinations of b_j and c_j with positive signs. This criterion points to the same LOG-CON form as before, though BWD does just as well as MSD by this test.

The second criterion was the t ratio, $c_j/\sigma c_j$. In three of the five observations in which (a) both regressions did not contain a negative sign, and (b) full BWD data existed, the values of this ratio were higher for BWD than for MSD. This does differ from the same test for b_j, suggesting the use of BWD regressions to estimate c_j. This makes sense because the advertising expenditure data are for the United States as a whole. But it is possible that the BWD values of t_{ej} are inflated by the poorer relationship for the sales data. And the standardized c_j are *relatively* larger compared to the standardized b_j in the BWD regressions. Also, four of the five F values for the advertising step (when it is second in the stepwise regression) are higher for the MSD regressions. The advantage of the BWD is not enough, if any, to shift to its use.

REFERENCES

1. James M. Ferguson, "Advertising Investment and the Theory of Entry," Unpublished paper, University of Virginia, 1965.
2. Irving Fisher, "Note on a Short-Cut Method for Calculating Distributed Lags," *Bulletin de l'Institut International de la Statistique*, 21, 3rd Session, (1937), 323-27. Also in Kristian Palda, *The Measurement of Cumulative Advertising Effects*, Englewood Cliffs, N.J.: Prentice-Hall, 1964.
3. ———, "Our Unstable Dollar and the So-Called Business Cycle," *Journal of the American Statistical Association*, 20 (June 1925), 179-202.
4. Gavin-Jobson Associates, Inc., *Liquor Handbook*, New York: Gavin-Jobson, annual.
5. Zvi Giliches, "A Note on Serial Correlation Bias in Estimates of Distributed Lags," *Econometrica*, 29 (January 1961), 65-73.
6. Leonard Hurwicz, "Least-Squares Bias in Time Series," In Tjalling C. Koopmans, ed., *Statistical Inference in Dynamic Economic Models*, New York: John Wiley & Sons, Inc., 1950.
7. Roy W. Jastram, "A Treatment of Distributed Lags in the Theory of Advertising Expenditure," *Journal of Marketing*, 20 (July 1955-56), 36-46.
8. L. M. Koyck, *Distributed Lags and Investment Analysis*, Amsterdam, The Netherlands: North-Holland, 1954.
9. Paul Lebland, "The Effect of Merchandise, Price and Weather on Department Store Advertising." Unpublished Ph.D. thesis, New York University, 1963.
10. Horace C. Levinson, "Experience in Commerical Operation Research," *Operations Research*, 1 (February 1953), 220-39.
11. Guy H. Orcutt and Donald Cochrane, "A Sampling Study of the Merits of Auto-regressive and Reduced Form Transformations in Regression Analysis," *Journal of the American Statistical Association*, 44 (September 1949), 356-72.
12. Kristian Palda, *The Measurement of Cumulative Advertising Effects*, Englewood Cliffs, N.J., Prentice-Hall, 1964.
13. Julian L. Simon, *How to Start and Operate a Mail-Order Business*, New York: McGraw-Hill, 1965.
14. ———, "Are There Economies of Scale in Advertising?" *Journal of Advertising Research*, 5 (June 1965), 15-9.
15. ———, "A Simple Model for Setting Advertising Appropriations," *Journal of Marketing Research*, 2 (August 1965), 285-92.
17. ———, "Advertising Expenditure Decisions," Unpublished paper, University of Illinois, 1966.
18. Lester G. Telser, "The Demand for Branded Goods as Estimated from Consumer Panel Data," *The Review of Economy and Statistics*, 44 (August 1962), 300-24.
19. ———, "Advertising and Cigarettes," *Journal of Political Economy*, 70 (October 1962), 471-99.
20. Harold Wattell, "The Whiskey Industry: An Economic Analysis," Unpublished Ph.D. thesis, New School of Social Research, 1954.
21. Herman O. A. Wold, "On the Definition and Meaning of Causal Concepts," Paper given at the Entretiens de Monaco, May 21-27, 1964.

OPTIMAL ALLOCATION OF COMPETITIVE MARKETING EFFORTS: AN EMPIRICAL STUDY

JEAN-JACQUES LAMBIN[*]

INTRODUCTION

There is probably no more difficult and complex problem in marketing than the allocation of the total selling efforts of a firm among the various marketing instruments that influence sales, such as advertising, price, product quality, and personal selling. From a theoretical viewpoint, this problem has been neatly solved and the formal conditions defining an equilibrium have been stated in a number of ways.[1] Dorfman and Steiner, for example, have derived a general rule which is claimed to be a useful guide for marketing programming; this theorem, however, so far has received little empirical verification.[2] Furthermore, implicit in the Dorfman-Steiner formula is the assumption that there is no reaction of competitors to the change in marketing inputs made by the firm, while in real market situations mutual interdependence is the rule, since the sales of any firm are also a function of marketing inputs of its rivals.[3] The neglect of competitive interdependence is of course a serious shortcoming.

The purpose of this article is to show how the Dorfman-Steiner theorem can be expressed in terms of market shares, relative price, advertising, and quality, and how it can then be converted into operational concepts by means of regression analysis, so that attention can be turned to the study of competitors' reactions to change in marketing pressure and especially in advertising. These objectives will be pursued by studying the case of a household durable product sold on three markets of Western Europe characterized by an oligopolistic structure.

This paper is divided into three parts. In the first one, a theoretical extension of the Dorfman-Steiner theorem that explicitly considers competitive effects is presented. In the second part, a description of the case studied, of the model, of the data utilized, and of the regression results is given. Using the optimization

[*] Associate professor of marketing research, Louvain University, Belgium. Part of this paper has been presented at the 1968 fall conference of the American Marketing Association. I am grateful to Miss Leboutte for programming assistance, and to K. S. Palda for his advice and comments on an earlier draft. Responsibility for errors remains mine.

[1] E. H. Chamberlin, *The Theory of Monopolistic Competition* (Cambridge, Mass.: Harvard University Press, 1933); R. Dorfman and P. O. Steiner, "Optimal Advertising and Optimal Quality," *American Economic Review* 64, no. 5 (1954):826–36; H. Brems, *Product Equilibrium under Monopolistic Competition* (Cambridge, Mass.: Harvard University Press, 1959); P. J. Verdoorn, "Marketing from the Producers' Point of View," *Journal of Marketing*, 23 (January 1956):221–35.

[2] As far as we know, a link between advertising marginal revenue product, price elasticity, marginal revenue, and marginal cost has been estimated, appraised, and analyzed in only two published contributions—Kristian S. Palda, *The Measurement of Cumulative Advertising Effects* (Englewood Cliffs, N.J.: Prentice-Hall, Inc., 1964), and Jean-Jacques Lambin, "Measuring the Profitability of Advertising: An Empirical Study," *Journal of Industrial Economics* 17, no. 2, (1969):86–103.

[3] Lawrence Friedman, "Game Theory in the Allocation of Advertising Expenditures," *Operations Research* 6, no. 6 (October 1958):699–709; H. D. Mills, "A Study in Promotional Competition," in *Mathematical Models and Methods in Marketing*, ed. F. M. Bass, R. D. Buzzell, et al. (Homewood, Ill.: Richard D. Irwin, Inc., 1961), pp. 245–89.

rule derived in the first section, I then try to determine whether the present allocation of the firm's marketing efforts is optimal. In the last part, an attempt is made to assess the interrelated impacts of the brand's advertising on the promotional activity of the competing firms; finally, the overall profitability of the advertising investment is evaluated.

I. THE SEARCH FOR THE OPTIMUM MARKETING MIX

The marketing manager who has to determine his marketing program faces a task similar to that of a production manager—allocation of scarce resources in a way that will maximize profit. Broadly speaking, the marketing inputs the firm can manipulate fall into three categories: sales price, promotional efforts (usually called "selling costs" or advertising), and quality variation. In the class of theoretical contributions to this problem, the Dorfman-Steiner rule appears to be a very useful tool for assisting management in marketing-mix decisions. In this section, I first briefly comment on the Dorfman-Steiner theorem and then derive a new version of it that comprehends competitive effects in the response estimates.

THE DORFMAN-STEINER THEOREM

Dorfman and Steiner proceeded in the following way.[4] Assuming that all the quantity produced is sold, they defined the company demand function in terms of three decision variables:

$$q = q(p,s,x) , \qquad (1)$$

where q = unit sales per time period, p = price of the product, s = advertising outlays per time period, and x = index of product quality. Assuming also that unit average costs c are a function of output and of quality, that is,

$$c = c(q,x) , \qquad (2)$$

the profit function is given by

$$\pi = pq - qc - s , \qquad (3)$$

or

$$\pi = pq(p,s,x) - [q(p,s,x)] \\ \times \{c[q(p,s,x),x] - s\} . \qquad (4)$$

The analysis can then be conducted as a problem in the maximization of a function with three independent variables. Necessary conditions for profit maximization are

$$\frac{\delta\pi}{\delta p} = \frac{\delta\pi}{\delta s} = \frac{\delta\pi}{\delta x} = 0 . \qquad (5)$$

Thus, taking the partial derivatives of equation (4), the authors define the equilibrium condition as

$$\frac{-q}{\delta q/\delta p} = \frac{1}{\delta q/\delta s} = q\frac{\delta c/\delta x}{\delta q/\delta x} , \qquad (6)$$

which reduces to

$$\eta_p = \mu = \eta_x \frac{p}{c} , \qquad (7)$$

where

$$\eta_p = -\frac{\delta q}{\delta p}\cdot\frac{p}{q} = \text{price elasticity} ,$$

$$\mu = \frac{p\delta q}{\delta s} = \text{marginal revenue product of advertising} ,$$

and

$$\eta_x = \frac{\delta q/\delta x}{\delta c/\delta x}\cdot\frac{c}{q} = \text{product quality elasticity} .$$

In words, equation (7) states that if the firm can manipulate price, advertising, and quality, it will find itself at equilibrium when the numerical values of price elasticity, marginal revenue product of advertising, and quality elasticity times price over average cost are equal.

In developing the proof of the theorem, I have not followed the Dorfman and Steiner article. Instead, I used the mathematical appendix which was added to the original article by editors of *Mathematical Models and Methods in Marketing* (Frank M. Bass, Robert D. Buzzell, et al., *Mathematical Models and Methods in Marketing* [Homewood, Ill.: Richard D. Irwin, Inc., 1961], pp. 214–29).

This is known as the Dorfman and Steiner theorem, and is simply an application of the marginal revenue-marginal cost equality rule.

THE MARKET-SHARE OPTIMIZATION RULE

One difficulty lies in the appropriate measurement of a given brand demand function. As pointed out by Telser,[5] the obvious measure in traditional economic analysis is sales of the firm. However, if sales are the dependent variable in a regression, there are a large number of predictors to be taken into consideration as independent variables. First the socioeconomic variables, such as the number of potential users, private disposable income, and product ownership; second, the company's own decision variables, such as price, advertising, product quality, and distribution rate; and third, the competitors' decision variables, such as their sales price, advertising, product quality, and distribution. Obviously, it is unlikely that reliable estimates of the separate effect of these factors are obtainable in a regression analysis, because of the collinearity problems usually met in econometric work.[6] This suggests that it is better to express the dependent variable in market-share terms, and the firm's decision variables relative to the decision variables of the other firms. This approach simplifies the basic model in reducing the number of variables to be taken into consideration and, in particular, in eliminating the socioeconomic factors which frequently exert the same influence on all brands. It also gives the

clearest picture of competition among brands.

Consequently, our task is to derive a new optimization rule, equivalent to the Dorfman-Steiner rule, that includes competitive effects. First, let the following definitions stand: $m = q/Q$ = brand i market share (ratio of brand i's physical sales to total industry sales); $p^* = p/P$ = relative price (ratio of brand i sales price to average market price); $s^* = s/S_i$ = relative advertising (ratio of brand i advertising outlays to competitive advertising outlays, excluding i); and $x^* = x/X$ = relative quality (ratio of brand i product quality index to average product quality index).

Let us rewrite equation (4), the profit function:

$$\pi = pq(p,s,x) - [q(p,s,x)] \times \{c[q(p,s,x)x] - s\} . \tag{8}$$

From the definitions given above, it follows that

$$\begin{aligned} q &= mQ , \\ p &= p^*P , \\ s &= s^*S_i , \\ x &= x^*X . \end{aligned} \tag{9}$$

Introducing these values into equation (8), one has

$$\pi = p^*PQm(p^*,s^*,s^*) - [Qm(p^*,s^*,x^*)] \times \{c[Qm(p^*,s^*,x^*),x^*] - s^*S_i\} . \tag{10}$$

Substituting into the equilibrium condition obtained in equation (6) the equivalent terms derived from equation (10), we have

$$\frac{-Qm}{(Q/P)(\delta m/\delta p^*)} = \frac{1}{(Q/S_i)(\delta m/\delta s^*)} \tag{11}$$
$$= Qm \frac{(\delta c/\delta x^*)(1/X)}{(Q/X)(\delta m/\delta x^*)} ,$$

[5] Lester G. Telser, "The Demand for Branded Goods as Estimated from Consumer Panel Data," *Review of Economics and Statistics* (August 1962), p. 300.

[6] E. Malinvaud, *Statistical Methods of Econometrics* (Chicago: Rand McNally & Co., 1966), pp. 181–219.

or, after simplification

$$-P\frac{m}{\delta m/\delta p^*} = (S_i/Q)(1/\delta m/\delta s^*)$$

$$= m\frac{\delta c/\delta x^*}{\delta m/\delta x^*}.\qquad(12)$$

Now, defining the following:

$$\eta_{p*} = -(\delta m/\delta p^*)(p^*/m) = \text{brand i's market-share elasticity with respect to i's relative price,}$$

$$\eta_{s*} = (\delta m/\delta s^*)(s^*/m) = \text{brand i's market-share elasticity with respect to i's relative advertising,}\qquad(13)$$

$$\eta_{x*} = (\delta m/\delta x^*)(x^*/m) = \text{brand i's market-share elasticity with respect to i's relative quality.}$$

We have, after transformation

$$\frac{\delta m}{\delta p^*} = -\eta_{p*}\frac{m}{p^*}; \quad \frac{\delta m}{\delta s^*} = \eta_{s*}\frac{m}{s^*};$$

$$\frac{\delta m}{\delta x^*} = \eta_{x*}\frac{m}{x^*}.\qquad(14)$$

Replacing these values in equation (12), after simplification, the new optimization rule becomes

$$\frac{p}{\eta_{p*}} = \frac{a}{\eta_{s*}} = \frac{\beta}{\eta_{x*}},\qquad(15)$$

where $a = s/q =$ advertising expenditures per unit sold, and $\beta = x^*\delta c/\delta x^* =$ weighted unit cost of a change in the relative quality index.

With Dorfman and Steiner, one may assume that the second-order conditions

are satisfied for a relative maximum.[7] A more detailed derivation of equation (15) is presented in the appendix.

In words, rule (15) states that, at optimum, the following equality must obtain (equation [18]).

We shall first concentrate our attention on price and advertising, assuming quality to be constant. The rule is

$$\frac{p}{\eta_{p*}} = \frac{a}{\eta_{s*}}.\qquad(16)$$

Equation (16) can be transformed as

$$\frac{\eta_{s*}}{\eta_{p*}} = \frac{a}{p}.\qquad(17)$$

This expression means that, at equilibrium, unit advertising outlay expressed as a percentage of unit sales price must be equal to the ratio of relative advertising and relative price market-shares elasticities. It is easy to see that such an optimum exists. Indeed, the ratio a/p is necessarily a number confined between 0 and 1. Furthermore, it has been shown that, at the optimum, absolute advertising-sales elasticity must be smaller

[7] Bass, Buzzell, et al., pp. 214–29.

$$\frac{\text{brand i's sales price}}{\substack{\text{i's market-share elasticity with respect}\\\text{to i's relative price}}} =$$

$$\frac{\substack{\text{advertising dollars per physical unit}\\\text{sold}}}{\substack{\text{i's market-share elasticity with respect}\\\text{to i's relative advertising}}} = \qquad(18)$$

$$\frac{\substack{\text{marginal cost of quality change times}\\\text{i's relative quality index}}}{\substack{\text{i's market-share elasticity with respect}\\\text{to i's relative quality}}}.$$

than one,[8] whereas a maximum profit price cannot occur unless $\eta_p > 1$. Therefore, the ratio η_{s*}/η_{p*} is also included between 0 and 1.

Next we consider the price and product quality relation expressed in equation (15):

$$\frac{p}{\eta_{p*}} = \frac{\beta}{\eta_{x*}}, \qquad (19)$$

where the numerator β is the weighted unit cost of a change in relative quality. This equation can be rewritten as

$$\frac{\eta_{x*}}{\eta_{p*}} = \frac{\beta}{p}. \qquad (20)$$

This expression means that, at equilibrium, the weighted unit cost of a quality change, expressed as a percentage of unit sales price, must be equal to the ratio of relative quality and relative price market-share elasticities. Here also, the rule is subject to the condition that the ratio of the two elasticities must be a number smaller than 1.

To summarize, it follows from equations (17) and (20) that the share of unit expenditures on a particular marketing instrument out of unit sales price is determined by the ratio of its own market-share elasticity to the relative price market-share elasticity. Basically, equation (15) is simply another formulation of the well known marginal principle, with one important difference however. The proposed rule incorporates estimates of competitive effect, and this theoretical extension encompasses the most common market situations. Our next objective is to see, on the basis of empirical evidence, how well this market-share optimization rule describes the actual behavior of competing firms.

[8] A. Rasmussen, "The Determination of Advertising Expenditures," *Journal of Marketing* 16 (August 1952): 537.

II. THE EMPIRICAL STUDY

The case studied is that of a consumer durable good sold in three European countries, or marketing areas, Germany, Benelux, and Scandinavia. These markets are dominated by three competing brands representing together about 90 percent of total industry sales. The product is a small electrical appliance, whose rate of ownership among households is as high as 75 percent. In this study, the analysis is confined to the marketing position of one of the competing brands.[9] In a mature market of this type, replacement demand constitutes the major part of new sales, and the firm's marketing and advertising efforts usually have little effect on increasing total industry sales, but rather tend to determine the distribution of the market between each brand and its competitors. Competition is therefore an essential determinant of the effectiveness of each firm marketing action.

THE MODEL

On the basis of these considerations, we can construct a simple market-share model.[10] Using the same notation as in

[9] The author is grateful to the firm for granting permission to publish this case study. At the request of the company, some figures have been modified, but without changing the conclusions reached.

[10] A number of competitive formulations have been developed in the literature: P. Kotler, "Competitive Strategies for New-Product Marketing over the Life-Cycle," *Management Science* 12 (December 1965):104–19; H. D. Mills, pp. 271–301; K. S. Krishnan and S. K. Gupta, "Mathematical Model for a Duopolistic Market," *Management Science* 13, no. 7 (March 1967):568–83.

The brand market-share models adopted here are estimated independent of one another. As a consequence, they cannot be utilized as forecasting instruments since they will not, in general, predict market shares that will sum to unity across all brands in the market. To have this condition fulfilled, the variables and coefficients should be sum constrained to unity. Thus, for each brand in turn, competitors' market shares are given by $(1 - m_i)$.

the first section, and the subscript i to designate the brand,

$$m_{i,t} = b_0 + b_1 m_{i,t-1} + b_2 p_{i,t}^*$$
$$+ b_3 s_{i,t}^* + b_4 d_{i,t}^* + b_5 x_{i,t}^* + u_t, \quad (21)$$

where $d_{i,t}^*$ stands for relative distribution, that is, the ratio of the rate of distribution of brand i to the average distribution rate of the product.[11]

This market-share model is dynamized, Koyck fashion,[12] by the introduction of a lagged dependent variable $m_{i,t-1}$ in the right-hand side of equation (21). This model has been used by Telser,[13] Palda,[14] Frank and Massy,[15] and Lambin.[16] The underlying assumption of Koyck's model is that the effect of each variable dies away to zero at a constant rate λ, following a decreasing geometric progression.[17] It can be shown[18] that the regression coefficient of $m_{i,t-1}$ is an esti-

mate of λ, here called the retention rate of the total marketing effort. Using this estimate, it is possible to calculate long-term elasticities for each marketing input.

All the variables of equation (21) are expressed in logarithms (base 10), and thus the regression coefficients b_2 through b_5 can be interpreted as constant elasticity coefficients. They measure the sensitivity of brand i's market share to a 1 percent change in each relative decision variable, other things remaining constant. Under the Koyck model assumption, we expect the coefficient of the lagged dependent variable (b_1) to lie between 0 and 1. Also we expect the sign of the relative price variable to be negative, and the signs of the relative advertising, distribution, and product quality variables to be positive.

THE DATA

The reported study covers the three marketing areas over a seven- to eight-year period of observation from 1959 to 1966. Each country is subdivided into three or four sales territories which can be considered to be homogeneous with regard to socioeconomic and marketing factors.[19] Therefore, by pooling time series and cross-sectional data within each country,[20] I obtained twenty-eight, twenty-one, and twenty-four yearly observations for areas 1, 2, and 3. Since each marketing area was under distinct management, somewhat different pricing and advertising policies have been followed during the period under study; in two markets, the product enjoys a much

---

[11] By distribution rate, I mean the retail availability of the product within each area. This variable is also expressed in percentages.

[12] J. M. Koyck, *Distributed Lags and Investment Analysis* (Amsterdam: North-Holland Publishing Co., 1954).

[13] Lester G. Telser, "Advertising and Cigarettes," *Journal of Political Economy* 70 (October 1962): 471–99.

[14] Palda.

[15] Roland E. Frank and William F. Massy, "Short Term Price and Dealing Effects in Selected Market Segments," *Journal of Marketing Research* 2 (May 1965):171–85.

[16] Lambin, pp. 86–103.

[17] For other similar approaches, see also Joel Dean, "Marketing and Productivity of Investment in Persuasion," *Journal of Industrial Economics* 15, no. 2 (April 1967):81–108; and M. L. Vidale and G. B. Wolfe, "An Operations-Research Study of Sales Response to Advertising," *Operations Research* 5, no. 3 (June 1957):370–81.

[18] Koyck's model (21), however, is expressed in logarithmic form and b_1, the regression coefficient of the lagged dependent variable, cannot be interpreted as λ exactly in the same sense that the parameter is used in the conventional Koyck model described above. See below, nn. 23, 36.

[19] The introduction of dummy variables (0,1) for each territory did not reveal significant regional differences.

[20] P. Balestra and M. Nerlove, "Pooling Cross Sections and Time Series Data in the Estimation of a Dynamic Model, the Demand for Natural Gas," *Econometrica* (July 1966), pp. 585–612.

higher distribution rate. This gives us a larger variability in the marketing input data on which to base the estimates of the demand function.

The sources of data vary among areas. In area 1, sales data, distribution rates, and sales prices came from a dealer panel, and can be considered to be very reliable. The dollar amount spent on newspaper, magazine, radio, and television advertising is available for the three leading brands over the whole period and by region. These data represent about 85 percent of the total advertising outlay in area 1. Point-of-purchase advertising data were not available. In the other two areas, the data came from the records of the firms, agencies, and professional or government sources. The product-quality variable is an index number included between 0 and 1. The values taken by this index are based on consumer survey results, and on subjective ratings given to each product model by the marketing staffs of firms and agencies. The general accuracy of the data collected is clearly higher in area 1 than in the other two areas. Since each variable is expressed in relative terms, one is forced to assume that the errors are self-canceling, but it is very difficult to verify to what extent this is an acceptable assumption. Consequently, we shall place more confidence in the results observed in the first marketing area.

THE REGRESSION RESULTS

Equation (21) was fitted with the help of a stepwise program for an IBM 360/40 computer.[21] Usually, the stepwise program eliminates variables which do not attain some degree of significance which is specified in advance. In this study, however, it was decided not to specify

any such level, but rather to evaluate the results on the basis of the various statistical criteria provided by the regression program.

The initial basic model takes into account all marketing instruments considered a priori as possibly exerting a specific influence on brand i's market share in each area. At the exploratory stage, a first regression was run to test this hypothesis. The results obtained showed that all the coefficients had the expected signs, except the distribution variable of areas 1 and 2 and the product-quality variable of area 2. Furthermore, these coefficients were less than one third their standard errors. These results are not very surprising, since relative distribution rates changed less during the sample period in areas 1 and 2 than in the other market. Thus, distribution did not show how much it affects brand i's market share in these two markets. The same remark holds for product quality in area 2. Consequently, we eliminated these three variables from the basic model, since such a move seemed likely to improve the quality of the fit.

The results obtained at the second stage are presented in table 1. Below each coefficient the standard deviation of the coefficient and the corresponding t-ratio appear. In the last row of the table are shown the principal criteria with which to evaluate the overall quality of the results. In each area, the fit of the regression, as measured by the unadjusted multiple determination coefficients, is 0.794, 0.341, and 0.753, respectively. All twelve regression coefficients have the expected signs; seven are significant at the 5 percent level or higher, and three at the 10 percent level;[22] the two remaining coefficients are

[21] The author gratefully acknowledges the services of the Louvain University Computer Center.

[22] One tailed t-test.

less than one half their standard errors. The coefficients of the three lagged market shares—called "goodwill"—are less than 1 and the range is 0.346 (area 3) to 0.678 (area 1). These last three coefficients are all significant at the 5 percent level or higher, and their contribution to the high correlation coefficient is very strong (as evidenced by the β coefficients not reported here). As suggested by

formance of area 2's regression. First, the results rest on fewer observations ($N = 21$) and the data were considered to be less reliable from the outset. Second, a graphic inspection of the sample data from area 2 revealed less variation in the various independent variables, and in particular in the advertising factor. These two elements combined prevent us from drawing any meaningful conclu-

TABLE 1

THE REGRESSION RESULTS

Variables	Area 1	Area 2	Area 3
Constant (b_0).....................	0.582	0.666	1.120
Goodwill ($m_{i,t-1}$)................	0.678	0.366	0.346
	(0.151)	(0.220)	(0.137)
	4.5***	1.7**	2.5***
Relative advertising ($s_{i,t}^*$).........	0.283	0.140	0.425
	(0.076)	(0.179)	(0.127)
	3.7***	0.2	3.3***
Relative price ($p_{i,t}^*$).............	−3.070	−0.829	−0.255
	(2.597)	(0.697)	(0.796)
	1.2*	1.2*	0.3
Relative distribution ($d_{i,t}^*$)........	....	....	0.439
	....	....	(0.252)
	....	....	1.7**
Relative quality ($x_{i,t}^*$)............	0.267	....	0.743
	(0.149)	....	(0.337)
	1.8*	....	2.2**
R^2............................	0.794ᵃ	0.341	0.753
F-test.........................	(4,23) 22	(3,17) 28	(5,18) 15
N............................	28	21	24

ᵃ Unadjusted for degrees of freedom.
* Significant at the 10 percent level (one-tailed t-test
** Significant at the 5 percent level (one-tailed t-test).
*** Significant at the 1 percent level (one-tailed t-test).

Palda,[23] this can be interpreted to mean that the cumulative action of past marketing efforts is an important explanatory factor in shaping current market shares. On the whole, the best results were obtained in areas 1 and 3. There are two possible explanations of the low per-

sion about the influence of the decision variables on brand i's market share in area 2. More unexpected are the low relative price elasticities observed in areas 2 and 3, which are less than one, although they have the expected sign.

The results have been tested for multicollinearity. Difficulties associated with a multicollinear set of data depend on the severity of the problem. As interdependence among explanatory variables grows, the correlation matrix approaches singularity. In the limit, perfect linear

[23] Palda, p. 14. See, however, n. 18 above. The estimates of the conventional λ obtained in a semilog model in the other independent variables are respectively:

0.712   0.398   0.455
(5.2)   (1.7)   (3.9)

dependence leads to perfect singularity on the part of the correlation matrix, and to a complete indeterminate set of parameter estimates. Farrar and Glauber[24] have proposed a systematic procedure for detecting the existence, measuring the extent, and pinpointing the locations and causes of multicollinearity within a set of independent variables. In order, the tests are (a) an approximate χ^2 transformation of the determinant of the correlation coefficients matrix to assess the presence and the severity of multicollinearity between the independent variables; (b) F-tests to indicate the dependence of a particular variable on other independent variables; and (c) t-tests and partial correlation coefficients to indicate the pattern of interdependence within the set of explanatory variables.

Applying these three tests to our data, we found χ^2 values inferior to their critical values at the 95 percent level in each area (see table 2), indicating that col-

TABLE 2

TESTS OF MULTICOLLINEARITY

Variables	Goodwill	Relative Advertising	Relative Price	Relative Distribution	Relative Quality
F-test:					
area 1....................	6.1	5.7	1.8	N.I.	2.2
area 2....................	0.9	1.0	1.6	N.I.	N.I
area 3....................	4.8	5.9	N.I.	0.8	3.4
t-tests and partial correlation coefficients:*					
Goodwill..............	....	3.04	0.76	N.I.†	−2.33
	....	−1.30	−1.35	N.I.	N.I.
	....	0.648	N.I.	1.65	−1.28
Relative advertising........	0.528	:..........	−2.27	N.I.	0.43
	0.300	:..........	−0.68	N.I.	N.I.
	0.140	....	N.I.	2.81	−0.33
Relative price.............	0.153	−0.421	....	N.I.	0.16
	−0.311	−0.162	....	N.I.	N.I.
	N.I.	N.I.	....	N.I.	N.I.
Relative distribution.......	N.I.	N.I.	N.I.	....	N.I.
	N.I.	N.I.	N.I.	....	N.I.
	0.339	0.523	N.I.	....	0.262
Relative quality...........	−0.430	0.088	0.032	N.I.	....
	N.I.	N.I.	N.I.	N.I.	....
	−0.269	0.071	N.I.	0.057	....
χ^2‡......................	Area 1—(6) 19.4		Area 2—(3) 3.1		Area 3—(10) 19.6

* Above diagonal—partial t-tests; below diagonal—partial correlation coefficients.
† N.I. = not included in the regression.
‡ At the 0.99 confidence level, the critical values of χ^2 for 3, 6, and 10 degrees of freedom are 11.3, 16.8, and 23.2, respectively.

²⁴ D. Farrar and Robert R. Glauber, "Multicollinearity in Regression Analysis—the Problem Revisited," *Review of Economics and Statistics* (February 1967), p. 92. I am indebted to Prof. L. Philips, Louvain University, who suggested the application of this test.

linearity is very weak. The F-tests show the variables to be relatively stable; only the lagged market-share variable in area 1 is moderately affected by collinearity. Partial correlation coefficients and associated t-ratios show no significant dependence among explanatory variables. We may conclude therefore, that multicollinearity is not a serious problem in this study.

A test for serial correlation by means of

the Durbin-Watson statistics is useless here for two reasons: (1) the random term is of time-space character, and (2) one of the independent variables is the lagged value of the dependent variable.[25] The residuals observed within each area are reproduced graphically in figure 1, so that a judgment may be made of their independence.[26]

in the first section. In this evaluation, it is assumed that on the whole the behavior of the firm is approximately optimum, our concern being mainly to verify to what extent the estimated relationships of table 1 give support to this assumption and to the normative implications of the rules. The implications of the regression results regarding the com-

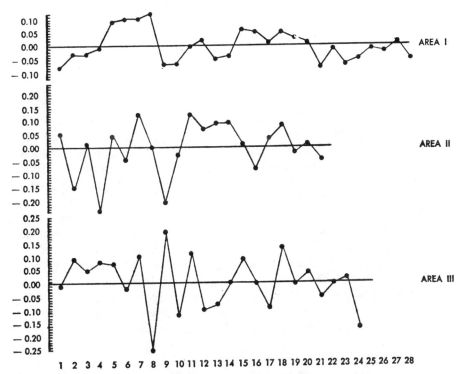

Fig. 1.—Analysis of residuals

III. ECONOMIC INTERPRETATION OF THE RESULTS

Having ascertained the statistical validity of the regression results, the estimates of table 1 may be used to test the market-share optimization rules derived

[25] Malinvaud, pp. 427–31.

[26] Several other familiar econometric formulations were fitted to the data (linear with and without lagged dependent variable, semilog in the advertising variables, data in first difference). The best results were those obtained with this Koyck log model.

petitive effects of advertising and the profitability in the long run of the firm advertising investment are then analyzed.

MARKETING MIX

The estimated short-term elasticities for each area are given in table 1 with their respective t-ratios. Clearly, the estimates from area 1 are the most reliable; consequently, the following discussion will be confined to the results observed in this area.

The market-share optimization rule derived in Section I is

$$\frac{p_i}{\eta_{p^*}} = \frac{a_i}{\eta_{s^*}} = \frac{\beta_i}{\eta_{x^*}}. \qquad (22)$$

This rule cannot be directly applied to our data, since β_i, the weighted marginal cost of a unit change in quality is unknown. However, we may calculate equations (17) and (20), which give us the implied values of a_i and β_i. We first turn our attention to the relative price and advertising relationship. The rule is

$$\frac{\eta_{s^*}}{\eta_{p^*}} = \frac{a_i}{p_i}. \qquad (23)$$

Using the short-term estimated elasticities we have $0.283/3.070 = 0.092$. This means that, at optimum, unit advertising outlays expressed as a percentage of sales price should be equal to 9.2 percent. To verify the plausibility of this ratio, the actual percentages observed in area 1 were calculated for the last ten years, using retail prices, mass media advertising expenditures, and physical sales. The ratios obtained lie in the range 6.9–13.4 percent, with a mean value of 12.5 percent for the last four years. Thus, according to our findings, the firm seems to have overspent on advertising. We must remind ourselves, however, that equation (23) is of static character, and that so far no allowance has been made for the lagged effects of advertising.[27] The evaluation of equilibrium in the long run will be discussed at the end of this section.

Let us now consider the competitive price-quality relationship. The rule is

$$\frac{\eta_{x^*}}{\eta_{p^*}} = \frac{\beta_i}{p_i}. \qquad (24)$$

According to our results, the ratio of the cost of unit change in quality to the unit price should be $0.267 / 3.070 = 0.0869$. This again means that the unit quality expenditures expressed as a per-

centage of price should be equal to 8.7 percent. Since $\delta c/\delta x^*$ is unknown, we cannot directly verify the plausibility of this ratio, but we can calculate the value of $\delta c/\delta x^*$ implied by the estimated elasticities. If we take the mean values of x^* and of p, and solve for $\delta c/\delta x^*$, we obtain

$$\frac{\delta c}{\delta x^*} = \frac{(0.0869) \cdot (\bar{p})}{\bar{x}^*} = \$1.97 . \qquad (25)$$

Since the price of the product is included between \$20 and \$25, this result seems reasonable.

On the whole, one may conclude that these results make sense. They suggest that the proposed optimization rules may give management some instructive and simple prescription to follow in its quest for the optimal marketing mix. To apply the rules, the only required estimates are the market-share elasticities for each competitive marketing variable. The estimation of these elasticities can be accomplished basically in two different ways—field or laboratory experimentation and analysis of historical data. In the second approach, the data obtained on a monthly or bimonthly basis from dealer or consumer panels are particularly useful and sufficiently accurate for the estimation of elasticities.

These rules cannot be applied in practice without qualification, however, and their limitations must be discussed. It is clear that the usefulness of elasticity as computed here is limited by the assumption that it remains constant over the range considered, while, in fact, it varies with the level of sales.[28] As a con-

---

[27] The introduction of long-run elasticities in equation (23) would yield the same result, since short- and long-run elasticities differ only by a constant of proportionality.

[28] For a discussion of this point, see G. David Hughes and Willard R. Bishop, Jr., "Some Quantitative Aids to Merchandise Management," *Journal of Retailing* 43, no. 3 (Fall 1967):10–21.

sequence, since these elasticities are variable magnitudes, these equations provide no general support for the prevailing industrial practice of fixing the advertising appropriation at a constant percentage of sales.[29] Because of this restriction, frequent updating of the model is a prerequisite to the application of the rules. Thus, as it is presented here, the model mainly describes the firm behavior. Nevertheless, these equations can quickly indicate to management whether the marketing mix accords with the marginal efficiency of each marketing instru-

firm is attempting to attain its optimal market share, its rivals are also pursuing the same objective.[30] The regression results of table 1 can also be used to evaluate and compare the intensity of competition by means of advertising in the three marketing areas.

Telser[31] has derived a very instructive relation which can be used here to determine the competitive advertising elasticity.[32] The relation is

$$\gamma = (1 - m)(\eta_s - \psi) = \eta_{s*}\theta , \quad (26)$$

where

$\gamma = (\delta m/\delta s)(s/m) =$ brand i's market-share elasticity with respect to i's absolute advertising outlay, $\quad (27)$

$\eta_s = (\delta q/\delta s)(s/q) =$ brand i's absolute sales elasticity with respect to i's absolute advertising outlay, $\quad (28)$

$\psi = (\delta Q_i/\delta s)(s/Q_i) =$ competitors' absolute sales elasticity with respect to i's absolute advertising outlay, where Q_i stands for competitive sales, $\quad (29)$

$\eta_{s*} = (\delta m/\delta s^*)(s^*/m) =$ brand i's market share elasticity with respect to i's relative advertising outlay, and $\quad (30)$

$\theta = 1 - (\delta S_i/\delta s)(s/S_i) =$ 1 minus competitors' absolute advertising outlays elasticity with respect to i's absolute advertising outlays. $\quad (31)$

ment; what is more important, the rules can also inform management of the direction, if not the exact magnitude, of changes in marketing inputs that will increase profit.

COMPETITIVE ADVERTISING ELASTICITY

In a highly interdependent market situation, an optimal strategy is that which yields a market share maximizing the company's net profit. It is clear that such a strategy cannot be developed by ignoring competitive reactions. While the

It is postulated in equation (26) that competitors may react to each other's advertising by changing their own advertising expenditure. Thus,

$$S_i = f(s) . \quad (32)$$

Now, if the firm operates in a stable market, as it does in the case of our product, one can assume that a change in a given brand advertising has no effect on total industry sales, and therefore all the increased sales of a given firm come necessarily at the expense of the other competing firms. In this case, it can be

[29] This restriction does not apply within the range of the observations used to compute these elasticities, however, since the constant elasticity model has given better results than the other models (see n. 6).

[30] Friedman, pp. 699–709; Mills, pp. 245–389.

[31] Telser, "Advertising and Cigarettes," p. 486.

[32] I do not follow here the notation adopted by Telser (see n. 31).

shown[33] that equation (26) simplifies to

$$\eta_s = \eta_{s*}\theta .\qquad(33)$$

Substituting the implied value of θ from equation (33) into equation (26), and solving for ψ, we have

$$\psi = -\eta_{s*}\theta[\,m/(1-m)\,] .\qquad(34)$$

Thus, to calculate ψ, the competitive advertising elasticity, the only additional information we need is an estimate of θ, since η_{s*} has already been estimated in the regression analysis whose results are in table 1.

In equations (26) and (33), it is clear that if θ is negative, brand i's market-share elasticity with respect to i's abso-

TABLE 3

COMPETITIVE ADVERTISING ELASTICITY

Areas	θ (1)	η_{s*} (2)	η_s (3)	ψ (4)
1	0.407	0.283	0.115	−0.046
2	0.424	0.041	0.017	−0.002
3	0.460	0.425	0.195	−0.037

lute advertising γ_s is also negative, even if η_{s*} is positive. A negative value for θ means that a change in brand i's absolute advertising (i.e., 1.0 percent) is met by a proportionally larger change in the absolute advertising of its competitors (i.e., 1.2 percent). As a consequence, γ also becomes negative, and brand i's advertising outlay cannot be justified on rational grounds. So the value of $(1-\theta)$ is a measure of the intensity of advertising competitive interdependence. In this case, since brand i's advertising investments are very high, we expect a positive value for θ.

To estimate θ, in each area a simple regression was run between $S_{i,t}$, com-

petitors' absolute deflated advertising outlays in period t, and s_{t-1}, brand i's absolute deflated advertising expenditures in the preceding period. Thus, it was assumed that the adjustment of competitors' advertising to a change in i's advertising is not instantaneous, but rather takes place with a lag of one period. The results obtained in each area are as follows:

$$\text{Log } S_{i,t} = 1.52 + 0.593 \text{ Log } s_{t-1}$$
$$(2.1)$$
$$N = 27 ; \quad R^2 = 0.392 ; \quad F = 4.5 ,\qquad(35)$$

$$\text{Log } S_{i,t} = 1.61 + 0.576 \text{ Log } s_{t-1}$$
$$(2.0)$$
$$N = 20 ; \quad R^2 = 0.435 ; \quad F = 4.2 ,\qquad(36)$$

$$\text{Log } S_{i,t} = 1.91 + 0.540 \text{ Log } s_{t-1}$$
$$(4.5)$$
$$N = 23 ; \quad R^2 = 0.687 ; \quad F = 20.6 .\qquad(37)$$

The estimated values of equations (33) and (34) can then be calculated for each area. The results are in table 3.

Several interesting conclusions about the competitive effects of advertising emerge from our analysis. First, absolute advertising sales elasticities are comparatively small, implying that large advertising expenditures are required to increase sales volume. The highest absolute elasticity is observed in area 3, where the rate of ownership of the product is the lowest. Second, market-share elasticities are relatively high in areas 1 and 3, indicating that relative advertising pressure is an important determinant of brand i's market share. Third, competitors' advertising appropriations seem to be very responsive to an increase in brand i's advertising outlay, and this is equally true in each marketing area. This finding, combined with the fact that a change in brand i's advertising

---

[33] See Telser, "Advertising and Cigarettes," pp. 485–86.

has a negative effect on competitors' sales, confirms the view of existing competition by means of advertising in these three markets.

PROFITABILITY OF THE ADVERTISING
INVESTMENT

Equation (33), discussed above, gives us an estimate of the absolute advertising-sales elasticity (see table 3, col. 3). We can use this result to evaluate the marginal-revenue product of advertising, which is a key parameter for the measurement of the advertising profitability. The following discussion will again be limited to the results observed in area 1. It should be recalled that the absolute advertising-sales elasticity is

$$\eta_s = (\delta q/\delta s)(s/q) .$$

Dividing the estimate of η_s by the ratio of the average sample advertising expenditures (av. s) to the average sample unit sales (av. q), and multiplying this result by p, brand i sales price, we obtain an estimate of the marginal-revenue product of advertising, here called μ. The result obtained in area 1 is

$$p\delta q/\delta s = \mu = \$1.245 .$$

From the Dorfman-Steiner theorem discussed in section I, we know that, at optimum, the marginal-revenue product of advertising should be equal to the value of price elasticity (see equation [7]). Since

$$\eta_p = \mu , \qquad (38)$$

it follows that

$$MC = p\left(1 - \frac{1}{\mu}\right) \qquad (39)$$

or

$$\mu = \frac{p}{p - MC} = \frac{1}{w} , \qquad (40)$$

where w is the gross profit margin (price less MC, marginal nonadvertising cost) expressed as a percentage of price.[34] In

this case, we do not know w with precision, and we estimate its order of magnitude at 30 percent. Therefore, the critical value of μ is $\mu^* = 1/0.30 = 3.333$. The estimated value of μ is much lower, and implies at the margin a negative profit contribution per dollar of advertising. To find a rational justification of the firm's past advertising effort, we are therefore induced to infer that brand i's advertising must have cumulative effects which are not measured by the short-term value of μ. This conclusion tends to support our previous statement on the long-term perspective of the firm's marketing policy, suggested by the highly significant coefficient observed for the lagged dependent variable in the regression model (see table 1); it also confirms our previous conclusions (see equation [23]). These findings strengthen our conviction that long-term advertising effects are, directly or indirectly, taken into consideration by management in setting the advertising appropriation.

As stated by Palda,[35] in the long run, the stipulation is that the present value of the last dollar invested in advertising should be equal to the present value of revenue generated by advertising, net of all nonadvertising costs. Thus,

$$\$1 = w\mu + \frac{w\mu\lambda}{(1+r)} + \frac{w\mu\lambda^2}{(1+r)^2} + \cdots \frac{w\mu\lambda^n}{(1+2)^n} , \qquad (41)$$

where r stands for the rate of return in percentage. For large n, equation (41) simplifies to

$$1 = w\mu \frac{1}{1 - [\lambda/(1+r)]} , \qquad (42)$$

[34] Net price to manufacturers, after dealer discounts.

[35] Kristian S. Palda, *Economic Analysis for Marketing Decisions* (Englewood Cliffs, N.J.: Prentice-Hall, Inc., 1969), pp. 190–91.

and can be rewritten as

$$w\mu = 1 - \frac{\lambda}{1+r}. \quad (43)$$

Multiplying both sides of equation (43) by $1/\mu$, one has

$$w = \frac{\delta s}{p\delta q}\left(1 - \frac{\lambda}{1+r}\right). \quad (44)$$

In section I, we derived an optimization rule relating price and advertising, where no allowance was made for the lagged effects of advertising. The rule was

$$\frac{\eta_{s*}}{\eta_{p*}} = \frac{s/q}{p}. \quad (45)$$

This rule can now be dynamized to take into account the cumulative advertising effects measured by equation (42). Solving equation (45) for p, gives

$$p = (\eta_{p*}/\eta_{s*})(s/q). \quad (46)$$

If we substitute equation (46) into equation (44), transposing and referring to definition (28), we obtain

$$\frac{\eta_{s*}}{\eta_{p*}} = \frac{\eta_s w}{1 - [\lambda/(1+r)]}. \quad (47)$$

This is the long-run optimization rule corresponding to equation (23), previously discussed. Let us now verify empirically the plausibility of equation (47), assuming a gross profit margin of 30 percent and a 7 percent rate of return. Introducing the estimates[36] of tables 1 and 3 in the right side of equation (47), we have

$$\frac{(0.115)(0.300)}{1 - 0.712/0.07} = 0.103,$$

whereas the ratio of the two elasticities is $0.283/3.070 = 0.0921$. This does not

[36] Regarding λ, the retention rate, we use here an estimate obtained in a semilog model (results not reported here). See nn. 18 and 23.

seem too far off from the optimum ratio. By solving equation (42) for r, we can calculate the rate of return of the firm's advertising investment:

$$r = \frac{w\mu + \lambda - 1}{1 - w\mu}$$

$$= \frac{(0.300)(1.245) + 0.712 - 1}{1 - (0.300)(1.245)} \quad (48)$$

$$= 0.132.$$

Should w, the actual percentage of gross profit, be smaller than 26 percent, the rate of return becomes negative. A rate of 13 percent, however, does not seem too unexpected.

To conclude, the empirical evidence provided by our regression results gives support to the market-share optimization rule derived in section I. Clearly, the results presented here are tentative with respect to their normative implications. Further work within the same framework may lead to other significant results.

CONCLUDING COMMENTS

The basic purpose of economic models in marketing is twofold: (1) to help management to think in a more analytical way about marketing decisions by providing new insights into the interrelated structures and into the economic implications of the problems, and (2) to give management a tool for testing its future decisions in order to determine a priori what outcome will result. In this article, I attempted to illustrate mainly the first objective, but the model presented in the first section lends itself to several practical applications. Basically, the model can assist management in four decison problems:

1. *Advertising Budget:* Given a certain market-share objective, and given several probable competitors' advertising expenditures levels

which are the corresponding required advertising budgets?[37]

2. *Spatial Allocation of Selling Efforts:* Given a fixed advertising (or marketing) budget, how should a firm optimally allocate these limited funds among the different marketing areas, taking into account profit and cost conditions of each market?[38]

3. *Sales Forecasting:* Having decided on the level of each marketing input present in the model, and given several probable competitive marketing strategies, what market share can one expect for the coming year? Given expected total industry sales, what are the sales volumes and the profits corresponding to these expected market shares?

4. *Marketing Strategy:* Having identified the marketing inputs most closely associated with past market-shares evolution, what marketing strategy should be adopted in each market? Does one have to concentrate efforts on pricing or on advertising? Does one have to reinforce the brand image, the distribution rate of the product, etc.?

So far, only the first problem has been explored by the firm with the help of this model. The procedure adopted follows closely the one proposed by Weinberg.[39] The recommendations made by the model confirmed a priori evaluations made by management. This is an interesting result displaying the analytical power of the model, and suggesting that a combination of managerial judgment and computerized systems should prove even more useful.

In using these results, we must of course keep in mind the limitations of econometric estimation.[40] Many difficulties met in regressions analysis, however, are caused by the poor quality of the data. It is clear that the reliability of the output depends closely on the accuracy of the input. I support the view that the reliability of econometric models could be significantly improved at a low cost, by setting up within the firms better record-keeping procedures of sales data per period, region, etc., and of advertising outlays per media, region, period, etc. This would give marketing research people valid statistical information to conduct similar studies and to peryiodicall update the results obtained, so that the remaining uncertainty will be progressively reduced.

APPENDIX[41]

DERIVATION OF THE MARKET-SHARE OPTIMIZATION RULE

Given a demand function

$$q_i = q_i(p_i, s_i, x_i) , \qquad \text{(A1)}$$

where q_i = brand i's physical sales, p_i = i's sales price, s_i = i's advertising outlays, x_i = i's index of quality, and a unit average cost function

$$c_i = c_i(q_i, x_i) . \qquad \text{(A2)}$$

The profit function can be written as

$$\pi_i = p_i q_i - q_i c_i - s_i , \qquad \text{(A3)}$$
or
$$\pi_i = [p_i q_i(p_i, s_i, x_i) - q_i(p_i, s_i, x_i) c_i] \\ \times \{[q_i(p_i, s_i, x_i), x_i] - s_i\} . \qquad \text{(A4)}$$

If one defines the following: $q_i = Q m_i$, $p_i = p_i^* P$, $s_i = s_i^* S_i$, $x_i = x_i^* X$, where

[37] Robert S. Weinberg, *An Analytical Approach to Advertising Expenditure Strategy* (New York: Association of National Advertisers, 1960).

[38] J. A. Nordin, "Spatial Allocation of Selling Expenses," *Journal of Marketing* 7, no. 3 (January 1943):210–19.

[39] Weinberg, pp. 16–87.

[40] Richard R. Quandt, "Estimating Advertising Effectiveness: Some Pitfalls in Econometric Méthods," *Journal of Marketing Research* 1 (May 1964): 1–60.

[41] I am indebted to Pierre Puyts, research assistant of Louvain University, for his assistance in developing the mathematical appendix.

m_i = i's market share, Q = total industry sales, P = average market price, S_i = competitors' advertising outlays excluding brand i's, X = average product-quality index, p_i^* = i's relative price, s_i^* = i's relative advertising, and x_i^* = i's relative quality, equation (A4) can be rewritten as

$$\pi = [p_i^* P Q m_i(p_i^*, s_i^*, x_i^*)$$

$$- Q m_i(p_i^*, s_i^*, x_i^*) c_i] \quad \text{(A5)}$$

$$\times \{[Q m_i(p_i^*, s_i^*, x_i^*), x_i^*] - s_i^* S_i\},$$

or

$$\pi_i = Q m_i(p_i^*, s_i^*, x_i^*)(p_i^* P - c_i)$$

$$\times \{[m_i(\ ), x_i^*] - s_i^* S_i\}. \quad \text{(A6)}$$

Necessary conditions for an equilibrium point are

$$\frac{\delta \pi_i}{\delta p_i^*} = \frac{\delta \pi_i}{\delta s_i^*} = \frac{\delta \pi_i}{\delta x_i^*} = 0. \quad \text{(A7)}$$

By taking the partial derivatives of equation (A6), one gets

$$\frac{\delta \pi_i}{\delta p_i^*} = Q \frac{\delta m_i}{\delta p_i^*}(p_i^* P - c_i)(m_i, x_i^*)$$

$$+ Q m_i \left[P - \left(\frac{\delta c_i}{\delta m_i} \frac{\delta m_i}{\delta p_i^*} \right) \right] = 0, \quad \text{(A8)}$$

$$\frac{\delta \pi_i}{\delta s_i^*} = Q \frac{\delta m_i}{\delta s_i^*}(p_i^* P - c_i)(m_i, x_i^*)$$

$$+ Q m_i \left[\left(- \frac{\delta c_i}{\delta m_i} \frac{\delta m_i}{\delta s_i^*} \right) - S_i \right] = 0; \quad \text{(A9)}$$

$$\frac{\delta \pi_i}{\delta x_i^*} = Q \frac{\delta m_i}{\delta x_i^*}(p_i^* P - c_i)(m_i, x_i^*)$$

$$+ Q m_i \left(- \frac{\delta c_i}{\delta x_i^*} \frac{\delta c_i}{\delta m_i} \frac{\delta m_i}{\delta x_i^*} \right) = 0. \quad \text{(A10)}$$

After multiplying equation (A8) by $\delta m_i/\delta s_i^*$ and equation (A9) by $\delta m_i/\delta p_i^*$, these equations simplify to

$$m_i Q P \frac{\delta m_i}{\delta s_i^*} = - S_i \frac{\delta m_i}{\delta p_i^*}. \quad \text{(A11)}$$

Similarly, multiplying equations (A9) and (A10), respectively, by $\delta m_i/\delta x_i^*$ and $\delta m_i/\delta s_i^*$ we obtain

$$- S_i \frac{\delta m_i}{\delta p_i^*} = \left(- m_i Q \frac{\delta c_i}{\delta x_i^*} \right) \left(\frac{\delta m_i}{\delta s_i^*} \right). \quad \text{(A12)}$$

From equation (A11) and (A12), we obtain

$$- \frac{P/\delta m_i}{\delta p_i^*} = \frac{S_i/Q}{\delta m_i/\delta s_i^*} = \frac{\delta c_i/\delta x_i^*}{\delta m_i/\delta x_i^*}. \quad \text{(A13)}$$

Now, let the following definitions stand: $\eta_{p_i^*} = (\delta m_i/\delta p_i^*)(p_i^*/m_i)$; $\eta_{s^*} = (\delta m_i/\delta s_i^*)(s^*/m_i)$; $\eta_{x^*} = (\delta m_i/\delta x^*)(x_i^*/m_i)$. If we substitute these values in equation (A13), replacing P by p_i/p_i^* and S_i by s_i/s_i^* and multiply through by m_i, we obtain

$$\frac{p_i}{\eta_{p_i^*}} = \frac{s_i/q_i}{\eta_{s_i^*}} = \frac{x_i^*(\delta c/\delta x_i^*)}{\eta_{x_i^*}}. \quad \text{(A14)}$$

Now, if we define $a_i = s_i/q_i$ and $\beta_i = x_i^*(\delta c/\delta x_i^*)$, we obtain

$$\frac{p_i}{\eta_{p_i^*}} = \frac{a_i}{\eta_{s_i^*}} = \frac{\beta_i}{\eta_{x_i^*}}.$$

NEIL' E. BECKWITH*

The sales responses of five competing brands to advertising were investigated, with parameters of the simple market response functions for all brands estimated jointly. The effectiveness of advertising was found to differ significantly among brands. Optimal advertising expenditures implied by the model were determined for each of the brands.

Multivariate Analysis of Sales Responses of Competing Brands to Advertising

INTRODUCTION

The measurement of advertising's effect upon sales has received considerable attention, but advertising and promotional expenses still represent a large expenditure for benefits of questionable quantity and kind. Uncertain measurement of advertising effectiveness makes rational determination of expenditures difficult. However, the potential profit from improved advertising allocation provides considerable motivation to search for a valid measure of advertising effectiveness.

This article reports on a study of advertising's effect upon sales of an inexpensive consumption good. The study explicitly considered:

1. Simultaneous competition between all major brands in a market, by estimating the covariance of the disturbances of the brands along with the regression coefficients
2. Use of more efficient estimators than ordinary least squares, which is consistent with the intended use of the parameter estimates to allocate advertising expenditures
3. Testing the model to confirm validity
4. Extension of the model to detect second-order effects, such as the response differences of individual product variants
5. Use of the estimated parameters in determining optimal advertising expenditures for the individual brands.

This study was aimed toward measurement of the

* Neil E. Beckwith is Assistant Professor of Business, Columbia University. The Marketing Science Institute gave assistance financially and in obtaining the data. The author is especially grateful to Professor Frank M. Bass, Purdue University, and to the two marketing executives of an unnamed firm for their candid comments and willingness to collect and release the data.

effect upon sales of decision variables, including total advertising expenditure for a firm's brands, allocation of advertising monies between brands, introduction of new brands, and discontinuance of promotion for existing brands. A model of the market response function was formulated, tested extensively, and then extended to obtain the parameter estimates necessary for different decisions. This article first considers multivariate methods of jointly estimating the market response functions for all brands.

STATISTICAL METHODS

Three different estimators are considered here, ordinary least squares (OLS), and two multivariate estimators, based upon the work of Zellner [28], which are generally more efficient than OLS. The iterative estimator will be denoted IZEF, the two-stage estimator, ZEF.

OLS Estimator

For brand i, one can assume a linear regression model of the brand's sales:

$$\mathbf{y}_i = \mathbf{X}_i\boldsymbol{\beta}_i + \mathbf{u}_i$$

where $\mathbf{y}_i$ is the vector of sales observations, $\mathbf{X}_i$ the matrix of observations of the explanatory variables, $\boldsymbol{\beta}_i$ the vector of coefficients to be estimated, and $\mathbf{u}_i$ the vector of disturbances. Using OLS, the coefficients of the response function of each brand can be estimated independently of the other brands by the well known estimator:

$$\hat{\boldsymbol{\beta}}_i = [\mathbf{X}_i'\mathbf{X}_i]^{-1}\mathbf{X}_i'\mathbf{y}_i.$$

The OLS estimators are not usually the most efficient (the variance of $\hat{\boldsymbol{\beta}}_i$ is not minimal) unless the disturb-

Journal of Marketing Research,
Vol. IX (May 1972), 168–76

ances, u, are uncorrelated between brands. If the disturbances are correlated, estimating the parameters of the response functions for all the brands jointly with the covariance of the disturbances between equations is usually more efficient.

IZEF Estimator

The basic idea of multivariate regression is to utilize Aitken's generalized least squares method on all observations of all brands in one regression. The set of M brands can be estimated by conjoining them:

$$\begin{bmatrix} y_1 \\ y_2 \\ \vdots \\ y_M \end{bmatrix} = \begin{bmatrix} X_1 & 0 & \cdots & 0 \\ 0 & X_2 & \cdots & 0 \\ \vdots & \vdots & & \vdots \\ 0 & 0 & \cdots & X_M \end{bmatrix} \begin{bmatrix} \beta_1 \\ \beta_2 \\ \vdots \\ \beta_M \end{bmatrix} + \begin{bmatrix} u_1 \\ u_2 \\ \vdots \\ u_M \end{bmatrix},$$

which is more simply denoted:

$$y = X\beta + u.$$

The disturbance vector u is assumed to have mean zero and covariance matrix, denoted Φ:

$$\Phi = E(uu') = \Omega \otimes I$$

where $\Omega = E(u_i u_i')$ is the matrix of contemporaneous covariances between the several brands; I the identity matrix of a size equal to the number of observations, T; and $\otimes$ the Kronecker product operation. Thus the covariance matrix Φ is of size MT and consists of M^2 diagonal submatrices, each equal to the corresponding scalar element of Ω times I.

If Ω, and thus Φ, were known, Aitken's generalized least squares estimator:

$$\hat{\beta} = [X'\Phi^{-1}X]^{-1}X'\Phi^{-1}y$$

could be used to estimate the coefficients. Since Ω is not known, Φ is replaced by its consistent estimator:

$$\hat{\Phi} = \hat{\Omega} \otimes I = 1/T[W \otimes I],$$

where W is the second moment matrix of the OLS residuals. This method is usually more efficient than OLS.

IZEF Estimator

The moment matrix of ZEF residuals can be used to reestimate Ω, then β, and so forth until convergence. This IZEF method is usually more efficient than OLS. IZEF is also more efficient than ZEF where the disturbances are highly correlated and the correlation between explanatory variables is low. It is a maximum likelihood estimator under the additional assumption of normally distributed disturbances [13, 27]. However, most of the properties of this estimator are not dependent upon assumed normality [18].

Estimator Choice

All three estimators are generally unbiased, so efficiency is the appropriate criteria for estimator choice. IZEF is almost always a better choice than OLS for

estimating models to be used for controlling advertising expenditures because of the increased efficiency in estimation of the coefficients.

Where lagged dependent variables are included among the regressors, all three estimators are biased for small samples but asymptotically unbiased as the number of observations becomes infinite. The IZEF estimator is asymptotically more efficient than either ZEF or OLS [21]. Thus IZEF may be used in anticipation of increased efficiency, which may or may not actually be realized for small samples with lagged variables.

The use of a more efficient estimating statistic does not imply that a more powerful test will necessarily be obtained than if a less efficient estimator had been used [17]. The relationship between estimating efficiency and test power is rather loose.

The use of IZEF estimators provides:

1. Maximum likelihood estimates under assumption of normality
2. Explicit accommodation of the covariance between brands
3. Usually more efficient parameter estimates, and therefore
4. Estimators appropriate for controlling advertising allocations.

For these reasons this study primarily reports IZEF estimates of market response functions [8].

BRAND COMPETITION

The estimation of the market response functions and the testing of the model follow a description of the investigated market.

The Market

The environment and modus operandi of the industry are described in order to argue for the assumptions of the analysis, to substitute for explicit identification of the industry and brands, and to emphasize the absence of many effects which often dominate the relatively weak effect of advertising.

Environment. The frequently purchased, inexpensive consumable good was at the stage of maturity where significant product innovations were not occurring. Consumption was seasonal, generally increasing over the period studied, and believed to be constant per capita. Three firms owned the five brands, denoted A through E, which shared 98 % of the industry sales in this highly developed country.

Product and packaging. All brands were packaged similarly, with distinctive brand labels on the package, and were offered in the same assortment of package sizes. Differences between brands were minor, and consumers were generally unable to identify brands in blind tests. Each brand was the aggregation of two popular subbrands (product variations). Brand D also included several less popular subbrands.

Distribution. All brands used the same two distribu-

Table 1
MARKET SHARE MODEL (1) PARAMETER ESTIMATES

Brand, i	OLS		ZEF		IZEF		
	$\hat{\lambda}_i$	$\hat{\gamma}_i$	$\hat{\lambda}_i$	$\hat{\gamma}_i$	$\hat{\lambda}_i$	$\hat{\gamma}_i$	R_i^2
A	.9966	−.0014	.9893	.0052	.9896	.0059	.983
	(.0072)[a]	(.0057)	(.0041)	(.0031)	(.0034)	(.0025)	
B	.9936	.0020	.9970	.0003	.9985	.0006	.920
	(.0064)	(.0048)	(.0033)	(.0023)	(.0031)	(.0022)	
C	.9798	.0130	.9805	.0132	.9848	.0117	.996
	(.0056)	(.0038)	(.0051)	(.0033)	(.0045)	(.0028)	
D	1.0027	.0024	1.0000	.0045	.9979	.0052	.991
	(.0044)	(.0053)	(.0028)	(.0030)	(.0025)	(.0026)	
E	.9894	.0161	.9907	.0133	.9911	.0107	.961
	(.0068)	(.0076)	(.0035)	(.0035)	(.0032)	(.0030)	

[a] Estimated standard errors are in parentheses.

tion channels. The larger one consisted of a chain of retail stores which offered all subbrands; the smaller one offered most subbrands.

Pricing. All brands were sold at uniform retail and wholesale prices. The price structure was constant during the period of observation. No price promotions or deals were offered to retailers or consumers.

Advertising. The firms advertised almost entirely in print, radio, and television.[1]

Primary demand. Advertising may have had a slight effect upon industry sales, but no substantial evidence was found to reject the hypothesis that total industry sales were independent of industry advertising. Market shares offered the advantage of being a measure of brand sales freer of seasonal influence.

Identification. The original intent of this study was to investigate the simultaneous determination of brand sales and advertising. However, no substantial evidence was found to contradict the assumption that current period brand sales did not affect current brand advertising [6]. Consistent with the one-month time interval for observation periods and with the lack of contrary evidence, it was assumed that brand advertising was not a function of current sales.

Transients. Four exogenous events occurred during the 48-month observation interval: the attempted acquisition of one firm by an extranational company, adverse Brand C publicity, the introduction of a new subbrand of Brand D, and a strike which disrupted distribution. The observations corresponding to these unusual transients were excluded from the data.

The problems of estimating advertising effects from aggregate data have been previously considered [3, 9, 25]. However, because of the absence of many common promotional and distributive variables, this market provides a better opportunity than normal for such an estimation.

[1] The effect of salesmen employed by each firm to call upon consumers and retailers was not included, nor was the spillover of extranational television advertisements. No other promotional variables were believed to be significant in this industry.

Model Estimation

The model assumed for all brands, i, in the absence of external transients, was that the market share, $MS_{i,t}$, is a function of lagged market share, $MS_{i,t-1}$, and advertising share, $AS_{i,t}$:

$$(1) \qquad MS_{i,t} = \lambda_i MS_{i,t-1} + \gamma_i AS_{i,t} + u_{i,t}.$$

This model accommodates a geometrically decaying effect of advertising by the inclusion of the lagged market share term. The use of distributed lag models reduced à la Koyck to include only one such lagged term has been popular among market investigators [19, 24, 26]. Some of the problems confronted by users of this type of model have also received attention [14, 16, 22].

The parameters of this model were estimated for the 35 homogeneous observations by the OLS, ZEF, and IZEF procedures. Estimates are listed in Table 1 for comparison. Only 2 of the 5 OLS-estimated advertising coefficients were significantly greater than zero, and one was estimated to be negative. Four of the five IZEF advertising coefficients were estimated to be significantly greater than zero. The ZEF estimates had larger estimated standard errors than the IZEF estimates. Also, the IZEF likelihood function was about 5 times that of the ZEF model and 10^5 times that of the model estimated by OLS. Thus the model estimated by IZEF was chosen for subsequent testing. The selected model of sales response was defined to be the conjunction of the IZEF-estimated model:

$$MS_{A,t} = .9896 \, MS_{A,t-1} + .0059 \, AS_{A,t} + u_{A,t}$$

$$MS_{B,t} = .9985 \, MS_{B,t-1} + .0006 \, AS_{B,t} + u_{B,t}$$

$$(2) \quad MS_{C,t} = .9848 \, MS_{C,t-1} + .0117 \, AS_{C,t} + u_{C,t}$$

$$MS_{D,t} = .9979 \, MS_{D,t-1} + .0052 \, AS_{D,t} + u_{D,t}$$

$$MS_{E,t} = .9911 \, MS_{E,t-1} + .0107 \, AS_{E,t} + u_{E,t},$$

an assumption of zero disturbance means:

(3) $$E[\mathbf{u}_t] = \mathbf{0}$$

and the IZEF-estimated matrix of covariances of disturbances between the brands:

$$(4) \quad E[\mathbf{u}_t\mathbf{u}_t'] = \begin{bmatrix} 65 & 20 & -1 & -43 & -52 \\ 20 & 54 & 1 & -41 & -46 \\ -1 & 1 & 11 & -5 & -6 \\ -43 & -41 & -5 & 61 & 39 \\ -52 & -46 & -6 & 39 & 82 \end{bmatrix} \cdot 10^{-7}.$$

The selected model utilized the simultaneity of the brands' sales in several ways. First, the dependent variable was brand market share, which was less affected than sales by seasonality and other exogenous variables that affected the brands proportionally to volume.

Second, the effect of advertising for each brand was assumed to be proportional to its current advertising share, which accommodated possible seasonal or other differences in responsiveness to advertising which affected all brands similarly. This also implied a decreasing return to scale for advertising expenditures.

Third, the covariance matrix of the disturbances accommodated the consistent interaction between brands. Disturbances at a particular time tended to cause the sales shares of Brands A and B to vary directly together—as evidenced by the positive covariance between them. Similarly, Brands D and E tended to vary together. Conversely, the negative covariances indicate that Brands A, B, and C were affected by disturbances oppositely from Brands D and E.

The usual equation-by-equation OLS estimation of the brands assumes that the matrix of disturbance covariances is diagonal. Since the dependent variable here was a proportion, market share, it was not possible for all brands to be independent. The assumption that all brands except one were independent would imply a very special covariance structure between that brand and all the others [23]. The IZEF multivariate estimation of the brands provided an estimate of the covariance, avoiding the necessity of assuming, perhaps implicitly, an arbitrary covariance structure.

Model Tests

One difficulty in determining the effect of advertising upon sales is the number of simple models which fit the (only set of available) data well. Many of these models would work as forecasting models, but not all are adequate for controlling advertising allocations [4]. The need for good parameter estimates, rather than good fit, required that the selected model be tested extensively. The model's estimated parameters were examined for plausibility, its residuals were tested for normality, its specification was tested by appending additional variables, and it was extended to estimate the response differences of individual product variants. These tests did not disprove the model for the original 35 homogeneous periods.

Parameter tests. A model must be rejected if false or unlikely statements can be deduced from the conjunction of the model and the data [2]. It was expected a priori that advertising effectiveness coefficients were positive and that the coefficients of the lagged terms were close to unity. The latter could not exceed unity for lengthy time intervals because the model would then diverge. In the present case, the 10 parameter estimates of the selected model (2) were all plausible, so the model was not rejected. Multivariate estimation tends to police the investigator, since estimates for all brands must be plausible in order for the model to be acceptable.

Residual tests. To test the residuals, it was assumed that they were from a multivariate-normal distribution with parameters (3) and (4) of the selected model. The means of the individual brands' IZEF-estimated residuals were not zero, so three aspects were tested: assumption of zero means, assumption of the estimated covariance matrix (4), and normality. Anderson [1] has specified the appropriate likelihood ratio test, the statistic for which has a chi-square distribution. It is not unlikely that the observed test statistic of 5.1 is from a χ_5^2 distribution.[2] Thus the residuals were not found inconsistent with the disturbance distribution specified in the selected model.

Specification tests. Lagged variable models should be tested for misspecification by including additional lagged terms among the explanatory variables. If the specified model is correct, the estimated coefficients of the appended variables should be small and the coefficients of the other variables should not be significantly different from those of the specified model. For the two models:

$$MS_{i,t} = \lambda_i MS_{i,t-1} + \alpha_i MS_{i,t-2} + \gamma_i AS_{i,t} + u_{i,t},$$

$$MS_{i,t} = \lambda_i MS_{i,t-1} + \alpha_i MS_{i,t-2} + \rho_i MS_{i,t-3} + \gamma_i AS_{i,t} + u_{i,t},$$

the estimates of λ_i and γ_i were not significantly different from the selected model, and the estimates of α_i and ρ_i were small (<0.13). These results did not disconfirm the appropriateness of the geometric decay implicitly assumed in the selected model.

Another specification test was based upon estimation of the selected model with an intercept term appended:

$$MS_{i,t} = \lambda_i MS_{i,t-1} + \gamma_i AS_{i,t} + \alpha_i + u_{i,t}.$$

None of the intercept terms, α_i, were estimated to be significantly different from zero, and none of the other coefficient estimates were significantly different from the corresponding values of the selected model. Thus the IZEF estimates of this model did not suggest rejection of the selected model because of misspecification.

[2] The test statistic was distributed as χ_{20}^2, but 15 degrees of freedom were lost by estimating the contemporaneous covariance matrix from the same data [15].

Table 2

SUBBRAND MARKET SHARE MODEL[a]

IZEF estimation	R_i^2
$MS_{A,t} = .9932\ MS_{A,t-1} + .0020\ AS_{A,t} + \hat{u}_{A,t}$ $\quad\quad (.0033) \quad\quad\quad (.0024)$	.985
$MS_{B,t} = 1.0007\ MS_{B,t-1} - .0030\ AS_{B,t} + \hat{u}_{B,t}$ $\quad\quad (.0038) \quad\quad\quad (.0025)$	.921
$MS_{C,t} = .9814\ MS_{C,t-1} + .0133\ AS_{C,t} + \hat{u}_{C,t}$ $\quad\quad (.0048) \quad\quad\quad (.0030)$	.996
$MS_{D1,t} = .9899\ MS_{D1,t-1} - .0008\ AS_{D,t} + \hat{u}_{D1,t}$ $\quad\quad (.0066) \quad\quad\quad (.0021)$	.970
$MS_{D2,t} = 1.0068\ MS_{D2,t-1} + .0068\ AS_{D,t} + \hat{u}_{D2,t}$ $\quad\quad (.0028) \quad\quad\quad (.0029)$	.998
$MS_{D3,t} = .9933\ MS_{D3,t-1} + .0000\ AS_{D,t} + \hat{u}_{D3,t}$ $\quad\quad (.0067) \quad\quad\quad (.0015)$	.988
$MS_{D4,t} = .9927\ MS_{D4,t-1} + .0066\ AS_{D,t} + \hat{u}_{D4,t}$ $\quad\quad (.0044) \quad\quad\quad (.0022)$	.980
$MS_{E,t} = .9911\ MS_{E,t-1} + .0129\ AS_{E,t} + \hat{u}_{E,t}$ $\quad\quad (.0032) \quad\quad\quad (.0031)$	.964

[a] Market shares for subbrands D1 through D4 are the shares of sales of their particular product class.

Furthermore, the estimates of the advertising coefficients, γ_i, were all significantly positive, which contradicted the alternative model that changes in market share were constant.[3]

Subbrand Differences

The selected model considered only the aggregate sales and advertising of each brand. The response to advertising of individual subbrands was investigated as a test of the appropriateness of the functional form (1) of the selected model. The extensions also demonstrated the ability of the model and the efficient IZEF estimators to detect second-order effects, such as response differences between individual subbrands.

Brand D was comprised of four popular subbrands, denoted D1–D4, plus a few others. An extension of the selected model to include subbrand equations was estimated (Table 2). The advertising coefficient estimates differed so as to suggest that D2 and D4 were featured in campaigns but that D1 and D3 were not. This inference was subsequently found to be substantially true (Table 3). Subbrand D2 was a fad within its major market segment during the observation period and the estimated coefficient of its lagged term was high (Table 2).

A new subbrand of Brand D, DN, was introduced in the nineteenth period. The previously selected model was extended to include two segments of Brand D, the new subbrand, and the sum of all other Brand D volume, DO. The IZEF estimate (Table 4) of the decay coefficient, λ_{DN}, for the new brand was quite low ($0.90^{12} = 0.28$ annual retention rate). This result suggested that

[3] The estimation of the model with an intercept term also indicated that the statistical anomalies caused by nonzero IZEF-estimated residual means for each brand did not significantly affect the estimation of the selected model.

Table 3

PERCENTAGE ALLOCATION OF BRAND D ADVERTISEMENTS

	Print	Radio	TV
Subbrand D1	11.9	9.9	4.6
Subbrand D2	38.7	33.1	44.0
Subbrand D3	1.9	1.1	1.9
Subbrand D4	14.4	25.6	33.1
New subbrand DN[a]	25.2	18.2	16.4
All other	7.9	12.1	0.0
	100.0	100.0	100.0

[a] All brands were averaged over the same time interval, so for the new subbrand, the indicated fraction is less than the actual fraction after its introduction.

the new subbrand obtained consumer trial but not continued repurchase.

Inferences about the new brand's advertising effectiveness or allocation of advertising effort between subbrands were impossible because of the aggregated Brand D advertising variable used.

The plausibility of the estimates obtained for these extensions of the selected model was interpreted as a confirmation of the function form (1) of the selected model.

IMPLICATIONS OF THE SELECTED MODEL

The selected model was extended to accommodate seasonal sales share differences of individual brands. The dynamic implications of the resultant model were compared to the actual sales shares of the brands. The normative advertising allocations were also determined for the brands under the assumption that each firm's objective was to maximize its discounted earnings stream.

Seasonal Market Share Model

The seasonality of the sales shares of the individual brands was accommodated by adding the average monthly residuals, $ms_{i,t}$, to the selected model.[4] The

[4] The selected model did not explicitly accommodate these differences. The estimation of such a model was attempted but the covariance structure of the selected model with monthly dummy variables appended could not be inverted using either the BMD inversion routine [11] or Garbow's SHARE AN 402 routine [10]. When this study was nearly completed, a seasonal model was estimated [7]:

$$MS_{i,t} = \lambda_{i,k} MS_{i,t-1} + \gamma_i AS_{i,t} + u_{i,t}$$

where $k = 1$ if t is a January, $k = 2$ if t is a February, etc. The $\lambda_{i,k}$ are not assumed to be the same for all months, k. For the five brands, the IZEF estimates of γ_i were 0.0046, 0.0029, 0.0139, 0.0014, and 0.0122 and the root products:

$$\left(\prod_{k=1}^{12} \lambda_{i,k} \right)^{1/12}$$

were 0.9897, 0.9942, 0.9856, 1.0001, and 0.9927. These were close to the coefficients in the selected model.

seasonal model was then defined to be the conjunction of (3), (4) and:

(5) $MS_{i,t} = \lambda_i MS_{i,t-1} + \gamma_i AS_{i,t} + ms_{i,t} + u_{i,t}$

where λ_i and γ_i are specified as in (2).

The forecast market share $\widetilde{MS}_{i,t}$ for each brand was based upon the actual monthly advertising share and upon the lagged value of the forecast market share:

(6) $\widetilde{MS}_{i,t} = \lambda_i \widetilde{MS}_{i,t-1} + \gamma_i AS_{i,t} + ms_{i,t}$

where λ_i and γ_i are specified as in (2). These forecast values are plotted with the actual market shares for each brand during the sample period and the following ten months in Figures 1 through 5.

Forecasting models such as (6), which iteratively base subsequent forecasts upon previous forecasts without the benefit of error feedback, are subject to gradual increases in the error. The forecasts are the market shares which would be expected if no exogenous transients (such as the Brand C publicity in Period 12) had disturbed the market process. The forecast can be started from any arbitrary period, as shown by the additional forecasts for Brands C and D.

Normative Inferences

Normative implications can be deduced from the functional form of the model. Where:

1. Advertising does not affect primary demand
2. Each brand i faces a response function such that:

$$MS_{i,t} = \lambda_i MS_{i,t-1} + \gamma_i AS_{i,t} + ms_{i,t}$$

3. Primary demand is constant, $M = 300$ units, for all future periods
4. For each brand i: $m_i = \$5.00 = $ incremental unit profit margin; $d_i = .008 = $ monthly cost of capital,

then the discounted earnings stream of each brand i

Table 4
NEW SUBBRAND INTRODUCTION MODEL

	IZEF estimation			R_i^2
$MS_{A,t}$	=	$.9903\ MS_{A,t-1}$ (.0041)	$+\ .0038\ AS_{A,t} + \hat{u}_{A,t}$ (.0030)	.985
$MS_{B,t}$	=	$.9969\ MS_{B,t-1}$ (.0041)	$-\ .0011\ AS_{B,t} + \hat{u}_{B,t}$ (.0029)	.923
$MS_{C,t}$	=	$.9810\ MS_{C,t-1}$ (.0051)	$+\ .0131\ AS_{C,t} + \hat{u}_{C,t}$ (.0033)	.996
$MS_{DN,t}$[a]	=	$.9020\ MS_{DN,t-1}$ (.0268)	$+\ .0012\ AS_{D,t} + \hat{u}_{DN,t}$ (.0015)	.994
$MS_{DO,t}$	=	$1.0057\ MS_{DO,t-1}$ (.0021)	$+\ .0017\ AS_{D,t} + \hat{u}_{DO,t}$ (.0022)	.999
$MS_{E,t}$	=	$.9917\ MS_{E,t-1}$ (.0034)	$+\ .0135\ AS_{E,t} + \hat{u}_{E,t}$ (.0035)	.964

[a] All three data series for the new subbrand DN were constrained to zero for the first 22 observation periods.

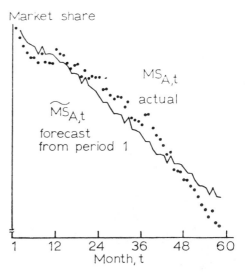

Figure 1
BRAND A MARKET SHARE FORECAST

could be maximized by advertising it at the optimal level:

$$A_{i,t}^* = \max\left[0, \left(\frac{M\gamma_i m_i(1+d_i)}{1+d_i-\lambda_i}\ A_{i,t}^0\right)^{1/2} - A_{i,t}^0\right],$$

where $A_{i,t}^0$ is the total advertising expenditure for all other brands.[b] Estimating the optimal advertising expenditure for brand i requires estimates of the primary demand, M, and the sum of advertising expenditures for all other brands, $A_{i,t}^0$, but not parameter values λ_j or γ_j for the other brands.

If each brand were advertised at its optimal level, the estimated parameter values λ_i and γ_i of the selected model (2) would infer a total disguised industry advertising level of $546, split among the brands:

Brand, i	Optimal advertising level, $A_{i,t}^*$
A	$ 0
B	0
C	167
D	144
E	235
Total	$546

The present value of the additional earnings stream was estimated to be less than the advertising expendi-

[b] This optimal advertising expenditure was deduced from the functional form of the sales response function, as in [5] for a slightly different function.

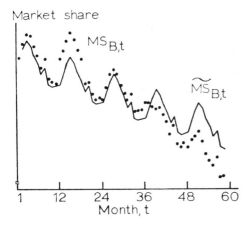

Figure 2
BRAND B MARKET SHARE FORECAST

ture for Brands A and B. Thus application of the normative theory to this disguised data suggested that some advertising monies should be reallocated from Brands A and B to Brand C. It is possible that at a

lower expenditure level the advertising effectiveness, γ_i, and the decay parameter, λ_i, might be sufficiently improved to justify advertising Brand A and/or B. If the firm cannot find such a level, the brands should be allowed to decay away without advertising support, then dropped when no longer profitable.

The theory, which is applicable to individual brands or subbrands, can be used to examine new products. The sales share of the new subbrand, DN, was estimated to decay much faster than that of the other subbrands. For similar advertising effectivenesses, the theory would imply that the other subbrands were better advertising investments than DN. This new subbrand might have warranted continued promotion if its advertising effectiveness were high enough to compensate for the rapid decay. Promotion of this particular subbrand was curtailed after extensive introductory advertising expenditures (Table 3).

Additional Periods Test

After this study was essentially completed, sales and advertising data for ten additional months (Periods 49–58) were received. The seasonal model (5) included assumption of the disturbance distribution parameters (3) and (4), so the hypothesis could be tested that the seasonal model errors for the additional ten periods, Table 5, were from a multivariate-normal distribution

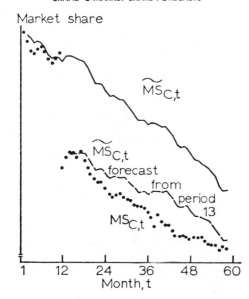

Figure 3
BRAND C MARKET SHARE FORECASTS

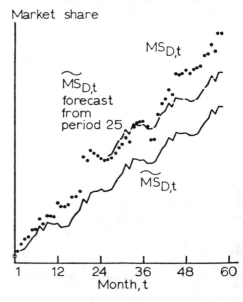

Figure 4
BRAND D MARKET SHARE FORECASTS

Figure 5
BRAND E MARKET SHARE FORECAST

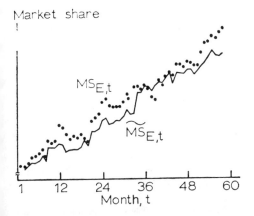

Market share

$MS_{E,t}$

$\widetilde{MS}_{E,t}$

1   12   24   36   48   60
Month, t

Table 5
TEN PERIODS' SEASONAL MODEL ERRORS[a]

Period, t	Brand, t				
	A	B	C	D	E
49	25	−21	6	−5	−11
50	−41	−19	−2	21	20
51	23	−10	4	−2	−16
52	−11	−11	−5	−19	42
53	−44	−7	−4	30	33
54	−25	4	8	−15	−21
55	12	15	9	2	0
56	−7	5	6	−8	2
57	−24	−8	16	58	−52
58	−15	7	−8	1	3

[a] All values are multiplied by 10^4.

with these parameters.[6] The appropriate likelihood ratio test statistic is distributed as χ^2_{20} if the errors are from the specified distribution [1]. Since the test statistic was 95.5, the seasonal model was found inconsistent with the new data under the added assumption of normality.

Brand B and Period 57 were temporarily excluded because the Brand B parameter estimates for the 10 additional periods (Table 6) and for the 35 original periods (Table 2) differed significantly, and because of the large errors (see Table 5) of opposite sign for Brands D and E in Period 57—the correlation specified in (4) was positive. The test statistic for the remaining observations was 18.0, which is not significant at the 10% level for a statistic distributed as χ^2_{14}, indicating that the remaining observations were consistent with the seasonal model.[7]

Throughout this study, Brand B consistently had the lowest coefficient of determination (R^2) of the brands. Data for the same month as Period 57 in the two previous years (Periods 33 and 45) were not available for use in estimating the selected model because of exogenous transients. Two industry marketing managers were not aware of any unusual or exogenous events surrounding Period 57 or Brand B. It was therefore concluded that the model and the added assumption of normally distributed disturbances were not consistent with the additional data.

Normative advertising for a brand is a function of the response parameters λ_i and γ_i of that brand. The

parameters must be sufficiently constant, in the absence of exogenous transients, so that the firm can base future advertising decisions upon the historically estimated parameters. Fortunately, where the firm can estimate competitors' advertising expenditures, it does not need the estimated response parameters for their brands. Thus, evidence of parameter instability for one brand, such as for Brand B, does not preclude use of the normative theory by the firms owning the other brands.

CONCLUSION

In this study the simultaneous nature of competition among the brands was explicitly acknowledged in three ways: (1) brand sales shares were used as the dependent variables, (2) the effect of advertising was assumed proportional to a brand's current share of all advertising expenditures, and (3) the covariance structure of the disturbances was utilized to estimate the consistent interaction between specific brand pair disturbances. The response functions of all brands were estimated jointly by multivariate regression to obtain an increase in estimation efficiency. The resulting estimates of advertising response were plausible and differed significantly between the brands.

Table 6
TEN-PERIOD SALES SHARE MODEL

IZEF estimation	R_i^2
$MS_{A,t} = \underset{(.0108)}{.9743}\, MS_{A,t-1} + \underset{(.0087)}{.0105}\, AS_{A,t} + \hat{u}_{A,t}$	.886
$MS_{B,t} = \underset{(.0170)}{.9450}\, MS_{B,t-1} + \underset{(.0117)}{.0347}\, AS_{B,t} + \hat{u}_{B,t}$	.750
$MS_{C,t} = \underset{(.0074)}{.9897}\, MS_{C,t-1} - \underset{(.1152)}{.0534}\, AS_{C,t} + \hat{u}_{C,t}$	.799
$MS_{D,t} = \underset{(.0072)}{1.0075}\, MS_{D,t-1} - \underset{(.0089)}{.0011}\, AS_{D,t} + \hat{u}_{D,t}$	.758
$MS_{E,t} = \underset{(.0087)}{1.0002}\, MS_{E,t-1} + \underset{(.0071)}{.0053}\, AS_{E,t} + \hat{u}_{E,t}$	.866

[6] The seasonal model assumed the same covariance matrix (4) as the selected model. This assumption ignores variance due to seasonal fluctuations. The statistic is appropriate for testing the consistency of additional observations with the seasonal model.

[7] The test statistic is biased by omission of the deviant observations, however.

The decay of advertising effect for a new subbrand was estimated to be plausibly and significantly different from that of existing subbrands. The investigation of the response of several other subbrands indicated significantly different advertising responses consistent with the known allocation of advertising between them.

The model assumed here was consistent with the data from which it was developed but was not consistent with all the data for the following 10 months under the added assumption of normally distributed disturbances. The important question for each firm is: in the absence of exogenous transients, are the market response functions for its brands sufficiently constant that the firm can utilize currently estimated parameters in future periods? If so, then the market response mechanism can be tracked adaptively by continual retesting and re-estimation of the model [12, 20]. The normative budgeting and allocation of advertising might then be implemented as a routine control function of the firm.

REFERENCES

1. Anderson, Theodore W. *An Introduction to Multivariate Statistical Analysis.* New York: John Wiley & Sons, 1950.
2. Basmann, Robert L. "On the Application of the Identifiability Test Statistic in Predictive Testing of Explanatory Economic Models," *The Indian Economic Journal,* 13 (October–December 1965), 387–423.
3. Bass, Frank M. "A Dynamic Model of Market Share and Sales Behavior," *Proceedings.* Winter Conference, American Marketing Association, 1963, 263–76.
4. ———. "Application of Regression Models in Marketing: Testing Versus Forecasting," Institute Paper No. 265, Herman C. Krannert Graduate School of Industrial Administration, Purdue University, December 1969.
5. Beckwith, Neil E. "Competitive Advertising," Institute Paper No. 225, Herman C. Krannert Graduate School of Industrial Administration, Purdue University, January 1969.
6. ———. "The Response of Competing Brands to Advertising: A Multivariate Regression Test," unpublished doctoral dissertation, Purdue University, June 1970.
7. ———. "Analysis of the Response of Competing Brands to Advertising Using Seasonal Models," unpublished paper, Columbia University, 1971.
8. ———. "Measuring the Effect of Advertising Upon the Sales of Several Brands," *Proceedings.* Fall Conference, American Marketing Association, 1971.
9. Cooley, R. H. "Practical Advertising Goals for Measuring Advertising Results," *Proceedings.* Fall Conference, American Marketing Association, 1963, 231–8.
10. Cooley, William W. and Paul R. Lohnes. *Multivariate Procedures for the Behavioral Sciences.* New York: John Wiley & Sons, 1962.
11. Dixon, W. J., ed. *BMD: Biomedical Computer Programs.* Los Angeles: Health Sciences Computing Facility, University of California, 1965.
12. Fitzroy, Peter T. "Some Adaptive Models for Sequentially Setting Advertising Budgets," paper presented at conference of the Operations Research Society of America. November 1968.
13. Goldberger, Arthur S. *Econometric Theory.* New York: John Wiley & Sons, 1964.
14. Griliches, Zvi. "Distributed Lags: A Survey," *Econometrica,* 35 (January 1967), 33–42.
15. Hogg, Robert V. and Allen T. Craig. *Introduction to Mathematical Statistics.* New York: Macmillan, 1965.
16. Jastram, R. "A Treatment of Distributed Lags in the Theory of Advertising Expenditures," *Journal of Marketing,* 20 (July 1955), 36–46.
17. Kendall, Maurice G. and Alan Stuart. *The Advanced Theory of Statistics,* Vol. II. New York: Hafner, 1961.
18. Kmenta, Jan and Roy F. Gilbert. "Small Sample Properties of Alternative Estimators of Seemingly Unrelated Regressions," *Journal of the American Statistical Association,* 63 (December 1968), 1180–200.
19. Kuehn, Alfred A. "How Advertising Performance Depends on Other Marketing Factors," *Journal of Advertising Research,* 2 (March 1962), 2–10.
20. Little, John D. C. "A Model of Adaptive Control of Promotional Spending," *Operations Research,* 14 (November–December 1966), 1075–97.
21. Maddala, G. S. "Generalized Least Squares with an Estimated Variance Covariance Matrix," *Econometrica,* 39 (January 1971), 23–33.
22. Martin, J. "Isolation of Lagged Economic Responses," *Journal of Farm Economics,* 49 (February 1967), 160–8.
23. McGuire, Timothy W., John U. Farley, Robert E. Lucas, Jr., and L. Winston Ring. "Estimation and Inference for Linear Models in Which Subsets of the Dependent Variable are Constrained," *Journal of the American Statistical Association,* 63 (December 1968), 1201–13.
24. Palda, Kristian S. *The Measurement of Cumulative Advertising Effects.* Englewood Cliffs, N.J.: Prentice Hall, 1964.
25. Quant, Richard E. "Estimating the Effectiveness of Advertising: Some Pitfalls in Econometric Methods," *Journal of Marketing Research,* 1 (May 1964), 51–60.
26. Telser, Lester G. "Advertising and Cigarettes," *Journal of Political Economy,* 70 (October 1968), 471–99.
27. Theil, Henri. *Economic Forecasts and Policy.* Amsterdam: North-Holland, 1965.
28. Zellner, Arnold. "An Efficient Method of Estimating Seemingly Unrelated Regressions and Tests for Aggregation Bias," *Journal of the American Statistical Association,* 57 (June 1962), 348–68.

During the GM strike, its competitors
changed their promotional budget differently
on 20 different models, thus revealing . . .

SALES EFFECTIVENESS OF AUTOMOBILE ADVERTISING

Robert D. Buzzell and Michael J. Baker

In the fall of 1970, a strike by the United Auto Workers stopped production of General Motors automobiles. During the 11 weeks of the strike, GM's competitors reduced their advertising and other promotional efforts substantially, apparently in order to conserve resources for the time when GM would return to the competitive fray. Did these cutbacks in promotional effort have any measurable effects on the sales of the automobile models that were available to consumers?

This paper summarizes the results of an analysis aimed at exploring the relationship between *changes* in advertising expenditures and *changes* in sales during the period of the strike. The inspiration for making this analysis was the recognition that the strike might be viewed as a "natural experiment," in which much greater changes occurred than those experienced during normal industry operations. Of course, the strike *was* an extraordinary event, and what happened then was, by definition, not typical of what can be expected to happen during more normal times.

In spite of this, analysis of the industry's experience during the strike may shed some light on the general question of whether, and to what extent, advertising exerts any short-run influence on the sales of automobiles—and, by extension, other consumer durables.

The UAW strike against General Motors began on September 14, 1970 and lasted until late November. As dealers' stocks were depleted, GM cars became virtually unavailable to buyers.

Sales of the company's overall product line, which accounted for around 45 per cent of total domestic registrations during the first nine months of 1970, declined to 40 per cent in October, 20 per cent in November, and 29 per cent in December (*Ward's Automotive Reports*).

Other automobile manufacturers responded to GM's plight by cutting back sharply on their promotional expenditures. These reductions in expenditures were not, however, uniform among different makes and models. "Selective adjustment" was apparently the rule. Thus, for example, among 20 selected makes and models covered in this study:

Advertising expenditures were reduced by 50 per

Robert D. Buzzell is executive director of the Marketing Science Institute, Cambridge, and professor of business administration at the Harvard Business School. Dr. Buzzell has combined a teaching and writing career with active participation in business management. He is a director of Management Horizons, Inc. and Lane Bryant, Inc. and a consultant to various firms and academic institutions, including Sears, Roebuck, Centre Europeen d'Education Permanente, and Istituto Studi Direzionale.

cent or more from 1969 levels for five models;

Expenditures were between 20 per cent and 50 per cent lower than in 1969 for six models;

Expenditures were *increased* over 1969 levels for six models, in one case by more than 100 per cent.

Retail sales of the automobile models available during the strike also varied widely. Most enjoyed at least some gains over 1969 figures, but several experienced significant declines in spite of the absence of the largest company in the industry from the market.

In light of the variability in both advertising expenditure levels and sales results for different makes and models offered by GM's competitors, there was a possibility of some relationship between the two factors. Did those models for which advertising was reduced most achieve lower rates of sales, relatively speaking, than competing models that maintained or increased their promotional spending? The nature of the relationship (if any) might give some insight into the role of advertising in the marketing of automobiles.

Does Advertising Sell Automobiles?

Even the most confirmed empiricists would agree that a statistical analysis of data should be based on some theoretical foundations. Before looking at the record, in other words, there should be some idea of what to look for. What do previous studies and generalized theories of consumer behavior suggest about the influence of advertising on automobile purchases?

A review of the few available published studies (Brown, 1961 and Smith, 1965) and some introspection led to the following views:

1. There is general consensus that advertising is *not* a dominant factor among the numerous controllable variables that influence either total automobile sales or the market shares of individual makes and models. Both published studies and the expressed beliefs of automobile marketers suggest that styling, performance features of individual makes, dealer facilities and reputation, and personal selling on the showroom floor all have much more to do with consumers' buying decisions than advertising does.

2. Not only is advertising a relatively minor factor among many that influence consumer purchases, but its effects may be so slight—at least in the short run—as to prevent meaningful measurement. Apparently, this was the line of reasoning that led GM to adopt in the early 1960's a system of evaluating the effectiveness of advertising based on measures of *communications* results (Smith, 1965).

3. Insofar as advertising *does* affect purchases, its influence is probably diffused over some period of time because the decision process for an automobile purchase usually stretches over several weeks or months.

4. The effects of automobile advertising, like those of most other types of promotion, are probably subject to diminishing returns.

If these beliefs about the role of advertising in the marketing of automobiles have any validity, it would not be surprising to find that there was *no* statistically significant relationship between changes in advertising and changes in sales for individual cars during the GM strike—particularly in view of the relatively short time period involved. If there *were* any measurable relationship, one would expect it to exhibit the "diminishing returns" phenomenon.

Sales and Advertising Estimates

Monthly registration figures for each make and model of domestically-produced automobiles are readily available from published sources. Estimates of advertising expenditures for each make/model were obtained from an industry source and they are believed to be the most accurate figures available. These figures cover expenditures in all major media, including advertisements placed by dealer associations as well as manufacturers' expenditures.

No data were available for sales promotion such as contests, premiums, dealer incentive programs, etc. Since these forms of promotional effort can be increased or decreased more flexibly than media advertising, it seems likely that *total* promotional spending was probably reduced somewhat more during the strike than is indicated in the figures. There is no way to know, however, how great the *differences* in sales promotion changes may have been among specific makes and models included in the analysis.

Advertising expenditure estimates were not available on a month-by-month basis. Consequently, the analysis is based on a comparison of changes between 1969 and 1970 spending for the September 1–December 31 period. This period corresponds closely to the new model introduction season in the industry.

Because of changes in automobile nameplates from 1969 to 1970, and differences in the nomenclature used in the sources of sales and advertising data, some effort was required to define the specific products to be included in the analysis. Also, data were not available for some makes and models in sufficient detail. For these reasons, the analysis was limited to 20 domestically-produced makes/models. To avoid disclosure of confidential data, the sales and advertising figures presented later are not identified with these automobiles by name or by company, but only on a coded basis.

Actual Results—Compared with What?

Since the experience of the industry during the GM strike is treated as a natural experiment, actual sales and advertising results during the period must be compared with some other set of figures in order to arrive at changes or differences.

The technique used in the study was to make projections of both sales and advertising expenditures for each of the automobile models included in the analysis. The projected figures were estimates of the most likely levels of retail sales and advertising outlays during the strike period *if no strike had occurred.* Four procedures were used in making the projections.

First, it was assumed that if there had been no strike, total industry sales in calendar 1970 would have amounted to 7,670,000 units. This was based on the forecast made at the National Association of Business Economists' conference held the day before the strike began. The figure of 7.67 million is virtually identical to the actual total for the 1970 model year (September 1, 1969 to August 31, 1970). Thus, it was assumed that sales in the last four months of 1970 would have been equal to sales in the last four months of 1969, if no strike had occurred.

Second, it was assumed that sales in each major automobile category would have represented the same share of total industry sales during the period September–December 1970 as they did in the period January–August 1970, except for the sub-compacts which were first offered in August 1970. The categories used in the analysis were those employed in *Ward's Automotive Reports*: high-price, medium-price, regular, intermediate, compact, and sports.

For the sub-compacts, actual share of industry sales for the period September–December 1970 (6.6 per cent) was used, and actual results during this period also were used to estimate the effects of the sub-compacts on other categories' sales. Another adjustment was made in the estimates of each category's share of total domestically-produced sales to allow for the exclusion of makes for which there was not sufficient sales data.

The third assumption was that each make/model would retain the same share of its category's sales in the months September–December 1970 as it had in the corresponding period in the previous year.

As noted earlier, advertising expenditure data were available only for four-month periods in 1969 and 1970. It was estimated that advertising expenditures for each make/model during the period September–December 1970, had there been no strike, would have been equal to the expenditures during the same period in 1969. The rationale for this was that since total sales would have been approximately the same as in 1969, expenditures would also have been set at the same levels as in the preceding year.

Michael J. Baker has had several years' experience in industrial sales management in the United Kingdom and has been a lecturer in marketing at Hull College of Technology. Professor Baker received his doctoral degree from the Harvard Business School. He is currently professor of marketing at the University of Strathclyde in Scotland. Dr. Baker has recently completed a study for MSI which is described in his working paper, "The Adoption of New Industrial Products: An Exploration of the Influence of 'Management Attitudes' on Acceptance of Two Industrial Innovations."

No reductions were made to allow for introductory spending on the sub-compacts. Since these new models were intended primarily to win sales back from imports, money spent to promote them was entirely separate from, and would have had very little impact on, budgets for established products.

On the basis of these assumptions, ratios of actual-to-projected sales and actual-to-projected advertising expenditures were computed for each of the 20 models. As explained earlier, the sales ratios are for individual months—October, November, and December 1970—while the advertising ratio is for the four-month period September—December. No sales projections were made for September, because the strike began in the middle of that month.

The ratios are shown in Table 1. They show, for example, that advertising expenditures for Model A were 24 per cent higher during the period September—December 1970 than was the projection for the same period on a no-strike assumption. Sales of Model A in October were 15.5 per cent higher than

projected sales for that month, 11.5 per cent higher in November, and so on.

Table 1 also shows logarithms of the ratios of actual-to-projected advertising. These logarithms were used in the statistical analysis of the relationship between sales ratios and advertising ratios.

Was There Any Relationship?

Inspection of scatter diagrams of the sales and advertising ratios suggested that (1) there *was* some relationship between them, and (2) there appeared to be a diminishing returns phenomenon operating. Accordingly, a regression equation was used as follows: Actual/Projected Sales = a + b LOG Actual/Projected Advertising.

Estimates of the coefficients of this equation were made for each month. That is, the equation was used to express the relationship between the advertising ratio and (1) the October sales ratio, (2)

Table 1

Ratio of Actual/Projected Advertising Expenditures— and Ratios of Actual/Projected Sales

Selected Make/Model Code Number	Actual/ Projected Advertising	Logarithm of Advertising Ratio	Actual/Projected Sales		
			Oct.	Nov.	Dec.
A	1.240	+.2151	1.155	1.115	1.094
B	1.340	+.2927	1.729	1.757	1.695
C	.980	−.0202	1.056	1.078	1.461
D	1.200	+.1832	1.768	1.071	.940
E	.970	−.0305	1.037	.902	1.057
F	.700	−.3567	1.204	.831	.974
G	1.988	+.6871	.905	.775	.842
H	1.560	+.4447	1.865	1.193	.946
I	2.390	+.8713	1.094	1.095	1.129
J	.350	−1.0498	1.151	.678	.697
K	.718	−.3313	1.284	1.092	1.152
L	.243	−1.4147	1.226	.583	.616
M	.665	−.4080	1.258	1.131	1.100
N	.948	−.0534	1.245	1.204	1.069
O	.700	−.3567	1.204	1.179	1.097
P	.410	−.8916	.980	.834	.736
Q	.390	−.9416	.738	.641	.618
R	.533	−.6292	.438	.484	.479
S	.690	−.3711	1.197	1.149	.902
T	.460	−.7765	1.051	.830	.782

Expenditure Ratio Period: September—December 1970
Sales Projection Ratio Period: Monthly—October, November, and December 1970.

the November sales ratio, and (3) the December sales ratio.

The results of the analysis are presented in Table 2, and a comparison of the estimated relationship with the actual figures for December is shown in Figure 1.

The statistics shown in Table 2 indicate that there was very little relationship between changes in advertising and ratios of actual-to-projected sales in October. But the relationship with sales *is* statistically significant in both November and December. Moreover, the big improvement in the degree of statistical association from October to November and the slight further improvement from November to December are consistent with expectations based on the assumption of a time lag in consumer response to promotion.

The estimated coefficients for the regression equations are very plausible. For example, the estimated relationship for December sales implies that:

If the ratio of actual/projected advertising for a given make/model was one—i.e., if expenditures were maintained at the same level as in 1969—the predicted ratio of actual/projected sales would be 1.04. This seems reasonable, in that the absence of GM from the market should enable other companies to achieve slight sales gains if they simply maintained their prior levels of promotion.

Progressively greater increases in advertising expenditures would produce smaller and smaller increases in sales. This is, of course, implied by the form of the relationship used in the regression analysis; but beyond this, the estimated coefficient seems reasonable. It implies, for instance, that a 20 per cent increase in expenditures would lead to a sales increase of around 5 per cent,

while a 50 per cent increase in expenditures would produce a gain of about 10 per cent.

As shown in Figure 1, the form of the estimated relationship implies that reductions in advertising expenditures were associated with proportionately greater decreases in sales than the sales increases that might have been expected from expanded promotional outlays. This, too, is consistent with the beliefs of marketing researchers in the industry, as expressed in correspondence and conversations with one of the authors. Note, too, that the agreement between actual sales results and those predicted by the regression equation—as shown in Figure 1— is much better for those makes and models that reduced expenditures than it is for those that spent more. One model, for which expenditures were nearly doubled, actually had a ratio of actual/expected sales of only .84 in December (See the data for Model "G" in Table 1.).

Discussion

The results of the analysis are rather clear-cut: there *was*, indeed, a statistically significant relationship between the ratios of actual-to-projected advertising during the GM strike and ratios of actual-to-projected sales during the last two months of 1970 for the models included in the study. Moreover, the nature and extent of the relationship, as estimated from the data, was consistent with *a priori* expectations.

How should these findings be interpreted? It is well known that statistical association is not necessarily an indication of cause and effect, and that

Table 2

Results of Regression Analysis:
Relationship of Actual/Projected Advertising Expenditures
and Actual/Projected Sales

Ratio of Actual to Projected Sales in:	Constant	Coefficient of Logarithm Actual/Projected Advertising	Corrected r^2	F	Significance Level
October 1970	1.228	0.196	.08	2.63	.12
November 1970	1.048	0.275	.29	8.72	<01
December 1970	1.038	0.278	.30	9.14	<01

statistical significance is not the same thing as managerial significance.

The statistical relationship shown in Table 2 and Figure 1 can be interpreted in at least two ways.

First, it may well be that advertising does influence enough buyers, over a period of two to three months, to act as *one* of the causes of automobile purchases. As stated earlier, this in no way implies that it is the only—or even one of the primary—factors affecting sales. But, given all of the other elements of the situation, which are more or less fixed in the short run, changes in expenditure levels could, indeed, lead to measurable differences in sales.

Second, it could be that changes in advertising expenditures reflected prior changes in sales of the various makes and models. That is, the cause-and-effect relationship might run in the reverse direction. It would seem that this interpretation is less plausible in the present case than the alternative because of the way the ratios of actual to projected advertising and sales were computed.

Insofar as 1969 levels of promotion already reflected the assessments of management about the sales potential of the various makes and models, changes from those levels are free of any "feedback" mechanism from sales results to expenditure decisions. Nevertheless, it is still possible that some kind of feedback relationship existed, with changes in sales during the later part of the 1970 model year influencing the budgets set for the early part of the 1971 model year.

Although interpretation of the results is, of course, ultimately a matter of judgment, it seems that the first alternative is more reasonable than the second. Thus, we believe that the experience of the automobile industry during the GM strike indicates that advertising *does* have a short-term effect on consumer buying—at least, reductions in promotional support tend to be associated with declines in sales. Whether or not it would have been profitable to maintain 1969 levels of advertising during the strike cannot, however, be resolved without incorporating cost and margin data to which we did not have access.

References

Brown, George H. *7th Annual Conference Proceedings*. New York: Advertising Research Foundation, 1961.

Smith, Gail. How GM Measures Ad Effectiveness. *Printers' Ink*, May 14, 1965, pp. 19-29.

Ward's Automotive Reports. Various issues.

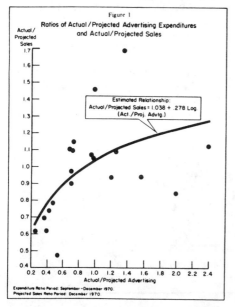

Figure 1

Ratios of Actual/Projected Advertising Expenditures and Actual/Projected Sales

Estimated Relationship:
Actual/Projected Sales = 1.038 + .278 Log. (Act./Proj. Advtg.)

Expenditure Ratio Period: September–December 1970.
Projected Sales Ratio Period: December 1970.

The research reported in this paper was carried out as a project of the Marketing Science Institute, Cambridge, Mass.

18th

ARF

ANNUAL

CONFERENCE

Nov. 13-14

New York Hilton

DARRAL G. CLARKE*

The measurement of the effect of one brand's advertising on the sales of another brand is accomplished using improved estimation procedures. The interpretation of parameter estimates is enhanced through transformation into sales-advertising elasticities. Normative implications of the model are investigated.

Sales–Advertising Cross-Elasticities and Advertising Competition

INTRODUCTION

This article focuses on the analysis of advertising competition in an industry. The approach followed is a synthesis and extension of previous studies by Bass [1], Beckwith [3], and Telser [13]. The study of advertising competition in the cigarette industry by Bass [1] is notable because the effects of the advertising of one market segment upon the sales of another market segment are explicitly expressed as sales-advertising cross-elasticities. The parameters of the structural form are specified a priori, rather than estimated, and are then tested against the reduced form estimates to ascertain the consistency of the structural form with the data. Although the a priori parameter ranges are not appreciably different than would probably be obtained through estimation, many readers have had difficulty in accepting Bass's results since the equations are underidentified. For purposes of this study, the major problem of this approach would be a severe restriction in the number of brands which could be considered in an equation system.

Beckwith's [3] study of five competing brands featured a much simpler equation system to estimate than did Bass's approach. Estimating a system of market share equations by an iterative technique, Beckwith obtained a set of statistically significant estimates of the coefficients of advertising share. Although these estimates were derived from a model which explicitly considered competition between brands, no explicit measure of the effect of the advertising of one brand on the sales of another was obtained. It is also important to note

that even the effect of a brand's advertising on its own sales cannot be compared across brands from Beckwith's results, as will be seen in this article.

Telser's study of the cigarette industry [13] was one of the earliest time series studies of advertising competition. Telser also deals with market share equations, and although his estimation procedure is not as powerful as Beckwith's, Telser obtains estimates of the sales-advertising elasticities for a brand on its own sales. Using these elasticities, it is possible to compare the effectiveness of the advertising of the various brands. Telser, however, does not develop a measure of the effect of the advertising of one brand upon the sales of another brand. The estimation procedure used extends the IZEF technique [16] used by Beckwith [3] to accommodate autocorrelated as well as cross-correlated residuals.[1]

DEFINING ADVERTISING COMPETITION

As Bauer and Greyser [2] have pointed out, one of the major obstacles to dialogue between economists and businessmen is the different meaning given to such words as "competition." To the economist, competition is closely tied to price. Telser states [14, p. xiv], ". . . a firm is said to operate in a competitive market if changes in its rate of sales exert no perceptible influence on the price of the product."[2] For the businessman, on the other hand, competition is felt to be present wherever

* Darral G. Clarke is Assistant Professor of Business Administration, Harvard Business School. He wishes to thank Professor Frank M. Bass for his assistance. Final drafts of this paper were partially supported by the Division of Research, Harvard Business School.

[1] The casual reader may wish to skip the next two technical sections and proceed to the concluding section on managerial implications.
[2] Telser is dissatisfied with this definition, but his new definition is also price based [14].

Journal of Marketing Research,
Vol. X (August 1973), 250–61

there are two differentiated, substitutable products, whether the differentiation is price, physical, or promotional.

The operational definition of competitive advertising effect used in this article generalizes the scope of competition from the price-bound concept of economics, while retaining the idea that a change in one variable must be associated with a perceptible change (or lack of it) in the other. The operational definition of advertising competition to be used is: *Brand A will be said to compete with brand B through advertising if a change in the advertising of brand A is associated with a change in the sales of brand B.* Note that this definition does not imply symmetry; the fact that brand A competes with brand B through advertising does not imply that brand B competes with brand A through advertising.

Using this definition of advertising competition implies the necessity of measuring the effect of the advertising of one brand on the sales of another brand and comparing the relative strengths of these effects from brand to brand. Hence, a unit of measurement that will not be distorted by the differing sizes of the sales and advertising expenditures of the brands is needed. Such a measure is the sales-advertising cross-elasticity, Θ_{ij}, which is defined as follows:

$$\Theta_{ij} = \frac{x_j}{q_i} \frac{dq_i}{dx_j},$$

where q_i is the sales of brand i, and x_j is the advertising of brand j. Θ_{ij} measures the percentage change in the sales of brand i for a 1 % change in brand j's advertising and is thus ideally suited for comparing the advertising effects for brands whose sales and advertising expenditures vary.

INVESTIGATED MARKET

By company request, the identity of the industry, as well as the actual data, cannot be published. Given this constraint, the major characteristics of the product and industry will be outlined in order that the reader may judge the appropriateness of the model.

The Product

The product is a low-priced, frequently purchased consumer good of the type predominantly sold in supermarkets. The product life cycle is at the stage of innovative maturity, since most of the growth in demand for the product is due to new brands. During the 8-year period being studied, unit sales of the product increased at an annual rate of about 4.5 %.

The Industry

The industry is dominated by less than 20 firms who account for over 90 % of the sales of the product. Each company offers multiple brands and product differentiation is the primary marketing strategy of the larger companies in the industry. In a related study [4] primary demand was found to be inelastic with respect to price. Price parity is maintained for generically similar brands throughout the industry. The product enjoys wide distribution in the marketplace, and a successful new brand will typically attain the same distribution level as the established brands in less than a year. All of the brands in this study had about the same level of distribution. Brand advertising is almost exclusively on a national basis. New product introduction in the industry is an important element of the marketing mix. During a 16-year period (including the study period of this article), the number of brands increased from 29 to 88.

The Data

The data which will be used in the analysis consist of the 8-year bimonthly sales and advertising histories of the total industry and the top 19 brands in the industry. Included among these brands are a number of brands which were introduced at or near the start of the study period, making the study of interactions between new brands and established brands possible.

MODEL

The brand market share equation system which will provide the basis for the study is defined as follows: Let t be measured in bimonths, and further let:

Q_t = industry sales at time t,
X_t = industry advertising at time t,
q_{it} = sales of brand i at time t,
x_{it} = advertising of brand i at time t,
f_{it} = seasonal dummy for brand i at time t,

$m_{it} = \dfrac{q_{it}}{Q_t}$, market share of brand i at time t,

$s_{it} = \dfrac{x_{it}}{X_t - x_{it}}$, "relative advertising" of brand i at time t.

Define the market share equation system as follows:

$$m_{it} = L_{0i} + L_{1i}m_{it-1}$$
$$\left. \begin{array}{l} \quad\quad + L_{2i}s_{it} + L_{3i}f_{it} + u_{it} \\ u_{it} = \rho_i u_{it-1} + \epsilon_{it}; \; |\rho_i| < 1 \end{array} \right\} \begin{array}{l} i = 1, 2, \cdots, N \\ t = 2, \cdots, T \end{array}$$

$$(1) \; E(\epsilon_{it}) = 0 \quad i = 1, 2, \cdots, N, t = 1, 2, \cdots, T$$

$$E(\epsilon_{it}, \epsilon_{jt'}) = \begin{cases} \sigma_{ij} & i, j = 1, 2, \cdots, N, \text{ and } t = t' \\ 0 & i, j = 1, 2, \cdots, N, \text{ and } t \neq t'. \end{cases}$$

ϵ_{it} are normal random variables.

Equation system (1) is a system of partial adjustment[3] brand market share equations which are contemporaneously correlated through the residuals. Such a model is treated in the econometrics literature as a system of seemingly unrelated regressions, see for example [11, 15, 16].

[3] If for each i, $\rho_i = L_{1i}$, each of these equations would be the reduced form of the distributed lag model commonly known as the Koyck model [15]. This restriction would unnecessarily complicate the estimation process.

Model (1) hypothesizes that current market share is a linear function of the previous period market share and an adjustment to current advertising share and seasonality. This is a simple and nonrestrictive hypothesis which should be easily satisfied in many industries. The simplicity of the model, however, makes it vulnerable to the effects of omitted variables. In this particular application long-term effects of advertising copy changes, slow changes in distribution level, general company policies, and so forth, necessitate the inclusion of the autocorrelated disturbance term. However, the most compelling reason for including the autocorrelated disturbance in the model is the inclusion of the lagged dependent variable in the set of independent variables.

> In the Koyck model it is well known that if the original error term is non-autocorrelated, the error term in the estimating equation will be autocorrelated. Equally well known is the fact that the ordinary least squares estimate of the coefficient of the lagged dependent variable will be inconsistent. Even if the model does not arise from a distributed lag, there is considerable evidence that the error term will still probably be autocorrelated [12, p. 329].

The inconsistency of the OLS estimates is also discussed by Maddala and Vogel and the direction of the bias is expressed by them as follows:

> ... ordinary least squares regression including a lagged dependent variable cannot distinguish between actual lagged adjustment and serial correlation in the disturbances. ... positive serial correlation in the disturbance biases the coefficient of the lagged dependent variable towards one and hence the speed of adjustment toward zero [9, p. 54].

The bias of which Maddala and Vogel speak would lead to an underestimation of the effect of advertising and an overestimation of the duration of the effect.

The disturbances of the equations are considered to be contemporaneously correlated since the dependent variables (market shares) are not independent. If all brands in the industry were included, it would be true that $\sum m_{it} = 1$. If this were the case in (1), one of two things would have to be done: (a) the effect of advertising could be assumed to be equal for each brand; (b) a constrained regression condition would have to be added to (1).

Alternative (a) is clearly a monumental assumption obviating the whole purpose of this study. Alternative (b) would further complicate an already complex estimation problem. Since only 19 brands are considered and their sum is considerably less than 1, this added complication is unnecessary. There is intuitive appeal to a loose dependence between the dependent variables which is most simply built into the model by assuming the disturbances of the equations to be contemporaneously correlated [3, 4].

A single dummy variable is used to account for seasonality in each equation, since a full set of seasonal dummies would require the addition of many variables

to the equation system. An OLS regression was run for each brand separately including the full set of seasonal factors. A single seasonal dummy was then defined for each equation approximating the effect of the five seasonals as closely as possible. A sign test on the residuals of each of the equations of Table 2 showed that seasonality was eliminated in most of the equations.

The individual brand market share equations are surprisingly rich in interpretation; most remarkably, they show that, through an extension of an approach used by Telser [13] in 1962, a complete set of sales-advertising cross-elasticities can be derived.

Omitting for the moment the seasonal and disturbance terms, the market share equation for brand i is:

$$(2) \qquad m_{it} = L_{0i} + L_{1i}m_{it-1} + L_{2i}s_{it}.$$

The derivative of the market share of brand i with respect to the advertising of brand j is seen from (2) to be:

$$(3) \qquad \frac{dm_i}{dx_j} = L_{2i}\frac{ds_i}{dx_j}.$$

Consider for the moment the left side of (3). Substitution of the definition of market share yields:

$$\frac{dm_i}{dx_j} = \frac{d}{dx_j}\left[\frac{q_i}{Q}\right] = \frac{1}{Q^2}\left[Q\frac{dq_i}{dx_j} - q_i\frac{dQ}{dx_j}\right]$$

Defining $Q = q_i + Q_i$ this becomes:

$$Q\left[\frac{dm_i}{dx_j}\right] = \frac{1}{Q}(q_i + Q_i)\frac{dq_i}{dx_j} - q_i\frac{dq_i}{dx_j} - q_i\frac{dQ_i}{dx_j}.$$

This expression further simplifies to:

$$(4) \qquad Q\frac{dm_i}{dx_j} = (1 - m_i)\frac{dq_i}{dx_j} - m_i\frac{dQ_i}{dx_j}.$$

Multiplying (4) by x_j/q_i yields:

$$x_j\left(\frac{Q}{q_i}\right)\frac{dm_i}{dx_j} = (1 - m_i)\frac{x_j}{q_i}\frac{dq_i}{dx_j} - m_i\frac{x_j}{q_i}\frac{dQ_i}{dx_j},$$

which in turn simplifies to:

$$(5) \qquad \frac{x_j}{m_i}\frac{dm_i}{dx_j} = (1 - m_i)\frac{x_j}{q_i}\frac{dq_i}{dx_j} - m_i\frac{Q_i}{q_i}\left(\frac{x_j}{Q_i}\frac{dQ_i}{dx_j}\right).$$

Let

$\gamma_{ij} = \dfrac{x_j}{m_i}\dfrac{dm_i}{dx_j}$ market share elasticity of brand i with respect to the advertising of brand j,

$\theta_{ij} = \dfrac{x_j}{q_i}\dfrac{dq_i}{dx_j}$ sales elasticity of brand i with respect to the advertising of brand j (as previously defined),

$\psi_{ij} = \dfrac{x_j}{Q_i}\dfrac{dQ_i}{dx_j}$ the sales elasticity of the industry excluding brand i's sales with respect to brand j's advertising.

Using these definitions and the fact that $Q_i/q_i = (1 - m_i)/m_i$, (5) becomes:

$$(6) \qquad \gamma_{ij} = (1 - m_i)(\theta_{ij} - \psi_{ij}).$$

Unfortunately, it is not possible to obtain an expression for Θ_{ij} and ψ_{ij} separately. It is possible to obtain bounds for Θ_{ij} and ψ_{ij}. Since ψ_{ij} is an aggregative measure of little interest in this presentation only bounds on Θ_{ij} will be derived.

Sales-Advertising Elasticity Bounds

Case I—Conservative estimate. Assume that the advertising of brand j has no effect on industry sales, i.e., $dQ/dx_j = 0$. Then any increase in sales of brand j will have to come at the expense of other brands. Then,

$$(7) \quad \frac{dm_i}{dx_j} = \frac{1}{Q^2}\left[Q\frac{dq_i}{dx_j} - q_i\frac{dQ}{dx_j}\right] = \frac{1}{Q}\frac{dq_i}{dx_j}.$$

Multiplying (7) by x_j/m_i yields:

$$\frac{x_j}{m_i}\frac{dm_i}{dx_j} = \frac{x_j}{m_i}\frac{1}{Q}\frac{dq_i}{dx_j} = \frac{x_j}{q_i}\frac{dq_i}{dx_j}.$$

Upon simplification and substitution of the elasticity definitions the conservative bound is obtained $\gamma_{ij} = \Theta_{ij}$.

Case II—Extreme estimate. If the effect of brand j's advertising is assumed to be concentrated on brand i's sales, i.e., $\psi_{ij} = 0$, the extreme effect of brand j's advertising on brand i's sales is obtained. Setting $\psi_{ij} = 0$ in (6) yields:

$$\gamma_{ij} = \Theta_{ij}(1 - m_i), \quad \text{or}$$

$$\Theta_{ij} = \frac{\gamma_{ij}}{1 - m_i}.$$

Range of Sales-Advertising Elasticity. Having thus derived conservative and extreme bounds for the sales-advertising elasticity, it becomes easier to understand the range of Θ_{ij}.

If $\Theta_{ij} < 0$, $\quad \dfrac{\gamma_{ij}}{1 - m_i} \leqq \Theta_{ij} \leqq \gamma_{ij}$.

If $\Theta_{ij} \geqq 0$, $\quad \gamma_{ij} \leqq \Theta_{ij} \leqq \dfrac{\gamma_{ij}}{1 - m_i}$.

In this particular application, Θ_{ii} is found in every case to be nonnegative and Θ_{ij} ($i \neq j$) was therefore negative. Although both bounds were computed for each brand, only the conservative bound is presented. (To find both bounds, see [4].)

The problem now remains to obtain an expression for the conservative bound γ_{ij}. From (3) and the definition of γ_{ij} it is seen that:

$$(8) \quad \gamma_{ij} = \frac{x_j}{m_i}\frac{dm_i}{dx_j} = L_{2i}\frac{x_j}{m_i}\frac{ds_i}{dx_j}.$$

For this industry the hypothesis that one brand does not respond to moderate advertising expenditure changes of another brand appears reasonable considering the large number of brands and the difficulty in obtaining accurate advertising data on competitors in less than one or two bimonths, a fact substantiated in corre-

lational studies done on the advertising histories. This "no response" hypothesis is expressed as:

$$\frac{\partial x_i}{\partial x_j} = \begin{cases} 1 \text{ if } i = j \\ 0 \text{ if } i \neq j. \end{cases}$$

Under this assumption, and defining $X = x_i + X_i$, ds_i/dx_j can be evaluated as follows:

$$\text{If } i = j \quad \frac{ds_i}{dx_j} = \frac{1}{X_i}\frac{dx_i}{dx_i} = \frac{1}{X_i}.$$

$$\text{if } i \neq j \quad \frac{ds_i}{dx_j} = \frac{-x_i}{X_i^2} = \frac{-s_i}{X_i}.$$

The conservative expressions for the sales-advertising elasticities are:

$$(9)$$
$$\frac{L_{2i}s_i}{m_i} \text{ if } i = j, \quad \text{and}$$
$$\frac{-L_{2i}s_i}{m_i}\frac{x_j}{X_i} \text{ if } i \neq j.[4]$$

For the case $i = j$, $\gamma_{ii} = L_{2i}s_i/m_i$ is the result obtained by Telser [13].

Some interesting properties of the expression for the sales-advertising elasticity, Θ_{ij}, are:

1. Θ_{ij} is a function of market share and relative advertising as well as L_{2i}. This very important property precludes drawing conclusions about advertising's effectiveness for various brands by comparing the magnitudes of the coefficients of relative advertising (L_{2i}) (or advertising share in similar equations). In brief, $L_{2i} < L_{2j}$ does not imply the advertising of brand i is more effective than the advertising of brand j either in terms of own- or cross-elasticities. (See example in applications section.)

2. Θ_{ij} is affected by the estimate of Θ_{ii} since $\Theta_{ij} = \Theta_{ii}s_ix_j/x_i$. If $L_{2i} = 0$, then $\Theta_{ij} = 0$ for all j. That is to say, if a brand's sales are not affected by its own advertising they are not affected by the advertising of other brands. If a brand's sales are not affected by its own advertising this does not preclude its advertising from affecting the sales of other brands.

3. The expression for Θ_{ij} assumes that all advertising is the same (as one would expect since only dollar expenditures are used), but the effect of advertising on all brands is not the same.

ESTIMATION

The problem now remains to obtain estimates of the parameters in (1). Ordinary least squares estimation of each brand equation is inappropriate since the set of regressors includes a lagged dependent variable and the

[4] An expression for γ_{ij}, assuming advertising response, can be found in Appendix A.

disturbances are autocorrelated. Since the equations are logically dependent, the consideration of each equation separately would be inefficient. Given the inappropriateness of OLS, a new estimation methodology was developed. This methodology is essentially a synthesis of Parks's approach to "seemingly unrelated regressions with autocorrelated disturbances" [11] and Maddala's observations about the advantages of iteration in the presence of dependence between estimates of parameters [8]. (In this case the estimate of the parameters in the market share equations are dependent upon the estimate of the autocorrelation coefficient.) This methodology was given the acronym SURWADI for "Seemingly Unrelated Regressions With Autocorrelated Disturbances (Iterative)."

SURWADI Estimation Procedure

Let
$$y_i = \begin{bmatrix} m_{2i} \\ m_{3i} \\ \vdots \\ m_{Ti} \end{bmatrix}, \quad X = \begin{bmatrix} 1 & m_{1i} & s_{2i} & f_{2i} \\ 1 & m_{2i} & s_{3i} & f_{3i} \\ \vdots & \vdots & \vdots & \vdots \\ 1 & m_{T-1i} & s_{Ti} & f_{Ti} \end{bmatrix},$$

$$\beta_i = \begin{bmatrix} L_{0i} \\ L_{1i} \\ L_{2i} \\ L_{3i} \end{bmatrix}, \quad \varepsilon_i = \begin{bmatrix} \epsilon_{2i} \\ \epsilon_{3i} \\ \vdots \\ \epsilon_{Ti} \end{bmatrix},$$

and, following Kadiyala [5], define:

$$P_i = \begin{bmatrix} (1-\rho_i^2)^{-1/2} & 0 & 0 & \cdots & 0 \\ \rho_i(1-\rho_i^2)^{-1/2} & 1 & 0 & \cdots & 0 \\ \rho_i^2(1-\rho_i^2)^{-1/2} & \rho_i & 1 & \cdots & \cdot \\ \vdots & \vdots & \vdots & & \vdots \\ \rho_i^{T-1}(1-\rho_i^2)^{-1/2} & \rho_i^{T-2} & \rho_i^{T-3} & \cdots & 1 \end{bmatrix}.$$

Then the equation for brand i in (1) can be written in matrix notation as:

$$(10) \qquad y_i = X_i\beta_i + P_i\varepsilon_i \qquad \begin{aligned} i &= 1, 2, \cdots N \\ t &= 2, 3, \cdots T \end{aligned}$$

where $u_i = P_i\varepsilon_i$ and

$$u_{1i} = (1-\rho_i^2)^{-1/2}\epsilon_{1i} \qquad t = 1, i = 1, 2, \cdots N.$$

The system (1) may be written as:

$$(11) \quad \begin{bmatrix} y_1 \\ y_2 \\ \vdots \\ y_N \end{bmatrix} = \begin{bmatrix} X_1 & 0 & \cdots & 0 \\ 0 & X_2 & \cdots & 0 \\ \vdots & & & \vdots \\ 0 & 0 & & X_N \end{bmatrix} \begin{bmatrix} \beta_1 \\ \beta_2 \\ \vdots \\ \beta_N \end{bmatrix} + \begin{bmatrix} u_1 \\ u_2 \\ \vdots \\ u_N \end{bmatrix}$$

or more compactly as:

$$Y = X\beta + U$$
$$E(U) = 0$$
$$E(UU') = \Omega.$$

Zellner [16] and Beckwith [3], among others, have considered the case $\Omega = \Sigma_c \otimes I$, where:

Σ_c is an $N \times N$ matrix expressing the covariance between disturbances in the various equations.

Σ_c is referred to as the "contemporaneous covariance matrix."

I is a $T \times T$ identity matrix.

$\otimes$ is the Kronecker or "direct" product [15, p. 303].

The conditions of (1) imply that Ω has a more complex structure, namely:

$$(12) \qquad \Omega = P(\Sigma_c \otimes I)P'.$$

If Ω is known and X is independent of u, the best linear unbiased estimator for β, $\bar{b}$ is:

$$(13) \qquad \bar{b} = (X'\Omega^{-1}X)^{-1}X'\Omega^{-1}y$$

and
$$\text{var }(\bar{b}) = (X'\Omega^{-1}X)^{-1}.$$

Because of the dependence of $\hat{\beta}$ and $\hat{\rho}$, the following iterative procedure is employed:

SURWADI Procedure

Step 1. For each i, estimate the autoregressive process. $\hat{u}_i = y_i - X_i\hat{\beta}_i$ where $\hat{\beta}_i$ is the OLS estimate of β_i in the regression (10). The parameter ρ_i is then estimated by:

$$(14) \qquad \hat{\rho}_i = \frac{\sum_{t=2}^{T} \hat{u}_{it}\hat{u}_{it-1}}{\sum_{t=2}^{T} \hat{u}_{it-1}^2}.$$

Step 2. Noting that

$$P_i^{-1} = \begin{bmatrix} (1-\rho_i^2) & 0 & 0 & \cdots & 0 \\ -\rho_i & 1 & 0 & \cdots & 0 \\ 0 & -\rho_i & 1 & \cdots & 0 \\ \vdots & \vdots & \vdots & 1 & 0 \\ 0 & 0 & 0 & -\rho_i & 1 \end{bmatrix},$$

use $\hat{\rho}_i$ to form $\hat{P}_i^{-1}$. Premultiplication of (10) by $\hat{P}_i^{-1}$ yields:

$$(15) \qquad y_i^* = X_i^*\beta_i + \varepsilon_i^* \qquad i = 1, 2, \cdots N$$

where $y_i^* = \hat{P}_i^{-1}y_i$, $X_i^* = \hat{P}_i^{-1}X_i$, $\varepsilon_i^* = \hat{P}_i^{-1}P_i\varepsilon_i$. The residuals from these transformed regressions are then used to estimate the contemporaneous covariance matrix $\hat{\Sigma}_c$. The general term in $\hat{\Sigma}_c$ is:

$$(16) \qquad s_{ij} = \frac{\hat{\varepsilon}_i'\hat{\varepsilon}_j}{T-K},$$

where $\hat{\varepsilon}_i = y_i^* - X_i^*\hat{\beta}_i$ and $\hat{\beta}_i$ is the OLS estimate of the ith transformed equation (15).

Step 3. Σ_c is an estimate of the contemporaneous covariance matrix Σ_c and the transformed equations (11) satisfy the GLS conditions, hence following (13), β is estimated:

$$\beta^* = [X^{*\prime}(\hat{\Sigma}_c^{-1} \otimes I)X^*]^{-1} X^{*\prime}(\hat{\Sigma}_c^{-1} \otimes I)y^*$$

$$(17) \qquad = [X'\hat{P}^{-1}(\hat{\Sigma}_c \otimes I)^{-1}\hat{P}^{-1}X]^{-1}$$
$$X'[\hat{P}^{-1}(\hat{\Sigma}_c \otimes I)^{-1}\hat{P}^{-1}]y.$$

Step 4. Compute the residuals from (17), i.e., $\mathbf{u}^* = \mathbf{Y} - \mathbf{X}\hat{\boldsymbol{\beta}}^*$, and from these residuals repeat steps 1 through 3. Continue the iteration until the estimates converge.

The properties of these estimates are not known, just as the small sample properties of the estimates obtained under the hypothesis that $\boldsymbol{\Omega} = \boldsymbol{\Sigma}_e \otimes \mathbf{I}$ are not known. Monte Carlo studies under this hypothesis by Kmenta and Gilbert [6] have been observed to be equivalent to the maximum likelihood estimators.

Experience with the SURWADI technique in [4] has shown the estimates to have smaller estimated standard errors than OLS estimates in most cases. Convergence of parameter estimates has been non-problematic. These observations are based on experience with more than 50 different equation systems of various specifications [4]. A Monte Carlo study of the small sample properties of this estimator is presently in the planning stages.

Estimation of the Sales Elasticities

The conservative bound for Θ_{ij}, as expressed in (9), is estimated by:

$$(18) \quad \hat{\Theta}_{ij} = \begin{bmatrix} \dfrac{1}{T-1} \displaystyle\sum_{t=2}^{T} \dfrac{\hat{L}_{2i}s_{it}}{m_{it}} & i = j \\[3ex] \dfrac{-1}{T-1} \displaystyle\sum_{t=2}^{T} \dfrac{\hat{L}_{2i}s_{it}x_{jt}}{m_{it}X_i} & i \neq j. \end{bmatrix}$$

Since the distribution of L_{2i} is unknown and $\hat{\Theta}_{ij}$ is a nonlinear function of the random variables $\hat{L}_{2i}$ and m_i, the distribution of $\hat{\Theta}_{ij}$ is unknown. The sample standard error of the estimates $\hat{\Theta}_i$, computed at each bimonth, is given in Table 3.

BRAND COMPETITION

The brands being studied can be cross-classified according to the manufacturer and their primary generic ingredient. If this is done, it will be possible to consider questions of intracompany and intercategory competition. The companies which manufacture the brands chosen are designated A through F, and the categories are numbered 1 through 7. (A more complete discussion of competition between companies and categories may be found in [4].) The distribution of the studied brands across companies and categories is shown in Table 1. Brands are named so that both the company and category can be determined (e.g., brand A34 is produced by company A, belongs to category 3 and is the fourth company A brand in the study).

The SURWADI estimates of the parameters of model (1) and the estimated standard errors of the estimates are presented in Table 2. Since the distribution of the parameter estimates is unknown, a t-test of significance is not appropriate. A heuristic definition of significance is used throughout the article: An estimate will be said to be significant if it exceeds its standard

Table 1
DISTRIBUTION OF BRANDS STUDIED

Primary ingredient categories	Companies						
	A	B	C	D	E	F	Σ
1	1	1	1				3
2	1						1
3	1	1					2
4		1	1	1		1	4
5			1				1
6	1		1			1	3
7	3	2					5
Σ	7	5	4	1		2	19

error by a factor of two or more.[5] The distribution of the estimates of the SURWADI procedure is unknown, but the small sample properties of any other estimator of (1) are also unknown (due to the presence of lagged market share). Furthermore, the OLS estimates would be biased (due to omission of the significant autocorrelation in many equations).

Using the heuristic definition, the coefficient of relative advertising is positive and significant for all brands but B11, A22, B43, A77, and B74. In no case is a coefficient of relative advertising negative and significant. Advertising is thus a significant factor in explaining the market share of most of the brands. In those cases in which the autocorrelation is low and the Kolmogorov-Smirnov test of the normality of the residuals is accepted at the .05 level (results appear in Table 2 as μ_t Normal — yes), advertising is the major factor in explaining market share behavior. In those cases in which the autocorrelation is significant, there are omitted factors affecting the market share behavior. Due to the SURWADI estimating procedure, however, the effect of these omitted variables is not attributed to advertising, as would have been the case if OLS estimation had been used. Model (1) is an acceptable description of the manner in which advertising affects market share for most of the brands. It is apparent, however, that if advertising affects the market share of brand B74, it does not affect it in the way (1) specifies. Misspecification is also a possibility for the other brands with high autocorrelation.

The limitations of Table 2 become apparent when one questions the competitive effects of advertising. Such questions as: Is the effect of the advertising of one brand on its own sales greater than the effect of another brand on its own sales? How much does the advertising of one brand affect the sales of another brand? The second question cannot be dealt with at all from Table 2 and, as will be seen, attempts to answer the first question

---

[5] By Chebychev's inequality [15, p. 63] the α-level for this test is $\alpha \leq .25$, assuming the actual distribution has a finite variance.

Table 2
RELATIVE ADVERTISING EQUATIONS

$$m_{jt} = L_{0j} + L_{1j}m_{jt-1} + L_{2j}s_{jt} + (seas) + \mu_{jt}$$
$$\mu_{jt} = \rho_j\mu_{jt-1} + \epsilon_{jt}$$

Brand	L_0	L_1	L_2	ρ	R^2	μ_t Normal?	Brand	L_0	L_1	L_2	ρ	R^2	μ_t Normal?
A11 (i)	.01987	.80161	.02918	.3545ᵃ	.7881	yes	C53 (i)	.00233	.91793	.03474	.0833	.8971	yes
(ii)		.0554	.0109				(ii)		.0366	.0090			
B11 (i)	.00245	.91272	.03007	.2195	.9379	yes	B43 (i)	.00128	.93763	.02201	-.1672	.9253	yes
(ii)		.0375	.0172				(ii)		.0368	.0117			
C11 (i)	.00043	.87925	.03760	.0687	.9462	no	C44 (i)	.02093	.58258	.03889	.5675ᵃ	.6340	yes
(ii)		.0326	.0115				(ii)		.0723	.0075			
A22 (i)	.03587	.32401	.01209	.9502ᵃ	.6608	yes	D41 (i)	.04006	.08960	.03623	.8255ᵃ	.2570	yes
(ii)		.0836	.0092				(ii)		.0804	.0083			
F41 (i)	-.00036	.89049	.07320	-.0818	.9447	no	A75 (i)	.00061	.44664	.43995	.5312ᵃ?	.8051	no
(ii)		.0383	.0162				(ii)		.0601	.0428			
A63 (i)	.00439	.85650	.02101	.3679ᵃ	.8455	yes	A76 (i)	.00164	.93648	.03840	-.1529	.9845	yes
(ii)		.0442	.0078				(ii)		.0187	.0129			
C62 (i)	-.00010	.87124	.07969	-.4555ᵃ?	.9960	no	A77 (i)	.00063	.92393	.03261	.3521ᵃ	.8461	yes
(ii)		.0128	.0053				(ii)		.0494	.0167			
F62 (i)	.00008	.93880	.06310	-.0074	.9799	no	B74 (i)	.00179	.89289	.00403	.4122ᵃ?	.9069	no
(ii)		.0176	.0057				(ii)		.0372	.0078			
A34 (i)	.00234	.79568	.11515	.4232ᵃ	.9137	yes	B75 (i)	.00126	.86681	.02873	.0832	.9579	yes
(ii)		.0409	.0201				(ii)		.0327	.0079			
B32 (i)	-.00019	.98891	.02061	-.0625	.9802	yes							
(ii)		.0214	.0085										

(Brands in the correlation matrix are in the same order as they are in the table.)
(i) Estimate
(ii) Standard deviation of estimate
ᵃ Significant at .05 level.
ᵃ? Heuristic significance only since residuals not normally distributed.

COMTEMPORANEOUS CORRELATION MATRIX

```
 1   1.000
 2    .130  1.000
 3    .335   .020  1.000
 4  - .210  - .120   .027  1.000
 5    .152   .062   .004   .019  1.000
 6  - .042  - .113  - .054   .339  - .144  1.000
 7    .014   .073  - .093   .045   .260   .056  1.000
 8  - .219   .044  - .189   .022  - .145  - .003   .160  1.000
 9  - .258  - .261  - .294  - .050  - .029   .065   .040   .138  1.000
10  - .285   .007  - .318   .210  - .067  - .037   .128   .267   .202  1.000
11    .060   .050   .381   .221  - .045   .055   .026  - .006  - .428  - .047  1.000
12  - .272  - .155  - .340  - .017   .255   .033   .058   .295   .232   .239  - .106  1.000
13    .418   .188   .254   .011   .160  - .078   .176  - .197  - .250   .133   .095  - .044  1.000
14  - .158   .025  - .295  - .390   .105  - .462  - .169   .030   .227   .114  - .077   .199  - .020  1.000
15  - .080   .069  - .012   .049  - .049   .061  - .292  - .392  - .250  - .060  - .084  - .089   .163  - .105  1.000
16    .125  - .298   .102  - .141   .101  - .124  - .131  - .280   .090  - .465  - .206  - .071  - .214   .067   .156
      1.000
17  - .104  - .226  - .115   .098   .101   .152  - .001  - .123   .291  - .142  - .017   .237  - .185   .100  - .222
      .326  1.000
18    .109   .368   .058  - .053  - .132  - .167   .199   .227   .005   .009  - .214   .016   .210   .149  - .032
    - .014  - .047  1.000
19  - .000   .099  - .085   .031   .044ᵈ  - ·¹¹2   .032   .216   .076   .051  - .135   .086   .168  - .101  - .037
    - .056   .003   .387  1.000
```

tion from Table 2 can be misleading. In order to answer these questions, it is necessary to know the sales-advertising cross-elasticities. Estimation of the sales-advertising cross-elasticities was performed as described in (18), and the conservative estimates are found in Appendix B. From Appendix B the percentage change in the sales of any brand associated with a 1 % change in the advertising of any other brand can be determined. In order to summarize the information in Appendix B, the following convention is adopted: A sales-advertising

Table 3
SUMMARY OF SALES-ADVERTISING ELASTICITIES

Brand	Θ_{ii}	Number of brands affecting			Number of brands affected		
		L	M	H	L	M	H
A11	.0486 (.007)[a]	18	0	0	9	2	7
B11	.0289 (.007)	18	0	0	15	1	2
C11	.0637 (.014)	12	3	3	17	0	1
A22	.0240 (.003)	18	0	0	12	2	4
F41	.1516 (.051)	7	5	6	16	1	1
A63	.0460 (.007)	18	0	0	11	4	3
C62	.3028 (.454)	4	4	10	17	1	0
F62	.2673 (.174)	1	1	16	17	0	1
A34	.1239 (.037)	12	4	2	17	0	1
B32	.0127 (.007)	18	0	0	17	0	1
C53	.0676 (.008)	18	0	0	11	2	5
B43	.0027 (.008)	18	0	0	15	2	1
C44	.0558 (.011)	18	0	0	12	3	3
D41	.0358 (.008)	18	0	0	15	1	2
A75	.0779 (.137)	17	1	0	16	1	1
A76	.0599 (.008)	18	0	0	13	2	3
A77	.0604 (.011)	13	4	1	16	2	0
B75	.0719 (.026)	15	3	0	15	1	2

[a] Parenthesized value is observed standard deviation of estimates of Θ_{ii}.

elasticity will be said to be:

high $\quad\quad\quad\quad |\Theta_{ij}| \geqq .1$
moderate $\quad .1 > |\Theta_{ij}| \geqq .05$
low $\quad\quad\quad .05 > |\Theta_{ij}| \geqq 0.$

Using this convention, the sales-advertising elasticities of Appendix B may be summarized as in Table 3.

Examination of the results in Tables 2 and 3 illustrate the danger of comparing the advertising effect of two brands on the basis of the estimated advertising coefficients:

Brand	$\hat{L}_{2i}$	Θ_{ii}
C62	.080	.303
A34	.115	.124!

The reason for this discrepancy is clear from the defini-

tion of Θ_{ii}: The effect of advertising is a function of the relative sizes of m_i and s_i as well as L_{2i}.

Further examination of Table 3 shows that the sales of six of the brands are affected by the advertising of at least one other brand in the "high" range. All but two of the brands exhibit a high effect on at least one other brand. A visual representation of the advertising effects in the industry is presented in the figure. Here an arrow indicates a "high" effect of the advertising of the brand at the tail of the arrow directed at the brand at the head of the arrow. The figure shows that there are numerous measurable effects of the advertising of one brand on the sales of other brands. By the definition of advertising competition presented in this article, it must be concluded that advertising is a competitive force in this industry.

As a further example of the use of sales-advertising elasticities and to gain a clearer picture of the degree of advertising competition, consider three generically similar brands A11, B11, and C11. The sales and advertising of these three brands expressed in terms of brand C11's sales and advertising, as well as the relevant cross-elasticities, are given in Table 4. Suppose first that each brand increased its advertising by 1%, and that the advertising of one brand had no effect on the sales of another brand, then the change in sales of each brand, Δq_i, would be:

$$\Delta q_i = \Theta_{ii} \frac{q_i}{x_i} \Delta x_i.$$

If, on the other hand, each brand increased its advertising by 1% and the sales-advertising elasticities are as in Table 4, the change in the sales of each brand, Δq_i^*,

BRAND COMPETITION MAP

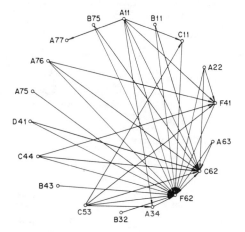

would be given by:

$$\Delta q_i{}^* = \sum_{j=1}^{3} \Theta_{ij} \frac{q_i}{x_j} \Delta x_j.$$

The resulting changes in sales under these two assumptions are given in Table 5 and indicate there is a great deal of advertising competition among the three brands. A11 is the largest selling brand in the industry, but if A11 increased advertising by 1%, its two major competitors could cut A11's expected sales *increase* from an 8.4% gain to only a 4.94% gain by increasing their own advertising 1%! From a managerial point of view, Table 5 makes it clear that, in this industry, the advertising of competing brands must be considered in setting advertising budgets. This competition has had important implications on the general level of advertising in the industry.

Market Positioning of New Brands

An analysis of the market positioning of new product categories can also be made from the figure. The brands can be divided into three groups:
1. New brands, category 6: A63, C62, F62
2. New brands, category 7: A75, A76, A77, B75
3. Older, established brands: Others.

The figure shows that the category 6 brands are highly affected by the advertising of the established brands, whereas the category 7 brands are relatively unaffected by the advertising of the established brands. This result is considered reasonable by researchers familiar with the industry.

Product Line Compatibility

A measure of the degree of cannibalization within company A's product line is also possible from the figure. Advertising of brand A11 affects the sales of brands A77 and A34. These are the only high sales-advertising effects in company A's portfolio, which implies a very nicely balanced product line. Given the large number of high effects which company A's brands impose on other companies' brands, this is quite remarkable.

NORMATIVE ADVERTISING IMPLICATIONS

Thus far, a model for measuring the effect of advertising on sales and an efficient procedure for esti-

Table 4
BRAND COMPETITION DATA

Brand	Sales	Adver-tising	Elasticities		
			A11	B11	C11
A11	17300	1070	.049	−.005	−.015
B11	5050	240	−.023	.029	−.002
C11	1000	100	−.177	−.044	.064

Table 5
SALES FOR BRANDS A11, B11, AND C11

Brand	Δq_i	$\Delta q_i{}^*$	$(\Delta q_i{}^* - \Delta q_i)/\Delta q_i \times 100$
A11	8.4	4.94	−41%
B11	1.45	.19	−87%
C11	.64	−1.57	−345%

mating the parameters of the model have been developed and the model has been applied to the study of the 19 brands. Consider now the use of the model to provide information for determining an optimal advertising policy. Only the problem of determining an optimal policy for a given period will be considered. An interesting treatment of the dynamic problem was made by Nerlove and Arrow [10]. Since most of the effects of advertising being measured last less than two years,[6] advertising will be considered as an expenditure and cost of capital considerations will be neglected.

Consider the case of maximizing the profit of a given brand without regard to budget constraints and product line considerations. If the effect of brand i on industry sales is assumed to be negligible i.e., $dQ/dx_i = 0$, an expression for the optimal advertising share for brand i is derived as follows. The response to a relative advertising expenditure s_{it} is

$$R(s_{it}) = \frac{L_{0i} + L_{2i}}{1 - L_{1i}} s_{it}.$$

$R(s_{it})$ is in terms of market share, thus the expression for the profit of brand i can be written as:

$$(19) \qquad \pi_{it} = Q_t R(s_{it}) v_i - x_{it}$$

where v_i is the gross margin of brand i. Since L_{0i} is nearly zero for all the brands, (19) is written as:

$$(20) \qquad \pi_{it} = Q_t v_t \frac{L_{2i}}{1 - L_{1i}} s_{it} - x_{it}.$$

Differentiating (20) with respect to x_i and setting the result equal to zero yields the value of s_{it} which maximizes the profit π_i. The maximum value of s_{it} is found to be associated with:

$$(21) \qquad s_{it}^* = \frac{X_t}{Q_t} \frac{1 - L_{1i}}{L_{2i} v_i} - 1.[7]$$

If the gross margin v_i were known, it would be a simple matter to compute the optimal advertising share and assess the past performance of the various brands. These data, unfortunately, are not available, but a manipulation of (21) allows a rough estimate of the

---

[6] The duration of the advertising effect n (in bimonths) is given by $n \leq \log (1 - p)/\log L_{2i}$ [7, p. 137] where p is the proportion of effect to be felt in the n periods.

[7] Since advertising share = $s_{it}/1 + s_{it}$ an expression for the optimal advertising share is inherent in (21).

Table 6
IMPUTED GROSS MARGINS

BRAND	v_i^*					v_i^*/p_i		
	BEGIN	END	MIN	MAX	MEAN	MIN	MAX	MEAN
A11	0.204	0.273	0.170	0.320	0.226	0.849	1.539	1.147
B11	0.091	0.124	0.080	0.146	0.106	0.447	0.739	0.581
C11	0.103	0.137	0.090	0.163	0.118	0.329	0.515	0.418
A22	1.688	2.319	1.473	2.693	1.930	5.477	8.653	6.803
F41	0.048	0.064	0.041	0.077	0.074	0.000	0.166	0.244
A63	0.200	0.260	0.176	0.308	0.226	0.455	0.767	0.587
C62	0.053	0.066	0.046	0.080	0.060	0.000	0.221	0.118
F62	0.032	0.041	0.027	0.049	0.036	0.100	0.176	0.138
A34	0.057	0.076	0.048	0.090	0.065	0.285	0.458	0.361
B32	0.017	0.023	0.015	0.028	0.020	0.085	0.134	0.113
C53	0.072	0.094	0.063	0.112	0.081	0.258	0.409	0.328
B43	0.090	0.119	0.079	0.141	0.102	0.420	0.621	0.508
C44	0.334	0.452	0.295	0.526	0.378	1.418	2.268	1.804
D41	0.805	1.061	0.694	1.262	0.903	3.403	5.704	4.475
A75	0.041	0.055	0.036	0.065	0.056	0.118	0.197	0.137
A76	0.053	0.069	0.045	0.081	0.059	0.188	0.303	0.238
A77	0.076	0.099	0.065	0.117	0.085	0.245	0.406	0.310
B75	0.143	0.198	0.121	0.237	0.167	0.424	0.775	0.641

optimality of a brand's advertising expenditures. Equation (21) is a relationship which is true if the brand is advertising optimally and if $dQ/dx_i = 0$. Assuming optimality of brand advertising, (21) can be solved for the gross margin. This value will be denoted by v_i^* and called the "imputed gross margin." Comparison of the imputed gross margin with the selling price will ow a rough test of the hypothesis that the brand is ing optimally advertised. Solving (21) for v_i^* yields:

$$(22) \qquad v_i^* = \frac{X_t}{Q_t} \frac{1 - L_{1i}}{L_{2i}(1 + s_i^*)}.$$

The imputed gross margins for the brands are presented in Table 6. To enable observation of trends in advertising expenditure levels, Table 6 presents v_i^* at the beginning and at the end of the study period as well as the mean value. It appears from other sources that the ross margin in this industry is between 30% and 50% f the selling price. If the ratio of imputed gross margin o selling price is compared with this range, the advertising expenditure level can be classified as under- or overadvertised. This information is summarized in Table 7 and reveals an interesting trend. At the beginning of the study period only four brands were overadvertised, while by the end of the study period eight brands were overadvertised. The advertising competition observed earlier in this industry is almost surely a contributing cause of this trend. Brands, perceiving a slipping market share and increased advertising by competitors, in turn increased their own advertising. While this change is too slow to be a factor in model (1), it has nevertheless had implications in determining the industry level of advertising. Evidence of this trend is the fact that the advertising to sales ratio nearly doubled during the study period. The strong relation-

ship between market share and advertising share observed in Table 3 forced management to increase advertising expenditures to maintain advertising share. The level of these increases has for a number of brands passed the point of diminishing returns. It is also indicative of the increased pressure to advertise that no brand had reduced its level of advertising commitment over the study period. Only three brands had advertising expenditures which averaged in the rough optimal range.

CONCLUSION

The major goal of this study has been to measure the competitive effects of advertising in an industry. The first step in this endeavor was the definition of advertising competition in operational terms. Two brands were said to compete through advertising if a change in the advertising of one brand was accompanied by a measurable change in the sales of the other brand. The sales-advertising elasticity was found to be a measure of advertising effect consistent with the definition.

A reasonable model was formulated on the basis of the nature of the industry and the restrictions imposed by data availability. An expression for the sales-advertising elasticity was then derived from the model. Following this derivation an iterative extension of the Seemingly Unrelated Regressions With Autocorrelated Disturbance: (SURWADI) procedure developed by Parks [11] was discussed. It was observed that the estimated variances of the SURWADI estimates in most applications were less than the estimated OLS estimate variances. Convergence of the SURWADI procedure was found to be nonproblematic in every equation system considered.

Table 7
ADVERTISING LEVEL OF BRANDS

Brand	Begin	End	Mean
A11	+	+	+
B11	R	+	+
C11	R	+	R
A22	+	+	+
F41	−	−	−
A63	R	+	+
C62	−	−	−
F62	−	−	−
A34	−	R	R
B32	−	−	−
C53	−	R	R
B43	R	+	+
C44	+	+	+
D41	+	+	+
A75	−	−	−
A76	−	R	−
A77	−	R	−
B75	R	+	+

+ = Overadvertised.
− = Underadvertised.
R = About right.

Application of the model to a collection of brands and managerial applications of the model including the optimal allocation of advertising were discussed. Examination of the cross-elasticities indicated that several brands in the industry are very sensitive to the advertising of other brands. Through the use of the imputed gross margins, computed assuming optimal advertising during the time period being studied, the industry changed from a generally underadvertised state to a generally overadvertised state. In summary, considerable empirical evidence has been presented showing that advertising influences not only the sales of the advertising brand but also the sales of other brands.

APPENDIX A

An expression for the cross-elasticities can be obtained if one hypothesizes a responsive model of advertising policy on the part of the brands.

Employing the well-known formula for the total derivative and (8) yields:

$$(23) \qquad \gamma_{ij} = L_{2i} \frac{x_j}{m_i} \sum_{k=1}^{N} \frac{\partial s_i}{\partial x_k} \frac{\partial x_k}{\partial x_j}.$$

In order to interpret (23), first consider $\partial s_i / \partial x_k$. Let $X = x_i + X_i$, then:

$$\frac{\partial s_i}{\partial x_k} = \frac{\partial}{\partial x_k}\left(\frac{x_i}{X_i}\right) = \frac{1}{X_i^2}\left[X_i \frac{\partial x_i}{\partial x_k} - x_i \frac{\partial X_i}{\partial x_k}\right]$$

$$= \frac{1}{X_i}\left[\frac{\partial x_i}{\partial x_k} - s_i \xi_{ik}\right],$$

where:

$$\xi_{ik} = \sum_{\substack{m=1 \\ m \neq i}}^{N} \frac{\partial x_m}{\partial x_k}.$$

Substituting this result into (23) produces a general expression for γ_{ij}, namely:

$$(24) \qquad \gamma_{ij} = L_{2i} \frac{x_j}{m_i} \sum_{k=1}^{N}\left[\frac{1}{X_i} \frac{\partial x_k}{\partial x_j}\left(\frac{\partial x_j}{\partial x_k} - s_i \xi_{ik}\right)\right].$$

The successful completion of this estimate of sales-advertising cross-elasticities requires an advertising response function. Since cross-correlations between brand advertising histories were low this approach was not pursued in this study.

Appendix B
SALES-ADVERTISING ELASTICITIES: TOP BRANDS
LOWER BOUND FOR SALES ADVERTISING ELASTICITY

1	.04860	−.00509	−.00150	−.01195	−.00357	−.00916
	−.00464	−.00382	−.00291	−.00196	−.01538	−.00433
	−.00905	−.00529	−.00334	−.00852	−.00311	−.00358
	−.00566					
2	−.02336	.02894	−.00179	−.01426	−.00405	−.01110
	−.00595	−.00451	−.00338	−.00221	−.01839	−.00516
	−.01068	−.00630	−.00398	−.01033	−.00375	−.00426
	−.00648					
3	−.17676	−.04426	.06369	−.10728	−.03146	−.08277
	−.04438	−.03559	−.02463	−.01651	−.13774	−.03809
	−.08043	−.04832	−.02993	−.07787	−.02836	−.03240
	−.04818					
4	−.01022	−.00277	−.00081	.02400	−.00194	−.00477
	−.00220	−.00196	−.00164	−.00108	−.00801	−.00233
	−.00476	−.00279	−.00175	−.00436	−.00162	−.00189
	−.00316					
5	−.24857	−.06460	−.01825	−.14659	.15146	−.11068
	−.05034	−.04588	−.03860	−.02626	−.18801	−.05323
	−.11211	−.06820	−.04099	−.10392	−.03865	−.04548
	−.07349					
6	−.03614	−.00982	−.00286	−.02223	−.00683	.04600
	−.00793	−.00703	−.00580	−.00379	−.02852	−.00817
	−.01670	−.00982	−.00624	−.01558	−.00580	−.00675
	−.01109					
7	−.49228	−.17032	−.03735	−.30620	−.09508	−.19422
	.30275	−.16901	−.02637	−.04572	−.35630	−.09182
	−.23178	−.13639	−.06715	−.19062	−.07343	−.08583
	−.11518					
8	−.61840	−.25622	−.10383	−.49050	−.15503	−.33995
	−.01225	.26727	−.19992	−.13624	−.50569	−.20761
	−.34359	−.17639	−.12731	−.19947	−.08479	−.11901
	−.39506					
9	−.13650	−.03273	−.00984	−.08229	−.02238	−.06423
	−.03802	−.02654	.12390	−.01178	.10541	−.02887
	−.06233	−.03646	−.02273	−.06119	−.02169	.02463
	−.03390					

Appendix B (Continued)

10	−.03108	−.00789	−.00236	−.01890	−.00543	−.01469
	−.00782	−.00596	−.00447	.01273	−.02428	−.00679
	−.01419	−.00836	−.00528	−.01369	−.00497	−.00569
	−.00866					
11	−.03206	−.00846	−.00245	−.01955	−.00597	−.01495
	−.00734	−.00638	−.00484	−.00324	.06762	−.00713
	−.01482	−.00875	−.00545	−.01382	−.00510	−.00594
	−.00938					
12	−.00307	−.00080	−.00023	−.00188	−.00054	−.00145
	−.00075	−.00059	−.00045	−.00030	−.00241	.00268
	−.00141	−.00082	−.00052	−.00135	−.00049	−.00056
	−.00087					
13	−.03060	−.00804	−.00236	−.01865	−.00560	−.01431
	−.00706	−.00591	−.00466	−.00306	−.02397	−.00682
	.05579	−.00829	−.00523	−.01324	−.00487	−.00561
	−.00896					
14	−.01486	−.00389	−.00114	−.00909	−.00273	−.00696
	−.00348	−.00292	−.00224	−.00149	−.01164	−.00330
	−.00683	.03575	−.00254	−.00647	−.00237	−.00274
	−.00432					
15	−.06190	−.01673	−.00491	−.03819	−.01162	−.02934
	−.01386	−.01193	−.00996	−.00653	−.04877	−.01406
	−.02859	−.01689	.07789	−.02681	−.00995	−.01148
	−.01911					
16	−.02756	−.00767	−.00226	−.01709	−.00537	−.01298
	−.00559	−.00515	−.00476	−.00308	−.02172	−.00638
	−.01279	−.00754	−.00482	.05990	−.00442	−.00513
	−.00904					
17	−.11264	−.03187	−.00934	−.07015	−.02203	−.05355
	−.02303	−.02086	−.01965	−.01259	−.08929	−.02654
	−.05268	−.03058	−.01971	−.04817	.06039	−.02105
	−.03697					
18	−.00032	−.00008	−.00002	−.00019	−.00005	−.00015
	−.00008	−.00006	−.00005	−.00003	−.00025	−.00007
	−.00014	−.00009	−.00005	−.00014	−.00005	.00016
	−.00009					
19	−.09022	−.02193	−.00666	−.05464	−.01497	−.04301
	−.02489	−.01704	−.01212	−.00779	−.07089	−.01949
	−.04112	−.02413	−.01534	−.04080	−.01454	−.01613
	.07187					

(Brands are in the same order as in Table 2.)

REFERENCES

1. Bass, Frank M. "A Simultaneous Equation Regression Study of Advertising and Sales of Cigarettes," *Journal of Marketing Research*, 6 (August 1969), 291–300.
2. Bauer, Raymond A. and Stephen A. Greyser. "The Dialogue That Never Happens," *Harvard Business Review*, 45 (November–December 1967), 2–12.
3. Beckwith, Neil E. "Multivariate Analysis of Sales Responses of Competing Brands to Advertising," *Journal of Marketing Research*, 9 (May 1972), 168–76.
4. Clarke, Darral G. "An Empirical Investigation of Advertising Competition," unpublished doctoral dissertation, Purdue University, 1972.
5. Kadiyala, K. Rao. "A Transformation Used to Circumvent the Problem of Autocorrelation," *Econometrica*, 36 (January 1968), 93–96.
6. Kmenta, Jay and Roy F. Gilbert. "Small Sample Properties of Alternative Estimators of Seemingly Unrelated Regressions," *Journal of the American Statistical Association*, 63 (December 1968), 1180–200.
7. Kotler, Phillip. *Marketing Decision-Making: A Model Building Approach*. New York: Holt, Rinehart and Winston, 1971.
8. Maddala, G. S. "Generalized Least Squares with an Estimated Variance/Covariance Matrix," *Econometrica*, 39 (January 1971), 23–33.
9. ——— and R. C. Vogel. "Estimating Lagged Relationships in Corporate Demand for Liquid Assets," *Review of Economics and Statistics*, 51 (February 1969), 53–61.
10. Nerlove, Marc and Kenneth Arrow. "Optimal Advertising Under Dynamic Conditions," *Economica*, 29 (May 1962), 129–42.
11. Parks, Richard W. "Efficient Estimation of a System of Regression Equations When the Disturbances are Both Serially and Contemporaneously Correlated," *Journal of the American Statistical Association*, 62 (June 1967), 500–9.
12. Taylor, L. D. and T. A. Wilson. "Three Pass Least Squares: A Method for Estimating Models with a Lagged Dependent Variable," *Review of Economics and Statistics*, 46 (November 1964), 329–46.
13. Telser, Lester G. "Advertising and Cigarettes," *Journal of Political Economy*, 70 (October 1962), 471–99.
14. ———. *Competition, Collusion and Game Theory*. Chicago: Aldine-Atherton, 1972.
15. Theil, Henri. *Principles of Econometrics*. New York: John Wiley and Sons, 1971.
16. Zellner, Arnold. "An Efficient Method of Estimating Seemingly Unrelated Regressions and Tests for Aggregation Bias," *Journal of the American Statistical Association*, 57 (June 1962), 348–68.

FRANKLIN S. HOUSTON and DOYLE L. WEISS*

This article reports the findings of an empirical investigation into the movement of competitive market share. Palda's cumulative advertising model is adapted to include a price variable, and the analysis is extended to a multibrand market. The statistical methodology employed in the investigation overtly recognizes the competitive interdependence of the brands studied and exploits this interdependence in its estimation procedures.

An Analysis of Competitive Market Behavior

INTRODUCTION

The importance of interbrand competition in determining the structure of product markets is well recognized by scholars working in the marketing area. Indeed, lucid discussions on the characteristics and proper implementation of "competitive (or adaptive) marketing strategies" can be found in almost any contemporary marketing management textbook. In few instances, however, have the competitive realities of the marketplace been recognized by empirical research on consumer choice and brand behavior. For notable and recent exceptions, see [2, 4].

This lack of emphasis on the competitive dimensions of marketplace behavior has not occurred without good reason. In many instances, competitive data have not been available to researchers. In other cases, the statistical methodology employed has caused competitive data series to be analyzed as if they were separate and independently generated series. The purpose of this article is to report the findings of research which attempts to overcome these limitations.

The models developed and analyzed below employ a Koyck [6] type distributed lag relationship between sales and the effects of advertising. Although this form of the relationship has been frequently analyzed by others, the models and analysis presented here extend the previous results in at least two dimensions: (1) they incorporate the effects of price along with that of advertising, and (2) the analytic structure used allows the competitive effect of multiple brands to be analyzed.

*Franklin S. Houston is Assistant Professor of Marketing, University of Missouri-St. Louis; Doyle L. Weiss is Visiting Professor of Marketing, University of British Columbia.

PRODUCT CLASS AND DATA SOURCES

The product studied is a frequently purchased, low cost, branded food item distributed in grocery stores and delicatessens. It is an item which is complementary to main dishes and is used as a sauce or seasoning ingredient. The market is dominated by three nationally advertised and distributed brands which, for purposes of this study, are treated as a three-brand market.

The data supporting the subsequent analysis have been compiled for the Chicago metropolitan market by the Family Survey Bureau of Chicago, Illinois and the marketing policy group of one of the principal firms in the industry. The purchase and price data analyzed represent the purchasing activities of 899 panel families purchasing the product across a 4-year period. The advertising expenditure data are estimates of total newspaper, magazine, radio, network television, and spot television advertising activities for the three national brands in the Chicago market for the same four-year period.

The data have been aggregated to provide 24 bimonthly observations of price, advertising expenditures, and volume for each of the 3 national brands (i.e., a total of 72 observations). Figures 1 through 3 illustrate the movement of the three variables over time.

THE ANALYTIC STRUCTURE

In the subsequent analysis, a model relating market share to price and advertising expenditures is fitted to the data described in the previous section. The model postulates a current period effect from price and advertising expenditures as well as a lagged effect from prior advertising expenditures. The lagged advertising relationship is hypothesized to be one of

Journal of Marketing Research
Vol. XI (May 1974), 151-5

Figure 1
MARKET SHARES

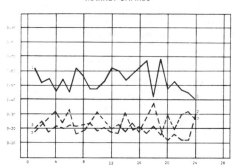

Figure 2
AVERAGE PRICE
(DOLLARS/OUNCE)

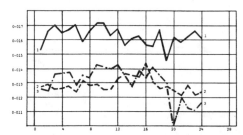

constant exponential decay, such as discussed by Koyck [6].

The reasons for using the Koyck transformation are straightforward. First, the product class is old and well established. Advertising expenditures are directed toward securing market share rather than focused on building primary demand. Second, the periodicity of the data and the rather long average interpurchase time (two months) will tend to obscure a more complex lag, if it does exist. Third and finally, the Koyck hypothesis is intuitively appealing and results in a reduced form which can be conveniently manipulated and tested.

The Model Development

The model is similar to Palda's [9] hypothesized model in that it also postulates a cumulative advertising function. It differs, however, in two respects:

1. Palda's model incorporated a single managerial decision variable—advertising, and

Figure 3
ADVERTISING EXPENDITURES
(IN THOUSANDS OF DOLLARS)

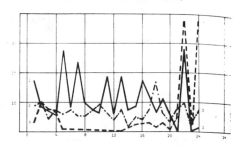

2. Palda's data base consisted of a single brand within a unique product class.

The structural model which hypothesizes a current price effect and cumulative advertising effect is:[1]

$$S_{B,t} = b_{B,0} + b_{B,1}\left[\frac{P_{B,t}}{\bar{P}_t}\right] + b_{B,2}\left[\frac{A_{B,t}}{\bar{A}_t}\right]$$

$$(1) \qquad + b_{B,2} \cdot \lambda_B \left[\frac{A_{B,t-1}}{\bar{A}_{t-1}}\right] + b_{B,2} \cdot \lambda_B^2 \left[\frac{A_{B,t-2}}{\bar{A}_{t-2}}\right]$$

$$+ \ldots + \epsilon_t$$

where:

$S_{B,t}$ = market share for brand B at time t,
$P_{B,t}$ = price ($\$/oz.$) for brand B at time t,
$A_{B,t}$ = advertising expenditures (thousands of dollars) for brand B at time t,
$\bar{P}_t$ = average price (weighted by volume) for period t,
$\bar{A}_t$ = $1/3 \Sigma_B A_{Bt}$,
ϵ_t = stochastic error term,
B = 1, 2, 3,
and $0 \leq \lambda \leq 1$.

When this equation is lagged one period, multiplied by λ_B, and subtracted from (1), the resulting equation is:

$$S_{B,t} = a_{B,0} + a_{B,1}\left[\frac{P_{B,t}}{\bar{P}_t}\right] + a_{B,2}\left[\frac{A_{B,t}}{\bar{A}_t}\right]$$

$$(2) \qquad + a_{B,3}\left[\frac{P_{B,t-1}}{\bar{P}_{t-1}}\right] + \lambda_B S_{B,t-1} + U_t$$

where:

---

[1] An alternative structure could contain cumulative effects of both price and advertising. Such a model was examined by Lambin [7] for consumer durables. Lambin's model, however, implies that the pricing and advertising effects decay at an equal rate.

$$a_{B,0} = b_{B,0}(1 - \lambda)$$
$$a_{B,1} = b_{B,1}$$
$$a_{B,2} = b_{B,2}$$
$$a_{B,3} = -b_{B,1}\lambda_B, \text{ and}$$
$$U_t = \epsilon_t - \lambda\epsilon_{t-1}.$$

The definitions for the variables in (2) remain as defined previously. The derivation of the multiplicative form of the model is similar to (2) with the variables defined as natural logarithms.[2]

Implications for Model Testing

If model (2) is a reasonable approximation of the true underlying structure of the market being studied, several conditions implied by its form and economic theory must be satisfied. These conditions are:

1. The price coefficient ($a_{B,1}$) for the model must be less than zero. This condition stems from the assumption that demand curves slope downward from left to right.
2. The advertising decay constants (λ_B) must be between zero and one. This condition results from the choice of a Koyck form for the lag relationship.
3. The complex coefficient for lagged price ($a_{B,3}$) must be greater than zero. This condition is implied by the form of the model and the two conditions immediately above.
4. The coefficient for current advertising expenditures ($a_{B,2}$) must be greater than zero.
5. Finally, because of the lagged structure $a_{B,3}/a_{B,1} = -\lambda_B$.

In summary, the conditions are:

(3) $a_{B,1} \leq 0,$

(4) $0 \leq \lambda_B \leq 1,$

(5) $a_{B,3} \geq 0,$

(6) $a_{B,2} \geq 0,$ and

(7) $a_{B,3}/a_{B,1} = -\lambda_B.$

Statistical Methodology

To explain the structure of existing interbrand competition, two forms of the model, one additive and one multiplicative, were developed and estimated. Initially the forms were estimated using ordinary least squares and a single equation to represent the three-brand market. Subsequent testing of the OLS results rejected the hypothesis that the coefficients of the model were equal across brands [3]. As a result, the analysis which follows postulates a separate equation for each of the three brands examined.

Joint generalized least squares (JT/GLS)[3] was used

to estimate the parameters for the multiple equation models. Estimation of the three equation (brand) models by means of ordinary least squares would implicitly assume that each brand's movement is independent of the remaining brands. The JT/GLS estimator, which recognizes and exploits any contemporaneous correlations existing across regression equations, was chosen for two reasons:

1. Because market shares were chosen as the dependent variables, an interdependent relationship across the three brands was assured.
2. The competitive nature of this market and its lack of primary growth also assure an interdependent relationship across the brands.

In addition, the explicit recognition of serial correlation is essential if one makes the standard assumptions about the behavior of the disturbance term in (1). This results because the Koyck transformation necessarily introduces serial correlation into the reduced form (2). Thus an adjustment for autocorrelation was incorporated, and the results in Table 1 were estimated by an iterative JT/GLS procedure which corrects for serial correlation.[4]

Finally, some of the parameter estimates for Brands 2 and 3, as presented in Table 1, are not significantly different from zero.[5] As a result, the estimation procedures were repeated with those parameters constrained to equal zero and a_{13} constrained to equal the first estimates of $a_{11} \cdot \lambda_1$ because of (7). These results are presented in Table 2.

ANALYSIS AND DISCUSSION

In general, the pattern of results obtained for the multiplicative and additive models are much the same, although the results for the multiplicative model are slightly stronger than those of the additive model. Therefore, most of the following interpretations and inferences could also be made for the additive structure, although they have been restricted to the multiplicative model in the interests of space and repetition.

Implications for Cumulative Advertising Effectiveness

The concept of a lagged or cumulative effectiveness for advertising expenditures is generally accepted by most marketing scholars, and some supporting empirical research has been reported [1, 2, 9]. The findings

---

[2]Note that a unit translation is made on the relative advertising variable prior to taking logs.

[3]JT/GLS, sometimes referred to as ZEF (Zellner's Efficient Estimator) and "seemingly unrelated regression," is more fully described in [2, 11, 12]. The name JT/GLS is due to Theil.

[4]The method employed was outlined in [5, 10]. The autocorrelation coefficients (ρ_B) were estimated from the residuals after four JT/GLS iterations. After correcting for $\hat{\rho}_B$, a new JT/GLS was performed. The computer program which accomplishes Zellner's procedure was written by Professor Houston.

[5]The JT/GLS estimators are asymptotically efficient and their small sample properties are generally stable. For some discussion and evidence of these properties, see [5].

Table 1
THREE COMPETING BRANDS—JOINT GLS WITH SERIAL CORRELATION CORRECTION ESTIMATES OF PARAMETERS

| | Parameter estimates | | "t" ratios | |
Variable	Additive	Multi-plicative	Additive	Multi-plicative
Brand 1				
Price (a_{11})	−1.157	−2.473	−8.45	−8.49
Lagged market share (λ_1)	.276	.496	1.31	2.11
Advertising (a_{12})	.016	.086	1.60	2.00
Lagged price (a_{13})	.566	1.894	1.71	2.39
Intercept	1.003	−.337	2.03	−3.97
Brand 2				
Price (a_{21})	−.486	−2.068	−1.46	−1.70
Lagged market share (λ_2)	.264	.256	1.20	1.14
Advertising (a_{22})	.042	.396	1.91	2.02
Lagged price (a_{23})	.434	1.958	1.26	1.53
Intercept (a_{20})	.147	−1.330	.46	−2.67
Brand 3				
Price (a_{31})	−.965	−3.670	−4.75	−4.24
Lagged market share (λ_3)	.109	−.031	.41	−.10
Advertising (a_{32})	.000	−.019	.02	−.13
Lagged price (a_{33})	.320	.679	.92	.45
Intercept (a_{30})	.768	−1.946	2.56	−3.73

reported in this article generally support earlier conclusions and present some additional evidence of a lagged relationship between market share and advertising expenditures. Unfortunately, however, the evidence is not strong and consistent for all three brands. The results for Brand 1 are the strongest and most consistent in this respect.

Examination of the results for Brand 1 (Table 1) shows all of the estimated parameters to be significant and of the proper sign. In addition, the hypothesis that $0 \leq \lambda_1 \leq 1$ can also be accepted for Brand 1.[6] As a result, the "a priori" conditions (3), (4), (5), and (6) have been met. Finally, the results in Table 2 show that imposing condition (7) caused little change in Brand 1's estimated parameters.

The estimates for Brands 2 and 3 (Table 1), however, are totally different from those for Brand 1. For Brand 2, the current period advertising coefficient ($a_{2,2}$) and the intercept term are significantly different from zero, while the price coefficient ($a_{2,1}$) is only marginally significant. For Brand 3, only the price coefficient and the intercept term are significant.

We would interpret the results to mean that Brands 2 and 3 have not been as successful as Brand 1 in creating a cumulative advertising effect. In fact, it

---

[6] A one-tailed test is appropriate for testing the coefficients of price, advertising, and lagged price. A two-tailed test is necessary for the coefficient of lagged market share, however, because of the restriction $0 \leq \lambda \leq 1$.

would appear that, not only is there no lagged effect from the advertising expenditures of Brands 2 and 3, but there appears to be no measurable effect from Brand 3's current advertising expenditures. Examination of the constrained estimates of Table 2 generally supports these observations.

Implications For Additional Research

Our findings, in general, support the theory that there can be cumulative time effects from a firm's advertising efforts. In addition, the differences in the findings among the brands suggest that marketing variables can play unique roles for individual brands. In the case of Brand 1, the cumulative effects of advertising are much stronger than they are for Brands 2 and 3. This would appear to indicate that Brand 1's management has been successful in developing an advertising associated stockpile of goodwill and the resulting "brand loyal" buyers.

Brand 2 has not been as effective as Brand 1 in stockpiling the effects of advertising. The rate of decay of Brand 2's advertising effectiveness is approximately 1.9 times that of Brand 1 and appears to be only marginally significant (Table 1). This conclusion is further substantiated by the effects from Brand 2's current advertising efforts as measured by the coefficient of current advertising expenditures. Brand 2 appears to receive more current period effect from its advertising expenditures than do either Brands 1 or 2.

Brand 3 appears to derive support for its sales mostly from its pricing policy. Examination of the data series shows Brand 3 to be the low-priced brand and to have the weakest market share position. Moreover,

Table 2
THREE COMPETING BRANDS— CONSTRAINED JOINT GLS WITH SERIAL CORRELATION CORRECTION ESTIMATES OF PARAMETERS

| | Parameter estimates | | "t" ratios | |
Variable	Additive	Multi-plicative	Additive	Multi-plicative
Brand 1				
Price (a_{11})	−1.094	−2.336	−8.10	−8.33
Lagged market share (λ_1)	.093	.276	1.23	3.55
Advertising (a_{12})	.018	.091	2.05	2.67
Lagged price (a_{13})	.319[a]	1.227[a]		
Intercept (a_{10})	1.319	−.424	8.27	−5.22
Brand 2				
Price (a_{21})	−.276	−1.404	−.95	−1.28
Advertising (a_{22})	.050	.416	2.38	2.28
Intercept (a_{20})	.441	−1.879	1.66	−13.48
Brand 3				
Price (a_{31})	−.726	−2.916	−5.92	−5.52
Intercept (a_{30})	.863	−1.895	7.91	−26.99

[a] Constrained estimate: $-\hat{a}_{11} \cdot \hat{\lambda}_1 = a_{13}$, $\hat{a}_{11}$ and $\hat{\lambda}_1$ from Table 1.

Brand 3 engaged in extensive product innovation toward the end of the data series time period. These efforts have recently been judged by *Business Week* [8] to be one of the ten largest marketing disasters of te 1960's decade. In such instances, an effective advertising program can only hasten sales erosion.

If the above inferences with respect to marketing policy effectiveness are true, a micro examination of the panel data from which our sample was aggregated should support them. For instance, one would expect to find different prices being paid by repeat buyers and buyers who are changing brands. Currently, the data are being assembled to test these and other implications.

CONCLUSION

This article has reported the results of an investigation into the effects of advertising expenditures on sales. In general, it has found some evidence to further support Palda's [9] and Bass and Clarke's [1] conclusions that the influences of advertising effects on sales are cumulative over time. These findings extend those of Palda's (and to a lesser degree, those of Bass and Clarke) by extending the analysis to a more competitive product class and including the effects of the price variable.

REFERENCES

1. Bass, Frank M. and D. G. Clarke. "Testing Distributed Lag Models of Advertising Effect," *Journal of Marketing Research*, 9 (August 1972), 298-308.

2. Beckwith, Neil E. "Multivariate Analysis of Sales Responses of Competing Brands to Advertising," *Journal of Marketing Research*, 9 (May 1972), 168-76.

3. Chow, Gregory C. "Tests of Equality Between Sets of Coefficients in Two Linear Regressions," *Econometrica*, 28 (July 1960), 591-605.

4. Houston, Frank S. "Competitive Brand Behavior: An Analysis of Market Share Retention, Relative Price and Relative Advertising in Aggregate Demand Models," unpublished doctoral dissertation, Purdue University, 1972.

5. Kmenta, J. and R. F. Gilbert. "Estimation of Seemingly Unrelated Regressions with Autoregressive Disturbances," *Journal of the American Statistical Association*, 65 (March 1970), 186-97.

6. Koyck, L. M. *Distributed Lags and Investment Analysis.* Amsterdam: North Holland Publishing, 1954.

7. Lambin, J. "Optimal Allocation of Competitive Marketing Efforts: An Empirical Study," *Journal of Business*, 43 (October 1970), 468-84.

8. "New Products: The Push is on Marketing," *Business Week*, 2218 (March 4, 1972), 77.

9. Palda, Kristian S. *The Measurement of Cumulative Advertising Effects.* Englewood Cliffs, N. J.: Prentice-Hall, 1964.

10. Parks, Richard W. "Efficient Estimation of a System of Regression Equations When Disturbances Are Both Serially and Contemporaneously Correlated," *Journal of the American Statistical Association*, 62 (June 1965), 500-9.

11. Theil, Henri. *Principles of Econometrics.* New York: John Wiley & Sons, 1971.

12. Zellner, Arnold. "An Efficient Method of Estimating Seemingly Unrelated Regression and Tests for Aggregation Bias," *Journal of the American Statistical Association*, 57 (June 1962), 348-68.

DAN HORSKY*

The purpose of this study is to formulate and test a model which can assess the impact of advertising on sales, rather than just produce sales forecasts. The proposed model, which incorporates many of the models and concepts previously suggested, is found through predictive tests to be consistent with empirical evidence.

Market Share Response to Advertising: An Example of Theory Testing

INTRODUCTION

The procedures followed in formulating and testing a model depend largely on its intended use. Managers commonly use models as forecasting tools, when forecasts about the phenomenon being studied are of interest, and as bases for management control systems, when controlling the phenomenon is the objective. When forecasting is the objective, almost any model which fits the data well and produces good forecasts can be accepted, even if the model is wrong in that it does not really represent the underlying process. However, when control is of interest, only a model (theory) which is not wrong can be expected to assess correctly the impact of changes in the control variables. Thus, in this case a high "goodness-of-fit" measure does not suffice; predictive tests aimed at rejecting wrong models must be applied. A case in point is the sales response to advertising relationship.

Because large sums of money are expended each year on advertising, the impact of advertising on sales is of major concern to most firms. In fact, the problem faced by the firm is twofold, first to establish the effectiveness of its advertising, and second to determine the optimal advertising policy to employ. Thus, a relevant model cannot just render sales forecasts, but must aid in the control of the sales process and serve as the basis for the determination of an optimal advertising policy. Use of a wrong model for this purpose may result in large errors on the part of management.[1]

Numerous empirical studies have been aimed at measuring the effects of advertising on sales and several distinct directions are evident. Palda [21] provided empirical support for the so-called carryover effects of advertising. He applied the Koyck [16] distributed lag structure, which is based on a geometric decay, to the analysis of yearly data. Bass and Clarke [6] tested several different lag structures and concluded that a nonmonotonic lag structure is more appropriate in the case of monthly data. These two studies represent the single equation approach. A multiple equation approach was taken by Bass [4], who addressed the notion of a two-way influence in the relation between advertising and sales by applying a simultaneous-equations regression approach. A different issue, the interaction between competing brands within the same industry, was addressed by Beckwith [8]. Each brand was represented by an equation and the set of equations were correlated contemporaneously; the estimation was performed with the aid of Zellner's [28] technique for seemingly unrelated regressions.

The model proposed herein represents a step back to single equation models. This approach is used in order to introduce a broadly based model which lends

*Dan Horsky is Assistant Professor, Graduate School of Management, University of Rochester. The author thanks Frank M. Bass for his assistance.

[1] An example of a wrong model, in this context, is when sales are postulated to be related linearly to advertising. It is a commonly used model which is found to fit data well. However, it implies no decreasing marginal returns to an investment in advertising. Its optimization therefore would suggest infinite advertising followed by infinite sales and profits—a sequence which is dubious at best.

Journal of Marketing Research
Vol. XIV (February 1977), 10-21

itself to the kind of rigorous testing required of a model to be used for control purposes. The model is found to be consistent with empirical evidence and to yield worthwhile managerial implications.[2]

MODEL SPECIFICATION

Sales of any brand are influenced by many factors, the more significant of which are:

1. The brand's advertising expenditure, both present and past.
2. The brand's other marketing activities such as pricing, product quality, new variety introductions, distribution, and dealer activities.
3. Industry factors such as the product's primary demand and competitors' activities.

The first two categories consist of variables that are controllable to a great extent by the firm, whereas the third category represents factors that are not. A general model of sales response should incorporate all the factors. However, in this study the marketing mix variables apart from advertising are assumed to remain constant. This restriction is imposed to facilitate the establishment of a theoretical basis for dealing with advertising to which the other activities can be added. The data base chosen for testing the model is selected so as to comply with this restriction.

In terms of the type of model to be proposed, several functional forms have been suggested in the past. One class consists of linear additive models in which the coefficient of any specific variable represents the marginal effects of a unit change in that variable. Another class is multiplicative models which are the demand counterpart of the Cobb-Douglas production function and in which the power of a variable represents the elasticity of sales with respect to that variable. Both types of models have been used widely, mainly because of their estimatable form. Linear regression can be applied directly to the first type and through a log transformation to the second. The main disadvantage of using these models in the context of this study is that known information about the nature of the process being examined is ignored.

Previous studies in the area of brand switching have shown that its pattern is either governed or well represented by a stochastic process. Massy [18], in a study of panel data, concluded first that individual consumers are well represented by a heterogeneous nonstationary zero-order switching model, and second that aggregation leads to a highly significant inference of a first-order Markov process. Though the second finding is not implied analytically by the first, it is an empirical finding which is also supported by Styan and Smith [25].

The Sales Process

On the basis of the foregoing findings, the initial assumption of this study is that the brand choice process of the *aggregated* population of consumers is a nonstationary first-order Markov process. If a two-brand market is considered (brand 1 and brand 2), the behavior of the aggregated population can be represented by the following sales equation:

$$S_{1,t} = S_{1,t-1} P_t(1|1) + S_{2,t-1} P_t(1|2)$$

where $S_{1,t}$ are the unit sales of brand 1 in period t and $P_t(1|1)$ is the conditional (transition) probability which represents the proportion of brand 1 customers, at period $t - 1$, who will repurchase the brand at t. It should be noticed, however, that this "flow" model involves an inherent assumption that the total industry sales remain a constant. Because this restriction is unrealistic for most industries, it is relaxed. The number of consumers purchasing the product class is allowed to vary and they are classified into two groups, consumers who have purchased the product in the previous period and new consumers. It is assumed that the "old" consumers switch among brands in accordance with the transition probabilities and that the new ones join the different brands in proportion to their present market shares. Suppose then that the new consumers all join at the end of the period and thus are unaffected by the transition process of that period. The total "flow" can be represented by:

$$(1) \quad S_{1,t} = S_{1,t-1} P_t(1|1) + S_{2,t-1} P_t(1|2) + (S_t - S_{t-1}) \frac{S_{1,t}}{S_t},$$

where S_t are the total industry sales in period t. Dividing through equation (1) by S_{t-1} and substituting $P_t(1|1) = 1 - P_t(2|1)$ leads to:

$$\frac{S_{1,t}}{S_t} - \frac{S_{1,t-1}}{S_{t-1}} = -\frac{S_{1,t-1}}{S_{t-1}} P_t(2|1) + \left(1 - \frac{S_{1,t-1}}{S_{t-1}}\right) P_t(1|2),$$

which is clearly equivalent to:

$$(2) \quad M_{1,t} - M_{1,t-1} = -M_{1,t-1} P_t(2|1) + (1 - M_{1,t-1}) P_t(1|2).$$

where $M_{1,t}$ is the market share of brand 1 at period t. It can be shown that equation (2) also would result if the new consumers enter the market at any time during the purchase period. Thus, on the basis of equation (2), the market share model is Markovian.

A Market Share Response to Advertising Model

It is now further hypothesized that the nonstationarity of the transition probabilities is a result of the effects of all marketing activities on the consumers. This general assumption is coupled with the following specific ones.

1. There are many brands in the product class, each with a relatively small market share. The industry

---

[2] Actual determination of the optimal advertising policy, based on the model presented here, is shown in [15].

is viewed, however, as having only two sectors, the brand of interest and the competition (which represents all other brands).

2. As the promotional activities, other than advertising, are assumed to remain constant, the only factor influencing the transition probabilities is advertising.
3. The effects of both past and current advertising expenditures are accumulated by the consumers in a "stock of goodwill." This stock can be increased by present and future advertising but is continuously decreased by its own depreciation.
4. The probability of switching to a competitive brand is a linear function of that brand's stock of advertising goodwill.

On the basis of these assumptions the following relation can be specified:

$$(3) \qquad P_t(1|2) = K_1' A_{1,t}',$$

where K_1' is the brand's coefficient of goodwill effectiveness and $A_{1,t}'$ is the brand's stock of advertising goodwill at period t. The advertising goodwill first is defined so as to be consistent with the definition of an investment:

$$(4) \qquad A_{1,t}' = (1 - \lambda_1) a_{1,t} + \lambda_1 A_{1,t-1}',$$

where $a_{1,t}$ is the brand's advertising expenditure in period t and λ_1 is the brand's rate of goodwill retention. Thus, though $(1 - \lambda_1) a_{1,t}$ yields a return on investment now, $\lambda_1 a_{1,t}$ will only become effective in the future. Equation (4) by expansion becomes:

$$
\begin{aligned}
(5) \quad A_{1,t}' &= (1 - \lambda_1) a_{1,t} + \lambda_1 [(1 - \lambda_1) a_{1,t-1} + \lambda_1 A_{1,t-2}'] \\
&= (1 - \lambda_1)[a_{1,t} + \lambda_1 a_{1,t-1} + \lambda_1^2 a_{1,t-2} + \ldots] \\
&= (1 - \lambda_1) A_{1,t},
\end{aligned}
$$

where $A_{1,t}$ is the Nerlove and Arrow [20] stock of advertising goodwill, which is defined by:

$$(6) \qquad A_{1,t} = a_{1,t} + \lambda_1 A_{1,t-1}.^3$$

Equation (3) can be rewritten with the aid of (5) and the definition of $K_1 = K_1' (1 - \lambda_1)$ as:

$$(7) \quad P_t(1|2) = K_1' A_{1,t}' = K_1' (1 - \lambda_1) A_{1,t} = K_1 A_{1,t}.$$

The interpretation of K_1 and its distinction from K_1' are rather interesting. Whereas K_1' represents the *total* future effectiveness of \$1 of advertising from the period of spending onward, K_1 represents only the *current* period's effectiveness.[4]

---

[3] Nerlove and Arrow [20] discussed the continuous version of this equation:

$$\frac{dA_1(t)}{dt} = a_1(t) - (1 - \lambda_1)A_1(t).$$

[4] This distinction also can be demonstrated directly by the summation of the current and future effects of \$1 of investment in advertising:

A development analogous to that of equations (3) through (7) is exercised for the competition. Their rate of retention is λ_2 and their advertising goodwill therefore is expressed by:

$$(8) \qquad A_{2,t} = a_{2,t} + \lambda_2 A_{2,t-1}.$$

Their counterpart to equation (7) is:

$$(9) \qquad P_t(2|1) = K_2 A_{2,t}.$$

When results (7) and (9) are substituted into equation (2) the basic model of this study emerges:

$$
\begin{aligned}
(10) \qquad M_{1,t} - M_{1,t-1} &= -M_{1,t-1} K_2 A_{2,t} \\
&\quad + (1 - M_{1,t-1}) K_1 A_{1,t}.
\end{aligned}
$$

With the aid of equation (10) it becomes even more apparent what the constant K_1 stands for. It represents the brand's increase in market share, for the current period, as the result of \$1 of advertising when, and only when, $M_{2,t-1} = 1$.

The model having been formulated, it is possible to elaborate on the implications of specifying a two-brand market, the brand of interest and its competition, when the latter is the aggregate of many brands. It is assumed implicitly that each \$1 of the competitors' advertising, regardless of the specific brand from which it originates, has an equal effect of K_2 on the brand's consumers, and vice versa. This is clearly a strong assumption which, unfortunately, cannot be avoided because of estimation problems when the number of brands is large. However, some justification for this assumption is that K_2 also can be construed as a measure of resistance to switch which the brand's consumers display when faced with competitive information—regardless of its specific source. A low K_2 therefore implies not only low effectiveness of competitors' advertising, but also a high measure of brand loyalty.

Some Desirable Properties

Empirical studies of panel data often report stationary or almost stationary transition probabilities. This finding can be explained here by the inherent stability over time of the goodwill values which is mapped through into the transition probabilities. Thus, for example, even if the brand's advertising is totally stopped, $a_{1,t} = 0$, there would still be an inflow of consumers to the brand as a result of past advertising, but at a reduced rate, as is evident from equations (6) and (10).

The incorporation of the goodwill of advertising in the model, apart from the foregoing reason and its consistency with investment theory, is also in keeping with the empirically founded lagged effects

---

$$
\begin{aligned}
K_1' &= K_1 + K_1 \lambda_1 + K_1 \lambda_1^2 \ldots = K_1(1 + \lambda_1 + \lambda_1^2 \ldots) \\
&= K_1/(1 - \lambda_1).
\end{aligned}
$$

of past advertising. The specific distributed lag structure assumed here is based on a geometric decay which, as pointed out previously, is appropriate when the time periods are years.

Elaboration as to interpretation of the K's shows another important property inherent in the model—decreasing marginal returns, in terms of gains in market share, to an increased expenditure in advertising. When $M_{1,t-1} = 0$, an additional \$1 of advertising increases the firm's market share by K_1, but in the next period when $M_{1,t} > 0$, an additional \$1 of advertising will increase its share by only $K_1(1 - M_{1,t})$. The property of decreasing marginal returns is clearly desirable in a model to be used for control purposes.

A commonly examined special condition is the "steady-state" condition. If that condition holds, equation (10) is equal to:

$$M_{1,t} - M_{1,t-1} = 0 = - M_{1,t-1} K_2 A_{2,t}$$
$$+ (1 - M_{1,t-1}) K_1 A_{1,t},$$

which leads to:

$$M_{1,t} = M_{1,t-1} = \frac{K_1 A_{1,t}}{K_2 A_{2,t} + K_1 A_{1,t}}$$

Thus, to remain in "steady state" the brand would have to retain its "effective" goodwill share, a result which seems very logical.[5]

Some Known Special Cases

Foremost among the special cases of the proposed model is the much quoted Vidale and Wolfe [27] model. If it is assumed first that $S_{1,t} = S$, implying a constant rate of total industry sales, second that $\lambda_1 = 0$, implying an instantaneous goodwill depreciation, and third that $P_t(2|1) = \beta$, implying stationary transition probability and consequently nondynamic competition, then equation (10) in its continuous version can be written as:

$$(1') \qquad \frac{dS_1(t)}{dt} = - S_1(t)\beta + [S - S_1(t)] K_1 a_1(t).$$

The replacement of K_1 by another constant k/S turns equation (11) into the Vidale and Wolfe model.

Another known special case emerges when a fourth assumption is added, that of $S - S_{1,t-1} = $ Constant, which implies, oddly enough, that the brand's sales remain unchanged or at least that the magnitude of $S_{1,t-1}$ is negligible with respect to that of S. Then,

by denoting $\gamma = K_1(S - S_{1,t-1})$, the discrete version of (11) is:

$$(12) \qquad S_{1,t} = (1 - \beta) S_{1,t-1} + \gamma a_{1,t}.$$

It is interesting to note that working under a completely different set of assumptions, and with a different parameter interpretation, Palda [21] arrived at the same equation. Though Palda has some specific assumptions about the model and its disturbance term, other studies often present (12) as a simple regression model.

THE DATA

To test the proposed model, an industry must be selected. To comply with the assumptions leading to the model, this industry should consist of many brands, each with a relatively small market share, and advertising should be their principal competitive weapon.

The cigarette industry during the years 1952-1970 was selected for study. In 1952 the first reports linking cigarettes to lung cancer were published. Presumably because of these reports the sales of filter cigarettes rose from 10% of the total industry sales in 1954 to 72% in 1967. An increase in the sales of menthol cigarettes was also evident. These increases prompted producers to introduce new brands in those categories. Further, beginning in 1965, filter and menthol cigarettes also were introduced under brand names traditionally associated with nonfilters. At about the same time, cigarette packages were required to bear the warning, "Cigarette Smoking May be Hazardous to Your Health," and the "equal time" provision was invoked to permit antismoking advertising. Eventually cigarette advertising was barred (by federal law) from radio and television as of January 2, 1971.

During the 19 years investigated there were six major cigarette producers, each making several brands. Their combined sales in 1966 were 99.7% of the total industry sales. With minor exceptions the relative prices of the different brands remained unchanged and "deals" were rare. Other promotional factors were not used to differentiate the brands. The distribution systems and the packaging were similar and there were no significant regional brands. Thus the major competitive device used in this industry was clearly advertising. Further, the advertising budgets were used to promote the sales of the specific brands and not the companies' total lines.

The sales and advertising data for the 35 best selling cigarette brands were published in *Advertising Age* [9-11]. The 12 leading brands in terms of sales in 1970 were selected for detailed analysis herein. In that year those brands amounted to 82.6% of the total industry sales. Additional details concerning these brands are given in Table 1.

PARAMETER ESTIMATION

As a first step in the empirical investigation a procedure for estimating the model's parameters must

---

[5] More general formulations of the model are also possible. First, the goodwill of equation (6) could be a nonlinear function of advertising. Next, the transition probability of equation (7) may depend on both firms' goodwills. Models in which the transition probability is specified as a function of both firms' advertising have been proposed by Kuehn [17], Telser [26], and more recently by Naert and Bultez [19]. Those works, however, do not incorporate the goodwill notion within the definition of the transition probability.

Table 1
THE 12 LEADING CIGARETTE BRANDS

No.	Brand	Category[a]	Introduction[b]	Market share 1952	Market share 1970
1	Winston	F	1955	—	15.8
2	Pall Mall	NF		10.8	11.1
3	Marlboro	F	1955	—	9.9
4	Salem	M	1956	—	8.6
5	Kool	M		3.0	8.4
6	Camel	NF		27.2	6.4
7	Kent	F		0.2	5.4
8	Tareyton	NF		3.2	4.1
9	Viceroy	F		0.7	3.8
10	Raleigh	F, NF		0.2	3.1
11	L&M	F	1954	—	3.0
12	Lucky Strike	NF		19.1	3.0
Total market share of 12 brands				63.4	82.6

[a] Category produced in 1952 (or year of introduction). Can be one of three: F (filter), NF (nonfilter), M (menthol).
[b] Introduction year if not produced in 1952.

be developed. Theoretically it may seem that if the left side of equation (10) is considered as the dependent variable, one could estimate K_1 and K_2 for any specific brand by linear regression of time series data. Unfortunately there seems to be no obvious measurement device for the stocks of advertising goodwill. To overcome this difficulty, $A_{1,t}$ and $A_{2,t}$ must be derived analytically in terms of other measurable variables. One such procedure would be the expansion of the goodwill equation (6) to:

$$A_{1,t} = a_{1,t} + \lambda_1 a_{1,t-1} + \lambda_1^2 a_{1,t-2} \dots,$$

and its substitution back into equation (10). However, this procedure raises serious problems. First, if too many lagged values of advertising are included, there might not be enough degrees of freedom left for the estimation process. On the other hand, there is no theoretical justification for truncating some of these terms. Second, even if the first issue is resolved, the independent variables would be highly correlated and the resulting estimates will not be efficient.

Thus a different procedure which does not require such expansion is developed. The market share equation (10) is lagged twice and the goodwill equations (6) and (8) once to provide the additional equations needed for the extraction of the two goodwill terms $A_{1,t-1}$ and $A_{2,t-1}$. Once these are expressed in terms of measurable variables, their substitution into equation (10) turns that equation into:

$$(13) \quad Y_{1,t} = K_1 X_{1,t} + K_2 X_{2,t} + \lambda_1 X_{3,t} + \lambda_1^2 X_{4,t}$$
$$+ K_1 \lambda_1 X_{5,t} + K_2 \lambda_1 X_{6,t}.$$

Appendix A details the exact forms of the dependent and independent variables of equation (13) and provides a discussion on their interpretation.

Equation (13) is clearly nonlinear in its parameters

and therefore their estimation requires use of nonlinear regression techniques.[6] Before such estimation takes place an error term must be added. It is assumed that its origin is not an equation error in model (10), but rather that an error u is associated with equation (13). It is further assumed that $u_t \sim N(0,\sigma^2)$. Theory regarding nonlinear estimation is offered in Appendix B.

The actual estimation was performed with the aid of an appropriate program.[7] In turn, each of the 12 leading brands served as brand 1 of equation (13) and all the other 34 were aggregated as the competition. The results for the different brands are given in Table 2. In 1965 brands 2, 6, 8, and 12 introduced filter cigarettes under the same brand names as their nonfilter cigarettes. This action could have caused a shift in their parameters, which therefore were re-estimated for the period 1952-64. For brands 6 and 12, Camel and Lucky Strike, the estimates did not change, but for brands 2 and 8, Pall Mall and Tareyton, significant changes were detected. As a result, the values in Table 2 for the latter two brands represent the 1952-64 period.

TESTING THE MODEL

Many alternative models of sales response to advertising have been proposed. Why is still another such model considered here? To answer this question on the basis of the criterion of a higher goodness of fit would be inappropriate given the intended use of the model for control purposes.[8] However, there are other, more appropriate criteria. In cases of nested alternative models (i.e., one is a special case of the other), tests can be conducted to determine whether the added complexity is worthwhile. If the models are not nested [e.g., 13] can be used to discriminate among the competing models. However, when the number of competing models is large, it would be desirable for the wrong ones (those which do not represent the underlying process) to be rejected at an earlier stage. The ability to reject a wrong model is attained by a *predictive test* in which a logical consequence derived from the theory is subjected to verification or falsification through empirical observation.

The philosophy of goodness of fit is well embedded in statistical theory, but predictive testing is a newer

---

[6] For an overview of nonlinear methods in econometrics, see [14].

[7] NONLINEAR written by Aird [1] is available on the Purdue University computer system and now also as part of the CDC SPSS package (version 6). The program uses a combination of iterative routines, primarily that of Fletcher [12], in its search for an optimum.

[8] For example, the ordinary least squares regression technique leads to R^2's which are higher than the ones obtained by any generalized least squares technique. However, the latter leads to more efficient estimates which in turn are more reliable when changes in the control variables are assessed.

Table 2
ESTIMATES OF THE MODEL'S PARAMETERS

No.	Brand	Advertising effectiveness		Advertising retention		R^2
		Brand $\hat{K}_1 \cdot 10^9$	Competition $\hat{K}_2 \cdot 10^9$	Brand $\hat{\lambda}_1$	Competition $\hat{\lambda}_2{}^a$	
1	Winston	2.07	1.53	0.33	0.30	0.96
2	Pall Mall	1.23	0.57	0.08	0.08	0.65
3	Marlboro	0.88	1.66	0.80	0.33	0.98
4	Salem	1.26	1.38	0.23	0.17	0.86
5	Kool	0.92	0.47	0.31	0.26	0.98
6	Camel	2.61	1.35	0.18	0.18	0.99
7	Kent	1.08	1.51	0.42	0.43	0.92
8	Tareyton	0.89	1.21	0.17	0.15	0.91
9	Viceroy	2.15	2.82	0.17	0.13	0.96
10	Raleigh	2.06	1.36	0.62	0.60	0.98
11	L&M	1.40	2.28	0.26	0.17	0.92
12	Lucky Strike	1.62	0.83	0.52	0.63	0.99

[a] Not estimated directly but computed by $\hat{\lambda}_2 = \hat{\lambda}_1 \hat{\psi}$.

concept. It has its foundations in the philosophy of logical positivism [e.g., 23] which does not permit labeling any model as a "true" model. However, though a model cannot be accepted, the degree of confidence in it increases if it is not rejected by a predictive test with a reasonable degree of falsification. Further, because the way to test a model is to try to falsify it, the more trials it passes, the higher the degree of confidence it attains.

Most of the models of sales response are acceptable on the criterion of goodness of fit. They achieve a high R^2 in estimation, and for the most part their estimates are significant. They also could pass some "weak" predictive tests such as logical signs for their estimates. However, except in the studies of Bass [4] and Bass and Parsons [7], none of these models were tested by "strong" predictive tests. The Bass and Parsons studies are in the context of simultaneous regression and closely follow the methodology developed by Basmann [2] for testing such systems.[9] A different methodology which relates to nonlinear regression is developed here and is used in testing the model.

Goodness of Fit

Goodness-of-fit tests are procedures which involve testing the fit of the data to a model by such measures as R^2, F, and t statistics. These tests are effective in ascertaining the forecasting power of a model. The results given in Table 2 indicate that the achieved R^2's are as good as any appearing in the past for other models in either the cigarette or other industries. The standard errors of the estimates obtained here, unlike in the case of linear regression, cannot be computed easily. Nevertheless, a test for the significance of the estimates can be conducted through an

hypothesis test. Theory with respect to hypothesis testing in nonlinear regression is given in Appendix B.

Test of estimates' significance. Suppose the contention that lagged advertising expenditures affect current sales is challenged. Then for the model represented by equation (13) the hypothesis to be tested is:

$$H_0: \quad \lambda_1 = 0, \quad \lambda_2 = 0.$$

The likelihood ratio ζ as defined by equation (B.3) of Appendix B implies here a ratio of two maximized likelihood functions, one corresponding to the non-constrained (unconditional) relation (10) and the other corresponding to the constrained (conditional) relation in which $\lambda_1 = \lambda_2 = 0$, so that:

$$(14) \qquad Y_t = K_1 X_{1,t} + K_2 X_{2,t} + v_t.$$

H_0 hypothesizes that there are two constrained parameters, $r = 2$; and the decision rule from equation (B.5) is at an $\alpha = 0.05$ significance level to reject H_0 if and only if:

$$\frac{SS(\bar{\theta})}{SS(\hat{\theta})} \geq \exp\left\{\frac{\chi^2_{0.05}(2)}{16}\right\} = 1.45.$$

$SS(\hat{\theta})$ for the unconstrained relation (10) is determined in the previous section and a simple linear regression is used to determine $SS(\bar{\theta})$ for the constrained relation (14). The values needed for the test of significance are shown in columns (i) and (ii) of Table 3. They indicate that for all brands H_0 could be rejected at the $\alpha = 0.05$ level, and for brands 5–10 H_0 also could be rejected at the $\alpha = 0.01$ level. Thus, it can be concluded that λ_1 and λ_2 are significant and that there is reason to believe lagged advertising expenditures affect current sales.[10]

---

[9] Bass [5] has been the main proponent of applying predictive testing to other marketing problems.

[10] Model (14) is in fact nested in model (13). A similar test was performed for K_1 and K_2 with similar results.

Table 3
VALUES FOR THE MODEL'S TESTS

		Significance test		Transition probabilities		Predictive test	
		$\dfrac{SS(\bar{\theta})}{SS(\hat{\theta})}$ (i)	C.V.[a] (ii)	$\bar{P}(1\|2)$ (iii)	$\bar{P}(2\|1)$ (iv)	$\dfrac{SS(\bar{\theta})}{SS(\hat{\theta})}$ (v)	C.V.[a] (vi)
No.	Brand						
1	Winston	1.88	1.58/2.03	0.11	0.53	1.84	1.82/2.38
2	Pall Mall	2.37	1.82/2.50	0.03	0.16	1.44	2.18/3.10
3	Marlboro	1.80	1.58/2.03	0.10	0.66	1.65	1.82/2.38
4	Salem	1.83	1.65/2.15	0.04	0.41	1.38	1.92/2.56
5	Kool	2.12	1.45/1.78	0.03	0.16	1.14	1.63/2.02
6	Camel	4.00	1.45/1.78	0.04	0.43	1.35	1.63/2.02
7	Kent	4.10	1.45/1.78	0.05	0.70	1.26	1.63/2.02
8	Tareyton	4.40	1.82/2.50	0.02	0.36	1.37	2.18/3.10
9	Viceroy	6.20	1.45/1.78	0.04	0.85	1.20	1.63/2.02
10	Raleigh	3.60	1.45/1.78	0.03	0.88	1.41	1.63/2.02
11	L&M	1.64	1.53/1.93	0.03	0.71	1.86	1.75/2.24
12	Lucky Strike	1.65	1.45/1.78	0.05	0.62	1.73	1.63/2.02

[a]Critical values for hypothesis rejection, when $\alpha = 0.05/\alpha = 0.01$ (the values vary as they depend on the number of observations).

Weak Predictive Testing

Closely related to the goodness-of-fit tests but more powerful are tests labeled here as weak predictive tests. These tests use as the criterion for validation the model's *reasonableness*. In these tests the signs and magnitudes of the estimates are examined for consistency with some obvious properties of the model's parameters. [11]

The first among such properties, for the model at hand, is non-negative signs for all its parameters because one could not expect negative signs for the effectiveness of advertising or its rate of retention:

$$K_1 \geq 0, \quad K_2 \geq 0, \quad \lambda_1 \geq 0, \quad \lambda_2 \geq 0.$$

The appropriate estimates in Table 2 support this contention. The second property is a zero to one interval for the rates of advertising retention:

$$0 \leq \lambda_1 \leq 1, \quad 0 \leq \lambda_2 \leq 1.$$

Again the estimates in Table 2 are supportive. The third and final property is a deduction from the fact that $K_1 A_{1,t}$ and $K_2 A_{2,t}$ represent the switching probabilities, and as probabilities they are restricted to values between zero and one:

$$0 \leq K_1 A_{1,t} \leq 1, \quad 0 \leq K_2 A_{2,t} \leq 1.$$

The lower limit is observed as it has been shown that $\hat{K}_1, \hat{K}_2 \geq 0$. As for the upper limit, to avoid the necessity of computing the switching probability for each period, a value that is greater than any of them is computed; if this value is smaller than 1, the test has been passed. By denoting:

---

[11] It is worth noting that holdout samples commonly are used to test models. This procedure, however, still belongs to the goodness-of-fit classification as it only tests the consistency of the parameters, without guaranteeing that the model itself is not "wrong" to start with.

$$\bar{a}_1 = \max_t \{a_{1,t}\} \quad \text{and} \quad \bar{A}_1 = \max_t \{A_{1,t}\},$$

the following inequality can be derived:

$$\bar{A}_1 \leq \bar{a}_1 [1 - \lambda_1 + \lambda_1^2 \dots] = \frac{\bar{a}_1}{1 - \lambda_1}.$$

An analogous inequality can be derived for the competition, and what needs to be tested is whether:

$$\bar{P}(1|2) = \frac{K_1 \bar{a}_1}{1 - \lambda_1} < 1, \quad \bar{P}(2|1) = \frac{K_2 \bar{a}_2}{1 - \lambda_2} < 1.$$

The values for this test are given in columns (iii) and (iv) of Table 3 and show that the requirements of this last weak predictive test also are complied with.

Strong Predictive Testing

Here the model's implications *per se* are used as *consistency* tests against the data from which the model was derived. The opportunity for such a test does not usually arise, but for certain nonlinear models it can be developed as a beneficial side effect.

To be more specific, equation (13) can be written as:

$$(15) \quad Y_{1,t} = \beta_1 X_{1,t} + \beta_2 X_{2,t} + \beta_3 X_{3,t} + \beta_4 X_{4,t} + \beta_5 X_{5,t} + \beta_6 X_{6,t} + u_t,$$

and β_1 through β_6 can be estimated directly from the data. However, if these estimates do not satisfy the relations implied for them in equation (13), an inconsistency has been found and the model has been falsified. Thus for the model presented by (15) it is desired to test the hypothesis that:

$$H_0: \quad \beta_4 = \beta_3^2, \quad \beta_5 = \beta_1 \beta_3, \quad \beta_6 = \beta_2 \beta_3,$$

which essentially is a test of an overidentified system. [12]

---

[12] Nonlinear models also can be just identified (i.e., in this context the number of parameters is equal to the number of independent

On the basis of the previously outlined hypothesis test, the likelihood ratio ζ for the hypothesis involves a ratio of two maximized likelihood functions, one corresponding to the nonconstrained relation (15) and the other to the constrained relation (13). The values required for this test are assembled in columns (v) and (vi) of Table 3. They indicate that though H_0 could be rejected for three brands (1, 11, and 12) at the $\alpha = 0.05$ level, it could not be rejected for any brand at the $\alpha = 0.01$ level. Thus, it can be concluded that the model could not be rejected by strong predictive testing. [13]

SUMMARY OF THE MODEL AND ITS TESTING

The model of market share response to advertising presented in equation (10) is formulated, on the basis of studies of panel data, as a Markov type of stochastic process. The brand-switching probabilities are assumed to be a function of the goodwill of advertising accumulated by the brand and its competitors. As the goodwills cannot be measured directly, a procedure for approximating them through other measurable variables is offered. This results in a transformed model, represented by equation (13), which is nonlinear in its parameters.

The intended use of the model is to aid in controlling the level of sales. A case is presented that a high goodness of fit would not suffice to determine the appropriateness of using a model for control purposes. Predictive tests must be applied which enable one to reject models on the basis of the inconsistency of their premises with empirical evidence.

The 12 leading brands of the cigarette industry were selected to form the data base against which the model would be tested because in that industry advertising is the principal competitive tool. In the tests the model not only exhibits good forecasting abilities but also withstands several predictive tests. The signs and magnitudes of the parameters are found to be reasonable, and its nonlinear form proves to offer a unique opportunity for testing the model's consistency.

MANAGERIAL IMPLICATIONS

Because of the nature of this study, the main objective of the empirical investigation was to test the model and not to examine the cigarette industry per se. However, as the model is shown to have not only theoretical foundations but also empirical support, managerial implications can be considered. Further, some of the findings can be compared with those of previous studies of the cigarette industry.

variables). In such a case, as in [3], only weak predictive tests of reasonableness can be performed.

[13] It should be noted that an hypothesis such as $\beta_5 = \beta_1 \beta_3$ cannot be tested by a simple t-test because, among other things, $E(\hat{\beta}_1 \hat{\beta}_3) \neq E(\hat{\beta}_1) E(\hat{\beta}_3)$ as $\hat{\beta}_1$ and $\hat{\beta}_3$ are, as any regression estimates, correlated.

In the model detailed in equations (6), (8), and (10), each brand is represented by four parameters, K_1, λ_1, K_2, and λ_2. The first two measure the total effectiveness of a brand's advertising and the last two measure the level of resistance its consumers display when faced with competitive advertising. The discussion here centers on the brands' advertising effectiveness and thus on K_1 and λ_1. They represent, to a certain extent, the immediate versus the long-run effects of advertising, and therefore the tradeoff between their values is explored. However, an investigation of whether the parameter values for a specific brand actually are the result of some intentions on the part of its management, or are traceable to some specific combination of advertising media, copy, or message used, is beyond the scope of this study.

The information of interest is presented in Table 2 which details the parameter estimates for the different cigarette brands. An initial observation can be made that the parameters vary considerably across brands and even within categories. Though this variation is known to be generally true for competing brands, it is of special relevance here because Peles [22] and Schmalensee [24] did pool cross-sectionally in their studies of the cigarette industry. Their results therefore should be construed as somewhat representative of the "average" brand.

Advertising Retention

The rate of yearly retention of advertising, λ_1, is shown in Table 2 to range from 80% for Marlboro to 8% for Pall Mall. The unweighted average across brands is about 35%. Peles [22], who studied the period of 1955-1966, found this average to equal 55%. Telser [26], who studied Camel, Lucky Strike, and Chesterfield for the period of 1912-1939, found the yearly retention rate to equal 80%. Thus, the rate of advertising retention found here is the lowest reported for the industry. It should be noted, however, that in the period analyzed by Telser these three brands had a combined market share of more than 75%, whereas in the period studied by Peles and in this report more than 30 brands were competing and major changes in consumer tastes were taking place. It seems, therefore, that in periods of greater consumer confusion—i.e., introductions of new brands, health scares, etc.—the rate of retention decreases.

Advertising Effectiveness

K_1 is defined as the brand's current gain, in terms of market share, to $1 of advertising, when $M_1 = 0$. However, not only the current gains are of interest, but also the future ones and, further, because advertising is expended in dollars, the dollar value of the gains is also relevant. Consequently, a few additional measures are needed. The first is K_1', which was defined previously as $K_1' = K_1/(1 - \lambda_1)$, and which measures both current and future gains in terms of

Table 4
MEASURES OF ADVERTISING EFFECTIVENESS

| | | Gains in market share | | Gains in dollars | | | Return on |
| | | Immediate | Total | Immediate | Total | Discounted | investment |
No.	Brand	$K_1 \cdot 10^9$	$K_1' \cdot 10^9$	G_1	G_1'	D_1	R_1
1	Winston	2.07	3.20	1.42	2.19	1.97	97%
2	Pall Mall	1.23	1.34	0.84	0.92	0.90	-10%
3	Marlboro	0.88	4.40	0.60	3.00	1.86	86%
4	Salem	1.26	1.64	0.86	1.12	1.07	7%
5	Kool	0.92	1.34	0.63	0.92	0.85	-15%
6	Camel	2.61	3.18	1.79	2.18	2.11	111%
7	Kent	1.08	1.86	0.74	1.27	1.15	15%
8	Tareyton	0.89	1.07	0.61	0.73	0.71	-29%
9	Viceroy	2.15	2.60	1.47	1.78	1.72	72%
10	Raleigh	2.06	5.40	1.41	3.70	2.96	196%
11	L&M	1.40	1.90	0.96	1.30	1.23	23%
12	Lucky Strike	1.62	4.38	1.11	2.24	1.98	98%

market share. The second and third measures are the dollar values of K_1 and K_1', which are equal to:

$$G_1 = K_1 g_1 \bar{S} \quad \text{and} \quad G_1' = K_1' g_1 \bar{S},$$

where g_1 is the gross margin for a unit of sales exclusive of advertising, and $\bar{S}$ is the mean of yearly industry sales during 1952-1970. In the context of the dollar values, the discount rate also should be considered, and so the fourth measure is the "discounted" dollar value of K_1' such that:

$$D_1 = g_1 \bar{S} \left[K_1 + K_1 \frac{\lambda_1}{1 + \delta} + K_1 \left(\frac{\lambda_1}{1 + \delta} \right)^2 \cdots \right]$$

$$= G_1 \frac{1 + \delta}{1 + \delta - \lambda_1},$$

where δ is the yearly cost of capital. The fifth and final measure is the total return on $1 investment in advertising which is defined as:

$$R_1 = (D_1 - 1)100.$$

The six different measures can be calculated with the aid of the values in Table 2. In the calculations the gross margin, g_1, is taken to be 15 cents a carton, and the yearly cost of capital before taxes, δ, as 18%. The values for the different brands are shown in Table 4.

The first observations which can be made concern the unweighted averages across brands. For G_1—the first year's contribution of $1 of advertising—this average is equal to $1.04. Peles found this value to equal $0.77. However, his rate of retention was higher than the one found here and, as a result, it would be more appropriate to make a comparison of the *total* contribution, as defined by G_1'. The average values are rather close, $1.6 here and $1.7 in Peles' study. As for the total return on investment in advertising, its average based on column R_1 is 50%.

The results are equally interesting with respect to

the individual brands. Raleigh, which all along consisted of both filter and nonfilter versions, is found to have the most effective advertising. Its total return on investment, based on D_1, is about 200%. Camel and Lucky Strike, two nonfilter brands, have a return on investment of about 100%. Three filter brands—Winston, Marlboro, and Viceroy—follow with only a slightly lower return of about 80%. Another two filter brands, L&M and Kent, have a considerably lower return of about 20%. Salem, a menthol brand, is just about breaking even and Kool, the other menthol brand, is already below that point. Pall Mall and Tareyton, the two other nonfilter brands, are trailing with negative returns of 10% and 30%.

The high rate of return found for Raleigh is somewhat misleading. Raleigh, which had on the average a third of the advertising budget of firms with similar market share, had stressed in its advertising its coupon campaign which actually offered an indirect price reduction. Thus, though the advertising figures for all other brands represent the great majority of their actual marketing expenditures, the figure for Raleigh represents a smaller part of that expenditure, the other part being the redemption of its coupons. To correct for this discrepancy, a number greater than unity would have to be subtracted from D_1 in the definition of the return on investment, R_1, thus reducing Raleigh's return.

The findings indicate that at least during part of the 1952-1970 period, Kool, Pall Mall, and Tareyton were overspending. These results also should be examined in light of the previous findings about the changes in the parameter values for the nonfilter brands after the introduction of filter cigarettes under the same brand names in 1965. Camel and Lucky Strike, whose parameters did not change, apparently continued to be perceived as nonfilters and had effective advertising all along as such. Pall Mall and Tareyton, whose parameters did change, apparently changed their "identity," and perhaps for the better as during the 1952–1964 period analyzed here their advertising was ineffective.

For the nine brands for which advertising seems a worthwhile endeavor, the previously analyzed measures do not tell the full story. They are defined to be "operational" as long as $M_1 = 0$, which usually is not the case. However, because the market shares of the brands are relatively small, the multiplication of these measures by $1 - M_1$ would not decrease them significantly. This is not true for the competitors' influence, because K_2 in equation (10) is multiplied by M_1 and a move from $M_1 = 0.01$ to $M_1 = 0.02$ would double the effect. Thus, although D_1 for nine of the brands suggests worthwhile investment in advertising, such investment will have decreasing marginal returns and further will increase the competitors' effectiveness. This tradeoff is the basis for determination of an optimal advertising policy for a brand.[14]

CONCLUSION

The objective of most marketing managers is not merely to make forecasts about the firm's sales, but also to control them. In this study a model which could serve that end is proposed. Several criteria for testing the model are suggested and the tests support the model. Moreover, the analysis of the model yields a considerable amount of managerially relevant information.

The generality of the model also makes it possible to incorporate other promotional variables apart from advertising by defining the goodwill so as to include all promotional variables. Further research in this direction is now in progress.

Finally, the model presented has lent itself to rigorous testing, and the lack of models of similar nature in past studies warrants further discussion. As shown, the ability to test the model was due to its nonlinear form. There is little likelihood, however, that one could directly specify a model which is nonlinear in its parameters. Here, only after several behavioral premises were postulated and *integrated* did the testable model emerge. A similar phenomenon, in a different context, occurred in Bass' study [3]. Thus, it appears that a behavioral rationale for a model is desirable, not only on philosophical grounds, but also in order to arrive at theories which can be tested thoroughly, and in turn to gain the user's confidence.

APPENDIX A

THE NONLINEAR MODEL

Equation (13) in its full detail is:

$$Y_{1,t} = K_1 X_{1,t} + K_2 X_{2,t} + \lambda_1 X_{3,t} + \lambda_1^2 X_{4,t} + K_1 \lambda_1 X_{5,t} + K_2 \lambda_1 X_{6,t}$$

---

[14] The optimization problem here is to maximize the discounted profits subject to equations (6) and (10). As the last two equations can be turned into differential equations, the optimization method applied by Horsky [15] is the optimal control theory.

where:

$$Y_{1,t} = M_{1,t} - M_{1,t-1}$$

$$X_{1,t} = (1 - M_{1,t-1})a_{1,t} \qquad X_{2,t} = -M_{1,t-1}a_{2,t}$$

$$X_{3,t} = (M_{1,t-1} - M_{1,t-2})\frac{M_{1,t-1}}{M_{1,t-2}}(\psi + Z_t)$$

$$X_{4,t} = -(M_{1,t-2} - M_{1,t-3})\frac{M_{1,t-1}}{M_{1,t-3}}\psi Z_t$$

$$X_{5,t} = -(1 - M_{1,t-3})\frac{M_{1,t-1}}{M_{1,t-3}}\psi Z_t a_{1,t-1}$$

$$X_{6,t} = M_{1,t-1}Z_t a_{2,t-1}$$

$$Z_t = \frac{(1 - M_{1,t-1})/M_{1,t-1} - \psi(1 - M_{1,t-2})/M_{1,t-2}}{(1 - M_{1,t-2})/M_{1,t-2} - \psi(1 - M_{1,t-3})/M_{1,t-3}}$$

$$\psi = \frac{\lambda_2}{\lambda_1}.$$

The independent variables of the equation, because of the complexity of their functional forms, cannot be fully interpreted. However, some observations can be made about these variables and their coefficients: first, $X_{1,t}$ and $X_{2,t}$ are linear functions of the current advertising and correspondingly their coefficients represent the advertising "effectiveness"—K_1 and K_2; second, $X_{5,t}$ and $X_{6,t}$ are linear functions of lagged advertising and correspondingly their coefficients are multiplications of the K_i's and the depreciation rate λ_1; third, $X_{3,t}$ and $X_{4,t}$ are not a function of advertising but a part of $X_{4,t}$ is a one-period lag of a similar part in $X_{3,t}$. Correspondingly, whereas the coefficient of $X_{3,t}$ is λ_1, that of $X_{4,t}$ is λ_1^2 which is smaller as $0 \le \lambda_1 \le 1$.

APPENDIX B

ESTIMATION IN NONLINEAR REGRESSION

The general nonlinear regression model can be represented by the following form:

$$(B.1) \qquad Y = f(X, \theta) + u,$$

where Y is the dependent variable, X is a k-component vector of independent variables, θ is a p-component vector of parameters, and u is a random disturbance term.

Estimation of the parameter vector θ commonly is based on the estimation criterion of either least squares (L.S.) or maximum likelihood (M.L.). However, if $u \sim N(0,\sigma^2)$, those two criteria lead to the same estimates and they have the statistical properties of M.L. estimators—consistency and asymptotic efficiency—and at the same time can be estimated by a L.S. estimation procedure. That is, given T observations on Y and X's denoted by Y_t

and $X^t = (X_{1,t},...,X_{k,t})$, the L.S. estimates are those that minimize the residual sum of squares (SS):

(B.2) $$SS(\theta) = \sum_{t=1}^{T} [Y_t - f(X^t,\theta)]^2.$$

The commonly used measure of goodness of fit, the R^2, is defined in this context as $R^2 = 1 - SS(\theta)/\Sigma_{t=1}^{T}(Y_t - \bar{Y})^2$.

HYPOTHESIS TESTING IN NONLINEAR REGRESSION

Suppose the p-component vector of parameters θ of model (B.1) is partitioned so that $\theta = (\theta_r, \theta_s)$, and that one wishes to test the hypothesis:

$$H_0: \quad \theta_r = \bar{\theta}_r,$$

where $\bar{\theta}_r$ are some externally provided constants or some functions of θ_s. Then, the likelihood ratio for this problem is given by:

(B.3) $$\zeta = \frac{L(X|\bar{\theta}_r, \hat{\hat{\theta}}_s)}{L(X|\hat{\theta}_r, \hat{\theta}_s)} = \frac{L(X|\bar{\theta})}{L(X|\hat{\theta})}$$

where $L(X|\bar{\theta})$ is the conditional maximum of the likelihood function given that $\theta_r = \bar{\theta}_r$, and $L(X|\hat{\theta})$ is the unconditional maximum of the likelihood function. It can be shown [see 14, p. 72-4] that (B.3) can be reduced to:

(B.4) $$\zeta = \left[\frac{SS(\hat{\theta})}{SS(\bar{\theta})} \right]^{T/2}$$

Equation (B.4) can be presented alternatively as:

$$-2 \ln \zeta = T \ln \left[\frac{SS(\bar{\theta})}{SS(\hat{\theta})} \right],$$

and it is known that under regularity conditions $-2 \ln \zeta \sim \chi_\alpha^2(r)$.
Thus for the hypothesis:

$$H_0: \quad \theta_1 = \bar{\theta}_1, ..., \theta_r = \bar{\theta}_r, \theta_{r+1}, \theta_{r+2}, ..., \theta_p$$

and at an α level of significance the decision rule is: reject H_0 if and only if:

(B.5) $$\frac{SS(\bar{\theta})}{SS(\hat{\theta})} \geq \exp\left\{ \frac{\chi_\alpha^2(r)}{T} \right\}.$$

REFERENCES

1. Aird, Thomas J. "Computational Solution of Global Nonlinear Least Squares Problems," Ph.D. dissertation, Purdue University, 1973.
2. Basmann, Robert L. "On the Application of the Identifiability Test Statistic in Predictive Testing of Explanatory Economic Models," The Econometric Annual of the Indian Economic Journal, 13, No. 3 (1965), 387-423.
3. Bass, Frank M. "A New Product Growth Model for Consumer Durables," Management Science, 15 (January 1969), 215-27.
4. ———. "A Simultaneous Equation Regression Study of Advertising and Sales of Cigarettes," Journal of Marketing Research, 6 (August 1969), 291-300.
5. ———. "Application of Regression Models in Marketing: Testing versus Forecasting," Institute for Research in the Behavioral, Economic and Management Sciences, Krannert Graduate School of Industrial Administration, Purdue University, 1969.
6. ——— and Darral G. Clarke. "Testing Distributed Lag Models of Advertising Effect: An Analysis of Dietary Weight Control Product Data," Journal of Marketing Research, 9 (August 1972), 298-308.
7. ——— and Leonard J. Parsons. "Simultaneous-Equations Regression Analysis of Sales and Advertising," Applied Economics, 1 (1969), 103-24.
8. Beckwith, Neil E. "Multivariate Analysis of Sales Response of Competing Brands to Advertising," Journal of Marketing Research, 9 (May 1972), 168-76.
9. "Costs of Cigarette Advertising: 1952-1959," Advertising Age, 31 (September 19, 1960), 126-7.
10. "Costs of Cigarette Advertising: 1957-1965," Advertising Age, 37 (July 25, 1966), 56-8.
11. "Costs of Cigarette Advertising: 1962-1970," Advertising Age, 42 (October 11, 1971), 28-30.
12. Fletcher, Richard. "Generalized Inverse Methods for the Best Least Squares Solution of Systems of Non-linear Equations," Computer Journal, 10 (1968), 392-99.
13. Gaver, K. M. and M. S. Geisel. "Discriminating Among Alternative Models: Bayesian and Non-Bayesian Methods," in Paul Zarembka, ed., Frontiers in Econometrics. New York: Academic Press, 1974, 49-77.
14. Goldfeld, Stephen M. and Richard E. Quandt. Nonlinear Methods in Econometrics. Amsterdam-London: North-Holland Publishing Company, 1972.
15. Horsky, Dan. "A Theoretical and Empirical Analysis of the Optimal Advertising Policy," Management Science, forthcoming.
16. Koyck, L. M. Distributed Lags and Investment Analysis. Amsterdam: North-Holland Publishing Company, 1954.
17. Kuehn, Alfred A. "A Model for Budgeting Advertising," in Frank M. Bass et al., eds., Mathematical Models and Methods in Marketing. Homewood, Illinois: Richard D. Irwin, 1961, 315-48.
18. Massy, William F. "Order and Homogeneity of Family Specific Brand-Switching Process," Journal of Marketing Research, 3 (February 1966), 48-54.
19. Naert, Philippe A. and Alain V. Bultez. "Logically Consistent Market Share Models," Journal of Marketing Research, 10 (August 1973), 334-40.
20. Nerlove, Mark and Kenneth J. Arrow. "Optimal Advertising Policy under Dynamic Conditions," Economica, 29 (May 1962), 129-42.
21. Palda, Kristian S. The Measurement of Cumulative Advertising Effects. Englewood Cliffs, New Jersey: Prentice-Hall, Inc., 1964.
22. Peles, Yoram. "Rates of Amortization of Advertising Expenditures," Journal of Political Economy, 79 (September-October 1971), 1032-59.
23. Popper, K. R. The Logic of Scientific Discovery. New York: Science Editions, 1961.
24. Schmalensee, Richard L. The Economics of Advertising. Amsterdam-London: North-Holland Publishing Company, 1972.

25. Styan, George P. H. and Harry Smith, Jr. "Markov Chains Applied to Marketing," *Journal of Marketing Research*, 1 (February 1964), 50-4.
26. Telser, Lester G. "Advertising and Cigarettes," *The Journal of Political Economy*, 70 (October 1962), 300-24.
27. Vidale, M. L. and H. B. Wolfe. "An Operations-Research Study of Sales Response to Advertising," *Operations Research*, 5 (June 1957), 370-81.
28. Zellner, Arnold. "An Efficient Method for Estimating Seemingly Unrelated Regressions and Tests for Aggregation Bias," *Journal of the American Statistical Association*, 57 (June 1962), 348-68.

AN OPERATIONS-RESEARCH STUDY OF SALES
RESPONSE TO ADVERTISING

M. L. VIDALE and H. B. WOLFE

Arthur D. Little, Inc., Cambridge, Massachusetts

(Received January 29, 1957)

This paper presents the results of studies for major industrial concerns on the sales response to advertising. A simple model of the interaction of advertising and sales is described that is consistent with the results of controlled experiments performed on a large number of products and several media. The model is based on three parameters: Sales Decay Constant, Saturation Level, and Response Constant. It has proved useful for analyses of advertising campaigns and for allocations of advertising appropriations.

OPERATIONS RESEARCH has not as yet found many applications in the field of advertising. Only a few papers[1-6] on the subject have appeared in the literature. It is difficult to obtain reliable experimental data. It is probably true that designing original advertising copy and making a priori estimates of the behavior of the buying public are not promising material for operations research; there do exist, however, problems that are of great interest to the advertising man and that can be studied quantitatively. For example:

1. How does one evaluate the effectiveness of an advertising campaign?
2. How should the advertising budget be allocated among different products and media?
3. What criteria determine the size of the advertising budget?

The last two questions cannot be answered without a knowledge of advertising effectiveness; this is where most of the difficulties lie and where research is most needed. Once the relation between sales response and advertising has been established, the optimum budget size and allocation can be determined.

During the past few years, the Operations Research Group at Arthur D. Little, Inc., has studied these problems and examined sales promotions for several large industrial concerns. In this paper we wish to present some generalizations that have been suggested by the results of our experiments.

We shall first describe the type of experimental results we have obtained, and then discuss a simple mathematical model consistent with our observations.

EXPERIMENTAL RESULTS: ADVERTISING PARAMETERS

IN ORDER to measure the sales response of individual products to advertising and to compare the effectiveness of various media, we have performed a large number of controlled experiments in which the intensity and type of promotion were varied. With the cooperation of sales and advertising departments and their advertising agencies, we have been able to run large-scale tests over considerable portions of the U. S. market. The results of the tests have in most cases been significant and reproducible. In the analysis of advertising campaigns, we have found it helpful to describe the interaction of sales and advertising in terms of three parameters:

1. *The Sales Decay Constant*
2. *The Saturation Level*
3. *The Response Constant*

We shall introduce these parameters by means of a few sales histories that exemplify them. The relations and the data in the examples are real. However, for reasons of industrial security, it has been necessary to conceal the types of products tested and, in a few cases, to paraphrase the advertising media.

Sales Decay Constant

In the absence of promotion, sales tend to decrease because of product obsolescence, competing advertising, etc. Under relatively constant market conditions, the rate of decrease is, in general, constant: that is, a constant per cent of sales is lost each year. Figure 1 presents the eight-year sales history of product A, plotted on a semi-logarithmic scale. This product exhibits a small seasonality in sales; however, over the years the sales have been decreasing exponentially. Figure 2 presents the sales history of a very seasonal product, B. Here again, the monthly sales, averaged over a full year, 'decay' at a constant rate.

This behavior, which we have observed in a great number of unpromoted products, leads us to introduce as a parameter the exponential Sales Decay Constant λ; that is, the sales rate at time t of an unpromoted product is given by $S(t) = S(0) \exp(-\lambda t)$. In the examples above, the Sales Decay Constants are 0.24 per year and 0.06 per year for products A and B respectively. As might be expected, the sales decay rate ranges from large values for products that become quickly obsolescent or products in a highly competitive market to almost zero for noncompetitive, well-established products.

Product C (Fig. 3) exhibits some interesting features when analyzed with this parameter in mind. The sales of this product were 'decaying' at a constant rate ($\lambda = 0.9$ per year) up to the beginning of 1953, when an article favorable to the product appeared in a popular magazine of wide circulation. Sales increased by a factor of five within a month. This level of sales, however, was not maintained, but began to decrease much more quickly ($\lambda = 4.7$ per year) than the original rate until it reached a new level, double that before the promotion. At this point, the Sales

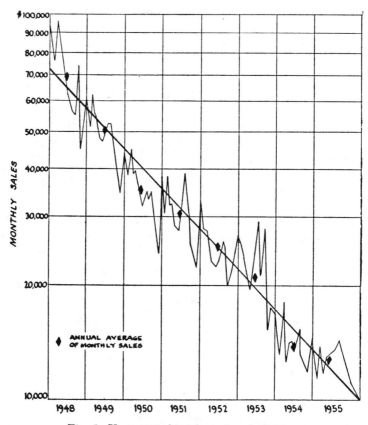

Fig. 1. Unpromoted product *A*—sales history.

Decay Constant returned to the original value of 0.9. Eight months later, the product was mentioned favorably in another popular magazine, and the same phenomenon occurred. Clearly, we are dealing here with two classes of customers: those who were induced to purchase after reading the magazine articles, but who soon lost interest in the product; and the 'normal' customers, who behaved much like the original customer population. Both articles succeeded in raising the number of 'normal' customers.

Saturation Level

The concept of Saturation Level is illustrated by the sales history of product *D*, Fig. 4. This product was promoted continuously for one year by weekly newspaper advertisements beginning in July 1954. In the first six months, sales rose 30 per cent and then leveled off, although the advertising campaign was continued for another six months. This additional advertising may have helped to maintain sales at the new level, but this effect cannot have been large, because the decay rate both before and after

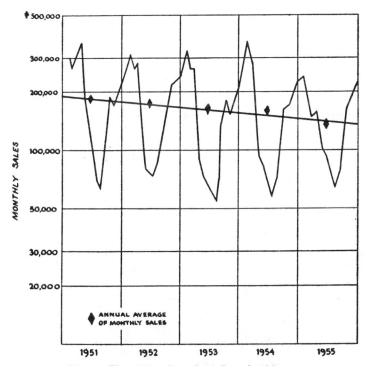

Fig. 2. Unpromoted product *B*—sales history.

the advertising campaign was small. We conclude that this campaign could have been considerably shorter and equally effective, and that beyond a certain point, it lost its value.

Figure 5 presents the sales history of product *E*. Because of the complexity of the sales responses, sales are here plotted on a cumulative scale.

- Area 1 received a spot radio commercial campaign for six months.
- Beginning at the same time, Area 2 received the campaign for twelve months.

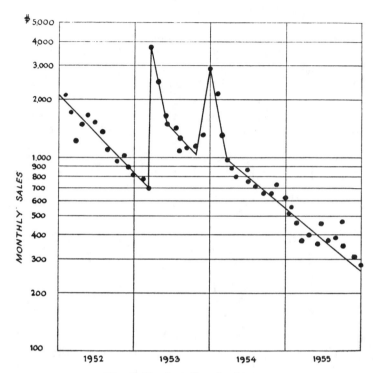

Fig. 3. Product *C*—sales history.

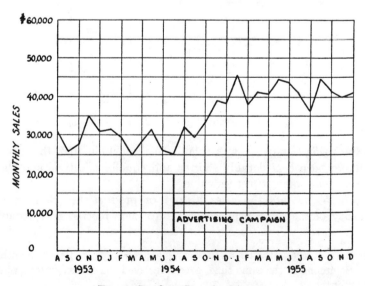

Fig. 4. Product *D*—sales history.

- At the end of the campaign in Area 1, Area 3 received the campaign for six months.
- Area 4 was kept as control and received no promotion.

In Areas 1 and 2, sales increased approximately 150 per cent over those in Area 4; the additional six months' promotion received by Area 2 did not increase sales further. Area 3 experienced a similar sales increase after the

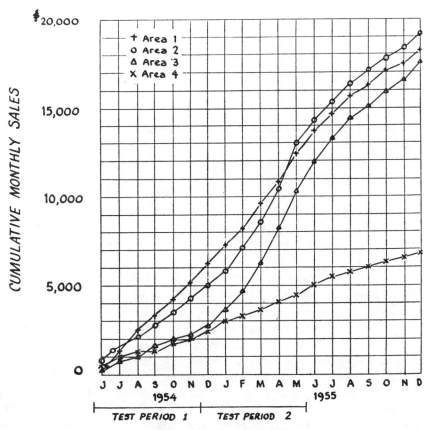

Fig. 5. Product *E*—sales history.

promotion started. Therefore, even though the advertising campaign was postponed for six months, it lost none of its effectiveness.

From the results exemplified in Figs. 4 and 5, we are led to describe the interaction of advertising and sales in terms of a second parameter—the Saturation Level, *M*, or practical limit of sales that can be generated. This Saturation Level depends not only on the product being promoted, but also on the advertising medium used; it represents the fraction of the

market that the particular campaign can capture. This Saturation Level
can often be raised further by other advertising media.

Response Constant

In addition to the Decay Constant and the Saturation Level, we need a
third parameter to describe the sales behavior of a product. We define the
Response Constant, r, as the sales generated per advertising dollar when
$S=0$. We note that the number of new customers who are potential
buyers decreases as sales approach saturation. When advertising is
directed indiscriminately to both customers and noncustomers, the effectiveness of each advertising dollar in obtaining new customers also
decreases as sales increase. In general, the sales generated per advertising
dollar, when sales are at a level S, is given by $r(M-S)/M$, where M is
the Saturation Level.

As an example, for product D the Saturation Level was \$42,000 per
month (see Fig. 4). The advertising expenditure was \$5,000 per month.
In 1954, before the start of the advertising campaign, monthly sales averaged \$29,000 or 70 per cent of the Saturation Level. The unsaturated
portion, or the percentage of the potential represented by noncustomers,
was 30 per cent. The new customers converted to the product as a result
of the July promotion increased sales by approximately \$3000 per month.
The Response Constant was therefore $r=(\$3000/\text{mo})/(0.30\times\$5000)=$
$2/\text{mo}$.

MEASUREMENT OF PARAMETERS

In the next section, we will present a model of the interaction of advertising and sales, based on the three parameters: Sales Decay Constant,
Saturation Level, and Response Constant. These parameters differ from
product to product and must therefore be determined separately for individual products. The Sales Decay Constant can be measured from the
sales data either before or after a promotion. The Saturation Level and
Response Constant can be determined from a detailed analysis of the sales
history, or when necessary, experimentally. We have found that test
promotions, when carefully designed with experimental controls and on a
sufficiently large scale, give results that are both significant and reproducible, though the degree of accuracy attainable is smaller than ordinarily
considered acceptable in many other fields of research. Product advertising, when effective, shows results within days or at most weeks, so proposed advertising programs can be thoroughly pretested. When as large a
market share as possible must be captured before competing products are
developed and marketed, it may be necessary to forego pretests. In such
cases, rough estimates of the three parameters can be made from a knowledge of past performances of similar products. As the campaign progresses

and the estimates of the parameters are improved, the campaign can be modified accordingly.

MATHEMATICAL MODEL

WE HAVE SEEN that the response of sales to a promotional campaign can be described by three parameters: λ, the exponential Sales Decay Constant, M, the Saturation Level, and r, the Response Constant.

A mathematical model of sales response to advertising, based on these parameters, is represented by:

$$dS/dt = r\, A(t)\, (M-S)/M - \lambda S, \qquad (1)$$

where S is the rate of sales at time t, and $A(t)$ is the rate of advertising expenditure. This equation has the following interpretation: the increase in the rate of sales, dS/dt, is proportional to the intensity of the advertising effort, A, reaching the fraction of potential customers, $(M-S)/M$, less the number of customers that are being lost, λS.

This model has been chosen because it describes in simple mathematical terms our experimental observations. Undoubtedly the probability of losing customers is decreased by advertising. Further experiments may prove that r and M are altered by changes in market conditions, by competing advertising, and by the introduction of new products. However, every increase in complexity requires the introduction of one or more additional parameters into equation (1). Since this model has been sufficient to describe the observed phenomena to the degree of accuracy allowed by the quality of our experimental data, there seems to be no reason at this time to complicate the picture unnecessarily. As our knowledge of advertising increases, it should be possible to improve this model and to develop more sophisticated theories.

From equation (1) we can derive several results that have proved useful in the design and evaluation of advertising campaigns:

Steady-state solution. We can determine the advertising effort required to maintain sales at a steady predetermined level by setting $dS/dt=0$. From equation (1), we then have $A = (\lambda/r)\, SM/(M-S)$. We see that the closer sales are to the saturation level M, and the larger the ratio λ/r, the more expensive it is to maintain the required sales rate.

Solution of equation (1). For a constant rate, A, of advertising expenditure, maintained for time T, the rate of sales is obtained by integration of equation (1):

$$S(t) = [M/(1+\lambda M/rA)]\{1 - e^{-(rA/M+\lambda)t}\} + S_0\, e^{-r(A/M+\lambda)t}, \qquad (t<T) \quad (2)$$

where S_0 is the rate of sales at $t=0$, the start of the advertising campaign. After advertising has stopped $(t>T)$, sales decrease exponentially:

$$S(t) = S(T)\, e^{-\lambda(t-T)} \qquad (t>T) \quad (3)$$

The sales response to an advertising campaign of constant intensity and of duration T is shown in Fig. 6.

The rate of sales increase is most rapid at $t=0$; as saturation, M, is approached, this rate is reduced. This means that the first advertising dollar expended is most effective, the second dollar is next most effective, and so on. A second implication of this advertising model is that for equal expenditures, a protracted advertising campaign is more profitable than a short, intense campaign. We have not yet tested this conclusion experimentally.

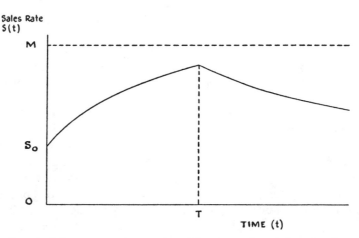

Fig. 6. Sales response to an advertising campaign of duration T.

Advertising Pulse

Many advertising campaigns are short and very intense. To get an expression for a single-pulse campaign of negligible duration we can integrate equation (1) to obtain

$$S(t) = M\, e^{-\lambda t} - (M - S_0)\, e^{-(ra/M + \lambda)t}, \qquad (4)$$

where S_0 is the rate of sales immediately preceding the promotion and a is the total advertising expenditure. The immediate sales increase resulting from the promotion is

$$S(0) - S_0 = (M - S_0)(1 - e^{-ra/M}). \qquad (5)$$

The total additional sales generated by this campaign are

$$\int_0^\infty [S(0) - S_0]\, e^{-\lambda t}\, dt = \frac{M - S_0}{\lambda}\, (1 - e^{-ra/M}),$$

which reduces to $(ra/\lambda)(M - S_0)/M$ for sales well below saturation. The total extra sales generated by the advertising campaign are therefore the immediate sales increase, multiplied by the mean life of the product, λ^{-1}. Also, given a choice of several products, the advertising campaign will generate the most sales for the product with the largest value of $(r/\lambda)(M-S_0)/M$.

ALLOCATION OF ADVERTISING BUDGET

WE HAVE DISCUSSED experimental results of sales response to advertising and have described a simple mathematical model that adequately fits our observations. Once the parameters are measured for individual products, the problems of advertising budget size and of the allocation of the budget among different products can be considered.

Advertising is a form of investment. Those products should be advertised that will result in a return on capital invested equal to or greater than the returns from other possible investments, such as new equipment and research.

As an example, let us consider the simple case of a family of products that might be advertised by short, intense campaigns. We define the following quantities:

a_k = total cost of the proposed advertising campaign for product k.
$R_k(t)$ = additional sales resulting from the advertising campaign.
$C_k(t)$ = rate of additional expenditures resulting from the advertising campaign. These include (a) the cost of the advertising campaign itself, (b) the cost of manufacturing and distributing the additional items sold.
I_k = return on capital invested in advertising product k. For example, \$100 at time t_1 is equivalent to \$100 $\exp[I_k(t_2-t_1)]$ at time t_2.

The sum total of expenditures incurred by the promotion of product k discounted at the rate I_k from the start of the advertising campaign $(t=0)$ is

$$\int_0^\infty C_k(t)\, e^{-I_k t}\, dt.$$

The additional sales resulting from the advertising campaign, also discounted at the rate I_k, are

$$\int_0^\infty R_k(t)\, e^{-I_k t}\, dt.$$

In order to determine the rate of return on capital invested in the promotion of product k, we equate expenditures and sales increases:

$$\int_0^\infty C_k(t)\, e^{-I_k t}\, dt = \int_0^\infty R_k(t)\, e^{-I_k t}\, dt. \tag{6}$$

Under the assumption that production and distribution costs are proportional to sales, we have

$$C_k(t) = f_k\, R_k(t) + a_k, \tag{7}$$

where f_k is the ratio of production and distribution costs to selling price. Assuming that the rate of sales of the unpromoted product decays exponentially at the rate λ_k, we have

$$R_k(t) = R_{0k}\, e^{-\lambda_k t}, \tag{8}$$

where R_{0k} is the instantaneous sales increase resulting from the campaign. Substituting (7) and (8) into equation (6), we obtain

$$a_k + \int_0^\infty f_k\, R_{0k}\, e^{-\lambda_k t}\, e^{-I_k t}\, dt = \int_0^\infty R_{0k}\, e^{-\lambda_k t}\, e^{-I_k t}\, dt.$$

Integrating and solving for I_k:

$$I_k = (R_{0k}/a_k)\,(1 - f_k) - \lambda_k. \tag{9}$$

It should be noted that the relation between R_{0k} and a_k is not linear, so the rate of return I_k is a function of the intensity of the advertising campaign.

Once the values of I_k are known, one can in principle select the products that may be advertised profitably. The rate of return considered acceptable by management varies considerably from company to company, but remains relatively constant in time.

We see that the amount of advertising appropriate to each product, and consequently the total advertising appropriation, can be determined once the I_k are known.

SUMMARY

In summary, we wish to stress the following points:

1. When carefully designed and executed, advertising experiments give results that are both reliable and reproducible. The degree of accuracy attainable is, however, considerably smaller than would be considered acceptable in many other fields of research. Product advertising gives quick results; the pretesting of proposed product advertising campaigns, therefore, is especially attractive.

2. The response of sales to advertising varies widely from product to product, but some generalizations are possible. The response of individual products to an advertising promotion may be characterized by two parameters: Response Constant and Saturation Level. A third parameter, the Sales Decay Constant, gives the rate at which customers are lost.

3. A mathematical model of sales response, based on these three parameters, has proved useful in the analysis of advertising campaigns. By means of this model one can compute the quantities needed to evaluate and compare alternate promotional campaigns.

4. A knowledge of sales response to advertising for each product permits one to evaluate the return that can be expected from capital invested in advertising for each product. With this information it is then possible to select profitable advertising programs and to estimate the optimum total size of the advertising budget.

We do not know whether the model of sales response discussed in this paper will prove applicable to all situations; our experience is limited to a few industries, and we have not tested all advertising media. It is our hope that as these studies progress and as the volume of experimental data grows, it will be possible to refine the model and thus increase its usefulness.

We wish to express our appreciation to SHERMAN KINGSBURY, GEORGE E. KIMBALL, and FRANK T. HULSWIT, who, in their studies of advertising effectiveness, first developed many of the ideas expressed in this paper and helped to demonstrate the value of the operations-research approach to sales problems.

REFERENCES

1. HORACE C. LEVINSON, "Experiences in Commercial Operations Research," *Opns. Res.* **1**, 220 (1953).
2. BERNARD O. KOOPMAN, "The Optimum Distribution of Effort," *Opns. Res.* **1**, 52 (1953).
3. JOHN F. MAGEE, "The Effect of Promotional Effort on Sales," *Opns. Res.* **1**, 64 (1953).
4. ROBERT DORFMAN AND PETER O. STEINER, "Optimal Advertising and Optimal Quality," *Amer. Econ. Rev.* **44**, 5 (1954).
5. R. S. WEINBERG, "Multiple Factor Break-Even Analysis," *Opns. Res.* **4**, 152 (1956).
6. A. A. BROWN, F. T. HULSWIT, AND J. D. KETTELLE, "A Study of Sales Operations," *Opns. Res.* **4**, 296 (1956).

ADVERTISING AND CIGARETTES[1]

LESTER G. TELSER

University of Chicago

I. INTRODUCTION

IN A study of the effects of advertising, cigarettes occupy a special place. The cigarette industry has become the traditional example of an industry in which advertising has posed a barrier to entry of new firms and becomes the main competitive weapon by which oligopolists seek to increase their relative shares. Yet despite the abundance of data, the industry's use of advertising has not been examined in detail.[2] This paper seeks to measure various aspects of competitive advertising to determine precisely how advertising affects sales. In the process, we obtain estimates of the rate of depreciation of advertising capital and the marginal rate of return on the advertising capital. These estimates place in perspective the extent of the competition among the cigarette companies by means of advertising.

Among the reasons why the cigarette industry is so frequently cited in discussions of advertising are, of course, the large advertising outlays by the cigarette companies and the important place the cigarette industry occupies in the economy. Table 1 shows the advertising outlays in the six categories for which the Internal Revenue Service reports the largest advertising expenditures. Since the first three categories include a wide range of products, the amount spent on advertising the goods in the latter three more homogenous categories—cigarettes, beer,

TABLE 1

ADVERTISING EXPENDITURES IN 1957,
BY SELECTED CATEGORIES

Category	Expenditures ($ Millions)
Department stores..............	426
Retail food stores.............	233
Drugs and medicine............	225
Cigarettes....................	210
Beer........................	209
Motor vehicles...............	195
All categories...............	7,666

Source: *The Source Book of Income* (Internal Revenue Service).

and automobiles—is all the more striking. Cigarettes are a sizable item in the consumer budget. In 1957, for instance, consumers spent more than $6 billion on this commodity, a figure which is about 2.1 per cent of their total expenditure. There are few other narrowly defined consumer goods that account for a larger fraction of consumption. Finally, cigarettes are widely used. In 1955, 47 per cent of the male population were regular cigarette smokers, and only 22 per cent had never smoked. Of the females, 27 per cent were in the first category and 65 per

[1] I am grateful to Zvi Griliches, Harry Roberts, and George Stigler for helpful comments and criticism. Responsibility for errors is mine. Computations were financed by the Ford Foundation Faculty Research Fund of the Graduate School of Business, University of Chicago. The computations were carried out by Lily Monheit and G. S. Maddala.

[2] The four main references are Reavis Cox, *Competition in the American Tobacco Industry* (New York: Columbia University Press, 1933); Neil H. Borden, *The Economic Effects of Advertising* (Chicago: Richard D. Irwin, Inc., 1942), chaps. viii and ix; William H. Nicholls, *Price Policies in the Cigarette Industry* (Nashville, Tenn.: Vanderbilt University Press, 1951); and Richard B. Tennant, *The American Cigarette Industry* (New Haven, Conn.: Yale University Press, 1950).

cent in the second.[3] Clearly the market for cigarettes is extensive and the advertising outlay large.

A more cogent reason for examining the advertising of cigarettes emerges from studying the history of the industry. The main point that comes out of such a study is the importance of advertising as the avenue of competition among the cigarette companies. Hence it is useful at the outset to summarize briefly the history of the industry. In 1911, the Tobacco Trust produced 86 per cent of the nation's cigarettes. Its dissolution in that year led to the creation of three cigarette firms: American Tobacco, Liggett and Myers, and P. Lorillard. In 1913 one of the successor companies, R. J. Reynolds, that had not obtained any cigarette business by the terms of the 1911 Consent Decree, entered a new brand, Camels. Because of its success, in about 1917 American Tobacco began the sale of a similar cigarette, Lucky Strike; and Liggett and Myers brought out Chesterfield. The first two brands enjoyed uninterrupted leadership from 1917 to 1953. In 1946 these three companies had a combined market share of 86 per cent (presumably a peril point so far as the Justice Department is concerned), and the Justice Department instituted antitrust proceedings. By 1960, the share of these three companies had declined to 70 per cent, probably the result less of antitrust action than the rise of filter cigarettes. Most of the decline in market share in this fifteen-year period was suffered by Liggett and Myers; and, in 1960, Lorillard was on the verge of replacing it as the third largest company. Two other

companies, Phillip Morris, and Brown and Williamson, became important during and after World War II.[4]

Since about 1923, prices of the major cigarette brands have been almost identical and price changes infrequent and simultaneous. Some price competition of an obvious kind emerged in the Great Depression when the ten-cent brands appeared. The four industry leaders reduced their prices, but even so the ten-cent brands persisted through the 1930's. By the end of World War II, these brands finally disappeared thanks to increased consumer income.[5]

Although advertising is widely believed to be the main avenue of competition among the cigarette companies, William H. Nicholls is the only one who has estimated its effect. Using his notation let

Y = percentage of American advertising to combined American and Reynolds advertising;

X = percentage of Lucky Strike sales to combined Lucky Strike and Camel sales.

For 1925–39 he finds

$$X = 18.9 + 0.548Y \quad (1)$$
$$(0.169)$$

and an adjusted correlation coefficient of .641. Omitting 1932, he obtains

$$X = 10.8 + 0.730Y \quad (2)$$
$$(0.236)$$

and an adjusted correlation of .561. He states that a similar regression for 1934–

[3] William Haenszel, Michael B. Shimkin, and Herman P. Miller, *Tobacco Smoking in the United States* (Public Health Monograph No. 45, Public Health Service, United States Department of Health, Education, and Welfare [Washington: Government Printing Office, 1956]).

[4] See Table 12.

[5] Monthly market shares of the ten-cent brands from January, 1931, to February, 1936, are shown in Borden, *op. cit.*, Table 34. From the beginning of this period to November, 1932, the share of these brands rose from zero to 23 per cent. Most of the increase followed a higher price of the standard brands that took effect on June 24, 1931. In January and February, 1933, the standard brands reduced their price, and by March the market share of the ten-cent brands had fallen to 7 per cent. Following

43 fails to show a significant correlation between the two variables.[6]

This line of analysis, however, has not been pursued. It is possible, moreover, to use the data obtained by Nicholls from the court record of the 1946 antitrust trial to deduce a number of results on the effects of advertising on competition and sales. First, we can see whether the firms made advertising outlays so large that marginal returns become negative with respect to advertising. (Finding negative marginal returns implies that a company spent more on advertising than its best interest dictates.) Second, we can estimate the rate of return on advertising capital by estimating the marginal sales effect of advertising capital and the rate of depreciation of advertising capital. The periodic advertising expenditures build up good will and increase sales for some period of time into the future. Thus advertising outlays are a capital investment that depreciates and that requires maintenance. The rate of depreciation of advertising capital is deduced from estimates of the consumer repeat-purchase probability. That is, it is widely believed that consumers display a certain amount of inertia in their buying behavior. Consumer inertia implies a relation between current market share, lagged market share, and relative advertising expenditure that allows estimation of repeat-purchase probabilities for consumers taken in the aggregate. The same theory makes it possible to estimate the propensity of consumers to transfer purchases from all other brands to a given brand and gives a direct measure of one aspect of the competition among brands. Finally, the relation between market share and relative advertising outlay implies upper bounds on the competitive effects of advertising. These analyses are made for the period before World War II.

The postwar period is more complicated because product changes became an important source of competition. Reports linking lung cancer to cigarette smoking were made public in 1952. By 1954, total cigarette sales were 92 per cent of the 1952 level. However, since 1954, sales have resumed their upward movement. Apparently the main effect of the cancer scare was to alter consumer preferences for various kinds of cigarettes without inducing large numbers to give up smoking altogether. Filtered and mentholated cigarettes became popular, and sales of the previously standard forms fell sharply. Cigarette companies have competed for consumer favor by introducing many new brands and varieties of cigarettes. This product innovation, together with advertising, is now the chief avenue of competition in the industry.

The theoretical literature on changes in taste and how firms adapt to these changes is sparse. Because no clear-cut theoretical burden is placed on the data, the analysis of the postwar period is a bit impressionistic. Nevertheless, the analysis of this difficult period does show that adaptations to changes in taste and relative advertising expenditures explain a large part of the variation of market shares for the six important cigarette companies of the postwar period.

II. RETURNS TO ADVERTISING

Measurement of the returns to cigarette advertising requires a model with relevance to the cigarette industry of the determinants of the advertising outlay. At this point, therefore, we need to draw

---

these price reductions, the share of the ten-cent brands rose to about 10 per cent, and it fluctuated around 12 per cent until 1940. Their share decreased steadily from 1940 to 1945 when they practically disappeared from the national market.

[6] Nicholls, *op. cit.*, p. 132.

together evidence on the nature of price competition in the cigarette industry and evidence on the reasons for advertising in the face of the seemingly collusive price policy in order to specify a mathematical model for estimating the returns to advertising.

The high concentration and the infrequency of price changes in the cigarette industry are facts beyond dispute. Hence the theory of perfect competition is of

TABLE 2

RELATIVE ADVERTISING EXPENDITURES
BY BRAND, 1929–43*

Year	Camels	Lucky Strike	Chesterfield
1929....	0.1640	0.9156	0.6159
1930....	.2996	.9364	.4003
1931....	.4393	.7133	.3860
1932....	.1086	.8021	.8413
1933....	.6933	.4032	.4352
1934....	.5975	.4030	.5122
1935....	.6248	.2962	.6312
1936....	.5891	.3760	.5528
1937....	.5541	.3310	.6523
1938....	.6037	.3273	.6051
1939....	.6558	.2756	.6337
1940....	.5886	.2872	.6845
1941....	.6062	.2988	.6461
1942....	.7410	.3056	.5159
1943....	.6438	.3352	.5559

* Relative advertising expenditures are defined as expenditures on the given brand divided by expenditures on all other brands. There are two sets of estimates; one is from Borden, *op. cit.*, Table 33, and the other from Nicholls, *op. cit.*, Tables 37 and 47. The differences are not large, and in those cases in which the Nicholls and Borden estimates differ the Nicholls estimate was used. Both sets of estimates exclude costs of radio programming and talent.

little help in explaining the behavior of the cigarette companies. Although this theory predicts that all firms in an industry will charge the same price for a given product, the observed price rigidity is incompatible with this theory, given year-to-year fluctuations in the price of tobacco leaf and other costs of manufacture. A pattern of price leadership emerged in the cigarette industry in the 1920's. In most cases, Reynolds was the first to announce a price change, and within a few days prices of the other stand-

ard brands were changed by the same amount. We shall examine the record of the cigarette industry to measure the effect of advertising on sales, but to study the effect upon entry by new firms would necessitate surveying a variety of industries.

Firms use advertising to persuade consumers to purchase their product, and it is not evident that they are concerned whether these new customers are new smokers or previous customers of rivals. However, given the price policy of the cigarette companies in which price competition seemed notably absent, there is the problem of explaining why firms compete by advertising. The existence of such competition is clear from Table 2, since relative advertising outlays did not remain constant from year to year.

Even assuming that the three firms whose advertising outlays are shown in Table 2 colluded explicitly or implicitly on price and fixed prices at the same level as would a single firm, it is not in their interest to suppress advertising altogether. Surely a monopolist may advertise to increase sales and, for the same reasons, three (or six) firms would advertise. In the real world, information is an economic good and advertising is a source of information.[7] This implies more intensive advertising of new than of established products, and the cigarette data bear this out. The percentage of urban households reporting the presence of at least one male cigarette smoker rose from 51 per cent in 1923 to 67 per cent in 1939. Over this seventeen-year period the number of urban households with at least one

[7] For an approach to advertising that stresses informational aspects see S. A. Ozga, "Imperfect Markets through Lack of Knowledge," *Quarterly Journal of Economics*, LXXIV (February, 1960), 29–52, and George J. Stigler, "The Economics of Information," *Journal of Political Economy*, LXIX (June, 1961), 213–25.

male smoker nearly doubled. From 1934 to 1939 the percentage of urban households reporting the presence of at least one female smoker increased from 17 to 27 per cent, and the absolute number of such households increased by 75 per cent in this six-year period.[8] Relative to the extent of the market, the advertising outlays were probably much greater in the earlier than in the later period. The combined advertising outlay of Reynolds and American reached a peak of $40 million in 1931 and thereafter leveled off to an annual rate of approximately $25 million until about 1953. Thus, during the period of rapid growth, the companies advertised to obtain new customers. As cigarette smoking became more widespread, relatively less was spent on advertising. Of course, the entry and exit of consumers explains the persistence of advertising even in a market of fixed size. Some additional evidence of advertising's informational role can be obtained by comparing advertising expenditures relative to sales before and after 1952, when reports linking lung cancer to cigarette smoking appeared and many new brands entered the market. From 1948 to 1951 the ratio of advertising to sales rose at an annual rate of 6.5 per cent; from 1953 to 1957 the annual rate of increase was 13.5 per cent.[9] Nevertheless, after the growth

in demand slackened in the 1930's, the relative advertising outlays of the three leading firms did affect market shares and, therefore, had a competitive effect.

Granted that it is not in the interest of the firms to suppress advertising altogether, there remains the question of why they did not collude on advertising. Suppose that the firms can agree on the total advertising outlay and that they decide to maintain constant shares of this total. An increase in market share need not result from larger advertising outlays, since a firm can attribute its larger sales to more effective advertising. Indeed, the argument for explicit collusion on advertising is the same as the argument for outright monopoly in another guise. Certainly a central marketing organization could have been more profitable than the existing arrangement. However, given the early history of the cigarette industry and the vigilance of the Department of Justice, such an organization would have been short lived.

We can construct simple models for estimating the effect of advertising on demand. Let us first treat the advertising as having its total effect within a single period. Let

q = sales of the firm
p = price
x = advertising outlay of the firm
X = advertising outlay of all other firms in the industry
C = total cost of the given firm as a function of its rate of output
R = net revenue.

By definition

$$R = pq - C - x . \qquad (3)$$

The demand for the firm's product is

$$q = F(p, x, X) . \qquad (4)$$

Suppose, in view of the preceding discussion, that the price is not a variable that

[8] Data on the percentage of households reporting the presence of at least one cigarette smoker are given in the annual reports of *The Milwaukee Journal. Consumer Analysis*. Figures on male smokers are available annually from 1923 and for female smokers from 1934. No surveys were published in 1932, 1933, and 1936. The figures may be regarded as estimates for the urban, not the rural, population. For the difference in smoking habits between the two see the reference cited in n. 3. Since the figures refer to households and not individuals, they may understate the fraction of smokers in the population.

[9] These figures are derived from microfilms of the *Source Book of Income* (Internal Revenue Service). These data give sales and advertising expenditures for corporations at the three-digit level.

the firm chooses but that it adjusts its advertising outlay to maximize profits. By a standard calculation, the necessary maximum condition is that

$$(p - C_q)\frac{dq}{dx} = 1, \qquad (5)$$

where

$$\frac{dq}{dx} = F_x + F_X \frac{dX}{ax}. \qquad (6)$$

Thus the change in sales per unit change in the firm's advertising outlay depends both on the partial effect on sales of its advertising, F_x, and on the indirect effect via changes in the advertising outlays of the other firms in the industry induced by a change in the firm's advertising outlay. On the basis of the preceding theoretical discussion, it seems plausible to expect that $F_X < 0$ and $F_x > 0$. If an increased x induces an increased X, then the net change in sales per unit change in the firm's advertising outlay, dq/dx, is less than the partial effect, F_x.

The sufficient condition for maximum profits requires that the second derivative of R with respect to x, or

$$R_{xx} = (p - C_q)\frac{d^2 q}{dx^2} - C_{qq}\left(\frac{dq}{dx}\right)^2$$

be negative. Since cigarette firms each operate several establishments of different sizes, it is plausible to assume that average cost is approximately constant, so that $C_{qq} = 0$.[10] It follows that the sufficient condition for maximum profits requires diminishing marginal sales effectiveness of advertising, that is, the second derivative of sales with respect to x must be negative. We can investigate the nature of the returns to advertising by fitting regressions of various forms to time series of sales, advertising expenditures and other variables. The result is

[10] See Nicholls, *op. cit.*, p. 199.

the best estimate of the firm's demand schedule, equation (4).

Table 3 gives the available data for the longest time period on annual sales of Lucky Strike and Camels and the advertising expenditures of Reynolds and American. The advertising data include an unknown, but probably small, amount of advertising on the other tobacco products of these two companies, besides, Lucky Strike and Camels. This measurement error might lead to downward-biased estimates of the effects of advertising on sales, but the effect will be small.

Perhaps a more serious problem is the lack of data that would allow us to measure the physical quantity of advertising instead of the dollar expenditures on advertising. The demand for cigarettes depends not so much on the dollar advertising outlays as on the number of advertising "messages" consumers receive. The firm buys space in magazines and newspapers or time on radio. To a first approximation, the number of advertising messages conveyed depends on the audience size of these media. For example, we may think of the number of messages conveyed by newspaper advertising as equal to the product of the number of pages purchased and the newspaper's circulation (as a proxy for readership). To estimate the number of advertising messages conveyed by newspaper advertising, therefore, we could divide the advertising expenditures in newspapers by the price per page and multiply the quotient by the circulation of the newspaper. Even this procedure, which requires information on advertising outlays by media and the price per unit of media services, is not ideal. First, we have no way of knowing how many of those in the audience of a given medium were exposed to the advertising. Estimates of radio audiences are admittedly crude approximations and do not give the number of those exposed to the advertising. Although the estimates of newspaper and magazine circulation are fairly accurate, they are also subject to error insofar as we wish to use these figures to estimate the number of advertising messages received. First, some fraction of the people who read the newspaper or magazine may not see the advertising of the particular product. Second, the readership of a mgazine or newspaper typically exceeds its recorded circulation. These two factors thus impart errors of measurement of opposite sign if our purpose is the estimation of the number of advertising messages received from newspapers and magazines. Time series on nominal advertising outlays thus neglect both the change over time of advertising rates and the audience size. There are reasons, however, for believing that advertising rates and audience size tend to move in the same direction over time; therefore, the error of measurement arising from the use of nominal instead of deflated advertising outlays is, to some extent, off-

TABLE 3

CIGARETTE SALES, ADVERTISING, REAL NATIONAL INCOME,
AND DEFLATED RETAIL PRICE OF STANDARD BRANDS

Year	Camels Sales (Billions of Cigarettes) (1)	Reynolds Advertising Outlay (Millions of Dollars) (2)	Lucky Strike Sales (Billions of Cigarettes) (3)	American Advertising Outlay (Millions of Dollars) (4)	Real National Income (Billions of Dollars) (5)	Deflated Retail Cigarette Price (1¢ per Package) (6)
1912	0.000	0.435	....	....	....	....
1913	0.035	0.682	....	....	86.3	23.6
1914	0.543	1.251	....	....	83.0	23.3
1915	2.425	1.901	....	....	89.4	23.0
1916	6.796	1.948	....	....	100.9	21.5
1917	12.253	0.708	....	....	102.7	22.8
1918	14.784	0.409	....	....	95.2	19.4
1919	21.032	5.356	....	....	96.6	20.3
1920	18.7	6.188	....	....	85.1	17.5
1921	18.4	8.042	....	....	71.3	19.6
1922	21.5	4.927	....	....	87.2	20.9
1923	30.1	5.342	....	....	100.0	20.6
1924	31.4	6.445	....	....	99.2	20.5
1925	34.2	10.100	13.7	8.8	103.1	20.0
1926	38.0	17.640	14.8	7.8	106.3	19.8
1927	38.4	19.473	19.1	12.7	107.3	20.2
1928	36.7	12.872	27.4	12.2	112.7	20.5
1929	37.2	9.934	37.0	13.7	119.2	20.5
1930	35.3	15.138	43.2	19.7	105.0	21.0
1931	33.3	16.057	44.5	23.7	90.6	23.1
1932	23.9	5.437	36.7	24.8	71.4	18.0
1933	25.6	14.896	36.7	14.6	71.6	20.8
1934	33.3	17.400	32.1	12.6	85.0	21.9
1935	39.4	14.471	30.7	10.5	96.8	21.3
1936	46.4	14.880	33.1	17.6	109.4	21.1
1937	47.7	14.962	34.5	10.2	119.9	20.4
1938	43.7	15.538	36.4	9.8	111.8	20.7
1939	42.8	15.363	38.4	9.7	122.1	21.0

Source: Cols. (1)–(4), Nicholls, *op. cit.*; col. (5), National income figures from *Agricultural Statistics 1952*, Table 633, and the United States Department of Commerce for recent years. The deflator is the Consumer Price Index, 1947–1949 = 100; col. (6), Nicholls, *op. cit., passim.*; the deflator is the Consumer Price Index, 1947–1949 = 100.

setting.[11] Even if the ratio of the percentage increase of audience size to the percentage increase of advertising rates is greater than one, so that the time series on nominal advertising outlays underestimates the increase in the number of advertising messages conveyed, the use of nominal advertising outlays would result in an upward-biased estimate of advertising effectiveness. Moreover, the introduction of radio in the late 1920's probably increased advertising effectiveness—all the more reason why the nominal advertising outlays give upward-biased estimates of advertising effectiveness.

To measure the nature of the return to advertising, we can calculate various regressions that have different implications about the form of the return to advertising and see which one best describes the data.[12] Four alternative forms are as follows:

$$q_t = A + Bx_t + Cy_t + Dp_t + Et \qquad \text{(i)}$$

$$q_t = A' + B' \log x_t + C' \log y_t \atop \qquad + D' \log p_t + E't \qquad \text{(ii)}$$

$$\log q_t = a' + b' \log x_t + c' \log y_t \atop \qquad + d' \log p_t + e't \qquad \text{(iii)}$$

$$\log q_t = a + bx_t + cy_t + dp_t + et, \qquad \text{(iv)}$$

where

q_t = sales in billions of cigarettes
x_t = advertising outlay in millions of dollars
y_t = national income divided by the consumer price index (1947–1949 = 100)

[11] *Printers' Ink* gives data on advertising rates and estimates of audience size by principle media for the postwar years. For newspapers and magazines the audience size is circulation and for television and radio the estimates are based on surveys of listeners. These data indicate a positive association between audience size and advertising rates.

[12] Polynomials use up too many degrees of freedom, have problems of collinearity, and were therefore not computed.

p_t = the retail price per package of a standard brand of cigarettes divided by the consumer price index
t = linear trend.

Since Chesterfield data are unavailable for the sample period, we cannot include X_t total advertising outlays by all the competitors of a given brand in these regressions. However, we can use the estimates of the coefficients of x to measure the net effect on sales of a change in the firm's advertising expenditure. That is, we can, estimate the effect on sales of advertising that takes implicit account of competitors' reactions induced by a change in the given firm's advertising.

We expect the coefficient of x_t and y_t to be positive, of p_t to be negative, and of t to be positive (because of the over-all upward trend in cigarette sales). The coefficients of the variables are estimated by least squares. Except for errors of measurement such estimates are unbiased, provided the firm is unable to make exact forecasts of its sales, and provided omitted variables are uncorrelated with those included. The inclusion of the trend term makes the expected values of the coefficients the same as would be found by taking first differences of the variables. In addition, for reasons given below, first difference regressions were calculated for (ii). The same price variable is used in Camel and Lucky Strike regressions because both brands had the same wholesale and retail prices. Prices did not change frequently, and most of the variation of the real price is due to changes in the deflator.

Equations (i)–(iv) differ in their implications regarding the nature of the returns to advertising. The second derivatives of sales with respect to advertising are

0	(i)	$bq(b-1)/x^2$	(iii)
$-B'/x^2 < 0$	(ii)	$b'^2q > 0$.	(iv)

Thus advertising has a constant marginal product in (i), a decreasing marginal product in (ii), and an increasing marginal product in (iv). In (iii) advertising has increasing, constant, or decreasing marginal returns according to whether b is greater than, equal to, or less than one. By deciding which of the four regressions best describes the data, we may learn whether firms choose to make their advertising outlay large enough to place them in the region of decreasing marginal effectiveness of advertising.

To see which of the four regressions gives the best fit, we compare the standard errors of prediction of actual sales. However, because (i) and (ii) are linear in the dependent variable whereas (iii) and (iv) are linear in the logarithm of the same variable, the standard errors between the two pairs are not directly comparable. The residuals are easily converted to a common base by calculating the anti-logs of the predicted dependent variables of (iii) and (iv).

Table 4 contains the regression esti-

TABLE 4

RELATION OF SALES, ADVERTISING, REAL INCOME, REAL PRICE, AND TREND[a]

Coefficients of	(i)	(ii)	(ii*)[b]	(iii)	(iv)
	R. J. Reynolds (Camels) 1913–39				
Advertising	.775	9.907	3.163	.473	.0246
	(.219)	(2.454)	(1.931)	(.286)	(.0244)
Real income	.309	72.5	60.0	2.14	.0084
	(.057)	(11.2)	(11.2)	(1.31)	(.0063)
Real price	−1.865	−64.95	5.32	−8.70	−.209
	(.533)	(23.93)	(16.33)	(2.79)	(.059)
Trend	.790	.018	....	.023	.029
	(.176)	(.153)		(.018)	(.020)
Constant	17.59	−50.76	1.143	7.760	4.140
R^{2c}	.938	.947	.622	.693	.675
d (Durbin-Watson Statistic)	.943	1.133	1.273		
s (standard error of estimate)	3.80	3.54	2.65		
	American Tobacco (Lucky Strike) 1925–39				
Advertising	1.212	41.776	12.781	.677	.0191
	(.302)	(10.244)	(8.98)	(.162)	(.0050)
Real income	.092	16.2	50.6	.259	.0014
	(.099)	(21.3)	(34.1)	(.338)	(.0017)
Real price	1.782	69.98	9.78	.960	.0252
	(1.279)	(60.38)	(25.64)	(.957)	(.0213)
Trend	1.144	1.136	....	.0214	.0216
	(.313)	(.308)		(.0049)	(.0052)
Constant	−49.56	−157.43	1.598	−1.401	.2082
R^{2d}	.794	.799	.306	.823	.799
d	1.533	1.605	1.020		
s	4.96	4.93	4.38		

[a] The dependent variable is sales of the indicated brand in billions of cigarettes. Data are shown in Table 3. Numbers in parentheses are standard errors of the corresponding coefficients.

[b] (ii*) is the regression on first differences of the same variables as in (ii). For Camels the period is 1914–39, for Lucky Strike 1926–39. The predictions using first differences are better for (ii*) than for (ii), as can be seen by comparing s's. For Camels, first differencing reduces the serial correlation of the residuals as shown by the increased value of the Durbin-Watson statistic; however, for Lucky Strike, first differencing increases the serial correlation of residuals. The constant terms of (ii*) are estimates of the trend coefficient and comparable to the trend coefficients of (ii).

[c] The 10, 5, and 1 per cent points with 4 and 22 degrees of freedom of R^2 are .288, .339, and .439, respectively.

[d] The 10, 5, and 1 per cent points of R^2 are .511, .582, and .705, respectively.

mates. These support the hypothesis that the advertising outlays were large enough to place the firms in the region of decreasing marginal effectiveness of advertising. According to the Reynolds regressions, the advertising coefficient in (iii) is less than one, indicating decreasing marginal effectiveness of advertising. The best regression is clearly (ii). Moreover, the Durbin-Watson statistic is larger for (ii) than for (i), which is consistent with the view that part of the serial correlation of residuals in (i) arises from the misspecification of the form of the regression in (i). One regression, (ii*), the first difference form of (ii), is clearly best on two counts. First, the standard error of prediction is lower for (ii*) than for any other regression of those considered. Second, the residuals of (ii*) have the lowest serial correlation, as shown by its having the highest Durbin-Watson statistic. Since the Reynolds data span a twenty-seven-year period, they are better suited to reveal the nature of the returns to advertising than the American data that cover only a fifteen-year period. Nevertheless, the American data clearly indicate a level of advertising high enough to place that company in the region of diminishing marginal effectiveness with respect to advertising. The R^2 of (iii) exceeds that of (iv), and b is less than one in (iii). Regression (ii) is better than (i) because its standard error of forecast is lower and its residuals show less serial correlation (a higher Durbin-Watson statistic). Although (iii) is a better predictor of the logarithm of sales than (ii) is of actual sales, (iii) is a much worse predictor of actual sales, since the mean squared error of predicting sales with (iii) is 63 per cent larger than (ii's) mean squared error. Thus (ii) is the best regression by these criteria. The regression (ii*) is not clearly better than (ii). Although its

standard error of prediction is lower, it shows more serial correlation of residuals. In view of the rather low serial correlation of residuals in (ii), this is not a surprising result, although it does differ from the same comparison with the Reynolds data.

One could use these results to estimate the marginal sales effect of advertising. However, advertising outlays probably affect sales even after the expenditures occur. Thus, the advertising outlays create a form of capital that continues to yield a return even in a period in which no current advertising outlays occur. It is more appropriate to estimate the marginal sales effect of advertising derived from a theory of investment by means of advertising. It is a simple matter to modify the necessary conditions for profit maximization and take into account the lasting effects of advertising.

Let r denote the marginal rate of return on advertising capital or good will. Assume that a one-dollar increment in advertising at the beginning of the first period generates an income stream $w_1, w_2, \ldots, w_t, \ldots$. The present value of this stream is

$$S = w_1 + \frac{w_2}{(1+r)} + \frac{w_3}{(1+r)^2} + \ldots + \frac{w_t}{(1+r)^{t-1}} + \ldots \quad (7)$$

The first term, w_1, is the marginal sales effect of the advertising in the first period. The w's in the succeeding periods are the marginal sales effects of the initial dollar increment of advertising. The optimal advertising outlay x is such that the marginal rate of return on the advertising, r, makes the present value of the stream of receipts imputed to the advertising equal one at the margin. Thus r is the marginal internal rate of return or the advertising and is the number to be estimated.

Suppose that w_t satisfies a simple difference equation as follows:

$$w_t - kw_{t-1}, \; w_t = k^{t-1}w_1 . \quad (8)$$

This means that a constant fraction of the marginal sales effect of the advertising in period $t - 1$ lasts into period t. Section IV gives empirical support to this hypothesis. Using (8), equation (7) simplifies to

$$w_1 \left[\frac{1 - \left(\frac{k}{1+r}\right)^n}{1 - \left(\frac{k}{1+r}\right)} \right] = 1 . \quad (9)$$

Since $w_1 = (p - C_q)dq/dx$, (9) reduces to (5) for $n = 1$. For large n,

$$w_1 = (p - C_q)\frac{dq}{dx} \approx 1 - \frac{k}{1+r}, \quad (10)$$

provided $k < 1 + r$. The rate of depreciation of the advertising capital is $1 - k$.

The marginal rate of return on advertising can be estimated from (10) for given estimates of the other terms of (10).

The above regressions, however, contain no information on k, since, except for the trend, they include no dynamic elements. One way of estimating k is to include lagged sales in the regression as follows:

$$q_t = a_0 + a_1q_{t-1} + a_2 \log x_t \\ + a_3 \log y_t + a_4 \log p_t + a_5 t . \quad (11)$$

This equation implies that an increase in x generates a series of increments in sales such that the increment in period t is a fraction a_1 of the increment in the preceding period. Thus the coefficient of lagged sales in this regression estimates k in (8). A second way of estimating (8) derived from repeat-purchase probabilities is discussed below. As it turns out, difficulties in using (11) to estimate k make the sec-

ond approach preferable. However, the difficulties in the first approach are themselves interesting.

For Camels (1913–39) we find

$$q_t = -60.14 + .41q_{t-1} \\ (.17)$$
$$+ 6.51 \log x_t + 48.03 \log y_t \quad (12) \\ (2.60) \qquad (14.17)$$
$$- 22.46 \log p_t + .42t . \\ (27.59) \qquad (.22)$$

The multiple $R^2 = .96$, $s = 3.11$, and the Durbin-Watson statistic $= .91$. The latter is, of course, merely a descriptive statistic in this case, since one of the explanatory variables is the lagged value of the dependent variable. For Lucky Strike (1926–39, omitting 1925 because sales figures are unavailable prior to that year), the regression equation is

$$q_t = -142.70 + .96q_{t-1} \\ (.22)$$
$$+ 7.36 \log x_t + 47.94 \log y_t \quad (13) \\ (9.93) \qquad (15.00)$$
$$+ 36.57 \log p_t - .42t . \\ (37.07 \qquad (.40)$$

The multiple $R^2 = .92$, $s = 3$, and there is a slight amount of negative serial correlation of the residuals.

An important point about equations (12) and (13) deserves comment. The most striking difference between the two regressions is that the trend coefficients are of opposite sign, and the coefficient of lagged sales is much larger in (13) than in (12). The explanation lies in the negative correlation between the *estimates* of a_1 and a_5. The correlations are $-.77$ and $-.85$, respectively, for Camels and Lucky Strike. This correlation means that the trend and lagged sales are highly correlated so that a reduction in the Camels trend coefficient increases the coefficient of lagged sales and an increase in the

Lucky Strike trend coefficient reduces its coefficient of lagged sales. This consistent pattern of results for the two regressions means that the coefficients of lagged sales cannot be reliably measured. Thus in the Camels regression, a reduction of the trend coefficient by 1.9 σ-units to zero increases a_1 by .25 to .66, an increase of 1.5 σ-units. For Lucky Strike an increase of a_5 to zero (1.05 σ-units) reduces a_1 by .2 to .76, a reduction of .9 σ-units of a_1. These results show the trade-off between the trend and lagged sales and indicate what would happen if the trend were omitted.

Since there is a tradeoff between the coefficients of trend and lagged sales, it is fair to ask why trend should be included in these regressions. The most important reason is that the trend serves as a linear deflator of advertising expenditures. In the discussion above, we saw that advertising might have become more effective over time because rates did not increase in proportion to audience size. Hence the trend can serve as a proxy measure of the increased effectiveness of advertising. Dropping the trend from the regressions results in an increase in the advertising coefficient, thus providing evidence in support of this view.

Keeping in mind the disturbing relation between the coefficients of trend and lagged market share, we may proceed to estimate the rate of return on advertising on the assumption that the actual advertising outlays maximized the present value of the returns imputed to advertising. Since sales are in billions of cigarettes and advertising is in millions of dollars, dq/dx is in thousands of cigarettes per dollar of advertising. Another minor point worth noting is that the derivative of the natural log of x is the reciprocal of x but that the regressions use common logarithms. Hence dq/dx is found by multi-

plying the coefficient of $\log_{10} x$ by $\log_{10} e$ = .43429.

The initial marginal sales effect of advertising is $(p - C_q) \, dq/dx$; we need an estimate of C_q. Because the companies each operated establishments of different sizes, it is plausible to believe that there were approximately constant average costs. Some data in Nicholls' study suggest that C_q is about one-half the net price to manufacturers after discounts and taxes.[13] The implied price elasticity to a profit-maximizing firm is about -2 given this estimate of marginal cost, a figure considerably larger than implied by the Camels regression.[14]

Using regressions (12) and (13), we now derive estimates of the marginal rate of return on advertising. Since the marginal sales effect of advertising varies from year to year as the level of advertising varies and as the net price changes, it is reasonable to estimate the marginal sales effect averaged over a number of years. The marginal sales effect of advertising averaged over the years 1925–28 and 1933–39 is 23 cents for Camels. Because of intrayear price changes, 1929–32 are excluded. According to (12) the estimated k is .41 and the implied r according to (10) is negative. Given this estimate of the marginal sales effect, a positive r requires k to exceed .77. Using the regres-

[13] Nicholls, *op. cit.*, gives cost estimates for 193 in Table 34 and for 1941 in Table 45. In 1932, the cost of leaf, direct factory costs, delivery costs, and depreciation and the cost of administration were 4 per cent of the net price to manufacturers after discounts and taxes. Selling and advertising costs were about 18 per cent of the net price. In 1941 these costs plus selling costs were 62 per cent of the net price to manufacturers. Advertising was 12.2 per cent, and selling costs were 4.8 per cent of the net price. Taking the marginal cost to be about 50 per cent of the net price seems a plausible estimate.

[14] For an estimate of the price elasticity between Lucky Strike and the competing brands, see Nicholls, *op. cit.*, p. 51, esp. n. 6. His estimates are of the same order of magnitude as implied by the text.

sion that excludes lagged sales, the mean marginal sales effect is 34 cents, and a positive r requires a k bigger than .66. However, the best regression for predicting the marginal sales effect of advertising is (ii*) (the first different form of [ii]) because it has the lowest standard error of prediction and because its residuals show the least serial correlation. Using (ii*), the mean marginal sales effect is 11 cents, and a positive r requires k at least equal to .89. Because of the tradeoff between the trend coefficient and the coefficient of lagged sales, we cannot have much confidence in the estimate of k implied by (12). These misgivings are confirmed by the estimates for Lucky Strike.

Using (13) the marginal sales effect of Lucky Strike advertising averaged over 1926–28 and 1933–39 is 34 cents. Given (13)'s estimate of $k = .96$, the implied r is 45 per cent! However, if the trend coefficient is assumed to be zero, the estimated k falls to .76, and the estimate of r is reduced to 15 per cent per year. If lagged sales are omitted from the regression, the mean marginal sales effect of advertising increases to $2.02, and the implied r is twice k. Given any reasonable estimate of k, the implied r seems much too high, even granting the greater effectiveness of Lucky Strike advertising. Thus in contrast to the results for Camels, the estimated k for Lucky Strike seems much too high. In addition, unlike the Camels results, (ii*) is inferior to (13) because it has a larger standard error of prediction and because its residuals show much more serial correlation.

The evidence thus indicates that the best estimate of the marginal sales effect of advertising for Camels is 11 cents derived from the first difference regression and the best estimate of the marginal sales effect of Lucky Strike advertising is 34 cents derived from (13). To estimate

k we use a different approach (described in detail in Sec. IV). Since consumers tend to repeat purchases of brands, they display a certain amount of inertia. Once Camels or Lucky Strike obtains a cohort of customers by means of advertising, the fraction of sales they retain from year to year is given by the repeat-purchase probabilities. Estimates of these repeat-purchase probabilities taken from Section IV are .83 for Camels and .74 for Lucky Strike. These repeat-purchase probabilities estimate k. Given these estimates, equation (10) implies that r was -6.8 per cent for Camels and about 15 per cent for Lucky Strike. Even the larger mean marginal sales effect of advertising for Camels implied by (12) makes r only 7.8 per cent. These estimates suggest that Camels spent too much on advertising during the sample period. Moreover, the best regression estimates for both brands do not yield very high r's. That the rate for Lucky Strike is larger than for Camels is undoubtedly due to the widely recognized advertising genius of George Washington Hill, president of the American Tobacco Company.

III. COMPETITIVE EFFECTS OF ADVERTISING

There are several ways of measuring advertising's competitive effects. First, we compare the residuals of the Lucky Strike and Camels regressions of the preceding section to see whether there is an inverse relation between the residuals. Second, we measure the correlation between advertising outlays on these two brands. Third, we include competitive advertising outlays in regressions to explain absolute sales of a given brand to see whether increased competitive advertising outlays reduce sales of that brand. Fourth, we estimate the relation between market share and relative advertising outlays. The latter approach gives the clearest picture of the competition among the brands and provides insights into other aspects of the problem that are discussed in the next section.

A first glimpse of the competition between the two brands is derived from a comparison of the residuals from 1925 to 1939 using the semi-log regressions of the preceding section. When Camels sales exceed predicted sales, Lucky Strike sales are less than predicted and vice versa. This inverse relation between the residuals occurs in eleven cases out of fifteen; and, of the four exceptions, one residual in every pair is close to zero. The semi-log regressions that include lagged sales lead to a similar conclusion. For 1926–39, the residuals are of opposite sign in nine cases out of fourteen; and, of the five exceptions, there are four cases in which one of the residuals of the pair is close to zero. These results indicate the presence of competition between the two brands resulting from all of the methods of promotion.

Increased advertising by competitors may be expected to reduce sales of a given brand. Hence we expect the coefficient of competitor's advertising in a regression designed to explain sales of a given brand to be negative. What is less obvious a priori is the relation between the advertising outlays of competitors. Perhaps the advertising outlays of the various brands move in step, implying a positive correlation between the advertising of a given firm and the advertising of its rivals. However, for 1925–39, there is a negative correlation between the advertising outlays of Reynolds and American. A 1 per cent increase in American's advertising was associated with a decrease of 0.32 per cent of Reynolds' advertising, and a 1 per cent increase of Reynolds' advertising was accompanied

by a 0.41 per cent decrease of American's advertising. The correlation between the logs of the advertising outlays of these two companies is $-.363$. This negative correlation suggests that the two firms avoided engagement in an advertising race, since a positive coefficient could lead to unprofitable escalation.

We can calculate regressions for Reynolds and American including part of the competitive advertising at least for the period 1925 to 1939. The results are:

Camels: $q_{1t} = -47.71$

$$+12.58 \log x_{1t} + .51 \log x_{2t}$$
$$\quad (8.48) \qquad\quad (6.19) \qquad\qquad (14)$$

$$+ 69.33 \log y_t - 33.66 \log p_t + .55t$$
$$\quad (11.4) \qquad\qquad (47.5) \qquad\quad (.16)$$

$R^2 = .899$

$$d(\text{Durbin-Watson statistic}) = .907$$

Lucky Strike: $q_{2t} = -59.84$

$$- 15.24 \log x_{1t} + 36.56 \log x_{2t}$$
$$\quad (15.9) \qquad\qquad (11.6()$$

$$+ 17.45 \log y_t + 132.66 \log p_t \quad (15)$$
$$\quad (21.4) \qquad\qquad (89.3)$$

$$+ 1.12t$$
$$(.31)$$

$$R^2 = .818 \qquad d = 1.675.$$

The coefficients of these two regressions are surprising. The coefficient of American advertising in the Reynolds regression is practically zero, and the omission of this variable would have little effect on the coefficient of the Reynolds' advertising outlay. Although the coefficient of Reynolds advertising in the American regression is negative as expected, omission of this variable increases the coefficient of American's own advertising because of the negative correlation between advertising expenditures of American and Reynolds. One difficulty with these regressions is that they fail to include advertising of Liggett and Myers, whose Chesterfield brand rivaled both Camels and Lucky Strike. Since advertising data for Liggett and Myers are unavailable prior to 1929, we shall study the competition among the three brands for 1929–39.

Instead of looking at the relation between absolute sales and advertising, we now study the relation between market share and relative advertising. Let m_{it}

$$m_{it} = L_{0i} + L_{1i}m_{it-1} + L_{2i}s_{it} \quad (16)$$

and defer to the next section the reasons for including lagged market share. The estimates of (16) are in Table 5. The estimated L_2's are all positive as expected and exceed the standard error except for Chesterfield. Interpretation of these results requires some simple algebra.

Let Q_i denote sales of all brands, excluding i. Hence total sales, Q, is $q_i + Q_i$.

TABLE 5

REGRESSION ESTIMATES OF MARKET SHARE ON RELATIVE
ADVERTISING EXPENDITURE, BY BRANDS, 1929–39*

BRAND	CONSTANT	COEFFICIENT OF		R^2†
		m_{t-1}	s_t	
Camels.......	.0477	.7356 (.1866)	.0909 (.0416)	.6948
Lucky Strike..	.0818	.5962 (.1279)	.1228 (.0300)	.8728
Chesterfield...	.0825	.6570 (.2645)	.0279 (.0624)	.4407

* The market share is the sales of the given brand divided by the sum of sales of Camels, Lucky Strike, and Chesterfield. From 1932 to 1939 sales of Phillip Morris, Old Gold, and the ten-cent brands ranged from about 18 to 27 per cent of total cigarette sales. These regressions assume that the competition of these brands had the same proportionate effects on sales of the three leading brands. For a discussion of this problem see Telser, "The Demand for Branded Goods as Estimated from Consumer Panel Data," *Review of Economics and Statistics*, August, 1962.

† Unadjusted for degrees of freedom. For two variables and eleven observations, the 10, 5, and 1 per cent significance levels of R^2 are, respectively, .4374, .5272, and .6838. The R^2 adjusted for degrees of freedom are .6185, .8410, and .3009, for Camels, Lucky Strike, and Chesterfield, respectively. See also Table 10.

denote the market share of brand i in period t, and let s_{it} denote the advertising outlay on the ith brand, x_{it}, divided by the sum of the outlays on all other brands, X_{it}. This measure of relative advertising expenditure simplifies the formulas for calculating the competitive effects and avoids some of the problems encountered in the use of nominal instead of appropriately deflated advertising expenditures. A regression using market share as a dependent variable can exclude relative price, since this was constant and equal to one for the standard brands considered. We shall estimate the following:

Since m_{it} is the ratio of q_{it} to Q_t, the differential of market share with respect to x_{it} is

$$Q\frac{dm_i}{dx_i} = (1 - m_i)\frac{dq_i}{dx_i}$$
$$- m_i\frac{dQ_i}{dx_i} = QL_{2i}\frac{ds_i}{dx_i}. \quad (17)$$

In this expression

$$\frac{dq_i}{dx_i} = \frac{\partial q_i}{\partial x_i} + \frac{\partial q_i}{\partial X_i}\frac{dX_i}{dx_i} \quad (18)$$

is the differential of the firm's sales with respect to its advertising, taking into account the effect on the advertising of its competitors induced by a change in its advertising. There is, therefore, a relation

$$X_i = h(x_i) \qquad (19)$$

that indicates the competitors' reactions to the firm's advertising. Similarly,

$$\frac{dQ_i}{dx_i} = \frac{\partial Q_i}{\partial x_i} + \frac{\partial Q_i}{\partial X_i}\frac{dX_i}{dx_i} \qquad (20)$$

$$\frac{ds_i}{dx_i} = \frac{1}{X_i}\left[1 - \frac{x_i}{X_i}\frac{dX_i}{dx_i}\right] = \frac{1}{X_i}\lambda_i, \qquad (21)$$

where λ_i is one minus the elasticity of response of competitors' advertising to a change in the given firm's advertising. Equation (17) simplifies to[15]

$$\gamma_{z_i} = (1 - m_i)(\theta_i - \psi_i) = \gamma_{s_i}\lambda_i, \qquad (22)$$

where

$$\gamma_{s_i} = \frac{s_i}{m_i}\left(\frac{dm_i}{ds_i}\right) = \begin{array}{l}\text{market share elasticity}\\\text{with respect to relative}\\\text{advertising}\end{array}$$

$$\psi_i = \frac{x_i}{Q_i}\left(\frac{dQ_i}{dx_i}\right) = \begin{array}{l}\text{competitive advertising}\\\text{elasticity}\end{array}$$

[15] Since $m_i = q_i \div Q$ and $Q = q_i + Q_i$,

$$\frac{dm_i}{dx_i} = \frac{Q_i(dq_i/dx_i) - q_i(dQ_i/dx_i)}{Q^2}$$

$$= L_{2i}\frac{ds_i}{dx_i}$$

$$Q\frac{dm_i}{dx_i} = \frac{Q_i}{Q}\left(\frac{dq_i}{dx_i}\right) - \frac{q_i}{Q}\left(\frac{dQ_i}{dx_i}\right) = QL_{2i}\frac{ds_i}{dx_i}.$$

This reduces to eq. (17).

$$\frac{x_i}{q_i}Q\frac{dm_i}{dx_i} = (1 - m_i)\frac{x_i}{q_i}\left(\frac{dq_i}{dx_i}\right)$$

$$- \frac{Q_i}{Q}\left(\frac{x_i}{Q_i}\right)\frac{dQ_i}{dx_i} = \frac{s_i}{m_i}L_{2i}X_i\frac{ds_i}{dx_i}.$$

Hence

$$\frac{x_i}{m_i}\left(\frac{dm_i}{dx_i}\right) = (1 - m_i)$$

$$\times \left[\frac{x_i}{q_i}\left(\frac{dq_i}{dx_i}\right) - \frac{x_i}{Q_i}\left(\frac{dQ_i}{dx_i}\right)\right] = \frac{s_i}{m_i}L_{2i}\lambda_i,$$

using (21). This equation becomes (22).

$$\theta_i = \frac{x_i}{q_i}\left(\frac{dq_i}{dx_i}\right) = \begin{array}{l}\text{absolute sales advertising}\\\text{elasticity}\end{array}$$

$$\gamma_{z_i} = \frac{x_i}{m_i}\left(\frac{dm_i}{dx_i}\right) = \begin{array}{l}\text{market share elasticity}\\\text{with respect to }i\text{'s adver-}\\\text{tising.}\end{array}$$

It is clear from (22) that if λ_i is zero, then γ_{z_i} will be zero, even if γ_{s_i} is positive. A zero value of λ_i means that a 1 per cent change in the given firm's advertising is met by a 1 per cent change in the advertising of its competitors.

The term ψ_i represents the effect on the sales of competitors of a change in i's advertising outlay. We can establish an upper bound on ψ_i by assuming that a change in i's advertising has no effect on total industry sales, that is, $dQ/dx_i = 0$. This means that all the increased sales of the given firm come at the expense of its rivals. This hypothesis implies that[16]

$$\theta_i = \gamma_{s_i}\lambda_i. \qquad (23)$$

Substituting the implied value of θ_i from (23) into (22) we find that

$$\psi_i \geq -\lambda_i\gamma_{s_i}\frac{m_i}{1-m_i} \geq -\gamma_{s_i}\frac{m_i}{1-m_i}, \qquad (24)$$

provided that $0 < \lambda < 1$. In fact, for Camels and Lucky Strike λ_i is nearly 1, and for Chesterfield λ_i is about .4. Hence upper bounds to the competitive effects are indeed given by the right-hand member of (24). The results are in Table 6.

[16] If

$$\frac{dQ}{dx_i} = 0 \text{ then } \frac{dm_i}{dx_i} = \frac{dq_i}{dx_i} \div Q$$

Hence

$$Q\frac{dm_i}{dx_i} = \frac{dq_i}{dx_i} = Q\frac{dm_i}{ds_i}\left(\frac{ds_i}{dx_i}\right) = \frac{Q}{X_i}L_{2i}\lambda_i$$

Therefore,

$$\frac{dm_i}{dx_i}\left(\frac{x_i}{m_i}\right) = \frac{x_i}{q_i}\left(\frac{dq_i}{dx_i}\right) = \frac{s_i}{m_i}L_{2i}\lambda_i,$$

which is (23).

Changes in Lucky Strike advertising had the largest effect on its two competitors, whereas changes in Chesterfield advertising had the least effect.

We may also assume that ψ_i is zero, so all increases in sales due to advertising come from new customers. Given this assumption, equation (22) establishes upper bounds for θ_i. The upper bound equals $\gamma_{s_i}/(1 - m_i)$. The numerical results are given in Table 6. Chesterfield has the lowest upper bound for θ_i.

These results are consistent with the fact that over the entire sample period

Strike advertising was positively correlated with the total spent by its rivals. However, the abrupt downward shift accounts for the over-all negative correlation between its advertising and its rivals' outlays. Over all, Camels advertising shows a slight positive correlation with the sum of its rivals' outlays. However, no abrupt shift occurs in the relation between Chesterfield advertising and that of its rivals. There is, in fact, a positive correlation between Chesterfield advertising and the sum of the outlays of Camels and Lucky Strike. One gets

TABLE 6

ESTIMATES OF γ_i, θ_i, AND ψ_i BY BRAND, 1929–39

Brand	$\bar{m}_i$*	$\gamma_{s_i} = \theta^l$	$\gamma_{s_i} \div (1 - \bar{m}_i)$ $= \theta_i^u$	$\psi_i^l = -\gamma_{s_i}$ $(\bar{m}_i)/(1 - \bar{m}_i)$	$\bar{s}_i \div$ $(1 + \bar{s}_i)$†
Camels.........	.3552	.1239	.1922	− .0683	.3202
Lucky Strike.....	.3581	.1802	.2807	− .1005	.3247
Chesterfield.....	.2867	.0554	.0774	− .0222	.3552

* $\bar{m}_i = \dfrac{1}{T} \sum_{t=1}^{T} m_{it}$. Hence $\bar{m}_i$ is the unweighted average market shares. The weighted averages are, respectively, .3588, .3540, and .2872.

† $\bar{s}_i \div (1 + \bar{s}_i)$ = the average of i's advertising expenditure relative to total advertising = $x_i + X_i$. These are weighted averages.

Chesterfield accounted for 35 per cent of total advertising of the three brands, whereas its market share was only 29 per cent. Table 6 also shows that the average advertising share of Camels and Lucky Strike was about the same and that their market shares were also about equal. Thus, relative to sales, Chesterfield spent the most on advertising with less effect than either Camels or Lucky Strike.

There is an interesting pattern of advertising outlays by these three brands. From 1929 to 1932, advertising on Lucky Strike relative to the total outlay on the other two brands was high; there was an abrupt shift to a lower level of advertising in 1933. From 1933 to 1943 Lucky

the impression from these figures that there was a closer competitive relation between the advertising on Camels and Lucky Strike than between any one of these brands and the Chesterfield expenditures.

IV. REPEAT-PURCHASE PROBABILITY

There is more to be learned from the relation between market share and relative advertising expenditure. In particular, if cigarette buyers exhibit inertia—that is, tend to repeat purchases of a given brand—then the relation between market share and relative advertising outlay results from a stochastic process that takes into account consumer propensities to repeat purchases and to transfer purchases from other brands to a given brand. The relation between market share and relative advertising expenditure allows us to measure the repeat- and transfer-purchase probabilities. The repeat-purchase probability estimates k (discussed in Sec. II) and tells us the proportion of an initial sales increment retained from one period to the next. Hence, 1 minus the repeat-purchase probability measures the rate of depreciation of advertising capital.

The sales of each brand come from three sources: (1) sales to those who have not previously bought the product; (2) sales to those who have previously purchased a competing brand; and (3) sales to those who are repeating their purchase. In this section we focus our attention on the latter two categories.[17]

Let the probability of repeating the purchase of a given brand be denoted by

a and let the probability of sales being transferred to the given brand from all other brands be denoted by β. Thus the market share of brand i at time t equals

$$m_{it} = am_{it-1} + \beta(1 - m_{it-1}) . \quad (25)$$

Both a and β are conditional probabilities. They indicate, respectively, the probability of purchasing brand i in period t conditional on having either purchased it in the preceding period or on having purchased some other brand in that period. Thus the product am_{it-1} is the part of the market share in period t due to purchases of brand i in both periods t and $t - 1$. Similarly, $\beta(1 - m_{it-1})$ is the joint probability of buying brand i in the current period and some other brand in the preceding period. Equation (25) is an example of a simple Markov process that gives considerable insight into the relations among the three standard cigarette brands.

Suppose that a and β are functions of the advertising outlay on brand i, relative to the sum of the outlays on all other brands. Thus

$$a_{it} = f(s_{it}) \qquad \beta_{it} = g(s_{it}) , \quad (26)$$

where, as in Section III, s_{it} designates relative advertising expenditure. These equations make the probabilities variables because they depend on relative advertising expenditures.

If data were available giving direct estimates of the repeat and transfer probabilities—that is, if we had figures giving the fraction of purchases of a given brand going to all other brands and back to itself—then f and g could be directly estimated. Unfortunately, such data are not available. However, by using the available figures on market share and relative advertising outlays, we can estimate the parameters of f and g indirectly.

---

[17] The model to be described assumes that the competition to the three major brands did not affect their market share. Thus the ten-cent brands, Phillip Morris, and Old Gold are assumed to have the same proportional effect on the sales of the three leading brands. Other variables affect absolute sales as we have seen, real income in particular. It is remarkable, however, that the income elasticities obtained from the best regressions of Camels and Lucky Strike, namely, (ii*) for the former and (13) for the latter in Sec. II, are quite close. Hence changes in income did not affect the market shares of these two brands. The estimates of income elasticities taken from eqs. (12) and (13) are virtually identical. Lack of data unfortunately prevents calculation of the Chesterfield income elasticity. Another favorable aspect for the analysis in terms of market share for the period 1929–39 is the absence of a marked trend in sales. Combined sales of the three brands increased at a 5.3 per cent annual rate from 1925 to 1950. However, the annual rate of increase from 1929 to 1939 was only 1.1. per cent. A fuller discussion of these issues can be found in the author's "The Demand for Branded Goods as Estimated from Consumer Panel Data" *Review of Economics and Statistics*, August, 1962. The estimation technique is described in the author's "Least Squares Estimates of Transition Probabilities," *Measurement in Economics*, ed. Don Patinkin (Stanford, Calif.: Stanford University Press, 1963).

A linear approximation to f and g in the neighborhood of the sample mean,

$$\bar{s}_i = \frac{1}{T} \sum_{t=1}^{T} s_{it},$$

is given by

$$a_{it} = a_{0i} + a_{1i}s_{it}$$
$$\beta_{it} = b_{0i} + b_{1i}s_{it}. \qquad (27)$$

The coefficients of s_{it} are the slopes of f and g at the sample mean s_i. Both slopes are positive if increased relative advertising increases both the repeat- and transfer-purchase probabilities. Substitute the linear approximations of f and g given by (27) into (25) and obtain

$$m_{it} = b_{0i} + (a_{0i} - b_{0i})m_{it-1} + b_{1i}s_{it} \\ + (a_{1i} + b_{1i})m_{it-1}s_{it}. \qquad (28)$$

ard errors are so large that there is little reason for rejecting the prior expectations regarding the signs of the coefficients.[18]

The collinearity is due to the presence of the product term $m_{it-1}s_{it}$ together with its factors in the same regression equation. To see this, write the product term as follows:

$$m_{t-1}s_t = P_0 + P_1 m_{t-1} + P_2 s_t + v_t, \qquad (29)$$

where

$$P_0 = \text{cov}(s_t, m_{t-1}) - Es_t Em_{t-1}$$
$$P_1 = Es_t$$
$$P_2 = Em_{t-1} \qquad (30)$$
$$v_t = (s_t - Es_t)(m_{t-1} - Em_{t-1}) \\ - \text{cov}(s_t, m_{t-1}).$$

TABLE 7

ESTIMATES OF a_{01}, a_{1i}, b_{0i}, AND b_{1i}, 1929–39

Brand	b_{0i}	$a_{0i}-b_{0i}$	b_{1i}	$a_{1i}-b_{1i}$	R^2	a_{0i}	a_{1i}
Camels......	.0735	.6641 (.6583)	.0438 (.4163)	.1314 (1.154)	.6954	.7376	.1752
Lucky Strike..	.2292	.1606 (.3310)	−.1585 (.2007)	.8124 (.5738)	.9011	.3898	.6539
Chesterfield..	−.1111	1.4125 (1.8568)	.3288 (.7340)	−1.1912 (2.894)	.4539	1.3014	−.8624

Thus the model implies that the current market share is a linear function of the lagged market share, relative advertising, and the product of the two.

Least squares estimates of the coefficients of (28) are given in Table 7. The coefficients confirm our expectations for Camels. However, b_{1i} is negative for Lucky Strike, and both b_{0i} and a_{1i} are negative for Chesterfield. Moreover, all of the standard errors are large relative to the coefficients. Thus the regressions show symptoms of collinearity among the explanatory variables. Indeed, the stand-

Equation (29) is an identity. Therefore, if v_t is approximately zero for every t, then a linear combination of the factors m_{t-1} and s_t with coefficients given by the P's nearly equals the product term $m_{t-1}s_t$.

[18] According to Nicholas Kaldor ("The Economic Aspects of Advertising" *Review of Economic Studies*, XVIII [1950–51], 1–27), the effect of advertising on repeat purchases should exceed its effect on transfer purchases. This implies that $a_{i1} \dots b_{i1}$. (A stable equilibrium thus relies heavily on the existence of diminishing marginal effectiveness of advertising.) Although his conjecture is verified for Camels and Lucky Strike as shown by the results of Table 7, the standard errors are too large to warrant placing much confidence in the tests. See esp. p. 18 in Kaldor's article.

There is evidence that v_t is approximately zero. Table 8 shows the least-squares estimates of the P's from (29) together with direct estimates of the P's in (30) derived from the sample means of m_{t-1}, s_t, and the sample estimate of the covariance between s_t and m_{t-1} (see also [33] below). Table 8 shows that not only are the least-squares estimates of the P's and direct estimates of the P's nearly identical, but also the R_2 of the least-squares estimates of equation (29) are nearly one. Hence the collinearity between the product term $m_{t-1}s_1$ and its two factors m_{t-1} and s_t is

Although the collinearity prevents reliable estimation of the a's and b's that determine the transition probabilities, we can measure the average values of the transition probabilities using the regression coefficients of Table 7 by substituting s_i and the estimates of the a's and b's into (27). Table 9 (A rows) gives these estimates. The results indicate that the average values of the repeat-purchase probabilities are substantially higher than the average values of the transfer-purchase probabilities. There are, however, still other ways of estimating these

TABLE 8

REGRESSIONS OF $m_{t-1}s_t$ ON s_t AND m_{t-1}, BY BRAND, 1929–39

BRAND	CON-STANT	COEFFICIENTS OF		R^2
		m_{t-1}	s_t	
Camels:				
Least squares estimates.....	−.1958	.5434	.3581	.9890
Predicted................	−.1747	.4845	.3581	
Lucky Strike:				
Least squares estimates.....	−.1815	.5362	.3463	.9865
Predicted................	−.1823	.5254	.3552	
Chesterfield....:				
Least squares estimates.....	−.1625	.6342	.2526	.9945
Predicted................	−.1634	.5696	.2867	

extreme. Collinearity has, of course, serious consequences if there are any errors of measurement in the data, since the errors become enormously magnified and can seriously distort the estimates of the parameters. It follows that not much can be made of the estimates of the a's and b's given in Table 7. It is worth noting that the extreme collinearity herein incountered is not an inevitable result in all cases in which we estimate transition probabilities indirectly by least squares. It is possible for v_t to be reasonably large for every t, thus reducing the collinearity, without being so large as to introduce much collinearity between s_t and m_{t-1}.[19]

probabilities. Moreover, the alternative approaches give the same estimates and increase our confidence in the estimates derived from Table 7.

In the preceding section we estimated the following:

$$m_{it} = L_{0i} + L_{1i}m_{it-1} + L_{2i}s_{it}. \quad (31)$$

This is nothing but equation (28) with the product term omitted. Hence the co-

[19] If advertising data were available for the 1920's then I suspect that the multicollinearity would be much reduced because there would be much more variability in both market share and relative advertising outlays. Although sales figures are available for all three brands since 1925, the advertising data becomes available only since 1929.

efficients of (31) are related to the transition probabilities in the following way:

$$L_{0i} = b_{0i} + (a_{1i} - b_{1i})[\text{cov}(a_{it}, m_{it-1})$$
$$- Es_{it}Em_{it-1t}]$$

$$L_{1i} = (a_{0i} - b_{0i}) + (a_{1i} - b_{1i})Es_{it}$$
$$= (a_{0i} + a_{1i}Es_{it}) - (b_{0i} + b_{1i}Es_{it}) \quad (32)$$

$$L_{2i} = b_{1i} + (a_{1i} - b_{1i})Em_{it-1}$$
$$= a_{1i}Em_{it-1} + b_{1i}(1 - Em_{it-1}).$$

Therefore, L_{2i} is a weighted average of the slopes of the repeat and transfer probabilities taken at the mean value of the relative advertising expenditure; and L_{1i} is the difference between the average repeat-purchase probability and the average transfer-purchase probability. Although one cannot obtain reliable measures of the coefficients of (28), estimates of the coefficients of (31) shed considerable light on the underlying parameters of the model. Table 5 gives the estimates of the coefficients of (31). Assuming $a_{1i} = b_{1i}$, we can use the results given in Table 5 to measure the repeat and transfer probabilities. The mean repeat and transfer probabilities are given in B rows of Table 9. The estimates are very close to those derived from Table 7. The largest discrepancy is Chesterfield; indeed this discrepancy increases the confidence in the method since otherwise the results would be too good to be true. The point, of course, is that a real test, as distinct from an exercise in arithmetic, must show some, but not too much, discrepancy between the hypothesis and the results.

There is still a third approach to the problem that confirms the interpretation of equations (31) and (32) and the estimates of the probabilities. Substitute v_{it} given by (30) for the product term m_{it-1} s_{it} in (28). This removes the linear component shown in (29) from the product

term. By so doing we attempt to measure the underlying parameters of the model by calculating v_{it} from (29) using the sample estimates of the theoretical coefficients of (29). Thus the P's are estimated not by least squares but as follows:

$$\hat{P}_{0i} = \frac{1}{T}\Sigma(s_{it} - \bar{s}_i)(m_{it-1} - \bar{m}_{it})$$
$$- \bar{s}_i\bar{m}_{it-1} \quad (33)$$

$$\hat{P}_{1i} = \bar{s}_i$$

$$\hat{P}_{2i} = \bar{m}_{it-1}.$$

TABLE 9

ESTIMATES OF AVERAGE REPEAT- AND TRANSFER-PURCHASE PROBABILITIES

Brand*	Average a	Average β
Camels:		
A	.822	.095
B	.827	.092
C	.822	.094
D	.770	n.a.
Lucky Strike:		
A	.733	.146
B	.742	.146
C	.737	.149
D	.879	n.a.
Chesterfield:		
A	.810	.076
B	.755	.098
C	.810	.076
D	.746	n.a.

* Source: row A, derived from Table 7; row B, derived from Table 5, assuming $a_{1i} = b_{1i}$; row C, derived from equation (34); row D, derived from "Least Squares Estimates of Transition Probabilities" assuming constant transition probabilities for 1926–43.

We then estimate

$$m_{it} = N_{0i} + N_{1i}m_{it-1} + N_{2i}s_{it} + N_{3i}v_{it}, \quad (34)$$

for which

$$N_{0i} = a_{0i} + (a_{1i} - b_{1i})\hat{P}_{0i}$$
$$N_{1i} = (a_{0i} - b_{0i}) + (a_{1i} - b_{1i})\hat{P}_{1i}$$
$$N_{2i} = b_{1i} + (a_{1i} - b_{1i})\hat{P}_{2i} \quad (35)$$
$$N_{3i} = a_{1i} - b_{1i}.$$

Given the estimates of the P's from (33) and the estimates of the N's from (34), estimates of the a's and b's are derived from (35). These estimates, however, turned out to be the same as found by the direct use of the product term $m_{it-1}s_{it}$ in (28). This result is not unexpected in view of the high collinearity and the close correspondence between the least squares estimates of the P's shown in Table 8 and the predicted values derived from (30). Moreover, the first three coefficients of (34) are close to the regression estimates of (31) for Camels and Lucky Strike. There are discrepancies for Chesterfield. Finally, the implied average values of the repeat- and transfer-purchase probabilities are very close to the ones obtained by the other two methods. The results are given in C rows of Table 9.[20]

The model proposed herein implies that an increment of sales decays at a rate equal to the repeat purchase probability. Thus w_t, the marginal sales effect of advertising in period t, satisfies a first-order difference equation as described in Section II. There is, however, an important point to be noted about the stochastic model. This model says that the rate at which an increment of sales due to advertising decays from period to period is not a constant, but that it depends

[20] This analysis was also carried out for the entire period 1929–43. Although the war years are hardly comparable to the prewar years, because of cigarette shortages and informal rationing, it is worth noting that the same conclusions reported in the test also hold for the extended period. However, the estimates of the coefficients of (28) are somewhat different as are the estimates of the repeat and transfer purchase probabilities. By including the war years we reduce the estimates of advertising effectiveness. The repeat purchase probabilities for the three brands are .817, .771, and .785, respectively, for Camels, Lucky Strike, and Chesterfield. The transfer purchase probabilities are .094, .135, and .138. These figures are comparable to the estimates given in Table 9. The multicollinearity is still too high to give any significance to the estimates of the a's and b's obtained from regression estimates of (28).

on the relative advertising outlay. There may be, in addition, a delayed response of market share to advertising. This would mean that the marginal sales effect of advertising satisfies a difference equation of second or higher order. We now investigate a second-order difference equation to see whether the main impact of relative advertising expenditure on market share comes in the period following the advertising outlay. From the regression equation

$$m_{it} = K_{0i} + K_{1i}m_{it-1} + K_{2i}s_{it} \\ + K_{3i}s_{it-1}, \quad (36)$$

we can decide whether the simpler model based on the first-order Markov process is adequate or whether a more complicated model is necessary.

Estimates of (36) for the period 1930–43 are given in Table 10. There is no consistent pattern of results. The coefficient of lagged s is negative in the Lucky strike regression and positive in both Camels and Chesterfield regressions. Moreover, for the latter two brands, K_{3i} exceeds K_{2i}; the difference between the two coefficients is sizable for Chesterfield. If there were a consistent pattern of results for the three brands, then we might be willing to accept the view that advertising has a delayed effect on market share. Indeed a sharper test of the hypothesis requires data for time periods shorter than a year, but even such a test is not relevant for deciding whether a first-order Markov process is adequate for annual data. Finally, the results given in Table 10 support the hypothesis of a first-order scheme. To see this, consider

$$m_{it} = H_{0i} + H_{1i}m_{it-1} + H_{2i}s_{it} \\ + H_{3i}m_{it-1}s_{it}, \quad (37)$$

which is equation (28) compactly written. Differentiate the current market share with respect to lagged relative advertising expenditure and obtain

$$\frac{\partial m_{it}}{\partial s_{it-1}} = \frac{\partial m_{it}}{\partial s_{it}}\frac{\partial s_{it}}{\partial s_{it-t}}$$
$$+ (a_t - \beta_t)\frac{\partial m_{it-1}}{\partial s_{it-1}}, \quad (38)$$

cient of lagged relative advertising expenditure. For Camels and Chesterfield there is an upward trend of relative advertising, and the positive coefficient of lagged relative advertising is consistent with this pattern. Moreover, K_{3i} exceeds

TABLE 10

MARKET SHARE ON LAGGED MARKET SHARE, RELATIVE ADVERTISING EXPENDITURE AND LAGGED RELATIVE ADVERTISING EXPENDITURE, BY BRAND, 1930–43

BRAND	CONSTANT	COEFFICIENTS OF			R^{2*}
		$m_{t-1,i}$	s_{ti}	$s_{t-1,i}$	
Camels...........	.0720	.6366 (.1846)	.0398 (.0434)	.0633 (.0391)	.7014
†.............	.0584	.7246 (.1890)	.0671 (.0429)	0	.6230
Lucky Strike......	.0887	.6457 (.1949)	.1112 (.0703)	−.0162 (.0690)	.7816
†.............	.0947	.6237 (.1634)	.0978 (.0397)	0	.7804
Chesterfield......	.0458	.6139 (.2204)	.0408 (.0520)	.0708 (.0521)	.5145
†.............	.0882	.6414 (.2277)	.0248 (.0526)	0	.4248

* For 14 observations and 10 degrees of freedom, the 10, 5 and 1 per cent levels of R^2 are, respectively, .450, .527, .663. For 14 observations and 11 degrees of freedom, the 10, 5, and 1 per cent levels of R^2 are .342, .420, and .567, respectively.

† Least squares estimates when lagged relative advertising expenditures are omitted. These estimates can be compared to the results of Table 5. By including the years 1940–43, we see that relative advertising expenditures have less effect on market share. In view of the radical change in the cigarette market caused by the war, these are not surprising results.

where a_t and β_t are the repeat and transfer purchase probabilities, respectively, at time t. Therefore,

$$\frac{\partial m_{it}}{\partial s_{it-1}} - \frac{\partial m_{it}}{\partial s_{it}} = \frac{\partial m_{it}}{\partial s_{it}}\left(\frac{\partial s_{it}}{\partial s_{it-t}}-1\right)$$
$$+ (a_t - \beta_t)\frac{\partial m_{it-1}}{\partial s_{it-1}}. \quad (39)$$

Since $a_t > \beta_t$ and both $(\partial m_{it})/(\partial s_{it})$ and $(\partial m_{it-1})/(\partial s_{it-1})$ are positive, the partial derivatives of current market share with respect to lagged advertising can be negative if there is a downward trend of advertising for the brand in question. For Lucky Strike, relative advertising expenditures did decline during the sample period; this explains the negative coeffi-

K_{2i} either if $(\partial s_{it})/(\partial s_{it-1}) > 1$ or if the difference between the repeat and transfer purchase rate is larger than the magnitude of $(\partial s_{it})/(\partial s_{it-1}) - 1$. Thus the upward trend of Camels and Chesterfield relative advertising expenditure accounts for the fact that K_{3i} exceeds K_{2i}.[21]

Hence we can accept the simple first-order Markov model as an adequate explanation of time path of market share.

[21] It is the pattern of relative advertising from 1930 to 1943 that is pertinent to the statements in the text. The aberration from the trend occurs in 1932 when Camels decreased its advertising by a large amount. Since the advertising figures are derived from estimates of the cost of advertising when it appeared, the possible lagged effect is not due to an interval between the appropriation of an advertising outlay and the actual appearance of the advertising.

The repeat-purchase probability measures the brand's capacity to retain sales. The magnitudes of the average values of the repeat-purchase probabilities are reasonable in view of the discussion of the measurement of the long-run marginal sales effect of advertising. In Section II we saw that k should be about 0.8 if we are to obtain reasonable estimates of the marginal rate of return on advertising capital. The estimates given in Table 9 imply that the marginal rate of return is either slightly negative or at most about 7.8 per cent for Camels and about 15 per cent for Lucky Strike. Another implication of the present approach is that the rate of depreciation of the advertising capital is not a constant since it depends on relative advertising expenditure.[22]

V. THE POSTWAR PERIOD

In the preceding analysis, the cigarette market exhibited product and price homogeneity. Except for the ten-cent brands, the three leaders, Camels, Lucky Strike, and Chesterfield, competed primarily by advertising. Even the smaller companies in the industry posed no serious threat to them and in fact adopted the same methods of competition. This made it possible to focus attention on a single variable—advertising. The analysis of the postwar period is complicated by the introduction of new varieties of cigarettes. In this section we study the

experience of the cigarette industry from 1946 to 1959.

Although one cigarette type accounts for most of the cigarette sales in the prewar period, many other varieties of cigarettes had been available to consumers for a long time. In the 1930's there were at least two mentholated cigarettes, Spuds (of Phillip Morris) and Kools (of Brown and Williamson). King-size cigarettes are even older, and two currently popular brands can trace their history to the 1930's. Indeed, in 1951, two king-size American brands, Pall Mall and Herbert Tareyton, accounted for more than 10 per cent of cigarette sales. Parliament, a filtered Phillip Morris brand, entered the market in 1945. In 1951 Brown and Williamson introduced Viceroy, a filtered cigarette. It is noteworthy that all these developments preceded announcement of reports linking lung cancer to cigarette smoking, which began to receive wide publicity in 1952. By 1954, the effect of these reports on smoking habits was manifested, since cigarette sales were 8 per cent below the 1952 level; sales of Viceroy, a filtered cigarette, rose sharply. There followed a rapid introduction of filtered and mentholated varieties. In the decade 1950–59, thirty-two brands of cigarettes, mostly new entries, had annual sales at one time or another of less than five billion cigarettes. Of these, six attained sales in excess of twenty billion cigarettes per year, and three were spectacular successes: two Reynolds' brands (Winston, filtered and non-mentholated, and Salem, filtered and mentholated) and one Lorillard brand (Kent, filtered and non-mentholated). There were two conspicuous failures: Hit Parade, an American filtered and non-mentholated brand that attained at one point annual sales of four billion cigarettes and was down to half a billion in

[22] The ratio of the transfer-purchase probability to the sum of the transfer-purchase probability and one minus the repeat-purchase probability is an estimate of the equilibrium market shares. For 1929–39 the resulting estimates are .356, .351, and .286 for Camels, Lucky Strike, and Chesterfield, respectively. The average market shares are .356, .354, and .287. What would be more interesting is a calculation of the equilibrium market shares given the relative advertising outlay in some year. Thus we could see the difference between the actual and equilibrium market share. Unfortunately such an estimate requires knowledge of the a's and b's that could not be reliably estimated from the available data.

1960; and Cavalier, a king-size Reynolds brand with a somewhat similar sales experience. Sales of regular cigarettes have fallen sharply. Of such brands, only Camels remain popular, although in 1960 it fell to second place after Pall Mall. Lucky Strike sales, although decreasing, still exceed 10 per cent of the total. Chesterfield, Phillip Morris, and Old Gold regular varieties are rapidly disappearing.

An index number can summarize these changes in product mix. There are six

lowest score and the newest type the highest score. Let q_{ijt} be sales of type j by company i at time t.

$$P_{it} = \sum_j z_j q_{ijt} \div \sum_j q_{ijt} \quad (40)$$

is an index of company i's product mix at time t. Similarly, one can construct an index for the product mix of the industry using as weights the industry sales of each variety. The resulting indexes by company are shown in Table 11. Until

TABLE 11

INDEX OF PRODUCT MIX, BY MAJOR COMPANIES, 1945–60

Year	R. J. Reynolds	American Tobacco	Liggett and Myers	P. Lorillard	Phillip Morris	Brown and Williamson	Total
1945....	1.00	1.10	1.00	1.00	1.08	1.92	1.10
1946....	1.00	1.11	1.00	1.00	1.03	2.71	1.08
1947....	1.00	1.13	1.00	1.00	1.03	2.68	1.09
1948....	1.00	1.15	1.01	1.01	1.03	3.05	1.12
1949....	1.01	1.20	1.02	1.03	1.04	2.58	1.14
1950....	1.01	1.27	1.03	1.02	1.05	2.68	1.18
1951....	1.01	1.35	1.03	1.02	1.05	2.73	1.22
1952....	1.01	1.43	1.16	1.07	1.11	2.77	1.29
1953....	1.03	1.49	1.29	1.39	1.37	3.10	1.42
1954....	1.20	1.55	1.45	1.56	1.41	3.23	1.59
1955....	1.47	1.56	1.66	1.80	1.74	3.25	1.76
1956....	1.82	1.59	1.96	1.92	2.11	3.13	1.93
1957....	2.20	1.62	2.13	2.58	2.36	3.45	2.20
1958....	2.44	1.65	2.23	2.91	2.53	3.56	2.38
1959....	2.67	1.71	2.30	3.19	2.69	3.65	2.53
1960....	2.81	1.74	2.32	3.26	2.85	3.75	2.63

main varieties of cigarettes listed in order of appearance on the market: (1) regular non-mentholated, (2) king-size non-mentholated, (3) filtered non-mentholated, (4) regular mentholated, (5) king-size mentholated, and (6) filtered and mentholated. Filtered cigarettes come in two sizes, regular and king-size, but we do not distinguish between them in the data. Nor do we take into account such recent developments as the introduction of imperial-size cigarettes, double filters, etc. Let z_j be the score of type j so that $z_j = 1, 2, 3, 4, 5, 6$, corresponding to the six types just listed. The oldest type has the

1952 there is a marked difference between the product mix of Brown and Williamson and its competitors. Some difference also appears between American and its competitors because of the success of the former's king-size brands. However, the gap between American and the others widens after 1952 because of American's failure to gain acceptance for its filtered varieties. The product mix of both American and Liggett and Myers remains close to the regular pole, although their market shares behave quite differently (see Table 12). From 1945 to 1960 American's share fell by 16 per cent whereas

Liggett and Myers' decreased by nearly 50 per cent. Although the wartime gains of the three smaller companies had largely disappeared by 1946, their combined share immediately reversed and began to increase.

Since product innovation is so important in the postwar period, we add a variable that measures product innovation to the same kind of regression we used

regular pole. A value of the index greater than 1 shows that the company is closer to the filtered and mentholated pole. Although one cannot decide a priori what the sign of the correlation between m_{it} and I_{it} should be, the positive sign for the Reynolds' correlation and the negative sign for the Brown and Williamson correlation, for example, means that the market shares of these two companies

TABLE 12

MARKET SHARES, 1945–60

Year	R. J. Reynolds	American Tobacco	Liggett and Myers	P. Lorillard	Phillip Morris	Brown and Williamson
1945	.223	.310	.219	.059	.116	.071
1946	.282	.364	.214	.046	.072	.022
1947	.298	.346	.213	.043	.071	.028
1948	.283	.350	.203	.048	.086	.029
1949	.282	.325	.197	.052	.101	.042
1950	.274	.313	.191	.055	.116	.050
1951	.279	.319	.177	.060	.110	.054
1952	.272	.329	.179	.063	.100	.057
1953	.266	.329	.168	.072	.101	.065
1954	.254	.332	.165	.067	.087	.094
1955	.261	.328	.157	.064	.083	.106
1956	.280	.316	.150	.058	.092	.104
1957	.288	.290	.146	.078	.093	.106
1958	.289	.267	.132	.119	.093	.100
1959	.308	.262	.123	.116	.092	.099
1960	.324	.257	.115	.110	.092	.102
Average	.281	.312	.168	.072	.094	.073

Source: 1945–49, Nicholls, *op. cit.*, Table 39; 1950–60, *Printers Ink*, November 18, 1952, January 9, 1953, January 15, 1954, December 31, 1954, December 30, 1955, December 28, 1956, December 27, 1957, December 26, 1958, December 25, 1959, and December 23, 1960.

to analyze market share in the pre-war period. Thus consider

$$m_{it} = J_{0i} + J_{1i}m_{it-1} + J_{2i}s_{it} + J_{3i}I_{it}. \quad (41)$$

The variable m_{it} is the market share of company i in time t and s_{it} is its relative advertising expenditure. The variable I_{it} is the measure of product innovation. It is the ratio of P_{it}, the index of product mix for company i, to P_t, the industry index.[23] If all companies have the same product mix, I_{it} is 1. It happens in this case that a value of I_{it} less than 1 signifies that the company mix is closer to the

and the indexes of product innovation both converged.

Estimates of the coefficients of (41) are shown in Table 14. For Reynolds, the simple correlation between market share

[23] An alternative measure of the product mix is

$$\sum_j z_j q_{ijt} \div \sum_{i,j} z_j q_{ijt}.$$

This measure is highly correlated with market share. In effect, I_{it} deflates this measure by market share to remove as well as possible a spurious correlation between market share and the index of product mix. I_{it} can also be regarded as a measure of the dispersion of the product mix among the companies.

and relative advertising expenditure is negative. However, the estimate of J_{2i} for Reynolds is positive. For American, however, both the simple correlation between these two variables and the regression coefficient of s_{it} are negative. By advertising, American failed to gain acceptance for its filtered brand or arrest appreciably the declining sales of Lucky Strike. The negative coefficient of rela-

tive advertising in the Brown and Williamson regression is surprising because of the positive simple correlation between s_t and m_t. Examination of the data, however, makes it clear that this company failed to increase its share toward the end of the sample period despite large increases in relative advertising outlays (see Tables 12 and 13).

The coefficients of lagged market

TABLE 13

RELATIVE ADVERTISING EXPENDITURE, BY COMPANY, 1945–59

Year	R. J. Reynolds	American Tobacco	Liggett and Myers	P. Lorillard	Phillip Morris	Brown and Williamson
1945	.211	.144	.308	.116	.246	.194
1946	.311	.216	.236	.112	.195	.149
1947	.434	.229	.291	.058	.187	.079
1948	.392	.230	.301	.102	.196	.046
1949	.343	.298	.224	.132	.217	.038
1950	.335	.295	.226	.135	.230	.032
1951	.341	.285	.249	.154	.192	.031
1952	.360	.294	.251	.153	.196	.010
1953	.331	.326	.232	.198	.160	.014
1954	.332	.297	.239	.216	.109	.055
1955	.322	.347	.187	.175	.139	.076
1956	.286	.260	.179	.102	.191	.199
1957	.267	.256	.166	.114	.176	.236
1958	.271	.308	.150	.191	.140	.160
1959	.291	.252	.178	.200	.150	.144

Source: 1945–49, Nicholls, *op. cit.*, Table 46; 1950, *Advertising Age*, July 13, 1953; 1951–59, *Printers Ink*, October 31, 1958, October 30, 1959, and September 9, 1960.

TABLE 14

REGRESSIONS OF MARKET SHARE ON LAGGED MARKET SHARE, RELATIVE ADVERTISING OUTLAY, AND PRODUCT MIX INDEX, BY COMPANY, 1946–59

COMPANY	CON-STANT	COEFFICIENTS OF			R^{2*}
		m_{t-1}	s_t	I_t	
R. J. Reynolds	.0965 (.0306)	.0839 (.0992)	.1112 (.0436)	.1394 (.0199)	.8552
American Tobacco	.1206 (.0691)	.4652 (.2306)	−.1796 (.1151)	.1037 (.0360)	.7704
Liggett and Myers	−.0612 (.0404)	.9791 (.0816)	.0621 (.0538)	.0483 (.0387)	.9803
P. Lorillard	−.0736 (.0222)	.1757 (.2645)	.1646 (.0784)	.1072 (.0298)	.8684
Phillip Morris	.0496 (.0709)	.3059 (.2665)	.1206 (.1126)	−.0073 (.0498)	.2390
Brown and Williamson	.1696 (.0517)	.4291 (.2817)	−.1158 (.0714)	−.0579 (.0180)	.8920

* The 10, 5, and 1 per cent significance levels are, respectively, .450, .527, and .663.

shares are all small in these regressions with the exception of Liggett and Myers. The high value for this company merely reflects the downward trend of its market share and the downward trend of its relative advertising outlay.

The ad hoc variable explaining most of the variation of market share is the index of product innovation. It fails only in the Phillip Morris regression, and indeed none of the explanatory variables are of much help. The company had a notable success with one of its brands, Marlboro. Prior to 1955, this was a standard brand with annual sales of less than a half-billion cigarettes. In that year it was converted to a filtered cigarette, and an advertising campaign showing a burly man with a tattoo was begun. By 1960 Marlboro cigarette sales were 22 billion, far ahead of Parliament, another Phillip Morris filtered cigarette introduced earlier. The regression estimates reflect these phenomena by giving a low multiple correlation.

Cigarette smokers could have chosen from among almost as large a variety of cigarette types as presently for at least a quarter-century. They chose to smoke one kind, the regular cigarette, almost to the exclusion of others. Some companies, whether by accident, because they could not gain acceptance for their regular brands, or by design, seemed to specialize in providing the less popular varieties. In 1952, there was a change in tastes and previously unpopular varieties became the vogue. Those companies that had marketed such varieties enjoyed a large increase of sales, but it is hard to explain their success as superior foresight. Some companies have not adjusted successfully to the new situation, although they were among the industry leaders of the past. Still other companies were quick to detect the change in tastes and became even more successful than their smaller competitors with long experience in providing the now-popular varieties. In spite of the changes in varieties and the upsetting of old loyalties, no new company has entered the cigarette industry. Although the market shares of the three leaders have declined and the industry is now in an unsettled state, competition among the established companies has taken on another dimension by product change.

VI. CONCLUSIONS

There are several conclusions one may draw from this study. First, the level of advertising was high enough to place the companies at the point where there were diminishing returns to advertising. Second, the advertising outlays built up a fund of good will that depreciated at a rate varying between 15 and 20 per cent per year. This rate of depreciation declines as the relative advertising expenditure increases. Third, the marginal rate of return on the advertising capital in the prewar period was about 15 per cent for Lucky Strike and about −6.8 per cent for Camels. According to another estimate for Camels based on a somewhat inferior regression, the marginal rate of return was 7.8 per cent. These rates are not so high as to cast doubt on the proposition that there was substantial competition among the companies by means of advertising. The direct estimates of the intensity of competition as measured by the transfer probabilities and the measures discussed in Section III confirm this view. In the prewar period Lucky Strike was the strongest brand, Camels was next, and Chesterfield was third.

The picture that emerges is one of competition by means of advertising, and I see no reason to doubt its effectiveness for some products, cigarettes being a case in point. The behavior of consumers in the market is consistent with the view that they demanded the advertising. The very low marginal rate of return on Camels' prewar advertising suggests that con-sumers can be supplied with more advertising than they want. In the postwar period, competition by product changes as well as by advertising became important. It remains to be seen whether the postwar period will settle down to the kind of stability that characterized the prewar period.

MANAGEMENT SCIENCE
Vol. 26, No. 12, December 1980
Printed in U.S.A.

EVALUATING AND IMPROVING RESOURCE ALLOCATION FOR NAVY RECRUITING*

RICHARD C. MOREY† AND JOHN M. McCANN†

The recruitment of enlisted men and officers under the All-Volunteer Force concept costs approximately $620 million per year; of this amount approximately $100 million are in advertising expenditures. However, recently Congress and the General Accounting Office have expressed considerable concern over the lack of justification for such expenditures. The issue is further complicated by the recent recruiting shortfalls by all the services and the debate surrounding registration and a possible return to the draft. Finally, results of most profit-oriented sales research are difficult to apply to improving military recruiting efficiency due to the difference in the levels of rapport and credibility necessary to convince a potential recruit to invest several years of his life.

This paper reports on modeling and implementation experience geared towards determining the proper allocation of resources between advertising and recruiters. This mix is especially crucial since Congress does not permit funds appropriated for advertising to be used for manpower or vice versa. The study consists of two parts: generation of response functions to estimate the number and mix of enlistments over time and geographically as a function of the various demographics, advertising expenditures and the number of recruiters; a nonlinear programming resource allocation model to improve the budget generation and budget execution capabilities in meeting and assessing the impact of the various multi-faceted quantity and quality goals. The basic model, with updating of the response function parameters, is being used by the Navy to aid in the generation and defense of its annual budget appropriations. Numerical results are given which are compared to the past allocations of the Navy and to results observed in industrial product marketing.

(ORGANIZATION DESIGN; NAVY RECRUITING; RESOURCE ALLOCATION)

1. Problem Perspective

The introduction of the All Volunteer Force (AVF) in July 1973 was accompanied by a dramatic increase in the level of effort expended to meet the various quantity and quality goals of the Armed Services. For example, the recruitment of enlisted men and officers with no prior service was budgeted at $620 million for fiscal year 1978. In addition, advertising expenditures for military recruitment have increased from $6.7 million in fiscal year 1970 to nearly $100 million in fiscal year 78. Even after adjustment for inflation this represents a tenfold increase.

These amounts were justified based on the postulated complementary nature of advertising in military recruiting, namely the stimulation of inquiries to a recruiter; the role of recruiters then was to "close the sale." It was argued that imbalances in either dimension would result in unmet quotas, either because of insufficient leads or the inability of recruiters to expend the necessary amount of time and resources with potential recruits.

These arguments notwithstanding, Congress and the General Accounting Office recently have expressed considerable concern over the lack of justification for the large

---

* Accepted by Arie Y. Lewin; received September 5, 1979. This paper has been with the author 2 months for 2 revisions.
† Duke University.

0025-1909/80/2612/1198$01.25

advertising expenditures (eg. see [1]). Indeed in the GAO report they conclude that "... few recruits can be traced to advertising and that the attitudes toward and images of the military have not changed greatly for the better or for worse." In addition, the same GAO report reported that only a small proportion of those who enlisted could be traced to an advertising lead. As a result large cuts in the funds allocated to advertising have been made. The issue has been further confounded by the recent recruiting shortfalls experienced by all the services, and the revived debate centered on registration for a possible return to the draft.

Responding to these concerns the Department of Defense selected the Navy, as a prototype for all the services, to begin an evaluation study aimed at improving the capability of all the Recruiting Commands to develop their budget needs and track their performance. In order to accomplish this, it has been necessary to gain a better understanding of the causal factors influencing the decision to enlist such as the size of the high school population, the unemployment rate, the levels and timing of advertising, and the numbers and locations of recruiters.

This type of comprehensive evaluation or audit is becoming increasingly popular in governmental and other not-for-profit entities (see eg. Charnes, Cooper and Rhodes [4] for models that address decision-making efficiency), where the audit is not restricted to merely examinations of financial transactions (and their representations in financial reports) but extends to an appraisal of the management and organization behavior. Hence, efforts such as these are aimed at increasing the accountability of the managers, particularly those whose mission and charter is assigned to them and there is not the freedom to redirect resources to other programs because they are more "profitable."

The amount of rapport and credibility necessary to convince potential recruits to enter into such a major commitment is the key feature that distinguishes recruiting research from that of most profit oriented sales research (e.g. that of Dorfman and Steiner, [5]). Relatively little published research in the open literature is available in recruitment marketing. There is a theoretical treatise by Chappel and Peel [3], some empirical work by Epps [6] and by Grissmer [7]. There are also several contractor reports (see e.g. C. Jehn and H. Carrol (1974) and Grissmer [8]) that were performed early in the post-draft environment. Finally, in terms of the tradeoff between advertising and personal selling in the marketing of industrial products, the empirical findings of Lilien [12] also provide some useful benchmarks.

2. The Navy's Recruiting Process

As was mentioned earlier, the Department of Defense funded the recruiting research under the premise that any techniques and insights developed would be available to all the services. In this regard it is noteworthy that, unlike the civilian sector, no big winner or loser can be tolerated in the long run among the various services in their recruiting.

Of the total recruiting bill of $620 million annually, the Navy receives approximately $125 million, based on two separate Congressional appropriations, one for recruiters and their support and one for advertising. These are then distributed over 1,305 stations, 43 districts and 6 areas. Of the total amount spent on advertising, a certain portion is allocated to national advertising agencies for a national campaign to increase awareness and generate leads; the balance of the advertising budget is allocated to the six areas to be used mainly for local advertising purposes. In the same manner the recruiters are allocated by headquarters to the individual areas which are then allocated to the district and station levels by an area commander using his best judgments. Hence, the basic decisions at the headquarters level, given the quantity and quality quotas to be met over the year, are:

(i) How much should the total advertising budget be?
(ii) What should be the geographical and seasonal distribution of the advertising?
(iii) How many recruiters are needed?
(iv) Where should they be assigned?

The outcomes of these decisions involve four measures: the number of leads generated, the number of enlistment contracts signed by high school graduates, the number of non high school graduate contracts and the number of shipments to Recruit Training Centers. The leads are formal inquiries and requests for more information utilizing coupons from magazines or direct mail campaign, toll-free telephone calls, etc. These are carefully tracked and managed by headquarters. The recruiters, following up on these leads, provide counseling, perform limited screening of the applicants and attempt to obtain a signed enlistment contract, i.e. a legal commitment to report for service within a specified period of time. Associated with this facet is the so-called Delayed Entry Program whereby those signing contracts can delay their actual date of entry for up to twelve months from the time of the contract signing. Hence, while advertising and recruiters have their impact on the timing, quantity and quality of contracts being signed, it is the shipments on which the quotas are based and shortfalls recorded.

3. The Enlistment Contract Prediction Model

In order to be able to determine the cost-effective split between advertising and recruiters, and aid in the budget generation and budget execution purposes, two separate modeling efforts were accomplished. First, it was necessary to develop and attempt to validate response functions which would be capable of predicting, on a geographical and seasonal basis, the total number and mix of contracts. These response functions would take as inputs the demographic characteristics of each particular region, e.g. its level of high school seniors, size of labor force, unemployment rate, etc. as well as the number of leads, the number of production recruiters in each region, and the dollars of advertising expended there. For the case of nationally placed television and radio ads, estimates of the dollars spent in each geographical region by month were made by the ad agency by prorating their budgets based on their "impressions" surveys.

Econometric methods were used to develop separate relationships for high school graduate contracts and for total contracts signed. In addition, the number of leads was related econometrically to a similar set of variables. Hence, there resulted a three-equation system: an equation with leads as the dependent variable, an equation with total enlistments as the dependent variable and leads as one of the explanatory variables, and a similar equation for enlistments by high school graduates.

Unfortunately however, the detailed geographical distribution of advertising expenditures had been measured for only two years, 1976 and 1977, resulting in only 24 monthly observations. Since such a short time series makes it difficult to estimate a model with more than one or two explanatory variables, observations were pooled to produce a combined cross sectional and time series data base. This resulted in 1032 observations (24 months times 43 districts). The technique of "Dummy Variable Regression" was used to pool the data by creating a dummy variable for each of the 43 districts as well as for each of the months. Hence, we permit each month and district to have its own unique level of enlistments and leads. In addition, two special events impacted both enlistments and leads, namely television advertising was extensively used in 1977 but not in 1976, and the GI-bill expired at the end of 1976. These events were handled by also using dummy variables, one for each event.

The method of Ordinary Least Squares (OLS) was used to estimate the parameters in the model. This method was used because it is widely known, produces best linear unbiased estimates, (BLUE), and permits statistical hypothesis tests. A possible criticism of OLS is that it is somewhat sensitive to outliers in the data. One approach to alleviate this potential problem would be to use a procedure which is more "robust," i.e. one which is not as sensitive to extreme values in the data, an example being the use of goal programming to minimize the sum of absolute deviations. Such procedures were not used because they do not produce BLUE estimates, they do not permit statistical tests (because the distribution of the estimates are usually not known), and it has not been shown that such methods dominate OLS except in certain circumstances.

The next problem faced was recognition of the fact that it had been the practice of the Recruiting Command to allocate advertising and recruiters based primarily on the size of the eligible population. This resource allocation procedure had introduced high correlations between advertising, recruiter enlistments, quotas, and size of labor force. This problem was somewhat attenuated by removing the allocation relationship from the data by dividing all of the variables by the level of labor force in each district. Hence, the dependent variable became enlistments and/or leads per labor force member.

The form of the regression model selected is shown below. Note the log linear form to capture the diminishing returns thought to be present and the use of the Koyck (see e.g. Parsons and Schultz, [13]) autoregressive term to account for the carry-over effect of past advertising and recruiters' efforts; the same type of model was also used for leads and high school graduate enlistments.

$$
\log\left\{\frac{E_{it}}{LF_{it}}\right\} = A_0 + A_1 \cdot D_1 + \ldots + A_{42} \cdot D_{42} + b_1 \cdot M_1 + \ldots + b_{11} \cdot M_{11}
$$

$$
+ C_1 \cdot Y + C_2 \cdot G + d_1 \cdot \log\left\{\frac{A_{it}}{LF_{it}}\right\} + d_2 \cdot \log\left\{\frac{R_{it}}{LF_{it}}\right\}
$$

$$
+ d_3 \cdot \log\left\{\frac{L_{i,t}}{LF_{i,t}}\right\} + d_4 \cdot \log\left\{\frac{E_{i,t-1}}{LF_{i,t-1}}\right\}
$$

$$
+ d_5 \cdot \log\left\{\frac{T_{it}}{LF_{it}}\right\} + d_6 \log\left(\frac{U_{i,t}}{LF_{i,t}}\right);
$$

$L_{i,t}$ = number of new leads from district i, period t.
$E_{i,t}$ = total enlistment contracts from district i, period t.
$HE_{i,t}$ = total number of high school graduate contracts from district i, period t.
$LF_{i,t}$ = labor force for ith district, period t.
D = district indicator variable.
M = monthly indicator variable.
Y = year indicator variable.

G = GI bill expiration indicator variable.

$A_{i,t}$ = total advertising and promotion expenditure in district i, period t.

$R_{i,t}$ = number of recruiters in district i, period t.

$T_{i,t}$ = total high school seniors in district i, period t.

$U_{i,t}$ = number unemployed for district i, period t.

The estimates of the slope coefficients, statistically significant at the 0.01 level, are given in the following Table along with their standard errors and t-statistics.

It might be mentioned that the single stage regression technique used is felt to be appropriate only for the quality, high school graduate enlistments since they are truly supply limited. The non-high school enlistments, accounting for some 25% of the total, tend to be demand limited (in contrast to supply limitations) since the Recruiting Command operates under quality constraints that limit the numbers of non-high school graduate recruits that can be accepted. Simultaneous multi-stage models that can capture the interplay between quotas, high school graduate enlistments and non-high school graduate enlistments could possibly be used to obtain estimates of elasticities for the demand limited group. It should also be noted that the standard assumptions concerning OLS are being made in this research (Johnston [10]), including homoscedascity and the assumption that the prediction variables are not perfectly correlated. When one works with nonexperimental data, correlations are usually encountered among the prediction variables. Unless these correlations are unity, the OLS assumption is not violated. Before performing the regressions, correlation analyses were performed to help highlight any potential problems in this area. In addition, it was found that, by normalizing the variables associated with recruiters, advertising dollars, high school seniors, etc. by the size of the labor force, much of the correlation present was removed; hence the variables utilized in the regression were all so normalized.

It should perhaps be mentioned in passing that high correlations among the variables usually results in large variances of the coefficient estimates. In such a case, failure to reject a null hypothesis concerning a coefficient may be because of multicollinearity. Since our final model only includes variables which were statistically significant, failure to include some variables does not necessarily mean that such variables are not important. It means that given the available data, the models could not distinguish their coefficients from zero (e.g., see Johnston [10]).

TABLE 1

High School Graduates Enlistments Model

Variable	Coefficient Estimates	Standard Error	t-value
$\log\{ \frac{A_{it}}{LF_{it}} \}$	0.073	0.020	3.65
$\log\{ \frac{R_{it}}{LF_{it}} \}$	0.391	0.095	4.12
$\log\{ \frac{T_{it}}{LF_{it}} \}$	0.356	0.113	3.15
$\log\{ \frac{L_{it}}{LF_{it}} \}$	0.051	0.015	3.40
$\log\{ \frac{HE_{i,t-1}}{LF_{i,t-1}} \}$	0.353	0.028	12.61

TABLE 2

Total Enlistments Model

Variable	Coefficient Estimate	Standard Error	t-value
$\log\{\frac{A_{it}}{LF_{it}}\}$	0.062	0.022	2.82
$\log\{\frac{R_{it}}{LF_{it}}\}$	0.291	0.084	3.46
$\log\{\frac{L_{it}}{LF_{it}}\}$	0.039	0.013	3.00
$\log\{\frac{T_{it}}{LF_{it}}\}$	0.458	0.100	4.58
$\log\{\frac{E_{i,t-1}}{LF_{i,t-1}}\}$	0.364	0.026	14.0

TABLE 3

Leads Model

Variable	Coefficient Estimates	Standard Error	t-value
$\log\{\frac{A_{it}}{LF_{it}}\}$	0.160	0.041	3.90
$\log\{\frac{T_{it}}{LF_{it}}\}$	0.611	0.137	4.46

The R^2's ranged from 72% for the high school enlistments to 67% for the total enlistments. Of the 55 dummy variables utilized to account for the monthly variation, district variations, different years, phasing out of GI bill, etc. only 24 of these were significant at the 1% level of significance; most of those were of the monthly type. More statistical details are available from the authors.

The next step was to decide how to use those results in the subsequent budget allocation scheme. Since the Navy Recruiting Command planned to use these models for allocating resources only among the 6 areas, one approach would have been to redo the regressions on area-level data. However, the short time-series could produce relatively unreliable estimates of the elasticities if the regressions were made at the regional level. Hence, the district-level data were utilized to obtain estimates of the elasticities. The method of fixed-value restrictions (Kmenta [11]) was then to obtain estimates of the area and seasonal dummies. In this method, the area-level elasticities are fixed at the values obtained in the district-level analysis.

After replacing the autoregressive term with the distributed lags, making the substitution for leads and collecting all of the non-controllable factors into one constant, P_{ij}, the area-monthly response function became, as a function of just the decision variables:

$$
\begin{aligned}
\begin{Bmatrix} \text{No. of HSG contracts} \\ \text{(in thousands) from} \\ \text{region } i, \text{ period } j \end{Bmatrix} = P_{i,j,2} & \begin{Bmatrix} \text{no. of recruiters} \\ \text{(in thousands) in} \\ \text{period } j, \text{ region } i \end{Bmatrix}^{0.391} \times \begin{Bmatrix} \text{no. of recruiters} \\ \text{(in thousands) in} \\ \text{period } j-1, \text{ region } i \end{Bmatrix}^{0.138} \times \begin{Bmatrix} \text{no. of recruiters} \\ \text{(in thousands) in} \\ \text{period } j-2, \text{ region } i \end{Bmatrix} \\[1em]
& \times \begin{Bmatrix} \text{Millions of dollars} \\ \text{of total advertising} \\ \text{in period } j, \text{ region } i \end{Bmatrix}^{0.081} \times \begin{Bmatrix} \text{Millions of dollars} \\ \text{of total advertising} \\ \text{in period } j-1, \text{ region } i \end{Bmatrix}^{0.029} \times \begin{Bmatrix} \text{Millions of dollars} \\ \text{of total advertising} \\ \text{in period } j-2, \text{ region } i \end{Bmatrix}
\end{aligned}
$$

$$
\begin{aligned}
\begin{Bmatrix} \text{No. of total contracts} \\ \text{(in thousands)} \\ \text{from region } i \\ \text{in period } j \end{Bmatrix} = P_{i,j,1} & \begin{bmatrix} \text{no. of recruiters} \\ \text{(in thousands)} \\ \text{in period } j, \\ \text{region } i \end{bmatrix}^{0.29} \times \begin{bmatrix} \text{no. of recruiters} \\ \text{(in thousands)} \\ \text{in period } j-1, \\ \text{region } i \end{bmatrix}^{0.106} \times \begin{bmatrix} \text{no. of recruiters} \\ \text{(in thousands)} \\ \text{in period } j-2, \\ \text{region } i \end{bmatrix}^{0.039} \\[1em]
& \times \begin{pmatrix} \text{Millions of dollars} \\ \text{of total advertising} \\ \text{in period } j, \text{ region } i \end{pmatrix}^{0.125} \times \begin{bmatrix} \text{Millions of dollars} \\ \text{of total advertising} \\ \text{in period } j-1, \\ \text{region } i \end{bmatrix}^{0.045} \times \begin{bmatrix} \text{Millions of dollars} \\ \text{of total advertising} \\ \text{in period } j-2, \\ \text{region } i \end{bmatrix}^{0.017}
\end{aligned}
$$

A discussion of attempts to "validate" these results is given in §5.

4. Budget Allocation Model

Having developed the enlistment contract response functions, the next step for arriving at the proper mix of advertising and recruiters was to optimize the level of each of these types of expenditures in order to achieve some stated set of objectives. Two different objective functions were used, depending on the mode selected by the user, i.e. a budget generation mode or a budget execution mode. In the first case the user provides a set of monthly or yearly quotas on total shipments, a quality constraint related to the minimum percentage of High School Graduate (HSG) enlistments permissible, together with a set of initial and terminal conditions. The user is then interested in the minimum total budget required, the optimal split between advertising and recruiting as well as the allocations of recruiters to areas and the allocation of advertising expenditures over time and by area. In the second case the user provides the separate budgets available for recruiters and advertising as well as the other inputs; the user is then interested in minimizing the sum of shortfalls from the stated quotas.

Since the quotas relate to shipments, and the advertising and recruiter efforts have their impacts through the response functions on contracts, it is necessary to be able to transform contracts into shipments; this was accomplished by utilizing the empirically observed delay factors associated with the Delayed Entry Program. In other words, based on a data analysis performed for all shipments over the years in question, by noting the date at which the enlistment decision was made, one could derive a lag distribution for the elapsed time between signing the contract and shipping. Hence, as exogenous inputs one has $(b_{j,v,k} : j = 1, 2, \ldots, 12; v = 0, 1, 2, \ldots, 12; k = 1, 2)$ where $b_{j,v,k}$ represents the fraction of all enlistment contracts of type k signed in period j, that convert to shipments v periods later. Note that $\sum_{v=0}^{12} b_{j,v,k}$ is generally less than 1 since some attrition occurs between contract signing and actual shipment.

Utilizing these delay factors, one can express the total number of shipments of all types in period j in the relationship:

$$
S_j = \sum_{k=1}^{2} \sum_{i=1}^{I} \sum_{v=0}^{12} (C_{i,j-v,k})(b_{v,j-v,k}) \tag{1}
$$

where $C_{i,j-\tau,k}$ is the number of enlistment contracts of type k signed in region i, in period $j - \tau$.

Hence, the objective function, in the budget generation mode, is to minimize the total expenditures needed, namely:

$$R \sum_{i=1}^{I} \sum_{j=1}^{12} X_{i,j} + \sum_{i=1}^{I} \sum_{j=1}^{12} Y_{i,j}$$

where
  R = the monthly cost per recruiter.
  $X_{i,j}$ = the number of recruiters assigned to region i, in period j.
  $Y_{i,j}$ = dollar amount of advertising expended in region i, period j.
The constraints relate to the national quotas, the terminal conditions desired, and the quality mix constraint. If Q_j $(j = 1, 2, \ldots, 12)$ represents the monthly shipping quotas for the decision year, then we have the nonlinear constraints $S_j \geqslant Q_j$ $(j = 1, 2, \ldots, 12)$ where the S_j's are defined as in (1). If P represents the quality constraint related to the minimum permissible percentage of high school enlistments (denoted by $k = 2$), then one has as this constraint:

$$\sum_{i=1}^{I} \sum_{j=1}^{12} C_{i,j,2} \geqslant P \sum_{i=1}^{I} \sum_{k=1}^{2} \sum_{j=1}^{12} C_{i,j,k}. \tag{2}$$

Next consider the impact of the initial conditions, in particular advertising expenditures and recruiting resources assumed to be in place shortly before the beginning of the decision horizon. Since a lagged effect was found between enlistments and past advertising and recruiter efforts, the initial conditions can affect the $\{P_{i,j,k}\}$ in the response functions derived earlier for the initial values of j. The actual modifications to the $P_{i,j,k}$ are determined by simply substituting the known advertising and recruiter levels into the earlier response equation to arrive at a new constant for the first few months in the decision horizon. The other initial condition relates to the assumed number of contracts already in the delayed entry pipeline from efforts expended prior to our decision year. These amounts have their impact in that they reduce the shipping quotas for the actual year in question since certain portions of these quotas will be satisfied from efforts expended earlier. Hence, the Q_j $(j = 1, 2, \ldots, 12)$ presented earlier are actually the net shipping quotas for the decision year, having made this adjustment.

Finally consider the terminal conditions needed due to our finite planning horizon. In order to recognize that recuiting does not end after our actual decision horizon, we add a set of shipping requirements for the year beyond the decision year that have to be met from contracts signed in the decision year; these are inputs from the user in that he may wish to increase, maintain, or decrease the size of the float. Hence, in addition to the Q_j's for the decision year, we add another set of inputs, namely Q_j $(j = 13, 14, \ldots, 24)$ and an additional set of constraints, namely $S_j \geqslant Q_j$ $(j = 13, 14, \ldots, 24)$. With these various types of constraints, the model in a budget generation mode will minimize the total yearly costs involved, provide the optimal split between recruiter effort and advertising, and yield the geographical and monthly distribution of both advertising expenditures and recruiters to meet the prescribed set of shipping quotas for the decision year, as well as satisfy the terminal conditions.

If instead it is desired to exercise the model in a budget execution mode, then the objective is to allocate a given advertising budget and a given recruiter budget in order to minimize the sum of shortfalls from stated quotas. Hence, the objective function becomes:
Minimize

$$\sum_{j=1}^{24} (Q_j - S_j)^+ \tag{3}$$

where x^+ denotes the positive part of x. Hence (3) will minimize the sum of shipment shortfalls over the two year horizon. Note that through the use of the positive part, there is no explicit penalty for a longfall; however, since longfalls consume resources in a non-productive manner, they will be discouraged by this formulation. The constraint set is that of the previous formulation, in addition to the budget constraints. In passing it might be noted that other objective functions could have been used, such as minimizing the sum of the squared deviations from the stated quotas, or minimizing the total horizon shortfall, i.e.

$$\text{minimize} \left(\sum_{j=1}^{24} Q_j - \sum_{j=1}^{24} S_j \right)^+ .$$

The final choice was made based on the feeling that it was important to meet the monthly quotas, due to a need to fill slots in the training schools each month, but that the use of the squared shortfalls objective would overpenalize such deviations.

5. A Partial "Validation" of the Models and Results to Date

To validate the combination of the response functions and allocation model, it was desired to exercise the programs using separate data for the most recent year. The validation strategy would have two parts: 1) first to test the predictive capability of the response functions to see if it would predict the shipments. that actually occurred reasonably well. 2) Secondly, using the optimization logic, to run both the budget generation and budget execution programs, with the appropriate initial and terminal conditions, for a subsequent year; the "optimized" results would then be compared to the results that actually occurred. Unfortunately, unavailability of the breakdown of advertising expenditures by month and area for the 1978 year precluded this type of validation. Hence a series of partial validations were performed. These included exercising the optimization program in a probationary mode where the computer competed with management in tightly designed decision situations. Each situation was limited in scope with the computer's solution and the manager's decision compared and any significant discrepancies reconciled. For example, the optimization logic was run at the area level (instead of at the national level) using the area budget constraints, and the allocations at the district level compared. This enabled the Area Commanders to apply their experience and intuition for their one area and not be overwhelmed by the tradeoffs between areas.

Another validation activity was to run the globally optimized (national/monthly model for 1977, the latest year for which complete data were available. While it was recognized that this was not a validation of the enlistment response functions, in that they had been generated to best fit the 1976–1977 data, it was of interest to compare the budgets generated with those actually expended. The same demographic conditions were used in the model as for the year in question, together with the identical "stocks" of advertising and recruiters present in the months before 1977.

In terms of the terminal conditions used in the test run, the optimization model was required to produce, in addition to the same number of new shipments for 1977 and the same quality mix as actually occurred, the same number of men in the Delayed Entry pipeline as actually occurred at the end of 1977.

The results of this test of the global model follow. Regarding the fit achieved by the enlistment response functions, we note in Table 4 that for the yearly totals, the model slightly overpredicts the actual shipments, most likely the result of the fact that no attrition factors (between contract signing and shipment) were available. However, in reality there is a small attrition factor (estimated at roughly about 1–3%) which is to be incorporated in the model when the data becomes available.

TABLE 4

Comparison of Fit Achieved for Contracts and Shipments Using Actual Demographic and Enlistment Data for 1977

	Actual Total Contracts	Predicted Total Contracts	Actual High School Graduate Contract	Predicted Actual HS Grad. Contract	Actual Total Shipments	Predicted Total Shipments
Jan.	7029	7022	4748	4745	8529	8605
Feb.	7239	7198	4729	4697	6833	6590
Mar.	7798	7849	5058	4944	5971	6295
Apr.	6397	6713	4139	4173	5051	5347
May	6195	6621	4028	4228	5802	6125
June	8251	8505	5579	5806	10203	11611
July	7812	7720	5194	5193	10667	12215
Aug.	8617	7956	5615	5347	11542	1219.
Sept.	7498	7690	4422	4796	11189	10467
Oct.	6013	5990	3784	3745	6815	7367
Nov.	6849	6838	4059	4046	5830	6291
Dec.	6926	6909	3972	4021	4206	3859
TOTAL for Yr.	86624	87011	55327	55741	92638	95966

The national model was run in a budget generation mode to determine the most cost-effective mix of advertising and recruiter expenditures for 1977. The optimization runs were made using the nonlinear programming MINOS Code (see Waren and Lasdon, [14]), where the number of geographical areas, periods, and types of expenditures resulted in 144 decision variables. The objective of the run was to minimize the total annual costs needed to meet the set of quotas actually in use for 1977. Since the enlistment response functions used only total advertising (in contrast to a breakdown of the various types of advertising) as the independent variable, it was assumed that the optimal advertising budget generated would be spent across the different media in the same percentages as in 1976–1977.

In addition to the same demographic variables, quality mix, initial and terminal conditions described earlier, the allocation logic was further constrained by the fact that it did not allow the number of recruiters to vary within a given area within the year; i.e., the optimization logic selected that single number of recruiters for each area that would be optimal for the entire year. This was to reflect the realities and difficulties in transferring recruiters from one area to another over a relatively short period of time.

The results of this exercise were that:

(i) it met the same set of quotas as were actually achieved in 1977 with a 6.6% reduction in yearly costs; this translated to a $5.7 million savings per year.

(ii) the optimal ratio of advertising costs to total costs changed from the 18.4% that actually occurred to 12.8%. In this regard it is interesting to compare this mix with the results of the ADVISOR 1 and ADVISOR 2 Programs (see Lilien [10]) aimed at understanding the mix between personal selling and advertising for industrial products. Based on surveys for 131 participating companies, covering such industries as machinery and equipment, chemical, fabricated material, etc., the median ratio of advertising to total marketing was 10.0%. Hence the 12.8% developed by the model seems in general agreement with the ADVISOR studies, if the analogy of obtaining enlistment contracts to that of obtaining industrial product contracts is applicable.

(iii) the model's allocation of the advertising expenditures over the year were on a proportional basis substantially less (41% compared to 65%) in the first half of the year than was spent in actuality, significantly more (35% compared to 14%) in the summer months, and about the same (24% compared to 21%) in the fall months. In addition there was a substantial increase in the advertising allocations for the months of January and December. Apparently there is a large pool of uncommitted eligibles in the summer months that the model claims will respond to advertising. In addition recent surveys have learned that high school seniors view the Christmas holidays as a key period in their career decision making process, which lends some credibility to the computer's recommendation.

(iv) the resulting area distribution of the total annual budget was very close to what occurred in 1977, for four of the six areas. For the other two areas the model suggested a transfer of some resources from one to the other; it is interesting to note that the Recruiting Command substantiated this recommendation based on its own internal studies dealing with relative propensities to enlist in the two areas.

The final partial validation effort has consisted of exercising the contract prediction equations, developed from 1976 and 1977 data, on recently acquired data for the first half of 1978. The error in the monthly forecasts for the nation as a whole averaged 4.12% and overpredicted enlistments. This points out that, while the model has some degree of credibility, other explanatory factors need to be investigated. These would include the effect of income differentials between civilian and military pay, the advertising expenditures of other services, the possible effects of quotas in holding down production (see Jehn and Shugart [9]), different propensities to enlist by area of the country, the urban-rural factors, and the availability of other special employment opportunities available to youths such as the Civilian Employment Training Program begun in early 1978. The use of these other factors will help eliminate the reliance on the district dummy variables to capture these effects, and remove any bias in the estimates generated.

6. Program Impact and Future Efforts

The model is now being used to help prepare the Navy's budget request to Congress for Fiscal Year 1982. Part of its value lies in being able to perform sensitivity analyses related to the impacts of various unemployment scenarios and the declining high school population on the size of the budget needed. It can also be used to help gauge the cost associated with varying the quality mix of the recruits, i.e. the minimum percent of high school graduates that can be accepted. It is noteworthy that the emphasis on recruiting high school graduates is related not only to the intellectual levels needed to complete training in the Navy's schools, but to the high correlation found between the high school degree and the perserverance needed to complete the enlistment contractual obligations.

Additionally the enlistment response functions generated, through the use of the sign and magnitude of the district dummy variables, can be helpful in highlighting those districts where field audits can uncover what recruiter techniques are particularly effective or ineffective. Also by rerunning the national optimization at the area level in a budget execution mode, it is hoped the model can provide some useful insights to the area commanders as to how he should allocate best his allotments from the national headquarters down to the district levels.

It is also being used to help prepare a five-year plan for the Recruiting Command whereby long range forecast of recruitment requirements are input and potential bottlenecks highlighted at an early stage. This is accomplished by running the program iteratively for each year, using the outputs from the run for the previous year as the initial conditions for the next run.

Future efforts being supported by the Navy include further validation work on the response functions, using more recent data and inclusion of the additional factors mentioned earlier; the number of response functions would be expanded to cover various mental categories for the recruits.

In order to help with the development of goals, the budget allocation model is also being expanded to optimize over the shipping quotas, now input as exogenous quantities. Under this scheme the decision maker could specify a yearly total quota, as well as some upper and lower bounds on the number of shipments that can be accommodated each month, and the optimization model used to determine the most efficient monthly and area quotas. Another extension contemplated is the disaggregation of the advertising budget into its various elements, i.e. local advertising, direct mail, TV, recruiter aids, etc. and its inclusion in the response functions and optimization program to improve on the effectiveness of the mix of advertising. Finally it is planned to expand the optimization model to consider a five year horizon so that it is able to tradeoff resource expenditures simultaneously over the various years to minimize the total expenditures needed. This type of capability is important, given the strong diminishing returns nature of marginal advertising and recruiters detected in the response functions.[1]

[1] The authors wish to acknowledge the capable computer support provided by David P. Robinson in the nonlinear programming area and the research assistant support of Varsha Rao.

This work was supported by the Office of Naval Research and the Navy Recruiting Command under Contract N00014-78-0440.

References

1. "Advertising for Military Recruiting: How Effective Is It?" Report to the Congress by the Comptroller General, FPCD-76-168, March, 1976.
2. CENTER FOR NAVAL ANALYSES, *Navy Recruiting in an All-Volunteer Environment*, Institute of Naval Studies Research Contribution 235, C. Jehn and H. Carroll, Arlington, Va., 25 April 1974.
3. CHAPPELL, DAVID AND PEEL, DAVID A., "Optimal Recruitment Advertising," *Management Sci.*, Vol. 24 (1978), pp. 910–917.

4. CHARNES, A., COOPER, W. W. AND RHODES, E., "Measuring the Efficiency of Decision Making Units,"
    European J. Operational Res., Vol. 2 (1978), pp. 429–444.
5. DORFMAN, R. AND STEINER, D. O., "Optimal Advertising and Optimal Quality," *Amer. Econom. Rev.*
    Vol. 44 (1954), pp. 826–836.
5. EPPS, THOMAS W., "An Econometric Analysis of the Effectiveness of the U.S. Army's 1971 Paid
    Advertising Campaign," *Appl. Econom.*, Vol. 5 (1973), pp. 261–269.
7. GRISSMER, DAVID W., "The Supply of Enlisted Volunteers in the Post-Draft Environment: An Analysis
    Based on Monthly Data, 1970–1975" in *Defense Manpower Policy* (editor: Richard V. L. Cooper),
    The Rand Corp., R-2396-ARPA, 1978.
8. ────── ET AL., "An Econometric Analysis of Volunteer Enlistments by Service and Cost-Effectiveness
    Comparison of Service Incentive Programs," General Research Corp., OAD-CD-66, 1974.
9. JEHN, C. AND SHUGART, W. "Recruiters, Quotas, and the Number of Enlistments," Center for Naval
    Analysis Report CNS 1073, 1976.
10. JOHNSTON, J., *Econometric Methods*, 2nd ed., McGraw-Hill, New York, 1972, p. 122.
11. KMENTA, JAN, *Elements of Econometrics*, Macmillan, New York, 1971, pp. 431–433.
12. LILIEN, GARY L., "Advisor 2: Modeling the Marketing Mix Decision for Industrial Products,"
    Management Sci., Vol. 25 (1979), pp. 191–204.
13. PARSONS, LEONARD J. AND SCHULTZ, RANDALL, *Marketing Models and Econometric Research*, North-
    Holland, Amsterdam, 1976, p. 169.
14. WAREN, ALLEN AND LASDON, LEON, "The Status of Non-Linear Programming Software," *ORSA*, Vol.
    27 (1979), pp. 431–456.

The Advertising-Sales Relationship in Australia

*Confidential data from 12 consumer-products firms
relate changes in market share
to changes in advertising share.*

Donald W. Hendon

The functional relationship sales = f (advertising) has intrigued businessmen, economists, and marketing scholars and practitioners for years. The literature abounds with studies. For example, Pearce, Cunningham, and Miller (1971) concluded after an extensive review of pre-1971 literature that promotional activity (including advertising) has some effect on aggregate consumption. However, five other variables have more influence on total demand than advertising has—the size and composition of the population, the level and distribution of personal income, technological changes, life-style changes, and various other social trends. Furthermore, these five phenomena and advertising interact with each other and affect demand and sales simultaneously.

Most advertisers are mainly concerned with the sales outcome of advertising, even though sales is only one of at least nine legitimate outcomes of advertising that can be measured. In descending order of desirability, and in ascending order of measurement validity, the basic advertising outcomes are as follows (Colley, 1961; Campbell, 1965):

(1) sales;
(2) market share;
(3) number of purchasers;
(4) distribution of product;
(5) distribution of the advertising vehicle or circulation;
(6) playback of attitude about the product;
(7) playback of attitude about the ad;
(8) playback of knowledge or awareness of the product;
(9) playback of knowledge or awareness of the ad.

Since the functional relationship between sales and advertising is difficult to measure validly, many advertisers use more valid measurements as proxy variables for sales. (Although such less desirable measurements as "recognition scores" have been criticized by such scholars as Palda [1966], Lucas and Britt [1963], and Lucas [1960], both Campbell [1965] and Hendon [1973] have maintained that any advertising outcome can be measured, even though the

validity of the different measurements ranges from high to low.) As a result, the Starch readership studies, which measure the ninth outcome, have many clients.

The literature dealing with determining the precise functional relationship between sales and advertising is small and has been overlooked by many marketing scholars and practitioners. For example, excellent work has been done by Metwally (1973), Lambin (1975), and Peckham (1972), although the latter uses the second most desirable outcome (market share) as a proxy variable for sales. This paper is concerned with acquainting larger audiences with this body of work and expanding upon the work of Peckham with empirical data from a small English-speaking nation.

Metwally's Australian Work

Metwally has written on the functional relationship between advertising and various outcomes. One of his most significant findings was published in the *Economic*

37

Record (1973). Table 1 shows the percentage of sales dollars devoted to advertising and the elasticity of demand coefficients for 20 product categories. The regression model $r = 0.00303c$ revealed a strong positive curvilinear correlation between the two. This is seen in $r = 0.86488$ and $|t| = 7.30957$.

Metwally explains the significant relationship by the "persuasive effect of advertising; the association between income-elasticity and scale of production on the one hand and between scale of production, marketing structure and advertising expenditures on the other hand, and by the association between income-elasticity, profit margins, and promotion expenditures."

Lambin's European Work

Lambin's work supports Metwally's choice of specific product classes rather than entire industries. Lambin feels that antitrust economists working with more aggregated industry data have attributed "evil" roles or socially undesirable effects to advertising, as seen in column 2 of Table

Donald W. Hendon is professor of administration at the College of Business Administration, Creighton University, Omaha. He holds Ph.D. and B.B.A. degrees from the University of Texas at Austin and an M.B.A. degree from the University of California at Berkeley. He has over 100 publications in 13 American and 8 foreign journals and in proceedings.

Table 1

Propensity to Advertise and the Income-Elasticities of Demand

Item	Advertising as % of sales	Elasticity
Food	.0081	0.761
Cigarettes	.0401	0.798
Alcoholic drinks	.0099	0.696
Toilet soap	.0101	0.395
Dental goods	.0532	1.442
Chemical goods	.0187	1.141
Pharmaceuticals	.0068	0.768
Women's toiletries	.0331	1.366
Clothing and drapery	.0120	0.969
Furniture	.0081	0.799
Household equipment	.0311	1.281
Paint	.0103	0.724
Petrol (gasoline) and oil	.0144	0.983
Rubber tires and tubes	.0112	0.924
Cars	.0663	1.791
Electrical goods	.0231	1.210
Refrigerators	.0162	1.182
Building materials	.0101	0.825
Travel and tourism	.0851	1.882
Entertainment	.0392	1.593

Source: M. M. Metwally, Australian Advertising Expenditure and Its Relation to Demand, *Economic Record* (June 1973), Table 5, 297. Used by permission of the author and the publisher.

2. Column 1 lists Lambin's version of the steps of the advertising process. Table 3 raises research questions to broaden the possibly oversimplified view inherent in each charge. Lambin concludes that most previous studies of the economic effects of advertising by a group of "antitrust economists" (see Telser, 1964; Comanor and Wilson, 1974) have attempted to relate advertising intensity directly to market performance. That is, they have tried to go directly from step 1 to step 6 in Table 2. As Lambin says, "because they relied on aggregate data (industry or total company advertising expenditures and sales), they could not capture the rich complexity of the managerial marketing decision process for individual brands." And so, in Table 2, column 3, he summarizes his conclusions about the effects of advertising at each of the six levels.

His conclusions are based on data from 16 product classes in 25 product markets, with 108 brand-nation observations (in 8 European nations) and 225 brand-years of

observations. Using the ordinary-least-squares method or one of its variants, he estimated three groups of behavioral relationships without giving the regression equations themselves:

(1) consumer demand in response to brand's and rival brands' advertising and in response to other marketing efforts;
(2) advertising appropriation in relation to its main determinants;
(3) rival-brand reactions to a brand's advertising, price, and product-quality changes.

Peckham's American Work

Peckham's work (1972) involves the two areas identified by asterisks in Table 3:
(1) "Does advertising influence consumer buying decisions?"
(2) "Are increased rival advertising outlays negatively related to a company's own sales or market shares?"

Table 2
The Advertising Controversy

Steps in the advertising controversy	Assumed roles or effects of advertising	Observed roles or effects of advertising
		Yes, but . . .
1 Advertising ◄	Large companies advertise in order to create a preference for their brands	they also use advertising to perform communication tasks required by the market situation;
		large-scale advertising has no built-in advantage for the large companies, although a threshold level exists that may privilege the deep purse
		Yes, but . . .
2 Consumer buying behavior	Consumers perceive real or apparent differences among brands and develop preferences	the advertising effect is modest in both absolute and relative value;
		consumers are less responsive to noninformational advertising
		Yes, but . . .
3 Barriers to entry	Preferences lead to brand loyalty, or consumer inertia, that constitutes a barrier to entry of new brands into the market	many other factors explain consumer inertia or loyalty;
		where consumer inertia is high, advertising intensity is not necessarily also high
		No . . .
4 Market power	Protected brand positions reduce active rivalry and give the company more discretionary power	we observed no basic incompatibility between the presence of intensive advertising in a market and the degree to which that market exhibits active rivalry,
		but . . .
		advertising escalation does not benefit the consumer as does a price war or a technological race
		No . . .
5 Market conduct	Discretionary power allows the company to ignore more tangible forms of competition (price and product quality) and lets it charge higher prices	consumer responsiveness to price and product quality remains high in advertising-intensive markets;
		a company may react to rival advertising by advertising, price, or even quality adjustments
		Yes . . .
6 Market performance	Higher prices result in high profits that furnish incentive to continue advertising	advertising increases the capacity of the company to charge higher prices to the consumer,
		but . . .
		no continuous association is observed between market concentration and advertising intensity;
		sales maximization under profit constraints seems to be the company's objective, although long-term profitability is likely for several brands

Source: Reprinted by permission of the Harvard Business Review. Exhibit III from "What is the real impact of advertising?" by Jean-Jacques Lambin (May–June 1975). Copyright © 1975 by the President and Fellows of Harvard College; all rights reserved.

Peckham's findings support Lambin's conclusions. Peckham uses the same simple, interesting, and yet mostly overlooked methodology used by Lambin to quantify the functional relationship between advertising and its second most desirable but second least valid outcome—market share. Since Peckham was a senior executive at A. C. Nielsen Company, he used confidential information from the Nielsen Retail Index on share of the advertising dollars spent (or ad share) and market-share data gathered over a 45-year period (1926-1969) for branded food, household, toiletry, and proprietary-drug products. Here are four of his findings:

(1) Table 4 shows a general correlation between advertising and sales. Peckham

Table 3
Statistically Testable Advertising Issues

1
Why do companies advertise?

Is there a positive and statistically significant relationship between advertising intensity, innovation density, and the degree of diversification of the product line?

Does advertising intensity vary with the size of the brand? Do large and small brands adopt different decision rules in setting their advertising appropriations?

Are advertising, price, distribution, and product quality substitutable and/or complementary marketing instruments for the company?

2
To what extent are consumers influenced by advertising?

Does advertising influence consumer buying decisions?*

How effective is advertising in creating artificial or spurious product differentiation? Are there constant, decreasing, or increasing marginal returns on advertising?

Can we observe the presence of threshold levels?

Does total industry advertising influence total market growth?

3
Does advertising create barriers to entry?

Is there a positive and statistically significant relationship between brand inertia rates and brand advertising intensity?

Does advertising create a reservoir of goodwill for the advertised brand?

Is there a significant difference in market instability for highly advertised brands and for little-advertised brands?

4
Does advertising dull corporate rivalry?

Are increased rival advertising outlays negatively related to a company's own sales or market shares?*

To what extent do companies adjust their advertising appropriations in view of the advertising decisions of their rivals?

To what extent do they react to rival brand advertising by means other than advertising – e.g., price or product quality adjustments?

5
Does advertising inhibit price and quality competition?

In advertising intensive markets, are prices and product quality significant determinants of sales and/or market shares?

Are advertising, price, distribution, and product quality substitutable and/or complementary marketing instruments for the company?

To what extent do companies react to rival brand advertising by means other than advertising – e.g., price or product quality adjustments?

6
What is the payoff on advertising?

Is there a positive and statistically significant relationship between market concentration and advertising intensity?

Do highly advertised brands charge, or have the capacity to charge, higher prices than little-advertised brands?

Is the brand's overall market performance compatible with short- or long-term profit maximization objectives?

* See text.

Source: Reprinted by permission of the Harvard Business Review. Exhibit II from "What is the real impact of advertising?" by Jean-Jacques Lambin (May–June 1975). Copyright © 1975 by the President and Fellows of Harvard College; all rights reserved.

Table 4
Dollar Sales and Advertising Trends of 58 Product Categories Studied by A. C. Nielsen Company, 1964 versus 1965

Category groups	Sales gain	Advertising gain
Top 17	+17%	+26%
Middle 23	+5%	0%
Bottom 18	−2%	−7%

Source: James O. Peckham, Sr., *The Wheel of Marketing* (Chicago: Nielsen, 1972), chart 62, opposite p. 25. Used by permission of the publisher.

ranked 58 major product categories by sales performance in 1965 versus 1964. The largest group—the middle 23—managed a consumer-dollar sales gain between 3 and 7 percent, or about the average 5-percent growth reported for all grocery-store sales in the United States. The lowest-ranked categories reported a sales gain of +2 percent or less and, as a group, averaged −2 percent. The fastest-growing group had sales greater than 7 percent (the top limit for the middle group) and averaged a sales gain of 17 percent over the 1964 level. There is a positive correlation between sales trends and level of advertising change for these groups. The fastest-growing categories had the greatest increase in advertising investment, and those groups with the weakest sales trend had a coincident cutback in advertising. Of course, this does not prove a cause-effect relationship.

(2) During the 15-year period 1946–1961, 12 of the leading brands in 34 product classifications lost leadership and were replaced by 12 new leaders. Eight of the 12 former leaders were challenged by a new or radically improved competitive brand having a demonstrable advantage to the consumer. The former leader in each of these 8 instances failed to equal or better the competitive product's improvement. Four of the losers—only half as many—lost out mainly because they allowed competition to outadvertise and outmerchandise them. These 4 equaled or bettered the competitive product's improvement.

Thirteen brands, or 60 percent of the 22 remaining brand leaders, maintained an ad share greater than market share throughout practically the entire 15-year period, and continued to lead at the end of the 15 years, in comparison to the 12 brands that lost their leadership position. While the 1946 ad share was less than the 1946 market share for another 4 of the brand leaders (or 18 percent), the ad share was sharply increased through 1961—in fact, it almost doubled. In only 4 of the brand leaders (or 18 percent) was the original high ad share allowed to fall, and in only one case (4 percent) was the ad share lower than the market share. Approximately 4 out of 5 brand leaders over the 15-year period, therefore, maintained an ad share consistent with their competitive position.

(3) Peckham concluded that the best insurance of staying on top is to consistently maintain one's ad share at a point ahead of one's market share—assuming that one also keeps one's product and its resulting advertising appeals up to date. Furthermore, one would expect an increase in market share during the second year if the ad share for a given brand exceeds the preceding year's market share, and conversely. Therefore, Peckham analyzed Nielsen data for the 15-year period 1950–1964 and found that in approximately 80 percent of the cases, [ad share > market share]$_{t-1}$ → [higher market share]$_t$, where t is the present year, and $t - 1$ is the previous year. Figure 1 shows the ad share and market share of all company brands combined for a ready-to-eat-cereal manufacturer. The changes in ad shares and market shares are in the same direction in every year of the period except for 1957. Peckham indicates that this firm is typical of the several hundred cases examined and lists five reasons for the 20-percent exception rate:

(a) a major price reduction relative to other brands;

(b) a more effective product-advertising story—for example, if the brand was improved or if the advertising got across to the consumer that the brand was improved, if there was a new use for the product, etc.;

(c) a brand with such an effective product-advertising story that it could continue to secure gains in market share without a competitive advertising budget (this is rare);

(d) a dynamic new competitive brand entering the market;

(e) a brand so weak in its consumer acceptance and product-advertising story that no amount of additional advertising support could stop the downward competitive trend.

(4) These reasons are nothing more than subjective conclusions and cannot be accepted without independent collaborative research. Fortunately, statistically significant relationships can be obtained through simple linear-regression analysis. Peckham applied this technique to the above-mentioned cereal firm. As the differential between the ad-share level versus the previous year's market share became less favorable (decreasing from +6.9 points in 1951 to +2.9 points in 1952 and still further to −7.6 points in 1953), the point change in market share as compared to the previous year also became less favorable.

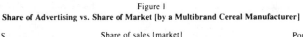

Figure 1
Share of Advertising vs. Share of Market [by a Multibrand Cereal Manufacturer]

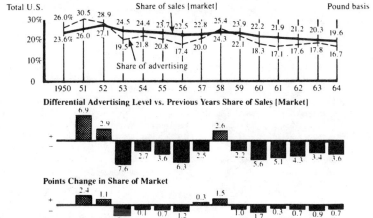

Source: James O. Peckham. *The Wheel of Marketing* (Chicago: Nielsen. 1972). chart 66. opposite p. 27. Used by permission of the publisher.

Figure 2
Share of Advertising vs. Share of Market [by a Multibrand Cereal Manufacturer]

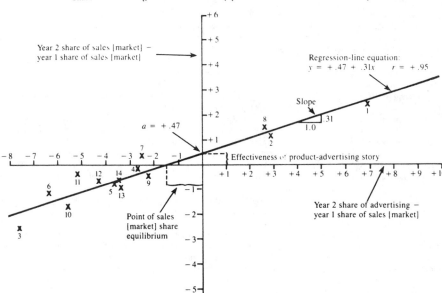

Source: James O. Peckham. *The Wheel of Marketing* (Chicago: Nielsen, 1972), chart 66.01, opposite p. 31. Used by permission of the publisher.

Furthermore, as the differential between the ad-share level versus the previous year's market share became more favorable, as it did between −7.6 points in 1953 and −2.7 points in 1954, the point change in market share as compared to the previous year also became more favorable. And so forth.

Thus, there appears to be a consistent relationship between changes in the independent variable (differential between the ad-share level and the previous year's market share) and the dependent variable (point change in market share). One can plot the pairs of points for each year, with the x axis representing the independent (advertising share, for short) variable and the y axis the dependent (market share or sales share, for short) variable. This is done in Figure 2 for the cereal manufacturer. Using the least-squares method, a simple linear regression line of the form $y = .47 + .31x$ was obtained. In other words, the

changes in share of sales (y) for this cereal manufacturer between any two years are equal to a constant of about one-half a percentage point (.47) plus .31 multiplied by the factor x (the number of points that ad share exceeds the previous year's sales share). The important thing to note here is the slope, +.31. If the slope were 0, the line would be flat, perpendicular to the x axis, and there would be no relationship between ad share and sales share. But the slope was +.31, which means that there was a change of +.31 in sales share every time there was a change of +1.0 in ad share. The higher the slope, the more that ad share affects sales share.

Peckham found the same kind of straight-line relationships (oblique to the x axis) for every brand. There was no case in which the slope was 0. Sometimes a negative slope was found, but for the most part slopes for most brands were positive.

Slopes are highest in the early stages of the product life cycle, and over a period of 20 to 50 years the slope of the regression line for most brands in the Nielsen data became flatter, although never 0. For example, most pre-World War I brands have flat slopes of .04 to .10. These brands now do very little advertising. Furthermore, after the fourth or fifth year of a brand's existence, the slope does not change much. It changes quite a bit during the first four years, however. After year 4, most marketing managers, through an intuitive or actual analysis of slopes of regression equations, know how much advertising is needed to generate the desired level of sales.

Although the slope does not change much after year 4, the y intercept does. The cereal manufacturer's y intercept is +.47. Therefore, the regression line cuts the y axis about midway between the point where the x and y axes meet and $+1$ on the y axis. This happens when $x = 0$, or when each year's ad share equals the preceding year's sales share. Peckham has interpreted this as the relative effectiveness of the product-advertising story as compared with competition. Here, the cereal manufacturer stands to gain about half a percentage point in sales share per year through maintaining an ad share merely equal to the preceding year's sales share, assuming all else remains equal.

Thus, unlike the slope of the regression line, which seems relatively fixed over fixed periods of time (after year 4), the y intercept can and does change from one year to the next as the following five things occur, according to Peckham:

(a) as the product was improved or when the advertising got across to the consumer that the brand was improved, that there was a new use for the product, etc. Here, the y intercept increases, and the regression line moves up a certain amount, paralleling the old regression line.

(b) as the price relationship to competition becomes more favorable, in which case the intercept increases, or less favorable to competition, in which case the y intercept declines, staying parallel again.

(c) as distribution is materially increased, in which case the y intercept increases, staying parallel again.

(d) as a strong new brand with a unique selling proposition enters the market, in which case, the intercept declines, again staying parallel.

(e) as the advertising message becomes more effective, in which case the y intercept increases, or less effective, in which case the y intercept declines, again staying parallel.

Furthermore, since we are dealing in market or sales shares, it should be kept in mind that the manufacturer's brand can secure an increase in the y-axis intercept by default if competition becomes less effective on any one of these five counts.

The Present Study's Australian Work

The present author was commissioned in 1974 by the Australian Association of National Advertisers to write a position paper on the economic effects of advertising for submission to a governmental regulatory commission (see Hendon, 1975). As a result of the success of the monograph, a follow-up effort by the author, again sponsored by the AANA, was successful. Twelve firms released sufficient confidential ad-share and market-share data for individual brands in response to the questionnaire shown in Figure 3 so that they could be included in the present study—Carnation Company (for an unspecified product); Cortalds Hilton, a hosiery manufacturer (for an unspecified product); Dulux, a paint manufacturer (for one of its architectural and decorative paint brands); Ford Motor Company (for one of its passenger motor cars); H. J. Heinz (for its canned soup); Johnson & Johnson (for its brand of women's sanitary tampons); Lever & Kitchen of the Unilever Group (for one of its heavy-duty washing-powder brands); Philip Morris (for an unidentified brand of cigarettes); Stafford-Miller, a toiletry manufacturer (for its denture-fixture brand); and three anonymous companies (a processor and marketer of consumer goods for an unspecified product, a food company for one of its canned-soup brands, and a food manufacturer for its brand of "continental regular packet soups excluding all instant soups").

Table 5 shows the changes in ad shares and market shares for these 12 firms. It should be noted that in order to preserve corporation secrets, the order in which the data are presented in Table 5 is not the same as that given in the text of this article. Table 6 gives the regression equations for these 12 firms, while Figures 4, 5, and 6 illustrate three regressions—firm A, which provided the author with the most data points; firm H, which had the steepest positive slope; and all 12 firms combined.

Figure 3
Questionnaire on Advertising's Usefulness

(1) Company name (optional):
(2) I wish to keep my name confidential. (Yes, no)
(3) Main business of Company:
(4) I wish to keep the information given in this questionnaire confidential. (Yes, no)
(5) You can contact me for more information if necessary. (Yes, no)

The following questions refer to just one product category. Please pick one product category which you feel would be useful for the purposes of the study, as described in the cover letter. Describe the product category in the space provided below.

(6) What were the total sales for your company in this product category? (1972, 1971, 1970, 1969, 1968, other years)
(7) What were the total industry's sales in this product category only? (1972, 1971, 1970, 1969, 1968, other years)
(8) What was the total advertising expense for your company for this product category? (1972, 1971, 1970, 1969, 1968, other years)
(9) What was the total advertising expense of the total industry for this product category only? (1972, 1971, 1970, 1969, 1968, other years)
(10) What was your market share in this product category? (1972, 1971, 1970, 1969, 1968, other years)
(11) What was your share of the total advertising dollars spent by the entire industry in this particular product category only? (1972, 1971, 1970, 1969, 1968, other years)
(12) Comment:
    (1) The data in Q. 6, 7, & 10 are based on Nielsen Index Plan information.
    (2) Advertising Expenditures relates only to Media (Television, Radio, and Press).

Source: Australian Association of National Advertisers, Sydney.

Table 5
Market Share$_t$ versus Market Share$_{t-1}$, and Advertising Share$_t$ versus Market Share$_{t-1}$ for 12 Australian Firms

Co.	'69 Mkt.- '68 Mkt.*	'69 Adv.- '68 Mkt.**	'70 Mkt.- '69 Mkt.*	'70 Adv.- '69 Mkt.**	'71 Mkt.- '70 Mkt.*	'71 Adv.- '70 Mkt.**	'72 Mkt.- '71 Mkt.*	'72 Adv.- '71 Mkt.**	'73 Mkt.- '72 Mkt.*	'73 Adv.- '72 Mkt.**	'74 Mkt.- '73 Mkt.*	'74 Adv.- '73 Mkt.**	'75 Mkt.- '74 Mkt.*	'75 Adv.- '74 Mkt.**
A	−1.4	−6.8	+1.5	+11.6	−0.6	+10.1	−1.4	+10.9	+3.1	−4.3	+3.0	+8.7	—	—
B	−1.0	+18.0	−5.0	+26.0	0.0	+25.0	+4.0	+30.0	—	—	—	—	—	—
C	+0.6	+14.4	+1.0	+11.8	+0.6	+15.8	+0.2	+12.2	—	—	—	—	—	—
D	+0.1	+5.9	+2.9	+6.6	+1.9	+5.1	+2.5	+1.2	—	—	—	—	—	—
E	+1.1	−7.6	+2.0	−8.8	0.0	−10.8	+5.1	−9.5	—	—	—	—	—	—
F	0.0	−4.6	+2.0	−9.3	0.0	−13.0	0.0	−15.5	—	—	—	—	—	—
G	+1.5	+13.1	−1.0	+11.6	+0.6	+15.6	+1.0	+9.0	—	—	—	—	—	—
H	−9.6	−13.7	+1.9	+1.0	−1.3	+1.9	−4.4	+6.3	—	—	—	—	—	—
I	+0.6	0.0	+0.1	+12.7	+1.9	+5.0	+0.2	−0.2	—	—	—	—	—	—
J	—	—	−3.8	+28.9	−1.0	+24.2	−0.9	+17.4	—	—	—	—	—	—
K	—	—	—	—	—	—	—	—	—	—	+8.8	+53.5	+1.6	+17.7
L	—	—	—	—	+4.2	+15.5	+4.8	+4.3	—	—	—	—	—	—

* y.
** x.

Source: Confidential data obtained from a survey conducted jointly by the author and the Australian Association of National Advertisers, Sydney, 1975. Companies' names are replaced by letters. To protect the anonymity of the respondents, the letters are not in the same order as are the companies as listed in the text of this article.

Implications

Special attention should be paid to the slopes. They range from −0.2337 for company J to +0.3885 for company H. The slope for all 12 firms was +0.0394, which indicates that advertising is only somewhat effective. Advertising seems to be a relatively weak variable in the marketing mix. Subjective speculations of the author for this weak relationship include the following:

(1) Group members offer resistance to any communication that advocates views contrary to the group's norms, including mass-communicated advertising messages (see Kelley and Volkart, 1952).

(2) The nature of commercial mass media in a free society leads the media (and the ad messages carried by those media) to espouse for the most part only such attitudes as were already virtually universal (see Klapper, 1940).

(3) Any persuasive message, such as an advertising message, is more likely to reinforce the existing opinions of its receivers than it is to change such opinions. At most, minor attitude changes may result. Seldom will any "ego-involved" attitudes be changed (see Klapper, 1960).

(4) Advertising is not very important to the majority of Americans (see Greyser, 1965).

(5) Word of mouth always intervenes in the communication process to offset changes advocated by the mass media, including behavioral and attitudinal changes advocated by advertising (see Klapper, 1960).

(6) In 17 studies summarized in *Psychological Abstracts* between 1954 and 1963, there was no correlation found between knowledge obtained from the mass media and behavioral and attitude changes (see Haskins, 1964).

(7) Asch (1955) reinforced the importance of word of mouth and personal influence by his famous experiment in which 37 percent of the subjects agreed with the group on length of lines even though they knew the group to be incorrect.

(8) The selective defense processes do not operate in word of mouth, while they do in the mass media. These processes operate to immunize us from communications not in accord with our existing attitudes and interests. Therefore, we can easily "tune out" an ad (see Arndt, 1967).

(9) Mass communication is less flexible

Table 6
Regressions for 12 Australian Firms

All companies: $y = 0.3051 + 0.0394x$
Company A: $y = 0.7408 − 0.0081x$
Company B: $y = −7.6181 + 0.2876x$
Company C: $y = 0.8033 − 0.0150x$
Company D: $y = 2.4854 − 0.1352x$
Company E: $y = 3.4602 + 0.1537x$
Company F: $y = 0.9081 + 0.0350x$
Company G: $y = 0.2415 + 0.0230x$
Company H: $y = −2.9129 + 0.3885x$
Company I: $y = 0.7604 − 0.0138x$
Company J: $y = 3.6013 − 0.2337x$
Company K: $y = −1.9591 + 0.2011x$
Company L: $y = 5.0306 − 0.0536x$

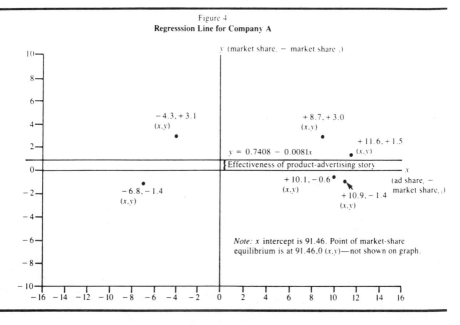

Figure 4
Regresssion Line for Company A

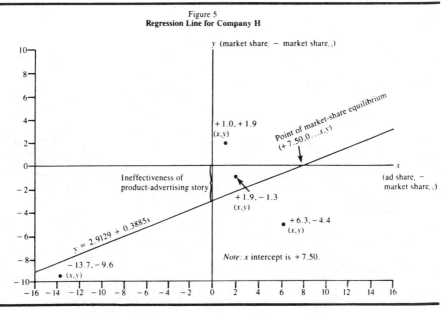

Figure 5
Regression Line for Company H

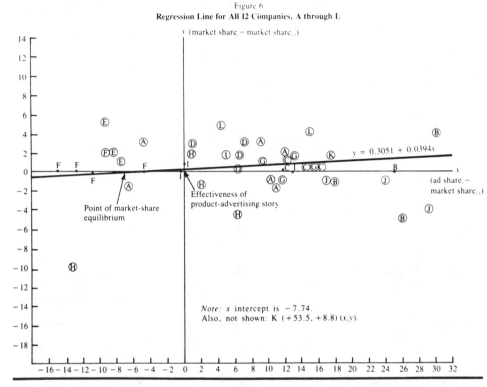

Figure 6
Regression Line for All 12 Companies, A through L

Note: x intercept is −7.74.
Also, not shown: K (+53.5, +8.8) (x,y).

than personal communication. Therefore, the mass communicator obtains feedback much later and has a more difficult time changing his communication when he finds it does not work (see Arndt, 1967).

(10) Personal sources are often in a position to offer rewards for compliance with their recommendations and punishments in the case of noncompliance, while mass-media sources are not in this position. This is because ads are not important to us, and we do not care whether we please the advertiser or not. Thus, word of mouth provides social approval to an innovation, while ad testimonials do not (see Arndt, 1967).

(11) Mass media can only provide factual information, while word of mouth can provide evaluative information, which we tend to trust more. This is because of the high credibility of the human source of the message as compared to the mass-media source. And the closer we get to making a purchasing decision, the more we need evaluative information (see Arndt, 1967).

Need for Additional Research

To the author's knowledge, there has never been a study that has revealed the aggregate slopes of more than one firm. All we have is Peckham's assurance that most American slopes are positive. It would be helpful to the advancement of marketing as a science if Nielsen revealed the aggregate slope for all its American and foreign firms over an extended period of time.

Until then, the only study that reveals slopes for aggregates of firms is this one.

Of course, this study was based on Australian data. Many will, therefore, feel that the results cannot be applied to the U.S. market. However, the author feels that U.S. and Australian advertising and marketing techniques and environments are similar. Therefore, he feels that the Australian results can and should be applied to the U.S. market. He hopes that the publication of these findings will spur other scholars and practitioners to reveal aggregated American information.

References

Arndt, Johan. *Word of Mouth Advertising: A Review of the Literature.* New York: Advertising Research Foundation, 1967.

Volume 21, Number 1, February 1981

Asch, Solomon E. Opinions and Social Pressure. *Scientific American* 193 (1955):31–35.

Campbell, Roy H. A Managerial Approach to Advertising Measurement. *Journal of Marketing* 24 (1965):5.

Colley, Russell H. *Defining Advertising Goals for Measured Advertising Results.* New York: Association of National Advertisers, 1961.

Comanor, William S., and Wilson, Thomas A. *Advertising and Market Power.* Cambridge, Mass.: Harvard University Press, 1974.

Greyser, Stephen A. Advertising the Institution. In *The A.A.A.A. Study on Consumer Judgment of Advertising.* New York: American Association of Advertising Agencies, 1965.

Haskins, Jack B. Factual Recall as a Measure of Advertising Effectiveness. *Journal of Advertising Research* 4 (1964):2–8.

Hendon, Donald W. How Mechanical Factors Affect Ad Perception. *Journal of Advertising Research* 13 (1973):39–45.

———. *The Economic Effects of Advertising.* Sydney: Australian Association of National Advertisers, 1975.

Kelley, Harold H., and Volkart, Edmund H. The Resistance to Change of Group-anchored Attitudes. *American Sociological Review* 17 (1952):464–65.

Klapper, Joseph T. *The Effects of Mass Media: A Report to the Director of the Public Library Inquiry.* New York: Bureau of Applied Social Research, Columbia University, 1940.

———. *The Effects of Mass Communication.* New York: The Free Press, 1960.

Lambin, Jean-Jacques. What Is the Real Impact of Advertising? *Harvard Business Review* 53 (1975):139–47.

Lucas, Darrell B. The ABCs of ARF's PARM. *Journal of Marketing* 25 (1960):9–20.

Lucas, Darrell B., and Britt, Steuart Henderson. *Measuring Advertising Effectiveness.* New York: McGraw-Hill, 1963.

Metwally, M. M. Australian Advertising Expenditure and Its Relation to Demand. *Economic Record* (June 1973):290–99.

Palda, Kristian S. The Hypothesis of a Hierarchy of Effects: A Partial Evaluation. *Journal of Marketing Research* 3 (1966):13–24.

Pearce, Michael, Cunningham, Scott M., and Miller, Avon. *Appraising the Economic and Social Effects of Advertising.* Cambridge, Mass.: Marketing Science Institute, 1971.

Peckham, James O., Sr. *The Wheel of Marketing.* Chicago: Nielsen, 1972.

Telser, Lester G. Advertising and Competition. *Journal of Political Economy* 72 (1964):537.

OPTIMAL ADVERTISING AND OPTIMAL QUALITY

By ROBERT DORFMAN and PETER O. STEINER*

Lawrence Abbott discussed some of the principles of quality competition in a recent issue of this *Review*.[1] Most of the conclusions obtained by Abbott and a number of other results of some interest can be derived more easily by approaching the problem of differentiated competition from a broader point of view than Abbott's, using rather simple analytic tools. We demonstrate the technique which we have in mind, along with some results of intrinsic interest, by applying the technique to a few problems including Abbott's.

1. *Joint Optimization of Advertising Budget and Price*

Theorem: A firm which can influence the demand for its product by advertising will, in order to maximize its profits, choose the advertising budget and price such that the increase in gross revenue resulting from a one dollar increase in advertising expenditure is equal to the ordinary elasticity of demand for the firm's product. The proof of this statement will be given immediately. As a clarifying preliminary we state that we mean by advertising any expenditure which influences the shape or position of a firm's demand curve and which enters the firm's cost function as a fixed cost, *i.e.*, a cost which does not vary with the quantity of output. This concept corresponds generally, but not exactly, to the usual concept of advertising. It includes expenditures on billboards, newspaper space, radio time, interior decoration of a place of business, air conditioning of sales space, etc. And now, the proof.

We consider a firm which makes two kinds of choice: the price of its product and the amount of its advertising budget. Assuming this to be so, the relationship between the quantity the firm can sell per unit of time, q, its price, p, and its advertising budget, s, can be denoted by the formula

$$q = f(p, s). \tag{1}$$

We assume that $f(p, s)$ is continuous and differentiable.

In order to determine the optimal price-quantity-advertising con-

* The authors are associate professor and assistant professor of economics, respectively, at the University of California, Berkeley.

[1] Lawrence Abbott, "Vertical Equilibrium under Pure Quality Competition," *Am. Econ. Rev.*, Dec. 1953, XLIII, 826–45.

stellation it is convenient for expository reasons to analyze the situation in two steps. In the first step we regard the quantity of output as fixed and specify the optimal price-advertising constellation for selling that predetermined quantity. Then we let quantity vary and seek its optimum. The advantage of this procedure is that cost considerations, other than the cost of advertising, do not enter the first step.[2]

Suppose, then, that price be changed by a small amount, dp, and advertising expenditure by a small amount, ds. The change in the level of sales will be the total differential of equation (1) or:

$$dq = \frac{\partial f}{\partial p} dp + \frac{\partial f}{\partial s} ds.$$

In order for quantity not to change as a result of these variations, dp and ds must be chosen in such a way that they have equal and opposite effects on quantity; so that $dq = 0$. That is,

$$dp = -\frac{\frac{\partial f}{\partial s}}{\frac{\partial f}{\partial p}} ds, \text{ assuming } \frac{\partial s}{\partial p} \neq 0. \tag{2}$$

The result of these variations is to change gross revenue by the amount qdp, change advertising expenditure by ds, and leave the volume of sales and aggregate production cost unchanged. The net effect on profit is, therefore:

$$qdp - ds = -\left(q \frac{\frac{\partial f}{\partial s}}{\frac{\partial f}{\partial p}} + 1 \right) ds. \tag{3}$$

Now we must consider two cases: first, where the original level of advertising from which the variations were measured was positive, and second, where the original level of advertising was zero. We now show that a positive level of advertising cannot be optimal unless the quantity in parentheses in equation (3) is zero. For, if that quantity were positive we could choose a negative value for ds (signifying a decrease in advertising) which would have the effect of making the whole expression positive. It would therefore indicate that a decrease in advertising and a compensating decrease in price (as specified in equa-

---

[2] This two-stage mode of analysis has, of course, no effect on the result. It is unnecessary from a purely mathematical point of view, since we could handle this as a problem in the maximization of a function of several independent variables. The procedure adopted makes the problem amenable to more elementary methods.

tion [2]) would increase profit. Hence, the original level of advertising was too large to be optimal. Similarly if the parenthesis were negative, slight increases in both advertising expense and prices would serve to increase profits.

Analogous reasoning for the case where the original level of advertising was zero shows that profits could not be maximized if the quantity in parentheses were negative. Thus we have a *necessary* condition for profit maximization at any level of output (and therefore at all levels). It is:

$$q \, \dfrac{\dfrac{\partial f}{\partial s}}{\dfrac{\partial f}{\partial p}} + 1 \begin{cases} = 0 \text{ if } s > 0, \\ \\ \geqq 0 \text{ if } s = 0. \end{cases} \tag{4}$$

Let us now define the ordinary elasticity of demand, denoted by η, by

$$\eta = -\frac{p}{q} \frac{\partial f}{\partial p}$$

and the marginal value product of advertising, denoted by μ, by

$$\mu = p \frac{\partial f}{\partial s}.$$

This last concept is simply the rate of increase of gross receipts as advertising expenditure increases, price remaining constant. Substituting these concepts for the partial derivatives in equation (4) we find:

$$-q \, \dfrac{\dfrac{\mu}{p}}{\dfrac{q}{p}\eta} + 1 \begin{cases} = 0 \text{ if } s > 0, \\ \\ \geqq 0 \text{ if } s = 0. \end{cases}$$

or, cancelling the p's and q's, multiplying through by η, and transposing:

$$\begin{cases} \mu = \eta & \text{if } s > 0, \\ \mu \leqq \eta & \text{if } s = 0. \end{cases} \tag{5}$$

This equation proves the theorem.

Furthermore, inequality of η and μ indicates the direction of change in price or advertising that will increase profits. If $\mu > \eta$, it will pay to increase advertising expenditure and price, as we saw in the discussion following equation (3). Inequality in the other direction leads to the reverse course of action in order to maximize profits.

Although the volume of sales, q, was assumed constant throughout this argument, the generality of the result is not restricted by this assumption. If a firm's position can be improved without changing its sales volume then, *a fortiori*, it can be improved if the possibility of changing sales volume is open to it. Therefore a condition which must be met if profit is to be maximized while holding volume constant must also be met if volume is permitted to change.

Figure 1 may help bring out the significance of this result. The figure consists of three parts, each representing a different conceivable situation. In each part the advertising budget, s, is measured horizontally. To each value of s there corresponds a certain price which maximizes

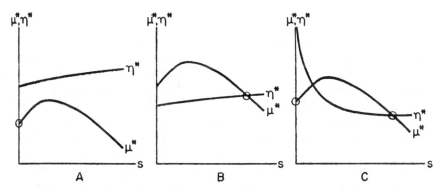

FIG. 1. OPTIMAL LEVELS OF ADVERTISING: ILLUSTRATIVE CASES.

profit regarding that advertising expenditure as given. To each such pair of advertising budget and optimal price there corresponds a certain elasticity of demand, which we denote by η^*, and a certain marginal value product of advertising, which we denote by μ^*. The three parts of Figure 1 show three possible ways in which η^* and μ^* may vary in response to changes in the advertising budget.

Our theorem shows that a nonzero level of advertising can maximize profits only if it corresponds to a crossing point of the η^* and μ^* curves. But not every crossing point, if there is more than one, is a profit maximizing point. Indeed, only points where μ^* crosses η^* from above correspond to profit maximization.[3] The circled points in the diagram indicate points of possible profit maximization.

What can be said about the shapes of the elasticity and revenue productivity functions portrayed? It seems plausible to assume that the effectiveness of advertising, indicated by the height of μ^*, increases initially but eventually shows decreasing returns. The effect of increased advertising expenditures on the elasticity of demand may work in either

[3] The proof is lengthy and, since it is fairly straightforward, it is omitted. It depends upon forming $\mu^* - \eta^*$ and finding its derivative in the neighborhood of crossing points.

direction,[4] and we offer no conjectures about it. In so far as the *existence* of an optimal level of advertising is concerned, the shape of the elasticity function is not critical. For if μ^* is ever greater than η^* (the necessary condition for advertising to pay at all), it must eventually cross it from above. This is because eventually μ^* will become less than unity, but η^* never will—by the classical arguments. In our illustrative figures we have arbitrarily drawn the elasticity curves as rising slightly in response to increases in advertising expenditures. It should be noted that changes in advertising budgets correspond to movements along these curves rather than to shifts of them.

A few market predictions follow at once from these considerations. In a perfectly competitive market the elasticity of demand for each firm's output is infinite. If we were to draw a diagram like Figure 1A for such a market, the η^* curve would be well above the top of the page. In this case the marginal value product of advertising is always less than the elasticity of demand and there will be no advertising.

At the other extreme are markets in which products are differentiated and in which product differences are important to consumers but are difficult for them to measure. Typically such markets offer a structure of prices for different brands. Either or both of two reasons conduce to relatively low elasticities of demand for the individual brands. First, there is a strong likelihood that the market structure will lead to retaliatory pricing if important changes in the structure of prices are attempted unilaterally. For this reason the relevant elasticity of demand may be approximated along a *mutatis mutandis* demand curve. Second, the price-brand preferences will reflect an uncertainty on the part of consumers which will make them reluctant to respond to changes in price differentials. To see this most clearly, imagine that consumers did know exactly what the differences between brands were worth to them. Then if any brand reduced its price it would immediately attract the "marginal" customers of other brands. Indeed we should have the case where the different brands were essentially competing commodities. But consumers' uncertainty blurs the sharp edge of preferences and replaces a cardinal ranking by something more like an ordinal one. The result is reduction in the effectiveness of changes in the price gaps between brands.

At the same time consumers' uncertainty has the effect of increasing the marginal effectiveness of advertising because consumers will not hold firmly to their appraisals of the relative merits of competing products. These circumstances are conducive to heavy advertising expenditure. Figure 1B would be typical of such a market.

[4] *Cf.* Neil H. Borden, *The Economic Effects of Advertising* (Chicago, 1947), esp. pp. 438, 850–51, 879.

A third important type of market occurs when product differentiation would not be important economically in the absence of advertising but when appropriate advertising can induce consumers to attach importance to the distinguishing characteristics of competing brands. Our previous conjecture concerning the effects of advertising on elasticity would not apply to this kind of market. Instead the elasticity of demand faced by any such firm would be infinite in the absence of advertising and would be decreased to finite levels by advertising. Figure 1C portrays the behavior of the curves in such a market. The perfectly competitive situation corresponding to zero or merely nominal levels of advertising would be transformed into the imperfectly competitive market corresponding to the circled intersection of the curves if aggregate profit were greater under the latter condition than under the former. Which of the two possible equilibrium situations is the more profitable will depend on the shape of the firm's cost curves and cannot be judged from this diagram alone.

In a monopolized industry as compared with an imperfectly competitive one both the effectiveness of advertising and the elasticity of the firm's demand curve are likely to be low. The appropriate level of advertising will depend very heavily on the special characteristics of the product, *e.g.*, necessity or luxury, major expenditure item or minor, closeness of substitutes, etc.

2. *Joint Optimization of Quality and Price*

In this section we find the optimal price-quality position for a firm which can influence its sales by modifying either the quality of its product or its price.

By quality we mean any aspect of a product, including the services included in the contract of sales, which influences the demand curve. The essential difference from advertising is that changes in quality enter into variable costs. Each conceivable quality will have a definite average cost curve, but there may be several different qualities with the same average cost curve. In this case we may assume that only that quality which has the most favorable demand curve will be given serious consideration. Thus we may assume that quality can be improved only at the expense of operating on a higher average cost curve. By quality improvement we mean any alteration in quality which shifts the demand curve to the right over the relevant range *and* raises the curve of average variable costs.

Now we can find the profit-maximizing conditions. Since the technique is parallel to that used in the preceding section we shall abbreviate the exposition. Consider a firm which produces a differentiated product whose quality can be measured (*e.g.*, in terms of horsepower, tensile strength, denier, etc.) and whose rate of sales per unit of time, continuous and differentiable function of price, p, and a quality index. We write as its demand function:

$$q = f(p, x)$$

The average cost of production, c, is a function of q and x:

$$c = c(q, x).$$

Just as in Section 1 we consider the effect on profit of arbitrary small changes in price and quality which have precisely offsetting effects on sales. This effect is expressed by the following equation, which is analogous to equation (3):

$$qdp - qdc = -q \left(\frac{\dfrac{\partial f}{\partial x}}{\dfrac{\partial f}{\partial p}} + \frac{\partial c}{\partial x} \right) dx.$$

By an argument similar to that following equation (3), the condition for profit maximizing equilibrium is found to be that the quantity in parentheses is zero, or:

$$-\frac{\partial f}{\partial p} = \frac{\dfrac{\partial f}{\partial x}}{\dfrac{\partial c}{\partial x}} .$$

This is the condition sought.

The left-hand side of this equation is the slope of the ordinary demand curve. The right-hand side measures essentially the rate at which sales increase in response to increases in average cost incurred in order to increase quality.[5] If the expression on the right-hand side of equation (6) is greater than that on the left, the indication is that an increase in quality will increase demand more than enough to compensate for the loss of sales that would result from an increase in price just sufficient to cover the increase in cost. Under such a circumstance quality should be increased.

Thus the general level of quality in any market depends on the relative magnitudes of two market characteristics and one technical characteristic of the product. Quality tends to be higher the greater the

---

[5] For example, if sales would increase by 100 units if the quality index were increased by one unit, and if this would raise average cost by $20, the right-hand side would be 5 units per dollar

sensitivity of consumers to quality variation (measured by $\partial f/\partial x$), the lower the sensitivity of consumers to price variation (measured by $\partial f/\partial p$), and the lower the effect on average costs of quality changes (measured by $\partial c/\partial x$). These are the three co-ordinate determinants of the general level of quality.

This analysis also suggests the conditions which conduce to quality variety in a market on the one hand and standardization on the other. If a market consists of a number of groups of consumers having identical demand curves but differing in their responsiveness to quality changes it will pay to provide different qualities at different prices. Similarly, if the groups are uniformly sensitive to quality changes but different in price consciousness (*i.e.*, if $\partial f/\partial x$ is the same for all groups, but $\partial f/\partial p$ differs among groups), there will be a range of qualities offered in order to exploit the differences in the demand curves. The analogy to discriminating monopoly is apparent. *A fortiori*, if, as frequently happens, those members of a market who have relatively high sensitivity to price changes have low sensitivity to quality and vice versa, then a spectrum of qualities will be offered. In all other cases, the commodity will tend to be standardized.

The optimizing condition of the quality variation case can be made more comparable to that for the price variation case by introducing the elasticity of demand with respect to quality variation, defined by the formula:

$$\eta_c = \frac{c}{q} \frac{\dfrac{\partial f}{\partial x}}{\dfrac{\partial c}{\partial x}}$$

This formula gives simply the ratio of the percentage change in demand to the percentage change in average cost, both induced by a small change in quality. If we multiply both sides of equation (6) by p/q and then multiply the right-hand side by c/c, we obtain

$$-\frac{p}{q} \frac{\partial f}{\partial p} = \frac{p}{c} \frac{c}{q} \frac{\dfrac{\partial f}{\partial s}}{\dfrac{\partial f}{\partial c}}$$

which, recalling the definition of the ordinary elasticity of demand, is equivalent to:

$$\eta = \frac{p}{c} \eta_c \tag{7}$$

3. *Joint Optimization of Advertising, Quality, and Price*

In Section 1 we discussed the equilibrium conditions for a firm which makes decisions with respect to both price and advertising expenditure; in Section 2 we dealt with a firm which makes decisions with respect to price and quality. The combined case, that of a firm which makes decisions of all three types, is probably of greater practical interest than either of these separated cases. This combined case presents no difficulties. We note that since advertising expenditure and quality can be varied independently a firm will not be in equilibrium unless it is in equilibrium with respect to each of these variables separately. Thus all of the preceding analyses apply and a firm will not be maximizing profits in the combined case unless its price, quality, and advertising expenditure are such that:

$$\mu = \eta = \frac{p}{c}\, \eta_c.$$

We here assume, of course, that advertising is at a positive level.

4. *Optimal Advertising with Fixed Prices*

Theorem: If the price which a firm can charge is predetermined by conventional, oligopolistic, legal or other considerations, and if the firm can influence its demand curve by advertising, it will, in order to maximize its profits, choose that advertising budget and the resulting rate of sales such that

$$\text{Marginal Cost} = p\left(1 - \frac{1}{\mu}\right).$$

The reader will notice that this formula is formally identical to the familiar relationship connecting price, marginal revenue, and elasticity where price is a variable of choice.

This is a simplified variant of the problem of Section 1. In order for an optimum to obtain, the advertising expenditure needed to increase sales by one unit must equal the profit on the marginal unit, *i.e.*, the excess of the given price over marginal production cost, MC. The equilibrium condition is then,

$$\frac{\partial s}{\partial q} = p - MC. \tag{8}$$

Since the marginal revenue product of advertising is

$$\mu = p\,\frac{\partial q}{\partial s},$$

equation (8) can be written

$$\frac{p}{\mu} = p - MC$$

which, after transposing and factoring out p proves our theorem.

By solving this formula for μ it can be seen that when advertising expenditure is optimized, the marginal revenue product of advertising equals the reciprocal of the mark-up on the marginal unit produced.

5. Optimal Quality with Fixed Prices

Theorem: If the price which a firm can charge is predetermined and if the firm can influence its demand curve by altering its product, it will, in order to maximize its profits, choose the quality such that the ratio of price to average cost multiplied by the elasticity of demand with respect to quality expenditure equals the reciprocal of the mark-up on the marginal unit. In symbols, the maximizing condition is

$$\frac{p}{c} \eta_c = \frac{p}{p - MC} .$$

This is Abbott's[6] problem and is a simplified variant of the problem discussed in Section 2. To solve it we notice that for profits to be maximized the marginal cost of production plus the total increase in quality cost necessary to sell one more unit at the given price must be equal to the given price. Furthermore, the average increase in quality cost necessary to sell one more unit at the going price is the increase in quality cost per unit increase in the quality index, divided by the increase in sales at the going price per unit increase in the quality index.[7] From these two considerations we have, at the optimal quality for the given price:

$$p = MC + q \frac{\frac{\partial c}{\partial x}}{\frac{\partial f}{\partial x}} . \tag{9}$$

Recalling the definition of elasticity with respect to expenditure on quality and inserting it, we obtain

$$p = MC + \frac{c}{\eta_c}$$

[6] Abbott, op. cit.

[7] To see this more clearly suppose that average cost will increase by $2 if the quality index is increased by one unit and that sales will increase by 10 units if the quality index is increased by one unit. Then a one unit increase in sales will result if quality is increased by 1/10 unit and this will raise average cost by $2/10 = $.20.

from which our theorem follows by elementary algebra. It may be noted that equation (9) appears to be the result given by Abbott.[8] It clearly conforms to common sense. What it says is that if a small increase, say Δc, in average cost suffices to improve quality enough to increase sales by one unit at the going price, then the total increase in production costs will be $q\Delta c$ (to increase quality of all units) plus the marginal cost (to produce one more unit) and this must be just equal to marginal revenue (price, in this case) in profit-maximizing equilibrium.

In a zero-profit group equilibrium without advertising $p = c$ and equation (9) shows that for each firm average cost exceeds marginal cost. Thus the firms are operating in the decreasing range of their cost curves, a result also noted by Abbott.[9]

6. *Conclusion*

There are good grounds for doubting the economic significance of the whole business of writing down profit functions (or drawing curves) and finding points of zero partial derivatives (or graphical points of tangency). Such devices are merely aids to thinking about practical problems and it may be an uneconomical expenditure of effort to devote too much ingenuity to developing them. Yet such devices are aids to clear thought and, if sufficiently simple and flexible, they help us find implications, interrelationships, and sometimes contradictions which might escape notice without them. Such aids are particularly needed in the field of nonprice competition. We hope that the techniques suggested here will be of assistance in developing this field and bringing out its connections with the theory of price competition. The examples we have solved above are not only of importance in themselves but, we hope, demonstrate the flexibility and convenience of the technique which we suggest.

[8] Abbott, *op. cit.*, pp. 837–38.
[9] *Ibid.*, p. 844.

Optimal Advertising Policy Under Dynamic Conditions[1]

By MARC NERLOVE and KENNETH J. ARROW

Advertising expenditures are similar in many ways to investments in durable plant and equipment. The latter affect the present and future character of output and, hence, the present and future net revenue of the investing firm. Advertising expenditures affect the present and future demand for the product and, hence, the present and future net revenue of the firm which advertises.[2] In a previous paper, Dorfman and Steiner[4] have given the necessary conditions for maximum net revenue when: (a) price and advertising expenditures are the only variables affecting the demand for the product; (b) current advertising expenditures do not affect the future demand for the product; and (c) the decision-maker is a monopolist who can determine both price and advertising expenditures. They have also extended their analysis to cover the case in which the quality of the product is variable.

In what follows, the Dorfman-Steiner model is extended to cover the situation in which present advertising expenditures affect the future demand for the product. It is shown that, under plausible assumptions, the necessary conditions for a maximum of the present value of future net revenues lead to a decision rule which is similar to a rule of thumb actually used by many firms. The Dorfman-Steiner model is a special case of the model presented here.

1. FORMULATION OF THE MODEL AND THE OPTIMAL PRICE POLICY

The demand for the output of an individual firm or of an industry depends on advertising expenditures in addition to the price of the product, consumer incomes, and the prices of competing or complementary products. Advertising expenditures may shift the demand function by adding new customers, those who may never have consumed the product before in the case of an industry, or those who have previously consumed the product of another firm in the case of an individual firm. Such expenditures may also alter the tastes and preferences of consumers and thereby change the shape of the demand function as well as shift it. For example, " brand " advertising may make the price elasticity of demand for the brand advertised lower

[1] The research on which this paper is based was supported in part by a grant from the National Science Foundation to Stanford University and in part by Contract Nonr-225(50) between the Office of Naval Research and Stanford University. An earlier draft with the same title by Nerlove was supported by the Department of Agricultural Economics at the University of Minnesota.

We are indebted to O. Brownlee, I. R. Savage, R. Strotz, F. V. Waugh, and S. Weintraub for helpful comments on an earlier draft.
[2] The idea that advertising is a form of investment occurs in Hoos [5].

than it would otherwise be. On the other hand, the attraction of new customers by means of advertising and the consequent broadening of the market may make demand more sensitive to price.[1]

Regardless of its precise effects on the demand function, advertising expenditure at any one time may be expected to lose its effectiveness in subsequent periods. An advertising campaign conducted now may bring a hundred thousand customers into the fold today, but next month or next year many of these will have drifted off. Other firms and other industries do not stand still but also commit funds to advertising; these campaigns in turn draw customers to the products or brands advertised and away from the product or brand initially considered. Furthermore, permanent changes in consumer tastes and preferences are difficult to effect; while a strenuous advertising campaign may induce a change in tastes and preferences for a time, there is a tendency for the preferences of consumers to return to their old pattern. On the other hand, the effects of a given advertising campaign, both upon the number of consumers and their tastes, tend to persist for a considerable period following the campaign, albeit, for the reasons given, to a steadily diminishing extent.[2]

One possibility of representing the temporal differences in the effects of advertising on demand would be to include a number of dated, past advertising outlays in the demand function. However, such an approach is not especially useful. A more promising analytical approach, and one which has considerable intuitive appeal, is to define a stock, which we shall call *goodwill* and denote by $A(t)$, and which we suppose summarizes the effects of current and past advertising outlays on demand. The price of a unit of goodwill, we shall suppose, is \$1, so that a dollar of current advertising expenditure increases goodwill by a like amount.[3] On the other hand, a dollar spent some time ago should, according to our previous argument, contribute less. One possible way of representing this lesser contribution is to say that

---

[1] See Borden [3], pp. 433–38.

[2] Vidale and Wolfe [10] present a large amount of empirical evidence that the effects of advertising linger on but diminish as time passes. As Waugh [11] has put it, " . . . old advertisements never die—they just fade away ". Vidale and Wolfe studied a number of situations in which an advertising campaign was run and then all further advertising ceased; they were thus able to ascertain the extent to which the effect of the campaign diminished over time.

[3] The assumption that the cost of adding to goodwill is always one, no matter at what level current advertising expenditures are carried on, is actually very unrealistic. At very high levels of current advertising expenditure resort must be had to inferior media so that the costs of adding a dollar's worth to goodwill must surely rise with the level of expenditure. One possible way of dealing with this problem is to set a finite upper bound to current advertising expenditure, below which we assume a proportional cost of adding to goodwill. This alternative has been discussed by Arrow [1]. Alternatively and more generally, one might introduce a non-linear cost function for additions to goodwill. This procedure has been used in Strotz [9] and Nerlove [8] in connection with optimal investment policies. Lack of one or the other of these assumptions leads to policies which may have a jump at $t=0$. Since we are primarily interested in the characteristics of the optimal policy after $t-0$, however, we shall restrict ourselves to the simpler, but more unrealistic case.

goodwill, like many other capital goods, depreciates. If we further assume that current advertising expenditure cannot be negative[1] and that depreciation occurs at a constant proportional rate, δ, we have

$$\dot{A} + \delta A = a \geq 0 \dots \dots \dots \dots \dots \dots \dots \dots \dots \dots \dots (1)$$

where a is current advertising outlay, a and A are understood to be functions of time, and the dot denotes differentiation with respect to time. Equation (1) states that the *net* investment in goodwill is the difference between the *gross* investment (current advertising outlay) and the depreciation of the stock of goodwill.[2]

We are now in a position to formulate our model: Let $q(t)$ be the rate at which purchases are made at time t, $p(t)$ the price charged, and $z(t)$ other variables not under the control of the firm such as consumer incomes, population, and the prices of substitute and complementary products. The quantity demanded is assumed to depend on $p(t)$, $A(t)$, and $z(t)$:

$$q = f(p, A, z) \ . \dots \dots \dots \dots \dots \dots \dots \dots \dots \dots \dots (2)$$

The rate at which total production costs, $c(t)$, are incurred is assumed to be a function of output:

$$c(t) = C(q) \ . \dots \dots \dots \dots \dots \dots \dots \dots \dots \dots \dots (3)$$

Let $r(t)$ be the rate at which revenue net of production costs and current advertising outlays accrues to the firm; then

$$
\begin{aligned}
r(t) &= pf(p, A, z) - C(q) - a \\
&= R(p, A, z) - a, \dots \dots \dots \dots \dots \dots \dots \dots \dots \dots (4)
\end{aligned}
$$

where R is revenue net of production expenses only. We assume that the firm attempts to maximize the present value of the stream of revenues net of both production expenses and advertising costs by appropriate price and advertising policies over time. That is, for a given initial value of A,

$$A(0) = A_o,$$

the time paths of p and A are chosen to maximize

$$V\{p, A\} = \int_0^\infty e^{-\alpha t} [R(p, A, z) - a] dt \dots \dots \dots \dots \dots \dots (5)$$

subject to (1), where α is a fixed rate of interest. Note that V is a functional depending on the whole time paths of p and A. The optimal policies must satisfy the initial condition $p(0) = p_o$ and $A(0) = A_o$.

It is important to note that the optimal policies need not be continuous functions of time. For example, suppose that A can be chosen

[1] One can conceive of a situation in which the effects of negative advertising expenditure on demand could be achieved, namely, where a firm advertises the product of a competitor. Unfortunately, to achieve the same effect on net revenue as negative advertising, one's competitor would have to pay double the amount of the expenditure to the firm in question. This is hardly plausible. For this reason, and since goodwill cannot be sold in any other way without selling the entire firm, we rule out negative current advertising expenditures altogether.

[2] The concept of exponentially depreciating goodwill was essentially introduced by Waugh [11]. It leads in the discrete case to a distributed lag model similar to the one employed by Jastram [6] which in turn was based on the work of Koyck [7].

without restriction such as (1) and that z is fixed. The initial stock of goodwill does not, then, constitute an effective constraint. Thus the optimal policies at any time will be made under the same conditions and must therefore be the same, i.e., constant. Since the optimal choice of A may not be A_o, there will be a discontinuity at $t=0$. The optimal policy will be to increase or decrease A at once to its optimal level and will therefore imply an infinite instantaneous rate of current advertising outlays, $a(0)$. For such paths, the integral in (5) must be interpreted with some care.

Since net revenue depends only on current price, it is clear that if there are no restrictions on price changes, the initial price does not matter. Furthermore, the maximum of V can be found by first maximizing it with respect to price, holding A fixed, and then maximizing the result with respect to A by an appropriate choice of the time path of a. Thus, optimal price policy is determined by maximizing current net revenue with respect to price, i.e., by equating marginal gross revenue to marginal production costs *at all times:*

$$(p - C') \frac{\partial f(p,A,z)}{\partial p} + f(p,A,z) = 0 \quad \dots\dots\dots\dots\dots\dots(6)$$

If we let $\eta = -\frac{p}{f} \frac{\partial f}{\partial p}$ be the elasticity of demand with respect to price, (6) can be written

$$p = \eta \ C'/(\eta - 1), \dots\dots\dots\dots\dots(6')$$

the usual price formula for a monopolist. If we solve (6) for the optimal price policy $\hat{p}$ as a function of A and z, $\hat{p}(t) = P(A,z)$, and insert the result in (5), we obtain a new problem, namely to maximize

$$V\{A\} = \int_0^\infty e^{-\alpha t} [\hat{R}(A,z) - a]dt, \quad \dots\dots\dots\dots\dots(7)$$

subject to (1) and the initial condition $A(0) = A_o$. Note that (1) determines a if A is given; hence, an optimal solution for A gives an optimal solution for a.

2. Determination of Optimal Advertising Policy[1]

Since A_o is fixed, maximizing the surplus

$$S\{A\} = V\{A\} - A_o, \quad \dots\dots\dots\dots\dots\dots\dots\dots\dots(8)$$

subject to (1) and $A(0) = A_o$ is equivalent to the problem stated in the previous section. Expanding (8) by means of (1) and (7), we have

$$S\{A\} = \int_0^\infty e^{-\alpha t} [\hat{R}(A,z) - A - \delta A]dt - A_o$$

$$= \int_0^\infty e^{-\alpha t} [\hat{R}(A,z) - \delta A]dt - [A_o + \int_0^\infty e^{-\alpha t} A \, dt] \quad (9)$$

---

[1] This section is largely based on the material given in [i].

Integrating the second term on the right by parts, we find

$$A_0 + \int_0^\infty e^{-\alpha t} A \, dt = A_0 + [e^{-\alpha t} A(t)]_0^\infty + \alpha \int_0^\infty e^{-\alpha t} A \, dt$$

$$= \lim_{t \to \infty} [e^{-\alpha t} A(t)] + \alpha \int_0^\infty e^{-\alpha t} A \, dt \ .. \ (10)$$

Substituting in (9), we obtain

$$S\{A\} = \int_0^\infty e^{-\alpha t} [\hat{R}(A,z) - (\alpha + \delta) A] dt - \lim_{t \to \infty} [e^{-\alpha t} A(t)] \, .. (11)$$

The function

$$\Pi(A,z) = \hat{R}(A,z) - (\alpha + \delta) A \dotfill (12)$$

may be called the net " profit " function; if goodwill were ordinary capital it would represent what was left of revenue net of production expenses after deduction of interest and depreciation charges on capital.

We make three assumptions:

Assumption 1: The limit $\lim_{t \to \infty} [e^{-\alpha t} A(t)]$ exists.

Assumption 2: The net profit has a unique local maximum at a value A^*.[1]

Assumption 3: For sufficiently large A, the net profit function is decreasing.

We first assume that z is constant, so that we are considering a *stationary environment*.

Under Assumptions 1–3, it can be shown that any optimal policy for constant z must be bounded;[2] for consider a policy, A, which is unbounded. By Assumption 3, we can find another policy $\tilde{A}$ which is bounded and for which $S\{A\}$ has a higher value. Let A_m be any value greater than A_0 for which the net profit function is decreasing for $A \geq A_m$. Then the policy $\tilde{A} = \min \{A_m, A\}$ is bounded, and by construction,

$$\Pi(\tilde{A},z) \geq \Pi(A,z) \dotfill (13)$$

for all t. Since $\tilde{A}$ is bounded,

$$\lim_{t \to \infty} [e^{-\alpha t} \tilde{A}(t)] = 0 \leq \lim_{t \to \infty} [e^{-\alpha t} A(t)] \dotfill (14)$$

It follows from (13) and (14) that $S\{\tilde{A}\} \geq S\{A\}$ where A is any unbounded policy. Thus the class of all *bounded* policies includes the optimal policy and we may restrict our consideration to bounded policies for which $\lim_{t \to \infty} [e^{-\alpha t} A(t)]$ vanishes.

---

[1] Arrow [1] deals with the more general situation in which the net profit function may have a finite number of distinct local maxima.

[2] Note, however, that the magnitude which is bounded is *goodwill*, not *current advertising expenditure*. It is perfectly possible for the latter to be unbounded even if the former is bounded.

B

To maximize $S\{A\}$, it is desirable to make $\Pi(A,z)$ as large as possible, subject to the constraints (1) and $A(0)=A_o$. Assumptions 2 and 3 imply that $\Pi(A,z)$ has a unique global maximum which is also the local maximum of Π with respect to A. This occurs at the value A^* which may be determined by solving

$$\frac{\partial \Pi(A,z)}{\partial A} = \frac{\partial \hat{R}(A,z)}{\partial A} - (\alpha+\delta)$$

$$=[P(A,z) - C'[f[P(A,z), A,z]] \; \frac{\partial f[P(A,z), A,z]}{\partial A}$$

$$- (\alpha+\delta)=0, \; \dots\dots\dots\dots\dots\dots\dots\dots(15)$$

for A where $P(A,z)$ is determined by solving (6) for the optimal price policy $\hat{p}$ as a function of A and z.[1]

We denote the solution to (15) as A^*; it is a function of z. Since z is, in general, a function of time, A^* has been defined as a function of time. We will refer to the policy

$$A(t)=A^*[z(t)] \; \dots\dots\dots\dots\dots\dots\dots\dots\dots(16)$$

as being the *instantaneously optimal* policy. This policy can be given a relatively simple form. Let $\beta = \frac{A}{f} \frac{\partial f}{\partial A}$, the elasticity of demand with respect to goodwill. If C' is expressed in terms of p, from (6'), (15) can be simplified to

$$\frac{A^*}{pq} = \frac{\beta}{\eta(\alpha+\delta)} \dots\dots\dots\dots\dots\dots\dots\dots\dots(17)$$

This is a dynamic counterpart of Dorfman and Steiner's main result [4].

What is the relation between the policy designed to maximize net profits at each instant of time and the optimal policy? First consider the case where $z(t)$ is constant over time so that the instantaneously optimal policy is a constant, $A^* =A^*(z)$. Clearly, the policy is optimal for $t > 0$, since

$$S\{A^*\}=\Pi(A^*,z)\int_{o+}^{\infty} e^{-\alpha t} \, dt = \frac{\Pi(A^*,z)}{\alpha} \dots\dots\dots\dots(18)$$

is as large as possible and not affected by what happens at the single point $t=0$, and since, for (17), $\dot{A}^*=0$, so that the constraint (1) is satisfied:

$$a^* = 0+ \delta \; A^* > 0 \dots\dots\dots\dots\dots\dots\dots\dots\dots(19)$$

---

[1] Equation (15) is a generalization of the result obtained by Dorfman and Steiner [4]. It states that at the optimal price (price equal marginal production costs), the marginal revenue from increased goodwill net of the marginal costs of producing the increased output should be equal to the marginal opportunity cost of investment in goodwill. To see this, note that the instantaneous rate of return on investment is α; the instantaneous decay is δ; therefore, if the firm invests a dollar now and spends it on advertising later, it makes α and saves δ. To put the matter another way, a dollar invested in a bond will yield $e^{\alpha t}$ in t periods, whereas a dollar invested in advertising will require $e^{-\delta t}$ further investment over the t periods to offset decay, the opportunity cost is $e^{\alpha t} - e^{-\delta t}$, so that the marginal opportunity cost at $t=0$ is $\alpha +\delta$.

where a^* is the current advertising outlay determined by A^*, for $t>0$. Thus, the key question is: what happens at $t=0$? If $A^* \geq A_o$, we either have a jump in A^* at $t=0$, in which case $\dot{A}(0)$ and therefore $a^*(0)$ are infinite,[1] or $\dot{A}^*=0$. In either case, the constraints are satisfied. On the other hand, suppose that $A^* < A_o$; then $A(t)$ has a downward jump at $t=0$ and $\dot{A}(0)$, and therefore $A(0)$ are $-\infty$, contradicting (1). We have proved:

Theorem 1: if A^* is a point at which $\Pi(A,z)$ reaches a maximum, and if $A^* \geq A_o$, then the optimal advertising policy for constant z is

$$a^* = \delta A^* \qquad \text{for } t>0,$$

and

$$a^* = \begin{cases} \delta A^* & \text{if } A^* = A_o \\ +\infty & \text{if } A^* > A_o \end{cases} \quad \text{for } t=0.$$

A^* is determined by equations (6) and (15).

Although goodwill can have an upward jump at $t=0$, as we have already observed it cannot have a downward jump in view of the constraint (1). What then is the optimal policy if $A^* < A_o$? Clearly, $\Pi(A,z)$ increases as we decrease A as long as A is greater than A^*; hence, the optimal policy must be to decrease A as fast as possible. The greatest rate at which this can be done is given by the equality in (1):

$$\dot{A} + \delta A = 0 \quad \dotfill (20)$$

or

$$A = A_o\, e^{-\delta t} \quad \dotfill (21)$$

At some time, $t=\tau$, $A(\tau)=A^*$, namely

$$\tau = \frac{1}{\delta}\, \log \frac{A_o}{A^*} \quad \dotfill (22)$$

Then the firm will be in the same position looking forward from τ as it would have been had $A^* = A_o$ to begin with; hence, the optimal policy will be to continue with the stationary policy $A(t)=A^*$. We have proved:

Theorem 2: If A^* is a point at which $\Pi(A,z)$ reaches a maximum, and if $A^* < A_o$, then the optimal advertising policy for constant z is

$$a^* = 0 \text{ for } 0 \leq t \leq \frac{1}{\delta}\, \log \frac{A_o}{A^*}$$

and

$$a^* = \delta A^* \text{ for } t > \frac{1}{\delta} \log \frac{A_o}{A^*}$$

where A^* is determined by equations (6) and (15).

The assumption of a constant z was used in the proofs of Theorems 1 and 2 only to establish that A^* satisfied (1) and that $e^{-\alpha t}A(t)$ approaches

[1] This is the difficulty referred to in footnote 3, p. 130. Modifying the model in either of the two ways suggested there would lead to a policy without a jump.

zero as t approaches infinity. Without any change in the argument, we state

Theorem 3: Let $A^*(z)$ maximize $\Pi(A,z)$ with respect to A. If

$$\text{(A)} \quad \lim_{t \to \infty} e^{-\alpha t} A^*[z(t)] = 0,$$

and

(B) $\dot{A}^*[z(t)] + \delta\, A^*[z(t)] \geqq 0$ for all t, then the optimal policy, $A(t)$, may be described as follows:

(a) for $A_o < A^*[z(0)]$, the policy consists of a jump at $t=0$ to $A^*[z(0)]$; $A(t) = A^*[z(t)]$ for $t > 0$;

(b) if $A_o = A^*[z(0)]$, then $A(t) = A^*[z(t)]$ for all $t \geqq 0$;

(c) if $A_o > A^*[z(0)]$, then $A(t) = A_o\, e^{-\delta t}$ for $0 \leqq t \leqq \tau$, and $A(t) = A^*[z(t)]$ for $t \geqq \tau$, where τ is a solution (if any) of the equation $A_o\, e^{-\delta t} = A^*[z(t)]$;

(d) if $A_o > A^*[z(0)]$ and $A_o\, e^{-\delta t} \geqq A^*[z(t)]$ for all $t \geqq 0$, then $A(t) = A_o\, e^{-\delta t}$ for all $t \geqq 0$.

In terms of current advertising expenditures, $a^*(0) = +\infty$ in case (a), and $a^*(t) = 0$ for $0 \leqq t \leqq \tau$ in case (c); otherwise, $a^*(t)$ is given by the left-hand side of (B).

If (B) does not hold, the optimal solution becomes complicated. It may become profitable to have $A(t)$ fall below the instantaneously optimal level, even at times when this policy does not violate (1), in order to prepare for later intervals in which (1) is violated. A special case of this problem, with no depreciation and a finite time horizon, has been studied in [2], and even in this case the algorithm cannot be described simply.

3. SOME COMPARATIVE DYNAMICS OF THE GENERAL SOLUTION FOR A STATIONARY ENVIRONMENT

At the level of generality of the model described in the previous sections, it is possible to discuss the effects of changes in the two parameters, α and δ, on the optimal stationary policies $\dot{p}$, a^* or A^*, and on τ, the time point at which these stationary policies are achieved, when z is assumed constant. To go further, it is necessary to specialize the model and we shall do this in the next section.

First note that α and δ enter symmetrically into equation (15) which determines A^*, and affect $\dot{p}$ only in so far as they affect A^*. Hence, as far as the effects of variations in the two upon either $\dot{p}$ or A^* are concerned, they are alike. Since $\Pi(A,z) = \dot{R}(A,z) - (\alpha + \delta)A$ has a unique maximum (both global and local) with respect to A, an increase in either α or δ must decrease the optimal stationary policy A^*. Analytically, the result follows from the fact that, at $A = A^*$, $\partial^2 \Pi / \partial A^2 = \partial^2 \dot{R} / \partial A^2 \leqq 0$.

The effect of a change in either α or δ upon the optimal price policy follows directly from the fact that an increase in either is equivalent to a decrease in A^*. Unfortunately, the effect of a decrease in A^* upon the optimal price depends upon its effect on the elasticity of demand, as is well-known. Hence, we cannot specify the result without more specific knowledge of the demand function.

Since A_0 is fixed, the effect of a change in α or δ upon τ, for $\tau > 0$, may be determined by differentiating (22):

$$\frac{\partial \tau}{\partial \alpha} = -\frac{1}{\delta}\frac{\partial A^*}{\partial \alpha}/A^* > 0, \text{ for } \tau > 0, \ldots\ldots\ldots\ldots\ldots(23a)$$

since $\delta > 0$, $A^* > 0$, and $\partial A^*/\partial \alpha < 0$.

$$\frac{\partial \tau}{\partial \delta} = -\frac{1}{\delta}\left\{\frac{\partial A^*}{\partial \delta}/A^* + \tau\right\}, \text{ for } \tau > 0, \ldots\ldots\ldots\ldots(23b)$$

which is positive or negative, according as

$$\left|\frac{\partial A^*}{\partial \delta}/A^*\right| \begin{array}{c} > \\ < \end{array} \tau, \text{ for } \tau > 0 \ldots\ldots\ldots\ldots\ldots\ldots(24)$$

since $\partial A^*/\partial \delta < 0$. Thus, an increase in the interest rate must always postpone achievement of the stationary policy A^*, but an increase in the depreciation rate may actually hasten it. The reason is simply that although an increase in the depreciation rate will lower A^* still further below A_0 (assuming that it is below so that $\tau \neq 0$), it also permits a faster approach with zero current advertising expenditures. It may be observed that $\partial \tau/\partial \delta > 0$ for τ sufficiently small, i.e., A_0 not too far above equilibrium, and negative in the contrary case.

The effects of changes in α and δ upon optimal current advertising expenditures in the case in which $\tau = 0$ (in other words, for the stationary part of the solution) may be found by differentiating (19):

$$\frac{\partial a^*}{\partial \alpha} = \delta\frac{\partial A^*}{\partial \alpha} < 0, \text{ for } \tau = 0, t > 0, \ldots\ldots\ldots\ldots\ldots(25)$$

and

$$\frac{\partial a^*}{\partial \delta} = \delta\frac{\partial A^*}{\partial \delta} + A^*, \text{ for } \tau = 0, t > 0, \ldots\ldots\ldots\ldots(26)$$

which is positive or negative, according as

$$\left|\frac{\delta}{A^*}\frac{\partial A^*}{\partial \delta}\right| \begin{array}{c} < \\ > \end{array} 1, \ldots\ldots\ldots\ldots\ldots\ldots\ldots\ldots\ldots(27)$$

that is, according as A^* is inelastic or elastic with respect to δ. Again, the ambiguity in the effect of a change in δ results from the fact that, although an increase in δ reduces the optimal A^* by increasing the opportunity cost of goodwill, such an increase also implies a higher level of current advertising expenditures to maintain any given level of goodwill.

4. SOME COMPARATIVE DYNAMICS OF THE SOLUTION IN A SPECIAL CASE

It is plain from the preceding discussion that not much can be said about the comparative dynamics of the solution to the optimal advertising problem in the general case. If, however, one is willing to set one's sights lower and specify particular forms for the demand and cost functions, a great deal more can be deduced. In this section it will be assumed that $\tau = 0$, that the total production cost function is linear in q, and that the demand function is of a particular *multiplicative form*,

$$f(p,A,z) = f_1(p) \, f_2(A) \, f_3(z) \dots\dots\dots\dots\dots\dots\dots(28)$$

For still more definite results, we will assume that the demand function is linear in the logarithms, which is a special case of (28):

$$f(p,A,z) = kp^{-\eta} \, A^\beta \, z^\zeta \dots\dots\dots\dots\dots\dots\dots\dots\dots(29)$$

Previously, the symbols η and β have been defined as the elasticities of demand ,with respect to price and goodwill, respectively; ζ is the elasticity of demand with respect to the variable, z,; if z is income, then ζ is the income elasticity of demand.

Theorem 3 assures us that the optimal policy for all t will coincide with the instantaneously optimal policy defined by (31) and (33) below, at least after a finite time period, provided A^* neither increases nor decreases too rapidly over time.

Since we are assuming that the total cost function is linear, the marginal cost is constant.

$$C' = \gamma, \text{ a constant} \dots\dots\dots\dots\dots\dots\dots\dots\dots\dots\dots(30)$$

Under the multiplicative assumption (28), η depends only on the variable p and β on A. Then, when (30) holds, (6') is an equation involving only p (and not A or z) so that

$$\hat{p} = \gamma \, \eta / (\eta - 1) \text{ is a constant with respect to } A \text{ and } z \dots(31)$$

Notice that (31) implies that η is also a constant with respect to A and z. Since the optimal price is surely not negative, we must have $\eta > 1$.

Under the assumptions (28) and (30), we can write, from (4),

$$R(p,A,z) = (p-\gamma) \, f_1(p) \, f_2(A) \, f_3(z)$$
$$= R_1(p) \, f_2(A) \, f_3(z) \dots\dots\dots\dots\dots\dots\dots\dots(32)$$

where $R_1(p) = (p = \gamma) \, f_1(p)$.

The price, $\hat{p}$, maximizes $R_1(p)$; let $\hat{R}_1 = R_1(\hat{p})$. Then $\hat{R}(A,z) = \hat{R}_1 \, f_2(A) \, f_3(z)$. If we now apply (15), we have

$$f'_2(A^*) = (\alpha + \delta) / \hat{R}_1 \, f_3(z) \dots\dots\dots\dots\dots\dots\dots\dots(33)$$

and the second-order condition for an optimum is that $f''_2(A^*) < 0$. If we differentiate (33) with respect to α, we have $f''_2(A^*) \, (\partial A^*/\partial \alpha) = 1/\hat{R}_1 \, f_3(z)$, and therefore

$$\partial A^*/\partial \alpha < \partial A^*/\partial \delta < 0 \dots\dots\dots\dots\dots\dots\dots(34)$$

For constant z, we can apply (25) to find

$$\partial a^*/\partial \alpha = \delta \, (\partial A^*/\partial \alpha) < 0 \dots\dots\dots\dots\dots\dots\dots(35)$$

If, on the other hand, we substitute (34) into (26), the sign remains ambiguous.

For any given p, $R_1(p)$ is a decreasing function of γ; hence, the maximum value, R_1, must also decrease as γ increases. Then the right-hand side of (33) increases with γ; since $f_2^- < 0$,

$$\partial A^*/\partial \gamma < 0 \dots\dots\dots\dots\dots\dots\dots\dots\dots\dots\dots (36)$$

To find the effect of γ on the price, p, we note that the latter is defined by the condition, $\partial R_1/\partial p = 0$, and that the second-order condition for a maximum is $\partial^2 R_1/\partial p^2 < 0$. Then, as usual, we have $\dfrac{\partial^2 R_1}{\partial p^2}\dfrac{dp}{d\gamma} + \dfrac{\partial^2 R_1}{\partial p \partial \gamma} = 0$. Since $\dfrac{\partial^2 R_1}{\partial p \partial \gamma} = -f'_1(p) > 0$,

$$dp/d\gamma > 0 \dots\dots\dots\dots\dots\dots\dots\dots\dots\dots\dots\dots (37)$$

To sum up, it has been established that, for multiplicative demand functions and constant marginal costs, price is constant with respect to income, the rate of interest or the rate of depreciation, and increases with marginal cost γ, the stock of goodwill decreases as the rate of interest or the rate of depreciation or the marginal cost increases, and current advertising outlay decreases as the rate of interest increases for fixed z.

We now move to the still more specific hypothesis, (29), that the demand function is linear in the logarithms. The second-order conditions now imply that $\beta < 1$. From (17), we now find that the optimal goodwill is a constant proportion of sales. But note that, since z may be changing over time, sales may not remain constant, in which case A^* will also change.

We may solve (29), (31), and (17) for A^* as a function of z:

$$A^* = \left[\frac{k \beta \gamma^{1-\eta}}{(\eta-1)(\alpha+\delta)}\right]^{1/(1-\beta)} \left(\frac{\eta}{\eta-1}\right)^{-\eta/(1-\beta)} z^{\zeta/(1-\beta)} \dots (38)$$

Thus A^* is a function solely of the time path of income and of the parameters, α, β, γ δ, η, and ζ. The parameter k may be thought of as defining the units of z; hence, we may set $k = 1$ without loss of generality.

If z is not held constant over time, the results given by (35) no longer hold because the effects of increasing income may offset the effects of changes in the interest rate or depreciation rates. Differentiating (38) with respect to time and substituting the result in (1), we find

$$a^*(t) = \left[\delta + \frac{\zeta}{1-\beta}\left(\frac{dz}{dt}/z\right)\right]A^* \dots\dots\dots\dots\dots (39)$$

where A^* is given by (38). We will suppose that income (or whatever other demand-shifter z is taken to represent) is changing or expected to change at a constant proportional rate, ρ, so that

$$\frac{dz}{dt}/z = \rho, \text{ constant} \dots\dots\dots\dots\dots\dots\dots\dots (40)$$

Under these conditions, it may easily be verified that the assumptions (A) and (B) of Theorem 3 are equivalent to the conditions,

$$\alpha > \zeta \rho/(1-\beta) \geqq - \delta, \quad \dots\dots\dots\dots\dots\dots\dots\dots\dots\dots\dots(41)$$

and these will be assumed in the following. (If the second inequality is reversed, then obviously the optimal policy is never to advertise.)

Thus, we may consider the effects of changes in seven parameters, α, β, γ, δ, η, ρ, and ζ, on optimal current advertising expenditure. Rather than discuss all the possible effects, however, we shall limit ourselves to the effects of changes in the interest and depreciation rates, α and δ, and leave the remaining analyses to the reader.

Differentiating a^* with respect to α, we find

$$\frac{\partial a^*}{\partial \alpha} = \left[\delta + \frac{\zeta \rho}{1-\beta}\right] \frac{(-A^*)}{(\alpha+\delta)(1-\beta)} = \frac{-a}{(\alpha+\delta(1-\beta))} < 0 \quad \dots(42)$$

so that an increase in the interest rate always reduces optimal current advertising expenditure. On the other hand, differentiating with respect to δ, we find

$$\frac{\partial a^*}{\partial \delta} = \frac{[(1-\beta)\, \alpha - \delta\beta] - \zeta \rho/(1-\beta)}{(\alpha+\delta)(1-\beta)} A^* \dots\dots\dots\dots\dots(43)$$

Thus, the effect of a change in the depreciation rate upon optimal current advertising expenditures depends upon the relationships among all the parameters.

More useful conclusions may be drawn by expressing optimal advertising expenditures as a ratio to sales. Let this ratio be σ; substituting for A^* in (39), from (17), we obtain

$$\sigma = \frac{\beta}{\eta\,(\alpha+\delta)} \quad (\delta + \frac{\zeta \rho}{1-\beta}) \quad \dots\dots\dots\dots\dots\dots\dots\dots(44)$$

If the value of σ computed from (44) is negative, then the optimal policy is zero advertising. Thus, assuming, as we have, that income (or any other demand-shifter) changes at a constant proportional rate (which may be zero) implies that firms should try to keep a constant ratio of sales to advertising. It is interesting to note that firms really do seem to follow a rule of thumb to this effect. Borden [3, pp. 721–22] reports that in 1935 the Association of National Advertisers found that of 215 companies investigated, 54 per cent. stated that their advertising appropriations were determined as a percentage of sales, either of the past year or expected in the year of the budget, and another 16 per cent. stated that their appropriations were guided in part by a percentage of sales.

The parameters of the model enter into the determination of the optimal ratio of advertising to sales in a much simpler manner than they do in the determination of the absolute level of optimal current advertising. It is therefore easier to discuss the effects of changes in these parameters on the optimal ratio. The derivatives of the ratio with respect to these parameters are given in the table below.

EFFECTS OF CHANGES IN α, β, γ, δ, η, ρ, AND ζ UPON σ

Parameter	Derivative of σ with respect to the parameter	Sign of the derivative of σ
α	$\dfrac{-\sigma}{\alpha+\delta}$	<0
β	$\dfrac{(1-\beta)^2\delta+\eta(\alpha+\delta)\zeta\rho}{\eta(\alpha+\delta)(1-\beta)^2}$	>0
γ	0	$=0$
δ	$\dfrac{\beta}{\eta(\alpha+\delta)^2}\left(\alpha-\dfrac{\zeta\rho}{1-\beta}\right)$	>0
η	$-\dfrac{\sigma}{\eta}$	<0
ρ	$\dfrac{\beta}{\eta(\alpha+\delta)}\left(\dfrac{\zeta}{1-\beta}\right)$	>0
ζ	$\dfrac{\beta}{\eta(\alpha+\delta)}\left(\dfrac{\rho}{1-\beta}\right)$	>0 if $\rho>0$ <0 if $\rho<0$

Note that changes in marginal cost have no effect, an increase in the interest rate or in the price elasticity of demand always reduces the ratio, and that an increase in advertising effectiveness or in the rate of growth of income always increases the ratio. The effects of a change in the depreciation rate, δ, always increases the proportion, in contrast to its effect on the absolute level which is ambiguous. The effect of a change in the income elasticity of demand depends on the sign of ρ.

5. SUMMARY

In this paper we derive optimal advertising and price policies for the individual firm under conditions of imperfect competition. Our model is simplified in the sense that it allows jump policies, which imply an infinite rate of current advertising expenditure, in the initial period. More realistic models may be developed by setting an upper bound on the rate of expenditure (Arrow [1]) or by introducing a non-linear investment cost function (Strotz [9] and Nerlove [8]). Our model has the advantage of considering contraction as well as expansion policies.

When no factors operate to shift the demand function independently of the firm's actions, we show that the optimal price and advertising policies are stationary after a certain point. The concept of goodwill, a stock related to the flow of current advertising expenditures, is introduced. We assume that this stock depreciates at a constant proportional rate, δ, and that the future is discounted at a constant rate of interest, α. Although we find that changes in α and δ affect the optimal goodwill in the same way, the effects upon current advertising expenditures and the time at which a stationary policy commences are asymmetrical.

Analysis of the special case in which demand is linear in logarithms and total cost is linear leads to more specific conclusions. We show that the optimal stationary solution implies a constant ratio of advertising to sales. Even in the non-stationary case, in which other factors operate to shift the demand function, the same result is obtained when these factors are assumed to change at a constant proportional rate.

Stanford University.

REFERENCES

[1] Arrow, K. J., " Optimal Capital Adjustment," chap. 1 in K. J. Arrow, S. Karlin and H. Scarf (eds.), *Studies in Applied Probability and Management Science*, Stanford, California, 1962.

[2] Arrow, K. J., M. Beckmann, and S. Karlin, " Optimal Expansion of the Capacity of a Firm," in K. J. Arrow, S. Karlin, and H. Scarf (eds.), *Studies in the Mathematical Theory of Inventory and Production*. Stanford, California, 1958, pp. 92–105.

[3] Borden, N. H., *The Economic Effects of Advertising*. Chicago, 1942.

[4] Dorfman, R. and P. O. Steiner, " Optimal Advertising and Optimal Quality," *American Economic Review*, vol. 44 (1954), pp. 826–36.

[5] Hoos, S., " The Advertising and Promotion of Farm Products—Some Theoretical Issues," *Journal of Farm Economics*, vol. 41 (1959), pp. 349–63.

[6] Jastram, R. W., " A Treatment of Distributed Lags in the Theory of Advertising," *Journal of Marketing*, vol. 19 (1955), pp. 36 ff.

[7] Koyck, L. M., *Distributed Lags and Investment Analysis*, Amsterdam, 1954.

[8] Nerlove, M., " Notes on the Identification and Estimation of Cobb-Douglas Production Functions," hectographed, University of Minnesota, 1958–59.

[9] Strotz, R. H., " Optimal Expansion Policies for the Firm," paper presented before the Econometric Society, New York City, December 28, 1961.

[10] Vidale, M. L. and H. B. Wolfe, " An Operations Research Study of Sales Response to Advertising ", *Operations Research*, vol. 5 (1957), pp. 370–81.

[11] Waugh, F. V., " Needed Research on the Effectiveness of Farm Products Promotions," *Journal of Farm Economics*, vol. 41 (1959), pp. 364–76.

Titles in This Series

1.
Henry Foster Adams. Advertising and Its Mental Laws. 1916

2.
Advertising Research Foundation. Copy Testing. 1939

3.
Hugh E. Agnew. Outdoor Advertising. 1938

4.
Earnest Elmo Calkins. And Hearing Not: Annals of an Ad Man. 1946

5.
Earnest Elmo Calkins and Ralph Holden. Modern Advertising. 1905

6.
John Caples. Advertising Ideas: A Practical Guide to Methods That Make Advertisements Work. 1938

7.
Jean-Louis Chandon. A Comparative Study of Media Exposure Models. 1985

8.
Paul Terry Cherington. The Consumer Looks at Advertising. 1928

9.
C. Samuel Craig and Avijit Ghosh, editors. The Development of Media Models in Advertising: An Anthology of Classic Articles. 1985

10.
C. Samuel Craig and Brian Sternthal, editors. Repetition Effects Over the Years: An Anthology of Classic Articles. 1985

11.
John K. Crippen. Successful Direct-Mail Methods. 1936

12.
Ernest Dichter. The Strategy of Desire. 1960

13.
Ben Duffy. Advertising Media and Markets. 1939

14.
Warren Benson Dygert. Radio as an Advertising Medium. 1939

15.
Francis Reed Eldridge. Advertising and Selling Abroad. 1930

16.
J. George Frederick, editor. Masters of Advertising Copy: Principles and Practice of Copy Writing According to its Leading Practitioners. 1925

17.
George French. Advertising: The Social and Economic Problem. 1915

18.
Max A. Geller. Advertising at the Crossroads: Federal Regulation vs. Voluntary Controls. 1952

19.
Avijit Ghosh and C. Samuel Craig. The Relationship of Advertising Expenditures to Sales: An Anthology of Classic Articles. 1985

20.
Albert E. Haase. The Advertising Appropriation, How to Determine It and How to Administer It. 1931

21.
S. Roland Hall. The Advertising Handbook, 1921

22.
S. Roland Hall. Retail Advertising and Selling. 1924

23.
Harry Levi Hollingworth. Advertising and Selling: Principles of Appeal and Response. 1913

24.
Floyd Y. Keeler and Albert E. Haase. The Advertising Agency, Procedure and Practice. 1927

25.
H. J. Kenner. The Fight for Truth in Advertising. 1936

26.
Otto Kleppner. Advertising Procedure. 1925

27.
Harden Bryant Leachman. The Early Advertising Scene. 1949

28.
E. St. Elmo Lewis. Financial Advertising, for Commercial and Savings Banks, Trust, Title Insurance, and Safe Deposit Companies, Investment Houses. 1908

29.
R. Bigelow Lockwood. Industrial Advertising Copy. 1929

30.
D. B. Lucas and C. E. Benson. Psychology for Advertisers. 1930

31.
Darrell B. Lucas and Steuart H. Britt. Measuring Advertising Effectiveness. 1963

32.
Papers of the American Association of Advertising Agencies. 1927

33.
Printer's Ink. Fifty Years 1888–1938. 1938

34.
Jason Rogers. Building Newspaper Advertising. 1919

35.
George Presbury Rowell. Forty Years an Advertising Agent, 1865–1905. 1906

36.
Walter Dill Scott. The Theory of Advertising: A Simple Exposition of the Principles of Psychology in Their Relation to Successful Advertising. 1903

37.
Daniel Starch. Principles of Advertising. 1923

38.
Harry Tipper, George Burton Hotchkiss, Harry L. Hollingworth, and Frank Alvah Parsons. Advertising, Its Principles and Practices. 1915

39.
Roland S. Vaile. Economics of Advertising. 1927

40.
Helen Woodward. Through Many Windows. 1926